REASONING & WRITING WELL

FIFTH EDITION

A Rhetoric, Research Guide, Reader, and Handbook

Betty Mattix Dietsch

Marion Technical College
Marion, Ohio

McGraw-Hill
Higher Education

Boston   Burr Ridge, IL   Dubuque, IA   New York   San Francisco   St. Louis
Bangkok   Bogotá   Caracas   Kuala Lumpur   Lisbon   London   Madrid   Mexico City
Milan   Montreal   New Delhi   Santiago   Seoul   Singapore   Sydney   Taipei   Toronto

Published by McGraw-Hill, an imprint of The McGraw-Hill Companies, Inc., 1221 Avenue of the Americas, New York, NY 10020. Copyright © 2009, 2006, 2003, 2000, 1998 by Betty Mattix Dietsch. All rights reserved. No part of this publication may be reproduced or distributed in any form or by any means, or stored in a database or retrieval system, without the prior written consent of The McGraw-Hill Companies, Inc., including, but not limited to, in any network or other electronic storage or transmission, or broadcast for distance learning.

This book is printed on acid-free paper.

2 3 4 5 6 7 8 9 0 DOC/DOC 1 5 4 3 2 1 0

ISBN: 978-0-07-338399-6
MHID: 0-07-338399-6

Editor in Chief: *Michael Ryan*
Publisher: *David S. Patterson*
Sponsoring Editor: *Christopher Bennem*
Editorial Coordinator: *Jesse Hassenger*
Marketing Manager: *Allison Jones*
Production Editor: *Alison Meier*
Media Project Manager: *Jessalyn Clark*
Design Coordinator: *Laurie Entringer*
Interior Design: *Maureen McCutcheon*
Cover Design: *Laurie Entringer*
Photo Research: *Brian J. Pecko*
Production Supervisor: *Tandra Jorgensen*
Composition: *10/12 Palatino by TBH Typecast, Inc.*
Printing: *45# New Era Matte, R R. Donnelley*

Cover image: © Royalty-free/Corbis

Library of Congress Cataloging-in-Publication Data

Dietsch, Betty M.
   Reasoning and writing well / Betty Mattix Dietsch.—5th ed.
     p. cm.
   Includes bibliographical references and indexes.
   ISBN-13: 978-0-07-338399-6 (alk. paper)
   ISBN-10: 0-07-338399-6 (alk. paper)
   1. English language—Rhetoric. 2. English language—Grammar. 3. College readers.
  4. Report writing. 5. Reasoning. I. Title.
  PE1408.D5437 2008
  808'.042—dc22   2008014427

The Internet addresses listed in the text were accurate at the time of publication. The inclusion of a Web site does not indicate an endorsement by the author or McGraw-Hill, and McGraw-Hill does not guarantee the accuracy of the information presented at these sites.

www.mhhe.com

IN APPRECIATION

This book is dedicated to my students, as well as the rhetoricians, composition theorists, and linguists upon whose work I build. To name them all would be impossible, but a few outstanding and influential names are in order, beginning with Aristotle (384–322 BC), who formulated rhetorical principles that are still widely used today. For his work in *Poetics,* Aristotle has been called the founder of literary criticism. Later Cicero (106–43 BC) and Quintilian (AD 40?–95?) developed and refined the process of argument.

I am also indebted to many twentieth-century critical thinkers and advocates of "plain writing," including John Dewey, Albert North Whitehead, E. B. White, William Strunk, William K. Zinsser, Jacques Barzun, Henry F. Graff, Edwin H. Newman, John Ciardi, Theodore M. Bernstein, Edward P. J. Corbett, John Langan, Judith Nadell, and Donald Murray. I appreciate, too, the work of Linda Flower, John Hayes, and Peter Elbow in formulating the basic steps of the writing process and that of Stephen Toulmin and Carl Rogers in argument.

CONTENTS IN BRIEF

CONTENTS

PART 4 Strategies for Critical Thinking, Evaluation, and Argument 206

Overview: Adopting an Attitude of Inquiry 208

PART 5   Critical Reading and Writing Strategies   284

PART 6 The Student Survival Guide 336

Overview: Fending Off the Wolves 338

BOOK II: THE RESEARCH WRITING GUIDE   417

BOOK III: THE READER   537

BOOK IV: THE HANDBOOK
A Guide to Grammar, Punctuation, Mechanics, and Usage   727

LIST OF FIGURES

The fifth edition of *Reasoning and Writing Well: A Rhetoric, Research Guide, Reader, and Handbook* is designed not only to help students meet and exceed the requirements of their colleges and employers but also to help them learn how to learn. Students need to become independent learners—able to analyze, synthesize, and evaluate, to think critically and to question thoughtfully. They also need to express ideas well, whether writing or speaking.

A core belief of the author is that students at all levels of preparedness can be encouraged and motivated to do their best through clear, logical instruction in plain English. The professional models in this textbook are interspersed with numerous student models to spur interest and provoke thought.

Whether you teach regular or advanced classes, you can select from this comprehensive array of stimulating and challenging materials. Economical, this text affords abundant material for a full year's composition, logic/argument, and research courses. For even more flexibility, chapters on oral presentations and visuals are included. Instructors can select just the lessons needed for their students.

NEW FEATURES

This edition of *Reasoning and Writing Well* is a keenly focused text that not only retains the best features of previous editions but also offers new topics, increased coverage of critical thinking, and the latest help with research. Among the many improvements are the following highlights.

New Chapter on Media and Visuals

"Understanding, Using, and Creating Visuals," chapter 20, analyzes ads and images, treating them as brief arguments. Guidelines for using copyrighted visuals and for creating effective visuals, including videos and statistical graphics, are provided.

Early Help in Using Quotations and Preventing Plagiarism

Part 2 has a new overview, "Plagiarism and Prevention," that alerts students to the dangers of plagiarism early and provides three ways to prevent it. Chapter 15, "Definition: An Introduction to Using Sources," explains how to use and cite sources of quotations and definitions in essays.

Updated Research Writing Guide with New APA Guidelines for Electronic References

Chapter R-1 has been expanded not only to help prevent plagiarism but also to provide assistance in determining the purpose of a research paper, selecting a topic, and maintaining objectivity. Chapter R-2 provides the latest guidelines for locating and using online and print resources at libraries. Tips for using vetted online subscription databases, free of charge, and criteria for evaluating the credibility of Web sites and documents are included. A new Internet directory lists reliable Web sites for research. Chapter R-4 contains not only updated APA models but also new APA guidelines for electronic references. Chapter R-5 has new material on interviewing.

New Help in Summarizing and Writing Critiques

"Writing a Critique," in chapter 21, offers increased help with summarizing and writing about reading. A critique of Frank McCourt's book *Teacher Man* shows how to analyze, interpret, and comment on a work.

Expanded Strategies for Critical Thinking, Evaluation, and Argument

Chapter 16, "Detecting Fallacies," contains new material on analyzing media. Chapter 17, "Examining Cause and Effect," has been moved to prepare students for problem solving (chapter 18) and argument (chapter 19). New chapter 20, "Understanding, Using, and Creating Visuals," emphasizes critical analysis and logical reasoning, as well as creating and using visuals in papers and reports.

New Features in "Effective Employment Writing"

Chapter 26 has several new sections to help in preparing materials for a job search, including "Video Clips for Résumés," "Ghosts of Electronic Messages," "Identity Thieves at Work and Other Dangers," as well as updated guidelines for e-mail. Two new Internet directories for employment research will help in finding reliable Web resources.

Increased Emphasis on Tone/Voice

The "voice of the writer" is an important thread running throughout the Rhetoric. Students learn how to create a friendly, sincere tone and build trust through attention to logic, accuracy, ethics, and appropriate word choice. "Making Oral Presentations," chapter 25, emphasizes credibility, enthusiasm, and trustworthiness, which are revealed in the speaker's persona and voice.

New Photos, Related Exercises, and Overviews

The updated interior design of *Reasoning and Writing Well* includes new part-opening photos and related practice writing exercises. The accompanying overviews summarize important concepts and present a perspective on lessons to come.

New Epigrams, Introductions, Examples, and Case Studies

New epigrams and introductions in several chapters relate writing to careers, as well as college writing. New examples have been sprinkled throughout the Rhetoric. Two new workplace case studies have been added.

Eighteen New Readings in Reader

The wide range of contemporary topics will hook readers' interest, provoke discussion, and stimulate ideas for writing. New arguments include "Last Rites for Indian Dead (Harjo), "Logging in Giant Sequoia National Monument" (Sierra Club), and English as an official language in the USA (Crawford, Krauthammer, Tabor).

New Thematic Unit: "The Work Ethic"

Employers frequently mention the lack of a work ethic in youthful hirees. Five new readings, including "Fun Ethic vs. Work Ethic" (Robert J. Samuelson) and "Dolores Dante" (Studs Terkel), reveal attitudes toward work and performance on the job.

Division into Four Books

For easier access, the fifth edition has been divided into four separate books: *The Rhetoric*, *The Research Writing Guide*, *The Reader*, and *The Handbook*.

Expanded Glossary of Usage

A quick reference to words that look alike, sound alike, or are commonly misused, the glossary clarifies words oftimes mistaken for similar ones.

Revised *Idea Book*

This unusually robust instructor's resource manual has been revised and enhanced to reflect the changes in the textbook. New elements also include answers to the new discussion questions in the Reader, quizzes, and model syllabi.

PROVEN FEATURES

BOOK I: THE RHETORIC

Student Friendly, Relevant, and Practical

Students consistently comment that the tone of the book is friendly and encouraging. Explanations are clear and the examples helpful. Every chapter cites benefits for students and applications in the workplace. Thirteen case studies, based on actual incidents offer insights into rhetorical situations and provide topics for writing. Case problems and exercises offer opportunities for discussion and writing. The three-chapter "Student Survival Guide" will help students prepare for exams, oral presentations, and employment.

Instructors have remarked that the author demonstrates the principles advocated, and the text is "almost self-teaching." Beginning with the rhetorical situation, this incremental approach covers fundamentals of the writing process before introducing writing strategies. The lessons, arranged from easy to difficult, prepare students for successive levels of writing.

In-Depth Coverage of Rhetorical Strategies and the Writing Process

The rhetorical situation is introduced in chapter 1 as integral to the writing process and is reinforced throughout the book. Students are asked to consider how the purpose, occasion, topic, audience, and voice of the writer influence writing and speaking. Step-by-step instructions explain the four stages of the writing process. These early chapters also include clear, specific help for focusing ideas with topic sentences, thesis statements, purpose statements, working outlines, controlling questions, and examples.

A Unique Revision Workshop

Four chapters are devoted to revision, editing, and proofreading. Chapter 5 explains the stages of revision and how readers can become their own editors. Chapter 6 discusses elements of effective paragraphs, including topic sentences, support sentences, and various orders. Chapter 7, "Restyling Sentences," explains five basic sentence structures and punctuation in those contexts. Voice of verbs, phrases and clauses, conjunctions, and parallelism are also explained. Chapter 8 provides in-depth coverage of denotation, connotation, positive words, negative words, courtesy words, and other influences on tone.

Emphasis on Ethics

"Writing and Ethics" is introduced in chapter 1. Chapter 3, "Learning to Think Critically," continues this emphasis. Chapters 16 through 19 link ethics to fallacies, evaluation, and argument. Chapter 25 discusses ethics and speaker credibility; chapter 26, ethics and accuracy of résumés.

Critical Thinking, Problem Solving, and Argument Coverage

Six chapters focus on critical thinking. Chapter 3 provides criteria for evaluating so-called facts, distinguishing inferences and value judgments from fact, and avoiding hasty generalizations. Chapters 16 to 18 explain how to recognize common logical and emotional fallacies, examine cause and effect, and apply problem solving to report writing and research papers. Chapter 19 shows how Aristotle's classic appeals of logos, ethos, and pathos can be combined in an effective argument. Chapter 20 analyzes ads and other media, viewing them as mini-arguments.

Critical Reading and Writing Strategies

A reading strategy in chapter 21 explains how to read essays critically, take notes, analyze, interpret, write reaction papers, and develop critiques. Chapter 22 analyzes the elements of literature, basic literary devices, and writing a literary analysis. Chapter 23 discusses and analyzes poetry, explaining figurative devices that students can use in their own writing.

The Student Survival Guide

This guide contains three comprehensive chapters to prepare students for essay and objective exams, make oral presentations, and write for employment. Unusually detailed, this guide has numerous examples to help students develop efficient study habits, give professional presentations, and prepare effective résumés, e-mail, and employment letters.

Exceptional Learning Resources and Study Aids

The Rhetoric includes a wealth of resources for individual and collaborative learning with numerous suggestions for generating topic ideas and practice activities. Case problems, peer review exercises, and small group discussion questions will help students strengthen their understanding of concepts and processes, analyze situations, and explore other points of view. Practical study aids—checklists, guidelines, and boxes—appear throughout. Icons in the margins point students to further coverage on Catalyst, McGraw-Hill's award-winning online reading, research, and writing resource.

BOOK II: THE RESEARCH WRITING GUIDE

This five-chapter research guide provides guidelines for objective research and writing a research paper using sources. Chapter R-1 explains how to plan research, schedule tasks, distinguish facts from ideas, and prevent plagiarism. Chapter R-2, edited by a university librarian, provides extensive help in locating reliable online resources, as well as library resources on the premises. Criteria for evaluating credibility of Web sites and material are included.

Chapter R-3 explains how to use sources, organize information, and draft a research paper. Summary, paraphrase, and quotation are explained at length. Detailed instructions and numerous examples will help students through every stage of writing a research paper and avoiding plagiarism. Included are a student outline and full-length annotated research paper, MLA style.

Chapter R-4 contains the latest Modern Language Association (MLA) and American Psychological Association (APA) formatting guidelines and documentation models. For easy access and clarity, each style is shown in a separate section and marked with a different edging. Chapter R-5 covers primary research: observation, interviews, and surveys, including a sample questionnaire, a student report of findings, and a student paper, based on observation.

BOOK III: THE READER

Forty-five engaging essays and short stories present diverse points of view. Organized by rhetorical modes, the Reader also includes a thematic table of contents. Convenient reference boxes at the ends of chapters in the Rhetoric suggest related readings. Maya Angelou, Charles Baxter, Suzanne Britt, Stephen L. Carter, Kate Chopin, Judith Ortiz Cofer, Charles Krauthammer, Daniel Henninger, William Raspberry, Robert J. Samuelson, Dan Shea, and John Updike are among the many authors represented.

BOOK IV: THE HANDBOOK

This simplified Handbook contains all the grammar references most first-year students will need. Rules and examples for parts of speech, punctuation, capitalization, abbreviations, numbers, and spelling are included. A glossary explains commonly confused terms. The Handbook also cites related chapters in the Rhetoric that explain usage, punctuation, and sentence structure. Grammar and usage worksheets, to supplement the Handbook, are provided in *The Idea Book*.

ELECTRONIC AND PRINT SUPPLEMENTS

The Idea Book: An Orientation and Resource Manual, 5th edition

This unusual instructor's manual, *The Idea Book*, is available online <www.mhhe.com/dietsch>. A print edition is available to instructors upon request. Both editions contain a wealth of materials to accompany *Reasoning and Writing Well*, 5th edition. *The Idea Book* was created for busy instructors and coordinators of community faculty to save time and promote quality instruction.

This unique 300+ page manual is packed with sample syllabi, lesson plans, practice exercises, visuals, quizzes, and other timesavers. For example, you can download the quizzes, add your own questions, and build your own quiz file. Included are teaching objectives, supplemental assignments, answers to exercises, grammar worksheets, teaching guides for selections in the Reader, and activity worksheets.

Online Learning Center Powered by Catalyst

The premier online tool for writing and research, Catalyst 2.0 features hundreds of interactive exercises, tutorials, reference materials, electronic bibliomakers for APA and MLA styles, and much more for both students and instructors. Marginal notes in *Reasoning and Writing Well* indicate specific URLs where Catalyst extends coverage.

The *Reasoning and Writing Well* Web site <www.mhhe.com/dietsch> is compatible with most online course management systems, such as WebCT and BlackBoard. For students the site provides 500 interactive grammar, punctuation, and editing exercises, as well as interactive activities focused on skills such as critical reading and evaluating Web sites. Answers to *The Idea Book* quizzes are available only to instructors.

A NOTE OF GRATITUDE

This book could not have been written without the generosity of the many students who have contributed their work. Heartfelt gratitude is also extended to my Marion Technical College colleagues, McGraw-Hill editors, local librarians, and especially OSUM librarian Betsy Blankenship for her suggestions in the fifth edition.

My thanks also go to the many reviewers who have helped us develop *Reasoning and Writing Well* over the years. The latest reviewers include Harryette Brown, Eastfield College; Anita Bryan, Northeast Mississippi Community College; Alisa Cooper, South Mountain Community College; Allison Cummings, Southern New Hampshire University; Carl C. Curtis III, Liberty University; Arnold R. Girdharry, Bridgewater State College; Kimberly Harrison, Florida International University; Richard Randolph, Kauai Community College; Linda Rose, Cerritos College; Leslie Vitale, Mott Community College; and Michelle W. Zollars, Patrick Henry Community College.

Betty Mattix Dietsch

BOOK I: THE RHETORIC

Writing in Context

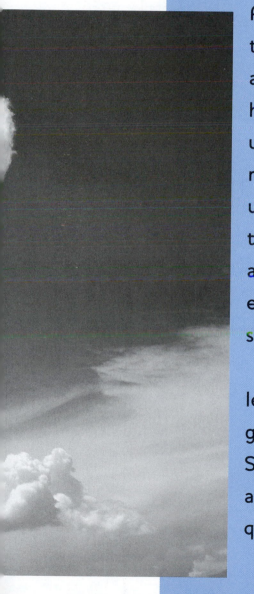

In about 450–425 B.C., Socrates, the Greek philosopher, strolled the streets of Athens, asking questions. As a citizen he felt a responsibility to help the people become wiser and better. Socrates believed that human goodness is founded on wisdom, but evil arises from ignorance. He believed that no one who was wise would do anything to harm himself over the long term and that most people who opt for evil are misled because the evil seems good at the moment.

Instead of lecturing or giving answers, Socrates would ask astute questions.

WRITING EXERCISE

1. Describe your thoughts as you examine the photo. Does it remind you of anything?
2. Do you agree or disagree with Socrates' premise in paragraph 1? Why? (Examine sentences 3 and 4.)

CRITICAL THINKING IN THE WRITING PROCESS

Questioning what you hear and read is essential to critical thinking and sound writing. When you hear a rumor or see mudslinging in a campaign ad, do you wonder "Is that really true?" When you watch commercials for medications, do you murmur, "Yes, but what about all the side effects?" When researching for a paper, do you ask, "When was the survey taken? Is it up-to-date? Does the author have credentials in that field?"

When you draft and revise, you use critical thinking skills as you puzzle over questions such as these: How should the introduction start? Is this topic sentence strong enough? Are these details relevant? Do I have enough support? What else needs to be said? How will the tone sound to the reader?

As you study this textbook and practice these concepts, your grasp of critical thinking will deepen. You will become more aware of the process of taking in data through your senses, interpreting, contemplating, inferring, and predicting. As you apply these skills in your writing classes, your grades will improve and your confidence will rise. So just keep on asking questions!

Reasons to Write and Ways to Start

In this age of remote controls, fast food, and instant messaging, many Americans have come to expect instant results by expending little effort. But learning to write well is neither quick nor effortless. *Rhetoric*, the art of writing or speaking effectively, implies study and practice. Assessing a rhetorical situation, prewriting, drafting, revising, and proofreading take considerable time and energy. For students who tend to learn just enough to

> Freedom to be your best means nothing unless you're willing to do your best.
>
> —Colin Powell, *Priorities*

pass a test, college and workplace writing will pose quite a challenge. That's the bad news.

For the good news, read on.

BENEFITS FOR YOU

You may take your ability to write for granted. But writing well is a skill that can improve the quality of your life. Here is a quick rundown of five benefits you can gain by learning to write well.

Writing Sharpens Thinking Skills

As you improve your writing skills, your ability to question, analyze, evaluate, and make decisions improves. You become not only more efficient in defining and sorting information but also more alert to possible cause-and-effect relationships. Your organizational skills also improve. You learn how to pin down wayward thoughts, draft quickly, and develop ideas effectively; how to digest and summarize information; and how to prepare an effective argument.

Writing Opens Opportunities to Learn

Writing is a process of discovery. As you write, you often discover thoughts and ideas that lie beneath the surface of your mind. Chances are that you'll become more aware of your beliefs and values—what is important to you. Your curiosity may sprout, spurring you to read and research new avenues. You become more alert to hasty generalizations, slick phrases, and common fallacies that often deter logical thinking.

Writing Nurtures Personal Development

As you deepen your awareness and improve your ability to express your thoughts, your self-confidence will rise. As you gain insights, your evaluation skills will improve, and you will become more skillful in setting priorities and objectives. Learning to write and speak well will give you power to direct your life into channels you may have once thought impossible.

Writing Helps to Establish Relationships

The ability to write well and cultivate a friendly written voice will help you establish and maintain relationships with friends, family, coworkers, and clients. As you learn to select positive words, de-emphasize negative ideas, and style sentences effectively, the tone of your e-mails, letters, and other writing will improve.

Writing Fosters Success in College and the Workplace

Skill in writing can help you succeed in college and advance your career. Writing skill can help you gain an interview, land a job, and earn a promotion. On the job you will be prepared to analyze and write about real concerns and problems, whether in e-mail, memos, letters, or reports. Learning to reason and write well is essential to your success.

ASSESSING THE RHETORICAL SITUATION

Every piece of writing has a context or circumstance surrounding it—called the *rhetorical situation*. To write effectively, consider the five elements of each writing situation: the *occasion, purpose, topic, audience,* and *voice*. If a writer or speaker neglects any element, the message may ramble, go astray, or miss the mark. Then the primary goal—to communicate clearly—will not be attained.

Occasion for Writing

The *occasion* is the event, condition, or need that causes you to write. On the job your writing may spring from a client's need, a problem with a supplier, or another complication that requires a written response. Considering the nature of the occasion that prompts writing or speaking will help you determine your writing purpose, audience, topic, and voice. Various occasions with different audiences call for different writing strategies. For example, the occasion of writing an e-mail to a friend is quite unlike that of sending a cover letter to a prospective employer.

The occasion for classroom writing has certain implications, depending upon the assignment. In-class writing is not expected to be as polished as out-of-class papers, where several revisions are expected. Usually, your instructor will give you a general purpose for a paper or presentation, but you choose the topic and the specific purpose. Often your classmates are the audience.

CHECKLIST **ASSESSING AN OCCASION FOR WRITING**

To assess an occasion for writing, ask yourself these four questions:

1. Why is there a need to write or speak?

2. What is required or expected?

3. What will be suitable for this situation?

4. What strategy will be effective?

Purpose for Writing

Purpose refers to a writer's reason for writing, which can be stated or implied. To be clear, expository writing should have both a general purpose and a specific purpose. Identifying your purpose early can help you focus your draft.

The General Purpose   Writing has four general purposes: *to inform, to persuade, to express,* or *to entertain.* Often these general purposes are combined. For example, most writing is intended to inform, but it also has a secondary persuasive element: to convince the reader that it is factual and reliable. Other writing is primarily persuasive, designed to argue a point and secure agreement, yet it is also informative. The degree of persuasion varies according to the occasion, purpose, audience, and voice.

Some writing is primarily expressive, allowing the writer to reveal feelings and opinions, often by recalling experience. Expressive writing may take the form of personal essays, journal writing, diaries, poetry, fiction, or plays. Yet you may also be expressive to a lesser extent in a business letter, report, or proposal, depending upon the rhetorical situation.

Although some humorous writing seems intended merely to entertain, it may also make a serious point. The clever use of humor can advance a point, as in the writing of Mark Twain. Abraham Lincoln used humor in his speeches to sway audiences to his way of thinking. A lighthearted approach captures the attention of readers and listeners. To be successful, humor must not be heavy-handed or derisive—otherwise, it tends to backfire.

The Specific Purpose   The specific purpose may be implied or stated. In literature the purpose is invariably implied in a theme that permeates the piece. In expository writing the purpose is usually stated directly for clarity, either in a topic sentence or in the thesis. In the introduction to *Watch Your Language,* Theodore M. Bernstein explains the specific purpose that directed the *New York Times* during his seven years as the assistant managing editor.

The first sentence below states Bernstein's specific purpose: to inform readers of the guiding editorial philosophy of the newspaper. The second sentence gives a valuable tip for assessing the audience.

> Today we think it well to make each issue as nearly self-sufficing as is reasonable so that the reader does not feel the need for a research staff to help him understand the day's news. Perhaps the best slogan a newspaper could post in its city room would be this: "Keep two readers always in mind: the high school sophomore and the man who has been marooned on a desert island for three months." Both of them, for different reasons, have to be told what it is all about.

Writing a Purpose Statement   A purpose statement is a helpful tool to focus the specific purpose, whether you are planning an essay, a research paper, or a report. A purpose statement can serve as a preliminary step to writing a topic sentence or a thesis statement. In the first example below, the general purpose is "to inform." The rest of the statement is the specific purpose.

- **Purpose:** To inform the reader of the advantages and disadvantages of TaxCut as opposed to Quicken.

- **Purpose:** To convince the reader that the way medical personnel are portrayed on television is often unrealistic.

Topic

Writing topics spring from real situations in the workplace and in daily life. Perhaps there is an incorrect shipment, an overdue payment, or a progress report for a contractor. Ordinary situations, injected with a bit of humor, can serve as the subjects of essays. Coping with contrary toddlers, mischievous pets, or disgruntled customers may provide topics. Or you might describe a hobby, a vacation, or a strange happening. Whether you write from experience or from research, this book will show you how to proceed.

> The first guideline for successful college writing is to *select a topic you care about.* The second is to *narrow the topic* so that you can focus the paper on one main idea and develop it well for your audience.

WRITING SUCCESS TIP: SELECTING AND NARROWING A TOPIC

Audience

Before starting to write, assess your audience: Who will be reading your writing or listening to your presentation? In the workplace your readers may be coworkers, clients, wholesalers, or others. In the classroom your instructor may assign an audience or suggest you write for your classmates. Or you might visualize a typical reader and write directly to him or her.

To accomplish your purpose, recognize, respect, and respond to your readers' needs. Knowing characteristics of their backgrounds, interests, and viewpoints will help you choose a suitable topic and devise an appropriate writing strategy. The more you can learn about the person or group who will be reading your writing, the more effective you can make it. *Writing that is addressed to no one in particular will lack a sense of purpose.*

1. **To whom am I writing?** What do I know about the age, gender, education, social class, economic status, interests, and attitudes of the readers? How will these characteristics influence my writing?

2. **Why will they read this writing?** How can they benefit? Will they gain information? Be entertained? What else? (Predicting the reactions of the audience will help you to capture their attention and maintain their interest.)

3. **How might they feel about the subject?** How will their feelings affect my word choice and writing strategy?

4. **How will they react to my point of view?** How should I approach the topic, directly or indirectly? (See chapter 19 on argument.)

5. **How much do they need or want to know?** How much should I say? What terms should I define?

QUESTIONS TO ASSESS AN AUDIENCE

A helpful tactic in assessing your writing audience is to deliberately shift your perspective from writer to reader. Try to put yourself into the reader's role—to feel and think as the reader might. In "Don't Blame the Editors," Sloan Wilson explains this dual role of writer/reader:

> Each of us is both writer and reader, and no reader has mercy for dullness. My editor, who as politely as possible had told me that my work was boring, had learned to speak for millions of readers, and I was grateful to him for making me clean up my act before putting it before the world's sleepy eyes. . . . Those listeners would start getting restless if I confused them; they demanded clarity above all else.

If a writer ignores readers and neglects their needs, they will respond by ignoring the writing. A keen awareness of how readers think and feel will assist you in shaping your writing purpose and in finding an appropriate voice.

The Voice of the Writer

The *voice* of writing is the presence of the writer as perceived by the reader. The writer's voice shapes the sound and the effect of the words. Writers' voices are influenced not only by their knowledge, experience, and beliefs but also by their biases or impartiality—how they *feel* about the act of writing, the reader, and the topic. A writer has many voices, and the voice selected for a rhetorical situation will affect how the audience responds.

To listen to the sound of your written voice, read your draft aloud. How do you sound? Confident? Knowledgeable? Encouraging? Amused? Critical? As you read chapter 2, you'll better understand how the choice of language affects the sound of a writer's voice.

UNDERSTANDING THE PROCESS OF WRITING

> www.mhhe.com/dietsch
>
> For general information related to the writing process, visit:
> Writing

Assessing the rhetorical situation is a preliminary stage of the writing process. This invisible stage requires thinking about why you are writing and how to shape ideas for a writing situation. Traditionally, the " writing process" has been divided into four stages that can be observed. Yet writing is rarely neat and linear, even though it may seem so at times. Most writers shuttle back and forth between stages.

Although there is no one way to write, there are ways to make writing easier, faster, and more effective, which you will find as you traverse this book. An excellent way to gain confidence is to dispel any myths you may have heard about writing. Then you will be less likely to become entangled in the "perfect draft" approach, expecting to perfect each sentence the first time. This method is tedious and exasperating. Those who use it proceed at a snail's pace. Nor will you be lulled by the false belief that inspiration alone can transform a first draft into a final draft without several revisions. High-quality papers re-

- **Prewriting.** The purpose of prewriting is to capture and preserve ideas. In this first stage of the writing process, you simply jot down ideas, whether in fragments, lists, or sentences.
- **Drafting.** While drafting, you develop, expand, and connect ideas. Drafting is a stage of discovery and exploration.
- **Revision.** During revision you rethink, refine, and develop ideas well. This third stage is ongoing—recurring whenever needed. You reshape ideas—expanding, deleting, clarifying, and reorganizing.
- **Editing/proofreading.** This final stage requires examining ideas, details, words, grammar, and punctuation—attending to matters *within each sentence.* Here the emphasis is on accuracy, correctness, and clarity.

FOUR STAGES OF THE WRITING PROCESS

quire much more than an hour or two of effort. They require considerable thought and multiple revisions.

THREE GUIDELINES FOR ETHICAL WRITING

In poetry and fiction authors create imaginary scenarios and characters. But in expository writing responsible writers present the truth: they do not fudge facts, mislead, or omit significant details. *Their purpose is to inform accurately, to express honestly, or to persuade ethically.* If they exaggerate to entertain or make a point, they make it apparent to the reader. Three basic guidelines will help you write ethically:

- Present facts clearly and objectively. Ads should not masquerade as news stories nor rumor as fact.
- State any possible risks that might harm the reader.
- Observe copyright laws and list sources appropriately.

Responsible writers select topics they know, either from experience or from research. They look at various views of an issue so that they can appraise it accurately and fairly. They tell readers, clearly, what they need to know. When citing the work of another, they give credit to the author and list the source data. Writers who follow these ethical practices respect not only the rights of authors but also the right of readers to know the truth.

See chapters 3, 11, and R-1.

This book will help you become more aware of the risks of using unethical shortcuts such as unqualified generalizations, stereotypes, fallacies, and plagiarism. You will learn to read critically—to question and analyze, to search for the real facts.

FOR YOUR REFERENCE
Study Skills

- **"Strategies to Prepare for Exams."** Includes reading tips, time management, reviewing, predicting exam questions, taking objective exams, and writing complete essay answers. See chapter 24.

- **"Critical Reading."** To increase reading comprehension and note-taking skills, see the strategy for critical reading, pages 291–293.

- **"Research Reading."** Explains summarizing, paraphrasing, and quoting research. Includes examples. See pages 443–452.

- **Handbook Directory.** For quick answers to grammar, punctuation, and usage questions, turn to the directory on page 728.

CASE PROBLEM: Responding to a Rhetorical Situation

Directions: Last night you went to a keg party just off campus. Three students spray-painted parked cars, but you just watched. Soon the police arrived, sirens screaming. The culprits threw down their paint cans and blended into the crowd. One can rolled near your feet, so you tossed it into the nearest trash can. Police questioned bystanders and noticed an orange smudge on your index finger. They handcuffed you and three guys, whose faces were misted with orange spray, and took you to the station. The three confessed; you were released. In a letter how would you tell the following people about the incident?

1. Your guidance counselor
2. Your best friend, who is doing her student teaching in a nearby town
3. Your parents

Listening to the Voice of the Writer

CHAPTER 2

> The skill of writing is to create a context in which other people can think.
>
> —Edwin Schlossberg,
> Founder of ESI Design

Schlossberg knows that for writing to be effective, it must have a context that stimulates readers to think. In your college classes, you also will be expected to create a context for writing. In other words, you write for a specific rhetorical situation. Knowing your audience and why you are writing will sharpen your ideas and enable you to present them in a clear, distinctive voice. How you sound on paper—how readers perceive a sense of your presence—is referred to as the *written voice.* A writer's voice radiates from the point of view, tone, and sentence style.

NOTICING THE WRITER'S VOICE

The written voice is like a mirror that reflects mind-set, personality, and knowledge of the topic. This voice also reveals an attitude toward the topic and the reader. A writer's voice may inspire liking and trust or dislike and distrust. A writer's voice influences the acceptance or rejection of ideas.*

A writer has many voices that vary according to the rhetorical situation. Between the *confidential voice* and the *academic voice* is a range of voices that differ in degree of formality. For college essays, you will be expected to have a clear, knowledgeable voice, perhaps informal and conversational, but not overly so. For research papers, most teachers expect an academic voice with a confident, objective tone, written in third person. Now let's listen to three very different voices.

See page H-3 for *person* of pronouns.

A Confidential Voice

In *I Am What I am . . . And Here's Why!* Cleo R. Ludwig, founder of the L-K restaurant chain, opens his biography with an intimate disclosure of feelings as a youth and later as an octogenarian. By using a confidential tone of voice, Ludwig treats the reader as a close friend with whom he shares secrets and personal opinions:

> When I was a small boy growing up, I felt that I didn't amount to much. Now, in the eighth decade of my life, I recognize the fallacy of that opinion. I know that it doesn't apply to me or anyone else. Because it is difficult to live with a feeling of worthlessness, I have tried to help my children, grandchildren and all the people with whom I've been associated to avoid such a self-assessment. Every human being has value, and sometimes those from the humblest origins have the most value. The history of America has proven this truth over and over. (1)

A Conversational Voice

In a conversational voice, Albert Payson Terhune tells how a mystery of disappearing lambs was solved. The morning after the lambs were missing, the collie Leggy was found, slashed and bleeding with a broken leg, still guarding the flock. Yet there were no strange animal tracks. That night the owner brought the flock near the house and watched to no avail. At dawn he entered the house, and Leggy dashed out. Two large eagles were each bearing away a lamb:

---

*I am indebted to Dona J. Hickey for her definitive work in *Developing a Written Voice* (1993).

> If one foreleg was disabled, his hindquarters still had the dynamic power of a racehorse's. Upward he sprang as the bird sought to heave itself and the lamb high enough for soaring flight. Five feet in the air Leggy's terrible jaws drove into the eagle's breast-plumage. They drove deep and hung on.
>
> It is one thing to bear off a fat little lamb. And it is quite another to sustain the raging weight of a seventy-pound collie. The eagle dropped its ba-a-ing prey. It smote with beak and claw at the dog. . . . The collie's weight brought the huge bird to earth, with a crash. . . . The dog's eyetooth had pierced to the eagle's heart and had ended the wild battle. ("The Critter")

Here Terhune uses adjectives and active verbs to describe the fierce battle between dog and eagle. His voice reveals admiration for the dog, which despite its leg in a cast and other injuries, was determined to protect the lamb.

An Academic Voice

In *Teaching Shakespeare in the High School,* Bertrand Evans, professor of English at University of California (Berkeley), uses an academic voice to provide guidelines for teachers and to give his professional opinion about the merits of teachings certain plays. Notice the impersonal tone, which focuses on facts, not personal feelings:

> *The Merchant of Venice* raises an issue of Christians and Jews, and to many individuals of both faiths the very fact that it does so makes the appropriateness of the play in public classrooms questionable. Areas of the United States differ, and communities within broad areas also differ. In certain communities teachers have found use of this play unthinkable; in others teachers have taught it closely and have reported no offense to sensitivities. (15)

Word Choice Influences Voice

www.mhhe.com/dietsch
For online resources related to word choice, check out:
Editing>Usage

Seasoned writers select words and a level of formality that are suitable for their audience. They think not only about the meaning but also about the sound of the words. When you write, it is important to consider not only the literal meanings of words but also the shadowy nuances—the subtle shades of meaning and feeling that accompany words. Some are as soft and soothing as a lullaby. Some words sound prickly; others crack like a whip. A writer's phrasing and tone influence how the audience perceives the message.

How Should a Writer's Voice Sound?

Readers expect a writer to be knowledgeable and reliable, to explain the topic clearly and accurately. Usually, readers are quick to sense incompetence, insincerity, arrogance, or dishonesty. To be respected and believed, your written voice should also reflect sincerity, integrity, and empathy for the audience. Warm, understanding words help readers relax and accept the message. Most readers want a receptive, understanding voice, one that does not talk down or sound smug or superior. Most important, they want a voice they can trust.

To better understand the written voice, think about what you do when chatting with a friend face to face. You automatically adapt your voice to the occasion, the topic, and the listener. Your tone is pleasant and friendly. You welcome your friend by your words and manner. When writing informally, you might think of the reader as a friend and use a similar tone.

CONSIDERING HOW CASUAL CONVERSATION DIFFERS FROM FOCUSED WRITING

In casual conversation the spoken voice tends to be more friendly and less purposeful than the written voice. Casual conversation ambles along, often wordy and repetitive, perhaps punctuated by witticisms. Fragmented and abbreviated, the conversation may become sidetracked from the point. Significant details may be omitted. When this happens, the listener may frown, raise an eyebrow, or ask a question.

In contrast, focused writing has a logical order—steadily advancing toward the point to be made. Since few writers have the chance to observe nonverbal feedback or to answer questions of the reader, they must exert more effort than conversationalists to be clear and diplomatic. To be effective, writing must be more specific, concise, and complete than casual conversation. The writer must monitor words carefully to avoid offending or miscommunicating. A keen ear for distinctions in usage and levels of formality is invaluable.

In college and on the job, you will be writing for different readers of e-mail, letters, reports, papers, and other documents. These pieces will require different voices, adapted to each occasion, purpose, topic, and audience. To achieve an appropriate voice, ask yourself three crucial questions:

- **Who will be reading this writing?** The motivation, interests, and values of the audience will influence how you shape your purpose. Think in terms of advantages: How can readers benefit? What approach will be effective and appropriate for the occasion?

- **What level of formality is appropriate?** Adapt your written voice to the occasion and the audience. Consider their expectations, culture, education, occupation, and gender.

- **Can I write reasonably about this topic?** Read your writing aloud. Does it sound fair, unbiased, and reasonable? Do the words say what you intend? Is the tone suitable? When you take a position or a particular point of view, do you present enough logical evidence to support your point and convince?

WRITING SUCCESS TIP: ASK THREE CRUCIAL QUESTIONS

CONSIDERING USAGE: STANDARD AND NONSTANDARD

With each technological advance, new generation, and fad, newborn words fly over the airwaves and into cyberspace. Dictionary publishers scramble to keep up by bringing out revised editions every few years. All dictionaries have two broad categories of usage: standard and nonstandard. For most audiences you will need standard usage for your writing. To determine the status of a word, consult a recent collegiate dictionary.

Standard Usage

To sound knowledgeable, a writer needs a command of standard usage. Most English words are standard usage, meaning they are widely accepted by educated speakers and writers. These words follow conventional spellings and rules of grammar. Standard usage varies widely, ranging from informal to formal words.

If a word in the dictionary has no usage label, then it is standard. Note, however, that some words have several meanings—both standard and nonstandard. So if you use the word, be sure to apply it in the context you intend. Some dictionaries provide examples showing usage. If a word is used primarily in conversation, it will be labeled *colloq.* or *colloquial, slang,* or *dialect.*

Sometimes the status of words changes. A word can also gain or lose acceptance as it acquires new meanings. For example, the word *punk* has several colloquial or slang meanings, but after *punk* was applied to a style of dress and music, that meaning became standard English. Often language is a mixture of the informal and formal, technical and nontechnical.

Nonstandard Usage

See chapter 26 for e-mail.

Throughout your early years, you have been taught to avoid nonstandard language. You have received instruction in using correct grammar, complete sentences, and standard spellings. You already know that fragments, misspellings, and certain words are taboo in most writing. So the chances are that you already have a good grasp of what constitutes nonstandard language.

Yes, nonstandard words are sometimes used to lend a sense of realism to poetry and fiction. But they are generally inappropriate in college and workplace writing. In fact, Bloomberg, the financial news and data company, filters electronic messages not only of its staff but also of traders and subscribers who use Bloomberg's desktop terminals. When profanity or ethnic, racial, or gender slurs are typed, a warning appears, and the user must reword the message before it can be sent.

Dialect and Regionalism   Words that are limited to a geographic area are identified as *dialect* or *regional.* This nonstandard usage can be difficult to understand. Dialect is the natural way some folks talk, using regionalisms such as "toted a poke full of greens" and "hit the road" or fractured grammar such as "didn't never" or "them books."

Where Are Keys to Usage Labels and Abbreviations Found?

The keys to usage and abbreviations are usually located in the introduction of a dictionary. Here are nonstandard usage labels and their common abbreviations:

- N.S. or nonstd. = nonstandard
- substand.   = substandard
- dial.   = dialect
- vul.   = vulgar (common)

When Dictionaries Disagree   Since the spelling and the status of a word can change in a relatively short time, consult an up-to-date dictionary. Even then dictionary makers may not agree on the status of a word. For example, *complected* is listed as "regional dialect" or "substandard" in several dictionaries whereas *Merriam-Webster's Collegiate Dictionary*, eleventh edition (2004) states, "Not an error, nor a dialectal term, nor nonstandard—all of which it has been labeled—*complected* still manages to raise hackles."*

If you are trying to decide whether or not to use a word of dubious status, it is safer to be conservative. Avoid the word lest the reader, unaware of the diversity in opinion, regard the word as an error. (Note: *Wikipedia* is not always reliable. Anyone can change a definition there.)

Three Vocabularies: Speaking, Writing, and Reading

A factor that complicates word choice for beginning writers is that most of us have three distinct vocabularies—one for speaking, one for writing, and one for reading. The spoken vocabulary is the smallest and least formal; rough drafts are often written at this level. The vocabulary for writing lies somewhere in between those for speaking and reading. Your final draft, after being revised several times, should contain this middle level, which uses standard words and grammar.

The reading vocabulary is the largest, most specific, and most formal. Sometimes students pull words from this vocabulary or use a word found during research but do not look up the meaning. This practice can result in confusion and error. Awareness of your own three vocabularies can help you select an appropriate voice for each rhetorical situation.

---

*By permission from *Merriam-Webster's Collegiate® Dictionary*, Eleventh Edition. Copyright © 2004 by Merriam-Webster, Incorporated (www.merriam-webster.com).

SELECTING A LEVEL OF FORMALITY

www.mhhe.com/dietsch

For further work on levels
of formality, visit:
Editing>Word Choice

To choose an appropriate level of formality, consider the rhetorical situation. Your choice will influence the sound of your written voice and how you are perceived by the reader. In college and workplace writing, three levels of formality—Informal English, Professional English, and Formal English—are used. All three levels follow the conventional rules of grammar.

LEVELS OF FORMALITY

Nonstandard	Informal English	Professional English	Formal English
Least ‑ ‑ ‑ ‑ ‑ ‑ ‑ ‑	_____	*Most*
Formal			*Formal*
(nonstandard grammar)		Standard grammar	

Informal Standard English

Most of your writing in college and on the job will require complete sentences. Although Informal Standard English may include a well-placed fragment once in a great while, verb forms, pronoun agreement, and other grammatical structures are always standard. To use fragments for a purpose, see page H-22 in the Handbook.

Dictionary entries usually label informal words, but not always in the same way; you may find either of two labels to denote *informal* usage:

- inf. = informal
- colloq. = colloquial (conversational or casual)

Informal Standard English is a language of conversation. You read Informal Standard English in many popular magazines, novels, short stories, poems, comics, ads, newspaper articles, and other writing. A *Wall Street Journal* article entitled "In 24-Hour Workplace, Day Care Is Moving to the Night Shift" uses Informal Standard English in the opening paragraphs:

> There are plenty of places to sleep at the Children's Choice Learning Center here, but nine-year-old Najah Finch isn't napping. Wearing a pink "I am Boy Crazy" T-shirt, she cartwheels around the floor, breaks for juice and popcorn, then settles down at the TV for a Muppet video. Najah's mom isn't due to pick her up for another three hours.
> At 3:30 a.m.
>
> —Barbara Carton

Did you note the conversational voice and the fragment "At 3:30 a.m."? Other clues to informality include the contraction *isn't* and the colloquial use of *mom* (mother). There are different varieties of Informal Standard English. Many business letters and printed materials require all sentences to be complete. The voice may be a bit more formal, as in Stuart M. Berger's *What Your Doctor Didn't Learn in Medical School:*

> The word *hypoglycemia* is the kind of six-syllable medicalese word that my patients hear and tell me: "That's Greek to me, doctor." Well, in the case of this word, it really is Greek! But just in case your ancient Greek is a tad rusty, let's review: *hypo* means "too little"; *gly* is the Greek root for "sugar"; and the suffix *-emia* means "of the blood." String them together, and you have "too little sugar in the blood." (The disease is the polar opposite of diabetes, which creates too much sugar in the blood.)

Watch the Pronouns   Did you notice Dr. Berger's use of the first person (*me*) and second person (*your*)? This usage is typical of Informal Standard English. Although Professional English and Formal English sometimes include the first person (*I, me, mine, we, our, us*), it is used only for a good reason. As a rule, these two levels do not include second person when written.

See page H-3 in the Handbook.

Mixing Levels of Formality   Once in a while, a writer may mix levels of formality, but only for a purpose. Making a switch *between* paragraphs, as Barbara Carton did, is easier than doing so within a paragraph, which requires more transition. As a rule, it is better and easier to use just one level of formality in business writing and academic papers.

Professional English

Professional English marks a writer as well-educated and knowledgeable. Certain audiences in the professional world expect a more serious, reserved, and authoritative voice than that found at the informal level. Some writers call this level Edited American English. Actually, the term *level of formality* is somewhat misleading. *Range of formality* would be more accurate, but no one calls it that. Professional English contains the most words, so it goes *unlabeled* in all dictionaries.

The hallmarks of Professional English are complete sentences, correct grammar, and standard word choice. This level of usage is found in many newspaper articles, textbooks, business reports, annual reports to stockholders, and much academic writing, including research papers. In the article on twenty-four-hour day care, Barbara Carton's voice changes in the fourth paragraph, where she switches to Professional English. (Note that there are no contractions or informal words.)

> As more single parents and working couples cope with a 24-hour economy, day care is making an uneasy transition to night care. Employers are building round-the-clock centers to attract and keep employees. State and local governments are also supporting extended-hour and night-care initiatives, partly because they feel obliged to help the single mothers they sent to work under welfare reform.

THREE LEVELS OF FORMALITY IN THE WORKPLACE

Informal Standard	Professional English	Formal English
memos	memos, e-mail	legal notices, letters
customer letters	bulletins	proposals
newsletters	newsletters, letters	laws, statutes
sales talks	bids, proposals	legal documents
letter reports	professional reports	technical reports
informal speeches	presentations	formal speeches
conversation	policies	policies
newspaper articles	contracts, forms	contracts, forms
e-mail	manuals	technical documents

Formal English

You may be familiar with Formal English. If enrolled in prelaw, paralegal, education, premed, nursing, data processing, engineering, or other such programs, you may read Formal Technical English in your textbooks. Or you may work in a profession where it is spoken and written daily.

Formal English may include foreign phrases, literary allusions, and specialized or technical terms unknown to the average reader. The sentence structure tends to be long and complex, written in third person. All of these characteristics tend to make the voice of the writer impersonal.

Formal English usually goes unmarked in dictionaries, but archaic words and foreign phrases are labeled. If you find the following labels, you will know the words are formal:

- arch.   = archaic (antiquated or rarely used)
- obs.   = obsolete (used chiefly before 1775)
- poetic (found in poetry)

Formal English is primarily written. It is the language of technical manuals, some college textbooks, professional journals, formal reports, many insurance policies, and legal and government documents. The following passage from a legal decision written by former U.S. Supreme Court chief justice Earl Warren is easier to understand than many other legal documents:

> The plaintiffs contend that segregated public schools are not "equal" and cannot be made "equal," and that hence they are deprived of the equal protection of the laws. Because of the obvious importance of the question presented, the Court took jurisdiction. Argument was heard in the 1952 Term, and reargument was heard this Term on certain questions propounded by the Court.

> The School Segregation Decision of 1954
> *Brown versus Board of Education of Topeka, Kansas*
> 347 U.S. 487–496 (May 17, 1954)

FIVE COMMON CONCERNS

Students who have been exposed to informal talk on television and elsewhere may use an overly casual written voice that is unsuitable for much college writing. Although slang, informal abbreviations, and colloquialisms give an air of friendliness, they may cause problems in clarity and create a poor impression in certain situations.

Slang and Abbreviations

Slang is a quick, cool way to show you belong to a group, but don't assume that all readers will understand. Since slang tends to be ethnic, occupational, generational, or other group–centered, some readers may be baffled by it. Some informal abbreviations are also indecipherable to many readers. For example, they may not have seen abbreviations used in singles columns (SWF) or in instant messaging (lol) or heard the latest teen talk.

www.mhhe.com/dietsch
For more help with slang and colloquialisms, go to: Editing>Clichés, Slang, Jargon, Colloquialism

Standard abbreviations that are not widely used may also be unfamiliar. And not all abbreviations require periods. Guidelines for using abbreviations vary according to the purpose and style manual used. For help with standard abbreviations, Modern Language Association (MLA) style, see page H-41 in the Handbook.

Misused Colloquialisms

Colloquialisms can add extra words and abruptly change the tone of writing. A sudden, unnecessary downshift to informality is jarring for the unsuspecting reader. Such shifts need to be made carefully and only for a sound reason. As you edit your college essays, watch for words that differ in the level of formality from the rest of your writing. If you find one, check to see that it serves a purpose. Otherwise, substitute a standard synonym.

COLLOQUIAL	STANDARD
"Toyota Is *Looking to* Build Hybrid in U.S. Plant" (headline)	Toyota Is *Planning* to Build. . . .
Brad is *looking to find* a job.	Brad is *looking for* a job.
Owen took the *stuff* out of his locker.	Owen cleaned out his locker.
Lily got a *good deal* on her iPod.	Lily's iPod was a *bargain*.
Liam downloaded *a lot* of songs.	Liam downloaded *many* songs.
Hope is an *awfully* good friend.	Hope is a *very* good friend.
When did Milo *get* married?	When *did* Milo *marry?*
Did you *get hired*?*	*Were* you *hired*? Did you *get* a job?

---

* *Get* is often used incorrectly as a helping verb. *Get* is a standard verb that requires a direct object, as in "Will you please *get* the mail?"

Other colloquial expressions to avoid in expository writing are listed below, along with standard alternatives:

COLLOQUIAL	STANDARD
got mad	became angry (or upset)
really good	very good, excellent
fun time	had fun
seeing as	since, because
fight (verbal)	argument, quarrel, spat

Switching Pronouns in Midsentence

www.mhhe.com/dietsch

For help with pronouns, visit:

Editing>Pronouns

When students write the way they talk, they may suddenly switch from first-person to second-person pronouns unnecessarily. An abrupt shift in person changes the point of view and disrupts the flow of the sentence. Consider this student's rough draft:

> Years ago *I* would start my vegetable plants from seed because it was much cheaper, and *you* could get a jump on the season. But as *I* expanded my garden, more and more plants were needed, too many to grow from seed. So *I* would go to garden centers, which is exciting. *You* can select from dozens of kinds and dream of big, red, ripe tomatoes.

See page H-5 in the Handbook.

Such unneeded shifts can be easily remedied by deleting each *you* and replacing it with an *I*. If you have this habit, beware of using *you* in academic writing except in process papers and business letters. Then use *you* correctly for a purpose.

Using Prescriptive Tone Appropriately

Just as a doctor prescribes medicine, a prescriptive writer offers advice, makes suggestions or requests, or issues a directive. Used appropriately, according to the rhetorical situation, prescriptive tone lends authority to a statement. Some prescriptive language is easily identified by the words *must, should, ought,* or *need.* Often such statements begin with an action verb because the subject is implied (*understood you*).

APPROPRIATE:

- **Business etiquette manual:** The boss, not the employee, *should* issue the first invitation to a lunch, dinner, or party.
- **Emergency:** [You] Call 911 now! (The subject is implied.)
- **Process paper:** First, [you] sand the surface and vacuum well.
- **Persuasive speech:** On the eve of the November election, *set* your alarm clock so that you have plenty of time to vote.

Yet prescription is sometimes unnecessary and undiplomatic. Inappropriate prescription can intrude, irritate, or inflame. As you read the examples below, think about each rhetorical situation and why prescription is inappropriate.

INAPPROPRIATE:

- **Order to roommate:** Next time be sure you lock the door!
- **Absolute generalization in a paper:** Setting goals *should* be a person's most important task in life.

Diplomatic Strategies

In a touchy situation, phrasing a statement as a question can soften the impact. Another effective tactic was shared by the most diplomatic director I have known. He uses three "magic" phrases to precede suggestions and advice: "I wonder if," "It might," or "You might try":

- *I wonder if* the battery could be low?
- It *might* be best to mow the lawn this morning; rain is predicted later.
- *You might try* waiting an hour and starting the engine one more time.

Note that two of the three statements do not include *you*. Using second person in ticklish situations can be unwise. If a person is testy or short-fused, you might try phrasing a suggestion or advice in third person with no reference to the individual. Or it might be wiser to say nothing at all.

PRACTICE

REWRITING SLANG, COLLOQUIALISMS, AND CONTRACTIONS

Directions: When you find slang, colloquialisms, or contractions below, rephrase the sentence into Professional English. If the sentence is already Professional English, mark with a C.

1. Tasha is looking to buy a riding horse.
2. Seeing as Milo has the lead in the senior play, he'll miss basketball tryouts.
3. Jaden's new car is really sweet.
4. Tara and Grace had a fun time at the flea market.
5. Yesterday Lance had a client who was a big headache.
6. In the employees' lounge are some awfully good cinnamon rolls.
7. That's a ballpark figure.
8. Connor made a lot of money on eBay selling flea market stuff.
9. I heard Owen and Faith got married last week.
10. Caleb was really mad when Maya started dating Liam.

LEVELS OF FORMALITY FOR DIFFERENT AUDIENCES (FOR GROUPS)

Directions: Read the case problems below. Then discuss which level of formality would be best for each audience. Cite reasons.

1. You are a newspaper reporter interviewing Colin Powell for a feature in the Sunday paper about his career. Which level of formality will you use?
2. You are a systems analyst, and your boss has assigned a systems project. He has asked for weekly memo reports. What level of formality will you use?
3. You are writing a cover letter to mail with your résumé. What level of formality will you use?
4. You are writing a television commercial for antifreeze. You want to appeal to everyone who drives a car, so you are featuring a mechanic at a local garage. Which level of formality will you use?
5. Imagine you are a physician writing an article that describes a new treatment for cancer. The article will appear in a medical journal that is read primarily by other doctors. What level of formality will you use?

Learning to Think Critically

Accuracy and Ethics

When CEOs of major corporations plead guilty to fraud, when well-known historians admit to plagiarism, and scams flood the Internet, one wonders what to believe. We live in an era in which propaganda, myth, and other misinformation often masquerade as truth. This climate of misinformation and moral relativism has influenced the programs and policies of our top business schools.

> Whatever is only almost true is quite false, and among the most dangerous of errors, because being so near truth, it is the more likely to lead astray.
>
> —Henry Ward Beecher (1813–1887)

Harvard offers a course entitled "Leadership, Governance, and Account-ability." The Columbia University Business School requires all students to take an ethics core curriculum. The Kelley School of Business at Indiana University created a twenty-page conduct code that follows corporate models, covering topics such as "cheating, fabrication, plagiarism, professional behavior with re-cruiters, and proper classroom manners." (*Wall Street Journal* 17 Sept. 2003: R9).

WHY ARE ACCURACY AND TRUTH IMPORTANT?

Regardless of your occupation, you need to know how to distinguish fact from inference and value judgment so that you can present yourself accurately on the job. If you will be working with patients, accuracy may mean the difference be-tween life and death. Inaccuracy and unethical conduct in other situations also pose risks to reputations and job security.

Chapter 3 lays the framework for critical thinking and writing from an eth-ical perspective. You will find guidelines and examples to help detect any over-statement, half-truths, or other misinformation in your own writing, as well as research material. (Chapter R-2 provides criteria for evaluating research mate-rial and Web sites.) But first, here are three excellent reasons for striving to be accurate and for maintaining high ethical standards.

Employers Expect the Truth

When you apply for your next job, you may be surprised by the questions aimed at your character—questions evaluating your values, principles, and ethics. Your résumé will be closely checked to uncover possible padding, exaggeration, or fabrication. Fingerprinting may be required and a thorough background check made. If any deviation from the truth is found, that is a prime reason for rejection.

Many recruiters say that they look for personal ethics and integrity in job candidates. Peter W. Schutz, former president and CEO of Porsche, AG has long advised: "Hire character. Train skill." Schutz is convinced that an employee's character greatly influences his or her work habits, reliability, and productivity (*Reader's Digest* May 2003).

An Audience Expects the Truth

Readers expect expository writing to be factual and reliable. They expect writ-ers to be knowledgeable, fair, and forthright. That includes *providing sources and using quotation marks to set off any material borrowed from someone else*. To copy someone else's writing and present it as your own is *plagiarism*.

See chapter R-4.

As writers, we are ethically obligated to check our facts and critically ex-amine our claims so that we provide accurate, up-to-date information. Whether you write college papers, reports, or letters, check to see that your writing is honest and reliable. Don't dance around the truth.

Truth Is the Cornerstone of Trust

When someone lies and those lies come to light, doubt and skepticism shatter trust. Throughout the ages, civilizations have accepted the basic premise that truth is the cornerstone of trust. Truth undergirds trust in business as well as social relationships. The handshake after a business transaction is a symbol of trust.

Businesses, partnerships, friendships, and marriages are built on truth and trust. Broken promises and contracts lead not only to ruptured relationships but also to legal problems and financial loss. Our courts take a firm stand on the need for truth in business and trade: Fraud, forgery, copyright infringement, slander, and other violations of truth are punishable by law.

SEARCHING FOR TRUTH

To present information accurately, a writer must separate established facts from various forms of opinion. This is not always easy because a statement may be a mixture of fact, theory, and faulty opinion. What is true in one instance may not be true in another.

www.mhhe.com/dietsch

For more help evaluating sources, go to: Research>Source Evaluation Tutor (CARS)

What Is an "Established Fact"?

An *established fact* is one that is observable or one that has been rigorously tested in other ways and finally accepted by most authorities in the field. We can observe firsthand and verify that certain conditions, creatures, or objects exist. Scientists in a laboratory can test to compare blood types, DNA, and other materials; they can repeat experiments by others to verify the results.

Surveys and polls, however, cannot be regarded as true for an entire population. They merely reveal what is true for the segment surveyed. Their results may or may not represent trends in the entire population, depending on the reliability and validity of the survey.

See "Surveys" in chapter R-5.

When you think something is probably true, consider whether or not it is an established fact. Can you verify it firsthand by seeing, hearing, smelling, tasting, or touching? Can you find reliable research or other evidence to *prove* it? If not, then it is still in the realm of theory or opinion. (A *theory* is an inference that may or may not be true; it has not been proved.)

Evidence Accepted as Fact in Court

The risk of perjury should keep witnesses truthful. Yet for honest witnesses there can still be problems in accuracy. Two eyewitnesses can disagree about the same event. Perhaps one did not see the entire event, or each interpreted it differently. Then too, recollections fade with time. Expert opinion seems to be reliable most of the time, but even experts disagree. Legally, fact is based on three types of evidence, sworn under oath:

1. Eyewitness reports
2. Expert opinion by an authority in the field
3. Material evidence (physical items that can be tested)

Without a doubt, material evidence is the most reliable of all. Hair, body fluids, DNA, fingerprints, voice prints, tire casts, and other materials can be carefully analyzed. Usually, the results are accurate, but once in a while human error does intrude. Even electronic devices are not foolproof. Temperature and other factors can hinder the performance of equipment, or someone may tamper with photographs, tapes, or other evidence. Determining what is true can be difficult.

Inferences Are Unproven

An *inference* is an assumption—an opinion—that is thought to be true but has not yet been proved. On a subzero morning, for example, a neighbor's car fails to start. This is the first time the engine has refused to budge. Since the gas gauge registers half full, he *infers* that the battery is weak. He calls a local service station for a quick charge. After that, the motor starts. A battery check reveals a faulty cell. Thus the inference has been proved to be a fact. Other inferences are tested and discredited.

As long as inferences are reasonable and not presented as facts, they seldom cause problems in writing. But sometimes beginning writers confuse inferences and facts, as in the following example about a hunting dog:

▶
> When his owner's red pickup truck approaches his pen, Buck realizes raccoon season must be here. During hunting season, his mind is strictly on tracking coon, but at other times his chief pleasure is chasing cats.

What are the problems here? First, dogs cannot understand the concept of "raccoon season" (although they might associate a truck with hunting). Second, the word *strictly* means 100 percent of the time, and it is doubtful that Buck thought about only one thing. Dogs are easily distracted by noises, other animals, and hunger pangs. The final statement—"his chief pleasure is chasing cats"—it is not an established fact but a value judgment. His chief pleasure might be eating.

Value Judgments and Point of View

Lew Wallace's familiar words, "Beauty is altogether in the eye of the beholder," point out the illusive nature of value judgments. Too often we regard our opinions as fact. Actually, they are perceptions, often influenced by emotion. Frequently, we assume other people have (or should have) the same values we cherish. Problems occur when value judgments masquerade as fact.

Value Judgment   A *value judgment* is an opinion about worth—an appraisal or evaluation. We often hear value judgments that rate appearance, skill, or value. Something may be labeled as plain or lovely, cute or garish, poor or excellent, worthless or valuable. Actions are deemed crude or refined, tactless or diplomatic, foolish or wise. Value judgments are imprecise and variable. These opinions can change with the times and differ from person to person or group to group, for example, political opinions.

But other types of value judgments stem from deep-seated beliefs about moral and religious values. These values influence what we consider good or bad, right or wrong, moral or immoral. They influence how we think, dress, and act, depending on the country, ethnic group, religious affiliation, political party, clan, or peer group. Deep-rooted values resist change. They influence group standards and individual points of view.

Point of View   The way someone perceives something is referred to as *point of view* or *perspective*. Both terms refer to either a way of thinking or to the physical angle from which an object is seen. Sinclair Lewis, in his early novel *Main Street,* describes two young women who see the town of Gopher Prairie through very different eyes. The impressions of Carol Kennicott, a city girl from Minneapolis, reveal her point of view:

> She glanced through the fly-specked windows of the most pretentious building in sight, the one place which welcomed strangers and determined their opinion of the charm and luxury of Gopher Prairie—the Minniemashie House. It was a tall lean shabby structure, three stories of yellow-streaked wood. . . . In the hotel office she could see a stretch of bare unclean floor, a line of rickety chairs with brass cuspidors. . . . The dining room beyond was a jungle of stained tablecloths and catsup bottles.

At the same time Bea Sorenson, "bored by farm work," walked along the other side of Main Street, thinking about the "excitements of city life" and the Minniemashie House. Her impression reveals very different judgments and a very different point of view:

> A hotel, awful high, higher than Oscar Tollefson's new red barn; three storied, one right on top of another; you had to stick your head back to look clear up to the top. There was a swell traveling man in there—probably been to Chicago lots of times.

Carol and Bea, coming from varying backgrounds, view the town differently. Later they make value judgments about Gopher Prairie, based on their points of view. Carol thinks: "I must be wrong. People do live here. It can't be as ugly as—as I know it is! I must be wrong." But Bea reasoned that even if she didn't receive a salary of six dollars every week, she would work for much less "to be allowed to stay here."

CHARACTERISTICS OF FACTS, INFERENCES, AND VALUE JUDGMENTS

Fact	Inference	Value Judgment
Act, deed, event, state or condition of reality	Assumption, generalization, or decision derived from evidence	Opinion or estimate of worth, an evaluation or rating
Objectively proved by observation, experiment, eyewitness, or expert opinion	Has not been proved; has possibility of being proved or discredited	Cannot be proved; will always be an opinion

Evaluating the Writer's Voice

Depending upon the rhetorical situation, the tone of a writer's voice may range from essentially *objective* to highly *subjective*. Some writing requires an impersonal voice that presents the facts squarely. The front pages of many U.S. newspapers, for example, carry factual reports in which writers attempt to relay news stories objectively. The purpose is to report what happened—not to push a particular view. The voice of objective writing is impartial—unslanted and unbiased. Readers seldom get a sense of the writer's opinion or personality.

In contrast, the purpose of editorial pages is to allow writers to express their individual points of view and opinions. In editorials, columns, and letters to the editor, writers interpret facts subjectively, based on their own political, ethical, and economic values. They offer opinions and judgments; they praise and criticize; they urge specific courses of action. Their written voices may carry conviction, indignation, anger, amusement, or appreciation.

A degree of subjectivity is inevitable in almost any writing, but it should be controlled and appropriate. Reading your draft aloud will help you to listen to your written voice and judge its impartiality.

WRITING TIP   Read your draft aloud and listen to your written voice. Does it sound calm and reasonable? Biased or impartial? A degree of subjectivity is inevitable in almost any writing, but it should be controlled and appropriate for the situation.

FOUR WAYS MISINFORMATION ARISES

As we grow up, we hear folk wisdom, propaganda, myths, superstitions, and other inaccuracies presented as fact. Steeped in these beliefs, we tend not to question them, and so we accumulate much misinformation without realizing it. Here are four ways misinformation commonly comes to be accepted as fact.

Expert Opinion Occasionally Changes

We all know that one should not swim for an hour after eating—or do we? This bit of advice was published by the American Red Cross over fifty years ago. A lifesaving manual claimed that a swimmer who ate immediately before a dip risked stomach cramps or even death. Now the *Journal of Health, Physical Education, and Recreation* disputes the idea of "stomach cramps." A prominent physical educator was quoted as saying that he had never seen a case of such stomach cramps, although he had seen thousands of persons swimming soon after meals. Medical opinions as well as other expert opinions sometimes change over the years.

A Small Survey Is Inadequate Proof

Sometimes we hear someone generalize after surveying a few friends or considering a few unusual incidents. It's the old story of "everyone else is getting a new prom dress but me." But a small sample is hardly a reliable survey (see chapter R-5).

Overstatement, stereotypic thinking, and generalizing from an unrepresentative sample can lead to the fallacy of hasty generalization. A *hasty generalization* is a broad statement, an inference, that lacks sufficient proof. A hasty generalization can occur when a *trend* or a *tendency* is overstated as if it were true for an entire group or population. Although assumed to be true, a hasty generalization is not an established fact. (This fallacy and others are explained in chapter 16.)

Facts Are Misstated or Overstated

Unintentional misstatement or overstatement sometimes occurs. We may not recall exactly what we read or heard. Or we may paraphrase, using synonyms that give an impression different from the one we intended. And some people exaggerate without being aware of it. For example, the student who wrote the following paragraph was convinced it was absolutely true:

> Lack of participation by the American people in their government is the number one cause for their loss of control over their own affairs. They say: "I don't care." "My vote doesn't matter." "I didn't have time to vote." These are some of the excuses given for not carrying out one of the most important rights given to the people, the right to vote.

Here a partial truth has been stretched ("number one cause"). This so-called statistic is not an established fact. The writer could have made the statement acceptable by adding one word: *possibly.*

Stereotyping Shuts Out Fact

A writer must be on guard against stereotypes based on gender, race/ethnicity, sexual orientation, age, religion, and the like. Stereotyping is pigeonholing, classifying someone or something, into a tight little box. A stereotypic belief supposedly typifies a group, place, issue, or event. Although the characteristic attributed to the group may be true for some individuals, it is not true for all. Consider the following statements carefully. Then mark each one true or false.

_____   1. Redheads have quick tempers.

_____   2. Men are stronger than women.

_____   3. Politicians can't be trusted.

If you marked all of the statements true, you have probably grown up hearing these stereotypes presented as fact. If you marked some false, you are to be congratulated on your growing skepticism. If you marked all false, you rate an A. Why are all three statements false? None allows for an exception. These statements are *absolute* or all-inclusive: they claim to apply 100 percent of the time. Think about it. Do *all* redheads in the world have quick tempers? Are *all* men stronger than *all* women? Isn't there even one politician who can be trusted? To further complicate matters, item 2 contains an *undefined term*. What kind of strength are we talking about—physical, emotional, intellectual, or spiritual?

Experienced speakers and writers avoid stereotypic thinking, for it is not only unfair and undiplomatic but also inaccurate. Stereotypes shut out new information that conflicts with old, embedded beliefs. Stereotypic thinking is a quagmire that can lead to charges of sexism and discrimination as well as hurt feelings.

WRITING RESPONSIBLY

Responsible writing presents the truth, and responsible claims are backed by adequate evidence. Readers should not have to grope through a fog of unsupported statements to determine the facts. Once you become aware of the slipperiness of fact, you can take three precautions to avoid misstatement: Limit your generalizations, use absolute terms accurately, and identify inferences and opinion.

Limiting Unsound Generalizations

To be accurate and useful in writing, generalizations must be factual. If they are overstated and too broad, they undermine your credibility. Thus you need to limit, or "qualify." *Qualifiers* are words or phrases that modify meanings and allow for exceptions. Qualified generalizations often serve as topic sentences and thesis statements. The generalizations below were used successfully as thesis sentences in student essays. (Qualifiers are italicized.)

- *Some* outstanding women have graced history with their heroic feats during battle.
- In today's hurried pace, the giving and receiving of love is *often* overlooked.
- Crash dieting *seems* to be the surefire approach to coping with obesity.

To limit an overly broad generalization for which you lack evidence, you may need a verb that indicates flexibility, such as *may, might, tend, seem,* or *appear.* Other qualifiers refer to indefinite numbers, such as a majority or a minority. Consider which one you are referring to, and state the indefinite number in an acceptable manner without overstatement.

Without thinking, it is easy to overstate. If in doubt, check a dictionary for fine distinctions in meaning. To indicate a *majority,* select a term that means *over 50 percent,* similar to those listed below:

most	largely	routinely	as a rule	principally
mostly	primarily	typically	generally	essentially
chiefly	mainly	usually	normally	ordinarily

To indicate a *minority* (less than 50 percent), use words that are less specific than those referring to a majority. Note, too, that the size of a minority can vary and influence word choice. For example, there is a big difference between *a few* and *many.*

WORDS TO INDICATE A MAJORITY OR A MINORITY

Small Minority		**Large Minority**	
rarely	relatively few	many	often
few	seldom	frequently	numerous
some	sometimes	oftentimes	countless
occasionally	several	profusion	plentiful

Using Absolute Terms Accurately

Absolute terms are inflexible words that state or imply *none* or *all.* These words mean zero or 100 percent. When you revise, examine every statement that contains an absolute term. Be sure you consider what the word means, not just what you intend. If you overstate a case by misusing an absolute, the reader will be apt to take the literal meaning unless you plant a clue that the statement is ironic or joking. The list below will help you recognize absolute terms:

all	always	everyone	no one
none	never	only	same
every	completely	exact	anything

Some verbs and adjectives are also precise and all-inclusive. Unless you have the evidence to support a hard-and-fast statement, look for an accurate alternative wording. When using the following words, think carefully, for they can lead to overstatement and misstatement:

DEFINITE	IDENTICAL	ONE OF A KIND	
is	exact	unique*	greatest
are	same	biggest	smallest
was	perfect*	worst	best

*There are no degrees of uniqueness or perfection. Something is either unique or not unique; perfect or imperfect. Phrases such as *very unique* or *very perfect* are incorrect. If in doubt about such usage, check a dictionary or style guide.

PEANUTS reprinted by permission of United Feature Syndicate, Inc.

Identifying Inferences and Other Opinions

In workplace writing and college assignments, you may be asked to "draw a conclusion" (an inference) from a set of facts, to "write a reaction" (see chapter 20), or to "interpret facts." To complete such assignments successfully, you need to know how to identify inferences and other types of opinion. Qualifiers like those below indicate inferences:

theory	seems	probably	apparently
conjecture	imply	possibly	suggests
indicate	infer	evidently	it appears

As you revise, check to see that no opinions are presented as facts. For example, a widely held belief that is unproved should be identified as opinion. Phrases such as "a common belief" or "the conventional wisdom" indicate the tentative nature of such statements. Other terms that identify opinion include the following:

current thinking	viewpoint	reaction	perception
appraisal	impression	feeling	folk wisdom
point of view	estimate	prediction	view

REVISING FOR ACCURACY

Whether you write a report, an essay, a research paper, or some other document, double-check every item to be sure it is logical and accurate. In the flurry of pinning down ideas during prewriting and drafting, it is easy to leave out a word, transpose a number, overstate a generalization, or commit some other blunder. Develop the habit of being thorough, of questioning information that doesn't quite ring true or seems suspicious. The following checklist should be helpful.

CHECKLIST   REVISING FOR ACCURACY

1. Are all data established facts?

2. Have inferences, value judgments, and other opinions been qualified?

3. Do any generalizations need to be limited?

4. Are all words accurate?

5. Does the tone sound appropriate?

6. Have any significant facts been omitted? Are any more needed?

Only when we learn to think logically and critically—to analyze carefully our own ideas as well as the ideas of other speakers and writers—can we begin to approach "the whole truth." That is what the writing process is all about.

FOR YOUR REFERENCE
Accuracy, Ethics, and Guidelines

- "Detecting Fallacies," chapter 16
- "Examining Cause and Effect," chapter 17
- "Constructing a Convincing Argument," chapter 19
- Compiling a résumé: see chapter 26
- Criteria for evaluating sources and Web sites: see chapter R-2
- Preventing plagiarism: see chapters R-1, R-3, and R-4

PRACTICE

FACT, INFERENCE, OR VALUE JUDGMENT?

Directions: Mark each item as fact (F), inference (I), or value judgment (VJ). If both fact and inference, mark I; if both fact and value judgment, mark VJ. Discuss any disagreement.

_____ 1. Great Britain is an island, not a continent.

_____ 2. Many exquisite bays line Britain's coast.

_____ 3. The beautiful white cliffs of Dover, overlooking the English Channel, are composed of chalk.

_____ 4. The Isle of Man lies in the Irish Sea.

_____ 5. If you mention hunting to a Brit, he or she will immediately think of fox hunting.

_____ 6. Most Americans are surprised to learn that a subway in London is an underground passageway for pedestrians.

_____ 7. If you want a delicious meal in London, order fish, not steak.

_____ 8. The Tower of London is the most fabulous sight in the city.

_____ 9. In the spring after a rain, Paris has a delicate, shimmering beauty.

_____ 10. The Louvre, the largest art museum and palace in the world, is located on the north bank of the River Seine in Paris.

Discovering and Developing Ideas

CHAPTER 4

I. PREWRITING STRATEGIES

Mystery novelist Agatha Christie often paused while washing dishes to jot down ideas for a story. The beauty of prewriting is that you can capture ideas however you like—on paper, at a keyboard, or with a tape recorder or other device. The purpose is simply to pin down ideas before they flit away.

> Most productive writers share the feeling that the first draft (and most . . . that follow) is an opportunity to discover what they have to say and how they can best say it.
>
> **Donald Murray, "The Maker's Eye: Revising Your Own Manuscript"**

The first stage of the writing process is a time of discovery—you search for wisps of ideas. Prewriting can condense swirling thoughts into words. Prewriting can help you find a topic or narrow a broad topic. In this first stage of writing, there is no need to think about order or correctness. To find out which prewriting strategy works best for you, you might try all five. Some students like to freewrite.

www.mhhe.com/dietsch

For online information about prewriting, visit: Writing>Prewriting

FREEWRITING

Freewriting, uncensored writing in fragments or sentences, is a good way to find a topic and details. Just turn off your internal editor and jot down ideas. To save time, set a timer for ten minutes. When it rings, stop, examine your catch, and develop whatever seems promising. Here is an example:

> ▶ What to write? There's so much debris in my mind. Clutter. What is signifi-
> cant? Let's see. Life is significant—very much so. Yet some individuals toss it
> away so lightly. Just last week two young guys carried out a suicide pact. They
> were drinking and doing drugs. A bartender heard them planning but didn't
> tell anyone. Thought they were just talking—old saying, you know, those who
> talk won't. But they often do. How sad. They jump into eternity without a
> parachute, not knowing where they will land.

This freewriting sample has unearthed three general topics: the value of life, suicide, and the possibility of life after death. The writer might take one of these topics as the subject for a second round of freewriting or *focused freewriting.* During a second round, the writer freewrites about one topic.

BRAINSTORMING

Brainstorming is often used to create new products, improve existing ones, or solve problems. By brainstorming for a class paper, you can find a topic, narrow it, and discover details to develop it. You might start by listing possible topics then jotting down ways to narrow or to branch off. For a group, using a chalkboard is helpful to record ideas and trigger more. *The secret of successful brainstorming is to think fast and forgo criticism.* All ideas are respected, no matter how wild. Remarks such as "That won't work" dampen enthusiasm and dam the stream of ideas.

WATER GARDENS

half barrels	landscaping a small pond	choosing fish and snails
molded ponds	selecting water plants	preventing algae
dig your own	building a waterfall	cost of materials
amount of labor	installing a fountain	legal liability

CLUSTERING

Clustering, devised by Gabriele Rico, is uncensored brainstorming combined with doodling. To begin, take a fresh sheet of paper and write a general subject in the center. Then circle the word. As each new thought bursts forth, jot it near the word that prompted it. Circle the new word. Next, draw a line between the two. Repeat the procedure. The sample cluster (fig. 4.1) began with the subject of birds. The central idea branched out, leading to the specific topic of birdwatching.

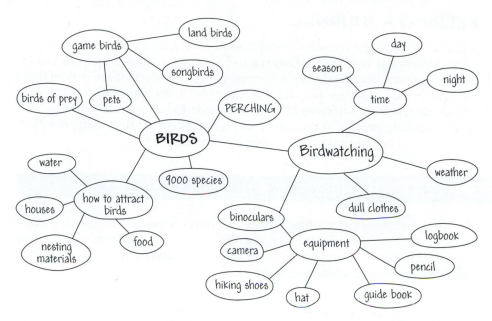

FIGURE 4.1 Clustering.

QUESTIONING

By questioning and thoughtful reflection, you can take notes on a significant incident or event and transform them into an essay. You might try projecting yourself into the role of a reporter. What questions could you ask other people? Or you might ask yourself: "How did this event influence me? What did I learn?" Questions like these can prod your thinking toward a meaningful conclusion. Whenever your writing stalls, ask more questions to restart the flow of details. The traditional "five Ws and an H" (who? what? when? where? why? how?) can be expanded to full-fledged questions:

- Who was involved?
- What happened?
- When did it happen? Where?
- How did it happen? Why?
- What can be learned?
- What is the subject like or unlike?
- How has it changed over time?

KEEPING A JOURNAL

A journal is useful for recording incidents, observations, impressions, and reactions. A journal is similar to a diary but includes more details. A journal can include anecdotes, quotations, funny stories, poems, or speculation. Any of these may jump-start ideas for writing. For example, a student who worked in a restaurant researched nonverbal communication for a report. By smiling and lightly touching patrons as she served them, she found her tips nearly doubled. Daily notes in her journal made writing the report easy.

II. DRAFTING STRATEGIES

www.mhhe.com/dietsch

For more coverage of drafting, go to:
Writing>Drafting and Revising

The second stage of the writing process, drafting, is the time to develop ideas and start thinking about focus and order. With each new draft, you will discover more details the reader might desire to know. You can begin by scanning your prewriting notes and selecting core ideas.

FLESHING OUT PREWRITING NOTES

Start writing wherever you wish—beginning, middle, or end of your draft. There is no need to worry about a thesis statement, transitions, or other concerns just now. Don't stop to correct errors or do anything that will disrupt your concentration. Just keep writing!

Turn Off Your Internal Censor

Let ideas sprawl over the page in any fashion that seems comfortable to you. Don't worry if your first draft wanders into byways. Unnecessary details and mistakes may litter the path of your main idea. That's fine, since this draft is for your eyes only. You can rearrange and delete later. If your inner censor will not allow you free rein, then circle suspicious spellings or mark questionable words. If a word or idea eludes you, just draw a short line and keep on writing. Carefree, you will be more apt to experience the fun of discovering what you know as you write.

When Ideas Disappear

As you roam the hills and valleys of your memory, collecting bits of experience (incidents, anecdotes, examples, and other specific details) for your exploratory draft, sometimes there is little to find. That may be the time to stop and take a short exercise break. Refreshed, you can return and restart. To refocus and find more material, try asking yourself:

- What might readers like to know?
- How might readers feel about the topic?

- How do I feel about the topic? Why?
- What else needs to be said?

FOCUSING AN EXPLORATORY DRAFT

Some writers do much of their prewriting and drafting mentally before they ever start to write. They have a distinct sense of purpose and audience, which enables them to focus their exploratory draft surprisingly well. A clear central idea unifies the material so that it progresses in a logical way and fulfills the purpose. Other writers know the general topic but circle aimlessly around it, unsure of the central point they will make. Pausing to limit the topic and write a thesis statement, however, can establish a direction for writing.

Limiting a Topic

To narrow a topic, focus on a part that you can develop well. Write more about less. To be manageable, a topic should be whittled down to fit the assignment and the rhetorical situation. The pyramid below shows how a very broad topic (top of the pyramid) can be limited.

Ohio

touring Ohio

touring the Ohio River

steamboats on the Ohio River

my steamboat ride on the Ohio River

Writing a Purpose Statement

When you have your topic clearly in mind and can state your purpose, that will save time in drafting. A purpose statement directs the flow of thought and provides the foundation for your thesis statement. First, jot down a brief description of your readers. This step will help to clarify your approach to the topic and the perspective you will take, as in these examples:

- **Audience for a letter to the editor:** Readers of the local paper who have never ridden a steamboat on the Ohio River.
- **Audience for a paper on litter control:** Voters who are concerned about the numerous cans and bottles littering city streets, roads, and highways.

Next start drafting a purpose statement. There are just two basic parts—the general purpose (italicized) and the specific purpose:

- **Purpose:** To *inform* readers about the scenic beauty of the Ohio River, the convenience of a steamboat trip, and the reasonable cost.
- **Purpose:** To *persuade* readers to vote for a bill requiring deposits on and recycling of all beverage cans and glass bottles.

CASE STUDY

NITA LIMITS HER TOPIC

Over the years Nita Jones has read about solar energy, but she wonders about recent discoveries. She suspects that her general readers are also hazy about the topic and may not care. She asks several classmates and verifies both inferences. How can she interest them? How might they benefit from reading about solar energy? She writes her questions and starts a list to narrow the topic.

Question: How might readers benefit by learning more about solar energy?
Limiting: general to specific

solar energy
practical applications for solar energy
solar heating for homes
solar heating during construction of new homes
solar heating for existing homes

As Nita reviews her list, she realizes that every reader is a potential home owner. At first she considers discussing applications for new home construction, but then she thinks about budget constraints. Few of her readers will be building their first home. Most will buy older homes and repair or remodel them. At this point, she briefly describes her audience and writes a purpose statement. Later she converts it into a thesis statement.

- **Audience:** College students who are potential buyers of existing homes and who are interested in comfort at a reasonable cost
- **Purpose:** To inform the reader of solar heating applications for existing homes and to evaluate practicality
- **Thesis statement:** Solar heating installations can reduce fuel bills and improve the value of an older home [states two advantages].

Drafting a Thesis Statement

The sooner you can write a tentative thesis statement, the fewer drafts you are apt to need. By pondering your purpose statement, you can convert it into your thesis, which states the main idea of the paper. A thesis can be expressed in just one sentence, or it may extend over several sentences. A thesis statement performs four specific functions:

FOUR FUNCTIONS OF A THESIS STATEMENT

1. Identify the subject.
2. State a claim, an approach, or an attitude.
3. Suggest the direction of the writing.
4. Set the tone.

www.mhhe.com/dietsch
For additional help writing your thesis statement, visit:
Writing>Thesis

Thesis statements come in all shapes and sizes. Throughout this book you will find various kinds and lengths. In the case study above, Nita cites two benefits. Michele Flahive's thesis below contains three aspects of the topic to be discussed:

Thesis: For the dedicated player, the challenge, the enjoyment, and the camaraderie make softball a game worth playing.

Topic: Playing softball

Claim: For the dedicated player, softball is worth playing.

Direction: The focus is on three main points—challenge, enjoyment, and camaraderie—in that order.

Tone: Middle level of formality

Positioning the Thesis Statement   Usually, the thesis statement is placed in the introduction of short papers. Sometimes it appears in the first sentence, but more often it is at the end of the opening paragraph. There it can forge a tight link to later paragraphs. In research or other long papers, the introduction may contain two or more paragraphs. In that case, the thesis sentence generally appears at the end of the introduction.

The three-part thesis statement is an easy way to start drafting. This basic thesis states the main points (usually three) in the order to be discussed. To start, just make a list and fill in the blanks below:

Topic: _____

Main points: _____

_____

_____

Thesis statement: _____

_____

DRAFTING A BASIC THESIS STATEMENT

FOR PRACTICE

First, choose a topic that can be divided into parts. For example, "Three reasons I chose _____ college/university." Write the topic in the top blank above. Second, think of reasons or aspects of the topic that will become main points. Arrange the points in least-to-most-important order. Third, condense and combine the items to make a complete sentence. This tentative thesis can help you make a scratch outline to organize a first draft.

Omitting a Thesis Statement   Some kinds of writing have a thesis that is never specified but is clearly implied. The omission is not a lapse. Careful planning and considerable skill are required to keep the controlling idea apparent without stating it openly. Omission of a thesis sentence is hazardous for a budding writer, especially for the kinds of writing often done in college. Most instructors expect an explicit thesis.

Dozens of different kinds of thesis statements appear in parts 2, 3, 4, and 5 of this book. You can find examples and explanations within the chapters as well as in the sample student papers.

Starting a Scratch Outline

www.mhhe.com/dietsch

For more coverage of outlines and outlining, go to: Writing>Outlines

A brief outline will help you focus your essay and save time. To start the outline, jot down your audience at the top of your screen (or paper). Then place your thesis statement next. Now scan your draft for clues to check the order needed. Perhaps an order of importance is unsuitable. For example, to explain a procedure or process, you will need to arrange the steps in chronological order. Or perhaps one of the other seven orders, explained below, would be best.

SCRATCH OUTLINE FOR A PROCEDURE OR PROCESS

> *Audience:* Someone who has never used varnish or achieved satisfactory results from refinishing furniture.
>
> *Introduction:* To achieve a satisfactory result when varnishing, you need to take much more care than when painting. Therefore, read and follow these instructions carefully.
>
> *Body:* (Chronological order)
>
> 1. Buy a new brush that will not lose bristles to apply the varnish. Old brushes, even though cleaned, still contain flecks of dried varnish that will loosen and leave bumps on the treated surface.
> 2. Remove the old finish and let dry or start with a new surface.
> 3. Sand the surface with various grades of sandpaper until very smooth.
> 4. Clean the surface thoroughly, then vacuum. Wipe with a rag moistened with turpentine. Let dry a few minutes.
> 5. Stir the varnish well with a new stir stick.
>
>   (Other steps omitted here.)
>
> *Conclusion:* (Mention benefits or make another appropriate comment.)

SEVEN BASIC WAYS TO ORGANIZE A DRAFT

To be clear, every completed manuscript needs a logical order. As you sort through your prewriting notes and write your first draft, watch for a dominant order to emerge. Look closely at the transitions you have included. Do they refer to time? To location? To cause and effect? Are some points more important than others? Or does your thesis statement contain a clue to a suitable order? Seven basic orders are commonly used and sometimes combined.

1. **Chronological order** (time): chronological/reverse chronological
2. **Spatial order** (space): organized by layout, design, direction, or location
3. **Order of importance:** least to most/most to least
4. **Order of generality:** general to specific/specific to general
5. **Order of formation:** whole to parts/parts to whole
6. **Order of complexity:** simple to complex/familiar to unfamiliar
7. **Order of materiality:** concrete to abstract/abstract to concrete

THE SEVEN BASIC ORDERS

Chronological Order

When dates or events are placed in a natural sequence according to *time*, this arrangement is known as *chronological order.* In process analysis you arrange the steps or stages chronologically (1, 2, 3, etc.). In a research paper, you may combine chronological order with other orders. Narratives usually move forward in chronological order, but not always. A sidewise shift in time may be indicated by transitions such as "meanwhile" or "at the same time."

Résumés are usually organized in *reverse chronological order.* This arrangement presents the most recent experience first, then goes backward, ending with the earliest.

Spatial Order

Organizing details according to location, layout, design, or direction is referred to as *spatial* order. For example, property descriptions use spatial order. In the essay "Through a Child's Eyes," the student writer describes her father, beginning with his head and moving down to his lap (see pages 84–85). Any of the following spatial orders (or their reverse) might be used in description:

head to toe	outside to inside	clockwise
bottom to top	north to south	circular
left to right	up and down	horizontal

Order of Importance

Newspaper articles typically use *most- to least-important* order, leaving the least important details until last. Editors know that readers often read only the first few paragraphs of an article or only the front page section. For other writing, *least- to most-important* order is often used. This order places the emphasis on the final point. You might use least- to most-important order in essays of division, classification, illustration, or argument.

Order of Generality

The order of generality can be effective to inform or to convince. You can begin or end with an observation, generalization, or basic principle, depending on the rhetorical situation. To use the *general-to-specific* (deductive) order, begin with the (general) basic premise, then supply enough specific details to support it. For example, a student wrote, "The magic of a carousel has a way of turning men and women into children again." Then she presented specific details to support her observation.

If the reader will need to be convinced, you can reverse the order to *specific to general*. This *inductive* order is often used in argument; the evidence is presented before the conclusion.

Order of Formation

The order of formation may be used in two ways: *whole to parts* or *parts to whole*. In problem solving, the whole-to-parts arrangement works well. You can present an overview of the topic before covering all significant alternatives, angles, or parts. You begin with a summary of a problem or an issue, then move on to look at the individual factors or aspects. In a basic argument, the whole-to-parts order is often used to describe the issue, followed by inductive reasoning (see chapter 18).

The whole-to-parts order can also be used to explain less complicated topics. For example, a student described an old rocking chair, starting with the general appearance and then going to the parts. He created an image of the old chair before explaining how it functioned in the life of his family. In some writing situations, this order can be reversed to move from the parts to the whole.

Order of Complexity

To explain a complex topic, you can use *the simple to the complex order* or *the familiar to unfamiliar order*. By starting with what readers already know and accept, you can orient them and establish rapport. Then they will be more comfortable and willing to explore the complex or the unfamiliar. If you were to begin with a difficult concept or highly technical material, some readers might refuse to read further.

Order of Materiality

To simplify a description, you can use *the concrete to the abstract order* to arrange core details. Other times you might use *the abstract to the concrete*. Concrete words refer to actual physical data about a condition, event, experience, object, animal, or person. Through our five senses, we can perceive evidence of these elements. Most of us are able to see, hear, touch, taste, and smell to obtain first-hand proof that concrete items exist. For example, tears are concrete—we can see them, feel them, even taste them. Sometimes tears indicate sadness, but sadness is an abstraction.

Abstract refers to ideas that have no physical referent; nothing material can prove they exist. We can think and talk about abstractions, but we *cannot* see, hear, taste, touch, or smell them. For example, patriotism, love, and integrity are all abstractions. The only way that we can infer they exist is to look for *concrete* evidence that *implies* their existence. Jeannine Caudill uses *abstract-to-concrete* order in "Mother Love."

Writers of description often move from the concrete to the abstract, presenting physical details about a subject before the symbolism. For example, you might briefly describe the Statue of Liberty before explaining its symbolic significance. For an essay of definition, you might use the reverse order, abstract to concrete. Then you would introduce an abstract concept, such as friendship or bravery, followed by concrete instances and examples.

DRAFTING AN INTRODUCTION

An effective introduction affords a graceful entry into a topic. Whether you draft your introduction first or last, make the first sentence notable. To arouse curiosity, cite an intriguing quotation, a striking statistic, or other novelty to lure the reader on. A wide array of introductions appear later in this book; here is a preview of five basic types.

> **www.mhhe.com/dietsch**
> For online help writing introductions, go to:
> Writing>Introductions

Setting the Scene with an Anecdote

An *anecdote,* or a brief narrative, can spark interest and set the scene. Telling *when* and *where* the experience happened will orient readers. Just a few carefully chosen details can give a sense of time and place:

My Worst Job

When I was sixteen, my cousin suggested I take a job where she worked. Because she liked the people and the wages, I hired on. The sight and sounds were overwhelming. Rows and rows of sewing machines whirred while hundreds of women worked at a furious pace. Finding an empty chair, the trainer demonstrated how to operate the machine and sew a facing on the bodice of a cotton dress. Since I had made my own clothes for years, the task was simple. Outwardly, the power sewing machines resembled the old Singer at home. But the motor was as much like my old machine's as a Mercedes' is like a Model T's. Careening around the curves, I hung onto the cloth and somehow guided it under the presser foot. By lunch time, however, I had mastered the machine and the two-minute task. Day after day for an interminable week, I repeated that mind-numbing procedure.

Overuse of the Pronoun *I*   Overemphasis on self can create wordiness and distract from the main idea. If your draft starts with *I*, you might move an adverb or prepositional phrase up front. Just one word, such as *yesterday, although,*

> **www.mhhe.com/dietsch**
> For more work with pronouns, go to:
> Editing>Pronouns

or *while*, will provide a smoother opening than a reference to self. Or you might invert the sentence, placing a phrase or clause before the main parts of the sentence.

OPENING WORDS TO SET THE SCENE

References to Time	References to Place
Five years ago I . . .	From my front window, I . . .
In 1999, I . . .	While working as assistant manager, I . . .
After I graduated	On Kelly's Island

WRITING SUCCESS TIP: THINK TWICE BEFORE OPENING WITH "I"

Using *I* as the first word focuses on the writer, not the reader, and can make writing sound amateurish. For example, a well-planned application letter for employment focuses on what the writer can do for the company. If, however, most sentences start with *I*, the interviewer may conclude that a supersize ego is not what the company needs.

Describing an Action or Event

Plunging the reader amid the action or a conversation will grab attention. At the same time, you can also impart vital details to give a sense of the setting. Notice how Kenny Patrick uses action verbs to describe how a fly fisherman carefully casts his bait. Then with vivid words he explains his fascination for the sport:

Hooked on a Tradition

Icy water swirls around the wading fly fisherman. With experience gained from thousands of casts, he deposits the tiny brown deer hair fly directly beneath an overhanging branch at the water's edge. His pulse quickens as he gently twitches the tip of the rod. Like a living being, the tiny fly dances across the surface.

Stating a Problem

Stating a problem can be a practical way to open. The purpose of Janet Edington's paper was to inform pet owners of ways to enhance the safety of animals when transporting them to the vet:

Safety First!

Pet owners are frequently faced with the challenge of transporting their animal friends to the veterinarian. This task can be not only nerve-wracking, but also hazardous, particularly if they are transporting a nervous cat or a large animal. In an automobile, an even-tempered pet can swiftly turn into a frightened, hostile enemy. The following suggestions are offered to spare anyone the battle scars I carry today.

Citing a Surprising Statistic or Striking Bit of History

You may be able to spur a reader's curiosity by opening with a surprising statistic or striking bit of history. The purpose of Kathy Cordle's paper was to inform classmates of a way, which worked for her, to stop smoking:

Kicking the Habit

Concern about the hazards of tobacco is not new. In 1604 King James I of England officially condemned the use of tobacco. An 1859 report about the dangers of tobacco stated that of the sixty-eight persons suffering from cancer of the mouth and throat in a hospital in Montpelier, France, all were tobacco users. In the United States during the early 1900s, admonitions such as "Don't smoke, or it will stunt your growth" and "Now that you are expecting, you'll have to lay off smoking" were common.

Disputing a Common Belief or Defying a Stereotype

The writer who surprises readers with a statement that disputes a common belief or an example that defies a stereotype will grab their attention. In the next paragraph, Paul Giacalone's purpose was to entertain his classmates. He begins by expressing a view that runs counter to the conventional notion that everyone should love the family dog. His offbeat perspective and critically amused tone surprises readers and hooks their curiosity.

The Trials of Tia

Recently my father brought home a very small and very ignorant animal. My parents named it Tia, and they have tried to convince me that it is a dog— I swear it is a rat. Actually, Tia is half rat terrier and half poodle—a strange-looking animal that has not been easy to train. Therein lies the nub of the problem.

WRITING AN EFFECTIVE CONCLUSION

An effective ending flows logically and smoothly from the body, giving a sense of completeness or *closure.* Such an ending seems appropriate for the purpose, the reader, and the topic. It does not rehash opinions or recite the obvious. No new material intrudes. Personal essays often end by sharing how the experience or event influenced the writer—the effect it had upon the inner self. Five basic ways to conclude are described here.

www.mhhe.com/dietsch
For online help writing conclusions, go to:
Writing>Conclusions

Referring to the Thesis

To provide a sense of completeness, writers often refer briefly to the thesis. Notice that this device is an allusion, *not* a repetition of the entire thesis. By reworking an old cliché and repeating key points, Nora Lee Corbett establishes *closure:*

- **Thesis:** We raise leghorn laying hens for their hardiness, longevity, and egg production.
- **Conclusion:** On our farm the chicken comes before the egg. And we have learned over the years that the best chicken according to hardiness, longevity, and egg production is the leghorn.

Ending with a Personal Response

Sometimes writers explain how an event affected them and confide in the reader. They may share feelings of sadness, embarrassment, satisfaction, elation, or another response, especially at the end of the piece. The student who described her "worst job" concluded this way:

> After a week of repeating the same deadly dull, two-minute procedure, my hands guided the cloth under the pressure foot automatically. But my mind was in limbo—I knew I could not continue unless I underwent a lobotomy. So at quitting time on Friday evening, I picked up my paycheck, inhaled the fresh air of freedom, and left with a light heart, knowing I would never go back.

Ending on a Note of Optimism

Adding a note of optimism can create a satisfying conclusion. The note might be one of encouragement to yourself or to the reader, or it might be a look toward the future. Kathy Cordle concluded "Kicking the Habit" with a congratulatory note to herself:

> Since November 7, I have not had one cigarette. Yes, there are times when I still want one, and I am struggling to drop those extra pounds, accumulated from eating all that candy, but I feel really good about myself. I am a winner!

Citing a Benefit

Sales letters often summarize the benefits, advantages, and value of a product or a plan. A college paper may conclude in a similar way. In ending her paper, Diane Zachman pointed out the benefits of a good manicure:

> The process of manicuring, when done correctly, gives your nails a vibrant, healthy appearance and keeps them from becoming weak and brittle.

Ending with an Unexpected Twist

A conclusion that creeps up on readers, catching them off guard, can surprise and delight. When well done, such an ending seems spontaneous and appropriate. A brief comment or fact can pose an absurdity or profundity that causes the reader to smile or think. Paul Giacalone ended with a twist in his paper about his parents' dog Tia:

> I feel the only solution to this problem is either I go or the dog goes. After I discussed this with my parents, they went out and bought me a set of luggage for Christmas.

Although a twist may be appropriate for personal writing, it is rarely appropriate for business writing. Customers, employees, and managers need to know what to expect and need to understand the writer's purpose early.

SELECTING A TITLE

If the muse smiles, you'll easily devise a clever title that is just right for your essay. But many of us have to wait until a draft is finished before settling on a title. The primary requirement is relevance to the central idea. A title should give at least a hint of what is to come and arouse the interest of the reader.

Some titles are specific, such as "The Myth of the Latin Woman." Others are more elusive and tantalizing, such as "Caterpillar Afternoon." Still others appeal to a need for information, as does "Write Your Own Success Story." These and other titles of essays in the Reader present a range of interesting approaches. To gain ideas, read some of these essays by professional writers.

PRACTICE

FREEWRITING TO FIND TOPICS

Directions: You might freewrite by beginning with one of the following phrases, or you might draft an essay based on item 8, 9, or 10:

1. I wish . . .
2. I wonder . . .
3. Tomorrow . . .
4. I can't . . . but I can . . .
5. Once I . . . but now . . .
6. When I see . . . , I remember . . .
7. My job is . . .
8. Describe your worst mistake. What have you learned from it?
9. What would you most like to do? How might you do it?
10. Sketch a career plan. What training or education will you need?

Revision Workshop

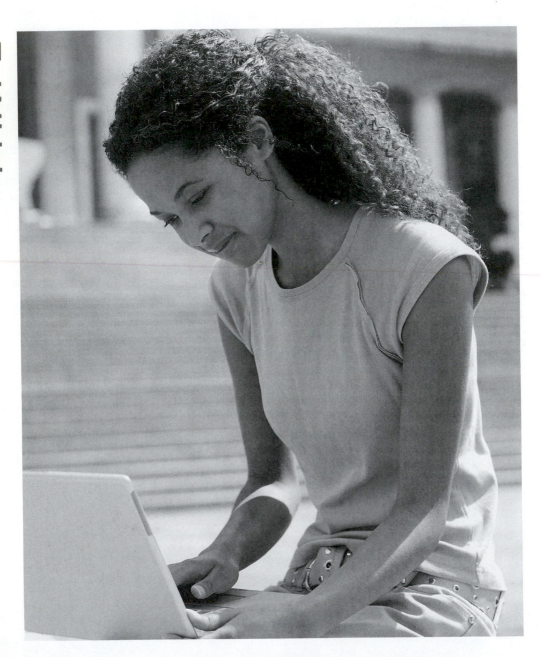

PART 2

Computers

Sending snippets of thoughts and
   greetings
to far-flung friends and those next
   door.
Zipping snapshots thru the ether,
intimate glimpses exposed.

Combing the cosmos, collecting
   data
and keywords to our lives,
expanding our realms, posing
temptations to take more than our
   due.

Write a paragraph describing your favorite spot to study, think, relax, or read. Give reasons. Then reread the paragraph aloud and revise until you are satisfied.

PLAGIARISM AND PREVENTION

Reputations have been destroyed by plagiarism. Well-known writers and biographers have admitted plagiarizing. Professors who committed this offense as long as twenty years ago and those who were negligent in advising students that plagiarized have been fired. In describing plagiarism cases at Ohio University, Robert Tomsho writes: "The affair raises questions about how well the nation's universities are teaching the fundamentals of research to foreign students." He says that this problem is also common among students born in the USA and comments, "Ethics specialists say it [plagiarism] represents a troubling erosion of standards" (*Wall Street Journal* 15 Aug. 2006).

Professional writing patched into a student paper is easily spotted. Instructors who suspect this blight can quickly find plagiarized phrases from Web sites by using a search engine. Ironically, many students regard plagiarism as insignificant, rather like downloading music free. But plagiarism is theft. The culprit can receive a failing grade and suspension or lose a job. The offense goes into his or her record.

Plagiarism is taking someone else's written work and misrepresenting it as one's own. Plagiarism can range from copying a few distinctive words to copying several pages without documentation. To give credit to the author, writers cite sources, following established rules (MLA, APA, or other style). They also summarize and paraphrase—restating the original material *in their own words.* When quoting (copying an author's words), they enclose those words in quotation marks.

A good rule of thumb is to vary your wording from the original as much as possible without becoming wordy or changing the meaning. With a good thesaurus, you can easily find synonyms to replace most major words. You also need to vary your sentence structure from the original. If difficult, then copy the necessary phrases and enclose in quotation marks. The Research Guide—chapters R-1, R-3, and R-4—explains and shows how to document the use of work that is not your own.

Revising, Editing, and Proofreading

> A writer's problem does not change. . . . It is always how to write truly and having found what is true, to project it in such a way that it becomes a part of the experience of the person who reads it.
>
> —Ernest Hemingway

Revision is much more than a hurried scan of punctuation and running a spell check. Revision is the process of refining writing—becoming more specific each run through—finding concrete details to reveal the facts of a topic and organizing them logically. You simplify and clarify by pruning out the nonessentials and supporting the main points, keeping your audience in mind.

College instructors expect several revisions of papers. Yet too many students skip or skimp on revision,

www.mhhe.com/dietsch

For a wealth of revision resources, check out: Editing

editing, and proofreading—turning in rough drafts instead of polished papers. Possibly in high school they wrote drafts the night before and did a minimum of proofreading. But in college much more is expected. A good way to revise your rough draft is to assume the role of an editor.

HOW DO YOU BECOME YOUR OWN EDITOR?

Someone once said that a writer must eventually become his or her own editor. This is even more true today when employees work alone at a computer. They are unlikely to have someone to mark errors and make suggestions. To become your own editor, evaluate not only the effectiveness of word choice and grammar but also the effectiveness of structure, logic, and development.

REVISION: STAGE THREE OF THE WRITING PROCESS

The goal of revision is to rethink and reshape your writing so that it effectively reaches your audience and accomplishes your purpose. Revision involves the larger aspects of the draft: the organization and presentation of ideas. The smaller items within sentences—word choice, grammar, spelling, and punctuation—are treated in the final stage of the writing process, editing and proofreading. Yet you can skip back and forth between stages, any way you wish. Many writers, however, find it easier and more effective to consider one aspect at a time.

FIVE MAJOR STEPS OF REVISION

Perhaps you revise in a hit-or-miss fashion that, more or less, works for you. The tips in this chapter should save you time and improve the quality of your writing. The secret of successful revision is this: repeat the process as often as needed.

Step 1. Acknowledge the Need for Revision

No matter how pleased you are with early drafts, keep looking for ways to improve them. After your euphoria wears off, you will find many imperfections. Judy DeGregario confides, "Anger erupted in me like hot lava when an editor met with me to critique. . . . I wanted to be petted and stroked like my calico cat. . . . Instead, the editor had informed me, in effect, that my writing had fleas. . . . After I cooled down, however, I realized the suggestions he offered me were invaluable. They were specific. They were accurate. They were true. I needed to hear them" (*The Writer* Apr. 2003).

Step 2. Look at the Big Picture

Print out your draft and read it quickly to determine the direction of your controlling idea. (It is difficult to do this on-screen, one frame at a time.) Then ask yourself: Is there just one main idea? Does it keep advancing steadily toward the final point? Is there a final point? Wherever you have doubts or wherever the main idea goes astray, place a check mark. If you are unsure about the effectiveness of the ending, write "What is my point?" "Do I allude to it?" Then revise later.

Step 3. Reread and Mark the Draft

Reread your printed draft silently and carefully. Mark it as you go but hold off on any drastic action. Just place parentheses around surplus or doubtful material. In the margins pencil notes and questions. If your draft has extra-long paragraphs, use brackets to divide logical units of thought into shorter paragraphs. Mark the changes on your working outline. Define terms unfamiliar to the reader and condense or delete wordiness. As you revise, ask yourself five questions:

See "A Strategy for Critical Reading and Prewriting," page 291.

- Is the level of language suitable for the purpose, occasion, and audience?
- Does the written voice sound appropriate?
- Are there any unsupported inferences or other errors in reasoning?
- Have any opposing arguments been treated fairly and objectively?
- Have I fulfilled the purpose? Should anything else be said?

WRITING SUCCESS TIPS: REVISING WITH A COMPUTER

Risky shortcuts while using a computer can devour time and elevate blood pressure. The following advice is based on hard-won wisdom:

1. **Print out a copy to revise.** Do not try to do all your revision on-screen. On a printed page, you will notice peculiarities that you may well miss on-screen. Marking your draft is essential.

2. **Save drafts often.** Why risk losing text when your screen freezes or a power failure occurs?

3. **Move text without losing it.** To be safe, insert the copied portion right away and save.

4. **Place drafts in a folder.** Saving early drafts under different file names, such as "Research 1" and "Research 2," allows you to retrieve deleted items if needed. To avoid confusion, place the drafts together in one folder.

5. **Back up your data.** If your computer were to die suddenly, would you be lost without your hard drive? Make a backup copy.

6. **Submit your latest draft.** It sounds so simple—but one student submitted a six-page formal report. After receiving a C−, he realized he had not submitted the final ten-page draft.

Step 4. Revise, Refine, and Question

Before you start to revise on-screen, renumber as "Research 2" and save your first draft—just in case you should want to retrieve items. Insert the changes. Then reread and revise. Any time you are ready to make significant changes, renumber and make a later draft. If you need more details, review your prewriting notes or do more research. To evaluate writing, ask questions such as these:

- What else needs to be said?
- What else might the audience like to know?
- Do any parts need to be trimmed?
- Are any details insignificant or irrelevant?

Step 5. Let the Draft Cool, Then Check the Focus

See chapter 2.

After the first revision, let your draft cool for half a day or more, if possible. Your thoughts need to settle so that new ideas can sprout. At least take a break and do something that requires you to move around. But be sure to set a time to return. Then, without looking at your paper or outline, jot down your audience and specific purpose. Has the purpose changed? Continue to ask questions to assess your draft:

- Is there one clear central idea throughout the paper?
- Are paragraphs arranged in a logical order?
- Does each paragraph have a transition to link back to the thesis statement?
- Are paragraphs well developed and interesting?
- Does the conclusion flow logically from the body?

REFOCUSING A DRAFT

As you revise, you may decide to narrow your topic or refocus it. You might try the pyramid method, shown on page 43, or you might refocus the title, create a new title, look for a fresh perspective, or revise your outline.

Focusing the Title

A focused title for expository writing not only sharpens the topic but also suggests the approach the writer will take. A focused title specifies and limits the topic, particularly for serious writing. Let's consider some examples of titles for research papers:

UNFOCUSED	FOCUSED
• Finding a Job	• Tips for Improving Your Résumé
• Buying a House	• Buying an Older Home Was Wise

The unfocused titles are so broad that the topics could not be covered adequately in a paper. But the focused titles offer a feasible scope and a direction for the main idea. For lighter topics, you may want to consider an amusing or playful title.

Creating an Intriguing Title

For personal essays and short stories, you may prefer an engaging title that provides just a hint of what is to come. Alliteration, assonance, and word play are often used to spice up titles, as in "The Baby and the Battalion," *Reader's Digest* (May 2007). Writer Doug McPherson, *The Writer* (May 2003), suggests using rhyming with clichés as a way to come up with an amusing title:

See chapter 22.

> Look through a book of clichés. . . . Turn "All's well that ends well" into "All's well that bends well" and you have a story [title] on yoga. . . . "Two heads are better than one" could become "Two beds are better than one." The story? How couples have trouble sleeping together because of snoring, nightmares, twitching, or other bedtime ailments.

Finding a Fresh Perspective

If your draft is just not going the way you intend, you might look for a different point of view, a fresh perspective on the topic. For example, P. M. Brady, in his comic strip "Rose Is Rose," shows Pasquale, tired of his toys, pleading for a new one. His father listens, then opens the door, hinting there is a big toy outside. Wading through newly fallen snow, Pasquale looks around and asks where the toy is. His father replies that Pasquale is standing in it.

We are all standing knee-deep in ideas for invigorating our writing. And like Pasquale, we often overlook them. Creativity involves taking everyday experience and transforming it. As writers we can step back to get an offbeat view of our lives. An ordinary topic can be enlivened by looking at it from an angle the reader does not expect. John Yeoman gave an amusing spin to an early experience by writing from the perspective of his two-year-old self:

Babysitting for Grandfather

Everyone except me was getting ready to go somewhere. Being the youngest of the family and a member in good standing of the club known as "the terrible twos," I was used to receiving a lot of attention. But that night my four-year-old sister, dressed in a lacy white dress and black patent leather slippers, was the center of attention. In her hands, she carried a beautiful bouquet of fresh flowers for her role in a wedding.

Outlining

www.mhhe.com/dietsch

For an electronic outlining tutorial, visit:

Writing>Outlining Tutor

Rather than committing mayhem on a draft, you can save time and effort by testing changes on an outline. Expand your scratch outline into a working outline on-screen. Then save and adapt as needed. Print out a copy to keep track of changes as you revise. This outline can be developed as needed. Some instructors require a formal outline, particularly for research papers. (See the model below.)

FORMAL OUTLINES

Formal outlines may be written in fragments or sentences. How detailed an outline is depends on the writer and the assignment, but here's a word of warning: Shy away from elaborate outlines. You can invest so much time and energy that you may be reluctant to revise. (For examples of outlines, turn to chapters 17, 18, and 29.) Both topic outlines and sentence outlines use the following format, with numerals and letters to distinguish parts and subparts:

I.
  A.
    1.
      a.
      b.
    2.
      a.
      b.
      c.
  B.
    1.
      a.
      b.
    2.
      a.
      b.
II. (Repeat as needed)
III. (Repeat as needed)

POINTERS FOR MAKING OUTLINES

- Begin with a large Roman numeral. Follow with a capital letter, then an arabic number.
- For subtopics, use small letters
- Use periods after each of the above.
- If you have an A, then you need a B. If you have a 1, then you need a 2. Otherwise, the section does not need a letter or number.

CLARIFYING THE DRAFT

After you are satisfied with the focus of the draft and the sequence of paragraphs, it is a good idea to check the sound. Read the draft aloud and listen. Be critical. How might some readers regard your point of view? How might they perceive your purpose? Is the main point clear, or might they misconstrue something? The following checklist will help you assess your written voice.

See chapter 2.

www.mhhe.com/dietsch
For further help moving through your drafts, check out:
Writing>Drafting and Revising

CHECKLIST   LISTENING TO YOUR WRITTEN VOICE

1.   Is your written voice appropriate for the occasion, purpose, and audience?

2.   Does your written voice sound knowledgeable?

3.   Might the reader misunderstand some of the words?

4.   Will a synonym improve the sound without changing the meaning?

Revising Sluggish Openings

Does your first sentence beguile readers, luring them to read on? If not, take a look at the sample openings in chapter 4 to stimulate ideas. Does your thesis statement need a little tinkering? Do readers have to stumble through unnecessary words, vague generalities, or other nuisances? To focus a thesis, try writing a purpose statement, as shown in chapter 1. Or you might leaf through part 3 and look at student papers at the ends of chapters. There you will see various openings and thesis statements.

Revising the Body

As you check the internal order within each paragraph, consider that all details should connect to one central idea. Usually, one sentence—the topic sentence—announces the subject of the paragraph and makes a claim. Supporting sentences provide evidence for the claim. They undergird the topic sentence with explanations, examples, anecdotes, reasons, and facts. If you should find more than one subject to a paragraph, you can either split it into two paragraphs or discard the less important idea.

See chapter 6.

　　　Skinny paragraphs may need to be fleshed out with more details. Or you may spot gaps in thought. A transitional phrase, sentence or even a paragraph may be needed to bridge ideas. (See *transition* in the index.)

CHECKLIST   REVISING PARAGRAPHS

1.   Is each paragraph organized around *one* central idea?

2.   Does each supporting sentence closely relate to the topic sentence?

3.   Do the sentences flow in a logical sequence?

4. Is a transition needed to connect any sentences?

5. Does any paragraph need more explanation, examples, or details?

6. If a quotation is included, is it enclosed by quotation marks? Is the source stated?

Revising the Conclusion

www.mhhe.com/dietsch

For online help with your conclusions, go to:
Writing>Conclusions

An effective conclusion gives a sense of completeness and leaves the audience with something to think about. The ending should flow logically and smoothly from the body and be consistent with the opening. An effective ending does not rehash opinions or belabor the obvious. No new material pops in unannounced. To see examples of conclusions, turn to chapter 4 or to the student papers at the ends of chapters 9–15.

EDITING AND PROOFREADING: STAGE FOUR OF THE WRITING PROCESS

During editing and proofreading, you attend to matters within the sentence. *Editing* refers to correcting the sentence structure and improving the word choice. *Proofreading* means examining grammar and punctuation. The goal in stage 4 is to clarify meaning and eliminate grammatical distractions so that the writing purpose can be achieved.

MAJOR TASKS IN EDITING AND PROOFREADING

www.mhhe.com/dietsch

You'll find numerous electronic tools to assist you in editing at:
Editing

An essential part of editing is looking closely at the meaning of each sentence as well as its structure. Proofreading requires a scrutiny of grammar, punctuation, and keyboarding errors. For more intense concentration, many writers separate editing and proofreading. Regardless, there is one guideline that is certain to be fruitful: Go through your revised printed draft three or more times. Editing and proofreading just once will not catch all the errors.

Marking the Revised Draft

After you have added all your revisions on-screen, save them, then run a spelling check. Next print out a clean, double-spaced copy to edit. Off-screen, you will be apt to notice more problems than on-screen. In the first round of editing, do not disrupt your concentration by consulting a thesaurus, dictionary, or handbook—that can come later. Just mark the spot and go on. Your first task is to find and mark items that interfere with clarity, completeness, and accuracy.

PROCEDURE FOR EFFECTIVE EDITING AND PROOFREADING

1. **Read every word.** After your second silent reading, read aloud to spot omissions, errors, and undue repetition. Listen carefully to the sound of the words. Are they pleasing, accurate, and appropriate?

2. **Mark the draft.** Use brackets to set off wordiness. If you notice an error in spelling or grammar, circle it. Place a check mark by any word or sentence you want to return to. Or devise your own system of marking.

3. **Revise sentences and improve wording.** Write changes on your hard copy. In the margins, list possible synonyms for dubious words. To select the best words, look up the meanings.

4. **Add changes on-screen.** After you finish marking your hard copy, make each change on screen.

5. **Print out a copy.** If your printed draft is quite messy, make a clean copy. Repeat the editing process as needed.

Making Sentences Clear and Concise

Reading sentences aloud will also help you to evaluate word choice and positioning of ideas. Important words should be placed in positions of emphasis— at the beginning or end of a sentence. To edit, underline the important words in your draft, then rearrange the sentence. Simply inverting the sentence and adding a comma will often improve the emphasis, as in this opening of a résumé cover letter:

DRAFT: I have developed a keen eye for detail, line, and color as an artist.

REVISED: As an artist, I have developed a keen eye for detail, line, and color.

If ideas are vague and lightweight, rethink them and restate in more specific words. You might ask yourself, "What do I really intend?" Shorten long rambling sentences by omitting unnecessary phrases: *sort of, color of, kind of, number of, in view of, type of,* and other wordiness. Watch, too, for passive voice of verbs, which adds extra words and numbs ideas. Try rewriting the sentence so that the subject is doing the action. Another way to clear out wordiness is to combine short related sentences:

DRAFT: Do you have short, choppy sentences? Are they related? Can they be combined into one sentence?

REVISED: If you find too many short, choppy sentences, try combining   See chapter 7.
            related ideas into one sentence.

Finding Fresh Language

Specific words, fresh language, and comparison enliven humdrum sentences. By choosing precise nouns and action verbs, you can create vivid images. Instead of using a general word such as *bee* or *roll,* you might say, "A large *bumblebee* lit on my blueberry muffin." Add power to verbs by making them specific. Instead of *went* through a red light, say *sped;* instead of *walked* down the street, say *strolled, ambled,* or *hurried.* Avoid overused words. And don't try to sneak slang or a pet colloquialism such as *mess up* or *stuff* past the reader by wrapping it in a set of quotation marks. Find a better way to say what you mean.

Create a Simile or Metaphor   Business and technical writing, as well as literature, employ similes and metaphors. These unusual comparisons use familiar images to lead readers to understand less familiar images. A *simile* is an explicit (or stated) comparison of two unlike items or ideas, using *like* or *as*. Let's take a look at these student similes:

· "My tires, *smooth as the soles of worn-out tennis shoes,* have tiny cracks in the sidewalls." (Kim Coffey)
· "Spade, whose pedigree was a mystery, had a tail eighteen inches long that *he could use like a whip.*" (John Spillman)

A *metaphor* is a figure of speech that contains an implicit (or suggested) contrast, such as "His last car *was a lemon.*" Notice that such metaphors contain *is* or *was*; they have no other signal words to announce them. Verbs, too, can act as metaphors: the motor *purred*; employees *support* their manager's decisions.

Experiment with Alliteration and Rhyme   *Alliteration* is the repetition of the initial (first) consonant sound. In a speech titled "Run-of-the-Mill Miracle," Gary Fenton used alliteration in the title (two m's). Later he commented on his daughter's birth: "No doubt about it. Having a baby is not easy. If it were, we would refer to it as leisure, not labor (two l's)."

Note too, that *leisure* and *labor* also rhyme, as does "No doubt about it." Alliteration and rhyme can be pleasing and emphatic as long as they are not overdone. Alliteration is easy to use; anyone can use it in titles or phrases.

EDITING AND PROOFREADING ON-SCREEN

1. **After adding your major revisions, print out a clean copy.** On-screen editing and proofreading carry the risk of overlooking errors you would normally notice on a printed page. Even after you think your text is error-free, print out a copy and proofread it carefully several times.

2. **As you make each change on-screen, check it off on your hard copy.** This way you will be less likely to omit corrections.

3. **After you make a change on-screen, read the sentence aloud.** This habit will help to ensure no words have been omitted and no extra ones have been left when text was moved.

4. **Before printing out your last draft, run a final spelling check.** Last-minute changes can cause errors. If you are not the world's best typist, typos could be lurking in your text.

PROOFREADING EFFECTIVELY

No significant piece of writing—whether a college paper, a report to a boss, or a business letter—can be considered complete until it has been carefully proofread at least twice for errors. Three times is better. Lapses in grammatical usage, punctuation, and spelling undercut your credibility as a writer and call into question your commitment to your work. In college these errors can lower your grade; at work they may damage your career prospects. We recommend that you:

- **Correct your graded papers soon after their return.** Look up words and errors. Correct every error. Look up misspelled words and write each one ten times to rivet the correct spelling in your mind.

- **Keep a list of errors pointed out in your graded papers.** Make a list of common errors you need to work on. Once you become aware of specific errors, you will be better prepared to avoid them.

- **Review the word pairs in the Glossary of Usage (page H-50).** These words are commonly confused because they look or sound alike. Examples: effect/affect, ensure/insure, all ready/already.

- **Learn the basic rules of grammar, punctuation, and spelling.** Don't ask someone else; you may get bad advice. Check your own work carefully. On the job you will be glad you did. You can start by memorizing the eight basic rules for using commas (pages H-24 to H-26).

- **Use a thesaurus and dictionary** to help in refining word choice.

PEER REVIEW: HELPING TO IMPROVE EACH OTHER'S WRITING

Published writers often receive input from writing groups, agents, editors, or reviewers. Peer review in a classroom provides similar help. These reviews not only enable class members to help each other with early drafts but also to sharpen their skill at identifying rough spots in their own writing.

The job of a peer reviewer is to pinpoint problems, not solve them. Revision, editing, and proofreading are the responsibility of the writer. When giving feedback, the reviewer should be tactful. Comments that are overly blunt, unduly critical, or vague can be worse than none at all. Before critiquing, you might ask yourself, "How would I feel if I received this feedback?"

The difference between callousness and tact often lies in the phrasing. Vague reactions such as "I don't like the opening" or "Confusing" or "Dull" are not very helpful. Responses should be fairly specific so that the writer understands where and what the problem is. Responses can be softened in three ways:

1. **Begin with a positive comment about the draft:**
   - This is an interesting topic.
   - That example is well developed (or funny or unusual).
   - The anecdote is delightful (or amusing or charming).
2. **Be tentative.** Offer comments as opinion, not a final decree:
   - This sentence *sounds* negative. Is that what you intend?

- This passage *seems* unclear. What do you mean? (If the person clarifies, say, "That's a good start. Why don't you write it down so you'll have it?")
- I *wonder* if this part might work better if moved over here? (Not "You ramble.")

3. **Ask polite questions:**
   - Where is the thesis? (Not "You don't have a thesis statement.")
   - Have you thought about the ending yet? (Not "There isn't any conclusion.")

SUGGESTIONS FOR PEER REVIEW

Writers who are mentally prepared to accept constructive criticism can learn much from peer review. Still, peer responses should not be taken as gospel. As you start to revise, evaluate the quality of each response and extract what is useful.

REVIEWERS: Consider one aspect of the writing at a time. Word your comments and suggestions thoughtfully and carefully. Identify concerns tactfully, but don't whitewash.

REVIEWEES: Keep an open mind. Be willing to consider suggestions. Ask about comments that seem unclear. Evaluate each suggestion thoughtfully. If in doubt, make an appointment with your instructor or the campus writing center.

WORKPLACE CASE STUDY

A SERIES OF STUDENT OUTLINES AND DRAFTS

Roger Moore's draft was revised eight times. The four examples here show key points of his progress. Roger wrote a first draft from his prewriting list, revised it, and decided it was still vague. To focus, he expanded the prewriting list to a scratch outline, listing the audience, purpose, and thesis statement. Note how he refined his thesis from a basic three-part version to a more subtle final version.

Scratch Outline   (Order of importance)

Audience: classmates
Purpose: to inform the class about swap meets and the people who attend
Title: Kinds of People Who Attend Swap Meets
Thesis statement: Jack and I have found that three general types of people come to swap meets to buy auto parts.
Body:
    Type A. Arrive in late afternoon and up till closing time. Nonbuyers.
    Type B. Are there at 4 a.m. Dealers. Get in the way.
    Type C. Come at 8 a.m. Family folks.
Conclusion

continued

WORKPLACE CASE STUDY

Using his scratch outline, Roger wrote drafts three and four. Dissatisfied, he revised the outline, switching the main points to chronological order. To refocus the internal order of each body paragraph, he renamed attendees and classified them according to "arrival, purpose, and behavior." With the structure of his paper firmly in mind, he wrote draft five, which follows the working outline.

Revision: A Working Outline   (Chronological order)

Title: Swap Meets
Thesis statement: My son and I have met three types of people who attend swap meets: early birds, buyers, and sightseers.
Body:
  1. Early Birds
     Arrival: 4 a.m.
     Purpose: Buy cheap for resale
     Behavior: Buy little. Give us a hard time
  2. Buyers
     Arrival: 8 a.m.
     Purpose: Find parts they need themselves
     Behavior: Pleasant, polite
  3. Sightseers
     Arrival: Late afternoon till closing time
     Purpose: Look around
     Behavior: Complaining, demanding
Conclusion: Swap meets are fun with Jack along. We make a little money and meet some interesting people.

Fifth Draft

Swap Meets

Jack, my son, and I have decided there are three types of people who attend swap meets—the early birds, the buyers, and the sightseers. Swap meets are like flea markets, except these swap meets are for car parts only. Set-up times usually start at 4 a.m. This is the time when the early birds try to buy our car parts. They hope to run across a good deal. They don't buy much.

The buyers don't arrive until 8 o'clock or thereafter. They usually look for hard-to-find parts to fix up an old vehicle they are working on. They take their time and hunt carefully through the boxes and piles of parts. They are serious buyers and do not give us a hard time. Some are almost like old friends—we see them regularly.

continued

WORKPLACE CASE STUDY

Sightseers generally come late in the afternoon, often at closing time. They are always complaining about something. Years ago we used to unload parts so they could see them, but then we noticed they would not buy anything anyway.

Swap meets are enjoyable because Jack and I get together, make a little money, and meet some interesting people.

Although Roger's fifth draft was focused and clear, it still needed additional details to provoke interest and provide support. Three more revisions yielded his final draft.

Final Draft

People Who Flock to Swap Meets

In the summertime my son and I load my panel truck with used auto parts and head for a swap meet every Saturday. Swap meets are like flea markets, except swap meets are for used car parts only. There Jack and I not only make a little money and enjoy our time together but also meet some friendly people and hear some fascinating stories.

As soon as we drive in at 4 a.m, before daybreak, the early birds begin flocking around the truck, often getting in the way as we unload and set up. They crowd around, hoping to find something and strike a good bargain. They are usually dealers, out for a fast buck. A few may offer to help unload, but most stand around, drinking coffee and giving us a hard time, joking and razzing us. They don't buy much.

The buyers arrive later, eight o'clock or so. They often look for difficult-to-find parts to repair a vintage vehicle. Working in their spare time, many are restoring a classic car in their garage. They like to tell us about it—how much it cost, how far along the project is, how it looked originally, and its history. We've heard some surprising stories about thousands of dollars being made from restoring an old, rusty junked car. One fellow claimed his 1946 Ford was once owned by a notorious bank robber, who used it in several getaways.

Some of the buyers return regularly; they are almost like old friends. Sometimes they bring their families along. They take their time, hunting carefully through boxes and piles of parts. They are serious buyers who ask how much a part costs. If they don't want it, they go on to the next display. Otherwise, they buy.

Sightseers usually come late in the afternoon, often near closing time. It seems they can always find something to complain about. Seldom do they find what they want, and they often become irritated when we are too busy loading the truck to help them. Some even ask us to unload so that they can look over the rest of the parts! Years ago we tried unloading the parts for them to see, but we noticed they would not buy anything anyway. They just wanted to sightsee.

Despite the little irritations, swap meets are still a good place to spend a leisurely Saturday, visiting with my son, meeting friendly people, and hearing interesting yarns.

CAN YOU EDIT FLABBY PHRASES?

Try your hand at editing wordy phrases that often clutter early drafts. The phrases below can be edited to one word. After you finish, check your answers with those at the end of the chapter.

1. In the immediate future
2. Actual truth of the matter
3. For this reason
4. Connected together
5. In the majority of cases
6. During the time which
7. At that point in time
8. Warning in advance
9. Absolutely free gift
10. Past history

IDEAS TO START WRITING

Directions: You might describe an incident, experience, or tradition, or try one of these options:

1. The job you would like to have in five years
2. Broken promises
3. An anecdote about a family holiday or vacation
4. An incident at summer camp, school, or work
5. The earliest childhood scene or event that you can recall

ANSWERS: "CAN YOU EDIT FLABBY PHRASES"

Answers may vary somewhat: *soon, truth, for* or *because, connected, usually, while, then, warning, gift, history.*

Improving Paragraphs

CHAPTER 6

> Writing and rewriting are a constant search for what one is saying.
>
> —John Updike

Clarity is the heart of effective writing. Yet first drafts rarely say exactly what we mean. To be effective, a paragraph must be centered on one idea and be well developed. The sentences must flow in a logical sequence. All this requires more than one revision.

Paragraphs vary according to purpose. Opening and ending paragraphs act as a frame for a piece of writing. Body paragraphs, as this chapter explains, present ideas and information. Transitional paragraphs provide connections. Sometimes a single well-developed paragraph serves as a complete essay.

PARTS OF AN EFFECTIVE PARAGRAPH

Understanding the basic parts of a paragraph and how they work will help you to revise effectively. Regardless of whether a paragraph stands alone or with others, it contains certain basic elements. For clarity, most expository paragraphs have a topic sentence.

The Topic Sentence

The *topic sentence* contains the main idea of a paragraph. This sentence tells the reader *what* will be covered and *why*. Some topic sentences also tell *where* or *when*. A basic topic sentence has two essential functions:

> www.mhhe.com/dietsch
>
> For more help creating topic sentences, check out: Writing>Thesis

1. *To limit the subject to one main idea* that can be developed in the paragraph.
2. *To make a claim, assertion, or statement of opinion.* This part of the topic sentence may be a belief, impression, generalization, or recommendation.

Let's consider a topic sentence that performs both these functions:

Uncle Jake, who came uninvited, was a difficult house guest.

The subject of the sentence is "Uncle Jake," and the claim is that he was "a difficult house guest." This topic sentence sets up the expectation that the writer will describe Uncle Jake's behavior. In the body of the paragraph, readers will expect support—examples of what he said and anecdotes of what he did—so that they can see for themselves how difficult Uncle Jake was.

Support Sentences

Support sentences explain the main idea of the topic sentence. They supply *evidence* to convince the reader of the soundness of the claim, assertion, or opinion. You might regard the topic sentence as an argument (view) to be proved. The support sentences supply proof in the form of facts, definitions, reasons, examples, or illustrations to back up the claim in the topic sentence.

The minimum number of support sentences is generally three or four; often there are more. As you search for support, keep in mind that *quality* is more important than quantity. A few excellent examples are worth more than a dozen mediocre ones. Established facts, definitions, and valid reasons provide credible evidence. Appropriate anecdotes and examples increase readers' interest, understanding, and conviction.

A Concluding Sentence

Some paragraphs have a third part: a *concluding sentence.* This final sentence may be a summary of the points made in the support sentences. It can also serve as a *clincher,* providing the paragraph with a sense of completeness by commenting on the subject in an interesting, surprising, or humorous way. In the following student paragraph by Bonita M. Goings, the concluding sentence serves as a clincher: First, it alludes to the topic sentence; then it makes a point.

> ### Climb Aboard!
>
> The magic of a carousel has a way of turning men and women into children again. As they approach the carousel house, their steps and their hearts suddenly become lighter. Tots tug at adult hands, eager to climb aboard this remnant from a fairy tale. The magnificent carousel stands with hundreds of lights reflected in mirrors on the brightly painted rounding boards. Adventurous riders select mounts from rows of prancing horses or from the menagerie of bears, big cats, goats, ostriches, rabbits, a zebra, a giraffe, or a hippopotamus. The timid and the elderly seem to prefer the sedate pace of the two chariots. When all riders are seated, the calliope signals the ride is about to begin. As the carousel gains speed, whirling faster and faster, the riders' faces are transformed by smiles. Their cares seem to disappear as they are charmed by the magic of the carousel.

POSITIONING THE TOPIC SENTENCE

Once you draft a topic sentence, your next concern is where to place it in the paragraph. Before positioning the topic sentence, consider its function and the effect you want to obtain. Will you place it at the beginning, the middle, or the end?

The Topic Sentence at the Beginning

Most expository paragraphs follow the direct approach: the topic sentence is placed at the beginning. There the topic receives more emphasis than it would in the middle, and the reader knows immediately what the writer will explain. Yet topic sentences sometimes wander into odd places. While revising this book, I was surprised now and then to find a topic sentence huddled in the middle of a paragraph for no apparent reason. Unless I found a reason to leave it there, I yanked it back to the beginning. Check your drafts to see that your topic sentences are in the most effective position for the purpose and audience.

The Topic Sentence in the Middle

Sometimes a writer may wish to take a leisurely path to the main idea. Then the topic sentence may appear in the middle of a paragraph. Placed there, the major idea receives less emphasis than it would at the beginning or end. In a paragraph of comparison, for instance, a topic sentence may be located midway between the two subjects. There it can identify the purpose and connect the items being compared. Or the topic sentence may be in the middle for other reasons, as in the following paragraph, which describes nonverbal communication:

> Mrs. Clark, who teaches math, is explaining an essential aspect of the subject. She notices that Fred is staring at her with unblinking eyes, his body taut and erect, his feet flat on the floor. She discerns no motion whatever from Fred. Do you think that Fred is listening to the lecture, evaluating what Mrs. Clark is saying? *If you think he is interested, you are wrong.* A young teacher unaccustomed to this posture might fall for it, but a more experienced educator would not. Fred has turned his teacher off and is using a cover-up technique to convince her that he is "all ears."

> —Gerard I. Nierenberg and Henry H. Calero,
> *How To Read a Person Like A Book*

Placing a topic sentence in the middle of a paragraph does carry a risk, however. The danger is that if readers are impatient or in a hurry, they may skim over the middle and miss the key idea. If the idea is important, place it at the beginning or end.

The Topic Sentence at the End

When placed at the end of a paragraph, the topic sentence acts as a summary. It presents the controlling idea that is implicit in the sentences that precede it. The following paragraph builds up to a concluding topic sentence that offers a startling and bleak statistic:

> Many illiterates cannot read the admonition on a pack of cigarettes. Neither the Surgeon General's warning nor its reproduction on the package can alert them to the risks. Although most people learn by word of mouth that smoking is related to a number of grave physical disorders, they do not get the chance to read the detailed stories which can document this danger with the vividness that turns concern into determination to resist. They can see the handsome cowboy or the slim Virginia lady lighting up a filter cigarette; they cannot heed the words that tell them that this product is (not "may be") dangerous to their health. *Sixty million men and women are condemned to be the unalerted, high-risk candidates for cancer.*

> —Jonathan Kozol, "The Human Cost of an Illiterate Society"

A topic sentence at the end of a paragraph requires the reader to look at the support before the main idea. Since the writer takes time to explain the reasons before making the claim, the readers are less likely to reject it. A topic sentence at the end can also let readers know how and why you arrived at a decision. (In the paragraphs above, the topic sentences have been italicized for emphasis.)

Unifying a Paragraph without a Topic Sentence

Not all paragraphs have a topic sentence. Nonetheless, the main idea must be clear. In narrative writing a topic sentence is often lacking, but a general point (or theme) is implied, as in the following paragraph:

> In the spring of 1948, in the first softball game during the afternoon hour of physical education in the dusty schoolyard, the two captains chose teams and, as always, they chose other boys until only two of us remained. I batted last, and first came to the plate with two or three runners on base, and while my teammates urged me to try for a walk, and the players on the field called, "Easy out, Easy out," I watched the softball coming in waist-high and stepped and swung, and hit it over the right fielder's head for a double. My next time at bat I tripled to center. From then on I brought my glove to school, hanging from a handlebar.

> —Andre Dubus, "Under the Lights"

The paragraph has no topic sentence, but its point is clearly implied and might be stated as "Without warning, I had become a good softball player." Using this inductive order (supportive details before the main point) provides interest by building to a climax. Another excellent reason for omitting a topic sentence is diplomacy. Some business letters, such as credit refusals, may not state the main idea directly. Instead, the refusal is *implied* in a subordinate clause. Unless there is a good reason to omit a topic sentence, however, include one.

CHECKING THE ORDER AND DEVELOPMENT OF PARAGRAPHS

You can organize a paragraph by any order that is clear and suitable for the purpose. For example, narrative and process paragraphs generally present events and steps in *chronological* order, the sequence in which they naturally occur. So it is important to make sure that each event or step is in the right order. Other kinds of order all contribute to clarity.

For seven orders, see chapter 4.

The student paragraphs that follow use strategies of narration, description, process analysis, illustration, and comparison/contrast. *Spatial* order, which locates parts or physical features, is explained in "Through a Child's Eyes," later in the chapter. Notice how the support sentences supply details that develop the main idea of each paragraph.

Narrative Paragraphs

Narrative paragraphs tell a story or relate an event or anecdote. The writer often sets the scene first, telling *who* or *what, when,* and *where.* Description, dialogue, or illustrations may be included to kindle interest and to clarify. Action verbs keep the story moving. Narratives often build suspense, reserving a surprise for the end. They may reveal rather than explain, letting the reader interpret the meaning, or they may direct attention to a social or political concern that has universal relevance (see chapter 9). The following student narrative by Suzanne Omaits suggests a fear we all might experience:

Home Alone

Quiet holds many eerie sounds. I never knew how many until I found myself alone one Friday night. Was that the wind rubbing a bare branch against the house, or was the front step groaning under someone's weight? To blot out the sounds, I turned on the television. But something compelled me to turn around. Dreading what I might see, yet afraid not to look, I slowly turned. For a moment I froze! Through the fogged glass, I saw a man's face pressed against the window pane, staring at me! Leaping to my feet, I flipped off the lights and TV. He began to pound on the window. Realizing he could still see me dimly, I ran to the back room and hid. After a moment I knew I had to get help. Shaking, I crawled back to the living room. My hands trembled so I could hardly dial the phone. Anxiously, I waited for the familiar voice of my neighbor. Suddenly the pounding stopped. Minutes dragged by until my neighbor arrived. After checking, he assured me the intruder was gone. Just then a car drove up. Never was I so glad to hear my parents call, "We're home!"

Descriptive Paragraphs

An effective description has a specific purpose; details are not just a pleasant filler. Significant physical details can capture the essence of a person, place, or object. Concrete words reveal perceptions obtained through the five senses: seeing, hearing, touching, tasting, and smelling. A single dominant impression can unify the details. In the next student paragraph, by Michael Schnitzler, the physical details about a chair and how it has been used down through the years yield a dominant impression of an affectionate family.

See chapter 10.

The Old Rocking Chair

In the corner of our living room sits an old wooden rocking chair. The chair is made of solid maple, varnished and trimmed in gold. The arms are worn smooth, as if someone had used the finest of sandpaper on the wood. On the edges of its arms, I can see indentations in the wood where little tykes did their teething. As I rock back and forth, the old chair squeaks and creaks; but the sounds are soothing. This rocking chair has served several purposes. It has helped to console our three children, countless nieces, nephews, and children of friends. It has rocked babies to sleep for naps and at bedtime. With its soothing rhythm, it has comforted and quieted them when they were restless or sick. Now that the children have grown older, the old chair is seldom used. Yet it sits patiently, awaiting the years when it will hold our grandchildren.

Process Analysis Paragraphs

Process analysis explains how to do something or how something happens. Chronological order is the clearest way to organize process analysis. Just list steps or actions in sequence as they normally occur. Include enough details for

See chapter 11.

the reader to understand. *If there is a risk during any part of the procedure, give a precaution early.* For conciseness and clarity, use second person (mainly the understood *you*). In the following example, which is directed to someone who has never used a coin-operated car wash, notice how student writer Kristi Gruber takes an ordinary topic and transforms it into an interesting paragraph:

How to Get the Best Shine from a Coin-Operated Car Wash

Whether your car is a prized possession or a necessary nuisance, it deserves an occasional wash. By following five simple steps, you can make your vehicle sparkling clean in just five minutes. First, vacuum the interior with the hose located outside the entrance of the car wash. Be sure the hose inhales every crumb, pebble, and gum wrapper. Second, drive into the wash cage. Third, before you add coins, read the directions for the wand. Then turn the dial to "Prewash." Add the coins and be ready to work fast. Fourth, spray all the exterior once to break up grime. Fifth, switch to "High Pressure Soap" and grip the wand tightly. As you move around the car, spray the top, hood, sides, wheels, and trunk. Sixth, change the mode to "High Pressure Rinse." To prevent streaking, rinse all suds off. Next, switch to "Spot-Free Final Rinse." This final step will prevent water spots and ensure a brilliant shine. If you are very dedicated to your four-wheeled friend, take time to wipe her off with the old bath towel you brought along. After that you will probably head down the highway only to be greeted with a gift from a passing bird!

Illustration Paragraphs

Illustration paragraphs—also called paragraphs of exemplification—present a *series* of examples to support the topic sentence. To maintain unity, every example is closely linked to the controlling idea. As you read the next student paragraph, notice the order Sharon K. Cleveland used for the examples:

The Fearsome Rabbit

Bathsheba was not the typical Easter bunny. Sheba was a Newfoundland flop-eared rabbit. Soon she grew into a fat fur ball. At maturity, she weighed 35 pounds—more than my two-year-old nephew! Our guests loved to watch her hop down the hall, then stand on her hind legs while she washed her face. With her long floppy ears hanging down, she had a sad, gentle look, which was deceiving. One day we came home to find her chewing on a camera bag that belonged to my husband. He yelled, "If I didn't love that rabbit so much, she would be dinner tonight!" Soon electrical cords, woodwork, wooden chairs, books, and other objects also bore the marks of her sharp teeth. As Sheba grew older, she developed a mean streak. One day our son, who was six, went near her litter box and came running—Sheba hopping close behind. As she nipped his bare heel, he screamed, "HELP!" After this incident she would hop toward him, and he would leap onto the couch. He had become afraid of her. Soon we took her to a farm that raises rabbits, where she seems fat and happy.

Comparison or Contrast Paragraphs

See chapter 14
for outlines.

Comparison includes both similarities and differences, while *contrast* refers to differences only. The key to writing a good comparison or contrast paragraph is first to select two subjects that might make an interesting pair. Then list specific, significant features of each, matching every detail you list for one subject with a corresponding detail for the other as student Peggy Walker did:

The Eye of the Beholder

This year when the first warm days of April began, I overflowed with energy. I wanted to make our family room as fresh as the spring buds outside. In a frenzy, I started to throw out one piece of junk after another, but each time Jerry would intervene to save a "treasure." First, I discarded a faded, cracked plate; but he rescued his family heirloom. Then I seized the tattered quilt; he returned his comforter for cold nights to its rightful place on the couch. Next I tossed out the stack of old *Time* and *Newsweek* magazines from the coffee table; he retrieved them because he might need a reference for a "current" event. And so it went. Finally, I said, "That sagging old couch we bought at a garage sale simply has to go!" But he objected sharply, "That's my favorite spot to watch football!" Refusing to argue, I stopped. But the first day he goes golfing, I'm calling Goodwill for an immediate pickup. . . . I may keep the plate.

Paragraphs of Definition

Sometimes a paragraph of definition is needed to explain the meaning and context of a word. A technical definition may specify the purpose and the function of a part or appliance. A literary definition may specify the root or origin of the word, the part of speech, and the standard meaning—or several meanings in different contexts. During practice writing, student Mark Jones speculated about the meaning and uses of the word *shaft*:

Words are fun to play with and think about. For example, *shaft* as a noun is a pole or long handle of a spear or other weapon. By that definition, an arrow could be considered a shaft, although it would seem strange to say we shafted a deer. The space shuttle might also be called a shaft. A pretty girl can wear a short dress and show a little shaft. The White House has many shafts; there are pillars at the entrance. *Shaft* is also used as a verb, but only in slang. If Bill shafted Al, then Bill did a wrong or injustice to Al. Bill did not hurl an arrow, spear, or space shuttle at Al, although Al has been hurt by Bill's action. *Shaft* is also the name of an old movie featuring a super-cool, super-bad bald man named John Shaft. If violent movies about super-cool, bad, bald men are not appealing, then paying five dollars to rent the film and not liking it would be getting the shaft.

Transitional Paragraphs

In the middle of an essay or paper, you may need more than just a signpost transition or embedded transition to bridge a gap—directing the reader to a shift in thought. A special paragraph of transition serves to connect two major ideas in a logical sequence. For example, Patty Seigneur wrote a brief transitional paragraph for a paper contrasting two good friends. Below is the paragraph she placed between her descriptions of Sue and June:

▶ Sue is a wonderful person and friend, but I found myself wanting a friend more like myself. Then I met June. Quickly, she and I became good friends. We both realized how alike we are and how much we enjoy each other's company.

Notice that only one signpost transition, *then,* is used in this transitional paragraph. But the writer repeats key terms and uses pronouns to establish clear *embedded* transition.

REVISION CHECKLIST: QUALITIES OF EFFECTIVE PARAGRAPHS

When you revise, you rearrange, add, and snip—polishing as you go. You check paragraphs to ensure interest, unity, completeness, and coherence. These four qualities contribute to clarity.

Interest

Does your opening sentence hook the reader's interest? If not, scan your prewriting; you may find an overlooked gem. Or can you approach the topic in an unusual way? What might readers like to know? A secret of good essay writing is to remember that readers like to be entertained; include anecdotes and offbeat examples. Supply action verbs and concrete nouns that enable the reader to share your vivid impression.

Unity

Does each paragraph focus on one major idea? *Do all of the support sentences closely relate to the topic sentence?* Support sentences amplify the major idea with examples, facts, statistics, opinions, or reasons. If a sentence lacks a connection, either establish one or discard the sentence. To check the unity of a paragraph, ask yourself four questions:

- What is the purpose (main idea) of the paragraph?
- Does each support sentence supply specific details?
- Does each support sentence help to explain the topic sentence?
- If not, what needs to be deleted or added?

Completeness

To be complete, a paragraph must supply adequate and appropriate information. But how much is enough? What is suitable? You, the writer, must decide according to each rhetorical situation. Whether your professor assigns a single paragraph or a lengthy paper, think about the purpose and the audience:

- How much are readers likely to know?
- How much more do they need to know?

- Why? How will the information be used?
- Are there enough examples, reasons, or anecdotes to be interesting?
- Is there enough specific support to make my point?

Coherence

You might think of a paragraph as a jigsaw puzzle—each piece must fit. If not, the paragraph lacks *coherence.* Do your paragraphs flow smoothly? Read them aloud. Are there gaps between the thoughts of sentences? Do you need transitions to connect them and show their relationship? You can add signposts or embedded transitions to bridge the gaps, or you can devise parallel structures.

www.mhhe.com/dietsch
For additional coverage of coherence, go to:
Writing>Coherence

Signpost Transitions   Like highway signs, signpost transitions direct the reader. Usually, these signal words and phrases appear at the beginning of sentences to indicate how the material fits with the preceding sentence. Just adding a word, phrase, or clause to indicate how the material relates to the preceding sentence often makes a paragraph clearer and easier to read.

- **To show time:** once, years ago, later, soon, now, today, then, before, when, while, after, meanwhile, as, next, first, second, and so forth
- **To add:** too, also, and, another, besides, in addition, furthermore
- **To show difference:** but, yet, however, still, otherwise, even so, although
- **To show similarity:** like, likewise, similarly, both, resemble, identical
- **To show effects or results:** because, for, therefore, as a result, since, thus
- **To emphasize:** in fact, indeed, above all, again, regardless, nonetheless
- **To point out examples:** for example, for instance

COMMON SIGNPOST TRANSITIONS

In the following student essay by Sonny Dyer, the italicized transitions show the passing of time:

Playing Possum

While defending an ambush position in Vietnam, I was run over by a tank. Hurt and bleeding, I was left lying in a rice paddy. My buddy, *after* routing the ambush against "Charlie" (the enemy), took off in pursuit, believing I was dead. *After an hour,* which seemed like an eternity, night fell. *A few hours later* the sky was pitch black. There was no moon or stars, just blackness. Suddenly I heard someone sloshing through the paddy. It was "Charlie." *As I lay there motionless,* I heard the Viet soldier rummaging through my Jeep. *After he finished with the Jeep,* he started to strip the dead. *Before I knew it,* he was standing over me. *While* lying there playing dead, trying not to breathe, I was sure he could hear the blood rushing from my wounds. Luckily for me, he was in a hurry and just stripped off my watch, flak jacket, lighter, and cigarettes. *After he left,* I took a big breath and let out a sigh of relief.

Hours later, as dawn broke, a patrol finally happened across my Jeep and discovered the bodies lying around. Tears came to my eyes as I heard a U.S. soldier call, "Medic, this one is still alive!"

Embedded Transition   Transition within a sentence is said to be "embedded." Four types of embedded transition are repetition of *key words, synonyms, pronouns,* and *natural relationships.* By repeating key words, substituting synonyms, using pronouns that refer to key words, and establishing natural links (spring/fall, in/out, farm/crops, etc.), you can knit sentences smoothly into a paragraph. Note how the four types of embedded transition make the following paragraph coherent:

> *My* mother was the eldest of *her* generation—of nine children—and came from a slightly more elevated social station in Jamaica. *She* had a high school education, which *my father* lacked. . . . Before emigrating, *Mom* had worked as a stenographer in a lawyer's office. *Her* mother, Gram McKoy, was a small, lovely woman whose English wedded African cadence to British inflection, the sound of which is still music to my soul. The McKoys and the Powells both had *bloodlines* common among *Jamaicans,* including *African, English, Irish, Scotch,* and probably *Arawak Indian.* My father's side even added a *Jewish strain* from a Broomfield ancestor.
>
> —Colin Powell, *My American Journey*

See chapter 7.   **Parallelism**   Parallel structures provide balance in writing and contribute to coherence. Undoubtedly, you already use parallelism in several ways: to balance items in a series, compound sentences, and pairs of related sentences, as well as to coordinate phrases and clauses. You may sense that parallelism smooths sentence structure and gives equal emphasis to coordinate ideas. To check the coherence and parallelism of paragraphs, read them aloud. The ear is often a better detector of imbalance and other irregularity than the eye. Note the parallelism in the following descriptive paragraph by student Nancy Smathers:

Through a Child's Eyes

A tall, husky man has long been a very special person in my life. *His hair is the color of bricks in a schoolhouse,* while *his eyes are the color of hickory nut shells. Above his eyes* he wears a permanent frown, but *in his smile* I can see his inner warmth peeking through. *When he speaks,* his voice sounds like a semi-truck going through a tunnel at a high rate of speed. The low, gravelly tones echo like a bouncing tennis ball in an empty room. *When he enters a room,* he resembles a bear just waking from its winter slumber. But *when he sits,* a lap appears that would never turn away a child who wished to crawl upon it. When sitting there, I can detect the faint scent of Old Spice. *His big, muscular arms* make me feel safe from any possible harm. *His huge, powerful hands* are *like vice grips,* but when wiping tears away, they are *like soft cotton.* As rough as this man appears *on the outside, on the inside* he is soft and gentle, just like a newborn kitten. . . . This very dear person is my dad.

Adjusting Paragraph Length

When Abraham Lincoln was once asked "How long should a man's legs be?" he replied, "Long enough to reach the ground." A similar answer comes to mind when students ask "How long should a paragraph be?" A paragraph should be long enough to cover the central idea well according to the needs of readers and their purpose in reading. As a general rule, avoid one- and two-sentence paragraphs or a series of short paragraphs. These tend to give writing a choppy, careless appearance.

Introductory paragraphs of short papers (500 words or less) usually range from three to five sentences. Introductions for research papers tend to be longer. Body paragraphs often range from five to eight sentences. Conclusions tend to be rather brief, perhaps three to five sentences. A one-paragraph essay may range from seven to twelve or more sentences.

Complexity of the subject also influences length; difficult subjects tend to require more explanation than easy ones. If a paragraph becomes quite long, consider the needs of the reader, the purpose of the writing, and the coverage required for clarity. If division is needed, look for a shift from one aspect of an idea to another.

GUIDELINES: DIVIDING LONG PARAGRAPHS

1. Divide when a paragraph has more than one main idea. Divide where the second idea or a shift to another facet of the major idea begins.
2. Divide where there is a lapse in time. Time provides a natural break. *Tip:* Look for transitions of time or a shift in verb tense.
3. Divide if there is a shift in person. First, check to see that the shift is necessary. If it is, that may be an excellent spot to divide. If the shift is unnecessary, revise the sentence. (See "Case of Pronouns," page H-3 and item 4, page H-5.)
4. In dialogue, start a new paragraph for each speaker.

What Exactly Is Clarity?

For writing to be clear, readers must be able to gain the meaning upon the first reading. True, they may need to reread for specific details, but the main idea should be apparent the first time. Clarity is the end result of knowing your purpose, correctly assessing the audience and occasion, selecting appropriate words, being complete, and connecting details to a central idea. Important influences on clarity are the level of formality, the voice of verbs, sentence structure, the length of sentences and paragraphs, and positions of emphasis (see chapter 7). Careful revision and editing will help to make your paragraphs clear.

PRACTICE

SMALL GROUPS: Evaluating Topic Sentences

Directions: Which sentences would make *good* topic sentences? Why?

_____ 1. My motto "play before work" received a severe blow this week.

_____ 2. The leftover macaroni and cheese in my refrigerator was covered with green mold.

_____ 3. Mary Todd married Abe Lincoln.

_____ 4. The older I become, the more I appreciate . . .

_____ 5. Overnight the amaryllis opened one large red trumpet.

_____ 6. Mr. Inskeep is my favorite teacher.

_____ 7. Computers are necessary for most workplaces.

_____ 8. A roommate who is a musician can be exasperating.

_____ 9. Cutting the Brazilian rain forest is causing weather problems.

_____ 10. Every Thursday night I watch my favorite TV program.

IDEAS FOR PARAGRAPHS

1. Describe a small object you own and its meaning to you.
2. Share a bit of advice given by a parent, grandparent, or other significant person. How did it influence you?
3. Describe a pet you once owned.
4. How has a certain book influenced you?
5. The day I almost . . .

Restyling Sentences

Truman Capote, one of the great writers of the twentieth century, realized the value of rules. He also knew that writers have to go beyond rules, listening to the sound of the written voice and varying their sentences, to achieve the desired effect. Learning the rules is just the beginning, for rules are simply guideposts to aid the writer. This chapter supplies the basic rules for creating and restyling sentences. As you write, you will learn to

> Writing has laws of perspective, of light and shade, just as painting does, or music. If you are born knowing them, fine. If not, learn them. Then rearrange the rules to suit yourself.
>
> —Truman Capote, interview, *Writers at Work: First Series* (1958)

rearrange basic sentence patterns and create new rhythms that are pleasing to the ear and meaningful to the reader.

The clarity of a message depends not only on the word choice but also on the sentence structure and punctuation. The kind of sentences you write depend upon the purpose.

THE PURPOSE OF SENTENCES

Understanding how sentences work will help you clarify, unify, and spark vigor into your drafts. The length of your sentences and the structures you use will depend on their purpose, the occasion, the topic, the audience, and the voice of the writer.

FIVE FUNCTIONS OF SENTENCES

The structure and content of a sentence is directed by its purpose and use. Sentences perform five general functions:

1. **Topic sentence.** The purpose of a topic sentence is to state the main idea of a paragraph. A topic sentence should not be overly long or complicated. (See page 75.)

2. **Support sentence.** The purpose of a support sentence is to provide information that reinforces and expands the main idea. Support sentences tend to be longer than topic sentences. (See page 75.)

3. **Concluding sentence.** The purpose of a concluding sentence (a "clincher") is to provide a sense of completeness to the paragraph. (See page 76.)

4. **Transitional sentence.** The purpose of a transitional sentence is to connect paragraphs in a sequence, to link ideas.

5. **Thesis sentence.** The purpose of a thesis sentence is to state the main idea of a piece of writing. Sometimes more than one sentence is required. A thesis sentence is similar to a topic sentence except that it contains the main idea of an entire essay or paper.

HOW LONG SHOULD A SENTENCE BE?

Sentence length is governed by purpose and content. Brief sentences quickly emphasize key points. Long sentences slow the pace, collect lesser details, and provide variety. Regardless of the length of a sentence, every word should count. Too many long sentences interfere with ease of reading and clarity. Too many short sentences, particularly in a sequence, can cause choppiness. Used well, short sentences can achieve four purposes:

- *Emphasize* information

- *Hasten the pace* of a sentence and convey urgency
- *Build suspense*
- *Conclude* with a snappy or witty comment

Since Elizabethan times, written sentences have been shrinking. In the 1600s the average sentence had about forty-five words. By Victorian times the average sentence was down to twenty-nine words. Now the average sentence in *ordinary writing* has seventeen words; in *technical writing* the average is twenty-one words, according to a survey by Rudolph Flesch. "Average" does not mean every sentence should be the same length. Vary your sentences according to their purpose.

STRATEGIES FOR EFFECTIVE SENTENCES

Effective sentences may be short or long, simple or complex, plain or ornate, depending on the purpose. To create strong suitable sentences, keep the rhetorical situation in mind. Although some sentences can do without certain parts of speech, a verb is always required.

CHOOSING AN EFFECTIVE VOICE FOR VERBS

Action verbs energize writing by showing movement, enabling readers to visualize an activity. For example, *ski, swim,* and *skate* evoke images of physical activity; *think, puzzle,* and *dream* indicate mental activity. Action verbs can be written in either the active or passive voice, depending on the rhetorical situation.

> www.mhhe.com/dietsch
> For more work with verb voice, go to:
> Editing>Verbs

Favoring the Active Voice

Strong action verbs in the active voice energize sentences. *Active voice* simply means that the subject of the sentence is *performing the action*. A verb is in the *passive voice* when the subject *receives the action*. Something or someone else is performing the act or deed, not the subject. Compare the two examples below:

ACTIVE VOICE: White-capped waves pounded the rocky cliff.

PASSIVE VOICE: The rocky cliff was pounded by white-capped waves.

Which sentence gives the sharpest image? What else do you notice? The sentence in active voice has just six words whereas the one in passive voice has eight words. Note that the passive voice requires a verb phrase (was pounded), not just one word. Although the passive voice is useful at times, it adds extra words and lessens the impact of a sentence. To make writing clear and direct, experienced writers usually prefer the active voice.

Replacing *Be* Verbs

Be, in all its forms, indicates a state of being, living, or existing on this planet. The main forms of the verb *be* are *is, am, are, was, were, be, been,* and *being.* For quick recall, you might practice saying them aloud. *Be* verbs, standing alone, do not show action. *Be* verbs are also used as helping verbs with action verbs. (See pages H-11 to H-15.)

Although *be* verbs are sometimes necessary, they often add extra words, diluting writing and weakening the effect. With a little thought, you can often replace a *be* verb with an action verb. This editing shortens and strengthens sentences. The following examples illustrate why action verbs are generally preferred:

BE **VERB:**   Lucille Ball *was* a comedienne who entertained millions with her movies and television show. (14 words)

ACTION **VERB:**   Comedienne Lucille Ball *entertained* millions with her movies and television show. (11 words)

CRAFTING SENTENCES AND PUNCTUATING

For most of your college writing, you will be relying on three basic sentence types: the *simple* sentence, *complex* sentence, and *compound* sentence. Used less often are the *compound-complex* sentence and the *periodic* sentence. All differ in purpose and use. A simple sentence highlights *one* idea.

SIMPLE: Interviewers may ask about weaknesses. (one independent clause)

COMPOUND: Interviewers may ask about weaknesses, but savvy applicants prepare for this question. (two independent clauses)

COMPLEX: Since interviewers may ask about weaknesses, savvy applicants prepare for this question. (dependent clause + independent clause)

By mixing and varying these three basic sentence structures according to the rhetorical situation, you not only add interest but also emphasize key points and clarify relationships between ideas.

The Simple Sentence

The research of Rudolph Flesch revealed that simple sentences compose about 70 percent of most expository writing. A *simple sentence* contains a subject (which may consist of more than one noun) and one or more verbs. The simple sentence is an *independent* clause—one complete thought that can stand alone.

www.mhhe.com/dietsch
For additional coverage of sentence types, go to:
Editing>Sentence Types

Elements of Simple Sentences   Every sentence must have a subject, whether implicit or explicit, and a verb. This basic unit conveys a complete thought. Most simple sentences contain other parts, including objects, prepositional phrases, other modifiers, and perhaps additional verbs:

- Eagles soar. (subject and verb)
- Eagles build *large nests.* (+ direct object)
- Eagles build large nests *in isolated places.* (+ prepositional phrase)
- *Usually,* eagles build large nests in isolated places. (+ adverb)
- Usually, eagles build large nests in isolated places and *lay two or three eggs.* (+ second verb and second object)

Understood *You*   Sometimes nouns and other words are omitted from a simple sentence, leaving one verb in the active voice to stand alone as a one-word sentence. For example, "Sit!" "Stop!" and "Heel!" are each a complete sentence. Although the subject of these brief sentences has been omitted, it is understood to be *you.* The omission makes the sentence quite concise—ideal for giving directions and orders or for explaining a procedure or process (chapter 11). Other sentences with *you* understood are longer. In the following examples, the understood subject is marked by brackets:

- [You] Turn left at the third stop light.
- To make excellent tea, [you] first heat the water to a rolling boil.

If just simple sentences are used, writing can sound dull. Every now and then, as you revise, look for ways to expand simple sentences into complex sentences. Or you might combine two simple sentences into a compound sentence.

The Compound Sentence

A *compound sentence* emphasizes related ideas of equal importance. It contains two main subjects and two main verbs. Usually, the two ideas are linked by a coordinating conjunction preceded by a comma, although a semicolon can be substituted, as in the third example.

- Mammoth Cave is the largest cave in the United States, *but* Carlsbad Caverns are the most colorful.

- William Zinsser advises placing "but" at the beginning of a sentence to "alert the reader . . . to any change in mood," *yet* this is a departure from traditional rules.

- An ancient Persian poem contains a reference to chess; a Persian book states that chess arrived there during the reign of King Chosoe-I Annshiravan (531–579).

Coordinating Conjunctions

These special words connect elements of equal rank, such as clauses, phrases, or nouns that are parallel. Since there are just seven coordinating conjunctions, you can soon memorize them. An acronym that will jog your memory is *fanboys: for, and, nor, but, or, yet, so.*

To choose a suitable conjunction for a compound sentence, look at the relationship of the ideas in the clauses. If the second clause adds additional information, use *and.* If the second clause contrasts with the first, use *but* or *yet.* If the second clause shows a cause-and-effect relationship with the first clause, use *for* or *so.* (*So* is more informal than the other six conjunctions and may be unsuitable for some writing.)

PUNCTUATING COMPOUND SENTENCES

If *both* clauses in a compound sentence are *four words or less,* you may join them with a comma. If one clause or both have *five words or more,* you have three options—according to the relationship:

1. **Comma and Conjunction.** Connect two related independent clauses with a *coordinate conjunction* preceded by a comma when transition is needed.

   - The hidden job market consists of an estimated eighty percent of available jobs, *but* most job seekers seem unaware that it exists.

2. **Semicolon.** When the ideas in a compound sentence are so closely related that no transition is needed, use a *semicolon* between independent clauses.

   - The hidden job market consists of an estimated eighty percent of available jobs; only twenty percent or so of the available jobs are ever advertised.

3. **Colon.** When the second clause of the compound sentence explains the first, join with a *colon.*

   - The astute job seeker carefully compiles search documents: most employers expect a résumé, cover letter, thank-you letter, and list of references.

www.mhhe.com/dietsch
For further coverage of comma use, visit:
Editing>Commas

Avoiding Fused Sentences and Comma Splices   A *fused sentence* occurs when punctuation is omitted between long independent clauses (sentences with five words or more). Add either a comma and coordinate conjunction or a semicolon between the two clauses.

FUSED SENTENCE:	A large multicolored rooster strutted along the city sidewalk people were in such a hurry that few noticed.
CORRECT:	A large multicolored rooster strutted along the city sidewalk, *but* people were in such a hurry that few noticed. (comma and conjunction)
FUSED SENTENCE:	His feathers glistened in the sunlight his red comb had a regal air.
CORRECT:	His feathers glistened in the sunlight; his red comb had a regal air. (semicolon)

Another error, the *comma splice,* occurs when long independent clauses are linked by a comma alone. Either add a coordinating conjunction or replace the comma with a semicolon.

COMMA SPLICE:	Terrariums are costly at a flower shop, they are inexpensive to make at home.
CORRECT:	Terrariums are costly at a flower shop, *but* they are inexpensive to make at home. (coodinate conjunction added)
COMMA SPLICE:	A sign read "High Water," however, one driver ignored the warning, and his car spluttered to a stop.
CORRECT:	A sign read "High Water"; however, one driver ignored the warning, and his car spluttered to a stop. (semicolon replaces the first comma)

The Complex Sentence

A *complex sentence* consists of an independent clause and one or more dependent clauses. The major idea appears in the independent clause; the minor idea appears in the dependent clause. To the untrained eye, a dependent clause may look like a complete sentence because both have a subject and a verb. But the dependent clause has a word at the beginning that makes the idea incomplete. Thus *a dependent clause is a fragment and cannot stand alone.*

FRAGMENTS (INCOMPLETE IDEAS)

When my cell phone rings

When the pilot tried to land the small plane in a field

SENTENCES (COMPLETE IDEAS)

When my cell phone rings, it plays "Bandana."

When the pilot tried to land a small plane in a field, the plane suddenly caught fire.

See "Relative
Pronouns,"
page H-8.

Adjective Clauses

Adjective clauses are dependent clauses that refer to nouns or pronouns. These clauses are easy to identify because they always start with one of five relative pronouns: *who, whom, whose, which,* or *that.* (Think: four *w*'s and a *t*.) An adjective clause may be essential or nonessential:

ESSENTIAL: The car *that Petra prefers* has four cup holders.
The man *who is wearing the navy suit* is Ken's uncle.

NONESSENTIAL: Mark, *who is my eldest brother,* jogs fifty miles weekly.
Risa's diamond, *which was bought at Higby's,* weighs one carat.

Did you notice that the sentences with *essential* clauses need no commas? But the sentences with *nonessential clauses require a pair of commas.* These commas act like tiny parentheses is to set off extra material that could be removed. To test whether or not a clause is essential, cover it with your hand and read the rest of the sentence. Does the basic meaning of the sentence change without the clause? If so, no commas are needed: the clause is essential. If the meaning does not change, set off the nonessential clause with commas.

**DISTINGUISHING
WHO, WHOM,
WHICH, AND THAT**

1. *That* is used to indicate *essential* information. Sometimes *that* can be omitted.
   That refers to people, animals, or things.

2. *Who* and *whom* refer only to people. *Which* can refer to animals or things.
   Who, whom, and *which* can introduce *essential* or *nonessential* clauses.

Adverb Clauses

Adverb clauses, like adverbs, tell *when, where, why, how,* or *under what conditions.* Adverb clauses begin with *subordinating conjunctions.* Some introduce reasons or explanations (because, since, whereas, although). After you learn to recognize the common subordinating conjunctions, you will be able to identify adverb clauses easily.

COMMON SUBORDINATING CONJUNCTIONS

when	although	if	as	whether
while	even though	until	as long as	before
where	so that	unless	as though	than
since	because	as if	after	whenever

An adverb clause may come before or after an independent clause in a complex sentence. Let's look at two versions of a sentence with the dependent clause italicized:

- *When a puma leaped onto the porch,* I slammed the door.
- I slammed the door *when a puma leaped onto the porch.*

Notice that the first sentence is more vivid because the ideas appear in chrono-logical order. Emphasis on *I* is also lessened within the sentence.

PUNCTUATING SENTENCES WITH ADVERB CLAUSES

1. **Introductory adverb clause.** When a long adverb clause (five words or more) appears at the beginning of a sentence, *place a comma after the clause.* If a misreading is possible, use a comma after a short clause.

2. **Concluding adverb clause.** When an adverb clause appears at the end, in a sequence of two events, no comma is needed.

The Compound-Complex Sentence

An expanded version of the complex sentence, the *compound-complex sentence* contains *two or more* independent clauses and *one or more* dependent clauses. Since compound-complex sentences tend to be long and complicated, they slow down reading and understanding. Therefore, they are used less often than other sentence styles. But in some cases a compound-complex sentence may be necessary.

If you construct a compound-complex sentence and find it cumbersome, you might consider two options: Divide the sentence into two sentences or create a complex sentence (subordinate one idea into a dependent clause). Both options allow for condensing, as shown here.

COMPOUND-COMPLEX: Ryan disagreed with other board members who wanted to raise the CEO's salary from $350,000 to $575,000 per year; nevertheless, he said nothing and raised his hand when most of the other members did. (34 words)

- **DIVIDED:**   Ryan disagreed with other board members who wanted to raise the CEO's salary from $350,000 to $575,000 per year. (19 words) Yet he said nothing and raised his hand when most of the other members did. (15 words)

- **COMPLEX:**   Although Ryan disagreed about raising the CEO's salary from $350,000 to $575,000 per year, he said nothing and voted for it. (21 words)

The option you choose will depend on the rhetorical situation and how much emphasis you need to place on each idea. To hear the differences in emphasis in the examples above, read them aloud.

The Periodic Sentence

A *periodic sentence* provides a refreshing change of pace, as well as emphasis. This sentence builds anticipation and suspense by presenting minor details before the major idea. This means the major idea always comes just before the period. The subject may appear early in the sentence, but *the verb is always delayed*. In "Rocky Mountain High," James Kelly uses a periodic sentence to emphasize an unusual item for sale:

> In Sandpoint, Idaho, a favorite refuge of disillusioned Californians, boutiques and craft shops flourish and stores sell wooden tubs for outdoor bathing.

James Herriot, a veterinarian well-known for his writing, used a periodic sentence at the end of his story "The Strychnine Episode at Darrowby":

> To me, the outbreak is a sad memory of failure and frustration. Fergus was my only cure. But over the years, when I saw the big dog striding majestically in his harness, leading his master unerringly around the streets of Darrowby, I always had one good feeling.

In this final sentence, Herriot builds to a climax, saying in one sentence what someone else might have said in three. Yet the periodic sentence is not an everyday sentence—it should be used to emphasize a significant idea.

POSITIONING ELEMENTS AND PUNCTUATING SENTENCES

Rearranging important words, phrases, or clauses can add variety and strengthen sentences. By moving an element to the beginning or end of a sentence, you place it in a *position of emphasis*. If you put important material in the middle, the reader may skim or skip it. To discern the best way to position sentence parts, rewrite the sentence in two or three ways, examine the differences, and read the results aloud.

Moving Sentence Parts and Adding Commas

When you change the normal order of a sentence (subject and verb are first), its sound and impact change. Usually, a comma is needed to set off the part that is moved.

NORMAL ORDER

- Joni clung tightly to the ropes as she started across the swinging bridge.
- The river swirled over large rocks far below.
- She focused on each narrow board and forced her feet over the empty spaces.

INVERTED ORDER, REQUIRING A COMMA

- Clinging tightly to the ropes, Joni crossed the swinging bridge over the abyss.
- Far below, the river swirled over large rocks.
- Focusing on each narrow board, she forced her feet over the empty spaces.

Did you notice that each change in the inverted order creates a more vivid image? Depending upon the purpose, you can also vary the normal order of a sentence by moving modifiers *within* the sentence. Such interruptions are set off with a pair of commas.

INTERRUPTED ORDER, REQUIRING A PAIR OF COMMAS

- I was astounded to see, outside my kitchen window, an unusual sight.
- A mother wren, angry at an inquisitive squirrel, was chasing him across the yard.

Notice that the interruption in each sentence builds suspense by delaying the key idea. As you revise, pause at times to think about ways to move modifiers to increase the effectiveness of your sentences.

Using Expletives

The English language includes two common expletives, *there* and *it*.* Expletives occupy space in a sentence but do not contribute to the meaning. As an expletive, *there* or *it* often appears at the beginning of a sentence. If you use either one in this way, check the sentence carefully to see whether the expletive increases the effectiveness of the sentence.

EXPLETIVE

- *There* is a yellow swallowtail butterfly on the patio.
- *It* is a fact that in preschool most boys lag behind most girls in verbal proficiency.

EDITED

- A yellow swallowtail butterfly is circling the patio.
- In preschool most boys lag behind most girls in verbal proficiency.

Yet an expletive sometimes adds zest to a sentence:

- *There* are no words to convey the depth of my appreciation.
- *It* is wonderful to see bright sunshine in November!

---

*In other contexts *there* can function as an adverb and *it* as a pronoun.

CREATING PARALLEL SENTENCE STRUCTURE

www.mhhe.com/dietsch

Further coverage of parallelism can be found at:
Editing>Parallelism

Parallelism is a balancing act, easily accomplished, that improves the grace and style of sentences. When you write compound sentences, the two independent clauses are parallel. The clauses have the same grammatical form (subject + verb; subject + verb). To create parallelism, you pair or match similar structures. Nouns are matched with nouns, active verbs with active verbs, passive verbs with passive verbs, and *be* verbs with *be* verbs.

There are different degrees of parallelism. Formal situations such as presidential speeches often call for precise parallelism with more repetition than informal situations, where part of the parallel structure is omitted. As you edit, be alert for instances of faulty parallelism. Reading your writing aloud will help you hear the awkwardness that results from nonparallel structures.

Parallel Pairs and Items in a Series

Regardless of whether pairs of items are single words, phrases, or clauses, all should be parallel just as in items of a series. Whenever you see a coordinating conjunction *(for, and, nor, but, or, yet, so)*, that is a clue that parallelism is required.

Parallel Nouns   In *Coping with Difficult People*, Robert Bramson often uses parallel nouns:

- "It pays to follow up any *complaint* or *suggestion* with an inquiry about what's happened."
- Your coping reply should be to ask, 'Is that a *decision* or just your *opinion* at this stage?'"

Parallel Adjectives   In the next example, Bramson uses three parallel adjectives that are not only parallel but also alliterative (all start with the same consonant sound of the letter *p*):

- "Three factors in the Complainers' view of the world combine to convert useful problem solving into complaining: They find themselves *powerless, prescriptive,* and *perfect.*"

Parallel Verbs   To be parallel, *verbs must be the same tense and the same voice.* Different tenses should not be mixed. Passive voice should not be mixed with active voice. The italicized verbs below are parallel.

- The slender aspens *were covered* with ice and [*were*] *bent* by its weight. (Both verbs are past tense, passive voice.)
- The students *are protesting* parking fees and [*are*] *requesting* free parking. (Both verbs are in present tense and active voice.)

Parallel Phrases   Related phrases, whether prepositional, infinitive, or gerund, should be balanced:

- *"For richer* or *for poorer, in sickness* and *in health"* (prepositional phrases)
- *To run a company profitably* and *to treat the environment responsibly* need not be conflicting goals. (infinitive phrases)

The final item in the series of gerund phrases below is not parallel. Yet it can be corrected easily:

NOT PARALLEL: Lee likes listening to music, taking long walks, and *also likes to work crossword puzzles.*

PARALLEL: Lee likes *listening* to music, *taking* long walks, and *working* crossword puzzles.

Parallel Clauses   A famous sentence from the Declaration of Independence contains three parallel clauses: "We hold these truths to be self-evident, *that all men are created equal, that they are endowed by the Creator with certain unalienable Rights, that among these are Life, Liberty, and the pursuit of Happiness."* (All the parallel clauses start with *that* and all contain the verb *are.*)

Parallel Comparisons

Comparisons formed by using *as* or *than* should be parallel. To balance, the two subjects being compared must have the same grammatical form:

- A *spelling check* (noun) is not as accurate as *careful proofreading* (noun).
- For most interviews, *wearing a suit* (gerund phrase) is safer than *wearing casual attire* (gerund phrase).

As you check your comparisons, look for faulty parallelism. Note how the imbalance in the first sentence below can be rectified in two ways:

NOT PARALLEL: It is wiser *to do* (infinitive phrase) class work throughout a semester than *cramming* (gerund) the night before an exam.

EDITED: It is wiser *to do* class work throughout a semester than *to cram* the night before an exam. (two infinitive phrases)

EDITED: *Doing* class work throughout a semester is wiser than *cramming* the night before an exam. (two gerunds)

Parallel Correlative Conjunctions

Correlative conjunctions work in pairs to link words, phrases, or clauses. These conjunctions add style and emphasis to a sentence by requiring parallel structure. Common correlative conjunctions include these five pairs:

either . . . or

not . . . but

both . . . and

neither . . . nor

not only . . . but also

Correlatives need to be in the correct place in a sentence to be logical and balanced. Place the correlative right *before* the word or phrase that it modifies:

NOT PARALLEL: *Either* you pay the fee for parking *or* a penalty.

PARALLEL: You pay *either* the parking fee *or* a penalty. (Each correlative precedes an article and a noun.)

NOT PARALLEL: *Not only* was the defendant charged with breaking and entering *but also* with resisting arrest.

PARALLEL: The defendant was charged *not only* with breaking and entering *but also* with resisting arrest. (Both of the correlatives precede prepositional phrases.)

PUNCTUATING SENTENCES WITH PARALLEL STRUCTURES

SIMPLE SENTENCES

Unless a simple sentence contains items in a series, there is *no comma* before the final conjunction. In the first set of examples, the parallel structures are italicized:

- The talk was *interesting, insightful,* and *inspirational.*
- The talk was both *interesting* and *inspirational.*
- David has been outstanding not only *in football* but also *in academic work.*
- He would either *pay* the ninety-six tickets or *go* to jail.

COMPOUND SENTENCES

Since compound sentences have two independent clauses, the final correlative conjunction is preceded by a comma.

- *Not* everyone received a bonus, *but* everyone received a raise.

CHOPPING OUT DEADWOOD

Ernest Hemingway's finished writing is sparse and clean because he worked long and hard to bring it to that state. Once Hemingway was questioned about how often he had revised the ending of his novel *A Farewell to Arms.* He said it had taken thirty-nine revisions. As you revise, don't hesitate to chop out the deadwood—the surplus words that litter sentences. Among the most common are unnecessary references to self.

OMITTING UNNECESSARY REFERENCES TO SELF

Self-confident persons sometimes refer to themselves often during conversation. In writing, however, this tendency should be monitored, lest it give the impression of an oversized ego. If *I* appears at the beginning of a sentence, the writer may be able to invert the sentence. Placing *I* in the middle of a sentence makes the reference to self less noticeable. Delete unnecessary words as long as there is no change in meaning:

DRAFT: I will graduate on June 12 and will be available for employment after that. (14 words)

EDITED: After graduation, June 12, I will be available for employment. (10 words)

When a rough draft has two sequential sentences that begin with *I*, try to combine the sentences and delete one of the *I*'s as well as extra words. Then check the edited sentence to be sure it is clear and complete.

DRAFT: I use Microsoft Office XP often at my present job. I also use C++ for some tasks. (17 words)

EDITED: At work I often use Microsoft Office XP and C++. (10 words)

Still another way to bypass *I* is to substitute *me* or *my* when a reference to self seems necessary.

DRAFT: I can type accurately, answer the telephone courteously, and perform basic accounting functions, as you requested in your ad for a receptionist. (22 words)

EDITED: My keyboarding skills, telephone etiquette training, and experience with accounts payable/receivable should qualify me for your position of receptionist. (20 words)

Sometimes a writer will go to another extreme: completely avoiding *I*, *me*, *my*, or *mine* by resorting to stilted phrases such as "the writer" or "the author of this paper." Experienced writers use *I* sensibly and sparingly.

DELETING USELESS PREPOSITIONAL PHRASES

See pages H-16 to H-17.

A string of unnecessary prepositional phrases may be another source of wordiness. If you find more than two prepositional phrases close together, check for wordiness. Although a string of these phrases may not affect clarity, there may be a more concise way to make your point. Consider the following examples:

DRAFT: A new type of compact, the Stallion II by CMG, was rated the safest in recent collision tests of compacts. (19 words)

> **EDITED:**   CMG's new Stallion II was rated safest in recent collision tests of compacts. (12 words)

Common phrases such as "this *type of* car" or "this *kind of* oven" or *"in the amount of $10"* may be shortened to "this car" or "this oven" or "$10."

CONDENSING ADJECTIVE CLAUSES

Sometimes there is little justification for an adjective clause, and the sentence can be made more effective by trimming the clause down to an appositive. Or you might substitute an adjective for an adjective clause. Consider the following examples:

> **DRAFT:**   Dr. Reddi, *who has been our physician since I was a child,* is going to retire. (adjective clause)

> **EDITED:**   Dr. Reddi, *our long-time family physician,* is going to retire. (appositive)

> **DRAFT:**   My Appaloosa mare, *which is only two years old,* placed first in the "Best-Trained Horse" trials. (adjective clause)

> **EDITED:**   My *two-year-old* Appaloosa mare placed first in the "Best-Trained Horse" trials. (adjective)

Parallelism

Directions: Make the italicized segments parallel.

1. Peach orchards dot the south-central shore of Lake Erie in Ohio, but *grapes are grown* along the eastern shore in New York.

2. Ohio's principal crops are corn, soybeans, and *sometimes wheat is also grown.*

3. Raising soybeans is much more profitable than *to raise corn.*

4. Canola, which yields an edible oil, is grown more often than ordinary rape, *yielding a similar oil.*

5. Many farmers who live near large cities have switched from planting grain crops *to vegetables.*

6. To produce a pound of meat on chickens costs much less than *producing* a pound of meat on beef cattle.

7. Collies are a favorite farm dog because they are intelligent, suited to herding, and *they are gentle with children.*

8. A well-trained collie can round up a herd of cows and see *that they go into the barn.*

9. Border collies range from 25 to 65 pounds whereas *Scotch collies range from 45–70 pounds.*

10. Border collie puppies often sell for $300 *and up to $600 each.*

Choosing Words That Work Well

> Words play an enormous part in our lives. . . . Words have power to [mold] . . . thinking. . . . Conduct and character are largely determined by the nature of the words we currently use to discuss ourselves and the world around us.
>
> —Aldous Huxley

The words we hear and use color our perception of the world around us. Words can encourage or discourage, gladden or sadden, soothe or inflame, strengthen or weaken a relationship, win or lose an election. The words of parents, teachers, and others help to shape our attitudes, values, and beliefs.

The words we choose influence the tone of our speech and writing—and how the listener or reader perceives them. If the words are inappropriate for the topic, audience, and occasion, they can create a negative impression and distort the intended message. Through study and reading aloud, you can increase your awareness of your written voice.

READING REAPS BENEFITS

Reading widely and often will help you acquire not only more knowledge and a larger vocabulary but also a deeper awareness of the nuances and subtle meanings of words. Through challenging reading, you can find new words and become more alert to variations in a writer's voice. This chapter will help you become more aware of delicate distinctions in word meanings and positive communication strategies. With careful editing, your writing will have more depth, diplomacy, and clarity.

I. EFFECTIVE WORD CHOICE

Selecting words is rather like shopping in an enormous supermarket. But instead of roaming the aisles for groceries, a writer thumbs through the pages of a dictionary or thesaurus, or goes online to search for the right words. The supply is plentiful, for the English language has more words than any other language. Whether a writer wants plain bread-and-butter words, sweet words, tart words, tasteless words, kosher words, gourmet words, or playful words—they are all there for the taking, free of charge.

MAKING THE MESSAGE CLEAR

How can you be sure that your writing is clear and appropriate? First, consider your audience and purpose. Choose words they will understand and words that fit the occasion. Second, *make sure you say what you mean in a diplomatic way.* Careless word choice can antagonize. Words should be clear and precise but not hurtful or irritating. A key to clarity is the cautious use of specific, concrete words. Avoid unnecessary value judgments.

Choosing Concrete Words Carefully

Concrete words describe actual details that can be perceived through the senses. You can *see* a purple crocus, the rings of a lunar eclipse, and the muted hues of a rainbow. You can *hear* the whir of a hummingbird's wings or the thump of a human heart. You can *smell* the fragrance of honeysuckle and the reek of an annoyed skunk. You can *touch* the fur of a baby rabbit and *feel* the grit of sandpaper. You can *taste* the sweetness of raspberry jam and the piquancy of horseradish. Concrete words stimulate the imagination and evoke vivid images, allowing the listener or reader to quickly understand what you mean.

QUESTIONS TO FIND CONCRETE WORDS

1. How does *X* look? Size? Shape? Color? Length of hair/coat?

2. Does *X* make a sound? Volume? Rate? Pitch?

3. How does *X* feel? Cool? Soft? Uneven?

4. Does *X* have a fragrance or odor? Fresh? Faint? Pleasant? Perfumed?

5. If *X* is edible, how does it taste? Sweet? Sour? Tangy? Acid? How does it feel on the tongue? Smooth? Satiny? Lumpy? Coarse?

6. Could the words offend the reader/listener? Is the topic too personal to mention?

Using Abstract Words Wisely

Abstractions are intangible concepts that lack a physical existence. Abstract words identify ideas, theories, or invisible qualities, such as *honesty, patriotism,* and *courage.* When you use abstractions, be prepared to provide concrete examples—specific instances with details. Otherwise, your audience will interpret your words in their own individual ways. Unexplained abstractions can make language vague and unclear.

You can steer away from meaningless abstractions by avoiding the use of *thing* and *stuff. Thing* is a shapeless blob of a word, the most abstract of all. *Thing* can refer to a monster or a gnat, a flask of poison or a glass of buttermilk, a viper or a star. *Thing* can mean a condition, quality, vegetable, animal, mineral—or any bit of matter on or off this planet. *Stuff,* in a colloquial sense, is an elastic word that can refer to objects, talk, or actions: "I picked up some stuff"; "Don't give me that stuff about being too busy."

Thing and *stuff* serve as substitutes for thinking. As you revise, watch for other abstract nouns and adjectives (*beautiful, terrible, great,* and the like). With thought and a thesaurus, you can replace worn-out words with concrete words.

Moving from General to Specific

Depending on the purpose, much writing can be made clearer and more interesting by editing general terms, such as *cat, dog,* or *horse,* and replacing them with specific terms, such as *black kitten, border collie pup,* or *sorrel stallion.* In the sentences below, note the different effects of general words and specific words:

GENERAL: A frog was in my garden.

SPECIFIC: A large leopard frog sat under a fringed canopy of parsley in my garden.

GENERAL: Bicycling is a good way to see fall leaves.

SPECIFIC: Bicycling on country roads lets me savor the brilliance of an Indiana autumn.

Specific words can create interest and imagery, but don't drench the reader with details unrelated to the purpose. And in some situations, a general word or a less specific word may be the better choice. Consider how specific you want to be. How will the words affect the audience?

Scholarly or Simple Words?

> A woman went up to Adlai Stevenson after a speech. Enthusiastically, she said, "Oh, Mr. Stevenson, I think your speech was absolutely superfluous!" He replied, "Thank you. I think I shall have it published—posthumously." "Fine!" she said. "The sooner, the better."

Leafing through a thesaurus, some students select scholarly or other unfamiliar words without consulting a dictionary. The results may be disastrous or unintentionally amusing. Even if used correctly, words may be inappropriate for a piece of writing. Novelist Kurt Vonnegut says: "Simplicity of language is not only reputable but perhaps even sacred. The Bible opens with a sentence well within the writing skills of a lively fourteen-year-old: 'In the beginning God created the heavens and the earth.'" Vonnegut recommends simplicity for most writing.

Lewis Thomas, an editor, physician, and contributor to the *New England Journal of Medicine,* used simple language to explain a complicated process in his book *The Lives of a Cell:*

> Everything in the world dies, but we know about it [only] as a kind of abstraction. If you stand in a meadow, at the edge of a hillside, and look around carefully, almost everything you can catch sight of is in the process of dying, and most things will be dead long before you are. . . .
>
> There are some creatures that do not seem to die at all; they simply vanish totally into their own progeny. Single cells do this. The cell becomes two, then four, and so on, and after a while the last trace is gone. It cannot be seen as death; barring mutation, the descendants are simply the first cell, living all over again.

Since Thomas is writing for a lay audience, he selects words they will understand. He begins with a statement about death and relates it to his readers. Then he compares the familiar process of death to that of cell division, which is unfamiliar. Because he supports the abstractions with concrete examples, the result is beautifully clear.

Timely Use of Technical Jargon

Technical jargon is the professional or formal language of a trade, profession, or group with a special interest. For example, medical jargon is used daily by pharmacists, physicians, nurses, and technicians. Technical jargon among peers rarely causes problems. But when a message is intended for a layperson, unfamiliar jargon will muddle the message. The resulting confusion could be dangerous. If you are wondering when technical jargon is appropriate, the answer hinges upon two questions:

- Can the jargon be clearly understood by the intended audience?

- Is there a sound reason for using technical language?

WORKPLACE CASE STUDY

WHAT'S THAT AGAIN?

Recently, a friend bought a tube of an over-the-counter hydrocortisone cream, which is widely sold in drug and department stores. The box carried these words: "Warning: For dermatological use only. Not for ophthalmic use."

She blinked and wondered if the average person would understand. Mentally, she revised the message to read, "Warning: Apply to the skin only. Do not use near or in the eyes."

MAKING MESSAGES APPROPRIATE

To receive the attention it deserves, a serious message should be worded well and correctly. Grammatical errors, trite language, and clichés can distract the reader and interfere with the writer's purpose. Two commonly overused and misused words are *a lot* and *get*.

Although *a lot* is frequently heard, it is informal. "Alot" is a common misspelling. Instead, you can use a synonym such as *many, much, several, various, some,* or *considerable.* The word *get* has numerous informal uses that are unsuitable for college writing, for example, "got married." *Were married* is standard English.

Another misused and overused word is *like.* In present-day slang, *like* often functions as a filler for gaps of thought in phrases such as "She, like, uses it in almost every sentence" and "He is, like, so hot." This usage can be jarring in writing and to listeners outside the peer group. (For questions of usage, see the glossary in the back of this book or a good dictionary.)

Tossing Out Trite Language and Clichés

www.mhhe.com/dietsch

For more help avoiding clichés, go to:
Editing>Clichés, Slang, Jargon, Colloquialism

Like favorite recordings, clichés become worn from overuse. Although they were once fresh and original, clichés have become familiar, ingrained in our daily language. Avoid common phrases that echo in your ears during casual greetings and small talk, such as—

richly rewarding	last but not least	never meets a stranger
each and every	tip of the iceberg	enclosed please find
to the tune of	ballpark figure	in this day and age

Many of William Shakespeare's brilliantly descriptive lines, written four hundred years ago, are now clichés. How many of the following have you used?

FAMOUS LINES	SOURCE
The naked truth	*Love's Labour's Lost*, V, ii, 715
A dish fit for the gods	*Julius Caesar*, I, i, 173
Parting is such sweet sorrow	*Romeo and Juliet*, II, ii, 184

Perhaps you are familiar with other timeworn phrases such as "fresh as a daisy," "happy as a lark," or "His bark is worse than his bite." For most conversations and some informal writing, a cliché now and then may be acceptable. In academic and professional writing, clichés rarely belong.

Denotations and Connotations

For years you have been looking up *denotations* in dictionaries. Denotations are the specific, literal meanings of words. If you look up *horsecar* in *Merriam-Webster's Collegiate Dictionary,* you will find two precise denotations: "1: a streetcar drawn by horses [1833] 2: a car fitted for transporting horses."* Denotations seldom cause confusion when writers know a language well and take time to edit carefully. Denotations seldom change. When they do, the changes often take place over a century or more, as in the example above.

Connotations are the imprecise impressions or emotional overtones we bring to words—the fuzzy associations beyond the denotation. Connotations are suggested meanings that vary by culture, occupation, education, region, generation, and gender. For example, men tend to use some words differently than most women, yet dictionaries do not make this distinction.

Connotative meanings can be illusive and difficult to pinpoint when they are not in dictionaries. Another complication is that some connotations change rapidly whereas others remain steady over the years. Connotations may also vary according to individual perceptions, which are shaped by experience and education. As you read the lists of unfavorable and more favorable words, think how they sound to you. Do you agree with the labels?

---

*By permission from *Merriam-Webster's Collegiate® Dictionary,* Eleventh Edition. Copyright © 2004 by Merriam-Webster, Incorporated (www.merriam-webster.com).

CONSIDERING HOW WORDS SOUND

Unfavorable	More Favorable
wrong	incorrect, inaccurate
failed	missed
mistake	error
advice	suggestion, recommendation
complained	reported, informed
claimed	stated
problem	concern, challenge
deal	bargain, offer, opportunity

Euphemisms

Euphemisms are words with overly favorable connotations. For politeness or to avoid confrontation, they may be substituted for direct words that might annoy. For example, the manager who bluntly evaluates work as "poor" or "careless" will undermine morale and productivity. But the manager who allows an employee to save face with euphemisms such as "needs to improve" or "you can do better" and who encourages with constructive suggestions will have a better chance of motivating.

If a euphemism is needed in a touchy situation, that is fine—as long as there is no deception. There is a big difference between tact and deceit. Much academic writing is direct and factual. Since euphemisms obscure reality, they are seldom advisable in student essays.

Negative and Positive Words

A negative word or an inappropriate word can contaminate an entire message, causing readers to misunderstand or become so irritated they stop reading. By including positive words, courtesy words, gender-free terms, and inoffensive phrasing, you can improve the tone, particularly for sensitive rhetorical situations.

Focusing on the Positive   During revision, the old adage "Tell them what you can do, not what you can't" is invaluable. Often an idea can be restated indirectly in positive words to soften unpleasant news, as in the examples below:

NEGATIVE: We are *out* of the HP Cwi23T tricolor inkjet print cartridges. They will *not* be available for three days.

POSITIVE: The HP Cwi23T tricolor inkjet print cartridges *will* arrive Thursday afternoon.

NEGATIVE: I *don't* have my paper finished. I had to work seven days last week.

POSITIVE: Professor James, although I worked seven days last week, I *do* have a typed draft. *May* I have another day to *revise*? Or would you *prefer* the rough draft now?

A strategy that will promote harmony in sensitive situations, along with positive words, is to ask suitable questions. When struggling to find a positive word, look up the negative word in a thesaurus and check antonyms. Sometimes we simply overlook positive words, such as the ones below:

advantage	courtesy	help	save
assistance	encourage	invite	succeed
benefit	enjoy	pleasure	success
cooperation	glad	prompt	win

WRITING SUCCESS TIPS: TACT AND DIPLOMACY

1. **Think about the rhetorical situation.** Will the reader be apt to disagree? Is the topic a sore point and apt to pose a risk? How will you proceed?

2. **Begin on a positive note.** Before discussing a negative item, you might thank the person for a previous favor or find an *area of agreement*. (See chapter 19.) If you offer a proposal, consider the benefits to the individual and to the company. Focus on long-term advantages that outweigh any short-term disadvantages.

3. **Choose words carefully.** Consider connotations. Might any words irritate or offend? Can you find a more positive word that has the same denotative meaning? (Consult a thesaurus.)

4. **Offer suggestions softly.** In some situations, consider prefacing a suggestion with a tentative phrase, such as *I wonder* or *You might*. These terms soften the impact of giving advice.

5. **Let your draft cool.** For touchy situations, wait twenty-four hours. Revise and edit before sending. If rushed, have a trusted friend or coworker react to the draft.

6. **Read/listen carefully to the receiver's response.** Do not argue. If you disagree, you might say, "Let me think about it" or "That's an interesting (or different) perspective."

Using Negative Prefixes   If you can't find a positive word and there is a reason to state a negative idea directly, then soften the impact with a negative prefix. There are nine common negative prefixes: *non-, un-, im-, in-, dis-, il-, ir-, a-, ab-*. All enable a writer to delete *not*. For example, instead of *not perfect*, you might say *imperfect* or *irregular*.

Using Courtesy Words   Words such as *please, may I, thanks, thank you, appreciate, appreciation, gratitude, your thoughtfulness, your generosity,* or *your effort* rally a positive response in the reader or listener. Conveying civility will enhance the tone and effectiveness of employment cover letters, other business letters, thank-you notes, e-mail, and other messages.

For emphasis, place courtesy words at the beginning and end of the document. As a safeguard, never send an e-mail, note, memo, or letter without rereading and reconsidering your word choice, as well as the spelling, grammar, and punctuation. When a situation is sensitive, take a day to mull over the best way to word the message.

II. USING INCLUSIVE LANGUAGE IN THE WORKPLACE

Just as society and culture change, so too does language. The Civil Rights Act of 1964 forced the U.S. Department of Labor to revise its *Dictionary of Occupational Titles* to eliminate sexist and ageist terms. Likewise, the Bureau of the Census modified 52 of the 442 categories of work. With this legislation came the idea that language should reflect equality by being gender-free or gender-neutral.

Other important changes that affect language in the workplace have occurred. To prevent lawsuits and other problems, many companies have enacted policies that forbid sexism, abusive language, and various forms of discrimination. Regardless of where you work, an understanding of inclusive language will enable you to interact and to write more effectively.

REPLACING SEXIST TERMS WITH GENDER-FREE TERMS

Although masculine nouns and pronouns (*he, his, him*) were used for centuries to include women, this usage is also outmoded. Other words are frowned upon because they carry sexist overtones, for example, *fireman, policeman, mailman.* But these forms have been dropped in favor of gender-free counterparts such as firefighter, police officer, and mail carrier. One way to avoid this faux pas is by writing in the plural, for example, "players . . . they." But the plural is not always possible. Then one "he or she," or one "his or her," is relatively unobtrusive. Often the best and simplest way is to use gender-free words, omitting any reference to gender.

PLURAL:	The *deans* are to bring *their* projected department budgets.
GENDER SPECIFIC:	Every dean should bring *his* projected department budget. (Correct only if all deans are male.)
GENDER FREE:	Every dean should bring *a* projected department budget.

Sexist	Nonsexist	
man, men (if applied to both sexes)	person, people	**REPLACING**
chairman	chair, chairperson	**SEXIST TERMS**
male nurse	nurse	
girl, gal, my woman	woman (adult)	
man and wife	husband and wife	

REPLACING OFFENSIVE TERMS WITH RESPECTFUL TERMS

In some high-stress jobs, crude and disrespectful language is not uncommon. As a result, many companies have created language codes of ethics. One policy forbids "unwanted, deliberate, repeated, unsolicited profanity, cussing, swearing, insulting, abusive or crude language." Penalties may include counseling or firing, depending on the case.* Definitions of verbal harassment and policies vary.

Although some words may not seem discriminatory, they may be unwise in regard to politeness and the law. The general advice is to avoid mentioning personal attributes, such as size, body parts, attractiveness, or age—even when joking. Careless jokes or teasing about absentmindedness, memory loss, or Alzheimer's are best avoided. And avoid any words that discriminate and disrespect on the basis of ethnicity, religion, race, or color.

TIMING THE DELIVERY OF MESSAGES

The timing, privacy, and delivery of a message influence its reception. For example, if you need to make an apology, don't wait a week or a month. The longer the lapse, the more resentment will grow. Draft and revise the message, even if you plan to deliver it in person. The right words don't always come fluently in tense situations.

Consider each rhetorical situation carefully and how the audience will be likely to perceive the message. Does it concern a sensitive issue? Should it be delivered in private? Should it be said face-to-face or written? When would be the best time to deliver the message? Poor timing and lack of privacy can affect reception. Some messages should be conveyed where they cannot be heard over cubicle walls or in restaurant booths.

Sometimes the rhetorical situation is best served by a prudent memo or letter. In some cases, a written message has three advantages:

---

*Rachel Emma Silverman, "On-the-Job Cursing: Obscene Talk Is Latest Target of Workplace Ban," *Wall Street Journal* 8 May 2001: B14.

- **Privacy.** (Do not send sensitive messages by e-mail; see chapter 26.)
- **Opportunity to revise.** You have more time to consider your words.
- **Record.** You can retain a copy for reference.

Wherever you communicate—in the workplace, in social settings, or at home—listen to the tone of your messages.

CHECKLIST   EDITING FOR CLARITY AND APPROPRIATENESS

The clarity and effectiveness of a message depend on how well you fulfill the purpose and tailor your writing to the audience. To be convincing, the written voice should sound knowledgeable, trustworthy, and appropriate.

1. Are the words clear, specific, and suitable for the audience? (See chapter 2.)

2. If you use abstractions, do you define or give examples or other support?

3. Do any words have negative connotations? Might they offend? (Read your message aloud and think how it might sound to someone else.)

4. Do any words seem trite?

5. Are any words repeated unnecessarily? If so, can you condense or find an accurate synonym?

PRACTICE

COLLABORATIVE LEARNING: Negative Connotations

Directions: Pretend you have had a mild disagreement with a family member. Later you overhear the person describing the exchange. Which terms below would you dislike hearing? Which would be acceptable? Do your group members agree or disagree? If so, why? (Consult a dictionary.)

dispute	quarrel	spat	scrap
hassle	difficulty	fight	row
tiff	altercation	fracas	brawl

EXAMINING NEWS HEADLINES

Notice how a slight difference in wording can change the tone. One item in each pair is an actual newspaper heading. Can you select the actual titles? Discuss your impressions with your group. (Answers are at the end of this chapter.)

1. (a) Broadcasters Fixate on Indecency

   (b) Broadcasters Focus on Indecency

2. (a) Disrespect of Our Judiciary

   (b) Lay Off Our Judiciary

3. (a) Admissions Bar Is Higher for Asians at Elite Schools

   (b) Is the Admissions Bar Higher for Asians at Elite Schools?

4. (a) Three Burglarize Neighbor's Home

   (b) Three Accused in Burglary of Neighbor's Home

5. (a) Exercise Can Keep Colds at Bay

   (b) Exercise Keeps Colds at Bay

WRITE A DESCRIPTION USING CONCRETE WORDS

Directions: In one paragraph, write a description. Give concrete details and examples. If you wish, describe one of the following topics.

1. An unusual pet

2. A family heirloom

3. A vehicle you use or have used

4. Your favorite footwear

5. Your favorite place when you were a child

ANSWERS: "EXAMINING NEWS HEADLINES"

The actual headlines are 1b; 2a; 3b; 4b; 5a.

Options for Organization

London Tower Bridge

Bridges in writing connect streams of thought and clarify ideas. These bridges—whether words, phrases, sentences, or paragraphs—link details and examples. In other words, *transitions* indicate shifts of meaning and relationships. Transitions can denote time and place, similarity or difference, addition, and emphasis. *Numerical transitions* indicate a sequence, such as in the steps of a process or events of a narrative.

In Part 3 you will have the opportunity to view ways that students and authors have used transitions and mixed writing strategies to enhance their writing.

WRITING EXERCISE

1. What intangible "bridges" have you built and enjoyed in your life? What invisible bridges connect you to others? Write a paragraph describing one.

2. Have you visited an unusual bridge? How would you describe it?

MIXING WRITING STRATEGIES FOR A PURPOSE

It was the best of times, it was the worst of times,
it was the age of wisdom, it was the age of foolishness . . .
it was the spring of hope, it was the winter of despair,
we had everything before us, we had nothing before us,
we were all going to Heaven, we were all going direct the other way—

Charles Dickens (1812–1870), *A Tale of Two Cities*

With these immortal words, Dickens opened his epic novel, which describes an eighteenth-century era. Dickens deftly combined various strategies in writing this masterpiece, rather like a master architect blends strategies for building an elegant bridge.

Seldom is one strategy adequate for any builder or writer. Although you undoubtedly combine various writing strategies, you can improve your organization, development, and style by studying part 3. Each chapter focuses on one major strategy of exposition, its chief purpose, and opportunities open to writers. To structure an essay, you have several rhetorical options. For example, your purpose might be to inform or to entertain by narrating an amusing anecdote. Your purpose might be to describe and preserve a memorable moment for your family history or to persuade readers to accept a point of view.

Think long and deep. You have a wellspring of experience to draw from and diverse thoughts to share. The more you write, read, and think, the more proficient you will become. Writing is a process of discovery. The result can be a delight to behold, a bridge to the minds of readers.

Writing Narratives

> Tell me a fact and I'll learn. Tell me a truth and I'll believe. But tell me a story and it will live in my heart forever.
>
> —Native American proverb

When you read a newspaper or watch televised news, you see and hear stories of real people and actual events. Stories impart information in a vivid way—stirring the imagination, eliciting empathy, and lending support to opinion. Magazines, histories, biographies, and college essays also use narration for a purpose. This chapter explains techniques of narration that have a wide range of practical uses.

PURPOSE OF NARRATION

You can use narration as a major or minor writing strategy. For example, medical personnel write reports of patients' conditions and progress. Managers keep brief histories of employees' performance. Law enforcement officers record the events that precede a crime and occur during an arrest. In college, you may write narratives not only in English, business, and technical writing classes but also in anthropology, psychology, prelaw, engineering, and other classes. Although these narratives invariably include description, narration is the major strategy.

General Purpose

An effective narrative recounts action for a purpose, according to the rhetorical situation. If the *general purpose* is to entertain and establish camaraderie, then it may not matter whether the account is fiction or fact. But when the purpose is serious—primarily to reflect, inform, or persuade—then the audience expects facts and should receive them. *Then the writer is obligated to put forth the unvarnished truth.*

Specific Purpose

To be worthwhile, every narrative must have a *point*—a valid reason to be told or written. Whether the point is stated or unstated, it should be apparent by the end of the story. If the purpose is to inform, the main idea, fact, or event is often stated first. When writers probe into causes or motives underlying an event or experience, they may place the point at the end. There they may provide an observation, insight, or lesson learned.

In "The Death of the Moth," Virginia Woolf begins by giving facts about moths, then narrates the brief experience of one moth. She compares the moth's struggle for life with that of all living things: "One could only watch the extraordinary efforts made by those tiny legs against an oncoming doom which could, had it chosen, have submerged an entire city, not merely a city, but masses of human beings . . ." As the moth struggles to live, Woolf is reminded of her own mortality and concludes with this insight:

> The struggle was over. . . . As I looked at the dead moth, this minute wayside triumph of so great a force over so mean an antagonist filled me with wonder. Just as life had been strange a few minutes before, so death was now as strange. The moth . . . now lay most decently and uncomplainingly composed. O yes, he seemed to say, death is stronger than I am.

Woolf's specific purpose is to share her wonder that so small a creature as a moth would struggle so hard to live—just as humans usually do.

ELEMENTS OF NARRATION

Every narrative has six basic elements: *where, when, who, what, how,* and *why* of an event. The answers to these questions and the narrator's point of view influence the effect of the story. The first four are usually answered early and easily when the writer sets the scene, giving the necessary background details.

Where and When

Where did the action take place? What era and time? Under what conditions? Typically, a writer begins by setting the scene of the action, event, or conflict. In fiction, however, the reader may be plunged into the action with little or no explanation. And the opening is the perfect spot to tuck a clue that foreshadows the climax.

Although readers need to know basic facts about the setting, they do not need long, involved descriptions that slow the pace for the reader. Essential details can be disclosed gradually as the story unfolds.

Who

Who was involved? A narrative usually revolves around people, although an animal may take the central role. The writer discloses significant characteristics and qualities of the participants, either explicitly or implicitly, often showing rather than telling. Dialogue can reveal a person's inner life, values, and insights. Personality and character are revealed by the way the person responds to challenges and interacts with others.

What

What happened? Action, conflict, and change are essential features of a narrative. Often the action hinges upon a physical conflict between persons (a feud or war), a person against nature (tornado or flood), or a person against an animal (attack by a cougar). Sometimes the conflict is internal. The individual must make a decision or solve a problem when information is incomplete, or there is no ideal solution.

How

How did it happen? The *how* of a narrative often involves cause and effect. To trace a cause, you might look at the effect and trace it backward. Then your first step is to describe the effect. Consider the short-term effect and any long-term effects (chapter 17). The second step is to look for possible causes. To start, you might ask these questions:

- What exactly was the effect? Was it short term, long term, or both?
- Who or what started the action that caused the effect?

- Could there have been more than one cause? Did a series of events result in the effect? (Complex problems seldom have a single cause.)
- How did the central participant respond?

Why

Why did it happen? The *why* of a narrative is the reasoning or motivation, usually of the central character, that propels the action. Yet the reader may not completely understand why the event happened until the very end. The factor(s) or influence(s) behind the action may seem hazy until you are heavily into examining the facts and revising. To explore why an event happened, you might ask these questions:

- What changes occurred? Who was responsible? Did the person take responsibility for his or her actions?
- Is there a change in attitude or a shift in values that directs behavior? (Examine dialogue, characters' thoughts, and actions.)
- What relationships, connections, or behavior influence the outcome?
- Why does the central character (or other character) act in a certain way?
- What motivated the person?

Point of View in Narration

The way the narrator tells a story influences its credibility. Is the narrator giving an eyewitness account or passing on something heard from someone else? How reliable is the narrator? How objective? How does the narrator regard the subject? From which angle or attitude?

Who is the narrator? In nonfiction, the writer is often the narrator. In fiction, an observer or one of the characters often acts as the narrator. If you observed the event firsthand, you might use a first-person point of view, depending on your writing purpose and the rhetorical situation.

First-Person Narration   First-person narration lends a sense of immediacy, giving the reader a front-row seat on the action. A firsthand account is often written in a conversational tone. Whether you choose first person (*I, me, my, mine, we,* or *ours*) or another perspective will depend upon your role. Is it your story or someone else's? Barb Bronson uses first person in her essay, based on experience. The first three paragraphs appear here:

Clipper Ship Mom

Unique and truly American, the clipper ship is a fast-sailing cargo ship whose shipmaster's talents have never been surpassed. My mother reminds me of those early ships and courageous sailors. Whenever the open sea of marriage gave warning of an approaching storm, Clipper Ship Mom would batten down the hatches and set her course in preparation for the rough voyage ahead. As a child, I watched helplessly as Clipper Ship Mom sailed to a hell where my father resided as gatekeeper.

Even when my father was sober, his behavior was unpredictable. Petty, trivial incidents would arouse his raging temper. But whenever he had too many drinks, it was like coming face to face with Satan himself. So many times I wished Mom would take us away to some safe place where we could hide. I also knew Mom had been taught to honor her marriage vows—for better or worse.

When I was fourteen I awoke to an argument which led to my father's yanking my mother to the front yard in her nightclothes and placing a gun to her temple as her five children watched. He told us to say goodbye to our mother; she was going to "meet her maker." Frozen with fear, we clung to each other as tears streamed down our faces. Looking to the heavens above, I whispered a prayer for God to spare her life. He must have heard the prayer, for after a while Dad calmed down, and we all went back to bed.

Mixing Writing Strategies   In this excerpt from "Clipper Ship Mom," Barb Bronson mixes writing strategies. She supports her thesis with comparison, description, and narration. Comparison begins in the title, "Clipper Ship Mom," and continues through the first paragraph. The second paragraph describes and summarizes the problem. The third paragraph narrates an episode. Comparison then reappears in the conclusion (page 159).

Third-Person Narration   Writers who are not personally involved in a story adopt a third-person point of view. They restrict pronouns to words such as *he, she, it, they,* and *them.* Third-person narration puts distance between the reader and the topic, producing a more detached voice than first person provides. A professional response, such as those found in many business and technical reports or research papers, usually requires third-person point of view. There the goal is to focus on facts and results, not on feelings or opinions. Reporters, biographers, and historians use third person in an objective way for various reasons.

The following third-person narrative recounts a disastrous 1981 accident at the Hyatt Regency Hotel in Kansas City. Think how differently a narrative of the accident by a first-person survivor would have sounded.

At 7:05 p.m. on Friday, July 17, 1981, the atrium was filled with more than sixteen hundred people, most of them dancing to the music of a well-known band for a tea dance competition, when suddenly a frightening, sharp sound like a thunderbolt was heard, stopping the dancers in mid-step. Looking up toward the source of the sound, they saw two groups of people on the second- and fourth-floor walkways, observing the festivities and stomping in rhythm with the music. As the two walkways began to fall, the observers were seen holding on to the railing with terrified expressions on their faces. The fourth-floor walkway dropped from the hangers holding it to the roof structure, leaving the hangers dangling like impotent stalactites. Since the second-floor walkway hung from the fourth-floor walkway, the two began to fall together. There was a large roar as the concrete decks of the steel-framed walkways cracked and crashed down, in a billowing cloud of dust, on the crowd gathered around the bar below the second-floor walkway. People were screaming; the west glass wall adjacent to the walkways shattered, sending shards flying over 100 ft.(30 m); pipes broken by the falling walkways sent jets of water spraying the atrium floor. It was a nightmare the survivors would never forget.

—Matthys Levy and Mario Salvadori, *Why Buildings Fall Down*

There may be a time when you decide to write in third person about your experience. Perhaps the topic is still hurtful, even heartrending. To gain distance and objectivity, you might write in third person about yourself, perhaps using a pseudonym. But first consider the nature of the experience. If a recent event has been traumatic, beware. You can become so entangled in emotion that you hit a writing block and lose the point.

WRITING A NARRATIVE PAPER

www.mhhe.com/dietsch

For online help writing narrative essays, visit: Writing>Writing Tutors> Narration

You have dozens of family stories just waiting to be told—some amusing, some sad, and some happy. Perhaps they are of pranks, other childhood experiences or those of older relatives, passed down from generation to generation. Here is your chance to preserve them. Or you might want to recount a friend's unusual experience.

Prewriting

www.mhhe.com/dietsch

For further coverage of prewriting, check out: Writing>Prewriting

A simple way to start prewriting is to list key events in the order they occurred. Leave an inch or so of space between items to insert related details later, as you think of them. Or you might prefer to mull over an episode and ask yourself:

- Who are the readers? How much do they need to know?
- Where should I start?
- What is the source of tension or conflict? (barrier, problem, decision)
- How did the experience influence me (or the central character)?
- What is the point of the narrative?
- Is there a lesson or moral?

MOVEMENT IN A NARRATIVE

The diagram below depicts how movement might flow from the beginning to the end of a narrative. The central character's motivation and reactions to events, as well as other factors, influence the pace and resolution at the end.

Opening   Climax   *End*

Events: 1   2   3

FIGURE 9.1

Drafting an Introduction

Lately some editors have advised writers that they have just five to ten seconds to hook most readers. As you prewrite, watch for a hook that will lure readers on. To begin an introduction to a narrative, you might ask yourself these questions:

- How should the story start? How can I grab the reader's attention?
- What is unusual, amusing, or ironic?
- Should I use first person or third person?
- How is the opening related to the point of the story?

www.mhhe.com/dietsch

Want more help with introductions? Go to:
Writing>Introductions

The purpose of the narrative will guide you in deciding whether to place the thesis at the beginning or end. Does the reader need to know immediately where the main idea is headed? For reasons of clarity and practicality, some rhetorical situations call for an early thesis. Other times the writer may delay the thesis, *laying a foundation to support the point of the narrative* and building to the peak of the action. Then the thesis comes at the end, where it can be stated or implied, depending upon the purpose.

Opening with Action and Emotion   An *action opening* often plunges the reader into the story with little, if any, explanation. The main participant or character is ensnared in a predicament or is faced with a decision that must somehow be resolved. The participant's emotions are often revealed. At the same time, the writer gradually sets the scene, identifying the place, time, and conditions. Necessary bits of information are imparted as the conflict continues and the suspense heightens.

Opening with a Quotation   If you find an appropriate quotation that *specifically* relates to your main idea, then you can easily tie it to the beginning of a narrative, using embedded transition. Be sure that any explanation does not delay the action unduly. Do not belabor the point of the quotation lest the reader perceive it as talking down. If you want to use a quotation that relates in a *general* way to your main point, then you will need to make the connection clear.

See chapter 15.

Opening with a Comparison   An unusual comparison in the title or first paragraph can hook the reader and serve as a unifying thread throughout the narrative. The comparison is introduced early and alluded to periodically. Sometimes a comparison may involve a symbol rich in connotations, as in "Clipper Ship Mom," earlier in this chapter. Note that along with this striking symbol, the writer used water imagery: matrimonial seas, rough seas, tears, and similar images in developing her paper.

Organizing a Narrative Paper

Narratives need a clear progression. Each event, detail, and scrap of dialogue should advance the narrative point and contribute to the unity. If you can limit the focus early, then it will be easier to decide what to include—and what to omit. Or if the white heat of inspiration seizes you, write down everything, then go back and delete extra details, no matter how interesting. Make sure that every detail helps to establish a coherent design.

In most narratives the action is presented in the order that it occurs. Sometimes, however, a writer may disrupt the chronology by a sudden shift to the past, or *flashback*. For example, you might begin a narrative at a dramatic moment near its chronological conclusion, then flash back to events leading up to this point. Keep in mind, though, that flashbacks are tricky to manage effectively because of the special transition and plotting required. As a novice writer of narrative, you may want to stick to chronological order.

Developing the Narrative Paper

As you develop a narrative, keep in mind the nature of the central character. It is usually advisable to look at people and events from a positive perspective but to be realistic. Human beings are a mix of negative and positive traits, and life is a blend of potholes, porcupines, and poppies. The following questions may be helpful to consider:

- Does the main character have a need or compulsion to reach a goal?
- Does the person have an internal or external conflict? A barrier to face?
- What will the person do?
- What is the darkest moment—the crisis? (It usually occurs about halfway.)
- How does the person react?
- What is the high point of the action—the climax?
- Does the person change or learn?

Dialogue   Selected dialogue can enliven a narrative, advance the action, and give clues to the personality of the speaker. Dialogue should have the ring of real conversation but move more quickly. Including actual words of participants can make the story come alive and ring true. The writer may edit the dialogue to make it direct and to the point, compressing, leaving those words that convey information and lend flavor to the narrative. Note, however, that it would be unethical to twist the words out of context and distort the intended meaning. Diane P. includes just one line of dialogue in the opening of her narrative:

> My first night in Houston, Texas, while visiting a friend, a hurricane hit. I slept through most of it. But when her brother yelled, "It's going to take the roof!" I awoke. As I sat up in bed, half awake, he dashed down the hall in his

underwear, headed for the front door. Then both doors of the house blasted open—even though they were dead bolted.

When writing dialogue, minimize the use of "he said" and "she said." As long as the identity of the person who is talking is clear, no other identification is needed. Just indent for a new paragraph with each new speaker, no matter how short the exchange. Set off the dialogue with quotation marks. (See "The Mulberry Tree," later in this chapter.)

Concrete Details and Action Verbs   The trick to writing an effective narrative is to nab the reader's attention and retain it by keeping the flow of details interesting. Include just enough *concrete details* of the setting and action to enable readers to visualize events and feel as if they know the people involved. Use vivid verbs, specific nouns, and modifiers that will appeal to your readers' senses not only through sight but also through hearing, touch, taste, and smell. Beware of including unnecessary description that slows the pace and distracts from the point of the narrative.

Building Suspense   Another way to keep readers interested is to build *suspense*. You can do this by hinting at something but withholding crucial details in order to reveal them at a strategic moment. You can also build tension by pacing your narrative so that readers are kept wondering what will happen next. By the end, however, all loose threads should be clearly connected and the conflict or problem resolved. This technique is not applicable to most workplace writing.

Writing a Conclusion

Although endings of narratives vary widely, every ending should have a sense of completeness. It should leave readers satisfied, convinced, empathetic, hopeful, amused, thoughtful, or wiser. Usually, the complication, problem, or conflict is resolved or alleviated at the end. To resolve matters successfully, the writer must tell enough but not too much. If an ending is too long and wordy, it may become tiresome or confusing. Underdeveloped endings may leave readers feeling disappointed or cheated. They should not be left hanging without a clue to the outcome.

www.mhhe.com/dietsch
If you want to learn more about conclusions, go to: Writing>Conclusions

Writing the ending of a narrative may be painstaking. In fact, you may attempt more than one before finally being satisfied. If in doubt about your ending, try asking these questions:

- What is my narrative point?
- Was there an unexpected result?
- Are there any loose ends to resolve?
- Does the ending seem complete?
- Does the voice of the narrator sound appropriate?

Ending with a Hint or a Hope   Even if the full story remains untold or the conflict is not resolved, there should be a clue so that readers can draw their own inferences. For example, in *Gone with the Wind,* Rhett is leaving Scarlett, and she is agonizing over his departure. Yet the reader is offered a hint and a hope that life will get better. The novel closes with these words:

> She could get Rhett back. She knew she could. There had never been a man she couldn't get, once she set her mind upon him.
> "I'll think of it all tomorrow, at Tara. I can stand it then. Tomorrow I'll think of some way to get him back. After all, tomorrow is another day."
>
> —Margaret Mitchell

Ending with a Surprise   An unusual incident or twist may bring a story to a satisfying close. The surprise ending contains something the reader does not expect. The surprise may be amusing, embarrassing, enlightening, romantic, or dramatic as long as it is appropriate. To be effective, the unexpected event should grow out of the action, problem, or conflict. For example, Shasta Scharf used a surprise ending that sprang from a key event in "Just a Walk" (at the end of the chapter).

See chapter 21.   **Ending with a Reaction**   Sometimes a narrative ends with a brief *reaction,* a focused response or thoughtful commentary. The reaction may mention influences, implications, or consequences of the action. There may be an attempt to explain an underlying motive. Columnists, biographers, historians, novelists, and other writers often explore motives that may have precipitated an event. Or the reaction ending may connect a personal experience to one with universal implications, as in "The Mulberry Tree," later in this chapter.

WRITING A NARRATIVE REPORT

A *narrative report* is written in response to the need for a record of a real situation or event. Before starting to write any report, consider the *purpose* and the *audience.* Why is the report needed? To whom is it directed? Will one person or several read the report? Might it become a public record? Considering these questions will help you judge the amount of detail needed, the level of language expected, and the degree of privacy involved.

Unlike personal narratives and fiction, a narrative report always has *a thesis at the beginning.* Reports do not withhold information to build suspense. In the workplace, the reader immediately needs to know the *purpose and scope,* which is the usual heading of the first section. This section tells why the report is being written and the range it will cover.

The body of a report also has a suitable heading. This major section explains the topic. The conclusion (use a heading) may summarize, recommend, or look to the future. For instance, research reports sometimes mention a need for future research. (See "How Research Papers and Research Reports Differ" in chapter R-5. An example of a report appears at the end of that chapter.)

REVISING A NARRATIVE

When revising a narrative, look at the larger items first. Check the shape of the story. Is the setting clear? Does the action flow well, or should some events be rearranged? Is the sequence of events clear, or are more transitions of time and place needed?

Watch for complicated sentences or cumbersome words that slow the pace unnecessarily. When the action is fast-paced, use short sentences. When movement slows, use longer sentences, combining ideas, to reflect the pace (like this one). The checklist that follows will also help you revise.

www.mhhe.com/dietsch
For general help with revision, check out:
Writing>Drafting and Revising

CHECKLIST   REVISING A NARRATIVE

1.   Does the narrative begin at a significant spot?

2.   Is the complication, conflict, or problem clear?

3.   Is the action arranged in the most effective order?

4.   Do major details advance the point of the narrative? Do minor details clearly relate?

5.   Does the pace of sentences reflect what is happening?

6.   Does the ending give a sense of completion?

TWO STUDENT PAPERS: NARRATION

The student writers of these two personal essays show unusual skill in their use of concrete detail, strong verbs, and dialogue. Betty Russell briefly sets the scene before the action begins. The point of her story appears at the end.

The Mulberry Tree

Mr. Grump's mulberries were big, plump, and tempting. At the edge of his yard stood two large trees, loaded with luscious blue-black mulberries. Although I would not have dreamed of stealing, I picked a few off the grass, and ate them; the other kids followed. The berries tasted so good.

There were eight of us—me, Alice, Dorothy, and Shirley, my sisters, and our friends, the four Smith sisters. I was ten years old and they were all younger. We often played at a vacant lot near our homes. There we would fill our cans at the "red haw" (hawthorn) tree. We used the red haws to string for neck-laces or for pretend food when we played house.

That afternoon, however, we had taken a different way to the red haw tree, past Mr. Grump's house. When we saw all those big dark berries going to waste underneath the trees, we decided to fill our cans. Then we thanked "Mr. Mulberry Tree" and ran home. Our mother washed the berries and put them in a big bowl for supper. That evening we piled whipped cream on the berries for dessert. We felt so proud because there were enough to treat the whole family.

Two days later all eight girls agreed it was time for more berries and cream. Our parents, thinking the trees were in the empty lot with the red haws, gave permission to go. To our dismay, when we reached the tree, there were no berries on the ground. Even the lower halves of the trees were bare of fruit. Lucy Smith and my sister Alice, tomboys of the group, climbed a tree, and started jumping and shaking the branches. Mulberries fell like black rain.

We had started to fill our cans, when suddenly a voice thundered, "What are you kids doing? I'm going to call the police. You are on MY property STEALING my mulberries!"

Within seconds Lucy and Alice slid down from the tree. The other kids were running in different directions. Alice grabbed five-year-old Shirley by the hand, and they ran toward home. I turned to pick up my can and, to my horror, saw Mr. Grump holding my seven-year-old sister, Dorothy, up by the back of her neck. Her feet dangled in the air.

"Let her go!" I shrieked.

"I'm going to hand you both over to the police," he yelled. He held her with one hand and tried to reach me with the other. We circled—he, trying to reach me and I, trying to reach Dorothy. But I could not get close enough to grab her without his grabbing me. So I ran up and threw the berries, can and all, in his face. He released his grip on Dorothy, and I snatched her hand.

As we cut across yards and down an alley, we could still hear Mr. Grump yelling. When we reached our yard, we slumped against the back of the garage to catch our breath. Our hearts seemed ready to leap out of our chests. How long we leaned there, I don't know.

Then we sneaked in the house. I hid in the closet under the stairs. Dorothy ran upstairs and hid with Alice under their bed. Shirley ran to the kitchen and clung to Mom like a second skin. When dinner was ready, Mom made us come out of our hiding places and demanded to know what we had done. No one said a word.

For two days we stayed in the house, expecting the police to come any moment and take us away. Our fear and guilt stayed with us for a long time. "Thou shalt not steal" was a commandment we never forgot.

QUESTIONS FOR DISCUSSION

1. What do you learn about the narrator in the first paragraph?
2. What strategy supplements narration?
3. What is the effect of including dialogue?
4. What is the effect of having the commandment in the last line?
5. Does this story remind you of another about a tree with forbidden fruit? What similarities do you see?

The second paper, by Shasta Scharf, is written in the third person. For the concluding paragraph, she shifts to first person for a reason.

▶ **Just a Walk**

Jimmy was seventeen the day he joined the armed forces. Fresh from the coal mines of West Virginia, with only a sixth-grade education and six weeks' survival training in Massachusetts, he was flown over 9,000 miles to Corregidor. Suddenly, his life became a battleground for survival. The day that General MacArthur left the Philippines, Jimmy shot his first enemy warrior. "This," he said, "was the first time I walked through Hell."

As the Japanese took possession of the Philippines, Jimmy was captured and the Bataan Death March began. Jimmy was near the head of the line. For over ninety days, he and the other U.S. soldiers suffered severe malnutrition, dysentery, malaria, and abuse as they walked to a prison camp. That was another walk through Hell. For three years, Jimmy was the camp interpreter. Being the interpreter gave him the chance to send messages to and receive them from the United States Army covertly. The Japanese never knew that "Jimpie," as they called him, was using their equipment for spying.

In 1945 Jimmy and the others left the Philippines via three "Hell Ships." Each ship was designed to hold 200 passengers. Over 1,700 men were crowded into quarters intended for 600. Only 482 men walked off the ships in Osaka, Japan. Poor ventilation, no food, no water, and no place to lie down had taken a heavy toll.

When Jimmy reached the United States, he was decorated for bravery and given a six-day pass to see California. He and three friends drove up to Mt. Shasta to ski. There he beheld "a sight that restored [his] sanity." With seven years of hell behind him, Lake Shasta and the snow-capped mountain in front of him, Jimmy came face to face with a young deer. Only five feet away, the fawn stared straight into Jimmy's eyes. Tears flowed down his cheeks as he gazed at the most beautiful scene he had encountered in his twenty-four years of life.

After his experience at Mt. Shasta, Jimmy's life became less chaotic. He went back to the dark, damp coal mines with his father and brothers. Since mining coal is a "filthy, unsafe job and most people do not live to regret their old age in the mines," Jimmy soon headed north to Ohio and the steel mills. . . .

Jimmy's dream included having a home, a wife, and a daughter, but after marrying "Kat," two sons were born within three years. He loved his sons, yet his heart yearned for a daughter, one who would never engage in combat or shoot another human being. One evening two years later, a girl was born to him and his wife.

The birth certificate was not signed until Jimmy got home from work after midnight, eight hours after the birth. As he stared at his newborn daughter in amazement, he whispered, "She is the most beautiful sight I have ever seen." Recalling that earlier moment of overwhelming joy and peace, my father named me Shasta.

QUESTIONS FOR DISCUSSION

1. Evaluate the effectiveness of Shasta's title. Give a reason for your opinion.

2. Contrast the death march and the drive up Mt. Shasta. Consider what awaited Jimmy at each place.

3. How are a new baby and a fawn similar? How are these two moments connected in the story?

4. Discuss the switch from third person to first person in the last line. Do you think third person throughout would have been more or less effective? Why?

5. Shasta could have ended with her father's death from black lung disease as his final walk through hell. Would this ending have been more or less effective? Why do you think so?

FOR YOUR REFERENCE Narrative Essays in the Reader	• "Sound and Fury," Dan Greenburg, page 542 • "Momma's Encounter," Maya Angelou, page 544 • "The Art of Acknowledgement," Jean Houston, page 549 • "Assembly Line Adventure," Lesley Hazelton, page 552

PRACTICE

WRITE A NEWS STORY

Directions: Assume you are a reporter for your campus or hometown newspaper. Write a news story, using the five *w*'s (pages 121–122). You may want to conduct interviews to gain specific details. The following suggestions may stimulate an idea you can use:

1. New construction, new business, or restaurant
2. Historical highlight: A story from the city's history
3. Profile of the president of the university or college
4. Student interviews about campus concerns
5. Plans for an activity such as May Day, a concert, or a pig roast

WRITE A FIRST-PERSON NARRATIVE

Directions: Select an incident from your experience that may have caused you to laugh, to cry, to run, to show courage, or to learn. Then do some prewriting about the key events, including your reactions. After that, write a unified paragraph or short narrative. Perhaps one of the suggestions below will help you to find a suitable topic:

1. A learning experience—gulp!
2. Your dog's list of New Year's resolutions for you
3. Finding a . . .
4. A wonderful day
5. Your cat's proposal for reorganizing the family household

TEN IDEAS FOR NARRATIVE PAPERS

1 An incident on the job (a narrative report)

2 A narrow escape

3 My first day on the job

4 A strange or embarrassing experience

5 Fatherhood/motherhood is . . .

6 My first taste of defeat

7   A prank that backfired

8   How my parents met

9   The secret in . . .

10   _____ weren't meant for . . .

Describing for a Purpose

Reporter Monica Torline has captured the essence of Tammy Taylor-Wells' personality when describing the diver's duties at the Columbus Zoo and Aquarium. Torline chooses sensory words that encourage readers to visualize the experience and accompany the diver in this underwater world by sharing her impressions vicariously.

> While volunteering at the Discovery Reef exhibit, Tammy has discovered an oceanic passion for a world of quiet beauty. She doesn't need a degree in marine biology to know that a stingray feels like "a soft, wet, velvet blanket," and she has seen the peaceful grace that exists in a sea turtle's eyes.
>
> —Monica Torline, "Under the Sea," *The Marion Star*

PURPOSE OF DESCRIPTION

Successful description has a rhetorical purpose, whether used on the job, in histories and biographies, or in fiction and poetry. Carefully selected details support the purpose. Description has four general purposes:

1. To provide information and stimulate understanding
2. To create imagery, a mood, or an aura of a place
3. To convince
4. To urge the listener to action

Usually description serves as a minor writing strategy, supplementing a major strategy, such as narration, process analysis, or comparison. This chapter, however, explains how description of concrete details can serve as a major writing strategy for various rhetorical situations.

WHAT EXACTLY IS DESCRIPTION?

Description is a recording of concrete details that you see, hear, smell, taste, or touch. On the job and in field research, we *observe, describe, interpret*, and *write* our perceptions of concrete details. This four-stage process enables us to relate the physical data we observe to the result or impression. Then we can contemplate its meaning and implications, whether it be a caterpillar or a proposed budget.

See "Caterpillar Afternoon," page 561.

In research and technical writing, writers use description to help readers understand the qualities and structure of physical objects, organisms, and phenomena. In an argument a writer may describe a shocking or heartrending incident in order to move listeners to action. Then description reinforces the thesis; factual details provide support for the major idea.

Creating a Dominant Impression

When description is the chief writing strategy, the details contribute to the dominant impression—the mood that remains throughout the piece for a purpose. Sensory details unite to produce the mood, such as delight, fear, or curiosity—adding interest as well as evidence. To determine the dominant impression you wish to create, reread your list of concrete details and think about why the topic is meaningful to you. What is the overriding idea or impression that will link the details? The idea need not be dramatic or earth-shaking; it need only be significant to you. You might ask yourself these questions:

- Why do I have a special fondness for the object?
- Did something about it cast a shadow on or change my life?
- How much do I want to say?
- Will that be enough? Will the ending seem complete?

Objective and Subjective Description

You can use objective or subjective description or a combination, depending on the purpose. The tone of an *objective* description is literal, factual, and fair—impartial and impersonal. In scientific and business writing, much description is based on unbiased, objective observation. The aim is to reproduce for the reader exactly what the writer observed without reference to the writer's feelings.

See page 232.

In *Thinking in Pictures*, Temple Grandin objectively describes a demonstration of a machine built by Robert Richardson of Prescott, Arizona, for desensitizing unrideable horses:

> The wild horse was placed in a narrow stall similar to a horse trailer, with two gentle horses in adjacent stalls . . . wild horses will panic when they are alone. The horse's head protruded through a padded opening in the front of the stall, and a rear pusher gate prevented him from backing up and pulling his head inside. Sand slowly filled up the stall. . . . It wasn't until the sand came up to his belly that he jerked slightly, but then he appeared to relax. He seldom put his ears back, which is a sign of fear or aggression, and he never tried to bite anybody. He was alert and curious about his surroundings, and he acted like a normal horse in a stall. . . . He was free to move his head, and eventually he allowed people to touch his face and rub his ears and mouth. Touching that had been intolerable was now being tolerated.

Paul Allen Dotson, Jr. drafted an objective description of a dining room light fixture. As he revised, he speculated about its meaning to him and realized it was more than just a beautiful object. There was a memory, an untold story behind it—one he did not want to tell. But by referring to the story and adding subjective details, he enriched the dominant impression.

The Crystal Chandelier

In the dining room of a house where I once lived hung a crystal chandelier. It was a gorgeous old-fashioned fixture with eight lights and numerous dangling crystals that sparkled with the colors of the rainbow. The chandelier had three settings: high, medium, and low. When it was set on high, my wife and I would entertain friends and relatives, balance our accounts, and write letters. When the chandelier was on medium, I would often lounge in a chair next to the stereo and listen to soft music while staring at the colors emanating from the crystals. Yet my favorite setting was low. There were nights I would arrive home before my wife and would prepare dinner for the two of us. When she would walk into the dining room, the colors from the crystals would shine on her hair; she would smile, and I would see the most beautiful woman in the world. Though we are no longer together, those moments under the crystal chandelier are among my fondest memories.

Although Paul merely hinted at the story in the last line, he enriched the description. Rarely is an entire story told. Someone once said that a story is like an iceberg: seven-eighths of it stays beneath the surface. The writer must decide how much to reveal.

Objective and Subjective Description

See page 232.

The tone of an *objective* description is literal, factual, and fair—impartial and impersonal. In scientific and business writing, much description is based on unbiased, objective observation. Its aim is to reproduce for the reader exactly what the writer observed without reference to the writer's feelings about the subject.

PLANNING A PAPER OF DESCRIPTION

www.mhhe.com/dietsch

For online help writing description essays, visit: Writing>Writing Tutors> Description

Whether you have toured Ravenna, Italy, looking at mosaics, or never ventured beyond your city's limits, you have stored numerous sensory impressions. Perhaps you recall a quiet afternoon spent fishing with your grandfather along a creek or an evening spent delivering newspapers after a three-day blizzard. Or perhaps you own something that has an unusual story. Think about the history of the item and its value to you; you might have a topic for an essay.

Prewriting

www.mhhe.com/dietsch

For further coverage of prewriting, check out: Writing>Prewriting

After you select a topic, think about who might like to read about it. At the top of your paper, jot down "Audience" and "Purpose" so that you can begin to focus your thoughts. Then mine your memory by prewriting details about your topic. When writing from experience, try asking yourself these questions:

- **AUDIENCE.** Who might be interested?
- **PURPOSE.** What is the point of the description?
- **Sight.** What specifically did I notice?
- **Sound.** What exactly did I hear?
- **Smell.** What did I smell? Did it remind me of anything?
- **Touch.** How did the item or object feel?
- **Taste.** Was taste involved? Could I compare the taste to something else?

Selecting a Vantage Point and Transition

You might think of a writer as holding a camera, aiming the lens in a certain direction to record an impression or a story. Wherever the writer is viewing the scene from is the *vantage point*. The writer may remain fixed in one spot or move around. A *fixed observer* describes only what can be seen from one position.

A *moving observer* describes a scene from more than one position. With each movement, the writer keeps the reader informed with transitional phrases, as Jeanne did in describing the antics of Giorgio (italicized below):

This dazzling winter morning Giorgio, our black and tan Corgi, was so excited that he ran, barking, from window to window. The snow had swirled high during the night, but he wanted to go outside. *I went from door to door* to find one that wasn't blocked by drifts. *When I let him out from the front porch,* he dived down the steps and disappeared! Under the drifted snow, he tunneled like a mole. Soon he reappeared, leaping like a dolphin, pawing the air as he came up! Then he disappeared again. He did this again and again, leaving a lugelike trail all around the front yard. He must have enjoyed frolicking because he stayed out quite awhile. When he came in, he looked like an abominable snow dog.

Imagine in your mind's eye the position from which you will view your topic. What would be the most interesting vantage point for the reader? Should you remain in one spot or move? Will you be close or distant? Will you observe for a few moments or over a span of time? What transitions will you need to keep readers informed of your movements?

See chapter 4.

DRAFTING A PAPER OF DESCRIPTION

Before you begin to draft, review your prewriting notes. Consider each item and whether or not it will contribute to the mood you aim to create. Mark only the details that will effectively convey the impression you have in mind.

www.mhhe.com/dietsch

For general drafting help, visit:
Writing>Drafting and Revision

Drafting an Introduction

A good introduction raises questions in the reader's mind: "What happened?" "Why is it significant?" "What kind of person is this?" "What sort of place?" Some openings create an image, taking readers directly to a scene with a short transitional phrase, such as "*In 1890 Central City* had dusty unpaved streets and 132 inhabitants, not counting 56 horses, 63 dogs, and 75 cats." Or a descriptive phrase may focus on a current scene: "*Nestled in a valley* . . . is a small village that still has a general store and a post office where patrons pick up their mail." Or a description may open with a striking comparison.

www.mhhe.com/dietsch

Want more help writing introductions? Go to:
Writing>Introductions

Developing a Description

An unusual viewpoint or perspective of an ordinary topic can arouse interest. In *Gift from the Sea*, Anne Morrow Lindbergh compares a shell, found on the beach, with a very different subjective impression:

> The shell in my hand is deserted. It once housed a whelk, a snail-like creature, and then temporarily, after the death of the first occupant, a little hermit crab. . . . Did he hope to find a better home, a better mode of living? I too have run away, I realize, I have shed the shell of my life, for these few weeks of vacation.
>
> But his shell—it is simple; it is bare, it is beautiful. Small, only the size of my thumb, its architecture is perfect, down to the finest detail. Its shape, swelling like a pear in the center, winds in a gentle spiral to the pointed apex. Its color, dull gold, is whitened by a wash of salt from the sea. Each whorl, each faint knob, each crisscross vein in its egg-shell texture, is as clearly defined as on the day of creation. . . .

> My shell is not like this, I think. How untidy it has become! Blurred with
> moss, knobby with barnacles, its shape is hardly recognizable any more. Surely,
> it had a shape once. It has a shape still in my mind. What is the shape of my life?

As Lindbergh describes the shell, it becomes a symbol of her life—an *analogy* that extends throughout the book. As she reflects, the images establish a thread of continuity, allowing the reader to sense her inner peace amid the problems of life. There is a tranquility, an acceptance of change, as she collects insights along with shells.

Organizing a Description

The organization of a description often arises naturally from a particular topic. If you describe an object, a place, an animal, or a person, then *spatial order* usually works well. In spatial order details are arranged according to space or location. For instance, to describe an Irish Setter, you might go from the head to the tip of the tail.

Chronological order, a sequence of time, may be used to describe the changes in a neighborhood or a person. Another possible order for description is from *abstract to concrete* or from *general to specific* (or vice versa). Or if a topic requires emphasis, you might go from *least-to-most important* or *most-to-least important.* For more about the seven basic orders, see chapter 4.

Writing a Conclusion

www.mhhe.com/dietsch

For online guidance on writing your conclusions, check out:
Writing>Conclusions

Successful endings give a sense of completion and satisfaction. In description, as in narration, the major point often appears at the end. The ending may be a brief summary that explains the point in an interesting way. Or the ending may sound an optimistic note as it looks to the future. A philosophical ending may relate physical details to an abstract thought. Anne Morrow Lindbergh is both optimistic and philosophical at the close of *Gift from the Sea:*

> The waves echo behind me. Patience—Faith—Openness, is what the sea
> has to teach. Simplify—Solitude—Intermittency. . . . But there are other
> beaches to explore. There are more shells to find. This is only the beginning.

Sometimes a surprise or twist ending is effective. Such endings require preparation. You cannot simply swoop down and attach an ending that is foreign to the description or story. You need to prepare the reader in small ways. Note that Paul mentions his wife early in "The Crystal Chandelier." He does not suddenly introduce her at the end. Effective endings are smooth; they grow out of whatever has preceded them.

REVISING A DESCRIPTION

When revising a description, choose words that convey sharp, clear images— vibrant verbs, specific nouns, and modifiers that crackle with meaning. The audience should be able to visualize the spot, object, or person and savor the other sensory details. The aim is not only to increase interest but also to enhance the dominant impression.

In *The Elements of Style,* E. B. White warns against the use of meaningless modifiers. He calls *very, rather, little,* and *pretty* "the leeches that infest the pond of prose, sucking the blood of words." Beware, too, of stacking adjectives in a series; use one if needed, seldom two, rarely three. Although the right adjective can convey an idea, an action verb can often convey it better.

www.mhhe.com/dietsch

For general help with revision, check out:
Writing>Drafting and Revising

CHECKLIST   REVISING A DESCRIPTION

1.   Does the opening line arouse interest for this audience?

2.   Is the vantage point suitable? Is any transition needed?

3.   Is the written voice appropriate? Should it be more personal or friendly?

4.   Is the imagery sharp and clear? Have I involved at least three senses?

5.   Are all details effective? Could their order be improved?

6.   Are most verbs in the active voice? Are nouns and adjectives specific?

7.   Is the dominant impression clear and effective?

8.   Does the ending seem complete?

TWO STUDENT PAPERS: DESCRIPTION

In the first paper, Jean Ice pays tribute to a favorite aunt. Her purpose is to inform, to preserve for her children this memory of an earlier family member whom they did not know. Jean uses the concrete-to-abstract strategy, describing appearance before personality.

Aunt Marzia

Marzia was an elegant lady. Even as a young girl, she exhibited unusual characteristics for a country lass. Her coal black hair glistened from regimental brushing and frequent shampooing. Her hair was a halo for a lovely face with arched eyebrows and curling lashes. Her eyes were light green or gray, depending upon the color of her apparel. Her high cheekbones gave her a slight resemblance to a Native American. Her mother was said to be of Indian ancestry.

Marzia was taller than most other women of this generation. She carried her height proudly. Her erect posture and uplifted chin gave her a regal air. Somewhat out of sync with her physical perfection was her quirky little walk. She turned each foot slightly to the side as she strolled the country lanes.

Marzia was different from other members of her family and from her classmates. The other schoolchildren wore plain homemade garments, but Marzia used her sewing skill to put tucks in her waists. She also put flounces in her skirts and attached lace or embroidery to her collars. Few people would have guessed her wardrobe was made from feed sacks.

Marzia adored her first name, but she abhorred the way it was pronounced "Marzie" by others. Even her older sisters Clara and Ara did not follow her wishes and mispronounced her name. This elegant lady was a perfectionist in many other ways. She seemed to believe it was her responsibility to reform others to her way of thinking. This was especially true of her nieces. There were only five of us, compared to many more nephews. She expected us girls to speak correctly, dress attractively, and excel in good manners. She tried to accomplish these objectives by correcting us whenever we made an error. Often I, the youngest niece, was overwhelmed by a miscue. Once I pronounced *chic* as "chick," confident that I was right. Consulting a dictionary, after she corrected me, proved how little I knew.

Marzia was well educated for her time and situation. She was graduated from high school when most students were satisfied to complete the eighth grade. She went to normal school and became a teacher in a one-room school. The school was on the outskirts of a very small town, composed mostly of people of color. Marzia prized her students, and they were very fond of her.

When Marzia decided to marry, she was forced to give up teaching; for years ago only single women were allowed to teach. Unlike her sisters, who married for security and a home of their own, Marzia married because of her love for a ne'er-do-well. Although he was short, unattractive, uneducated, and rough of manner and speech, he had a jolly personality, which attracted the young ladies. But even Marzia could not contend with the old demon—liquor. After three years of silent grief, she divorced this man. She was the only member of her family to be divorced.

Marzia lived a long and productive life in spite of the divorce. She was greatly loved by all her younger kin, who were so different from her. When Aunt Marzia died, we all missed her so much. Nobody ever took her place in my life; no one else reminded me that I could do better.

QUESTIONS FOR DISCUSSION

1. Is Jean's dominant impression implicit or explicit?
2. How is the claim that Marzia is different and "elegant" supported?
3. Jean mixes writing strategies. How? What order is used in her last three paragraphs?
4. What type of ending does she use?

In the second paper, Neil Roberts combines description and narration with cause and effect. His purpose is to inform readers of how to cope with a yellow jacket attack.

Yellow Jacket Attack

Four weeks have passed since I was stung in our front yard while home alone. Almost immediately my arm numbed and my eyes swelled. Dizzy and unable to drive, I called an ambulance to go to the emergency room. At the time I didn't know what had stung me. A follow-up visit to an allergist verified that I have an allergic reaction to yellow jackets and bald-face hornets. He told me that if stung again, I have a 60 percent chance of an equal or worse reaction (i.e. dizziness, a drop in blood pressure, swollen eyes, lips and fingers). He advised keeping medication on hand and an Epipen (self-injecting medication device) with me if I travel. If stung, I'm not only to inject myself but also go to an emergency room within an hour.

Last weekend Kim and I were working in the same area, cleaning up the plank walk, preparing to put preservative on the wood. As Kim reached down to clear leaves away, yellow jackets zoomed out of a hole in the ground. About 15 feet away, I heard her yell, "Run, Neil, run." We both flew inside, but so did a half dozen yellow jackets. Although she was wearing sweatpants, the yellow jackets still managed to sting her three times on the legs. Finally, armed with fly swatter and insect spray, we dispatched the last of the intruders.

My allergist's recent instructions in first aid were put to good use. Antihistamines minimized her discomfort. The stings were painful for awhile but the local inflammation went away after thirty-six hours, and she did not have any other symptoms. Because yellow jackets live in the ground, wasp spray was of little use in getting rid of what turned out to be a large nest. In the end Kim got her revenge by pouring boiling water down the hole. RIP, yellow jackets.

The final sting was yet to come. Medical bills arrived: $500 for the ambulance; $2400 for emergency room treatment; plus a visit to the allergist, an allergy test, and medicine. Yes, a yellow jacket sting can cost well over $3000! Fortunately, insurance covers most of it. From what I can deduce from the abstruse medical statements, the insurance company told the hospital they were out of their minds and paid them about $700. I expect my out-of-pocket costs for medicine and co-payments to the ambulance, hospital, and allergist will amount to about $200. Pity those who are uninsured and have to bear the full brunt of health care costs when an incident like this occurs.

QUESTIONS FOR DISCUSSION

1. What dominant impression does Neil create in his description of the yellow jacket attack?

2. What order is predominant in the first paragraph?

3. What do you notice about the verbs in the second paragraph?

4. Find the fragment in paragraph three. Rate its effectiveness and your reason for this rating.

5. Can you find the transition that bridges the gap between the attack and costs?

PRACTICE

IDEAS FOR WRITING A PARAGRAPH

Directions: Be specific, using concrete words and vivid verbs. End with a thoughtful comment, perhaps about the function, meaning, or qualities of the object or person, *so that your paragraph has a point.*

1. Describe the vehicle you are driving or riding. What is the dominant impression of you in or on this vehicle?

2. Describe a prized object. Why is it special?

3. Describe the contents of your purse (if you have one). What is the dominant impression to a casual spectator?

4. Describe someone you know. What predominant qualities does he or she have?

5. Describe your favorite piece of old clothing. Why is it special?

TEN IDEAS FOR DESCRIPTIVE PAPERS

1   A special moment

2   My first job

3   Riding a cable car in San Francisco

4   A favorite place to be alone

5   The most courageous (or some other quality) person I know

6   Riding the rapids in Colorado

7   My neighborhood

8   The first time I . . .

9   Earliest childhood memory

10   The best dog I ever had

Explaining a Process

Writing clear, concise directions is not always easy even for the professional. Perhaps you have worked with inadequate or nonexistent instructions and know how frustrating that can be. One young man, lacking any instruction, began a welding job only to find the equipment was different from that used on his previous job. He ruined $400 worth of equipment the first night. To write clear directions, you need to explain the process.

> It is far easier to discuss Hamlet's complexes than to write orders which ensure that five working parties from five different units arrive at the right time equipped with proper tools for the job.
>
> —G. B. Harrison

WHAT IS PROCESS ANALYSIS?

Regular occurrences in the natural world—such as digestion, icicles, and hurricanes—involve processes. A *process* is a series of steps, stages, phases, or natural changes that lead to a result. You engage in a process whether taking a shower, brewing coffee, or driving a car. On the job you may explain a procedure to a new worker, show someone how to operate a machine, or write instructions for operating software.

In *process analysis* you describe a series of actions, operations, or changes. A paper of process analysis may explain how to do something, how a condition develops, how an organism grows, or how a phenomenon evolves. For clarity, explain the process in the order that changes or events normally occur.

Directions for Procedures

The simple experiments you conducted in high school science and chemistry labs were procedures. When you assemble shelving or pour a concrete patio, you also perform a procedure. To ensure good results, you follow the instructions carefully. If any steps are omitted or the order is reversed, the deviation may mar the final result. Some procedures, such as operating a chain saw, require warnings so that users take precautions. *Include a reason for each precaution so that users will take heed.*

Other kinds of processes require multiple sets of directions, all of which have phases, steps, or stages. For instance, the production of steel and the publication of a book involve many processes and people. The *audience* for directions consists of the people who will be performing the procedure.

WORKPLACE CASE STUDY

ETHAN SOLVES THE OFFICE LOUNGE PROBLEM

The sink of the employee lounge is usually stacked full of dirty dishes. The room smells of stale coffee grounds. Green mold grows on uneaten lunches in the refrigerator. Although employees are assigned days to tidy the room, they often forget. Those who remember may wash only the dishes. Ethan has been asked to devise a new system.

After careful thought, Ethan gives each office employee a copy of a quarterly assignment sheet with his or her day marked in red and tacks a copy in the lounge. In a memo he asks the employees to add this date to their calendars. On the refrigerator, he posts a sign that reads: "On Fridays all lunch containers and open soda will be discarded." On a cupboard, he posts the following notice:

continued

Daily Cleaning Procedure

On your assigned day, please clean between 3 and 5 p.m. Then no one will be using the lounge. The following procedure will save time. (It should take 10–12 minutes.)

1. Close the drain and fill the sink with hot water.
2. Add detergent and let dishes soak.
3. Clear the table and counter of debris. Wash them off.
4. Wipe the microwave inside and out.
5. Wash dishes, rinse, and stack on drainboard.
6. To prevent fire, unplug coffeemaker. Dispose of grounds.
7. Wash and rinse coffeemaker.
8. Dry dishes and put in cupboard.
9. FRIDAY: Throw out all lunch containers and open soda cans in the refrigerator. Wipe up crumbs and spills in the refrigerator.

The system has worked well. Grumbling about clutter and odor has stopped. The lounge is a much more pleasant place to sit and relax.

Use Second Person for Clarity   Directions for a procedure should be clear and concise. Therefore, they are usually written in second person with *understood you*. Each step begins with an active verb: "*Insert* the tab . . . ," "*Open* the chamber . . . ," "*Lift* the switch. . . ." Most instructions should be more than a brief list, unless there is a sound reason to limit. They should explain according to readers' general level of knowledge. On the job, steps of a procedure are often simplified and numbered.

Process Descriptions

Students in all academic disciplines analyze processes and write *process descriptions*. For example, you might interview a patient, write a case history, and describe the onset of a health problem. Or you might explain how a hobby grew into a successful business or explain a process to a group touring a factory.

The purpose of a process description is to describe a procedure, natural phenomenon, or other process for an audience who would like to know more about it. They will *not* be performing the process. First, you supply enough details to provide an overview. Then you state the function of each step or stage and explain how each fits into the process. Process descriptions are often written in narrative form, using either first- or third-person pronouns.

See page H-3.

Using First Person   Student writer Janice D. uses first person and past tense to begin the story of how her rock garden evolved:

▶ **Gardening with Rocks**

Rock gardening wasn't something I gave much thought to until a few years after we bought a house. I can remember the seller pointing out an overgrown bush in the front of the weedy yard, trying to use that as a selling point. Later my husband and I agreed "that will have to be the first thing to go." The first year we were so busy inside we didn't do much outside except to mow the lawn and kill the weeds. But over the next few years, we began to beautify the outside as well. We started small with a tree here, a few flowers and a rock there, which led to our lovely rock garden of today.

See "Caterpillar Afternoon," page 561.

Using Third Person   Process descriptions that are not drawn from a writer's personal experience are usually written in the third person. Present tense verbs in *active* voice are used for actions that recur: "The mollusk *opens* its shell . . . ," "Each year the tree *grows* new rings," "The furnace *melts* the glass. . . ."

TRANSITION IN PROCESS ANALYSIS

A *transition* is a word, phrase, sentence, or paragraph that connects ideas or informs the reader of what is ahead. Transitions indicate shifts of meaning and relationships of time, location, sequence, similarity or difference, certainty or uncertainty. *Signpost transitions* appear at the beginning of sentences. This method is generally used in procedures. *Embedded transitions* appear at other places in a sentence, as explained in chapter 13.

For process analysis, use transitions that indicate *chronological* order. Distinguish between major and minor steps. For major steps, use *numerical* transitions (*first, second, third,* and so forth). For substeps, use other transitions of time, such as *then* or *next.* (Two or three *first*'s and *second*'s would be confusing.)

TRANSITIONS TO CLARIFY A PROCESS

To Emphasize Major Steps or Stages		To Indicate Substeps	
first	(begin)	next	then
second		after that	later
third		while	when
fourth		meanwhile	as soon as
fifth	(finally)	during	after one hour

WRITING A PROCESS PAPER

www.mhhe.com/dietsch
For online insight into process papers, visit: Writing>Writing Tutors> Process Analysis

The purpose of a process paper can be to provide directions for a procedure or to describe a process, according to the assignment. To fulfill either purpose, you first need to estimate how much readers know about the topic and whether they are likely to have performed or witnessed the procedure or process.

This estimate is particularly important when writing directions. It will help you gauge not only the amount of explanation needed but also the need for *pre-*

cautions and reasons at strategic points. At tricky or risky points, include a reason for the step. For example, "Follow directions carefully *to obtain a smooth finish.*" Otherwise, some users may take unwise shortcuts.

Selecting a Topic and Prewriting

The topic for a process paper should be based on your personal experience or observation unless you plan to do research. The topic should be complex enough that readers won't find it obvious. You may find that narrowing the topic is essential: even a fairly simple process paper can become surprisingly lengthy. To develop your thinking skills, avoid a recipe or any other process you have learned from printed instructions.

www.mhhe.com/dietsch

For more coverage of prewriting, go to:
Writing>Prewriting

The quickest way to start is to make a scratch outline, listing the steps or stages in chronological order. Leave spaces to jot in brief explanations and insert necessary precautions or warnings at the beginning and at strategic points—not the end. *Many readers will not read the entire set of directions before they start.*

Drafting an Introduction

The length of an introduction to a process paper may vary, depending on the purpose for writing and the assignment. Particularly for directions, state the finished product or result of the process in the introduction. If you dive into the first step with no thesis statement, readers may become confused. The thesis should identify the process, make a claim, and specify the result, product, or benefit for the reader:

www.mhhe.com/dietsch

For general help writing introductions, check out:
Writing>Introductions

- White-water rafting can be an enjoyable experience for the beginner who is well prepared. (Claim/result: enjoyable experience)
- Setting up a backpacking tent correctly can net a good night's sleep. (Claim/result: good night's sleep)

The following student introductions illustrate just two of many options for an introduction.

Generalization Followed by Restriction

An accurate generalization may be used for the beginning of a process analysis. Patricia Jones Black opens with a generalization followed by a restriction. Safety is her key idea. Since Patricia's introduction is only two sentences long, she chooses to combine it with the first point.

How to Process Green Beans

Home-grown green beans can be served year round when they are properly processed and stored. By following the twelve steps listed here, you can safely take green beans from the garden to the table several months later. First, pick beans that are plump and tender. Three to five pounds of beans will be needed for each quart to be processed.

Historical Opening   Melinda Ham selected an unusual topic that carries a hint of nostalgia. She begins by describing the slow-paced life of pioneer days (a life without television, computers, or expensive toys).

▶
Apple-Head Dolls: A Remnant of Yesteryear

Years ago when life was less complicated and most families lived miles away from their nearest neighbors, family entertainment was more often homespun than manufactured. Children had to invent their own games. Parents frequently made toys for their children out of natural materials because cash was scarce. One popular homemade toy was the apple-head doll. These dolls had wizened faces, like very wrinkled old people, with a variety of expressions. By following these simple instructions, you, too, can make an unusual doll for a child in your family.

Combining Second Person with Third Person   Note that Melinda begins the introduction by using third person. Then she skillfully switches to *second person in the middle of the final sentence* of the paragraph. This way she makes the pronoun shift smoothly.

Developing a Process Paper

As you draft, keep a specific audience in mind so that you will know how much explanation is needed. If you are writing directions, ask yourself, What points might be difficult, unclear, or risky? Present the steps in an orderly sequence so that the reader can understand and possibly duplicate the procedure. At the beginning, specify the equipment and material necessary to complete the process. In her paper on making apple-head dolls, Melinda Ham explains the process clearly, using numerical transitions and active verbs to indicate major steps. Her transitions are italicized here:

▶
First, gather the necessary materials. An apple and cotton balls are needed for the face, hair, and beard of a male doll. Or you may wish to make a pair of dolls, male and female. The apple should be large because the head will shrink later. The body consists of a fine-gauge wire coat hanger, a large paper clip, clean cotton rags (an old sheet, pillowcase, or shirt), varnish or shellac, and scraps of fabric for clothing. Other items needed are a sharp paring knife, pliers, a small bowl, a bottle of pure lemon juice, plain table salt (not iodized), and about eighteen inches of heavy thread or fine cord.

Second, make the face of the doll. With the paring knife, thinly peel the apple. *Then* carve out the tiny eye sockets, nose, mouth, and ears. *After the head is carved,* place it in a small bowl. Pour one-fourth cup of lemon juice over the apple. Let set for thirty seconds, *then* rotate so that all sides are covered with juice. Wait one minute. To make the eyes, press two apple seeds horizontally into the carved sockets.

Aging is the *third* step. Unbend the paper clip, leaving the smallest "hook." Push the straight end of the clip into the top of the core down through the apple. *When the wire emerges,* bend it about an inch to make a right angle to support the apple. Loop a length of heavy thread over the top hook and tie a knot. *Next* suspend the thread from a window catch, away from direct sunlight, where the apple can hang for two to four weeks. *When the desired "wrinkling" occurs,* apply a thin coat of clear shellac or varnish to prevent further deterioration. Let dry overnight.

Fourth, add "hair" to the head. For a male, pull apart a cotton ball to form a beard. Glue around the jawline. A narrow strip of cotton around the back will form a fringe of hair around a bald spot. For a female doll, a large cotton ball (or two) will be needed for her hair, which can be arranged as desired.

Making the body is the *fifth* step. Use pliers to twist a thin wire coat hanger into a simple stick figure. Wrap strips of rags around arms and legs to give a rounded effect. Secure the rag strips with rubber bands or adhesive tape or both.

Creating clothing is the *sixth* step. Design simple clothes for the dolls. The male doll might wear a simple dark suit with a white shirt and perhaps a cap or hat. The female doll might wear a tiny apron, shawl or cape, sunbonnet, and long dress.

The final step is attaching the head. Attach the apple head firmly to the neck wire. Twist the clip wire tightly around the body wire so that the apple head will remain upright. If wire shows, cover with a necktie, shawl, or scarf.

Writing a Conclusion

An effective conclusion to a process analysis provides a sense of completion, often by referring specifically to the result of the process. If possible, end on a positive note. Even if the results of a procedure are negative, you might summarize what was learned, refer to a benefit or emotion, or add a bit of humor. Melinda ends by pointing out what makes apple-head dolls special:

> Apple-head dolls are not only easy to make, but unusual. The face and expression of each doll will vary somewhat. The clothing can vary greatly. Apple-head dolls make attractive and distinctive gifts.

Revising a Process Paper

Clarity and completeness are the main qualities to check for as you revise your process paper. The following questions should be helpful.

CHECKLIST   REVISING A PROCESS PAPER

1. Who is the audience? (*Tip:* On your outline list age, experience, and any other relevant characteristics of the audience. Refer to the list as you revise.)

2. Does the introduction establish the purpose and point out the product or result of the process?

3. Are necessary precautions included at appropriate spots?

4. Are reasons included at strategic points?

5. Do transitions clearly distinguish major steps as well as substeps?

6. Is each step or stage of the process discussed in sufficient detail?

www.mhhe.com/dietsch
For online guidance on writing your conclusions, check out:
Writing>Conclusions

www.mhhe.com/dietsch
For general help with revision, visit:
Writing>Drafting and Revising

7. Are the steps arranged in chronological order?

8. Does the conclusion complete the paper in a satisfying way?

A STUDENT PAPER: PROCESS ANALYSIS

The purpose of Keith Witzel's paper is to explain how to replace a defective electrical outlet safely. He directs the paper to the average homeowner with relatively little experience in home repairs.

▶

Replacing an Electrical Outlet Safely

Many people refuse to replace defective electrical connections in the home, either because of a lack of knowledge concerning the proper procedure or from fear of creating a fire hazard. By following a few simple guidelines, however, almost anyone can make minor repairs safely.

Most electrical circuits in the home are made up of general lighting circuits of either 15- or 20-amp circuits. These are the circuits used for small appliances, lamps, television, and others. These items are connected into the general lighting circuits by plugging into the wall outlet receptacles. If one of these receptacles becomes defective, it is a safe and simple process to replace it by following five main steps: First, assemble the necessary materials; second, shut off the house current; third, remove the receptacle; fourth, install the new receptacle; fifth, restore power and check the operation of the new receptacle.

First, assemble the necessary materials. These include a pair of needle-nosed pliers with a jaw approximately two inches long, tapering to a pointed end; a slotted screwdriver; a utility knife; and a new receptacle rated at 15 amps or 20 amps as required.

Second, shut off the power to the circuit that contains the defective receptacle. This is done by turning the main switch (marked on handle) to the "off" position on the circuit breaker or fuse box. Check to make certain that the electricity is off by trying to operate appliances in various locations of the house. They should not function.

Third, remove the cover plate from the defective receptacle by turning the screw in a counterclockwise direction. Remove the two screws that hold the receptacle outlet to the utility box (the small metal box mounted in the wall), and pull the receptacle from this box. There will be a white insulated wire, a black insulated wire, and possibly an uninsulated ground wire (depending on the age of the structure) attached to the receptacle. Remove these wires and discard the used receptacle.

Fourth, install the new receptacle and replace the cover. Before installation, inspect the black and white wires to ensure that each end is free of insulation for approximately five-eighths inch and the ends are formed into loops. These loops should be made in a clockwise direction. The purpose is to ensure that the wire is secured around the screw as the screw is tightened.

After that, install the wires to the new receptacle. The white wire is connected to the silver-colored side of the receptacle and the black wire to the brass-colored side. Tighten each screw firmly. Next, connect the uninsulated wire (if used) to the green screw on the bottom of the receptacle. Push the receptacle into the utility box and tighten, using the screws supplied with the new receptacle. Remount the receptacle cover, being careful not to overtighten this screw, which could cause the cover to crack.

Finally, restore power to the house and check the receptacle to see that it is functioning properly. If not, check to see that you have flipped all breaker switches.

If each of these steps is followed closely, you will have not only the satisfaction of doing the job yourself but also the satisfaction of saving the cost of an electrician.

QUESTIONS FOR DISCUSSION

1. Is Keith's paper a set of directions for a procedure or a process description? How do you know?

2. What transition does he use to indicate the substep of step four?

3. Does he provide any precautions or warnings? Where?

4. What type of ending does he use?

5. How clear do you find Keith's analysis? Is any step or substep unclear? If so, how might it be clarified?

- "Fast Track to Perfection," Ian Dunbar, page 574
- "Write Your Own Success Story," Carol Carter, page 578
- "How to Get Out of a Locked Trunk," Philip Weiss, page 584
- "How Do You Know It's Good?" Marya Mannes, page 589

FOR YOUR REFERENCE
Process Analysis Essays in the Reader

PRACTICE

WRITING IDEAS FOR PARAGRAPHS

1. How to prune a shrub neatly and safely
2. Making homemade ice cream
3. How to bathe a dog with little fuss
4. How to make a paper airplane that will fly
5. How to tie a shoe (as explained to a five-year-old child)

TEN IDEAS FOR PROCESS PAPERS

Describe or explain:

1   How to start a chess club for schoolchildren

2   A natural process you have observed (butterfly hatching, erosion of a beach, aging of an oak tree, or other)

3   A procedure that you perform at work

4   How to water-ski

5   How to bathe a bedridden patient (or an infant)

6   How to make a minor household repair

7   Burglar-proofing your home

8   Grooming a horse for show

9   How to have a successful garage sale

10 How to refinish furniture

Selecting Effective Examples

CHAPTER 12

> Example moves the
> world more than
> doctrine.
>
> —Henry Miller

For nearly fifty years Charles Schulz entertained Americans with the exploits of Charlie Brown, Snoopy, Lucy, Linus, and other characters in *Peanuts*. Schulz based many of his daily comic strips on examples taken from his own experience. For instance, Charlie Brown's fear of rejection from the little red-haired girl originated from a refusal to a marriage proposal that Shulz once endured.*

---

*Brendan I. Koerner, "Good Grief! Charlie Brown Says, So Long," *U.S. News & World Report* 27 Dec. 1999: 28.

PEANUTS reprinted by permission of United Feature Syndicate, Inc.

In the comic strip reprinted above, Charles Schulz depicted an incident from his boyhood. Then he reacted, and explained what friendship meant to him. You might say that he derived a statement of his philosophy of life.

PURPOSE OF EXAMPLES

An effective example can explain, convince, or lure a reader on. The right selection of examples can help you demonstrate your knowledge—whether in an employment application letter, a technical report, an essay exam, or a paper. Examples are valuable for explaining a concept, illustrating a problem, or supporting a reaction for papers in psychology, law enforcement, business management, literature, composition, philosophy, and other fields.

See chapter 21 for reaction papers.

ELEMENTS OF ILLUSTRATION

To illustrate or to exemplify simply means to clarify through example. You include impressions, facts, statistics, or expert opinion to lend substance to your writing, according to the rhetorical situation. The key is to choose examples that count, that enable your audience to understand what you mean and to see that you know what you are talking about. On the job you might use illustration to persuade, as in a proposal or grant application. In an academic paper or a personal essay, you might use illustration to explain (see "Envy" at the end of this chapter).

Various examples may relate an incident, compare, describe, or explain for a purpose: *Anecdotes* are brief stories, often humorous. An *analogy* is an extended comparison. *Historical examples* usually describe people or events. *Literary allusions* are examples taken from literature. *Hypothetical examples* are conjectures—supposedly true. However, real examples drawn from life are the most interesting and convincing illustrations.

WRITING A PAPER OF ILLUSTRATION

For a paper of illustration, you have a wide range of topic choices and organizational strategies. Select a topic you can develop with interesting examples. Then arrange the examples in an order that reflects your purpose.

www.mhhe.com/dietsch

For further information about illustration, go to: Writing>Writing Tutors> Exemplification

Prewriting

The topic may be concrete or abstract, according to the assignment. When something is concrete, it is detectable through at least one of the five senses, often more. You can see, hear, feel, smell, or taste it. If you write about an abstract principle, you can clarify it with concrete examples familiar to the reader. You can cite a variety of examples as long as they all have a central thread.

www.mhhe.com/dietsch

For more coverage of prewriting, go to: Writing>Prewriting

Excellent illustrations can often be lifted from everyday life. For instance, if you have a family heirloom, memento, or special gift (possibly a music box), you might find a topic there. Perhaps your great uncle has a collection of old coins. What do these objects represent to your family? Or perhaps your home has an unusual feature: a tower room, a secret room or stairway, or something else. Perhaps the house was once a one-room school, barn, or stop on the Underground Railroad. What is the story behind it?

Once you have chosen a topic, prewrite to form a pool of details. To start your creative juices flowing, write your topic at the top of a clean sheet of paper. Then jot down every idea that dives into your mind—anything that might be used as support. If you know the topic well, you will soon have a page of examples and details. To start prewriting, the following questions will be helpful:

- Why am I interested in the topic?
- What examples can I recall?
- Who is connected with the topic?
- Did he or she have a favorite saying, mannerism, or habit?
- How has he or she influenced me? Can I give an example?
- What changes have occurred; how do I feel about the changes?
- What is my main point?

Finally, draft a thesis that makes a point about your topic, ideally one that is unfamiliar to your readers.

Organizing and Developing a Paper of Illustration

To organize and develop your paper, choose an order, select examples, and weave explanation with examples, all the while focusing on your purpose and considering your audience.

See chapter 4.

Order   To organize a paper of illustration, select an order that suits your purpose and topic. You might organize examples chronologically or according to importance or in any other way that will advance your point. As you read the student papers in this chapter, notice the organizational strategies. Dixie O'Rourke combines chronological order and contrast:

Envy

I. *Introduction.* Age ten: Staring through window. Envy, resentment, and fear influence Dixie's childhood.

II. *Body*

    A. Junior high: Was learning to control feelings of envy.

    B. Age thirteen: Sudden change in perspective.

    C. Today: Envy seldom occurs.

III. *Conclusion.* Focusing energy in a positive way.

Other topics can be organized according to an order of importance. For a paper about exotic pets, you might move from familiar examples to surprising ones. For a paper on natural cures for common ailments, you might move from cures for minor ailments to cures for life-threatening ones. This way the examples increase in interest.

Relevant, Accurate, and Sufficient Examples   Every example you include should be *relevant* to your thesis, illustrating your main point in some way. Resist the temptation to include an example just because it is odd or funny. Illustrations should illuminate a point. Irrelevant examples distract from the thesis.

Check to see that examples are *accurate.* In attempting to be humorous or to dramatize a point, writers sometimes embellish examples, but extravagance can sabotage logic. An example may be dramatic, but it should not be too far-fetched or unusual—the one-in-a-million variety. To palm off an atypical example as typical is unethical. If you generalize from an example, it should be *typical of its class.* When researching, consider the source of your statistics. Is it reliable? Is the information up-to-date?

How many examples will be sufficient? The answer depends on the nature of your thesis and the weight of the examples. The sheer number of examples is less important than their quality. Select impressive examples that will provide strong support for your thesis. A controversial or debatable thesis will require several high-quality examples to convince a skeptical audience. As a rule, when examples are brief, you need more than when they can be developed in detail.

Weaving Examples with Explanation   As you draft, try to find an interesting approach to your topic. You might start with a series of short examples, eye-catching details drawn from everyday life. To connect the examples to your thesis, you will need to interlace them with explanation. Bryan Vaughn weaves example with explanation as he describes his perceptions of happiness:

During my childhood, happiness meant anything from having waffles for breakfast to being able to stay outside after the streetlights came on, catching lightning bugs and playing tag. Early in my adolescence, happiness seemed to take on another meaning. Driving fast was my new source of happiness. I discovered that a motor could be affixed to just about anything. My first few inventions were just this side of lethal. When I consider these vehicles, it's a wonder I'm still alive today. I rode go-carts, three-wheelers, snowmobiles, motorcycles—anything I could put gas in, I drove.

During mid-adolescence, my perception of happiness changed again. Sports became my passion. For me, nothing could compare with the exhilaration of being part of a winning team. Our football team was the defending state champion. Our basketball team finished third in the state, and our baseball team was the conference champion. Happiness was being one of the main players on every team and having the potential to play college sports and possibly having a career in professional sports.

But those dreams ended during a football game when I received a severe spinal injury. After two months in the hospital, I was sent home—handicapped, but thankful. At this time happiness took on yet a new meaning: I was just glad to be alive and able to walk. . . .

As my life began to return to normal, I saw a new source of happiness. One day I saw, parked in front of a Sunoco station, a red 1969 Pontiac GTO Judge. That same day I bought "The Judge" and spent every spare minute working on it. . . . But later an old man drove out in front of me without warning and wrecked my happiness. . . . Although I bought another car, it was not the same as the Judge.

Now that I have matured to a ripe old twenty-two, the word *happiness* means much more than ever before. . . .

Writing a Conclusion

The conclusion for a paper of illustration, as with any essay, should provide a satisfying close. Ending on a positive note, especially after the recounting of a painful experience, is gratifying for the reader. Barb Bronson ends "Clipper Ship Mom" (see chapter 9) by continuing the comparison and expressing gratitude:

> My clipper ship, my mom, has endured many rough storms. Every day I thank God that my mother stood fast. Words can never express how lucky I feel to have her. At the present Clipper Ship Mom and crew continue to sail steadfastly on course, but on different seas.

In a paper about a series of failures she faced, Phyllis Parks ends on an optimistic note, providing some specific examples of current successes:

> Despite the failures I have experienced, all phases of my life have not been grim. My daughter from my first marriage has grown into a beautiful, healthy young lady. Fifteen months ago my new husband and I were married. I am also enrolled in college classes. Now I truly feel successful.

Sometimes writers repeat their introductions in slightly different words or to summarize their body paragraphs. But try to find a more satisfying conclusion.

www.mhhe.com/dietsch
For general coverage of writing conclusions, visit: Writing>Conclusions

Consider explaining a particular insight, noting an advantage, offering a suggestion, or expressing an opinion that is supported by your examples. Leave readers feeling they have learned something from the examples.

Revising a Paper of Illustration

www.mhhe.com/dietsch

For online revision guidance, check out:
Writing>Drafting and Revising

After your first draft has cooled a bit, go back and read through the examples carefully. Try to distance yourself from each one so that you can evaluate it impartially. As you make revisions, consider the principles you have learned so far. The following checklist will help you revise.

CHECKLIST   REVISING A PAPER OF ILLUSTRATION

1. What is the main point of the paper? Is the point clear?

2. Is each example relevant, accurate, and valid?

3. Does each example add substance to my claim?

4. Do the examples create interest?

5. Are there enough examples?

6. Are examples arranged in a clear, logical order? Or could the order be improved?

TWO STUDENT PAPERS: ILLUSTRATION

In the first paper, Anita Ketcham describes her hobby in an unusual way, blending explanation with example. Her purpose is to entertain as well as to inform.

Bathtub Solitude

An avid tennis player can be found lobbing away on the court; a woodworker may enjoy crafting furniture in a workshop; a gardener may relax by tending flower beds. I, too, have an enjoyable hobby—one that is not only relaxing and challenging but also educational. Like tennis, woodworking, and gardening, my hobby is done in the best possible place. That is why I do crossword puzzles in the bathtub.

As a mother of four young children, I rarely find time to sit down. Any time I do take for myself is soon interrupted. Mom sitting down is like a red flag waving, signaling a parade of little feet. This is why the bathtub is the perfect place to relax while working puzzles. There I cannot answer the telephone or pour a glass of milk or dress a Barbie doll. Those tasks have to wait. For a half hour, I escape to my own private retreat. Although it's not like Hawaii or the Bahamas, yet I am totally alone with my book and my bubbles, and it seems like heaven. The toughest problem I have to face is a six-letter word for supplication.

Working crossword puzzles is challenging. My favorites are the large "challenger" puzzles because the clues are difficult, requiring considerable thought. Still, I enjoy matching wits with the puzzlemaker. Some words can have several meanings and the clues can be ambiguous. A good puzzle solver learns to look at clues from different angles. For example, a five-letter word for the clue "drop a line" could be *write* or *angle,* but the answer the puzzlemaker wanted was *erase.* "Iron clothes" could be a clue for *press;* however, *armor* was the answer. A very difficult clue can be frustrating, especially for a puzzle printed in a newspaper because answers are not available until the next day. Although I rarely complete a difficult puzzle, I always try to improve my skills in order to do better with the next one.

Working crossword puzzles is educational. By using a dictionary often, I have expanded my vocabulary. Words such as *hirsute* and *litigious* have been added to my lexicon—as well as the word *lexicon.* And where else but in crossword puzzles could one find such a plethora of insignificant information? I know that Guido's note is an *ela,* but I do not know who Guido is. I know that the answer to "Roman bronze" is *aes* and that Caesar's road is an *iter,* should anyone ask. Not all of the knowledge I have gleaned from crossword puzzles is this trivial; some I have even found useful. Knowing that Siam is the former name of Thailand and that Istanbul was once Constantinople has helped me to defeat my husband during heated games of *Jeopardy.* He thinks he is married to a genius! I will never tell him my secret.

For my soon-to-be birthday, my husband will probably give me a bottle of bubble bath, the latest copy of *Dell Championship Crosswords,* and an hour to myself. Then I can enjoy some peace and quiet, sharpen my wits, and discover words new to me. All knocks on the door will be ignored. I will come out only when my toes are too wrinkled to stay longer.

QUESTIONS FOR DISCUSSION

1. Look at Anita's opening. What expectation does she set up with the first three brief examples?

2. What comparisons do you see in paragraph two?

3. What is the purpose of examples in paragraphs three and four?

4. Look at Anita's ending. How do the examples function there?

Next, Dixie O'Rourke offers a series of extended personal examples to show how she learned to control her emotions.

Envy

One evening without warning, envy crept into my young heart. The year was 1967. The place was a backyard ice rink at the home of my best friend, Sylvia. Although the time was only 5 p.m., dusk had already settled. Sylvia had just gone inside to eat dinner with her family in their comfortable brick home in a pleasant neighborhood.

Outside I continued to cut figure eights and spin on the ice while Sylvia ate dinner. As I paused to catch my breath, I found myself staring through the dining room window. Inside, the brightly lit room appeared warm and friendly as the family gathered around the table. Sylvia's father stood at the head, reading from the family Bible.

As I continued to window peek, I felt an overwhelming surge of envy and ill will. Suddenly, I was resentful not only of Sylvia's many possessions but also of her intact family. I longed to live like Sylvia. This flood of painful feelings changed not only how I felt toward her but also how I felt toward myself. The contentment of my childhood had shattered: I was ashamed of my house, my family, and myself.

Only ten years old, I was unable to deal with these new feelings of inferiority and kept them locked tightly within. I feared losing my best friend; I was afraid that if I told Sylvia how I felt, she might not like me anymore. I also feared telling my grandparents (with whom I resided); they might feel hurt and angry. So I told no one.

By junior high school, the feelings of shame and resentment had begun to diminish. Although I still felt pangs of envy when my friends flaunted their possessions, I had learned to control the envy so that it did not overwhelm me. The technique was simple—nothing new. I would count my blessings and thank God for each and every one of them. My grandparents had set a good example for me.

When I was thirteen, a sobering experience brought my perspective into a more realistic focus. During the school lunch hour, a group of students, whom I envied, gathered in front of the malt shop across from the school. This particular day the group welcomed and invited me to go with them to a carnival at a shopping center across town. The plan was to meet after school the next day and walk to the carnival. Knowing my grandfather's second job took him near the area, I offered the group a ride.

When school let out that afternoon, I ran home to plead for a ride and money for the carnival. Smiling, my grandmother lifted the lid of an old blue sugar bowl and gave me several silver coins. The next day grandpa drove his old Chevrolet, freckled with rust, to the school; and five of us piled in. When we reached a large parking lot, my friends hurried off toward the carnival without a word or backward glance to either of us.

Grandpa locked the car doors, bid me goodbye, and started toward the factory. As I watched him fade into the crowd, my eyes watered. Not one person had thanked him for the ride or waited for me. The envy I felt for that group fled. Suddenly, I felt proud of my grandfather even though he wore bib overalls and carried a lunch bucket. I felt fortunate to have both my grandparents.

Although I still feel a twinge of envy now and then, I no longer have the strong feelings of my youth. As my values have changed, I have focused my energies in a positive direction; presently, I'm working full time and attending classes for a nursing degree. Over the years, I have learned to subdue envy and to make the most of what I have.

QUESTIONS FOR DISCUSSION

1. What do you notice about Dixie's opening?

2. How does she set the scene for the reader?

3. What do you notice about Dixie's vantage point? (See the second paragraph: "outside," "inside.")

4. What incident causes a sharp shift in Dixie's perspective?

5. Examine her conclusion. What do you notice?

- "Fruitful Questions," James Sollish, page 595
- "Road Rage," Vest, Cohen, & Tharp, page 597
- "Going for Broke," Matea Gold & David Ferrell, page 603
- "Refuse to Live in Fear," Diana Bletter, page 608

FOR YOUR REFERENCE
Illustration Essays in the Reader

PRACTICE

IDEAS FOR WRITING

1. A pet food company is seeking winsome cats and dogs to be featured in television commercials. Write a letter explaining why your pet should be featured. Include examples of behavior and training.

2. Recently you purchased a home. Near the back fence, on a neighbor's property, stands an apple tree. Several limbs extend over the fence. Rotten apples, covered with insects, dot your lawn. Bees have stung your children twice. Legally, you can cut the tree back to the fence line, but for the sake of diplomacy, you prefer to talk to the neighbor. Map out your strategy by prewriting.

3. Describe a seemingly small incident such as a chance meeting or a sudden impulse that influenced your life.

4. Describe your first ride on a roller coaster.

5. Write an article for your campus newspaper using humorous examples to spoof a campus condition or a consumer product.

TEN IDEAS FOR PAPERS OF ILLUSTRATION

1. How my view of work has changed

2. Soothing upset restaurant patrons is an art

3. How my parents' divorce affected me

4. What are good manners?

5. Adversity can be an asset

6. Perils of baby-sitting

7. Common gardening mistakes

8. Ways to attract hummingbirds

9. View the wonders of West Virginia (or another state)

10. My grandmother's perseverance (or someone else's)

Classification
Sorting into Categories

CHAPTER 13

> Out of clutter, find simplicity.
>
> —Albert Einstein

PURPOSE OF CLASSIFICATION

Classification allows us to establish order in our lives and to function effectively. In daily living we classify, selecting categories according to our needs in various situations, rhetorical or otherwise. Perhaps as you clean out the attic, you find an old stack of comic books, long forgotten, handed down through the family. You are surprised to see that all the covers are still intact. "Hmm—maybe they are valuable," you murmur. You sort them into piles, grouping according to the title: *Batman, Superman, Flash, Green Hornet, Justice League, Donald Duck, Uncle Scrooge, Scamp, Mickey Mouse, Smokey Bear, Woodsy Owl, Junior Woodchucks,* and *Metal Men.*

Whether you look for a job by scanning the classified ads, file documents on your computer, sort your laundry, stock shelves in a store, or consider investments according to risk, you classify.

WHAT IS THE BASIS OF CLASSIFICATION?

Classification is a method of sorting—grouping and dividing—items or ideas logically. To classify various pieces of information, you look for a common feature that certain items have—a shared *principle of selection*—that marks them as

Unclassified Buckeye Fans

■■■◻◻■■◻■◻■◻◻■■◻■◻■■■■

Classified Buckeye Fans

Casual Fans   Concerned Fans   Ardent Fans

◯◯◯◯◯◯   ■■■■■■■■■■■   ■■■■■■■■

FIGURE 13.1 Classification of Buckeye fans.

belonging to a group. To fit into the group, each item must have this similarity. Then, if needed, you can subdivide the group, making finer distinctions as to relationship.

Everything on this planet can be classified in some way. The millions of species are divided into five formal classifications or kingdoms: animals, plants, fungi, bacteria, and algae/molds. And each one is subdivided into categories. For example, one category is *felines*—big and little cats, both wild and domesticated. Felines can be subdivided according to species: tigers, lions, panthers, and others. Each species can be further subdivided into kinds, such as albino tigers, Bengal tigers, and Siberian tigers.

Student writer Jane Tinker humorously classifies Ohio State Buckeye football fans, dividing them into three groups, according to their degree of "Buckeye Fever" (later in this chapter). Her principles of selection are "casual fans," "concerned fans," and "ardent fans" (see fig. 13.1).

WRITING A PAPER OF CLASSIFICATION

www.mhhe.com/dietsch

For online help writing classification essays, visit: Writing>Writing Tutors> Classification

A paper of classification not only groups and divides but also analyzes, describes, and explains. The purpose and the way the topic is approached determine the order. As you choose a topic, consider the rhetorical situation, especially the way you will treat the topic. Regardless of whether you adopt a serious or light tone, your written voice should be appropriate and the development should be ethical.

Ethical Concerns

As you prewrite and draft, think about your written voice and how it may sound to readers. Beware of applying negative labels—such as ageist, sexist, racist, or ethnic stereotypes—that might be hurtful to any particular group. Be creative and original, if you wish; but strive for objectivity and fairness. As you classify, you might ask yourself these questions:

See chapter 3.

- Are the categories suitable for the purpose, audience, and assignment?
- Is the word choice appropriate?
- Have I avoided stereotyping and other unsound generalizations?
- Is the main idea of my paper presented ethically?

For example, a nursing student writes a research paper that classifies certain illegal drugs; the purpose is to warn readers of dangers in usage. She consults numerous sources written by authorities in the field. Then she summarizes the evidence, describing the effects of the drugs in an objective tone and warning of possible side effects. Thus written, her development of the topic would be balanced and ethical.

But if another student were to write an essay on a similar topic without doing valid research, then the topic would be inappropriate and the development unethical. Although the student might interview several friends, then classify the various recreational drugs they use and describe the euphoria-inducing effects they experience, apparently with no negative side effects, the survey would be unreliable. It would be merely the opinion of a small group, not necessarily fact or representative of users as a whole. Effects of drugs can vary from person to person; and side effects can be incremental, perhaps not showing up until much later. And human memory is not always reliable.

Shaping a Topic to the Purpose and Audience

Chances are that you already have a lode of details to be mined and classified that you can use for an interesting informative essay. If you have a collection or hobby, you might classify the objects you have accumulated over the years, perhaps record albums, pedal cars, or video games, pointing out little-known facts, bits of history, and the value of the collection. Or perhaps you live near a scenic area with little-known features that might attract tourists (including the reader). If you were to write a brochure, what features would you describe and how would you classify them?

1. **Classify items according to the purpose and audience.** Have a reason.
2. **Avoid overlapping parts or categories.** Be clear-cut.
3. **Make each part or category large enough to contain a significant number.** Have a minimum of three items or details in each category.
4. **Make all parts parallel.** All items in a category should be similar, having a common principle of selection. Then they will be parallel.
5. **Organize all parts or categories to fit into one logical system.** All the parts should fit together into one organized whole.
6. **Arrange in a logical order.** See "Seven Basic Orders," page 47.

GUIDELINES: CLASSIFICATION

Student writer Patricia Rush described her observations of a restaurant buffet. Her writing purpose was to amuse; her audience was her classmates. She classified "Annoying Eaters of America" as "inspectors, critics, conversationalists, and gulpers." Here is how she described the fourth group:

Gulpers are the Indianapolis drivers of the table. To prepare for the race, they pile their platters high, thus cutting down on stops for refueling. They are determined to finish the meal first, even at the cost of indigestion. Stuffing their mouths and chomping, they shovel in the food and wash it down with great gulps of water. When every scrap is gone, they sometimes take a morsel of bread and swab their platters clean. Often their belches can be heard throughout the restaurant. Gulpers are usually males in ragged T-shirts and dingy jeans. For them, these garments may have more than one use; gulpers sometimes finish by wiping their hands across their chests or thighs.

With a topic in mind, you can use any of the prewriting and drafting techniques you learned in chapter 4. Still another way can be helpful: the "because" technique.

Prewriting with the "Because" Technique

www.mhhe.com/dietsch

For further coverage of prewriting, go to:
Writing>Prewriting

If your topic can be divided into advantages, benefits, or reasons, you might try the "because" technique to simplify your prewriting. Just ask a question about the topic, then answer "because. . . ." Jot down your answer and ask "What else?" Repeat the sequence until you have enough material. After that, group the details logically into main points.

Let's assume you have a fourteen-year-old daughter, Kim, who has been invited to go for a drive with Brad, the sixteen-year-old next door. But you are convinced Brad is a reckless and irresponsible driver. Simply stating your belief and forbidding Kim to go may not carry much weight with her. You need evidence to support the claim and reinforce your decision. Prior to your talk, you use the "because" technique to help you classify relevant facts into main points:

QUESTIONS	ANSWERS
1. Why does Brad seem rude and immature?	*Because* he insulted a neighbor who reprimanded him for backing into her driveway and almost hitting her cat. He has yelled crude comments to neighborhood children on bikes and scared them by coming too close.
2. Why does Brad seem irresponsible?	*Because* I have seen him speed on city streets, run stop signs and red lights. He brakes sharply, squealing his tires.
3. Are there any other reasons?	*Because* he has put several dents in his car although he's had it only three months. He backed into his mother's car last week.
4. What else?	*Because* he has been cited for speeding twice.

Your prewriting could continue until everything you know about Brad's driving has been listed. Then you could analyze the details and divide them into categories such as *rudeness, carelessness, speeding, ignoring traffic rules,* or in other ways.

Organizing a Classification Paper

Perhaps the most common order for a paper of classification is some order of degree: simple to complex, least to most important, easy to difficult, and so forth. To make a case against Brad as a driver, you might organize points from the least to most dangerous aspects of his driving.

BRAD IS A RECKLESS AND IRRESPONSIBLE DRIVER:

1. *Because he is careless.*
   He almost hit the neighbor's cat in her driveway.
   Last week he backed into his mother's car.
   His car has several dents in it after only three months.

2. *Because he is rude and immature.*
   He told old Mrs. Smith to shut up when she reprimanded him.
   He yells crude comments at children on bikes and drives too close to them.

3. *Because he speeds.*
   He has had two speeding tickets.
   He drove 50 mph on a street posted at 35 mph.
   He turns corners too fast, squealing his tires.

4. *Because he often ignores traffic signs and signals.*
   He turns quickly without signaling to other drivers.
   He drove through a stop sign last week.
   He sometimes drives through red lights.

Drafting a Thesis Statement

The next step is to draft a tentative thesis. A first draft might be a brief claim: "You can't go out with Brad for four reasons." But the tone is inappropriate and specifying all the reasons in the thesis would prove unwieldy. A second stronger draft might read: "Brad is an immature driver who lacks consideration and judgment." Then you could make an outline listing the main points you intend to make.

www.mhhe.com/dietsch
For online help with your thesis statement, check out:
Writing>Thesis

Developing Main Points and Embedding Transition

As you draft, develop your main points with specific evidence—facts, reasons, and examples. Each paragraph should support the claim made in the thesis. And each paragraph should have a clear link to the thesis, either through signpost or embedded transition. Subtle transition is the mark of a proficient writer.

In the following example, Mark Brady begins by stating an opinion. In the second sentence he gives facts. Next he cites three reasons (italicized) to support the claim made in the first sentence:

Upland bird hunting in Ohio is in a sad condition. Populations of three game birds—the ring-necked pheasant, the blue grouse, and the bobwhite quail—have dwindled. Three main factors for this decline are *the kind of hunters, increased pollution,* and *clearing of woods and underbrush for farming.*

Note how Mark creates a direct link from each of his body paragraphs back to the thesis. In other words, he embeds his transition:

▶ Along with the good *hunters* in the fields are a number of ignorant *hunters* who shoot every bird they can, despite the fact that they are exceeding the daily bag limit. . . .

The second reason for the dwindling bird population is the *increased pollution* in our environment. . . .

The *farmer* is probably the biggest reason for declining bird populations. . . .

Again, in his conclusion, Mark reinforces each of his initial main points by alluding to the thesis:

▶ Frankly, most of those concerned seem to contribute to poor hunting conditions. The *nonsportsman hunter* takes home more birds than allowed. The *manufacturers who make pesticides and weed sprays* sometimes fail to adequately check the long-term effects of products upon birds and their eggs. Many *farmers* clear their land and plow in the fall, not leaving cover or grain for the game birds. Surely we must work to solve this problem before it is too late.

Mark does an excellent job of connecting his thesis to the main points of his paper, using all four kinds of embedded transition: repetition of key terms, synonyms, pronoun and antecedent, and natural relationships.

FOUR KINDS OF EMBEDDED TRANSITION	1. **Repetition of key terms:** hunters, increased pollution
	2. **Synonyms:** ignorant hunters, nonsportsman hunters
	3. **Pronoun and antecedent:** hunters/they
	4. **Natural relationships:** pollution/manufacturers/pesticides/sprays, nonsportsman/bag limit, farming/farmers

STUDENT ESSAY STATING MAIN POINTS IN THE THESIS

Michele Flahive briefly states three main points in the thesis. She uses embedded transition to establish clear links from the thesis to body paragraphs. These links mark the path of the main idea and provide unity. Note how she repeats a key term (italicized) in the first sentence of each body paragraph:

Diamonds: A Girl's Summer Friend

▶ As the batter walks up to the dusty plate on the diamond, she scans the outfield. Spying a vacancy between left and left center, she knows this is the best area to hit the ball. While the pitcher gets ready, the batter stands in position, watching every move. In a slow pitch, the ball sails off in a perfect arc, dropping right where the batter wants it. With heart pounding, she swings the aluminum bat and cracks the ball. Quickly, she runs three bases, listening to the cheers of teammates and hoping to reach home plate before the ball. For her the *challenge,* the *enjoyment,* and the *camaraderie* make softball a game worth playing.

The first game of the season seems always to pose a special *challenge.* The players often feel a bit rusty and nervous. Just walking onto the field and up to bat that first time takes strength of will. But once the umpire yells, "Play ball," the nervousness melts away and determination flows in. Enthusiasm for the game takes over.

Enjoyment of softball is the heart of the game. After a long day of work or school, it is a pleasure to leave the stress behind and walk out onto the diamond. Since both teammates and crowd are just out for an evening of recreation, there is no great pressure to win. The fun and action provide a refreshing reward at the end of a day.

The challenge and enjoyment would be incomplete without the *camaraderie* of teammates who share the same passion for a rousing game of softball. And when a member is feeling down for missing a ball or for striking out, words of encouragement flow from other members. Then too, there is a sense of unity as everyone plays together in the infield and outfield, backing each other up as needed.

As August slowly winds to an end, so must the summer softball season. It can be a sad time for many die-hard ball players who must leave the diamond and put away their gloves. Yet some players take heart, for not only does autumn bring bright foliage and cool evenings, but it also heralds the fall softball season!

Did you notice how Michele sets the scene and pulls the reader right into the action at the very beginning? With just a few concrete details, she creates an image of the dusty plate, batter with pounding heart, aluminum bat, sound of the bat hitting the ball, perfect arc, and cheers. This vivid description helps the reader to relive what she feels and sees as she walks up to the batter's box. Examples also help readers share the emotions that pervade the game.

Making Main Points Parallel

When main points are parallel, the resulting balance strengthens transition, sentence structure, and unity. In the example below, note how Joanne M. Pohlman begins each main point with the same type of structure, a gerund phrase (italicized). Each main point in the body explains the matching point in her thesis:

See chapter 7.

THESIS: As a volunteer member of the National Ski Patrol, I earn the opportunity to meet many interesting people, learn challenging skills, and spend time with my family.

PARALLEL POINTS: 1. *Joining the Central Division of the Patrol* has acquainted me with approximately eighty other patrollers. . . .

2. *Becoming a member of this national organization* takes more than being a proficient skier. My training. . . .

3. *Being able to ski with my family* is the main reason I chose to become a patroller.

Writing a Conclusion

www.mhhe.com/dietsch

For online help with your conclusions, visit:

Writing>Conclusions

A conclusion should flow logically and smoothly from the main idea. As a result, the reader should gain a sense of completeness or closure. To provide a satisfying ending, writers often allude to the thesis, as Joanne Pohlman does. At the end of the paper about skiing, she repeats the name of the organization and expresses appreciation:

> Finally, I feel fortunate to belong to the National Ski Patrol. Although I receive no wages, I do gain new friends, invaluable skills, and a closeness with my family that is priceless.

Revising the Paper

www.mhhe.com/dietsch

For general help with revising, check out:

Writing>Drafting and Revising

A paper of classification is more complex than those discussed in earlier chapters. The checklist below should help you to revise your paper successfully:

CHECKLIST   REVISING CLASSIFICATION PAPERS

1. Has the topic been narrowed to one item?

2. Is the introduction focused and interesting?

3. Do the main points follow the order set up in the thesis statement?

4. Are the main points linked with the thesis?

5. Are the main points parallel?

6. Are the main points well supported with specific details and examples?

7. Does the internal order of each paragraph flow well?

8. Can clarity be improved? Is more transition needed?

TWO STUDENT PAPERS: CLASSIFICATION

In the first paper, Nicole Vanderkooi's purpose is to inform, and her classmates are her audience. Her thesis (fourth sentence) is much different from the previous ones; it is all-encompassing. Although Nicole makes several generalizations, notice that she qualifies them.

The Melting Pot of New Orleans

The sweet voice of jazz and spicy smell of Cajun cuisine capture Nicole's senses as she strolls through the French Quarter of New Orleans in the bright sunshine. On the corner of Bourbon Street sits a homeless man, cross-legged, playing his harmonica. Occasionally, a passerby drops a few coins or a dollar bill in his soiled cap. People from every walk of life seem to wander these cobblestone streets.

Tourists dot the avenues of New Orleans. At daybreak they begin to roam the high-priced novelty shops and spacious old plantations surrounding the area. Frequently, a woman is escorted by an overburdened man and a trusty guidebook. Often dressed in walking shorts, they sport "I survived New Orleans night life" T-shirts and sun visors or sunglasses. Before sundown nocturnal pleasures begin, enticing sightseers to partake in Cajun feasting and boisterous drinking.

In a horse-drawn carriage, a tourist reclines, listening to the gentle clip-clop of hooves and the driver's southern drawl. Carrying briefcases, three businesspeople stride past shops, apparently bent on another destination. In a jewelry store, a couple examine pendants, intent on a possible purchase. In an art gallery, a sightseer from New York purchases yet another work, possibly for his loft.

Draped with tattered overcoats and wearing tennis shoes, the homeless of this elusive city often wear weathered grins amid week-old whiskers. Many of their daily hours are spent collecting tips, as they stand on street corners, providing the pleasure of hearing their sultry saxophones. The night brings them home to humid, stagnant alleys and alcoves. These bumbling creatures usually walk alone, accompanied only by their instrument and a bottle, enclosed in a brown paper bag.

Yet another colorful feature of this Louisiana melting pot is the local businessman. Often attired in a single-breasted black suit, an ivory silk shirt, and a brilliant tie, this worldly person exudes professionalism and sophistication. Finding him in a trendy coffee shop, drinking a black brew from a small cup, is not unusual. At night he often dines at a specialty restaurant and listens to the rhythms of jazz. His companion may be a colleague or a breathtaking, well-dressed woman.

New Orleans graciously accepts the prize for the most captivating city in the U.S.A. There an array of sights and sounds—musical vagrants, inquisitive visitors, and local residents—catches the eye and captures the heart.

QUESTIONS FOR DISCUSSION

1. How many types of people does Nicole classify?

2. How does Nicole link body paragraphs to her thesis?

3. What kinds of specific details does she use to describe each of her categories?

4. How does Nicole establish closure in her ending?

5. How would you describe her tone?

In the next paper, Jane Tinker classifies Ohio State football fans into three categories. Her tongue-in-cheek tone and adroit use of concrete details enable readers to share her amusement.

Buckeye Fever

Every autumn for the past twelve years, I have witnessed an outbreak of "Buckeye Fever" in my neighborhood. The ailment seems to hit victims in varying intensities. They are the casual, the concerned, and the ardent fans of the Ohio State Buckeyes.

The mildest strain of Buckeye Fever is evident in the casual fans. When time permits, they enjoy watching the game on television or listening on radio. But if time is limited or the weather turns sunny and warm, they forsake the game without a second thought. If given tickets, they will go—they may even buy them occasionally. The casual fans usually know the names and numbers of a few star players. Some casual fans feel that if the Bucks lose the game, an afternoon's viewing time is wasted. Casual fans are not interested in watching the Saturday night replay, for they already know the result.

Buckeye Fever hits concerned fans with moderate severity. They watch or listen to every Buckeye game possible. With buddies they enjoy seeing the Bucks on television. Enthusiastic, the concerned fans enter into the game, yelling and screaming as excitement mounts. If they have to miss a game, they will tape it on the VCR to watch later. They will purchase tickets to a game if readily available, but they will not stand in line for hours. They know the names and numbers of all starting players and are also aware of the opponent's capabilities. If Ohio State loses, the concerned fans are very disappointed, but not upset if the game was well played.

The ardent fans have contracted a serious case of Buckeye Fever. This strain may be terminal to some relationships. On Friday nights, the ardent fans are planning and preparing their elaborate tailgate lunches for the next day's game. Saturday mornings they rise early to proudly display their scarlet and gray flags in a prominent place and to beat the traffic jam to home games or any other within driving distance. Their tickets have been purchased either by waiting long hours in line or by knuckling into scalpers.

Dressed in their red sweaters and gray pants, the ardent fans anticipate the glory of Buckeye victory. They know the names, numbers, and personal statistics of all fifty team players as well as the high school players being recruited for next season. Later the ardent fans watch the replay to relive moments of victory. Depending on the outcome of the game, the Buckeye coach is either a saint or a bum. When the Bucks lose, the ardent fans are furious; then they become depressed. The depression may last until the following Tuesday, when they begin to anticipate the upcoming game.

Despite the degree to which a fan catches the fever, they all agree that football can be a very exciting game to watch. And for them, no team is more exciting than the Ohio State Buckeyes.

QUESTIONS FOR DISCUSSION

1. How does Jane's introduction differ from Nicole's?

2. What principle of organization has Jane used for her paper?

3. Where has Jane used embedded transition to link body paragraphs back to her thesis?

4. Why do you think Jane devotes more attention to her final category than her first two?

5. How does Jane's ending differ from Nicole's?

PRACTICE

Classification

Directions: Analyze the statements below and classify them according to the listed categories.

cliché   common belief   myth
old saying   superstition   fad
stereotype   tradition   trend

_____ 1. "Punks" dye their hair unusual colors such as green, orange, or purple.

_____ 2. Groups of people who ride motorcycles and wear black leather jackets are dangerous.

_____ 3. Red sky at night; sailors' delight
              Red sky in morning; sailors take warning.

_____ 4. Down through the ages, our family has baked Christmas fruitcakes.

_____ 5. When a couple divorce, the mother should receive custody of very young children.

_____ 6. To win at bridge, select a seat that is parallel with the bathtub in the house.

_____ 7. Money is the root of all evil.

_____ 8. According to Greek legend, Cerberus guarded the underworld, the realm of Hades, devouring anyone who tried to leave.

_____ 9. Don't make mountains out of molehills.

_____ 10. The middle class is gradually disappearing.

COLLABORATIVE LEARNING: CLASSIFICATION

Directions: Select the word in each group that is not in the same category as the other three words. Then compare your selections with those of other group members. Discuss disagreement. You may use dictionaries.

1. orange   2. gannet   3. putter
   kiwi   petrel   baseball bat
   lemon   dodo   tennis racquet
   ugli   trogon   hockey stick

4. lace
    snowflake
    frost
    water

5. crocus
    daffodil
    zinnia
    tulip

6. lobo
    sheltie
    wolverine
    coyote

7. wombat
    kangaroo
    opossum
    aardvark

8. daisy
    violet
    chrysanthemum
    echinacea

9. arrowroot
    fennel
    holly berries
    juniper berries

TEN IDEAS FOR CLASSIFICATION PAPERS

To develop your topic well, you should have a definite audience in mind. In the suggestions that follow, some possible audiences are mentioned.

1 Classify the groups you belong to and explain why each is meaningful to you. *Audience:* Your parents who want you to study more.

2 Classify small cars (or some other vehicles) and evaluate them. *Audience:* Assume you are writing for readers of *Consumer Reports*.

3 For the home gardener, classify and describe hardy perennials that thrive in the sun, partial shade, or full shade.

4 Annoying drivers

5 Students in your classes

6 Hazards in buying a used car (or anything else)

7 Commercials that irritate

8 Types of homes available in the price range you can afford

9 Classify and evaluate local restaurants

10 Kinds of patients/clients/customers

Comparison
Explaining Relationships

A striking comparison can capture the essence of an idea in a single sentence. Comparing an abstract idea with a concrete image, as in the proverb above, explains the resemblance in a de-lightful way. We smile or sigh and think "How true." *Comparison* includes both likeness and difference with an emphasis on likeness. A *contrast* shows or emphasizes differences.

> Happiness is like a sunbeam, which the least shadow intercepts.
>
> —**Chinese proverb**

In daily living you frequently use comparison and contrast in making purposeful choices. Whether you purchase a car, clothing, or cell phone, you undoubtedly compare and contrast the features of various brands before making your decision. On the job you may purchase supplies, screen applicants, preview software, or perform other tasks that require comparing prices, qualities, or features. Daily we weigh advantages against disadvantages, pros against cons, possibilities against difficulties in order to make wise decisions.

PURPOSE OF A COMPARISON OR CONTRAST PAPER

Every paper needs a specific purpose, a valid reason for a comparison or contrast, according to the rhetorical situation. The fact that an instructor assigns the paper is not a purpose. The comparison or contrast should illustrate a point the writer wishes to make. The point may be placed at the beginning or the end of the paper.

Determining a Purpose

To determine your specific purpose, try asking yourself, "Why might the audience like to read about this topic?" What is the point? When a topic is unfamiliar to readers, your purpose in comparing and contrasting may be to inform them of significant relationships and distinctions between the two subjects. When the topic is familiar, your general purpose may be informative; but to hold readers' attention, you need to present specific insights or a fresh perspective. You might entertain, as well as inform, by presenting the features of the two subjects in an amusing way.

When the general purpose of comparison or contrast is to persuade, you shape a specific strategy to influence readers toward a certain viewpoint. For example, an employee might write a proposal comparing a present procedure to a proposed new procedure, weighing advantages and disadvantages (if any). The specific purpose would be to convince readers that the new procedure would save time and money.

See "Writing a
Purpose State-
ment," chapter 1.

Selecting a Suitable Topic

Regardless of the subjects you choose to contrast or compare for this paper, they must have something in common. *They should be of the same species, class, or category.* For example, there would be no practical reason to compare hockey to stock car racing, for you would be unable to find opposing points to match for a logical purpose. But if you wanted to compare different kinds of race car designs, you could find logical points of comparison or contrast. To avoid boring the reader, steer away from predictable topics and stereotypes.

1. **Find a common ground.** The two topics must have something in common so that you have points of likeness and difference to c-ompare.

2. **Avoid general topics.** Broad, general topics such as "city life versus country life" can lead to stereotypes and unsupported generaliza-tions. Write from firsthand experience on specific topics you know.

3. **Familiar topics.** Don't tell the audience what they already know. Present new information or a fresh perspective to create interest or amusement.

4. **Unfamiliar topic.** Compare the unfamiliar topic to one they already know. The topics must have a significant relationship that affords points to compare.

5. **Intriguing title.** Try looking at the topic from an unusual angle. For example, your title might be "What Kind of Bait Do Blue Gills Really Like?" Then compare using night crawlers to using your own spe-cial dough balls.

TIPS FOR SELECTING TOPICS

ANALOGY: A SPECIAL KIND OF COMPARISON

Although the subjects of a comparison or contrast are usually of the same species, class, or category, a writer may choose to make an imaginative comparison—*finding unusual likenesses in things that are of completely different categories.* In "The Attic of the Brain," biologist and essayist Lewis Thomas compares the uncon-scious human mind to the attic of a house. In "Snapping the Leash," journalist Murray Kempton compares the darker forces of human nature to "a raging tiger" that each individual "spends [his or her] life building a cage to pen . . . in."

Such imaginative comparisons are similar to simile and metaphor. But when extended over the course of a paragraph or an essay, comparisons like these become *analogies.* To be effective, an analogy should be consistent, apt, and fresh. It should also help readers see the subject in a new light. Note how the analogy of "cowboying" is used to illuminate the work of a writer:

> Both jobs—writing and cowboying—take up the whole mind and heart. . . .
> A good hand on a ranch requires vigilance, acute powers of observation,
> readiness to anticipate what might go wrong or what's coming next, a taste for
> recklessness, intuitive skills, patience, and what cowboys look for when they
> buy a horse: a lot of heart. Aspiring to those qualities as a rancher, I can only
> hope my writing will benefit as well.
>
> —Gretel Ehrlich, "Life at Close Range"

Analogies are often used to help explain abstract ideas in scientific and tech-nical writing. If you use an analogy, make sure that it has a clear explanatory purpose. Readers may not see the point of an analogy that is used primarily for decoration or entertainment.

WRITING A PAPER OF COMPARISON OR CONTRAST

www.mhhe.com/dietsch

For further guidance on writing comparison or contrast essays, visit: **Writing>Writing Tutors> Comparison/Contrast**

In composing a paper of comparison or contrast, you examine relationships between elements, distinguish their similarities and differences, and organize them in a logical order that reflects your purpose.

Gathering Information and Prewriting

If you were to compare two cars, the purpose might be to determine which one would better suit your needs and to inform an interested reader. To gather information, you might visit showrooms, talk to sales representatives, and drive the two cars. You could quote and identify the source in general terms such as "One salesperson said that. . . ." If, however, you were to read *Consumer Reports* or another publication, you would need to supply specific documentation, as explained in chapters 28 and 29.

www.mhhe.com/dietsch

For additional information on prewriting, go to: **Writing>Prewriting**

To save time, prewrite details in parallel lists. Simply head two columns with the selected topics, then skip a space and start listing. Each time you write in a detail for one item, add a corresponding detail for the other. Placing the details side by side will make the lists parallel.

	HONDA CIVIC HYBRID	TOYOTA PRIUS
Features:	_____	_____
	_____	_____
	_____	_____
Price:	_____	_____
mpg:	_____	_____
Warranty:	_____	_____
Styling:	_____	_____
Handling:	_____	_____
Comfort:	_____	_____
Maintenance:	_____	_____

Next, classify details into categories. These categories can act as main points in your paper. For example, the price, expected cost of maintenance, and cost of operation (mpg) could be grouped under the category of economy.

After prewriting and grouping details, focus your paper with a thesis statement. Check to see that it (1) identifies a specific topic, (2) indicates similarity and/or difference, and (3) sets up an order of main points. Although not all thesis statements are this explicit, many instructors prefer such a clear focus, as in the following examples:

- **THESIS:** Although the Chevrolet Lumina and the Ford Taurus are similar in several respects, they vary in comfort, performance, and cost.

- **THESIS:** Whether I am in the mood for an exhilarating challenge or a leisurely ride through the woods, I have horses for each mood. (Kathy Burton)

- **THESIS:** Despite obvious differences, the two series *Earth's Children* and *The Hitchhiker's Guide to the Galaxy* have much in common. (Melissa Baker)

Organizing a Paper of Comparison or Contrast

The *block* and *alternating* methods are two basic ways to organize parallel points of comparison or contrast. For an easily understood topic, the block method is simple and suitable. This order lists all the pertinent points about the first subject in one block of parallel details, then lists the points about the second subject in corresponding order. This balanced arrangement ensures that the details are easy to follow.

BLOCK OUTLINE OF CONTRAST

I. *Thesis statement:* Mr. Courtney and Mr. Graham, my former neighbors, contrasted greatly in appearance, demeanor, and friendliness.

www.mhhe.com/dietsch
For help outlining, check out:
Writing>Outlining Tutor

II. Mr. Courtney

   A. Appearance

      1. Meticulous. Clothes perfectly pressed.

      2. Clean-shaven. Hair neatly groomed.

      3. Short, trim, and muscular.

   B. Demeanor

      1. Solemn. Never seemed to smile. Eyes glared.

      2. Never out except to care for lawn. Swore and hurried.

      3. Children afraid of him. He scowled when greeted.

   C. Friendliness

      1. Unfriendly.

      2. Protected his privacy.

III. Mr. Graham

   A. Appearance

      1. Clothes never hung quite right.

      2. Hint of a beard. Hair untidy.

      3. Tall and rather heavy.

   B. Demeanor

      1. Always smiling. Kind eyes.

      2. Often outside. Hummed, sang, worked in rose garden.

      3. Charmed children. Pitched ball, played hide and seek.

   C. Friendliness

     1. Regarded as grandparent by children.

     2. Concerned, a real neighbor.

 IV. Conclusion

For a complex comparison, the alternating method is an effective way to organize. You explain comparable points paired in parallel order. In other words, you alternate the subjects. Because of frequent shifts from subject to subject, the alternating method requires more transition than the block method.

OUTLINE OF CONTRAST (ALTERNATING SUBJECTS)

 I. Introduction

 II. Appearance

   A. Mr. Courtney

   B. Mr. Graham

 III. Demeanor

   A. Mr. Courtney

   B. Mr. Graham

 IV. Friendliness

   A. Mr. Courtney

   B. Mr. Graham

 V. Conclusion

When only similarities are discussed, the pattern can be similar to one of the preceding examples for contrast. When you include both similarities and dissimilarities, the structure of the comparison becomes more complicated. Usually, similarities are discussed first, unless there is a reason for reversal.

www.mhhe.com/dietsch

Want more coverage of introductions? Go to:
Writing>Introductions

Drafting an Introduction

The introduction sets the stage for the two subjects by revealing what, where, how, and when. A narrative opening is an easy and effective way to set the stage for a comparison or contrast. Terri Bloomfield uses narration, presenting a few graphic details to describe a sudden change in her life.

My Life after Dealing with Death

As I pushed my Fiero up to sixty-five miles an hour, the possibility of being killed in an automobile accident was miles of thoughts away. Being young, I felt invincible—why should I worry about an unpleasant subject like death? In a few days, however, I had to confront that topic in an instant. On August 18, 1993, my best friend and my cousin were killed in an automobile accident. The realization of how quickly life can be snatched away changed my life, starting the moment I met death face-to-face.

Developing a Comparison or Contrast Paper

The order in which you develop your parallel points in a comparison or contrast depends upon the purpose and the audience. One technique, order of familiarity, starting with the familiar and going to the unfamiliar, is quite effective, allowing less explanation than the reverse requires. You use analogies, anecdotes, or examples to flesh out ideas before moving to more complex points. A topic that involves physical description will need numerous concrete details to support the main points.

In the next example from "My Two Neighbors," Betty Fetters' precise descriptions enable the reader to visualize two individuals, see beyond outer appearances, and appreciate their own good neighbors.

Mr. Courtney was a meticulous person who seemed to reflect this quality in every aspect of his life. His clothes were always perfectly pressed, his face clean-shaven, and his hair neatly groomed. His short frame was trim and muscular despite his age. He seemed always to wear a solemn expression; I never once saw him smile. His glaring eyes echoed his disgust with people and his contempt for life.

Seldom did I see Mr. Courtney outdoors except to care for his lawn. Despite the swearing and hurrying to get the job done, his yard was the best tended in the neighborhood. Local children never went near his house because they knew that the slightest transgression would be met with angry retribution. Mr. Courtney was a private person, and everyone treated him and his property with the respect he so vehemently demanded.

Many times a greeting to Mr. Courtney would be answered with an angry scowl. Mr. Courtney was indeed an island unto himself. Every encounter with him would remind me of another, much more gentle, man—a very dear friend who had taught me the value of friendship and the real definition of the word *neighbor*.

Note that after the first block of details, Betty smoothly introduces the second block with "would remind me of another, much more gentle man . . . ," leading into a description of Mr. Graham:

If judged by first appearance, Mr. Graham would not have made a very good impression. His clothes, although neatly pressed, never hung quite right on his tall, rotund body. He seemed always to have a shadow of a beard, and his hair usually looked as if he had started to comb it but had been interrupted. He was, however, always smiling; and his love for people and life was reflected in his eyes.

Many times I would hear Mr. Graham singing or humming while he worked in his garden or trimmed his rosebushes. He always worked with the same patience and deliberation, nurturing and caring for each plant. With this same calm concern, he charmed the children of the neighborhood. It was common to see him pitching a ball, playing hide-and-seek, or sitting on his porch with a group of children at his feet. The children regarded him as a grandparent and treated him with great respect, as did everyone in the neighborhood. He was a real neighbor to all, friend or stranger.

Transition to Indicate Similarity or Dissimilarity

As you move from detail to detail while comparing or contrasting, you will need special transitions to indicate shifts in meaning. For your convenience, here are some transitions that point out likeness or difference:

SIMILARITY		DISSIMILARITY	
also	too	but	yet
and	both	in contrast	on the other hand
again	similarly	however	on the contrary
likewise	in addition	still	although
besides	then too	conversely	nevertheless

Now and then you may need a *transitional sentence* to bridge a gap in thought. For example, after discussing one horse, you might supply a sentence of transition to introduce another horse: "Whereas Rocket looked as if he had been groomed for the Kentucky Derby, Skip had the careless air of a beachcomber." Two other tips you may want to consider: (1) Place *also* or *however* within a sentence rather than at the beginning, where they may sound tacked on or out of place. (2) Substitute *too* or *then too* to avoid overuse of *also*.

Writing a Conclusion

www.mhhe.com/dietsch

If you want additional coverage of writing conclusions, go to:
Writing>Conclusions

When the purpose of a comparison is to inform, a brief summary may be in order. In her conclusion, Betty Fetters not only summarizes but also shares insights gained from experience:

> Although Mr. Graham died a year ago, his memory will live in the hearts of the people who were lucky enough to have known him. For me, he made it easier to accept the Mr. Courtneys of the world. Mr. Graham knew the secret of happiness, and the values that he taught will remain a part of my life forever.

For a serious topic, a change of perspective can provide just the right note for ending. Terri Bloomfield concluded with this thought:

> After witnessing the death of my cousin and best friend, I cherish life much more. I know firsthand that life is precious and fragile. Now I never take today or tomorrow for granted. I feel as if I must appreciate life not only for myself but for my cousin and my friend, too.

REVISING A PAPER OF COMPARISON OR CONTRAST

www.mhhe.com/dietsch

For general revision resources, go to:
Writing>Drafting and Revision

As you revise your paper, keep your outline handy and your audience in mind. The outline will help you to maintain the balanced order that comparison and contrast require. Thinking of the audience will help in selecting words and in knowing how much to explain. Strive for originality. Concrete nouns, vivid adjectives, and verbs in the active voice will invigorate your descriptions. Yet trite expressions sometimes infiltrate papers of comparison and contrast. Few readers enjoy frayed phrases like these:

different as day and night   a different story altogether

like two peas in a pod   are worlds apart

spitting image of his father   looked like twins

If you find common, overused expressions in your draft, get out a thesaurus and dictionary. Select a fitting synonym and rephrase the sentence. If needed, add examples of interest. Read your paper aloud so that you can hear the flow of sentences and check to see that transition is adequate. The checklist that follows will help you to find possible trouble spots.

CHECKLIST | **REVISING A PAPER OF COMPARISON OR CONTRAST**

1. Is the thesis clear and specific?

2. Is the order of points in the thesis the same as their order in the body?

3. Are main points and paragraph details arranged in parallel form?

4. Does every paragraph have a topic sentence?

5. Does every topic sentence have adequate support?

6. Does the conclusion seem complete?

7. Have I fulfilled the purpose of the comparison or contrast?

8. Does anything else need to be said for this audience?

TWO STUDENT PAPERS: COMPARISON

In the first paper, Jeff Patten contrasts two books by the same author. Jeff's purpose is to inform. His audience consists of readers who enjoy historical fiction.

I, Claudius and Claudius the God

In 1934 Robert Graves published a rather lengthy book of historical fiction entitled *I, Claudius*. The novel was written in such a manner as to have the reader believe it was an autobiography of the Roman emperor Tiberius Claudius Drusus Nero Germanicus. *I, Claudius* takes the reader from the emperor's earliest childhood remembrances up to the year 41 AD, when he became emperor of the Roman Empire. It is there, minutes after Claudius's ascent to the throne, that the book ends.

This abrupt ending seemed to demand a sequel, and in 1935 Graves published *Claudius the God*. This second "autobiographical novel" chronicled the life of Claudius from his ascent to the throne to his murder. Although each of the novels was written about the same person, by the same author, there are few similarities. *I, Claudius* and *Claudius the God* seem similar only in the basic form in which they are written. They differ in readability, style, and entertainment value.

The two books resemble each other only in narrative autobiographical form. The reader experiences the life of ancient Rome, narrated through the thoughts and words of the emperor Claudius. Graves has an almost mystical way of making the reader feel as if the emperor Claudius had penned the words himself. The novels provide accounts of the seedy, scandalous lives of the ruling Caesars. Greek and Latin phrases reveal careful research. The historical accuracy makes the novels seem authentic.

There the resemblance ends. *I, Claudius* is an easily read, thoroughly engrossing book. Readers receive the impression of a smooth, flowing manuscript. They are led chronologically, with a few pauses for reflection, through the turmoil and pageantry of the Roman Empire and its rulers. *Claudius the God,* however, is a rather choppy, disjointed work. Readers are required to leap from one story line to another with little or no hint of a chronological advance. One can only speculate as to the reason. Yet one thing is certain. The readability and style of *I, Claudius* are far superior to its sequel.

Style is a significant difference between the two novels. Although both manuscripts were thoroughly researched, the historical data are presented in two very different ways. In *I, Claudius* the facts are colorful; the pompous and elegant lives of the ruling class make for fascinating reading. In contrast, the facts presented in *Claudius the God* seem dry and mundane; furthermore, the story line makes for dull reading.

The net result of these differences makes the books unequal in entertainment value. *I, Claudius,* whatever its historical worth, is a very good story. Even readers who ordinarily do not enjoy histories or autobiographies will likely enjoy this novel because it is so entertaining. The sequel, however, is a chore to read—much like reading a history textbook.

If it were not for the many weaknesses of *Claudius the God,* the set would make worthwhile reading. Robert Graves's prowess as a poet and distinguished writer shines brightly in his first novel but fails miserably in the second.

QUESTIONS FOR DISCUSSION

1. What is the function of Jeff's first two paragraphs?

2. How are the two novels alike? How are they different?

3. What method of organization does Jeff use?

4. How would you characterize the tone of Jeff's essay?

5. Comment on the conclusion.

In the second paper, Rosy Erdy pays tribute to her parents. She looks at her parents' few similarities and many differences, then makes an important point at the end. Her purpose is to inform; she envisions an audience of descendants who will read this comparison in the family history.

▶ ### Parents through a Child's Eyes

In this modern age when divorce is more common than not, my parents are in the minority. They have lived contentedly for nearly half a century despite distinctive differences in childhood backgrounds, political views, and personalities. Some folks might view them as ordinary, but to me they are very special, and I want my descendants to know more about them than their photos in the family album reveal.

The old axiom "opposites attract" certainly seems true in regard to Mom and Dad. Despite a physical resemblance, their differences far outnumber their likenesses. Born only a year apart and now in their middle seventies, my parents both have thinning, silver-colored hair. Both are less than average height: Mom refers to herself as "petite." Dad, with a smile, says he is "not tall."

The childhood backgrounds of my parents were certainly not alike. Growing up, Mom lived only in the city whereas Dad knew only the life on a farm in the 1920s and 1930s. Mom was the first of her family to graduate from high school; Dad went to work immediately after completing the eighth grade at a one-room school. A strong religious environment influenced Mom whereas no visible religious commitments existed in Dad's family. Shortly after their marriage, however, Dad adopted Mom's religion. He still attends church regularly with her, but only half-heartedly.

My parents' political differences became quite apparent when I was very young because Mom is a loyal Democrat and Dad is a proud Republican. Every four years after a presidential election, they return from the polls loudly declaring that it is fruitless to vote. They know that the vote of one cancels out the vote of the other, but still they vote each year.

My parents' greatest difference is in personality. Mom has always been more friendly and outgoing whereas Dad tends to be shy. Mom seems to be always laughing, even with tears in her eyes, but Dad is more serious. Mom demonstrates affection freely; Dad has difficulty in letting his emotions show. Years ago, Mom administered discipline, while Dad stayed in the background. Afterward he would give us hugs and smiles on the sly.

Mom is forthright and open, but Dad is soft-spoken and reserved. Mom seems to have a strong opinion on everything; Dad tends to be quiet and easily swayed. No one in the family needs to worry about anything because Mom does it for us. If Dad ever worries, he keeps it well hidden. Privacy is not a word in Mom's vocabulary; it seems to be her God-given right as a mother to know everything about her family. On the other hand, Dad quietly respects everyone's privacy.

Despite their many differences, my parents have been steadfast in their devotion to each other and to the family. As a result, my brother and I have been greatly influenced by the blending of their differences. From our wonderful parents, we have gained a balance and stability that has been transmitted to our own families' lives.

QUESTIONS FOR DISCUSSION

1. What is the effect of including similarities? What would be the effect if Rosy had included only differences?

2. Which method of organization does she use?

3. Notice that she mixes a few first-person references with the third person. Are these necessary and effective? Why or why not?

4. Are her examples convincing support for her claims?

5. How would you describe the tone of the essay?

6. Comment on her conclusion.

<table>
<tr><td>FOR YOUR REFERENCE
Comparison and Contrast Essays in the Reader</td><td><ul><li>"That Lean and Hungry Look," Suzanne Britt, page 630</li><li>"The Stubborn Twig," Monica Sone, page 633</li><li>"Mother Tongue," Amy Tan, page 638</li><li>"Fun Ethic vs. Work Ethic," Robert J. Samuelson, page 643</li></ul></td></tr>
</table>

GROUPS: Selecting a Topic for Comparison

Directions: Would the topics below be suitable for a 500-word paper of comparison? Mark them as suitable (S) or unsuitable (U). Compare your answers and discuss.

_____ 1. The courage of two United States presidents who faced monumental decisions.

_____ 2. Two pets I have owned

_____ 3. Before and after: stay-at-home mom, then career woman

_____ 4. Good and evil

_____ 5. Tipping versus nontipping

IDEAS FOR PRACTICE WRITING

Directions: Select a topic from the list below (or one of your own) to contrast in a paragraph. Prewrite by making parallel lists of details.

1. Two routes to a destination
2. Two methods of fishing
3. A date you enjoyed and one you did not enjoy
4. Two appliances you have owned
5. Two pets (same species) you have owned

TEN IDEAS FOR COMPARISON OR CONTRAST PAPERS

1 Profit: a garage sale or eBay?

2 Two reviews of a ballgame (favor the team you like)

3 Buy or lease a car?

4 Two attitudes toward a family heirloom

5 Your life and your grandmother's or grandfather's life

6 Life before attending college and after

7   Life before and after losing weight

8   Two versions of an accident

9   Two cars I have owned

10   Two athletes in the same sport

Definition
An Introduction to Using Sources

CHAPTER 15

> The beginning of wisdom is the definition of terms.
>
> —Socrates (470–399 BC)

PURPOSE OF DEFINITION

Learning to write clear definitions will sharpen your thinking and enable you to be more precise and accurate. Definition at the right time can dissolve misunderstanding, improve communication, cut costs, and promote safety. On the job you may write definitions in procedures, policies, or reports. You may need to simplify a technical definition and restate it in words the lay reader can understand, both on the job and for college research papers.

On exams you may write formal sentence definitions or longer extended definitions. Definition can also be used in personal essays. For example, "In the Joys of Workaholism," Jim Sollisch defines "workaholic trance":

> Recently I had a bout of workaholism. Let's call it an episode. I binged on work for about four months. And while I'm not yet ready to attend a 12-step WA meeting, I am concerned about how easily I fell into a workaholic trance. It was a delicious mix of adrenaline, caffeine, self-importance and a heady rush of focus. Gone was the indecision. Suddenly I was a verb—and not one passively constructed. I was all action. It was invigorating to be riveted to a single purpose—like a rock climber without ropes. (*Wall Street Journal*, 3 Mar. 2007)

FORMAL SENTENCE DEFINITION

A writing instructor had just explained formal sentence definition to his freshman composition class. Turning to a student who seemed half asleep, he said, "Nick, will you please define mammal for me?"

Suddenly awake, the student stammered, "Er . . . a mammal is hairy; uh . . . it has a hard skeleton and provides milk."

With a twinkle in his eye, the instructor replied, "So far, you have not ruled out the coconut."

A formal sentence definition is a complete sentence that classifies an item or an idea and differentiates it from other members of its class. More complete than dictionary definitions, which are fragments, formal sentence definitions have four parts:

1. The term to be defined
2. A *be* verb—usually *is* or *are*
3. The classification (genus, class, or species)
4. The distinguishing features or characteristics

Below are two illustrations of the parts of a formal sentence definition. Note that the copied words, from *The Oxford American Dictionary*,* are enclosed with quotation marks.

TERM	VERB	CLASSIFICATION	DISTINGUISHING FEATURES
A pelican	is	a "large, water bird of warm regions	with a pouch in its long bill for storing fish."
Lynxes	are	wildcats "with spotted fur,	noted for [their] keen sight" and tufted ears.

Identifying Sources, Quoting, and Paraphrasing

When you copy someone else's words, whether from a dictionary or other source, you are required to provide documentation. To avoid plagiarism, identify the source and enclose the copied material with quotation marks. Or you may prefer to restate or paraphrase the passage in your own words. For example: A pelican is a big water bird with *skin between its toes* and a *stretchable bag* beneath its bill for catching and stowing fish.

Minor words such as *a, an, the, with* and other prepositions can be reused without quotation marks, but supply your own words when possible. Generic words that do not have synonyms (*water, bird, bill,* and *fish*), do not require quotation marks when copied. If you need help, use a thesaurus to find synonyms.

See chapter R-3.

---

*From *Oxford American Dictionary*. Copyright © 1980 by Oxford University Press, Inc. Used by permission of Oxford University Press, Inc.

Chapter R-3 of "The Research Writing Guide" explains how to use sources. Brief guidelines are provided here. A safeguard while note-taking is to enclose all copied words with quotation marks so there is no confusion later. Include the page number in case you need to go back and check something. To avoid plagiarism, you are required to provide the following documentation:

1. Enclose short quotations with quotation marks.

2. *Indent* all lines of long quotations of five lines or more. (No quotation marks.)

3. Specify the name of the author and the source. (Check with your instructor for the preferred format, MLA or APA.)

4. If you omit any words from the middle of the quotation, use ellipses [. . .] to indicate the omission.

NOTETAKING AND DOCUMENTING SOURCES

Prewriting a Formal Sentence Definition

To start prewriting a formal sentence definition, choose a concrete topic. Then ask yourself three questions about the topic:

- What distinguishing features do all items in the class have?
- How can similar items be ruled out?
- What purpose or function does the item serve?

Two precautions will help you to sidestep common errors when writing formal sentence definitions:

1. *Do not define a term by repeating the term or using a derivation.*
   Avoid: A keystone is the key stone in an arch.
   Instead: A keystone is the central wedge-shaped piece at the top of an arch that holds the other stones in place.

2. *Avoid the phrase "is when" or "is where."* This usage is ungrammatical.
   Avoid: A greenbelt *is where* a band of parks, farmland, or unused land surrounds a community.
   Instead: A greenbelt is a band of parks, farmland, or unused land surrounding a community.

Start with a familiar object such as an apple. Consider: Which classification does an apple belong to? How do apples differ from other members of the class, such as plums, pears, and peaches? What are the distinguishing features of apples? Write a complete sentence that includes all four parts of the formal definition:

(continued)

WRITING A SENTENCE DEFINITION

WRITING A
SENTENCE
DEFINITION
(continued)

Term	Verb	Classification	Distinguishing Features
An apple	is	a/an _____	_____

An apple is a fruit, of course, but you might be more precise by stating the purpose: edible fruit. You might be more specific by giving its taxonomic category, the rose family. At first you may jot down features such as red and round. (Are all apples red? Round?) After you finish, see the example at the end of the chapter.

WRITING A PAPER OF EXTENDED DEFINITION

The purpose of a paper of extended definition is to explain a term or concept clearly in an *original* way. Just as it sounds, the definition continues throughout the paragraph or paper. You can draw examples and anecdotes from your own experience or that of someone you know to provide support. Research is generally limited to dictionaries, thesauruses, and short quotations. If needed, you may include your own sentence definition or a dictionary definition, properly documented.

Selecting a Topic and Consulting Sources

To learn as much as possible from writing a definition paper, select an abstract topic. What do you feel strongly about? How does the topic relate to you? How does it affect your principles and values? How much support can you provide for your thesis? You will be wise to sidestep Herculean topics such as "time," "democracy," and others that are very broad. If you choose a term you have learned in another class, do not merely summarize other people's ideas—develop your own.

To gather ideas about your topic, consult two or three very large dictionaries. Especially helpful is the unabridged *Oxford English Dictionary*, a set of several volumes, that traces the history of words introduced into the English language since AD 1150. In the OED you may find an unusual detail to serve as an attention-getter for your introduction or for an example in your paper. You might trace the history of a word whose meaning has changed over the years.

First, narrow the topic so that it can be covered adequately in the assignment. For instance, "discrimination" would be too broad. One student limited this topic to "prejudice against short men." He gave examples of how he copes with shortness through elevator shoes, hairstyles, and dress. Then he explained how these changes have improved his life and gained him respect.

www.mhhe.com/dietsch

For additional help on prewriting, go to:
Writing>Prewriting

Prewriting and Organizing a Paper of Definition

Next, consult your dictionary notes and think about them. Then prewrite to unearth examples, anecdotes, comparisons, cause-and-effect factors, or changes in meaning. Clustering is particularly helpful for prewriting about an abstract concept. To review the seven basic ways to organize, turn back to chapter 4. The two sample scratch outlines below are arranged according to order of importance.

EXAMPLE I: PROFESSIONALISM AT A GOLF CLUB

a. Ethics = respect

b. Customer service

c. Accuracy of records

d. Dress of personnel

EXAMPLE II: MY PROCRASTINATION

a. Examples: Cause

b. Effects

c. How I am overcoming

Including a Dictionary Definition for a Purpose

Seldom is a dictionary definition needed in a paper of extended definition. If you should wish to expand a dictionary definition, however, you would have a valid purpose. When citing a definition, you need to weave the definition into the text by providing adequate transition. The basic examples that follow will not be suitable for every writing situation, but you may be able to adapt them to fit your paper.

- Although *Webster's College Dictionary* defines _____ as "_____," this definition lacks _____.

- According to Webster's *New World Dictionary,* _____ is "_____" but that definition does not adequately explain _____.

Drafting a Special Kind of Introduction

Opening with a quotation is one of the easiest ways for a beginning writer to achieve a polished introduction. A relevant quotation can set the tone and indicate the focus of the paper. The quotations that open the chapters of this book show how to format and document a quotation that precedes your main text. Notice that because the quotations are indented and set apart from the text, quotation marks are not needed. The author's name appears beneath the quotation. Inclusion of the source is optional. Include dates of works written *before* the twentieth century.

Establishing Transition   To forge a link from an introductory quotation to the text of your paper, embed transition in your first sentence. You can repeat a key term from the quotation or use a synonym or related word to establish a clear link. Try to be subtle. A direct reference, unless cleverly done, can mar the opening and stamp the work as that of an amateur. With thought, you can avoid weak transitions, such as "In this quotation . . . ," "As stated in the quotation above, . . . ," or "I think the above quotation means. . . ."

In the following example, the student writer (who prefers to remain anonymous) uses an embedded transition in her first sentence. A related word (*alcoholism*) echoes a word in the quotation (*drunkenness*). Note, too, that the first sentence here is a formal sentence definition.

Living with an Alcoholic

Drunkenness . . . spoils health,
dismounts the mind, and unmans men.
                —WILLIAM PENN

Alcoholism is a disease caused by continual heavy drinking of alcoholic beverages. In the acute and chronic stages, alcoholism consists of symptoms ranging from the obvious to the obscure. Usually, it is not difficult to recognize a person who is inebriated; generally, staggering and slurring of speech are apparent. Accompanying neurological disorders such as tremors (shakes), hallucinations, and seizures are easily discerned. Hidden to the naked eye is the damage endured by the liver, stomach, and pancreas. Not only is excessive drinking devastating to the physical and mental health of the alcoholic, but it is also devastating to the alcoholic's family.

Living for eighteen years with my father, who was a severe alcoholic, was much like living with Dr. Jekyll and Mr. Hyde. The alcohol would turn my kindhearted, loving father into a brutal, hateful monster. Because of my father's unpredictable behavior, high anxiety and fear were normal, everyday emotions for me.

Did you notice that the first paragraph is written in *third* person? The writer gives general background information before narrowing the topic to the alcoholic's family. In the second paragraph, she shifts to *first* person because it reveals specific details about her life. See how she eases the shift from third person to first with a gerund phrase ("Living . . . with my father").

Did you note the simile in the second paragraph? The phrase "like living with Dr. Jekyll and Mr. Hyde" not only sets up a striking comparison but also establishes a natural relationship with "unmans men" in the opening quotation.

Developing an Extended Definition

Depending on the subject and purpose, a paper of extended definition may be developed by almost any strategy or combination of strategies—description, process, comparison, examples, or explanation. To find details and develop your paper, consider these five basic techniques of extended definition.

Operational Definition   To define an operation, the writer tells (a) what the object being defined does, (b) how it works, and (c) the basic principle underlying its performance. For example, a one-sentence operational definition might state that a refrigerator is a mechanized box, powered by electricity or gas, that circulates coolant to a condenser to chill food, medicines, or other items. An expanded operational definition would explain in detail how a refrigerator works. Operational definitions are often used in technical writing.

Defining by Comparison   Comparison is useful for explaining abstractions, such as emotions. If you can find an object to compare an idea or emotion to, then this technique will help to clarify your definition. In the following example, Marjorie Holmes begins with concrete images before going to abstract feelings:

> What feeling is so nice as a child's hand in yours? [It is] so small, so soft and warm like a kitten huddling in the shelter of your clasp. A child's hand in yours—what tenderness it arouses, what power it conjures up. You are instantly the very touchstone of wisdom and strength.

Defining by Synonym   In defining by synonym, a writer provides another word or phrase that has the same meaning. The synonym can be included either in parentheses or as an appositive:

- Rocky Collins will fight F. G. Jones for the bantamweight (112 to 118 pounds) world title.
- At one time many people believed that human intelligence could be judged by phrenology, the study of the shape of the skull.

Defining by Negation   Another effective technique of definition is *negation* (denial). The writer begins by telling what the term is not. In a paper entitled "Fear of Failure," Phyllis Parks uses negation in her opening sentence:

> *Failure* is not a pretty word. The very mention of it creates images and feelings of someone who is inept and incompetent. The word itself strikes fear in my heart. Sometimes my life has seemed as though it has been one failure after another. But with time has come an appreciation for the value of failure.

In *Faith of My Fathers*, Senator John McCain begins his definition of *glory* by explaining what glory is not. Then he describes what glory means to him:

> Glory is not a conceit. It is not a decoration for valor. It is not a prize for being the most clever, the strongest, or the boldest. Glory belongs to the act of being constant to something greater than yourself, to a cause, to your principles, to the people on whom you rely, and who rely on you in return.

Weaving Example with Explanation   A lone example without interpretation may be of little use to readers. You cannot assume that every reader will see the connection you intend. You need to link the example to the main idea and comment appropriately. Chris Layman, a student writer, first uses negation. Then he weaves example with explanation in an extended definition of honesty:

> "Do as I say, not as I do," my parents would often say as I was growing up. However, admonitions such as this often fade from the mind whereas examples form lasting impressions. As children grow they need models to follow. They need to determine how they will live their lives, what their values will be,

and how they will treat other people. A father is a model that his children depend on to learn how to act within their society and to form their own set of values.

Recently, my young son and I were in a store when he noticed a $100 bill lying on the floor. I had always told my son to be honest; now I could show him what honesty meant. Together we went to the store manager and put the money in his care, hoping the rightful owner would return to claim it. This incident allowed me to act as a role model for my son, and it set an example I hope he will follow throughout his life.

Writing a Conclusion

www.mhhe.com/dietsch

For general conclusion resources, visit: Writing>Conclusions

A conclusion for a paper of definition should be brief and appropriate. One way to end is with a formal sentence definition. Another is to allude to an opening quotation. A third way is to summarize changes and end on a positive note.

Closing with a Formal Sentence Definition   Debby Ketcham concludes her paper with a formal sentence definition. The definition is followed by a sentence of summary and another of comment:

▶ Finally, poise is an inner mental balance, the ability to face new situations calmly, to hold one's temper, to cope with stress, and to deal with embarrassment. All these situations require a control over emotion and the ability to present a calm, tactful, polite manner. Poise is truly a valuable trait.

Alluding to an Opening Quotation   A reference to the beginning creates an "echo ending" and establishes closure. Using this technique, Penny Amrine repeats parts of a quotation by Joseph Conrad in her conclusion. In the last sentence she provides a formal sentence definition:

▶ My loneliness did indeed wear a "mask." For months I had endured its "naked terror" without being able to identify its misleading appearance. Loneliness for me was life without intimate friends and relatives to lean on for love and companionship.

Ending with a Personal Lesson   Those of us who successfully survive a painful experience often extract a lesson, a bit of wisdom. The student who wrote "Living with an Alcoholic" summarized her insights:

▶ Over the years I have tried to educate myself on alcoholism. Counseling has helped me to understand how alcoholism victimizes the entire family. Now, at age 33, I realize that despite how it seemed at the time, my father was only a human being who was consumed by a dread disease.

The last line reveals the writer's compassion as well as her intellectual and emotional growth since those early years of torment. The implicit note of forgiveness and the gentle tone provide a positive ending to a wrenching topic.

- **Use quotations for a purpose**. Readers enjoy a bit of wisdom or a humorous insight but dislike a patchwork of quotations.
- **If you use multiple quotations from different sources, be sure they fit well**. Writing is simpler when you keep quotation to a minimum.
- **Avoid stereotypes and clichés**. They are rarely needed.
- **Use a dictionary definition only for a logical reason**. Have a purpose, such as to clarify further or to disagree.

GUIDELINES FOR EXTENDED DEFINITION

Revising a Paper of Definition

To revise a paper of extended definition successfully, you need to examine its many facets. If you include a quotation, whether a dictionary definition, lines from a poem, or a bit of wisdom, check to see that the material *is copied exactly as written*. The checklist below will enable you to scrutinize other parts of your paper.

www.mhhe.com/dietsch

If you want general revision help, go to: Writing>Drafting and Revision

CHECKLIST   **REVISING EXTENDED DEFINITIONS**

1. Is the topic narrow enough to be defined in a short paper?

2. Have important terms been defined if they are apt to be unfamiliar to the average reader?

3. Are all definitions necessary?

4. Do formal sentence definitions (if any) conform to the standard four-part format?

5. Does every detail, definition, and quotation support the thesis?

6. Are quotations worked smoothly into the text so that their point is clear in the paper? Has proper credit been given to each original source?

7. Is the organization of the paper clear?

8. Is the closing effective?

TWO STUDENT PAPERS: DEFINITION

Jeannine Caudill talked to her friends before she wrote the following paper, which is based on their experience as well as hers. Her purpose is to explain a term not found in the dictionary. Skillfully, she states several axioms (universal truths). Three questions begin her introduction.

▶

Mother Love

Love cannot be forced, love cannot be
coaxed and teased. It comes out of
Heaven, unasked and unsought.
                    —PEARL BUCK

What is mother love? Is it a feeling, an emotion, or the dedication of an entire lifetime? Is it bad or good, imaginary or genuine? One thing is certain; mother love is difficult to define, especially to those who have not experienced it. None of the dictionaries seem to think *mother* and *love* should be combined into the phrase *mother love*. Yet there is motherhood, mother lode, and mother-land. Could any of these words be more fitting to combine with *mother* than the word *love*?

Psychiatrists define mother love, doctors prescribe it, lawyers divide it, children bask or drown in it, and fathers observe it. Perhaps even a mother cannot define it, but some still try. Love as only a mother can feel begins for some women with the first knowledge of pregnancy. For others, it comes with beholding the charm of their own soft, sweet-smelling baby. The baby does not have to be beautiful to inspire great love. Perhaps mother love at this stage of life is a myriad of feelings: infant dependency, mother's pride of accomplishment, and primitive emotions that have been basic to the human race since its beginning. Whatever the reasons, loving a baby seems very easy.

The real growth of mother love begins later. Much of the time during a child's life, no one seems to love him or her except the mother. True mother love develops over many years and through many trials. When a toddler throws a fit in a store, shouts a loud "No," or dampens a neighbor's carpet, mother love is put to a test. But even in this stage, the child is very appealing to her. Here a new facet of love begins, pride in the child's independence.

The early school years strain the most patient mother. After the thumb-sucking, leg-hugging, insecure years come the years of grade cards, teacher conferences, show and tell, and four hundred papers to be praised and hung up.

Many older mothers say to younger mothers, "If you think things are bad now, just wait till he's a teenager!" But the young mothers often counter with "Nothing could be worse." This lack of foresight must be a tool of Mother Nature. Otherwise, only the very brave would dare to have a child.

Mother love seems never to end. It usually begins with the birth of a child and continues to encircle and entwine the mother's heart down through the years. Strangely enough, the only person who can appreciate the real meaning of mother love is a mother.

QUESTIONS FOR DISCUSSION

1. What do you notice about Jeannine's introduction?

2. Examine the first sentence of the second paragraph. What do you notice about the sentence structure?

3. Do Jeannine's examples ring true? Why or why not?

4. What does she do before she comments?

5. How would you describe the tone of the essay?

In the following paper, Ron Willetts opens with a quotation and provides not only the author but also the source. Then he cites a dictionary definition and the parts of speech for the word *work* for a significant reason: to expand upon its meaning as a noun and as a verb. In the first main point, he uses narration and explanation to illustrate his early view of work. He defines later views by explanation, associations, and examples.

Changes in My View of Work

My friend there is a Hell . . . when a man has a family to support, has his health, and is ready to work, and there is no work to do. When he stands with empty hands and sees his children going hungry, his wife without the things to do with. I hope you never have to try it.
—LOUIS L'AMOUR, *THE WALKING DRUM*

The *Oxford American Dictionary* defines work as a noun that means "Use of bodily or mental power in order to do or make something, especially as contrasted with play or recreation." Work is also defined as a verb: "to perform work, to be engaged in bodily or mental activity."* Over the years I gradually learned to understand these concepts, but only when I became unemployed for an extended period did I understand L'Amour's definition.

When I was very young, work was not a verb, it was a noun, a place to go and a place to leave. My grandfather would come home from work in the evenings, and we would go through a ritual. As he drove his truck into the garage, I would be waiting. He would pick me up, and somewhere between the truck and the house, I would remove the hat from his head and transfer it to mine. Once inside, he would place his dinner bucket on a chair, and I would rummage through it for the leftover cookie, banana, or candy bar that was always there. At that time in my life, I did not have to worry; all my needs were taken care of.

When I became a young adult, the word *work* took on a new meaning. It was not only a noun, but suddenly a verb, a task to be performed for which one received some form of remuneration. This definition began to form when I was in the eleventh grade and began helping the janitors after school during basketball season. For sweeping the classrooms and dusting the teachers' desks, I received a modest sum and attended the home games at no cost. Thus work became associated with money. And money became closely associated with girls, cars, entertainment, and other necessities. At this time, work was a necessary evil, for it took time away from my social life.

When I became older, I found the word *work* had to be redefined once again. Along with being a place to go and an activity to perform, work became a goal. This new meaning became associated with other words such as wife, insurance, children, house, and friends. Between 1975 and 2000, work was no problem for me. If I changed jobs, the longest period of unemployment was two days. Once I quit one job on Friday and started a new one the following Monday.

---

*From *Oxford American Dictionary.* Copyright © 1980 by Oxford University Press, Inc. Used by permission of Oxford University Press, Inc.

In 2000, however, the story changed. Due to economic conditions, I became unemployed after working at a company for fifteen years. That company and my coworkers were as much a part of my life as my own family. I felt rejected and depressed. The severance pay ran out. The unemployment benefits were exhausted. The retirement fund vanished, and the bills began to pile up. I was no longer able to provide for my family. But then I thanked God we were living in modern times when it was acceptable for a married woman to work. Although my wife's income did not pay all the bills, it did allow us to feed the family and keep the electricity turned on.

Being unemployed for over two years creates a situation that at times is almost unbearable. Perhaps the worst part is being told that one cannot be hired because he is overqualified and undereducated. Being told that one could perform the task, but would not be satisfied with the job is enough to make a person ill. A man needs to be able to provide for his family.

Yes, my friend, there is a hell—I know, for I have been there. It is my sincere hope that I am the last person that has to define the lack of work as hell.

QUESTIONS FOR DISCUSSION

1. Discuss the use of the dictionary definition in the introduction. Would the paper have been as effective without it? Why or why not?

2. What do you notice about the examples? How would you rate their effectiveness?

3. Briefly summarize the changes in Ron's viewpoint.

4. What causes are specified?

5. Discuss the effectiveness of this ending. What device does he use?

<table>
<tr><td>FOR YOUR REFERENCE
Definition Essays in the Reader</td><td>
• "In Praise of the Humble Comma," Pico Iyer, page 647
• "On Being 17," David Raymond, page 650
• "The Handicap of Definition," William Raspberry, page 653
• "The Insufficiency of Honesty," Stephen L. Carter, page 655</td></tr>
</table>

PRACTICE

COLLABORATIVE EXERCISE: Discerning Genuine Definitions

Directions: Identify the satisfactory definitions in the list below and mark with an S. Mark the unsatisfactory ones with a U. Discuss why they are unsatisfactory. (You may consult a dictionary.)

1. Honey is a sweet gooey substance that is delicious on breakfast cereal.
2. A sprinkling can is a utensil that is not a bucket, dishpan, or bowl.
3. A book is like a little golden door to opportunity.
4. The gemsbok of southern Africa is a large antelope with long, sharp, straight horns and a tufted tail.
5. "Monopoly" is a table game that resembles life because you trade, buy, and sell.
6. *Morale* refers to the condition of the spirits of individuals or employees.
7. The ruffed grouse, sometimes called "partridge" or "pheasant," is a North American game bird with spotted brown feathers.
8. A dandelion is a small edible weed with fuzzy yellow flowers and saw-toothed leaves.
9. Dissatisfied means not content.
10. A fruitcake is a cake that contains fruit.

COLLABORATIVE WRITING: Formal Sentence Definition

1. Appoint a recorder to jot down the comments of the group. Define one of the terms below in a formal sentence definition:

   dog   cow   cucumber   chair   couch

2. Ask each other questions to limit the term and identify the essential features. For example:
   a. How does a dog differ from a wolf or coyote?
   b. What kind of dog? Prairie dog? Wild dog? What?
   c. What is the purpose of the dog?
   (*Note:* You may want to limit the term to watch dog, police dog, Seeing Eye dog, hunting dog, or another kind of dog.)

3. Revise. Does the definition have all four parts? Does it read smoothly?

4. Repeat the procedure, using another term.

POSSIBLE ANSWER FOR WRITING A SENTENCE DEFINITION (PAGES 193–194)

An apple is an edible fruit of the rose family that can be red, yellow, green, or multicolored; the small seeds are encased in a core connected to a flexible stem at the top and at the blossom end.

TEN IDEAS FOR PAPERS OF DEFINITION

1 What is customer service?

2 What is integrity?

3 What does a college degree really mean?

4 What is maturity?

5 Procrastination

6 Attitude: victim or winner?

7 A family value

8 Appreciation

9 Discrimination (What kind?)

10 Responsibility

Strategies for Critical Thinking, Evaluation, and Argument

PART 4

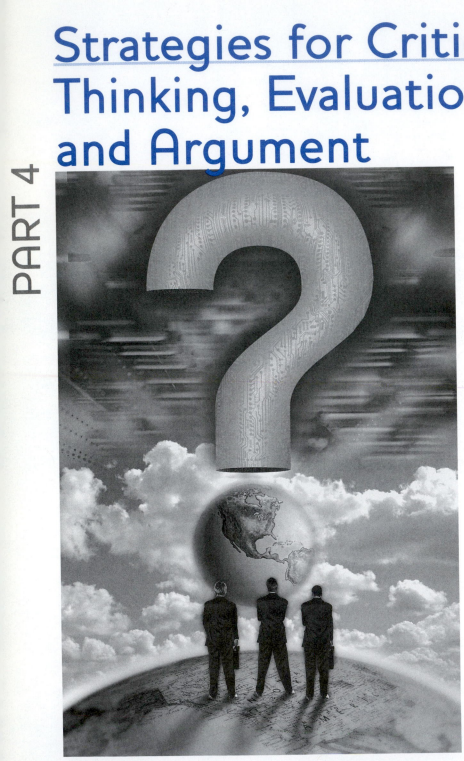

Around the world, heads of state, politicians, and ordinary citizens ponder immense questions that affect our future and possibly the survival of the human race. Perhaps the most worrisome are the following issues: As droughts spread and populations increase, what can be done to alleviate the looming water shortage? If logging in rain forests and our national parks were stopped, would this help? How can forest fires be better controlled? How can hunger be curbed? How accurate are estimates of climate change? Will the melting of glaciers and icebergs cause flooding of our shores? How much can be done to slow global warming?

These and other issues can serve as topics for research and argument and help to hone your logical reasoning, problem-solving, and argumentation skills.

WRITING EXERCISE

1. What global issue especially concerns you? Why?

2. Describe a problem that you were able to resolve satisfactorily.

ADOPTING AN ATTITUDE OF INQUIRY

To examine a problem or issue objectively, our minds need to be open to new information and differing points of view. That requires putting aside preconceived notions, listening attentively, and asking questions—adopting an *attitude of inquiry.* Then we can avoid rash decisions. For example, it is all too easy to fasten on one cause of a problem and fail to look further. But *complex problems seldom have a single cause.*

In part 1 you were introduced to critical thinking and the need for questioning to obtain accurate and complete information. Parts 2 and 3 supply checklists and other questions to help you organize, develop, and revise your drafts. Part 4 continues this emphasis and raises these questions:

1. How can you separate fact from fallacy?
2. How can you pinpoint cause and effect?
3. How do you go about solving problems logically?
4. How do you organize an effective argument?

Chapter 16, "Detecting Fallacies," explains common logical fallacies and fallacies that ignore the issue. Chapter 17, "Examining Cause and Effect," takes a close look at the relationships between cause and effect and the two fallacies that often result. Chapter 18, "Solving a Problem," discusses how to become more objective and how to apply Dewey's method of problem solving. Chapter 19, "Constructing a Convincing Argument," explains three classic appeals and how to organize an effective argument. Chapter 20, "Understanding, Using, and Creating Visuals," shows how to analyze and interpret visuals, use them in presentations, and create your own.

The Reader contains several thought-provoking essays that discuss factors that may influence the future of our country and the world.

Detecting Fallacies

CHAPTER 16

> Doubt is often the beginning of wisdom.
>
> —M. Scott Peck,
> *The Road Less Traveled and Beyond*

You've probably seen dozens of dubious news stories circulating on the Internet, but how many have you questioned? Do you accept them at face value, or do you wonder "Is that really true?" or "Is it a myth?" To determine whether such reports are fact or fiction, visit <www.urbanlegends .com> or <www.snopes.com>. Or you can type keywords into Google to see what other sources report.

To protect yourself from misinformation, deceptive arguments, and other fallacies, follow four precautions:

- **Develop a healthy sense of skepticism.** Don't believe everything you hear or read. The most convincing lies contain at least a few grains of truth.

- **Ponder what words really mean.** Broad terms such as *natural* and *eco-friendly,* appear on cereal, napkins, detergent, and other products, but the U.S. government has yet to define them. Many long-time brands sport the word "new," but seldom do they say what is new. (New is not necessarily better. The quality may have been cut to save on cost of production.)

- **Look for the sponsor or author, place, and date of claims.** Lack of documentation raises doubt about credibility and validity.

- **Check out a claim before you accept it as fact.** Can you find the same information in a reputable source? For example, the Better Business Bureau at <www.bbb.org> provides prevention tips to avoid scams, lists of reputable charities and businesses, and other helpful information.

Studying the common fallacies will help you to spot distortions in research as well as in daily life. Then you will be better prepared to avoid them in your own writing.

LOGICAL FALLACIES

Logical fallacies are false beliefs, based on errors in reasoning. These fallacies are often caused by omission, oversimplification, or exaggeration. We may overlook, de-emphasize, or overemphasize a significant factor in a situation or event. Then we may make incorrect assumptions. Unless you stop to think and question, the errors may seem plausible and persuasive.

Logical fallacies can be found in everyday conversation, talk shows, chat rooms, political speeches, advertising, published writing, and student papers. Histories, biographies, and other works may contain distortions, misinformation, or fabrications. There are six common logical fallacies:

1. Card stacking
2. Either/or fallacy (Fallacy of false alternatives)
3. False analogy
4. Hasty generalization
5. Non sequitur
6. Post hoc fallacy

Card Stacking

Card stacking (stacking the deck) is an act of slanting, distorting, or fabricating facts to suit the speaker's or writer's purpose. This fallacy involves misrepresentation, either intentional or unintentional. Although card stacking is unethical, scientific researchers have been known to fudge facts in order to support an illogical conclusion. To save time, they may take unethical shortcuts or falsify data. Or they may select only the facts that support a theory, omitting other evidence. Sooner or later, such practices are generally discovered and discredited.

But what are we to make of polls and studies from reputable sources that report widely varying results? As you gather data, be aware that research methods can be flawed in various ways. The way that questions are worded can influence the answers. Then, too, if respondents are asked to recall data or events, they may not remember. The size and kind of population samples may also vary, resulting in skewed data. Keep in mind that the *sample must represent the general population to produce reliable results.* (See "How Can One Be Objective?" in chapter 18 and "Observation" in chapter R-5.)

Sometimes students unintentionally "stack the deck" while doing research for papers. They may have too few sources to provide objective coverage. Insignificant details may be exaggerated or significant details underemphasized. Important facts may be omitted through carelessness or insufficient research.

Either/Or Fallacy (Fallacy of False Alternatives)

The either/or fallacy assumes there are only two sides to an issue or two alternatives for a problem when there are actually more. On bumper stickers you may have seen this fallacy in slogans such as "Make love, not war" and "America: Love it or leave it." Basically, the either/or fallacy presents the writer's view as the only correct alternative.

The either/or fallacy is a simplistic judgment that can occur from glancing at a problem and jumping to a conclusion. For example, office seekers often oversimplify our country's policy-making process with statements like this: "Either elect me and have a truly democratic government or elect one of my opponents and continue as we are." This either/or claim overlooks the possibility of change by other elected officials.

False Analogy

The fallacy of *false analogy* hinges upon an invalid comparison. Just as an invalid check will not clear a bank's requirements, neither will a false analogy clear a test of logic. In this fallacy two cases or items are compared and assumed to be similar although they are basically different. A conclusion that is true for one is assumed to be true for the other.

The fundamental problem with a false analogy is that it ignores a basic difference in the two cases. For example, a few years ago a group of citizens who lived in an earthquake-prone state argued for underground rail systems, pointing out that such systems have worked well in other states. The analogy was false, however, since the successful systems were located in states with little earthquake activity. A false analogy can be revealed by pointing out a significant difference.

Hasty Generalization

A *hasty generalization* is a broad general statement that lacks adequate support. The writer misstates, exaggerates, or minimizes the facts. Hasty generalizations are assumptions that occur in various ways. Three of the most common are (1) presenting inferences as fact, (2) stereotyping, (3) taking a small or atypical sample of a group and generalizing about a larger group or population. Beware of phrases such as "everyone knows," "obviously," or "the fact is" when inadequate proof is offered.

Hasty generalization can be averted by careful, accurate word choice to reflect the facts. You can identify opinions and qualify generalizations so that they are accurate. You can avoid absolute terms unless adequate evidence is available. When conducting research, you can secure a representative sample.

See "Writing Responsibly," chapter 3.

A hasty generalization may resemble the non sequitur somewhat (both contain inferences), but the hasty generalization does not set up a false cause and effect as the non sequitur does. Nor does the hasty generalization refer to specific instances as the non sequitur does.

Non Sequitur

Translated from Latin, the phrase *non sequitur* simply means "it does not follow." Such fallacies contain faulty assumptions about cause-and-effect relationships. In other words, a cause is asserted for an effect, but the effect "does not follow" logically from the cause. Non sequiturs may use words such as *because, therefore,* and *if . . . then* in attempts to persuade someone to do something. A student may claim, for example, "I should get an A on this paper because I spent thirty hours working on it and handed it in two days early." But the quality of the paper does not necessarily follow from either of the two reasons offered for the high grade.

Non sequiturs may appear in predictions: "Because Marilyn vos Savant is listed in the *Guinness Book of World Records* as having the highest IQ on record, she would make an excellent president." The fallacy here is in assuming that the chief requirement for the presidency is stellar intelligence. Jimmy Carter, for example, is highly intelligent, but many historians do not consider him to be among the more effective presidents.

Post Hoc Fallacy

One evening in New York City, so the story goes, a small boy kicked a lamppost. At that moment the lights went out all over the city; a power blackout had occurred. Yet the boy thought he had caused the power failure. This kind of thinking illustrates the *post hoc fallacy:* because one event follows another, the first is assumed to have caused the second. But there is no evidence of a connection:

FACTS:	Event A: Boy kicked lamppost. Event B: Power blackout.
POST HOC FALLACY:	A caused B. (Because event B followed event A, A is assumed to have caused B.)

The full Latin name of this fallacy is *post hoc ergo propter hoc,* meaning "after this, therefore because of this." Although no proof is offered, this fallacy assumes that one event or condition was caused by another. The truth is that the two events or conditions only *correlate,* meaning they exist together but do not interact upon or influence one another. Post hoc fallacies also occur in superstitions.

THE PATTERN OF SUPERSTITIOUS THINKING: A POST HOC FALLACY

Part 1. Superstition: Handling toads causes warts. (A causes B.)

Part 2. Because Shawn handled a toad and the following week a wart appeared on his thumb, the toad caused the wart. (Therefore, A caused B.)

To avoid confusing the fallacies of cause and effect, notice that post hoc involves two events that occur in a sequence whereas the non sequitur has only one. If a statement contains both fallacies, label it post hoc. For your convenience, the following list summarizes the main distinctions between post hoc and non sequitur.

POST HOC	NON SEQUITUR
• Two sequential events or conditions (A apparently caused B)	• Only one fact or event plus an inference
• No proof that the first event caused (or will cause) the second	• Only an opinion, often a prediction

FALLACIES THAT IGNORE THE ISSUE

Americans are bombarded every day with emotional fallacies that ignore the issue. When we drive past a billboard, open a magazine, or turn on a television set, we are exposed to clever propaganda—usually appeals to believe, buy, or donate. Such appeals rely on emotion, not logic, to sway the audience. The appeals are not always in our best interests, for they often ignore significant issues:

- Is the claim an established fact?
- Will buying the product improve my health or my life?
- Will the donation actually go to a worthy cause or will most be withheld as overhead and administrative costs?

Understanding these fallacies can help you to resist them and detect them in your research and writing. This is not to say that all emotional appeals are to be avoided. Some may attempt to persuade honestly and fairly. *But an emotional appeal should not conflict with logical thinking.* In an argument, an emotional appeal may be warranted, but the emotion should be controlled and the appeal should be ethical. Deceit is never acceptable. Eight fallacies that ignore the issue are explained here:

1. Red herring
2. Begging the question (circular argument)
3. *Argumentum ad hominem*
4. Straw man
5. Bandwagon
6. Plain folk appeal *(ad populum)*
7. Testimonial and
8. Glittering generality

Red Herring

The fallacy of *red herring* drags in a side issue or irrelevant point to distract the audience from the main issue. This fallacy is rather like the tactic that burglars in old movies often used, carrying steak along to throw to the watchdog before robbing the mansion. In the red herring fallacy, the writer suddenly tosses the reader a "bone," an irrelevant point, to avoid proving the original claim. In other words, the subject is abruptly changed in order to divert attention from the real issue.

Using the red herring fallacy, a speaker or writer attempts to prove a point by leapfrogging to an irrelevancy. For example, "The mayor is a man of integrity; he is a church member and a fine family man." But the discerning listener or reader knows the mayor's church membership and family status are not evidence of integrity. No real proof has been submitted.

Begging the Question (Circular Argument)

When a question is "begged," the issue or subject under discussion is ignored. In the fallacy of *begging the question* or *circular argument,* the claim is simply repeated in different words, not discussed or explained. No evidence or reason is offered for the claim. For example, "Football is entertaining because it is such an enjoyable sport," or "Irrelevant courses such as Latin are a waste of time." The proposition is simply assumed to be true.

Students sometimes beg the question when writing essay answers on tests and exams. They try to disguise the fact they lack the answer.

Argumentum ad Hominem

In an *ad hominem* argument, a person's character or appearance is assaulted. Name-calling, mudslinging, and smear tactics are all forms of *argumentum ad hominem* ("against the man"). A sly variation of ad hominem uses derisive humor to discredit. A personal characteristic that is irrelevant to performance becomes the subject of joking. Former president Gerald Ford was ridiculed for his lack of physical coordination and former vice president Dan Quayle for his misspelling of *potato*. Neither characteristic pertained to the ability to perform in office.

Straw Man

The *straw man* fallacy involves an erroneous or trumped-up charge. This fallacy ignores the truth. The claim can be easily refuted by presenting proof and showing the belief to be false. A classic case occurred in a Midwestern town in the 1950s. A whispered attack claimed that a retired bank president, a mayoral candidate, was a member of the Communist Party. His opponents circulated a story that he held "weekend 'Red' meetings in a party house beside his pond." When citizens demanded the sheriff investigate, he discovered the host and a bunch of buddies enjoying their weekly poker game. There was no evidence of communist activities.

Bandwagon

The bandwagon fallacy urges everyone "to jump on the bandwagon," to go along with the crowd. This fallacy uses the "everyone's doing it, so you should, too," argument. Peer pressure is exerted to exploit the desire to belong to a group or to do what other people are doing. The bandwagon fallacy also pushes the belief that the majority knows best.

Ads and commercials using the bandwagon appeal often show large groups of happy people using and enjoying the same product. For example, a commercial may feature entreaties such as "Join the Pepsi Generation." The bandwagon fallacy focuses on common ties of family, nationality, race, age, religion, gender, job, or special interest. Thus the propagandist may call upon us as United States citizens, Polish Americans, Catholics, Protestants, men, women, baby-boomers, truck drivers, or members of another group to do something.

Plain Folk Appeal (*ad Populum*)

The plain folk or *ad populum* appeal ignores the issues of class differences and interests, instead stressing core beliefs and values the audience is presumed to share. The plain folk appeal emphasizes similarity to ordinary people or so-called average citizens. She or he may wear casual clothing, participate in everyday activities, and adopt similar speech habits to show that "I'm just a regular guy" at heart—despite making a huge salary. Political candidates often appear standing with their spouses and children or riding a horse at their ranch.

Testimonial and Improper Appeal to Authority

Because Tiger Woods gives a testimonial for Nike apparel, a television viewer may be convinced to purchase some. Other athletes have plugged a variety of goods from shaving lotion to snuff. The *fallacy* inherent in a *testimonial* is the assumption that something is true or good just because a well-known person says so. No proof is offered. Never forget that unless stated otherwise, the person giving the testimony has been paid by the sponsor.

Political testimonials for candidates are often given in election campaigns. Although a well-known public figure may endorse a relatively unknown candidate, we should keep in mind that endorsements are a form of patronage, an exchange of political favors. In student writing, testimonials seldom appear, but a related fallacy sometimes occurs—improper appeal to authority.

An *improper appeal to authority* is the giving of testimony by well-known persons about a particular field in which he or she is unqualified. When a so-called authority, lacking relevant credentials, claims something is true, that is deception. For example, when physicians, researchers, or other professionals step outside their fields of expertise, their claims become meaningless. In writing papers, consider the qualifications of the researcher as well as the validity of the claim.

Glittering Generality

Glittering generalities proffer fuzzy phrases that sound good but lack substance. In other words, these vague generalizations "glitter," but have little meaning. A glittering generality contains an undefined term. If people were called upon to define the term, they might respond with different definitions. For instance, what is a "red-blooded American"? The "American way"? "Good government"? "Old-fashioned goodness"? All of these phrases can be stretched to mean whatever a writer wants.

Glittering generalities often contain virtuous words such as *freedom, liberty, loyalty, progress, truth, honor, justice,* or *fairness.* These words suggest ideals that all "good" people believe in. Politicians often use glittering generalities to appeal to our sense of fair play, brotherhood, or patriotism.

TRANSFER

Transfer is a device of association that uses the connotations of words and images to direct our senses and responses. Transfer plays a significant role in fallacies that ignore the issue. For example, negative transfer is often used to disparage opponents, as in *ad hominem* and straw man whereas positive transfer appears in the other six fallacies that ignore the issue.

Positive transfer is designed to carry pleasant connotations over to products, ideas, or people. Positive transfer presents products in the most attractive way possible with appealing names, good-looking people, and endearing scenes. These scenes are designed to stimulate enjoyable feelings and convince us to accept ideas, buy products, or donate funds.

CHECKLIST   CRITERIA FOR EVALUATING CLAIMS AND APPEALS

To determine the difference between a fallacy and a legitimate claim or appeal, ask yourself these key questions:

1. Is the claim entirely truthful and accurate?

2. Does the writing represent the claim fairly? Objectively?

3. If precautions are needed, are they clearly stated?

4. Does the appeal contain a sly attempt to manipulate by ignoring the issue?

5. Does an appeal to emotion conflict with logical reasoning?

ETHICS: DEALING WITH FALLACIES

Fallacies are dishonest arguments that cheat on the facts, ignore the underlying issue, or use an overdose of emotion to beguile an audience. Although there may be temptations to resort to fallacious persuasion, this path is unwise from both an ethical and a practical standpoint. Ethically, we have the obligation to give readers and listeners the facts. In the long run, deception is invariably impractical. Chances are the truth will eventually emerge, and the reputation of an unethical writer or speaker will be tarnished.

You may become fascinated by finding and categorizing fallacies, but if you find it difficult to label a particular case, don't worry. Recognizing deceit, manipulation, and misstatement is what is important, not the label. By learning about fallacies, you can develop healthy skepticism as well as thinking skills.

This chapter is much more than an intellectual exercise. The most important lesson is to *apply* your learning. Thinking skills can be applied almost anywhere. Critical thinking is valuable in writing and revising papers, in your personal life, and in the workplace. Critical thinking can improve your self-image and professional image. Critical thinking used wisely can give you *power*.

PRACTICE

SMALL GROUPS: Acceptable or Hasty Generalizations?

Directions: Mark A for acceptable generalization or H for hasty generalization. Discuss your answers.

1. Pit bulls are killers.
2. Women tend to score higher on vocabulary tests than men.
3. Most teenage drivers today are more reckless than those of other decades.
4. Left-handed folks are better at arithmetic than right-handed.
5. Beef is a versatile and nutritious food.

CASE PROBLEMS: Analyzing Logic

Directions: In small groups read the following cases aloud. Then discuss the main points and implications. Decide if the logic is valid or invalid. Give reasons for your decisions.

1. Is there a curse on presidents who are elected every twenty years, in years ending in zero? Since William Henry Harrison, elected 1840, all but one of the presidents elected in twenty-year cycles have either died in office or been shot: Abraham Lincoln, elected in 1860; James Garfield, elected in 1880; William McKinley, elected in 1900; Warren G. Harding, elected in 1920; Franklin D. Roosevelt, reelected in 1940; John F. Kennedy, elected in 1960; Ronald Reagan, elected in 1980 (seriously wounded but recovered). Just one other president died in office: Zachary Taylor, elected in 1850. Which fallacy is revealed in the idea of a curse?

2. After the November 2000 presidential election, Katherine Harris, Florida secretary of state, was disparaged by some journalists for her stand on ballot counting. Robin Givhan of the *Washington Post* described Harris at a press conference: "Her eyes, rimmed in liner and frosted with blue shadow, bore the telltale . . . spikes of false eyelashes. Caterpillars seemed to rise and fall with every bat of her eyelid, with every downward glance." What two fallacies are present in this comment?

3. In an essay entitled "Blue Jeans Are Here to Stay," a student made the following claims. Discuss their validity.

    > The atmosphere at business meetings . . . is more casual when people dress in blue jeans. The fact that everyone feels comfortable eases the tension. Conversation is easily developed; ideas and thoughts flow more freely. The second factor that makes blue jeans popular is their quality. Everyone likes the thought of receiving the best value in clothing for the right price. Blue jeans have this feature. They are purchased for reasonable prices and provide excellent wear. . . .

The most influential factor that causes people to buy blue jeans is their comfort in wearing. Most people like to feel good in the clothing they wear. Blue jeans are made to give this feeling to all who wear them. There is an exact size to provide everyone with a unique fit. Then they are pleased with themselves and present a cheerful attitude toward life.

COLLABORATIVE LEARNING: Identify the Fallacies

Directions: Identify the fallacy or propaganda device in each example.

1. As a burglar entered a home, a black cat dashed across the room. The burglar opened a wall safe, emptied it, and continued to search. Suddenly, he was confronted by two policemen with drawn guns. At that moment he realized the cat was a bad omen. (The safe had an alarm.)

2. Mike wrote an argument paper using information from only two sources: a paid political advertisement and three pamphlets from the National Rifle Association. Discuss any problems you see in his sources and the quality of his evidence.

3. Excerpt from a student theme: "The mature person is *continuously* open, flexible, curious, and active." (*Hint:* See a dictionary.)

4. A ninety-year-old woman makes her own wine using whole grapes. Recently she had a minor stroke, but is now completely recovered. She attributes her recovery to drinking three small glasses of her homemade wine daily. Do you agree with this reasoning? Why or why not?

5. Four-year-old Jill Smythe has won twenty beauty contests. Her mother has enrolled Jill at a school of dance, for she believes that Jill will become a movie star. Discuss this path of reasoning and where it leads.

Examining Cause and Effect

> Our least deed, like the young of the land crab, wends its way to the sea of cause and effect as soon as born, and makes a drop there to eternity.
>
> —Henry David Thoreau, *Journal*, March 14, 1838

Thoreau's observation reminds us that a single decision, action, or event can cause far-reaching effects. The relationship between cause and effect can be more intricate and extensive than we may imagine. Sometimes we lack complete information and see only part of an effect. Or we may assume a connection between two events where none exists. Or we glimpse only *short-term effects* while significant *long-term effects* remain hidden for years.

All the while there is the ever-present risk of blithely underestimating the repercussions of certain acts and of making unwise decisions based on unproved assumptions and ill-founded predictions.

PURPOSE OF CAUSAL ANALYSIS

The purpose of causal analysis is to determine whether or not a cause-and-effect relationship actually exists. If it does exist, precisely what is the connection between the cause and the effect? What happened to bring about the change?

Causal analysis allows you to reflect on an experience or event and to learn from the past. With study and practice, you can improve your ability to analyze cause-and-effect relationships. You can question doubtful information and withhold judgment until adequate proof of the final cause is available.

On the job you may analyze cause-and-effect relationships, then give input into decisions that will influence the profit or loss of your company. According to the rhetorical situation, you may write a recommendation, proposal, or report, based on your causal analysis. The greater your knowledge and insight, the more accurate the analysis will be.

THE ACCIDENT

Lisa was walking within the pedestrian lane of the large plant warehouse where she worked. The warehouse seemed even more noisy than usual. She was unaware that behind her a tow-truck driver violated company rules when he failed to sound his horn before coming around a corner. The next moment she heard the roar of a motor and glanced back. The vehicle hit her. A searing pain darted down her right leg. She crumpled and fell to the floor.

Lisa was rushed to the hospital, where a leg fracture and several deep cuts were treated. She was kept overnight. The emergency room physician said she would be unable to work for eight weeks. A witness to the accident corroborated Lisa's report, saying she was in the safety lane. The driver did not sound his horn before coming around the corner very fast. Losing temporary control of the vehicle, he swerved into the safety lane and knocked her to one side.

Activity

Assume the role of the supervisor. Write a summary of the accident in your own words and recommend action. The tow-truck driver was newly hired; he has worked only three days. The plant provides no training for tow-truck drivers.

WORKPLACE CASE STUDY

WHAT IS CAUSAL ANALYSIS?

A *cause* influences or changes something or someone. The resulting change is called the *effect. Causal analysis* is an examination of effects that have one or more causes (conditions that may have contributed to the effect). To resolve a question of cause and effect, explore all the conditions that might have caused the effect. Since you already know the effect (by observation), start by noting its significant features. Then work backward through the chain of cause and effect. Describe the related condition(s). Then list possible explanations. Next, test each explanation and eliminate as many as possible. That should lead you to the cause(s). If not, keep searching.

For example, the supervisor of a department that spray-paints washing machines notices that the finish is uneven. He wonders what condition could have caused this effect. Has an atmospheric change occurred? Is there a mechanical defect? Has human error interfered? Was the batch of paint too thin? Could multiple causes exist? Only after he has ruled out all other possibilities will he be able to pinpoint the cause(s).

STEPS IN CAUSAL ANALYSIS

1. Specify the effects. Separate from the presumed cause.
2. Examine the conditions that existed.
3. Ask whether or not these conditions could have caused the effect(s).
4. Think about possible explanations. What might have happened?
5. Test your theories. Did the presumed causes actually produce the effect?

A Reversed Chain of Cause and Effect

To trace a simple cause, start with the observed effect(s) and work *backward* through the chain until you find proof of the cause. In the example below, the gas hot water furnace requires electricity to operate the pump and thermostat.

EFFECT →	Condition →	Possibilities →	Test →	CAUSE
House is cold	<Furnace not working	<Electricity off?	(no)	
		<Gas line plugged?	(unlikely)	
		<Gas line shut off?	yes*	<Bill unpaid*

---

*Since the pilot light cannot be lit, you assume that the gas has been shut off. Checking through old bills reveals three are unpaid. But until you check with the gas company, you do not have actual proof of the cause.

Logical Principles of Cause-and-Effect Relationships

As you explore possible cause-and-effect connections, examine the logic of your conclusion or inference. Is it reasonable, sensible, and sound? Or has an error occurred? To be valid, a claim of causal relationship must be based on two essential standards.

TWO PRINCIPLES OF LOGIC IN CAUSE AND EFFECT

- The cause is able to produce the effect.
- Other causes that might have produced the effect have been ruled out.

Two Fallacies to Avoid in Analyzing Cause and Effect

A systems analyst says that the most frequent mistake in logic that his team makes is to assume that because one event follows another, the first caused the second—even though there is no proof. This assumption is the *post hoc* fallacy; chronology is mistaken for causation. Events in a sequence do not always have a connection.

Another fallacy of cause and effect is the *non sequitur* (meaning *it is not necessarily true*). A non sequitur is also an assumption, but it does not involve the timing of events. Non sequiturs often occur in predictions. For example, it was once widely said that "a Catholic will never be elected president." Yet John F. Kennedy became the first Roman Catholic president of the United States. This common belief was disproved.

See chapter 16 for fallacies.

If we keep in mind that much of what we "know" is actually inference, theory, value judgment, or myth, we are more likely to pause and seek evidence before leaping to conclusions about why something happened.

WRITING A PAPER ANALYZING CAUSE AND EFFECT

A paper of causal analysis allows for a wide range of topics to be organized and developed in various ways. Every time you inquire about *how* or *why* something happened, you begin causal analysis. To prewrite, you might sketch a reverse chain of cause and effect as shown in the earlier diagram. Keep in mind the following principle: *Complex events, conditions, or situations seldom stem from a single cause.* Therefore don't halt your search too soon. You may find more than one cause.

www.mhhe.com/dietsch

If you want further guidance on writing cause-and-effect papers, check out: Writing>Writing Tutors> Causal Analysis

Planning a Cause-and-Effect Paper

After you have sketched a cause-and-effect chain, consider how to organize details. The big question is this: *"What does the audience need to know?"* Your answer will help you decide what to include and where to start. Then set up a scratch outline in a way that seems logical. To begin, consider the following questions:

- Was there a single cause and single effect? Or were several factors involved?
- Will the major emphasis be on the specific phenomenon (cause)? Or will it be on the consequence (effect)?
- What kind of order will work best?

Chronological order is often simplest and most efficient. This way you discuss the cause before the effect. Sometimes *reverse chronological order* is used with effect before cause. If you have multiple causes and/or multiple effects, you may need to organize your main points by order of importance. Several possible strategies are presented here. If one seems to fit your topic, adapt it as needed.

www.mhhe.com/dietsch
For help outlining, check out:
Writing>Outlining Tutor

STRATEGIES FOR CAUSE-AND-EFFECT PAPERS

A. SINGLE CAUSE WITH MULTIPLE EFFECTS

I. Introduction (specifies the cause, then the effects)

- *Claim:* High consumption of soft drinks containing sugar and caffeine contributes to overweight, other health problems, and mild addiction.

II. Body (most- to least-important order)

A. Describes/explains effect no. 1: overweight

B. Describes/explains effect no. 2: other health problems

C. Describes/explains effect no. 3: mild addiction

III. Conclusion

B. SINGLE EFFECT PRODUCED BY MULTIPLE CAUSES

I. Introduction (specifies the effect, then the final cause)

- *Claim:* Many farmers in the South are decreasing the acreage allotted to tobacco in favor of vegetable crops because fresh produce sold to urban markets yields more profit.

II. Body (chronological order: sequence of related events)

A. Cause no. 1: Nicotine has been identified as a cause of cancer.

B. Cause no. 2: Many people have ceased smoking because of possible health hazards.

C. Cause no. 3: Prospects for future tobacco markets are dimming.

D. Cause no. 4: High prices of fresh produce promise lucrative returns.

III. Conclusion

continued

C. MULTIPLE CAUSES AND MULTIPLE EFFECTS (block method)

   I. Introduction: who, what, and where?

      • *Claim:* (state causes, then effects)

   II. Body (explanation of causes and effects)

     A. Causes

     B. Effects

   III. Conclusion (may be recommendations)

D. SERIES OF LINKED EVENTS (alternating method)

   I. Introduction (related events in a sequence)

      • *Claim:* During a heavy fog on . . . many drivers sped and failed to maintain a safe distance between cars, causing wrecks and a pile-up that blocked Interstate . . . for nineteen miles.

   II. Body (cause and effect alternated)

     A. Cause no. 1: heavy fog

     B. Effect no. 1: decreased visibility

     C. Cause no. 2: speeding too close to other cars

     D. Effect no. 2: drivers were unable to stop quickly (continue as needed)

   III. Conclusion

STRATEGIES FOR CAUSE-AND-EFFECT PAPERS *(continued)*

Drafting an Introduction

The introduction may take various forms, depending on the emphasis and kind of causal relationships. For example, you might begin with a *narrative,* possibly an eyewitness account of an accident, then go on to describe the cause and effect(s). Your thesis could then link the cause with the effects you will focus on.

    Or you might open by describing a specific effect, showing why it is important or interesting to consider what caused it. You might explain the effect by classifying *examples* and presenting *illustrations.* Or you might provide an overview of the causal relationship or suggest that the causes or effects will be surprising. Watch for a hook that will make your analysis meaningful for your readers.

See chapter 4.

www.mhhe.com/dietsch
For general help writing introductions, check out:
Writing>Introductions

Developing a Paper Analyzing Cause and Effect

Your purpose will help you to devise a suitable writing strategy to develop your paper adequately. Most topics will require a thorough explanation with specific details and examples that reflect the purpose. Usually, the primary purpose of causal analysis is to inform or to persuade. Even when the purpose is informative, the paper will still have an *argumentative edge,* or element of persuasion. It may range from a hint to much more. In short, whether *implicitly* or *explicitly,* you will argue for your claim that a cause has led or will lead to an effect. (The difference between an informative and a persuasive paper of causal analysis is a matter of degree and strategy, not necessarily content.)

To support your claim, you need convincing proof. For example, you might contend that action should be taken to keep sixteen-year-olds from driving after midnight because of an extremely high rate of accidents for that age group. To make your claim plausible, you would have to produce valid research and possibly expert opinion to indicate that the hours after midnight are a dangerous time for sixteen-year-old drivers to be out on the roads.

Writing a Conclusion

See chapter 4.

The conclusion of a cause-and-effect paper summarizes the consequence or result. It may mention a repercussion, influence, benefit, or implication for the future. Or there may be an allusion to the title or opening that establishes closure, as in "Silver Lining," below. Regardless, the ending should flow from the description of cause and effect and give a sense of completeness.

Revising a Cause-and-Effect Paper

www.mhhe.com/dietsch

For general revising help, visit:
Writing>Drafting and Revision

As you start to revise your cause-and-effect paper, look at the larger items first. Pay particular attention to the strategy, logic, and writer's voice. After you are satisfied with these aspects, check the smaller aspects, as explained in chapter 5.

The checklist below should be helpful.

CHECKLIST REVISING A CAUSE-AND-EFFECT PAPER

1. Does the strategy emphasize the purpose?

2. Is the evidence adequate to support the claim?

3. If not, have I qualified my statements (with *seem* or *appear*, for example) to allow for chance?

4. Could another contributing cause exist?

5. Is the voice impartial and fair?

6. Is the connection clear? Have I explained enough?

TWO STUDENT PAPERS: CAUSE AND EFFECT

College students and others on tight budgets will empathize with Jo Rae Sloan. The purpose of her paper is to inform. She begins with the cause and explains the effects.

Silver Lining

To a nineteen-year-old girl, owning her own vehicle oftentimes seems alluring. But once the dream becomes a reality, the resulting responsibilities may seem overwhelming at times. Several months ago I had an opportunity to buy a pickup truck with help from my mother. Having my own transportation is convenient, and I do take pride in my Chevy pickup; yet the upkeep and expense can be exasperating.

Before I bought a truck, I had to schedule my activities around the other family members. I had to borrow my mother's car and worry about the possibility of putting a dent in the fender before I returned. Now I can hop in my Chevy and go whenever I need or wish without a care. I am a cautious driver and have insurance. Although I still park in a far row of parking lots, away from other vehicles, I no longer worry about possible dents.

When I drove someone else's car, I did not really care how it looked. Once I owned my own vehicle, however, my feelings changed. I take pride in my Chevy truck. When I first purchased it, I took it to a body shop for a new paint job with stripes and for window tinting. Now I vacuum my truck every week as well as wash and wax it regularly. All this takes time and effort. The work and expense are much more than I bargained for.

In the "good old days," all of my extra cash went for clothes, cosmetics, and anything else I wanted. Not now—every cent seems to go to my truck. The expected expense is bad enough, but the unexpected expense can be heartbreaking to a full-time student with a part-time job. Insurance takes a big chunk of my earnings. Filling the gas tank is another regular expense, along with the cost of oil and periodic maintenance. The unexpected expense of a new tire, a muffler system, and other repairs has been formidable. Thank goodness, I live at home and don't have to make payments to a car dealer. My mother is willing to wait for a payment when necessary.

As a result of buying my truck, I have been forced to budget—I haven't bought any new clothes since graduation last June. Although I seldom have more than a few dollar bills and some silver lining my pockets, I have a wonderful sense of independence. My Chevy truck has transported me from adolescence to adulthood.

QUESTIONS FOR DISCUSSION

1. What is the single cause of the effects Jo Rae describes?
2. How do her expectations compare with reality?
3. How does she feel about the effects at times? What is her overall feeling?
4. Does Jo Rae use the block or the alternating method of organization?
5. What is the effect of placing advantages before disadvantages?
6. What is the effect of the title? To what old saying does it allude?

In the next paper, Mary Ann Holvik also describes a single cause that produces multiple effects. Her purpose is to explain the difficulties of her job and the unexpected benefits she reaped.

Why Would Anyone Want to Be a School Bus Driver?

Often when two people are introduced, they initiate conversation by inquiring about each other's occupation. For six years my answer to that question produced raised eyebrows and caused my new acquaintances to exclaim, "You couldn't pay me enough to do that job!" Then I would explain that driving a school bus had rewards other than the usual monetary compensation: mastering a machine, enjoying nature, and participating in children's lives.

Achieving control of the school bus was an arduous task. I had to learn a maintenance routine which included checking all oil and fluid levels, inspecting all hoses and belts for signs of wear, and verifying that all lights and warning buzzers were functional. The most difficult aspect was backing the bus, 38 feet long, from a narrow country road into a still narrower driveway. Yet I derived great satisfaction from knowing the children on the bus were safe because it was in top running condition, and I was confidently in control.

Nature rewarded me for my early morning hours with a spectacular array of sunrises, which fired the deep-textured woods and fence rows with iridescent colors. Although I had grown up in the country, I never tired of watching the trees, wildflowers, and farm crops grow, blossom, and display the triumphant colors of a purpose fulfilled. Under the cover of vegetation, animals and birds carried on their daily lives, unabashed by the passing of so many curious eyes. The children and I enjoyed sights such as a buck deer bounding across an open field, a skunk hunting for his insect breakfast, a flock of Canadian geese flying in formation, and a hawk carrying away his prey with victorious cries.

The children, however, were my constant source of delight. The younger ones were always eager to share their concerns with me. I became a doll fashion adviser and new clothes admirer. I sympathized with the losing Little League team and empathized with the disappointed owners of bologna sandwich lunches. I patched dozens of scraped knees and critiqued hundreds of home-work papers. Grade cards were presented for approval; and, occasionally, love notes were dropped surreptitiously into my lap by red-faced little boys.

Older students generally remained aloof until desperation brought them to me, seeking advice about dating or dealing with unreasonable parents. For homecoming queens I saved newspaper pictures, and I congratulated teams for their athletic feats and scholastic achievement. And I worried over their safety each weekend when carloads of teenagers jammed the downtown square. Although I do not have any children of my own, I have loved several hundred boys and girls who made me a part of their lives.

If, like my new acquaintances, I had considered only the hard work involved in my job, then I would not have been a school bus driver. Of course, I received a monetary reward, but my real rewards were the physical discipline of driving, intimacy with nature, and the trusting love of the children.

QUESTIONS FOR DISCUSSION

1. What is the cause in Mary Ann's paper?

2. What are the effects?

3. How does Mary Ann use description to convey her feelings about her job? Which examples do you find most vivid? Why?

4. What order is used to organize details relating to children? To organize main points?

5. How would you describe the voice of the paper?

FOR YOUR REFERENCE
Cause-and-Effect Essays in the Reader

- "The Rebirth of Civility?" Daniel Henninger, page 661
- "Why Marriages Fail," Anne Roiphe, page 664
- "The Teacher Who Changed My Life," Nicholas Gage, page 668
- "Cut," Bob Greene, page 673

IDEAS FOR A CAUSE-AND-EFFECT PARAGRAPH

1. Haste makes waste
2. How learning to save (or not save) has affected my life
3. Honesty is the best policy
4. How an error in judgment caused . . .
5. How learning to _____ led to . . .

GROUP EXERCISE: Writing "If . . . Then" Statements

Directions: Discuss the claim and the implications that *logically* follow. Then write a series of inferences derived from each claim (three have been started).

1. In 1998 a Canadian business group got a permit to export water from Lake Superior to Asia. After an outcry in Canada and the United States, Ontario canceled the permit in 1999. Now Global Water Corp. of Vancouver, British Columbia, has secured a permit to take water from a lake near Sitka, Alaska, to sell to China. Alaskans granted the permit because they regard water as a renewable resource.

   Claim: Alaska should not be allowed to export water to a foreign country.

   • If Alaska exports water, then there will be _____ water available to _____.

   • If a _____ should occur in the lower United States, then _____.

   • If Alaska continues to export water over the years, then _____.

TEN IDEAS FOR PAPERS OF CAUSE AND EFFECT

1 Good intentions—unexpected consequences

2 The influence of my favorite teacher

3 Peer pressure in high school

4 The effects of fatherhood on a sports enthusiast

5 The effect of a telephone stalker on my life

6 How reading influenced me

7   Effects of being the oldest of _____ children

8   Influence of my stay-at-home mother

9   A father's example

10 The effects of being raised in a _____ neighborhood

Solving a Problem

CHAPTER 18

> A problem well stated
> is a problem half solved.
>
> —Charles F. Kettering

Wherever you live or work, problems arise. The way the problems are resolved affects your family, your life, and your work. Effective problem-solving skills not only lead to practical solutions and peace of mind but also give applicants an edge in job interviews. They have the confidence and skill needed to manage malfunctions of equipment, mistakes by personnel, customer complaints, delays in deliveries, or other snafus that can mean profit or loss for the company.

This chapter shows you, step-by-step, how to combine various writing strategies into an effective format for problem solving. You can use this basic format in writing memos, e-mail, letters, reports, or research papers, according to the rhetorical situation.

DEWEY'S METHOD OF PROBLEM SOLVING

John Dewey, a twentieth-century educator, devised an effective problem-solving method, based on the scientific method (which has seven steps). Dewey omitted the step of formulating a hypothesis—which can hinder objectivity. The researcher who hypothesizes may find only support for the theory and halt the search too soon, thereby overlooking evidence against it.

Dewey's six-step procedure has been widely adopted and adapted by educators, business personnel, and others. The purpose is to describe the problem, identify possible alternatives for solving or alleviating it, and select a practical solution. A simplified version appears here:

1. **State the problem.** Identify it.
2. **Define the problem.** Limit its scope. Examine its history.
3. **Formulate criteria.** Devise standards to measure the problem.
4. **Propose alternatives.** Consider possible solutions.
5. **Evaluate alternatives.** Apply criteria to rate the options.
6. **Recommend action.** Select the best possible solution(s).

Finding practical solutions was Dewey's chief concern. His primary criterion for evaluating an option was "Will it work?" He went to great lengths to be objective.

ETHICS: HOW CAN ONE BE OBJECTIVE?

To be objective, we must be willing to relinquish old biases, to question and seek the truth. Basically, there are two general ways to obtain information: firsthand and secondhand. Both ways can present problems in terms of objectivity. Although we observe something firsthand, we may see only part of it and think we saw 100 percent. Or we may misinterpret the meaning, make incorrect inferences, and treat them as fact. Information gained secondhand is also subject to error and distortion. So how can we become as objective as possible and minimize chances of error?

1. **Reserve judgment.** We can study both sides of an issue and consider all facets of a problem before stating an opinion. Before making decisions, we can gather as many facts as possible and weigh them carefully.
2. **Strive to be impartial and fair.** We can remain open to new information, welcome different perspectives, and watch for errors in reasoning.

3. **Qualify generalizations and avoid overstatement.** We can distinguish   See chapter 3.
   inference and value judgment from fact. We can check our facts.

4. **Keep in mind that no one is immune to mistakes.** Although we think
   we understand something, our information may be only partial. Although we may tell what caused something, what affects it now and
   what may affect it in the future, or how it affects something else, vital
   information may be missing. This awareness should keep us not only
   humble but also alert.

WRITING A PROBLEM-SOLVING PAPER

A problem-solving paper combines various writing strategies into a basic format
that is suitable not only for some short papers but also for some research papers.
The outline on page 234 is based on Dewey's method of problem solving. Although you and your peers may use the same general pattern of organization,
you will make individual decisions according to the rhetorical situation.

Selecting a Topic and Prewriting

To find a topic for a problem-solving paper, you might begin by considering   www.mhhe.com/dietsch
your experiences, including work-related projects. Or perhaps you know of a   For more help choosing
family, a neighborhood, a community, or a city facing a problem. The problem   a topic, visit:
should be significant, yet not too technical or complex. It should have at least   Writing>Prewriting
three alternative solutions. That does not mean all alternatives must be feasible.
Two or more can be ruled out, but one must provide a means to alleviate or to
resolve the problem. Sometimes all alternatives may be needed. If the problem
cannot be alleviated, look for another topic.

As you search for details to use in a problem-solving paper, watch for
changes, cause and effect, side effects, risks, advantages and disadvantages.
Note that changes may be negative or positive and their effects may be simple
or complicated. Advantages and disadvantages may be short-term or long-term.
Asking questions will speed your search.

QUESTIONS TO DISCOVER DETAILS FOR PROBLEM SOLVING
- What exactly is the problem?
- When was it first noticed?
- What or whom does it affect?
- What are its effects (Signs, symptoms, characteristics?)
- How far does it extend? (Scope?)
- What were the causes? (History?)
- What, if anything, has been done to alleviate the problem?
- What other alternatives exist?

- What are the advantages and disadvantages of each alternative?
- What is the best alternative? Or will a combination be needed?

Caution: Beware of oversimplification. Complex problems seldom have a single cause.

Organizing a Problem-Solving Paper

Dewey's method of problem solving furnishes an easy and effective way to organize information clearly. You can adapt this method to most problems. Using the six steps, you can start a scratch outline. Steps 1 and 2 form the introduction of the paper. Steps 3, 4, and 5, form the body. Step 6 forms the conclusion. Then you can convert your scratch outline into a working outline.

WORKING OUTLINE

I. Introduction
   A. Attention-getting detail
   B. Summary of the current problem (description)
   C. History of the problem (narration, using chronological order)
   D. Identification of the causes (cause-and-effect order)
II. Body
   A. Specific criteria to evaluate the alternatives (classification)
   B. Alternative 1 and evaluation of effectiveness (order of importance)
   C. Alternative 2 and evaluation of effectiveness (order of importance)
   D. Alternative 3 and evaluation of effectiveness (order of importance)
III. Conclusion
   A. Recommendation, citing best alternative (or combination)
   B. Relevant comment

TRANSITION IN A PROBLEM-SOLVING PAPER

See chapter 17.

A problem-solving paper requires transitions to signal cause-and-effect relationships. To direct the reader, place appropriate transitions near reasons why an event happened or a description of how it affected another event or situation:

therefore	one difficulty	an offshoot	one part
thus	an outcome	a consequence	one complication
affected	one effect	a by-product	one influence
two factors	an outgrowth	as a result	one proposal
three aspects	influenced	contributed	changed

www.mhhe.com/dietsch
For general help writing introductory paragraphs, go to:
Writing>Introductions

Drafting an Introduction

Problem-solving papers can begin in several ways. You might open with an appropriate quotation or a brief dialogue that illustrates a vital aspect of the problem. Another way is to start with a narrative that describes the problem; then you might describe cause and effect. Keith Zuspan describes an incident that happened where he worked:

Preventing an Expensive Problem

One of the most recent crises at _____ State Headquarters in _____ occurred in the executive building. A twenty-five-year-old air-conditioning unit failed to maintain the required cooling level in this large complex. When such an event occurs, it is imperative that the Building Operations Supervisor take action immediately. The supervisor must be able not only to recognize the potential risks but also to correct the problem in the least amount of time and in the most efficient manner.

The introduction of a problem-solving paper sets the stage for the identification of criteria and a discussion of alternatives.

Identifying Criteria

To check decisions and to evaluate possible solutions to problems, we need to develop criteria. By identifying our own specific criteria, we can measure the existing alternatives and make more logical decisions than we might otherwise make.

What Are Criteria?   You may be used to terms such as "guidelines," "specifications," or "company policy," instead of criteria. Yet all those terms refer to criteria that are used to weigh decisions and evaluate alternatives. *Criteria* are simply the factors that influence decision making and problem solving.

Daily life offers many opportunities to apply criteria. For instance, when planning a major purchase, you use criteria to weigh the advantages and disadvantages of comparable products. Before buying a new television set, you might consider some, or perhaps all, of the following criteria:

- screen size
- brand name
- price
- warranty
- quality of sound
- high definition
- flat-screen options
- sharpness of details

A criterion (the singular of *criteria*) is *one* standard, rule, principle, or test used to evaluate a decision or proposal. For example, *Merriam-Webster's Collegiate Dictionary,* Eleventh Edition, defines *criterion* as "a standard on which a judgment or decision may be based."*

Dewey's first criterion—"Will it work?"—is a factor in solving any problem. Time is another important criterion to consider. Other common criteria are listed here:

---

*By permission from *Merriam-Webster's Collegiate® Dictionary,* Eleventh Edition. Copyright © 2004 by Merriam-Webster, Incorporated (www.merriam-webster.com).

- Is it cost-effective?
- Is it safe?
- Is it practical?
- Is it legal?

- Is it ethical?
- Is it fair?
- Is it appropriate?
- Is it beneficial in the short run? Long run?

Stating Criteria   To identify criteria, ask: "What factors will influence this decision?" Perhaps the simplest way to specify criteria is to pose each criterion as a question. In her paper Nancy Miller used that tactic:

> Making our house more energy-efficient required careful consideration. When the alternatives to this problem were evaluated, three main questions were asked. First, what is the cost? Second, how energy-efficient is the alternative? Third, will the alternative raise the equity in our home?

Another example was written by a mother who had recently lost her job through a layoff. Carol Walkins specified three concerns in her job search—day shift, pay scale, and location:

> A major problem that I faced was the possibility of having to work the evening or midnight shift if I found employment in another factory. With two elementary school children, I needed to be at home in the evenings in order to spend important time with them. Since my family depends on my income, I also had to find a job that would provide a pay scale similar to that of my former job. Location was another factor to be considered. My husband works locally, and we own our home. Therefore, moving was not an option.

For clarity in a problem-solving paper, some instructors prefer that students state criteria before alternatives. Regardless, do not confuse criteria with alternatives. *Criteria* are the factors or considerations that govern decisions. Alternatives are the options for action—possible solutions. In other words, criteria provide a means to weigh the benefits and risks of an alternative.

Proposing and Evaluating Alternatives

Usually, a problem-solving paper presents at least three alternatives. Perhaps two of the choices can be eliminated, leaving one that can best solve the problem. This does not mean that every problem can be solved with one alternative. Perhaps a combination will be needed. Or perhaps the best that can be done is to alleviate the problem.

After alternatives are determined, each possibility is evaluated according to criteria. In this fifth step, advantages and disadvantages become apparent. Upon a first glance, an alternative may seem to be a practical solution to a problem. After research and analysis, however, hidden disadvantages may emerge.

To evaluate alternatives for a paper, research the feasibility of each one. Do not assume there are no disadvantages. To be objective, a paper must specify disadvantages as well as advantages. (An omission of either would constitute card stacking. See chapter 16.) Then evaluate the alternatives according to the criteria. Note that a problem may have a short-term alternative and a long-term solution. When Carol analyzed her problem of unemployment, she found both:

> My first alternative was to collect the nine months of unemployment compensation that I qualified for. I could accomplish my household tasks during the day, leaving the evenings free for my children. Collecting unemployment and saving on sitter's fees would compensate for the weekly paycheck. Although the idea of staying home was appealing, collecting an unemployment check would be temporary and not a real solution to the problem.
>
> A second alternative was to go job hunting. Although it seemed like a logical solution, I knew that a good job would be difficult to find at this time. To secure factory work with daytime hours would be almost impossible. Daytime office jobs were available, but I lacked the training needed to qualify. I realized that it was unrealistic to expect to find a suitable, well-paying job locally.
>
> A third option was available, however. Because I had lost my job due to foreign trade, I was eligible for a new federal program under the Trade Readjustment Act. This program would pay for college tuition for two years as well as books and supplies. I could attend day classes while the children were in school. The plan would also pay a small allowance for living expenses for up to one year if grade and attendance requirements were maintained. Although this option would require a drastically revised family budget, I knew I could manage.

Carol combined steps 4 and 5 of the problem-solving method: she proposed an alternative, applied criteria, and evaluated. This order enabled her to avoid undue repetition. The parallelism of her points helped to make the paper clear and easy to read. The details prepared the audience for the conclusion.

Writing a Conclusion

The end of a problem-solving paper presents the recommendation the writer has prepared the reader to accept. In other words, the selected solution should flow logically from the discussion of alternatives. Some conclusions contain a call for action, perhaps pointing out the consequences of inaction. In his paper about the air-conditioning problem on the job, Keith Zuspan concluded by making a recommendation:

> Repairing the existing air-conditioning unit would, in fact, be the most efficient and economical method of regaining the desired environmental controls required for the complex. It is also the writer's opinion that by utilizing the in-house building mechanics to complete this project, additional money could be saved.

Other conclusions, like the ending of Nancy Miller's paper, summarize the action already taken and explain how a solution fits the criteria:

> After reviewing the three alternatives, we chose the third, which proved to be the most cost-effective as well as energy efficient. By purchasing the siding and windows together, we received a discount. The new furnace also proved to be energy-efficient, and we saw a sizable reduction in heating expense in the

www.mhhe.com/dietsch

For general assistance writing conclusions, check out:
Writing>Conclusions

first year after installation. This third option has also increased the home's equity dramatically, although part of the increase is due to inflation. In 1972 we paid just over seven thousand dollars for the house; and now, three decades later, the house is worth over seventy-five thousand dollars.

Revising a Problem-Solving Paper

www.mhhe.com/dietsch

For more help with revision, visit:
Writing>Drafting and Revising

See chapter 5.

To produce your best work, allow plenty of time for revising, editing, and proof-reading your problem-solving paper. Proofread for mechanical errors at least two or three times. After entering corrections on-screen, run a final spelling check—a vital step that will catch last-minute typos. The following checklist will help to ensure that you check strategic points:

CHECKLIST   **REVISING A PROBLEM-SOLVING PAPER**

1. Is the problem clearly defined in the introduction? Are the causes and pertinent history of the problem explained?

2. Are specific criteria for evaluating alternative solutions identified? Are these criteria reasonable and adequate?

3. Are different alternatives for solving the problem identified and described?

4. Is one alternative recommended? Is it clear why this solution is best?

5. Is the conclusion effective? Does it flow logically from the body?

6. Have transitions been used effectively?

STUDENT PAPER: PROBLEM SOLVING

In this paper, Chris Hafley proposes a solution to a problem facing his community:

A Plan for Quality Emergency Care

In the small northwest Ohio city of _____, the city fire department provides emergency medical care for its residents and township residents. In the past decade, a need for more advanced prehospital intervention has developed. To provide better medical care, the city council elected to send ten (of twenty) Advanced Emergency Medical Technicians to paramedic school at Sandusky Providence Hospital.

Before these ten people graduate and begin to function as paramedics, a dilemma must be resolved as to how the rescue squad will respond to possible life-threatening medical and trauma emergencies. With only one paramedic on duty as part of a two-person team, it would be almost impossible for the squad to function properly and respond efficiently to all calls twenty-four hours a day. Therefore, a committee has been organized to investigate four possible solutions.

The criteria set up by the investigational committee for review of the recommendations were availability, training, and cost-effectiveness. The first solution suggested was to respond with an ambulance and two police officers. But the officers' level of medical training is limited to basic first aid and CPR training. They would not be much help with patients needing advanced life support. To upgrade all the officers' training to at least Basic Emergency Medical Technician would involve considerable expense to the city. This method would be the most expensive option of the four, costing initially $30,000 to certify all eighteen officers. There are many times, however, when officers are out on call and thus are unavailable.

The second option would be to arrange for one additional paramedic to be on call at home for twenty-four hours a day. This plan would cost approximately $27,000, but it would be the most effective as far as availability is concerned.

The third option would be to dispatch an additional ambulance as a backup system for the first ambulance. After researching this option, more people favored it than any of the others because of quality of assistance and cost-effectiveness. Personnel on the ambulance already have the necessary training. Availability, however, would be a problem at times since the ambulance personnel make numerous out-of-town transfers.

The fourth option would provide for the fire department pumper to respond along with the ambulance. Research shows that this alternative would be the most cost-effective. The idea is to have two firefighters cross-trained as Basic Emergency Medical Technicians. There would be two firefighter EMTs on each shift. This option would cut down the number of personnel to be trained and would be the least expensive way for the city to provide the additional staff to assist in medical emergencies. The initial cost would be about $12,000 for training. An advantage to using the firefighters would be that they are usually available to respond to medical emergencies with the ambulance.

After all the information was compiled and the alternatives were reviewed again and again, the review committee recommended both options three and four be implemented. Thus if the firefighters were unavailable, the second ambulance might possibly provide a backup.

QUESTIONS FOR ANALYSIS

1. Does the paper provide a clear description of the problem?
2. Are the criteria clear?
3. Does the order of alternatives seem appropriate?
4. Are alternatives evaluated according to the criteria?
5. Does the conclusion seem logical and complete?

**FOR YOUR REFERENCE
Problem-Solving
Essays in the Reader**

PRACTICE

SMALL GROUPS: Identifying Criteria

After you read Patricia Davis's introduction below, brainstorm possible criteria that would influence the final decision. One group member should record them. Then examine your criteria and decide which are most important.

▶

A Pet for Aunt Emily

My aunt, although eighty-three years old and rather frail, is still able to care for herself. Aunt Emily lives alone in her own home on a limited income. Ordinarily, she is quite independent and self-sufficient, but last week she surprised me. When I dropped by, she asked for advice. Confiding that she was lonely, she explained she needed companionship and was thinking about getting a pet. But she was unsure about what sort of animal would be best for her. She asked me to help in deciding what kind of pet would be the most enjoyable and suitable.

SMALL GROUPS: Case Problems

Directions: Select *one* of the authentic cases below. Steps 1 and 2 of Dewey's problem-solving method are given. Supply steps 3, 4, 5, and 6.

1. You are on the committee to plan the office Christmas party. You are instructed to eliminate past problems or cancel! In past years, employees have bought gifts for the owner of the firm. Some buy expensive gifts and appear to be currying favors, which causes grumbling. The owner gives everyone a small ham and provides a lunch of finger food and fruit punch. Someone always spikes the punch. Some employees have become rowdy and amorous. Devise a plan to prevent similar problems.

2. You are a software sales rep. While at a trade show, you meet a woman who asks if you still have the same sales manager, J. D. Smith. When you reply "Yes," she tells about her boyfriend buying software out of J. D.'s home. You mull over the pros and cons of telling the owner, whom you trust. You do not trust J. D. because of his office pranks and complaints behind the owner's back. What else should you consider? What do you decide?

3. Your neighbors often stay out until 2:30 a.m. on weekends. They leave their Doberman tied out in the backyard, where he howls—keeping you awake until they take him in. You do not know if he is hungry or lonely. The dog does not recognize you, but from a distance he seems fairly friendly. What are your alternatives? What risks are involved?

TEN IDEAS FOR PROBLEM-SOLVING PAPERS

1. A problem on the job

2. Keeping your car safe from theft

3. Staffing athletic programs on a low budget

4. Stress management for nurses, police officers, or . . .

5. Finding child-care for working parents

6. Stray animal control

7. Adjustment to college after _____ years

8. Good nutrition on a low budget

9. Breaking the nicotine habit

10. Maintaining an exercise plan

Constructing a Convincing Argument

CHAPTER 19

> The best argument is that which seems merely an explanation.
>
> —Dale Carnegie

Hardly a day passes without your persuading someone of something. It may be as trivial as convincing a friend to try a new restaurant or as significant as convincing an interviewer you are qualified for a position. On the job you may write a proposal, a request for new software, a grant application, or other document. In a college class you may be asked to write a persuasive essay, a reaction paper, or a paper of argument. Skill in argument and persuasion will enable you to become a more effective writer and speaker, both in college and in the workplace.

THE PURPOSE OF ARGUMENTATION

Argumentation is reasoned persuasion. Although there are many types of arguments, the general purpose of any serious argument is to persuade the audience to accept a belief, adopt a policy, or enact a decision, proposal, or law. In the strictest sense, the term *argument* refers to an assertion that is based on logic and proof, a rational appeal to the intellect. To be effective, an argument must contain adequate evidence to buttress the claim and convince.

But facts alone may not persuade. People often act on perceptions and instincts that are not always logical. When a problem arises, you may have a practical solution and all the relevant facts, but unless you can tap into your audience's priorities and needs, your proposal will probably be rejected. For that reason, many arguments contain not only rational appeals but also ethical and emotional appeals. This chapter explains a classic argument model that is flexible and practical. It can be adapted in various ways for papers, presentations, proposals, and other uses.

THREE CLASSIC APPEALS USED IN ARGUMENT

Aristotle, the early Greek philosopher, defined three kinds of appeals that make up an argument: *logos* (logic), *ethos* (ethics or moral character), and *pathos* (emotion). Aristotle realized that logic alone is not always sufficient to persuade an audience. To be convincing, you must also gain credibility—the trust of your listeners or readers. To succeed, you must be perceived as honest, fair, and responsive to moral obligations. Aristotle called this the appeal to *ethos*. In *Nicomachean Ethics*, he explains:

> Virtue then is twofold, partly intellectual and partly moral, and intellectual virtue is originated and fostered mainly by teaching; it demands therefore experience and time. Moral virtue on the other hand is the outcome of habit, and accordingly its name *éthike*, is derived by a slight variation from *éthos*, habit.

> —from *On Man and the Universe: Metaphysics, Parts of Animals, Ethics, Politics, Poetics.* Louise R. Loomis, Editor

Logical and ethical appeals are often enough to convince on some issues, but unless emotion moves an audience to act on other issues, the argument will be in vain.

You can identify the three classic appeals by the questions they raise with readers:

- **Logical appeal.** Is the claim or petition factual and reasonable? True or false? Practical or impractical?

- **Ethical appeal.** Is the claim just or unjust? Honest or dishonest? Right or wrong?

- **Emotional appeal.** Do the words arouse such feelings as empathy and sympathy? Do they cause the reader to care about the subject?

The Logical Appeal

In most rhetorical situations, you will be expected to base your conclusions on sound reasoning and adequate proof. A logical argument appeals to the mind, using evidence, reasons, and examples to support a claim or proposition. Logical appeals are based on facts, sound inferences, and working theories. Reliable evidence may include established truths, primary sources, statistics, expert opinion, or personal experience.

Established Truths   Some evidence is so solidly grounded that no reasonable person will seriously debate it. In the examples that follow, the first three are *established facts,* which have been conclusively proven. The fourth example has been accepted as fact, based on the existing evidence.

- **Historical fact.** Meriwether Lewis and William Clark explored the northwestern United States from St. Louis to the Pacific Ocean.
- **Geographical fact.** The Mississippi River is joined by the Missouri, Illinois, and Ohio Rivers before it flows down to the Gulf of Mexico.
- **Scientific fact.** When a heavy object is dropped, it falls to the ground.
- **Scientific theory regarded as fact.** The sun's gravitation attracts the planets and keeps them in their paths. Stars are held on course by the pull of heavenly bodies.

www.mhhe.com/dietsch

If you'd like more help gathering sources, check out:
Research

Primary Sources   Research that is gathered firsthand carries more credibility than that filtered through secondary researchers. If you can obtain relevant documents, letters, autobiographies, or other primary source materials, these can lend strong support to your argument. Or you may choose to gather evidence firsthand yourself. For further explanation and suggestions, see chapter R-5, "Field Research: Observation, Interviews, and Surveys."

Statistics   Reliable statistical findings from recognized and reputable authorities can strengthen your argument. To be reliable, the findings should be based on samples that are representative and random. Yet some widely quoted findings are neither random nor representative, as explained in chapter R-5.

Another problem in reliability occurs when the researcher who is under extreme pressure, such as meeting a deadline, falsifies results. When you find unusual conclusions, check to see if the results are consistent with those of others in the field. Unless an experiment can be duplicated under controlled laboratory conditions by qualified researchers, it cannot be accepted as evidence.

See "Evaluating the Reliability of Internet Sources," chapter R-2.

Expert Opinion   The opinion of a recognized authority in a field generally conveys credibility and enhances an argument. If you decide to use expert opinion, check out the person's qualifications first. Here the Internet is an invaluable and speedy resource for checking on well-known authorities. Interviewing can also be helpful for local issues. For instance, if you were arguing for a proposal to thwart break-ins and burglary, then the chief of police, sheriff, or mayor could be credible sources.

Personal Experience   The personal stories of people who have been involved in an accident, a tragedy, or a natural phenomenon such as a tornado can be powerful. A detailed description of such an event can have a strong emotional impact and buttress a logical argument. Personal experience stories should be used to supplement logical evidence, not supplant it. The experience should be significant and have a definite and relevant point.

Important Considerations   When you are presenting inconclusive evidence, avoid confusing theory with fact. Be accurate and precise so as not to overstate and weaken your case. For a reference list, see "Using Tentative Words to Discuss Findings and Theories," page 443.

Inferences are often confused with fact, and generalizations are often made from an invalid sample. To construct a flawless argument, you need to be able to recognize pitfalls in logic. For a further discussion of what constitutes reliable evidence, see chapters 3 and 16.

The Ethical Appeal

Ethical appeals are designed to strike a responsive chord in the minds of the readers, entreating them to do what is right, good, fair, and best. *Ethics* can be broadly defined as a set of moral values—principles of conduct for an individual, group, profession, or society. Sound ethics are essential for a well-constructed argument.

To be ethical, an argument must respect the rights and needs of the audience. In other words, deception to obtain a selfish aim is unethical—and often illegal. For example, a pastor of an Ohio church persuaded several elderly couples to donate their life savings to his church. However, he spent the money for expensive cars and other luxuries. Eventually, he was convicted of fraud and sent to prison.

An ethical appeal requires you to first demonstrate comprehensive knowledge of your subject. *You have an ethical obligation to give the reader the whole truth,* not just proof that will make your side of the argument *seem* convincing. In other words, if there are disadvantages to your proposal, you need to be honest about them. Second, you must approach the subject in an even-handed way, presenting differing viewpoints accurately and fairly. Your written voice must sound reasonable, controlled, and concerned.

The Emotional Appeal

Emotional appeals stir the feelings of readers with figurative language, connotation, and anecdote. Such appeals can be powerful, for they bypass the intellect. Emotional appeals work best, however, when used in moderation. They should also be ethical. Do not use an emotional appeal that gives you any misgivings or uneasiness. If an emotional appeal is overdone or if it conflicts with a logical or an ethical appeal, then the emotional appeal is inappropriate and unethical.

Using the Three Appeals

Credible persuasion rests on a blend of established facts and ethical reasons, sometimes bonded with a bit of emotion. To be effective, all three appeals must be appropriate for the rhetorical situation. The bulk of your argument paper should be a logical appeal, based on sound logical proof. But keep in mind that credible persuasion rests on a blend of facts and ethical reasons, often bonded with suitable emotion. To be effective, all three appeals must harmonize.

As rhetoricians from Aristotle to Stephen Toulmin, Carl Rogers, and others have indicated, ordinary claims and assertions (unlike mathematical equations) are rarely clear-cut and undeniably certain. The claims and conclusions of such arguments are probable, according to the weight of known or submitted evidence. And their reception may vary, depending on the audience.

WORKPLACE CASE STUDY

"YOU GOT A TIGER BY THE TAIL!"

Matthew Resome was a programmer at XYZ Company. Matt was a quiet guy with an excellent work record who got along well with other employees. For three years he had tried to work through the right channels to improve wages and working conditions. But neither had changed despite the fact that the company's sales had increased 55 percent during those years.

When Matt contacted the National Labor Relations Board (NLRB), they said that if he could secure seventy-five signatures on a petition, then they could come in and conduct a vote to unionize the plant. The company would have to provide a room with a booth where employees could come during work hours. Matt secured the required signatures, and two NLRB representatives conducted the vote at the plant. The vote failed.

The next morning J. B. Smith, the plant manager, told his assistant to fire Matt. The assistant, who had attended law school, refused. Using a *logical* appeal, he warned, "You can't do this. Federal laws prohibit discrimination against peaceful and acceptable union activities. You got a tiger by the tail! Let it go."

But four days later, the irate plant manager called Matt in and stated: "Your job has been phased out. We don't need you any more. You can clear out your desk and leave right now." Matt contacted the NLRB.

Activity

Assume the role of the NLRB investigator. Examine Matt's work record and investigate the events preceding the firing. Summarize the situation and write a letter to J. B. Smith. Inform him that to prevent legal action, the company must reinstate and reimburse Matt for all lost wages. The company has thirty days to consider the offer.

Used wisely, emotion can motivate. In the Workplace Case Study, the assistant could have stressed the emotional appeal more. Instead of hinting with "You got a tiger by the tail!" he could have been more direct by saying, "You might lose your own job over this firing. Be careful." Then the boss might have listened.

Dodging Fallacies   For an argument to be effective, the logic must be impeccable. A writer who misquotes, transposes statistics, misdiagnoses cause and effect, or lapses into hasty generalizations may be perceived as careless, uninformed, or manipulative. If the words disparage one opponent and favor the other, the argument is slanted and biased. Although name-calling, exaggeration, or other blunders may be discounted in conversation, readers are unlikely to be so patient or forgiving. Let's consider two fallacies from student papers:

- The most annoying thing in the world is to pick up the telephone after a long day at work and find a telemarketer at the other end of the line.
- A military draft service would solve the United States' problems.

Both assertions are hasty generalizations. Certainly there are greater annoyances than telephone interruption, and no one action could possibly solve the numerous problems faced by the United States. Another common fallacy is assuming that a complex problem results from a single cause. Rarely does a complex problem have only one cause. For example, presidents are often blamed for problems existing long before they took office. The truth is that many factors influence complicated problems.

A final precaution to keep in mind is that an analogy cannot constitute proof. *Although valid analogies are useful for explanation, they prove nothing.* For an explanation of common logical fallacies and propaganda appeals (emotional fallacies), see chapter 16, "Detecting Fallacies."

1. **Alert the audience to a problem by using suitable emotion.**
2. **Use restraint.** Do not overstate. Exaggerated appeals can backfire.
3. **Do not circumvent an issue.** Focus your argument on the issue. Answer all of the opposition's points with solid evidence and reasons.
4. **Do not oversimplify.** Guard against either/or alternatives.
5. **Avoid conflicting appeals.** Contradiction undermines arguments.
6. **Show and tell.** Use examples and anecdotes to illustrate and heighten interest.
7. **Read aloud to check for objectivity.** Evidence should be presented honestly without slanting or manipulation. The writer's voice should sound fair and trustworthy.

GUIDELINES FOR USING PERSUASIVE APPEALS

UNDERSTANDING OPPOSING VIEWS AND OVERCOMING OBJECTIONS

A key factor in shaping an argument effectively is to consider the degree of resistance to the claim: *Will the audience show reluctance, firm opposition, or downright hostility? What objections will they raise? Why?* Study the opposing view so that you can know the objections that will likely arise. Then you can prepare and organize your argument well.

Researching both views of an issue provides an opportunity not only to weigh the facts but also to consider the priorities, values, and attitudes of the audience who disagree. Sometimes they may agree with a proposal, but not act. Then your first task is to discover the *area of resistance* and determine why they are reluctant. The second task is to prepare a persuasive strategy to overcome their objections and resistance.

UNDERSTANDING OPPOSING VIEWS

> Two landowners were involved in a boundary dispute that dated back to their grandfathers' time. Years before, a rail fence had been erected by one grandparent and moved by the other. At last one man consulted a lawyer. Relating the history of the argument, the client presented one view of the dispute. The lawyer assured him that the law was on his side and asked when he wanted to sue. The client replied, "Never, I just gave you the other guy's version."

Once you understand the opposing view, you can decide how to shape the argument to emphasize advantages and benefits. For example, voters may agree that more money is needed to fund local schools, but they may resist voting for a bond levy. How do you convince them that the proposed benefits justify the expense? An appeal combining logic, ethics, and emotion might be the most effective:

Several of our school buildings are over seventy-five years old. They are drafty and expensive to heat; those big windows have single panes. The frames rattle. The electrical wiring is inadequate; there are not enough outlets for computers. Plaster has fallen from some ceilings. Building now will avoid expensive renovations and save money in the long run, for construction costs continue to climb.

The buildings are also overcrowded. For instance, in one building a class meets on the auditorium stage, another in the lunchroom, and two meet at the ends of halls. The children are distracted by passersby, and the acoustics are poor. The children have no place to put their coats.

Our children deserve better. They deserve a place where they can concentrate and do their best. Our children are the future leaders of this country. Surely, we need to give them a chance for optimum learning. Won't you dig down in your pocket to come up with the extra dollars to make this dream come true? Vote yes for the school bond levy!

1. How much does the audience know about the topic?
2. How strong is their disagreement or resistance?
3. If they agree on a proposal, why are they reluctant to act?
4. What is important to them?
5. What is important to me?
6. What change can I reasonably expect in the audience?

QUESTIONS TO ANALYZE AN AUDIENCE

WRITING A CLASSIC ARGUMENT PAPER

Aristotle's three strategic appeals are still widely used today. His early work and the innovations by later rhetoricians have evolved into a classic format that can be altered in various ways. Depending upon the purpose, the topic, and the audience, the structure can be adapted for various occasions and types of claims.

Claims of judgment set forth an opinion that is significant and logical. Ethical judgments evaluate the facts and decide whether something is beneficial or harmful, humane or inhumane, moral or immoral. Explained here are five basic types of claims, including judgments.

www.mhhe.com/dietsch

For electronic assistance writing an argument, go to:
Writing>Writing Tutors>
Argument

FIVE BASIC CLAIMS MADE IN ARGUMENTS

1. **Claim of judgment.** What is the writer's position on the issue? Why? What are the criteria and evidence upon which the judgment is based? What is ethical?

2. **Claim of interpretation.** What do the facts mean? What are the implications?

3. **Claim of cause.** Why did something happen? Why is it the way it is? To be valid, a hypothesis must provide the simplest and best explanation.

4. **Claim of value.** An appraisal or rating of worth. For example, aesthetic claims evaluate the value of music, art, or literature. To be valid, the appraisals are based on criteria.

5. **Claim of policy.** What should be done? What is the best alternative to solve the problem? What will work? What is the most practical solution? Or are there several acceptable alternatives?

Selecting a Topic

The topic for an argument paper should be controversial and significant. This means it should have at least two points of view. It should involve more than a simple question of fact or personal preference or definition of terms. For example, to argue vaguely that U2 is better than the Beatles would be futile because this judgment hinges on personal taste. But a paper that contains adequate support and criteria to evaluate the characteristics of both musical groups could yield a logical argument.

Before a controversy can be resolved, the participants must share a view—agree on a *basic premise underlying the argument*. For example, two students could agree that a college diploma should signify competency even though they disagree about how competency should be measured. Because they agree on this basic belief, a logical argument could be constructed.

To write effectively about a value-laden topic, you must be open-minded, fair, and alert. Topics such as gun control, abortion, and religion carry emotional baggage that make them difficult to argue for three reasons: (1) rarely do the opposing views agree on a basic premise; (2) sources are often slanted toward one view; and (3) you must sift the evidence while keeping your own biases under control. Other topics for argument may have inherent hazards, too. For your consideration, some typical problems that students wade into are listed here:

COMMON HAZARDS IN SELECTING TOPICS FOR ARGUMENT

1. **The topic is too broad.** Subjects should be narrowed to a claim that can be supported and discussed well in the allotted length.

2. **The topic is strictly informational.** A paper of argument does more than collect information. You strive to convince the reader of the claim.

3. **Adequate support is unavailable.** If a topic is recent, you may find little data available. If a topic is heavily laden with emotion, you may find bias and fallacies in the sources.

4. **A common ground is lacking.** Some heated topics lack an area of common agreement. (A deadlock would result.)

5. **The topic is hackneyed.** Sometimes students resurrect old papers or debate notes from high school. An important reason for assigning a paper of argument is to spur you to think and learn.

Typically, instructors groan when they see old, overused topics such as capital punishment, legalizing illicit drugs, and the like. To be significant, a topic does not have to have worldwide or national implications—it may be a campus, community, or neighborhood issue. Such topics can yield fresh material.

CRITERIA FOR SELECTING AN ARGUMENT TOPIC

1. Is there disagreement about the subject or an area of resistance?
2. Is the issue significant and challenging?
3. Can I obtain enough factual information?
4. After research, will I be able to thoroughly understand the issue?
5. Can I write about the topic in a fair, objective tone?

www.mhhe.com/dietsch

For general prewriting coverage, visit:
Research>Prewriting

Gathering Information and Prewriting

The more knowledgeable and sophisticated the audience, the more they will insist on adequate proof of a claim. Yet a writer seldom has all the facts at hand to attain a comprehensive view of a controversial topic. Many argument topics and assignments will require research of several sources. An exception might be a paper that takes a position on a literary work, and the writer consults just the work itself. To focus a search for information, you might begin by posing a controlling question.

Drafting a Controlling Question

A controlling question narrows the search for information and establishes the focus of a paper. This question limits the topic and aids in finding suitable source materials. After you write your controlling question, check to see whether or not it performs these two vital functions:

1. Identifies the *specific* topic and scope.
2. Specifies the *direction* of the research.

For controversial topics, the wording of the question should receive special attention. The words should be fair and objective. Notice how a few words can change the tone of a question:

BIASED: Should students be *forced* to take achievement tests *every year?*

NEUTRAL: Should achievement tests *be given yearly?*

A neutral controlling question will help you to analyze a controversy fairly. Rereading the question from time to time will aid you in withholding judgment until key facts and implications are clear. The researcher who maintains an open mind is more likely to appraise an issue impartially than is one who leaps to a quick decision.

Searching for Reliable Sources

To gain an accurate overview of an issue, you need to gather evidence to support both points of view. Understanding varying views is necessary to shape a convincing argument. To compare accounts and judge credibility, read from several sources. Not all sources are authoritative or reliable. Some may contain incorrect or outdated information, logical fallacies, or bias.

As you select books, look at the back cover, in the foreword, or in the introduction for the writer's credentials. Is he or she an authority in the field? Then scan a few pages and listen to the tone of the writing. Does it sound objective or biased? Does the coverage seem slanted? Do the significant points of the controversy seem to be covered? If you find inconsistencies or differing interpretations, jot down page numbers and authors. These discrepancies should be mentioned in your paper.

To research a local issue, you might interview the people involved and read newspaper accounts. To research a topic in a specialized field, consult journals or trade publications for technical information and opinions of authorities. Popular magazines may give brief factual overviews of issues, but the treatment may be incomplete. (Also see "Selecting Suitable Sources" and "Evaluating the Reliability of Internet Sources" in chapter R-2.)

www.mhhe.com/dietsch

For electronic help evaluating sources, go to:
Research>Source
Evaluation Tutor (CARS)

Note-Taking and Critical Reading   While interviewing and reading, gather facts, statistics, expert opinion, cause and effect, reasons, and examples that constitute support for *both* sides. You will need to know the points of the opposing side so that you can refute them effectively. If you cannot answer the opposition's points by citing stronger evidence and better reasons, then your argument will not be convincing.

Take care to represent differing views fairly. That does not mean you give them equal space; you condense their main points. Try to spot anything that seems illogical, biased, or irresponsible. Write your notes in the margins of a copy or on cards. For detailed suggestions for critical reading, see chapter 21.

Making Con/Pro Lists   To simplify the task of organizing the chief points of a controversy, list pros and cons as you read. To separate evidence against and for the proposition, write *con* and *pro* at the top of a sheet of paper. List proof in two vertical columns, placing parallel points side by side. Leave plenty of white space between items to add notes. Follow each item with the name of the author and page number. This identification will save time later. The lists will resemble those below except that actual points and answers will be listed:

CON	PRO
Main point (Barnes 140)	Agrees with facts, then disagrees about implications (Aker 39)
Main point (Barnes 141)	Objection and answer (Berry 149)
Main point (Smith 33)	Objection and answer (Conroy 12)

Stating a Position

After listing the significant points of disagreement, select the soundest viewpoint. Then write a claim to indicate this position on the issue. The claim is your thesis statement. The tone is usually serious and much firmer than that of an ordinary thesis. To draft a claim, you can rewrite your controlling question and explore its implications. You might even decide to take a position of compromise, as shown below:

CONTROLLING QUESTION: Should English be declared our official language?

Con: The USA does not need an official language.

Pro: English should be declared the official language of the USA.

COMPROMISE: The USA should have two official languages: English and Spanish.

Or when an issue is heated, the writer might use the controlling question as the title to create a zone of neutrality. This zone allows the writer to present and evaluate the evidence before declaring a position in a *delayed thesis*. This *indirect approach* lowers the temperature of the argument and encourages consideration of differences. Nonetheless, the writer needs to have a clear thesis in mind to avoid vagueness and rambling. Understanding the opposing view will assist you in focusing your persuasive strategy.

Planning the Shape of an Argument

There is no "one size fits all" strategy of argument. Arguments come in all shapes and sizes, depending on the rhetorical situation. Thus a writer is left to devise a strategy that will accommodate the situation in the best possible way. The structure of a logical argument consists of four basic parts: (1) making a claim (stating the purpose), (2) anticipating objections from readers, (3) countering objections by supporting the claim with solid evidence, and (4) submitting a conclusion derived from the evidence. When possible, a fifth part—a point of agreement (common ground)—is often included to lend a fair, objective tone.

FIVE ELEMENTS OF A LOGICAL ARGUMENT

Claim: The position on the issue as revealed in the thesis statement. The claim is often referred to as the "proposition."

Common Ground: What underlying view is shared? What do the opponents agree on?

Objections: Points of disagreement. Understanding the main points of the opposition will help the writer to answer objections effectively.

Evidence: The support for the claim: facts, reasons, examples, or other proof.

Conclusion: The end of an argument invariably restates the claim. The conclusion may also urge the reader to act.

To organize an effective argument, first consider whether to use direct or indirect order. In other words, will an early or a delayed thesis be most effective? How the five parts of the argument are arranged and developed depends on the implications of the topic and the probable impact on the audience. Think: How will the proposition be received by readers?

Direct Approach   If your readers are likely to be well informed and only mildly opposed, you may decide to be direct and bring out the proposition or proposal early. Then the thesis can be stated in the introduction. Here is an example of a proposition that would likely meet with little resistance from employees who will readily accept change:

Early thesis: A new system of billing will speed up the collection process and save an estimated $50,000 annually in collection costs.

Indirect Approach   An indirect plan, on the other hand, allows you to delay your thesis until much later in the paper. A delayed thesis allows you to consider the main points of the other side before mentioning your points. This arrangement sets the stage for a congenial discussion. Often it is wise to treat an argument as a misunderstanding or as a difference in perception. This low-key approach is less likely to be perceived as threatening or combative. Any hint of antagonism, sarcasm, impatience, or superiority will undermine your stand. Negative undertones can sabotage the flawless logic of an argument.

Readers who are likely to be uninformed or hostile will require more facts and reasons than will readers who are well informed. You may need to lay extra groundwork for your recommendation. The stronger the objection, the more time you will need to prepare them to accept the proposition. As long as the path of an argument is clear, the thesis statement may be postponed until the body or conclusion.

Delayed thesis: Genetic engineering of food crops is beneficial and safe.

Sometimes, however, a thesis is implicit (unstated). Still, the argument is focused on one unmistakable conclusion. Since arguments with implicit theses require considerable skill, they are best left to experienced writers. Most instructors require an explicit thesis to aid in establishing the direction of an argument. Regardless of the type of argument you write, stress the benefits, advantages, and strengths of your proposal.

CHECKLIST   PLANNING AN ARGUMENT

1. What does the audience believe about the issue?

2. How does the audience feel about the issue?

3. Which order will be most effective: direct or indirect?

4. What kind of title will be most effective?

5. Are the points of view clearly labeled?

Presenting Opposing Viewpoints   To set the tone for a calm, courteous discussion, place the opposing view *before* your own. This method acknowledges the main points of the opposition and shows that you have considered the evidence. This arrangement is akin to listening, indicating a willingness to suspend judgment. Placing your points afterward gives them more emphasis.

When you are *for* an issue, the argument seems simpler to organize. *You take the pro side of the issue and place it second:*

(Opposing view) Opponents of gambling

(Pro view) Proponents of gambling

But when you are *against* an issue, setting up the terminology takes more thought. The order of the viewpoints is *reversed.* (Just remember that your view always comes second.) To prevent possible confusion in your notes, clearly label points of view and place them at the top of your lists of points:

> *(Other view)* Proponents of yearly achievement testing

> *(My view)* Opponents to yearly achievement testing

To prevent confusion, identify each view *every time a shift from one side to the other occurs.* Four pairs of possible transitions appear below:

| (con) adversaries | opponents | critics | opposition |
| (pro) advocates | proponents | supporters | sponsors |

Select either *one pair* of terms or *two closely related pairs* and repeat them throughout your paper for clarity. To provide variety, you might substitute *opponents* for *the opposition.* But abrupt shifts to dissimilar pairs would be distracting; the puzzled reader would have to stop and reread.

When selecting labels for viewpoints, beware of slanting. For instance, a student writing about sex education called the opposition "right wingers" while labeling the other side "proponents." This mismatch of terms not only lacked parallelism but also revealed bias. Likewise, avoid the terms *liberals* and *conservatives.* These words have been bandied about so much their meanings have blurred. In some contexts, they have also taken on negative connotations.

LABELING POINTS OF VIEW

Block and Alternating Organization   After clearly identifying the points of view, consider whether to present the argument in block or alternating (point-by-point) form. An outline is essential to keep the argument on track. There are two basic ways to set up a controversial topic. The simplest is the block method. This way the main points of the opposing side appear in one chunk right after the introduction. One paragraph is usually adequate for this *summary of the opposing view.* Then in the next several paragraphs, you answer *all* the points raised and submit *evidence* to support your reasoning. The block method has an advantage in tone. Describing the opponent's view first not only conveys a sense of fairness but also postpones disagreement.

When an issue is complex, the alternating method is clearer than the block method. The alternating pattern pairs one of the opposing points with one of yours, arguing back and forth, emphasizing your answers. (In fig. 19.1 each box represents a paragraph.) A possible disadvantage of alternating is that disagreement emerges earlier than in the block method. Then too, the alternating method requires extra transition.

Usually, main points are arranged in least- to most-important order so that the argument gradually builds. An unanswered point would pose a serious flaw. If you cannot answer a point adequately and decide to reverse your

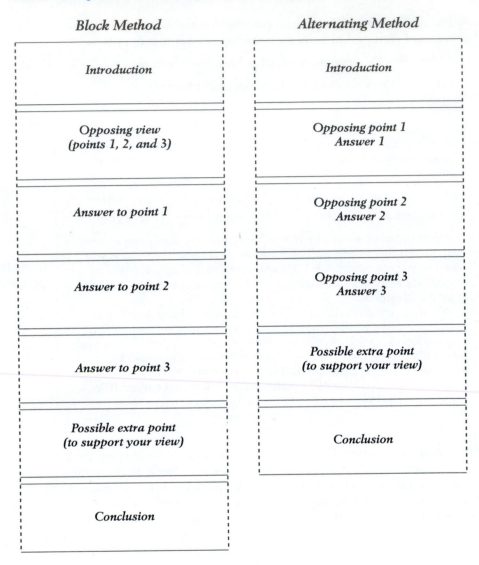

FIGURE 19.1 Ways to organize an argument.

original position in the argument, that is fine. It shows you have an open, logical mind.

To maintain an objective tone, try to avoid personal involvement in the argument. Two tips should be helpful: (1) Use third person, not first. (2) Try putting yourself in the role of a reporter writing a news item. This role should help you to distance yourself from the topic and avoid slanting.

QUESTIONS FOR SHAPING A CONTROVERSIAL TOPIC

1. What is at stake? Is there a hidden agenda?
2. Is there a common ground?
3. Where is the best spot for the proposition? (Direct or indirect order?)
4. Is a definition needed?
5. How much background information will be needed?
6. Can any concessions be made?
7. What are the advantages to accepting the proposition?
8. Are there disadvantages?
9. Will the block or alternating method be more suitable?
10. What is the best way to conclude the argument?

Drafting a Neutral Introduction

The purpose of an introduction is to present a factual overview of the argument and set a neutral tone. The introduction describes the issue and its origin, cause(s), and history. The introduction tells *when, who, what, how,* and perhaps *why,* defining the area of disagreement. The appeal is primarily logical. If readers are familiar with a topic, background information may be brief. If a topic is unfamiliar, the introduction should be more detailed. In the first example below, the writer describes a local problem that had been aired extensively by the media:

Curbing Overpopulation of Deer by "Harvesting"

The rapid growth of deer herds in Sharron Woods and Blacklick Park in Central Ohio poses problems. With no predators, the deer have multiplied to the point where they have stripped the woods and run out of food. Samuel B. Randall, attorney for Metro Parks, estimates that in the 700 acres of Sharron Woods, 375 deer live, which is "10 times the number the park can support." The controversy is over the means by which the deer herds will be decreased. One alternative is to let nature resolve the problem. Other alternatives are to use birth control or to move the deer. A fourth alternative, "harvesting," has led to requests for intervention. Recently, a Franklin Court judge declared he had no jurisdiction over the case (Candisky 1).

In the next student introduction, Pamela J. Van Camp begins with a definition, then gives logical reasons why so many people are turning to alternative medical treatments. At the end of the paragraph, she introduces the element of risk.

Alternative Medicine Has a Healthy Attraction

Alternative medicine is a term that describes nonconventional medical practices such as chiropractic, meditation, yoga, acupuncture, and herbal remedies. In the past two decades in the United States, more and more people are seeking alternative treatment. One reason for this growing trend is that people are looking for effective medical help without the side effects that often come with conventional medicine (Peeke 92). They are also attracted by the

mind-body connection that alternative therapies claim to address for their total health (92). Many of the alternative medicine patients are well-educated
people who pay for treatments out of pocket (Patel 49–50). Some are terminally ill and desperately seeking a cure even though it may carry a risk.

Finding Common Ground

Agreement sets the scene for mutual respect. A point of agreement or *common
ground* increases the chances that a proposition will receive thoughtful consideration from readers who disagree. Common ground can be a shared interest, a
belief, an understanding, or a goal. Psychologist Carl Rogers is generally cred-
ited with this form of argument, which aims to decrease hostility on a divisive
question.

A common ground prepares the reader for a reasonable argument. In a paper about aspartame, Rita Fleming provides facts and advantages before presenting disadvantages:

> Nearly "180 times sweeter than sugar," aspartame is the most popular low-
> calorie sweetener available today. Each year over "100 million Americans con-
> sume carbonated beverages, iced tea, desserts, presweetened cold cereal and
> other products" sweetened with aspartame (Farber 52). NutraSweet has been
> referred to as a "dieter's dream" since it contains few calories, and many prod-
> ucts containing aspartame have been labeled "low calorie" (*Sweeteners* 49).

To settle on a common ground, a writer not only presents facts but also listens to the connotations of words. Ill-chosen phrases can inflame feelings. But
tactful words create an air of peaceful deliberation.

Acknowledging and Clarifying Points of Agreement

While analyzing the main points of the opposing view, watch for a way to grant
a point or clarify what you mean. To show agreement with the opposition's
point, acknowledge it with a word or phrase such as *certainly, granted, it is true,
proponents agree,* or *advocates recognize.* Then present the related pro point. The
following phrases or similar ones might be used according to the purpose:

- It is true that . . . but . . .
- Proponents realize that . . . , yet they believe . . .
- Supporters recognize . . . ; still they do not acknowledge . . .
- This is not to say that . . . but to . . .
- _____ argues that . . .
- _____ claims that . . . but [include evidence] reveals . . .
- In short, the opponents believe . . . because . . .

Agreeing before disagreeing is not only fair but also tactically sound. Rita
Fleming extends the common ground of her argument by conceding a point
(italicized):

Many consumers assume that when the FDA approves a product, it is safe for them to use. *True, aspartame has been generally accepted as harmless, and many people use it with "no apparent ill effects,"* but others do "complain of side effects." According to Richard Wurtman, a neuroscientist at the Massachusetts Institute of Technology, aspartame has been linked to "numerous side effects." Some of the most common are "seizures, migraine headaches and mood swings" (*Macleans'* 31, 32).

Refuting Opposing Points

To refute means to show that the information of a claim is irrelevant or just partly true or completely false. In answering opposing points, avoid any hint of disrespect or antagonism; be respectful and friendly. When you show respect for the opponent's points, your chances for acceptance of the proposition will increase. To be convincing, a writer needs adequate evidence. The opinion of just one authority is inadequate; multiple sources are required. Opinion must be substantiated by facts, reasons, and examples. As a rule, the more evidence, the more convincing the argument, but do not oversell.

Select the most noteworthy points of the argument. Use quality evidence. Weak evidence will not support a claim for very long. Careful readers will be apt to spot distortions, omissions, quotations taken out of context, or other problems. There must be solid proof that the proposition is logical, beneficial, and ethical. Only a sound, ethical argument will stand up under intense scrutiny. Examining the student paper at the end of the chapter will help you see how to refute points well.

Writing a Conclusion

A conclusion is the final nail in the building of an argument. The conclusion should be sound, appropriate, and complete. It should not stray into irrelevancies, fail to take a stand, or end abruptly. It should leave the reader persuaded that the reasoning is valid and worthy of consideration. If action is advocated, the tone should convey a sense of immediacy, a feeling that impels the reader to act. Rita Fleming closes with a reference to risk:

Although the FDA has allowed aspartame to remain on the market, a look at the history of this chemical raises severe doubts about its long-term safety for everyone. The risks of using this product regularly far outweigh any advantages.

To be forceful and complete, most arguments need a restatement of the thesis. Restatement redirects the reader's attention to the claim, as in the following example. Kathy Kerchner writes:

Finally, the use of restraints is a prime concern in geriatric facilities. Research on physical or mechanical restraint use is vague, and more is needed. For many confused residents, restraints are harmful in the long run. If a restraint not only denies freedom and dignity for the aged but also leads to disorientation, then justification for use must outweigh possible consequences. Caregivers should exhaust all other alternatives before applying a restraint and continue to reevaluate its need from time to time.

Kathy's ending is one of compromise. She realizes that there is no one solution for all situations or all patients at all times. Still, she takes a firm stand, pointing out the dangers of long-term use of restraints.

Revising an Argument

Reviewing your outline will help you check the organization of your paper. Could the order be improved? Would any section or subsection fit better in another spot? Reread the paper and check it with the outline as you go. Do you see any discrepancies? This method forces you to look more closely at work that has become familiar. Using a checklist will help you guard against omissions.

CHECKLIST   REVISING AN ARGUMENT

1. Is the issue clearly defined?

2. Does the introduction have a neutral tone?

3. Has a common ground been established?

4. Are points of view clearly identified?

5. Are main points of the opposition presented fairly?

6. Is adequate evidence presented to refute each opposing point?

7. Is the logic sound and ethical?

8. Is the language calm and rational?

9. Does the conclusion restate the position?

10. Is the organization clear to the reader?

In summary, to build an effective argument about a controversial topic, you should (1) define the disagreement, (2) find the area of resistance or dissent, (3) respect the audience, and (4) ensure that evidence is logical and ethical.

STUDENT PAPER: CLASSIC ARGUMENT

See chapter R-3.

This paper is presented in the MLA format for research papers without a cover page. The pages are reduced to show proportional margins for an 8½- by 11-inch page. The paper is by Bethany Shirk, who researched her questions on the legality of high-decibel noise and the effects of noise on human health.

www.mhhe.com/dietsch

For other student-written arguments, go to:
Writing>Sample Argument
Papers

Shirk 1

Bethany Shirk

Professor Nancy Gilson

Communications 112

1 February 2007

Automobile Stereo Speakers: Turn Them Down

For decades the right of United States citizens to turn the volume of their automobile stereo speakers to any decibel level has been an issue. Although the federal Noise Control Regulation of 1995 governs noise emitted from vehicles, including "amplified music," enforcement varies across the nation. The law states that "neighborhood noise" is left to local police and city councils ("Noise Control"). In many communities, police have been slow to enforce noise ordinances. Often they just issue a warning and tell the offender to turn down the music.

Numerous large cities across the USA have drafted strict codes that spell out violations and have begun to enforce them. A Rochester, N.Y., ordinance states: "No person shall operate . . . any motor vehicle . . . that the sound level emitted . . . exceeds 80 decibels either: 1) At a distance of 25 feet or more from . . . the vehicle . . . on a public street or sidewalk . . . park or other public place; or 2) At or beyond the property line . . . on private property. . . . Any motor vehicle used in . . . violation of this section shall be towed" (Sheveloff).

Other cities have drafted codes that specifically spell out violations and have begun to enforce them. For example, in Pittsburgh,

Shirk 2

Buffalo, New York City, and Chicago, police can impound offending vehicles and impose expensive fines ("Cut Volume").

Viewpoints of citizens generally fall into two directly opposed groups. Those who drive with high-powered stereos going full blast believe they have the right to play their music as loud as they like. Those outside the car often say the level of sound is rude, unsafe, and threatening to their health.

For some drivers, pumping up the stereo is a form of entertainment. Dallas Wilson, who works in an electronics store and competes in car stereo sound competitions, said, "I will drop the windows, and I will crank my stereo to a point where I can enjoy my music at a loud volume" ("Aurora"). Although playing loud music is enjoyable for some people, many others believe the negative aspects outweigh the positive.

Those for stricter enforcement of laws limiting car stereo sound believe that it is not only inconsiderate but also unethical and unhealthy to pollute the environment with unnecessary noise. One group, the Noise Pollution Clearinghouse (NPC) is seeking to advance the "ethic of the commons." They think that noise polluters mistakenly extend "their own private property rights to that [air space] which is publicly owned or cared for." In other words, no one has the right to infringe on other people's rights by making loud noises that disrupt peace of mind and sleep ("Protecting").

Proponents of strict enforcement also point out that sound from car stereos can be dangerous not only to the offender but also

Shirk 3

to other drivers on the road. Excessively high volume prevents the driver from hearing horns of other cars or sirens of emergency vehicles such as fire trucks, police cars, and ambulances. Thus he or she may not move out of the way. Nor can the driver hear approaching trains over throbbing stereo speakers. Adjusting volume controls and driver distraction can also lead to tragic accidents.

The most common danger is to human health. Hearing is at risk when an individual is exposed to excessively loud noise over a length of time. Over twenty-eight million people in the United States already have impaired hearing, and more than a third of the cases are believed to have been partly caused by loud noise. Hearing loss is not limited to the elderly. Nancy Nadler, director of the noise center at the League for the Hard of Hearing in New York City, says that "Hearing loss is also affecting younger people" (Colino).

Excessive noise contributes to many health problems other than hearing loss. According to the EPA, various research studies reveal that high noise levels in humans can increase headaches, "susceptibility to minor accidents," "reliance on sedatives and sleeping pills," and "mental hospital admission rates." Other associated conditions are "colds, changes in blood pressure, other cardiovascular changes," digestive problems, and fatigue ("Effects of Noise").

Many studies have linked noise pollution with hypertension, low birth weight, and impaired immune function (Colino). Arline Bronzaft, professor emerita of psychology at Lehman College, New

Shirk 4

York City, explains, "A person's pulse rate and blood pressure increase; adrenaline surges. In addition, William Clark, PhD, reports there is medical evidence that excessive noise has caused heart attacks in individuals with existing cardiac injury (Wilson 77). The medical journal *Thorax* reported four cases of "lung collapse triggered by loud bass music." Three of the victims attended concerts; the other was in a boom car using a 1,000 watt bass system (Citizens).

Yet in 2005 Ford and Volkswagen equipped some models with 1000 watt stereo systems. Similar systems by Sony and others can be purchased and installed. The MTX Audio Jackhammer Superwoofer is a 320-pound speaker that can handle 12,000 watts. It "is designed to be even louder than a Boeing 747 at takeoff" (Citizens).

In the <u>Los Angeles Times,</u> Ted Rueter commented, "Well there is no peace when a boom car is around. These brutal excruciatingly loud cars can be heard for more than a mile. They can shake your windows and furniture. . . . Noise levels have risen sixfold in major U.S. cities in the past 15 years, and automobiles are the largest source of noise" (Rueter).

Finally, excessive volume from car stereos is not just a breach of etiquette and ethics. It is much more serious. Excessive noise can damage hearing and health. High-decibel sound can also cause accidents involving other drivers on the road. Cities and communities without noise control ordinances should outlaw extremely loud sounds from car speakers. Then police should be advised to ticket those who violate the law and infringe upon the rights of other citizens.

Shirk 5

Works Cited

"Aurora Fighting Cars That Go Boom." <u>Chicago Tribune</u> 26 March
    1996: 1.

Citizens Coalition Against Noise Pollution. "Boom Cars." 14 Mar.
    2007 <http://www.noiseoff.org/boomcars.shtm>.

Colino, Stacy. "Sounding Off about Noise." <u>American Health for
    Women</u> Oct. 1997: 64.

"Cut Volume on Whining." <u>Chicago Sun Times</u> 30 Sept. 1998: 41.

"Effects of Noise." 1997. Environmental Protection Agency. 13 Mar.
    2007 <http://www.epa.nsw.gov.au/soe/97/ch1/15.htm>.

"Noise Control Measures." 1997. Environmental Protection Agency.
    13 Mar. 2007 <http://www.epa.nsw.gov.au/soe/97/ch1/
    15_5.htm#0_15_5_6_0_0_0>.

"Protecting the Commons." n.d. Noise Pollution Clearinghouse.
    15 Mar. 2007 <http://www.nonoise.org/commons.htm>.

Rueter, Ted. "Today's Boom Cars Are Nothing If Not Acoustic Ter-
    rorism." <u>Los Angeles Times,</u> 27 March 2002.

Sheveloff, Micah. "Opposition Making Noise." 2003 <http://www
    .transalt.org/press/media/2003/030901audio.html> 12 Mar.
    2007.

Wilson, Brenda L. "All Quiet on the Noise Control Front." <u>Governing</u>
    Sept. 1990: 77–78.

QUESTIONS FOR DISCUSSION

1. Where is Bethany's thesis statement located?
2. Is there a common ground in this argument?
3. Does she use block or alternating order?
4. Would another order be more effective? Why or why not?
5. Does the argument give the opposing view a fair hearing?
6. Examine the conclusion. What does she do here?
7. What types of appeals do you see?
8. The EPA entries of Bethany's works-cited list are for government publications. How does this kind of entry differ from most?

FOR YOUR REFERENCE
Argument Essays in the Reader

- "Last Rites for Indian Dead," Suzan Shown Harjo, page 678
- "Logging in Giant Sequoia National Monument,"Sierra Club Task Force, page 681
- "Wal-Mart's Big City Blues," Dan Levine, page 685
- "The War on Wal-Mart," Steven Malanga, page 688
- "We Have No 'Right to Happiness,'" C. S. Lewis, page 693
- "The Pursuit of Happiness: Four Revolutionary Words," Andrew Sullivan, page 697
- "The Official English Question," James Crawford, page 703
- "In Plain English: Let's Make It Official," Charles Krauthammer, page 707
- "Speaking English Preserves Our National Heritage," Nathan Tabor, page 709

PRACTICE

WRITING EXERCISE: Examining Opposing Points of View

Directions: Select a topic. Write two paragraphs from two *contrasting* points of view. Separate the paragraphs and indicate the person speaking. Be biased and emotional if the occasion calls for it.

1. *Animal control.* Your town council is considering hiring an animal control officer because of complaints about stray cats, bats, and raccoons. You are a citizen with high property taxes who thinks the officer is unnecessary. You have varmint-proofed your home yourself and cats are not a problem. Next, write the view of a citizen who has had flowers dug up, sleep disturbed, and a car scratched by cats. Raccoons have invaded his attic, and he is afraid they may have rabies.

2. *Deadline.* At 4:30 p.m. your boss hands you ten pages of a draft with numerous red-penciled changes. The typed project report is due at 8 a.m. tomorrow. He plans to revise the last six pages while you correct the first ten pages. You have a dinner date and know the job will take at least an hour. You normally work until 5 p.m. Write your boss's view and your view.

3. *Dental charge.* A busy dentist has a policy that if a patient misses an appointment without canceling, a minimum charge of $25 is added to the bill. A woman who missed her appointment because she took her injured child (who suffered a broken arm) to the emergency room is protesting the extra charge. Write the dentist's view, then her view.

4. *Broken window.* A ten-year-old has just batted a softball through the thermopane window of a neighbor's house. It landed on the dining room table while she was entertaining dinner guests. One guest received a nick on the face from flying glass. Write the batter's version of the event and then the neighbor's.

5. *Ball game.* Imagine you are two reporters writing accounts of the same game. One reporter favors the hometown team; the other does not.

WORKPLACE ISSUES FOR DISCUSSION

1. You do not have quite enough money to buy your lunch. Is it all right to borrow $5 from your cash register and return the money after you are paid that evening? (You will be returning after dinner to work overtime.) Why or why not?

2. Is it all right to use your company's computer to print ten posters for a garage sale you are planning? Why or why not?

3. Is it ethical to use the company computer during work time to send several e-mail messages to friends? To chat online? Give reasons for your answer.

4. Two office mates (one is married) are having a romance that has affected their productivity. Should the employer intervene?

5. In a foreign country where bribes are a part of the economic system, is it all right for an American factory owner to offer a bribe to a purchasing agent? Why or why not?

TEN IDEAS FOR PAPERS OF ARGUMENT

1. Should more nuclear power plants be built?

2. Should e-commerce be taxed?

3. Should cross-species cloning be banned?

4. Should schools score children on height and weight?

5. Should the military draft be reinstated?

6. Should classes for gifted students be required?

7. Should the growing of tobacco be subsidized?

8. Should lawmakers overrule courts in life-support cases?

9. Should the legal driving age be raised to seventeen?

10. Should search bots on the Internet be restricted?

Understanding, Using, and Creating Visuals

CHAPTER 20

> A picture is worth ten thousand words.
>
> —Frederick R. Barnard

You have probably heard a variation of this proverb, which is often attributed to Confucius, a Chinese philosopher (551?–479 BC). The truth is that in 1921 Frederick R. Barnard of New York conceived an early version: "One look is worth a thousand words." That version appeared in Chinese writing on posters to hawk the benefits of advertising on streetcars. In 1927 Barnard changed the wording to "A picture is worth ten thousand words" to advertise baking soda.

The more you analyze ads, cartoons, commercials, and other visuals, the more your critical thinking skills will improve. Just keep in mind that many of these visuals are brief arguments, designed to hook your emotions and sway your judgment. You will also gain insights into how they influence our culture and how to use visuals to your advantage in presentations and documents.

UNDERSTANDING VISUAL IMAGES

Visual images appear almost everywhere: atop grocery displays, computer screens, and buildings; in magazines, newspapers, and shop windows; on cereal boxes, television sets, and trains; along highways on signs and billboards. Daily we are confronted with visual content designed to persuade us to do something, think a certain way, or buy a product.

Analyzing Advertisements, Comics, and Cartoons

Advertising is a multimillion dollar business, and clever ads abound. To understand these visuals, first identify the service or product and the source (sponsor, service, or producer). Knowing the source will enable you to consider the image of the company or organization and the slant of the message. For example, the Sierra Club has long advocated conservation of natural resources, and this position influences their messages.

Some television commercials are puzzling on first, second, or even a third viewing. Perhaps you recall the one of a man who enters his kitchen and sees Abe Lincoln, wearing a stovepipe hat, and a beaver seated around a chess board. The beaver is eating pancakes. This surreal visual and the dialogue do not explain the purpose of the ad. The sponsor, Takeda Pharmaceutical, surveyed viewers and found they had to watch the ad "six to nine times" before they fully realized what was happening. Viewers were expected to infer—within thirty seconds—that this was a dream sequence and that sound sleep could be obtained by taking the sponsor's product, Rozerem (*Wall Street Journal*, 27 Nov. 2006).

While you enjoy (or endure) commercials and ads, consider the nature of the claims. Do the claims sound reasonable? Are facts or statistics cited? Is adequate evidence provided? Are any risks or warnings stated, particularly in ads for pharmaceuticals? The Federal Trade Commission's truth-in-advertising law requires ads to be fair, factual, and based on evidence. Any risks or side effects must be stated.

A more subtle influence on consumers are print ads that release a fragrance when scratched or opened. Avon has long employed this method, including scented pages in catalogs. The purpose is to connect the brand, beyond the image and words, to the customer's senses. Although producing scented ads is expensive, the trend has increased in recent years.

To make political statements, some visuals use appeals that combine bits of truth with irony and exaggeration. Witty, derisive statements chip away at the dignity and image of the subject. Comic strips, such as "Doonesbury," and political cartoons often employ humor and exaggeration to make biting statements. To analyze these visuals, identify the central character and the situation. Is the wit sarcastic, ironic, or satiric? Is it derogatory? What point is being made? Then decide if the point is valid and significant.

Finally, categorize the type of appeal. Like a formal argument, the brief arguments in visuals employ three persuasive appeals, which are often combined. A logical appeal solicits a reasoned response; this is an appeal to the intellect. An ethical appeal beseeches the viewer to do what is right and good. An emotional appeal seeks to trigger personal feelings, perhaps self-indulgence, indignation, sympathy, or another emotion. Emotional appeals are made not only through images and words but also through scented ads.

- **Logical appeal:** "Vote for Tom Smith for township trustee. Tom has 20 years' experience managing his own local business." (Appeal to reason)
- **Ethical appeal:** "Donate to the Children's Fund" (Appeal to values)
- **Emotional appeal:** "Enjoy the luxury of a New-Age Spa in your own home!" (Appeal to feelings)

See chapter 16.

CHECKLIST   ANALYZING AND INTERPRETING VISUALS

1. Who or what is the topic?

2. Who is the intended audience?

3. Who is the sponsor or producer (writer, artist, or photographer)?

4. What is the purpose of the visual?

5. Do the elements of the visual support the purpose?

6. Consider the caption and any other information. Does the content seem accurate and adequate? Are the claims and any risks fairly stated?

7. What inferences can be drawn from the visual?

How Do Visuals Influence the Viewer?

Each of us views photos and other visuals through the window of our own personal experience. Our frame of reference—a perspective shaped by our values, beliefs, abilities, and culture—influences how we perceive and interpret. In other words, we may all observe the same scenario, but we do not perceive it or interpret it in exactly the same way. Some will notice details that others overlook; some will have the experience or education to better comprehend what is happening.

When a strange object, unlike anything we know, is pictured or represented, we often pause. Our minds usually start flitting through the files of our experiences, searching for something similar so that we can classify the unidentified object. For this reason effective writers and speakers consider the audience and

See chapter R-1.

estimate their knowledge of and reaction to a visual. Omission of *audience analysis* can result in confusion or miscommunication.

Sponsors often use attractive animals and charming children in ads and commercials to appeal to a general audience. Purina has featured a pet cat, standing upright, mimicking its owner's stretching exercise. The Aflac duck and the Hartford stag advertise insurance. The Dreyfus lion, "Prowling for Growth," is featured on financial pages. Surprising is a full-page ad by America's Oil & Natural Gas Industry with the caption "A breath of fresh air." The ad shows a pretty preteen, head back and eyes closed, amid drifting snowflakes. What seems to be the implication there?

Other ads and commercials are aimed at a more adventurous audience. A shampoo ad shows two young women with long hair, bouncing up and down on a mattress display labeled "Do not touch." Still others show risky antics on ski slopes, speeding motorcycles on wet roads, and cars racing down twisting roads. One commercial shows a car moving atop the edge of a building, then vaulting into a river. Taboo and bizarre activities gain attention and thrill some viewers while others are repulsed. Viewers, however, often remember the action, not the product.

In *Can't Buy My Love: How Advertising Changes How We Feel and Think*, Jean Kilbourne ends her analysis of messages in car advertising with the following observation:

> As always, taken individually, the car ads are funny, silly, exciting, sometimes breathtakingly clever, and seemingly insignificant. However, they have a cumulative direction and a cumulative impact . . . the car in commercials has gone from being a symbol of power to the actual source of power (the engine that pumps the valves in our hearts), from a symbol of sex to an actual lover, from a conduit to relationships to the important relationship itself, and from a prized possession to the very emblem of oneself. The car ads are an important part of a world in which things are becoming ever more, and people ever less, important.

USING VISUALS IN ORAL PRESENTATIONS AND DOCUMENTS

Effective visuals provide not only eye appeal but also evidence and emphasis. They are a way to compress and illustrate data for oral presentations and documents. For example, colorful graphs and charts can show comparisons and trends. Yet visuals should not be overused; every visual should have a clear purpose.

Interpreting and Explaining Visuals

The amount of interpretation and explanation needed for a presentation or document will vary according to your topic, purpose, occasion, audience, and type of visual. Graphics citing statistics may require more interpretation than ads, drawings, or photos. Usually, a reference to the graphic and a brief explanation accompanies a chart, graph, or table. Highlights are summarized and the main point or result is stated.

In an oral presentation, as well as a document, specify the subject of each visual, its significance, and the source. Enlarge the visual so that it can be seen from the back of the room. To heighten interest, begin by asking a question or two of the audience. For a lay audience, summarize complicated and technical visuals in plain English. Define unfamiliar terms.

As you study the principles for creating effective visuals and examine the examples that follow, you will be better prepared to select an appropriate format and to gauge the amount of explanation needed for your visuals.

Guidelines for Using Copyrighted Visuals and Sources

To avoid copyright infringement, always give the source and date of borrowed text, drawings, photos, charts, graphs, tables, maps, or other visuals. It is illegal to publish or to post copyrighted material online without the owner's permission. That includes logos, symbols, ads, cartoon characters, and any other figures that are copyrighted. Permission for such use usually requires a fee. For online or on-site business use or commercial distribution of visuals, contact the copyright owner.

If you are using statistical visuals in a research paper or report for a class, just list the source and date. If you gather common information made available to the public, either online or otherwise, state the source and date. No permission or documentation is required for software clip art or special fonts. Brief video clips, such as commercials or excerpts from a newscast that identify the source, may be taped and used in a class presentation without permission or more documentation.

USING VIDEO CLIPS

You might include a short video in a class presentation if the clip directly relates to the purpose and develops the main idea. The clip should serve as support, not as a substitute for preparation. For example, a one- or two-minute video might be included in a seven-minute presentation, depending on the assignment. The clip should be smoothly integrated, with no undue pauses or unnecessary remarks.

Video clips are versatile, but the content should be carefully monitored before presentation to a class or to the public. Frivolous personal videos that are posted in blogs or on social networking sites may be regretted. Employers often visit these Web sites to check out job applicants.

Video clips can be used as a training tool in sports, exercise classes, seminars, and workshops or by individuals. Studying a video clip can help to perfect a golf swing, tennis return, dance routine, or interviewing technique. Realtors and homeowners regularly use online videos to show property for sale. An artist might use a video clip to present a 'Statement of Purpose" to describe the genre, influences, and evolution of his or her work to gain a gallery showing or to interview for a position.

Video clips can also be used as an innovative job search tool to accompany a résumé for some positions—but only if done well. In fields such as broadcasting, advertising, and public relations, a video clip could be appropriate for job seekers who are confident and professional. A video reflecting these qualities can help to gain an interview. In fields such as medicine or law that focus primarily on knowledge (education and experience), a video would be of less value.

Some employers conduct virtual interviews via a remote PC-based video camera. To prepare for video clips and job interviews, see chapter 25, "Making Oral Presentations," as well as "Challenging Interview Questions" and "Video Clips for Résumés" in chapter 26. For help with telephone and face-to-face interviews, including types of questions, also see chapter R-5.

CREATING EFFECTIVE VISUALS

Before planning a visual, consider the topic, purpose, and audience. The general purpose of a visual for academic or professional use is to arouse interest and provide pertinent information in an easily assimilated format. Select images that illustrate the points well for your purpose and audience. The subject of each visual should be easy to discern, and any message within the visual should be clear and large enough to read easily.

Appropriate visuals support major points and lend interest to presentations and documents. Keep visuals simple; eliminate distracting details. If tempted to interject a funny visual into a presentation or report, consider the visual and the audience carefully. Humor should be low key, inoffensive, and tied to the purpose. Shy away from exaggerated political cartoons and off-color dialogue, which can distract and offend.

GUIDELINES FOR CREATING VISUALS

1. **Focus on the central image.** Avoid clutter and unnecessary items. Limit the amount of text.

2. **Connect the text to the image.** The caption and other words should directly relate to and support the main idea.

3. **Consider using bullets to emphasize important points.** Use fragments with bullets, not sentences.

4. **Make visuals neat and attractive.** Plan layouts that are clear and pleasing to the eye. Use color for a purpose; for example, red for emphasis.

5. **Check the visibility of captions and text.** Black and other dark letters show up better than pastels. Use a large, easy-to-read font. To ensure visibility during a presentation, check from the back row of seating.

Examine your text to find prime spots for a few visuals. Too many visuals can distract from the purpose. Devise an appropriate caption for each visual by identifying the subject and making a brief statement. Link any text to the visual by supplying adequate explanation and transition. Locate the visual near its introduction.

CREATING STATISTICAL VISUALS

To create statistical visuals (tables, charts, and graphs), first obtain data to support the purpose of your document or presentation. In other words the visuals should help to clarify, explain, and enhance your main idea. Research may be done firsthand by conducting a survey or interviews or secondhand by finding and using data collected by someone else.

This chapter shows examples of graphics based on research and explains how the data were collected and organized. The use of copyrighted materials and quotations is also shown and briefly explained. For more help, see the Research Writing Guide later in this book. The guide also provides in-depth help in narrowing a topic and finding and using electronic and print sources.

Principles for creating statistical visuals have evolved over the years into traditional formats. Those principles are still generally followed in class papers, proposals, reports, financial pages, and business presentations. With computer software you can create colorful graphics that look professional. Hand-drawn charts or graphs are unsuitable for an oral presentation or typed document. (If you do not yet use such software, go to the campus computer lab and seek assistance.)

The preliminary process of organizing and preparing common captions and headings, using software such as Microsoft Excel, is the same for tables, charts, or graphs. The basic process has five steps:

- Obtain or import raw data, usually into a spreadsheet.

- If the data is complex, summarize it in a one-, two-, or three-dimensional table with headings. This data table can be used as a formal table or as the base for creating charts or graphs.

- Insert a text box in the lower part of the spreadsheet and enter source and date.

- Refine the data table as needed, depending on the format selected for the graphic. The refinement may vary according to the software used.

- Cut and paste the graphic into your word-processing document.

BASIC PROCESS FOR PREPARING STATISTICAL GRAPHICS

Although variations and hybrid formats of graphics have arisen, due to variance in software, most tables, charts, and graphs still retain certain standard features:

1. **Numbering.** Graphics of a single type are labeled in a sequence, as Chart 1, 2, or 3 or as Table 1, 2, or 3. For mixed types use Figure 1, Figure 2, and so forth. This label normally appears outside the graphic.

2. **Reference in the text.** Every figure is preceded by a sentence in the text or a parenthetical reference. Example: "In figure 2 the EPA mileage is shown for highway and in-city driving for . . . or (see fig. 2)."

3. **Location.** A graphic should be placed following where it is first mentioned, on the same page if possible.

4. **Lines set off graphics.** Formal tables, charts, and graphs are separated from the text by lines. In addition, the entire graphic may be set on a pale block of color. (See fig. 20.1.)

5. **Caption.** Every statistical graphic, except an informal table, requires a caption that identifies the subject. Other information may be included.

6. **Decimals.** Use decimals, not fractions, unless decimals are not customary for the topic.

7. **Vertical scale (axis).** Measurements of temperature, percentages, and other quantities are usually placed on the left side. The measurement is printed above or beside the scale.

8. **Horizontal scale (axis).** Measurements of time (often months or years) are usually placed parallel to the lower edge of a chart or line graph. The designation or name is placed below.

9. **Key.** If needed, a key or legend is supplied, usually to the right of the data or near the lower edge of the graphic.

10. **Source and date.** The source and date appear nearest the lower edge.

Tables

If you have data that would be difficult to comprehend in a paragraph and would be unsuited to a chart or graph, consider using a table. This way numerical data are arranged in columns with headings. The major differences between a formal table and an informal table are size and complexity.

The chief function of a *formal table* is to compare and contrast large quantities of statistics. Formal tables of less than one page are separated from the text by a line at the top and bottom. Larger tables, without lines, are located alone on a separate page. A formal table is numbered "Table 1" unless included in a sequence with other graphics that are labeled as figures. Figure 20.1 shows the results of a personal survey of seven banks. Because each of the banks is obviously the source of the information, no other source is listed. But a note is needed to specify the locale and date because bank services and fees can vary by region and season.

If your draft of a table seems too large and the information too complex for the reader to grasp easily, you can divide it logically into two or more related tables. A brief explanation can follow each table or appear after the final table.

A short *informal table* can be integrated into the text, using the basic table insertion features built into most word-processing software. No figure number or

Bank Services and Fees*

Bank	Free Checking Minimum Balance	Other ATMs	Phone Transfer	Overdraft Transfer	Returned Check	Certified Check
Chase	$25	$1.50	free	$7	$ 6	$10
Commercial Savings	$25	$2.00	free	$3	$25	$25
Fahey	$100	$1.00	free	free	$32	$5
Fifth Third	$50	$1.50	free	$9	$33	$10
National City	$500	$1.50	free	$10	$30 – $36	$5
Ohio State	$50	$1.50	free	NA	$30	$4
United	$25	$0.80	$3 each	$1	$30	$3

*Marion, Ohio, September 2007

FIGURE 20.1 Example of a formal table.

lines are needed because the table becomes part of the text. The introductory sentence(s) may cite the source and date along with a brief explanation, or that information may come below the data. When the subject and purpose are given in the introductory sentence, a caption can be omitted.

CHECKLIST   CONSTRUCTING TABLES

1. Is a table the best way to show the quantity and kind of information?

2. Are items grouped in a logical and appropriate order?

3. Do the headings reflect the content of the columns?

4. Are necessary subtotals and totals included?

5. Are all numbers accurate?

6. Are the source and date included?

7. Is each table introduced and explained as needed?

8. Do formal tables have numerical labels and captions?

Bar Charts

The purpose of a bar chart is to compare sets of data. Bars can be arranged horizontally or vertically, depending on the quantity being measured and the space needed for names. For example, braking distance would be depicted best with

GUIDELINES FOR CREATING TABLES, CHARTS, AND GRAPHS

1. **Group data in a logical sequence, in the way you wish readers to recall it.** Tables usually display data chronologically, alphabetically, or logically by importance. Let your purpose guide the order.

2. **Use suitable headings.** The heading should reflect the kind of data indicated in the column, bar, line, or section. Eliminate any category that is not directly related to the purpose.

3. **Use consistent categories and formats.** For example, if some quantities are in pounds and others in metric tons, convert to the same measurement, one that your readers will understand. Use consistent data formatting: align rows, columns, and decimal points so that they are neat and clear.

4. **Use standard abbreviations and symbols.** Keep the graphic concise. Include information that will be helpful to the reader.

5. **Introduce and explain the graphic in the text.** State the purpose. An explanation can come after the graphic.

6. **Precede a note with an asterisk.** In addition, a prior asterisk, placed after the caption or item, will alert the reader to the note.

the bars running horizontally, just as cars go. A comparison of interior sound levels of cars could be depicted with the bars running upward, parallel to the vertical scale that shows the rise in decibels. Placing bars logically helps to clarify the chart for the viewer.

The vertical scale on a bar chart can indicate percentages, temperature, dollars, gallons, tons, or other quantities. The exact amount, especially for dollars, is often stated above each wide solid bar. In that case, the horizontal scale shows upright bars, at evenly spaced intervals, perhaps showing the names of comparable companies.

A *simple bilateral bar chart* illustrates positive and negative values to show, for example, gains and losses in earnings for a company. The vertical scale not only ascends from zero but also descends below zero. A bilateral chart uses upright bars to indicate gains. Bars running downward below zero indicate large losses. To indicate gains, the dollar amount is listed above each upright bar. Losses are preceded by a minus and placed beneath each inverted bar.

A *grouped bar chart* compares sets of data for multiple subjects. A set of two or three narrow bars, distinguished by color, diagonal lines, or otherwise, represent each subject. These narrow bars ordinarily indicate an approximate amount on the scale because there is not enough space above each bar to print the amount. For figure 20.2, the information was collected online by visiting all the available sites displaying data on 2008 compact cars. For a valid comparison, just the compacts with the same number of cylinders and type of transmission, using regular gasoline, were selected. The first bar in each set indicates mileage for highway driving. The second bar indicates mileage for in-city driving.

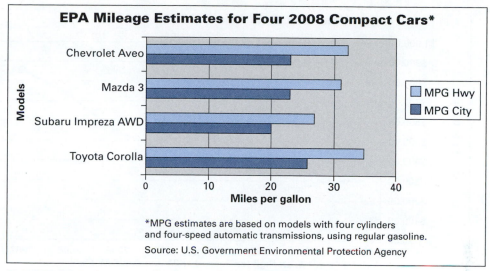

FIGURE 20.2 Example of a grouped bar chart.

Line Graphs

The standard function of a *single line graph* is to show a trend, a change over time (weeks, months, or years). The time scale is placed horizontally across the lower edge. The vertical scale is placed on the left edge to indicate quantities. For percentages the scale normally begins with zero, as shown in figure 20.3. The data for this graph was found online by searching the words *historic gold prices.* Finfacts of Ireland lists the "high," "low," and "close" prices for December 31 of each year from 1800 to the present. For figure 20.3 just the high prices of years 2000 to 2007 were used.

A *complex line graph* compares trends of two to five items. To show the high, low, and closing year-end gold prices, we could have started with figure 20.3 and added two lines across the graph, one for the low price of the day and one for the closing price. The three lines would be distinguished by color or labels under each. If color were used, a key would be required.

Pie Charts

The function of a *single pie chart* is to illustrate the relation of a whole item to its parts. A pie chart allows comparison of the parts. The small circular chart is divided into sections that are sized according to the percentage or quantity each represents. The percentages should total 100 percent.

Various colors, diagonal lines, or other means can be used to distinguish sections of a pie chart. The most important item normally comes right after the 12 o'clock position, as in figure 20.4. The percentage of each section is often

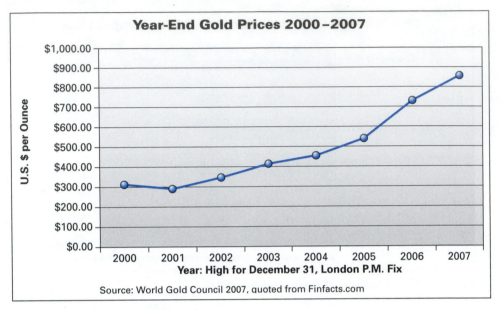

FIGURE 20.3 Example of a single line graph.

FIGURE 20.4 Example of a pie chart.

printed on its slice of the pie. If the slice is too small, the percentage is placed with an arrow just outside the slice. Slices are put in descending order, clockwise, unless there is a logical exception. In figure 20.4, the source and date in the caption identify the portfolio, mix of funds, and time. This chart was compiled from data provided by Shefali Anand in "Mixing It Up" (*Wall Street Journal*, 10 Sept. 2007).

A pair of pie charts side by side perform two functions: (1) show how each subject is related to its parts, and (2) compare the two subjects. To illustrate and compare more complex data, consider using a table or bar chart.

CHECKLIST   **CONSTRUCTING CHARTS AND GRAPHS**

1. Does each graphic clearly reflect its purpose? Is it suitable for the amount and kind of data shown?

2. Are the graphics labeled numerically in a sequence?

3. Does each one have a clear, identifying caption?

4. Are the scales clear, consistent, and divided into equal segments?

5. Does the size of each pie chart section correspond to the percentage it represents?

6. Do the percentages in a pie chart add up to 100 percent?

7. Are the source and date provided for each graphic?

8. Is a key needed?

New Versions and Hybrid Graphics

With the evolution of software, various versions of charts and graphs have blossomed. Some innovations are merely small changes in appearance and layout. Sometimes a measurement scale is placed on the right side instead the left. Instead of being vertical, a bar chart is often horizontal so that the labels identifying the bars can be placed on the left for easy reading.

Hybrids may contain various combinations of graphics. For example, a list and a bar chart might be combined, as shown in figure 20.5. Notice that this chart is copyrighted and requires permission for its use. The following sample introduction shows how to cite the source and excerpts of information that are borrowed.

Sample Introduction   A survey of the "500 most visited sites," *AARP Bulletin* (May 2007), revealed interesting differences in the favorite online destinations of older and younger adults, as shown in figure 20.5.

To see more examples of graphics, check the financial pages of large newspapers, newsmagazines, and journals. In the periodical section of a campus or

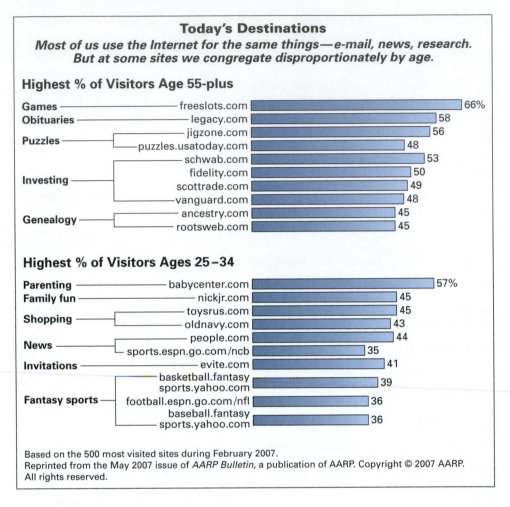

FIGURE 20.5 Example of a hybrid graph.

public library, you can easily find dozens of traditional and hybrid graphics. *Note that the simpler the graphic, the easier for the reader to understand.* If you are tempted to innovate when creating graphics, consider not only appropriateness but also whether the changes will enhance the clarity and ease of reading. If not, use a traditional format.

CREATE A GRAPHIC

Directions: Select one of the options below and create a graphic, following the guidelines in this chapter.

1. Survey the prices for a doughnut, Danish roll, and a small of cup of coffee in six or more local restaurants. Compile the results into a table with a caption. If a restaurant does not carry one of the items, mark NA (not available).

2. Create a grouped bar chart to compare the price of your tuition, textbooks, and lab fees for last year and this year.

3. Create a pie chart showing how your salary or allowance is allocated for one month. For example, what percentage goes for income taxes? Tuition? Books? Housing? Food? Utilities? Transportation? Clothing? Leisure? Other?

4. If you or your parents own your home, create a simple line graph showing how the property taxes have increased in the past four or five years for this residence. Or if you rent, you might show how rent has increased for the past several years.

5. Collect information online from various sites and compile an appropriate chart or graph of your choice. (If a site has already compiled such a graphic, do not copy it. Choose another topic and create your own graphic.)

Critical Reading and Writing Strategies

"Reading without thinking is as nothing, for a book is less important for what it says than for what it makes you think."
Louis L'Amour,
The Walking Drum

Of all the books you have read, which one stands out the clearest in your mind? Why? How has it influenced you?

Reading and Responding to Essays

> . . . the unexamined life is not worth living.
>
> —Socrates, in *Apology*, Plato

Essays appear in magazines, in blogs, and on editorial pages of newspapers. In college classes you write essays—compositions setting forth your point of view. An essay is a short literary composition that focuses on one major idea. Essays range all the way from lighthearted spoofs to political commentary to serious argument. Essayists reflect, reminisce, discuss incidents, or argue about daily life, trends, justice, values, and other subjects. Their words may echo nostalgia or disgust, cheerfulness or sadness, cheekiness or humility. Often the ideas in essays are universal and timeless, connecting people around the world and down through the ages.

As you analyze and evaluate essays, you will become more aware of the many options that are available to writers. At the same time, you will be developing your critical thinking skills, which will help you focus ideas, refine word choice, and write with conviction.

PURPOSE OF ESSAYS

The chief purpose of an essay is to explore an idea and reflect upon it—to think critically. Sometimes an essayist may simply seek a means of fresh expression, not necessarily agreement. Other essayists seek to inform or entertain. Others attempt to persuade the reader to agree with a position on an issue.

Personal Essays

Personal (informal) essays often expose a human frailty or condition and attempt to elicit empathy or sympathy from the reader. The essayist, like a friend, shares personal details, opinions, and biases. Other essayists go against popular opinion in an attempt to surprise, shock, or arouse public indignation. Still others use humor not only to entertain but also to make a point.

You can identify personal essays by their conversational tone, self-disclosure, humor, freshness, and casual structure. They often appear to be spontaneous as they meander in and through a subject or circle it, coming closer and closer to the heart of the discussion. Others move along a time line, narrating an incident. Personal essays tend to be subjective and honest, inspiring trust in the reader.

In *The Art of the Personal Essay,* editor Phillip Lopate explains:

> The hallmark of the personal essay is its intimacy. The writer seems to be speaking directly into your ear, confiding everything from gossip to wisdom. . . . At the core . . . is the supposition that there is a certain unity to human experience.

Formal Essays

Formal essays usually have an earnest purpose and tighter structure than personal essays. The tone of a formal essay is generally impersonal, factual, and solemn. Typically, the language is refined and restrained, logical and well-supported. The essayist seeks to stimulate thought and persuade the reader to agree or at least consider a point of view.

Cynthia Ozick, in "Portrait of the Essay as a Warm Body" (*Atlantic Monthly* Sept. 1998), describes a "genuine" essay as a "fireside [chat], not a conflagration or a safari." Ozick says these essays have power, derived from an alluring use of language. She explains, "I may not be persuaded by Emersonianism as an ideology, but Emerson—his voice, his language, his music—persuades me."

HOW DO ESSAYS DIFFER FROM SHORT STORIES?

Like fictional works, essays often contain figurative language and symbolism. Sometimes these devices are so cleverly used that the essay may seem like a short story. So how can you distinguish the two? First, check to see how the piece is categorized. In a magazine or book, turn to the table of contents or introduction. Consider that essays tend to be self-expressive and idea-centered. They often express an opinion about a significant topic. Stories, however, have a theme, which is invariably implicit. Rarely is there a direct attempt to share an opinion, as in an essay.

Point of View and Voice in an Essay

The perspective of the writer usually permeates an essay, although other viewpoints may be present. The way the topic is viewed affects the voice you hear from the printed page. This written voice may sound informal or formal, humble or arrogant, friendly or cantankerous, cheerful or cranky—just as the human voice reflects a range of emotion. Once in a great while, an essayist will assume a *persona*, a fictitious narrator, to tell a story. To determine how the words should be taken, seriously or in jest, you need to listen carefully to the tone of the written voice.

In "A Ride through Spain," a descriptive essay by Truman Capote, the reader hears a light, conversational voice like that of a friend. Capote writes from the point of view of a passenger on the train. His written voice reveals enjoyment of the experience. The opening and ending of this informal essay appear here:

A Ride through Spain

Certainly the train was old. The seats sagged like the jowls of a bulldog, windows were out and strips of adhesive held together those that were left; in the corridor a prowling cat appeared to be hunting mice, and it was not unreasonable to assume his search would be rewarded.

Slowly, as though the engine were harnessed to elderly coolies, we crept out of Granada. The southern sky was as white and burning as a desert; there was one cloud, and it drifted like a traveling oasis. . . .

It was like a party, and we all drifted back to the train as though each of us wished to be the last to leave. The old man, with my shirt like a grand turban on his head, was put into a first-class carriage. . . .

The train moved away so slowly butterflies blew in and out the windows.

Figurative Language in an Essay

Comparisons in the forms of metaphor, simile, and analogy are often used in essays and other nonfiction writing. In the excerpt from "A Ride through Spain,"

Capote uses concrete images and figurative language, which enable the reader to share the train ride vicariously. Frequent similes ("sagged like the jowls of a bulldog") and other images enable the reader to visualize the trip and to sense the camaraderie of fellow travelers.

Assonance and other devices of sound contribute to the imagery and movement. An example of assonance appears in the last sentence. Here the sounds of the words reflect the movement of the train: the long *o* in *so* and *slowly* slows the rate of speech as do the three syllables of *butterflies* and the phrase *in and out the windows*. In fact, the language is rather like that of a lyric poem.

See chapter 23.

Satire and Irony in an Essay

Essays are usually nonfiction. They often appear in op-ed columns, meditations, memoirs, diaries, journals, and letters. But some essays are fiction. They may appear in such forms as fables, parodies, satire, or others. For example, in 1729 after three years of drought and poor crops, Jonathan Swift wrote a satire entitled "A Modest Proposal." The essay raised quite a stir because many people took it seriously. The offending segment follows:

> I have been assured by a very knowing American of my acquaintance in London, that a young healthy child well nursed is at a year old a most delicious, nourishing, and wholesome food, whether stewed, roasted, baked, or boiled; and I make no doubt that it will equally serve in a fricassee or a ragout.

Although the general populace did not understand Swift's bitter irony, "A Modest Proposal" became famous. It is still widely read today as a classic example of satire.

CHECKLIST   ANALYZING POINT OF VIEW AND VOICE

1. Whose perspective is presented?

2. How would you describe the sound of the written voice?

3. How is the subject treated? Seriously? Sympathetically? Ironically? With sly ridicule? How?

4. Does the voice seem overly biased? Reasonably objective? How so?

5. How did you react to the way the topic was treated?

CRITICAL READING AND WRITING

In college classes you may be asked to respond to an essay, short story, or other piece with a "summary," a "paper of reaction," or a "critique." A summary is the simplest response, merely showing that you understand the main ideas and the connections between the ideas. A paper of reaction and a critique require not only summary but also analysis, commentary, and possibly evaluation.

TASKS IN RESPONDING TO READINGS

- **Summarize:** *To condense, giving only the chief points in your own words.* The purpose of a summary is to set forth the main ideas and explain relationships between ideas. Usually, a summary is 25 to 50 percent as long as the original (chapter R-3).

- **Paraphrase:** *To restate , in your own words, sentence by sentence.* The purpose of paraphrasing is to clarify, yet not lose the gist or the context. Use only when needed. Paraphrasing is time consuming; it can cause wordiness (chapter R-3).

- **Quote:** *To copy someone's work and to give credit to the author.* That requires quotation marks and source identification (chapter R-3).

- **Analyze:** *To examine the parts of a whole.* Analysis goes beyond a summary. You may be asked to look closely at the structure and style, including figurative language. The purpose is to explain how the author achieves the effect/result.

- **Comment:** *To explain, illustrate, or remark.* May contain an opinion.

- **Evaluate:** *To rate, appraise, or judge.* The purpose is to attach a reasonable opinion of value or worth.

Evaluating What You Read

Emotion can color the perceptions of a writer as well as a reader. In some descriptive, expressive, or entertaining essays, generous emotion may be appropriate. In an argument, however, emotion should be restrained so that the tone is reasonable and convincing. The critical reader's task is to spot any bias, illogic, or inaccuracy. This task requires knowledge, objectivity, and awareness of common fallacies and methods of propaganda. Responding to an argument requires the reader to analyze the line of reasoning and evaluate the quality of the evidence. In other words, you read critically and decide whether or not the argument is adequately supported and convincing.

CHECKLIST   **RESPONDING TO AN ARGUMENT**

1. Does the writer give the opposing belief a fair hearing? Or is the opposing view distorted?

2. Is the argument well-organized and clear?

3. Is the argument complete? Have all objections been answered?

4. Does the writer present enough support to refute the opposition's points?

See chapter 19 on argument.

5. Does the conclusion summarize the thrust of the argument?

Critical reading requires you not only to examine and weigh ideas but also to consider their implications. You consider cause and effect, as well as relationships between ideas. With a skeptical eye, you contemplate the writer's analysis, interpretation, or argument—while waiting to form your own opinion. To be fair to the author, you hold off making a judgment until all evidence has been carefully reviewed. With an open mind, you scrutinize inferences, data, results of studies, claims, reasons, examples, or whatever the author offers for support.

A Strategy for Critical Reading and Prewriting

Critical reading can be divided into three stages: prereading, rereading, and prewriting. Throughout this procedure, you will be trying to gauge the *reliability* of any quoted sources, to judge whether or not you can believe everything the author presents.

Stage 1: Prereading A good place to start is with a brief background of the author. A synopsis of an author's background can give you a sense of the culture and era that influenced the essay, as well as personal information about the author.

- **Read a biographical sketch.** Background material may appear in a preface, introduction, or epilogue. Encyclopedias also contain biographical sketches of well-known authors. Or type the name into a good search engine, such as Google. Examine the writer's credentials. Is he or she an authority in the field? What else has the author written?

- **Look for the date of the essay.** A biographical sketch may yield the year an essay was written. Some essays may refer to events, which can help to determine the year. Then ask yourself whether or not the message is timely or dated. Some essays, regardless of age, remain timeless and *universal*. They continue to have relevance down through the centuries. Others soon become outdated.

- **Read the essay quickly.** To gain an overview and impression, preview the piece. A quick reading can improve your comprehension and retention during the second reading.

Stage 2: Rereading Take your time so that you can read every word. The purpose of rereading is to examine the ideas and support the author presents.

- **Consider the title and other clues.** Essay titles often identify the topic and suggest an attitude or point of view. Sometimes a title is deliberately misleading. Watch for clues that point to double meanings or layers of meaning. As you read the body of an essay, think how it fits with the title.

- **Look for the thesis.** If the thesis is elusive, look at the first and last paragraphs. Once in a while, a thesis is unstated and implied—with just a hint in the title or elsewhere.

- **Note any headings, subheadings, or italicized phrases.** These spots contain ideas the author wishes to call attention to. Also watch for repetition. Are any names repeated or ideas echoed?

- **Watch for the unusual.** If you find an odd description or an apparent meandering, ask yourself how this relates to the main idea. An analogy or some other bit of symbolism may be hiding there.

- **Consider point of view and tone.** Try to view the subject through the author's eyes. Read the entire piece before making a judgment. Consider how the writer's voice sounds. Does it seem serious, joking, or ironic? What values underlie the piece? For example, how does the author regard responsibility? Sanctity of human life? Other universal concerns?

www.mhhe.com/dietsch

For electronic resources on prewriting, check out: Writing>Prewriting

Stage 3: Prewriting   Prewriting will help you to question and clarify ideas. You can make prewriting notes in the margins or on a note pad or laptop computer as you read. Later you can use these notes to start your draft.

- **Underline.** Mark the thesis, key points, and any related clues. Then ask yourself, "What is this essay about?" Keep in mind that the first idea may merely introduce the topic. The main idea may come later.

- **Star any definitions or copy them.** Circle unfamiliar words and look them up. These notes will help you to understand and link details in the text.

- **Question.** Place a question mark beside any information that omits significant details or raises doubt. Write out brief questions. Then watch to see if the author answers your questions.

- **Watch for sources.** Does the author provide sources of information cited? If the essay cites research, ask questions: "Who did the study? When? Was the sample representative? Has anything been pulled out of context?"

- **Look for the premise of an argument.** Where is the starting point or basis of the discussion? On what vital point does the argument hinge? For example, the *premise* of an animal rights proposal might be the belief that animals have a right to enjoy their lives. From this premise, the proponents might argue that animals should not be eaten. But opponents might argue that this view conflicts with the traditional belief that humans should rule over animals and eat certain ones. If opposing factions cannot agree on a premise, they will be unable to convince the other side.

- **Write a synopsis or make an outline.** In your own words, summarize the content of the essay in a paragraph or two. Scan each topic sentence so that all key ideas are included. Or if you prefer, make a brief outline. Either technique will help to clarify your understanding.

- **Restate the thesis.** Ask yourself, "What is the author's thesis?" Try to reduce the main point of the essay to one or two sentences. This restatement should clarify the focus.
- **Check out new or doubtful ideas further.** If a reading topic is unfamiliar, find out what other authors have written about it. A quick search of periodicals in the library or on the Internet will usually yield information. If a claim differs from the general thinking of experts in the field, does the writer provide sufficient support to be convincing?

Keeping a Writer's Journal

As you read in your classes, you might keep a journal of ideas for future writing. When you find a topic that interests you, jot it down along with your thoughts. Note writing strategies that you particularly like. When two writers offer different perspectives on the same subject, comment. Think about how the ideas connect. Combining ideas logically is synthesis, a critical thinking skill.

Copy any quotations you might use in future writings and enclose them in quotation marks. Check carefully to see that all words and punctuation are accurate. Note the sources and page numbers. (See page 158 to avoid plagiarism.)

WRITING A PAPER OF REACTION OR ESSAY EXAM ANSWERS

In your college courses, you may be asked to write short reaction papers and exam answers that *respond to ideas* in essays, short stories, histories, or other readings. Your task then is to analyze the reading and contribute an *informed opinion.* The opinion should be based on facts and reasons. Any emotion should be controlled and appropriate. A written reaction is expected to be logical, clear, and complete.

A paper of reaction rarely requires further research. Usually, you are expected to study only one reading and draw from your own experience. If you do consult outside sources, however, proper documentation is always required. For help with using sources, see chapters R-3 and R-4.

> www.mhhe.com/dietsch
>
> For a wealth of electronic writing resources, go to: Writing

Two Types of Reactions

A reaction paper or an essay exam answer requires a thoughtful response to the writer's ideas. The purpose is to present a point of view and persuade the audience that the response is sound and reasonable. In one or two pages, you either comment or argue a point.

A Commentary   A reaction may be a *commentary* that considers *how* the reading presents the main idea. For example, you might discuss the originality of the piece, insights of the author, and the humor, if any; then give your response. On weightier matters, you consider the facts and possible consequences or implications of the main idea. Does the idea have relevance for you personally or for your field of study?

When appropriate, you might allude to historical figures or literary characters or cite quotations. You might compare or contrast, discuss cause and effect, give real-life examples, or organize in any way that is effective. There is no single way to organize a reaction.

An Argument   A reaction is often an argument that examines, interprets, evaluates, and states an opinion. To be effective, an argument requires specific facts and reasons to defend and support a stand on an issue. Although a reaction paper or an exam answer may not be a full-fledged argument, an element of persuasion is inherent in many assignments. When an assignment is not explained, you may have to interpret it, as in the following example:

- React to the ethical questions William Raspberry raises in "The Handicap of Definition." *Here you are to consider questions of responsibility and of right and wrong. Then comment and supply reasons for your opinion.*

Other assignments clearly call for an argument. They require you to take a position, defend it, and provide logical reasons:

- React to "The War on Wal-Mart." *Do you agree or disagree with Malanga's thesis? Why?*

Those and similar questions are the sort to consider in your reaction paper. When you disagree, you can summarize the main points of the opposing view. Then you might cite an example from the essay, dispute it, and present support for your view.

Prewriting and Outlining

To expand your prewriting notes, look at your questions in the margins. Did the author answer them? If not, you might raise them in your draft. Did any of the author's statements seem doubtful or inconsistent? Were you impressed by any descriptions or insights? Can you think of further comments to make? Asking yourself more questions will help you to expand your prewriting notes and start drafting.

QUESTIONS FOR PREWRITING

1. What is the main point of the essay?
2. Is the support convincing? Why or why not?
3. Has the writer omitted any significant facts? Are there implications or possible side effects that should be discussed?
4. What is especially interesting or challenging?
5. Is there any aspect I particularly like or dislike?
6. How does the author's voice sound?
7. How do I feel about the values underlying the essay? Why?
8. Might the ideas in the essay be applied to my field of study?

To make your draft go quickly, expand your working outline. If you haven't started an outline yet, just copy your thesis at the top of a clean sheet. Underneath, list your main points. Leave spaces between the points to add subpoints later. If a definition is required, write it on the outline. This framework will establish the direction of the paper. The outline below was drafted in reaction to a short story for a literature class paper.

Drafting

There is no one way to start a draft, but it helps to know where you are going. Look over your working outline. Will you be writing a commentary, argument, or combination? What order is indicated? Revise your outline so that it clearly reflects a suitable order.

www.mhhe.com/dietsch
You can find advice online regarding drafting at:
Writing>Drafting and Revising

Writing a Commentary   To begin a commentary, you can identify the author and title of the work, then add a statement about the piece. (*Tip:* In your prewriting notes, find the one-sentence summary of the author's main point.) When you agree with an author, you might comment on a significant point or statement, the research, or an example. Or you might discuss the implications for you and your future career.

Consult your working outline and prewriting notes for details and examples to develop your paper. The ending of a reaction paper can be brief, just a few well-stated sentences that give a sense of closure.

Question: Define *poetic justice* and explain how it functions in the "The Lady and the Tiger." What outcome would you predict?* Why? [In this short story by Frank Stockton, the main character has a chance to live and marry a lovely woman if he opens the right door. Behind one of the three doors lurks a tiger.]

WORKING OUTLINE:

Definition **1.** Poetic justice—goodness is rewarded and evil is punished, often ironically.

Thesis **2.** I think the tiger will come out the opened door.

Reasons **3.** Why do I think so?
   a. Hints about "poetic justice." (Give examples)
   b. You can't believe the king—or his daughter? (Example)
   c. The princess is "semi-barbaric." (Explain)
   d. Nothing indicates she loves him so much she'll give him to another woman. She is jealous. (Give example)

Ending **4.** Allude to "Nor hell a fury like a woman scorned." William Congreve, *The Mourning Bride* (1697) [Give the original source, regardless of where you find the line.]

*The word *predict* implies a reaction. The question calls for an opinion that will provide a logical outcome to the story.

WORKING OUTLINE FOR A PAPER OF REACTION

Planning an Argument   If you disagree with an author, then you need to construct a reasonable argument and provide adequate support. Before plunging into the fray, list pros and cons on your outline. In the first paragraph, identify the author and title and summarize the issue or controversy. The tone of this description should be neutral. Next, briefly summarize the author's position, taking care to be fair. After that, give your rebuttal, answering the main points of the other side. Cite facts and other logical support. Use a summary ending, restating your thesis. (See chapter 19.)

Revision and Editing

www.mhhe.com/dietsch

For a wealth of revision and editing resources, check out:

Editing

Before you revise and edit a paper of reaction, it is often helpful to reread the directions for the assignment. Then as you revise, check to see if have fulfilled every one of them. Examine the organization, development, and logic of your paper. Would any sentence be more effective if moved elsewhere? Does more need to be said at any point? Is there needless repetition? Are the words clear?

Read your paper aloud to hear how your written voice sounds. Is the tone consistent with your purpose? Do you sound objective and knowledgeable? Can you find a better way to express an idea? Use a dictionary and a thesaurus to help you refine words so that you say what you intend in a suitable tone.

Edit each sentence with care. Even though you may have run a computer check for spelling, grammar, or punctuation, *proofread your paper carefully.* Software will not pick up all errors, and some packages may disagree with the rules your instructor advocates. Don't guess about spelling corrections—take a few seconds to open an up-to-date dictionary and check.

CHECKLIST   **REVISING A REACTION PAPER**

1. Is the thesis clear?

2. Is the order clear and logical?

3. Do I go beyond a summary and actually contribute to the discussion? Does my opinion sound informed?

4. If I am disagreeing, have I responded to all the writer's points?

5. Is my defense well supported?

6. Are facts correctly stated?

7. Are inferences logical and identifiable?

8. If there are allusions to other writers' works, have I given credit? If I consulted outside sources, are they properly documented?

9. Is my written voice appropriate?

10. Is there anything else that should be said?

ANNOTATED STUDENT REACTION PAPER

A college philosophy class was assigned a short paper of reaction with topics drawn from readings discussed in the classroom. One of the topics was to react to the philosophy of Martin Buber and to give practical applications. Scott Allen discusses the implication of Buber's beliefs for classroom teachers. He presents impressions, draws comparisons, and points out applications.

A Reaction to Martin Buber's Philosophy

Summary/Comparison

Source identified

    Martin Buber's philosophy, as set forth in *Between Man and Man,* seems similar to Plato's in many respects. Although the philosophers disagree about the source of goodness, they both believe that goodness is an absolute, quite distinct from people. They believe we strive to attain goodness by making wise choices. Buber's philosophy has important applications for teachers.

    Buber feels that the formal teaching of values is worthless. Nonetheless, he believes that the teacher presents a selection from the real world and acts as a model to the pupil (indirect teaching). Buber develops the concept of "inclusiveness," which is the complete realization of the submissive person (i.e., the student).

    To develop the mental powers to make good choices, Plato suggests the [direct] study of mathematics, philosophy, and other disciplines. Plato attempts to outline an ideal society where everyone can live peacefully and develop to the fullest capacity.

Reaction and Implications

Comments

    In the educational situation, this inclusiveness means that educators must beware of the dangers of such a relationship. They must refrain from arbitrariness and must exercise responsibility in interpreting the real world to the pupil. I agree: Teachers should consider the needs and rights of their pupils and try to respond in a way that will benefit them. This goal requires not only responsibility in the selection of classroom material but also fairness in grading, settling disputes, and other situations which arise. I concur with Buber's theory about the teaching of values: values are caught, not taught. A teacher should be of good character and should act as a role model for students.

Quotation

    How can educators accomplish this responsibility? Buber says they can do it by "conscious and willed selection." In other words, educators should know *Restatement* what they want to achieve and select the proper means to achieve it. They should examine their basic principles and understand what is happening—not merely what they think they are doing. They must be objective as well as responsible.

Quotation

    Finally, Buber believes that "Life lived in freedom is personal responsibility or it is a pathetic farce" ("Education," sec. 3). Rousseau, in a similar vein, says that pupils are obliged to develop their intellectual powers to learn a vocation and provide for themselves. Like Buber, Rousseau is greatly concerned about

Summary

the educator's responsibility of keeping evil away from pupils. This idea of personal responsibility involves intellectual self-discipline as well as physical self-discipline, but it helps us to gain self-respect and stature in the eyes of others. It also helps us to find a purpose beyond ourselves—and perhaps that is what life is really all about.

Conclusion

Comment

In short, although Buber's traditional Judeo-Christian philosophy will not appeal to Ayn Rand fans or existentialists with leanings toward Nietzsche or Sartre, I believe it provides an excellent set of principles for undergirding education.

WRITING A CRITIQUE

In some college classes you may be asked to write a *critique*. That term refers to a critical discussion, an opinion of a work, perhaps a film, play, essay, or memoir. You may be asked to evaluate specific aspects or to simply react to the work. Critiques are usually short, just one or two pages, depending on the assignment. This kind of writing provides an introduction to research writing, which also requires critical reading and evaluation.

Steps in Writing a Critique

Writing a critique is not difficult if you like the work. Just be careful that you don't overdo the praise. If you did not like the work, then you'll need more thought to weigh your words and decide how to phrase them appropriately. To start prewriting, list what you liked and then list what you disliked. Then jot down reasons and examples. To draft a critique, the following procedure is helpful:

1. Identify the title of the work and the author.
2. Specify the type of work, whether it is an essay, memoir, biography, or other genre.
3. Summarize the main ideas in your own words. Vary your sentence structure from the original. (See tips for summaries in chapter R-3.)
4. Include a few direct quotations to convey the flavor of the work. Enclose these word-for-word citations with quotation marks.
5. Describe a few interesting examples in your own words. If needed, include the author's exact phrasing, enclosed in quotation marks.
6. Evaluate the quality of the information, especially if it is an argument. Does it seem reliable, factual, and reasonable? Do you agree or disagree? (For help, see chapters 16 and 19.)
7. Give your opinion or estimate of the work. Be honest, but also be fair.

A Critique of *Teacher Man*

As you read the critique below, watch for words that indicate opinion. Where do you hear the first hint of how the writer feels about the book? Does the writer like it, dislike it, or have mixed feelings? Does the appraisal sound fair?

Teacher Man

If you open *Teacher Man*, a memoir by Frank McCourt, and read a few pages, you'll likely be lured on by the friendly voice of an Irishman who begins by poking fun at himself. Formerly, he labored on the wharf, but now he's teaching at an intercity school. As his life story unfolds, he drops the amused facade and shares dark secrets from his "miserable" past, as he apparently does with strangers at a pub, where he swigs pint after pint. This is not a pretty tale. It is the sad story of a soul who has rejected God early in life and gone on alone, finding occasional solace in the beds of strange women. So why should the reader continue reading?

Blended in this painfully honest tale are some compelling moments when McCourt hits on novel ways to engage his streetwise students. For example, they are so good at writing fake excuses from home that he asks them to write excuses from Adam or Eve to God. Surprised and delighted, they take up their pens to write original and thoughtful essays. The principal walks into the classroom during the session and is impressed.

Yet "Teacher Man," as they call him, is seldom able to keep order or teach the fundamentals of English. He doesn't know the parts of speech and "nothing about diagramming" a sentence. Instead, he tells stories of his "miserable childhood" to keep the students quiet. The highlights of the book are the many vignettes of students: Augie, the class nuisance, whose muscular father invades the classroom, "lifts Augie into the air, carries him over to the wall, bangs him, repeatedly, against the wall." No wonder this teacher never reported another student's misbehavior and gave passing grades to all who attended class.

Sylvia, a black student who wants to be a doctor, endures jeers of "Hey, Doc, you scrape yourself an' you find that honky skin?" Bob, who never brings a pencil or paper and who says that reading the textbook does "not fit into his plans," entertains the class. And there is Ken, a Korean boy who "hated his father" and whose mother later wrote a letter to him at Stanford, saying "unless he had straight A's in his courses, he was not to come home at Christmas." To these and other emotionally needy students, "Teacher Man" reaches out, even years later when they meet. That seems to be the chief redeeming aspect of his life.

After nineteen years of marriage, McCourt's wife divorces him. He does not blame her but regrets that he seldom sees his eight-year-old daughter. Although he has few friends, he somehow manages to interview well and finally lands a teaching position at a prestigious high school. After thirty years of teaching at several schools, he retires—still lonely—to the solitary life of a writer. Perhaps the saddest aspect of all is that McCourt, once a devout Catholic, seems to have learned so little from his mistakes. Let's hope he has gained satisfaction from writing this haunting book.

FOR YOUR REFERENCE
Essays in the Reader

PRACTICE

ONE-MINUTE REACTIONS

Directions: Select one of the following topics or another and write until your instructor tells you to stop.

1. Are you satisfied or dissatisfied with your state's highways? Why?
2. What is the most annoying problem in your neighborhood or city?
3. What is your favorite make of automobile? Why?
4. How would you describe the president? Why?
5. Did you ever get into mischief in school? How did you react?

SUMMARY

Directions: Write a short summary of "Refuse to Live in Fear," by Diana Bletter, located on page 608 in the Reader. Restate the reading in your own words and condense by at least 50 percent. Include the main ideas, a quotation, and a one-sentence paraphrase. You may consult a thesaurus and "Writing a Summary," chapter R-3. Revise your work carefully, using this checklist:

1. Are the title of the reading and the author stated in the first sentence?
2. Are all specific major words restated except those copied in the quotation?
3. Is the sentence structure varied so that it is not repetitive of the original?
4. Is the quotation significant? Is it enclosed by quotation marks?
5. Is the paraphrase significant? Does it avoid plagiarism?

TEN IDEAS FOR REACTION PAPERS

All of the essays mentioned below are located in the Reader. Or you may prefer to react to another essay of your choice.

1   Respond to "Road Rage." Have you ever experienced a similar incident? What did you do?

2   Respond to "Mother Tongue," by Amy Tan. Summarize her conclusions. Do you think her experience was unique, or does it have widespread implications? Why?

3   In "The Handicap of Definition," William Raspberry discusses the effects of stereotypes on black children. Do you agree or disagree with his thesis that we define our success by our beliefs and goals? Why?

4 React to "Why Marriages Fail," by Ann Roiphe. Can you cite any other reasons that marriages fail? Can you expand on Roiphe's points?

5 React to Jean Huston's "The Art of Acknowledgment." Have you ever had a similar experience? How did you cope?

6 React to "The Rebirth of Civility?" by Daniel Henninger.

7 Read the three essays on English as an official language and then react. What is your opinion and why?

8 React to "Fun Ethic vs. Work Ethic," by Robert J. Samuelson. Do you agree or disagree with his thesis?

9 Describe your reaction to a hardship as a child. Has your perception changed over the years? If so, how?

10 Select any other essay you wish and react to it.

CHAPTER 22

Reading and Responding to Short Stories, Novels, and Plays

> Genuine literature informs while it entertains. It manages to be both clear and profound.
>
> —"Author's Note,"
> *The Collected Stories
> of Isaac Bashevis Singer*

The written word can be more alluring than a video or a movie screen. Readers enter a virtual world, created on the screen of the mind. There we explore new ideas and sensations, meet intriguing characters, and participate in an exciting plot vicariously. By turning the pages, we experience the unfamiliar and untried without facing the risks of reality. We can laugh at the foolishness and smile at the cleverness of human behavior and thought.

Through literature we can learn more about our universe and its inevitable laws of cause and effect. We can view the results of personal decisions, wise or unwise, that change lives. From characters who undergo tremendous hardship and succeed, we can take courage. We may be inspired to overcome obstacles in our own lives and expend the effort to succeed.

Literature can help us to distinguish the insignificant from the significant—to gain a truer perspective of reality and insight into our own values. By sharing moments of human experience through literature, we are prompted to reflect on the shape and direction of our own lives. With thought and deliberation, we are better prepared to make wise decisions.

THE HUMAN CONDITION

Literature encourages us to think and consider concerns that arise from the *human condition,* which all people experience. Regardless of our culture, race, or creed, we share universal concerns: We wonder about the purpose of life and other vital questions:

- What is happiness?
- What responsibilities do we have for each other? For animals? For planet earth?
- What causes conflict between people who love each other?
- Should I risk danger to protect someone else's life?
- What is ethical? What is moral?

THE ROLE OF THE READER

Many people assume a literary work has a single meaning or interpretation. The truth is that there is no one right answer about what a work means. Often a piece of literature is subtle, containing meanings of which even the author is unaware. Meaning is not limited to the text of a work; the reader plays an active role. As we read, we view ideas through our own window of experience—interpreting, inferring, evaluating—creating meaning. Our view is colored by our individual perception of the world, the topic, the treatment of the text, and the voice of the narrator.

Although readers create meaning to some extent, this is not an invitation to pull a passage out of context and distort it. To be valid, an interpretation must be supported by evidence and logical reasoning. This chapter explains an analytical approach that is applicable to short stories, novels, and plays.

How Do Short Stories Differ from Novels?

Time in a short story is compressed, often limited to a week or a day or less. Since short stories have just a few pages for the action to unfold, every word must count. Every detail is there for a reason. Descriptions and images are pared to the essential, and there are few characters.

Sometimes the meaning is puzzling upon a first reading. Often the meaning is implicit, to be derived by the reader, who examines events, symbols, phrasing, and dialogue. The reader must be alert for clues cleverly concealed throughout the plot. Plain, seemingly ordinary little stories are often not ordinary at all; they contain clues that reveal surprising intensity and depth. Although similar clues exist in novels, the clues are seldom so important to the meaning as in the short story.

What Are the Major Characteristics of Novels?

A novel generally covers a much longer period than a short story or play. Novels of epic proportions may chronicle the life of the main character and the lives of descendants over several generations. Divided into chapters, novels usually have complex plots and subplots with several characters. The main characters tend to be well developed; the reader learns of their quirks and peers into their personal lives. The action may take place in various locales, often far-flung. Yet the skillful author weaves all the elements together into a compelling tale that has unity and coherence.

The opening of a novel may contain lengthy description and proceed at a slower pace than that of a short story or a play, where the action begins at once. The leisurely pace of some novels is due to the narrator's revelations about characters and a smaller percentage of dialogue. Once the conflict is introduced and the main character is beset with a problem, decision, or moral dilemma, the pace of a novel picks up. In the latter half, conflict builds to a climax, and the situation is usually resolved.

How Does Reading a Play Differ from Reading a Novel?

Plays are meant to be seen and heard. When you read a play, you are more or less on your own. Reading a play is rather like using a flashlight to view the action instead of watching it performed on a well-lit stage. You can't see the expressions on the faces of the characters or hear the intonations in their voices. In a novel there is a narrator who usually drops hints or explains from time to time. In a play there is usually no narrator.

Plays are often divided into one to three acts, which are divided into scenes. An introduction may precede the first act. Never skip this opportunity to preview the background, the plot, or other aspects. If the author is well known, you can consult an encyclopedia or look for a biography or a review of the play. Otherwise, you are handed only a list of characters before the action begins.

Scenes may shift abruptly with only a note such as "Venice. A street." Entrances, exits, and other sparse notes appear at intervals in parentheses. As you read, you are forced to rely chiefly on the words of the characters, which may be deceptive. A character may not tell the truth, or the words of the play may be from a different era. Shakespeare, for example, often uses common words, but they may have different meanings and connotations than do the same words today. Therefore, the reader is often obliged to interrupt the passage and consult a footnote to understand.

At times it is helpful to read puzzling bits of dialogue aloud and try to imagine the action in your mind's eye. What seems to be happening? Watch for subtleties and layers of meaning. Consider the craftsmanship of the play. Three important features to keep in mind are—

- **Sequencing of scenes.** How do scenes vary? For example, comedy may slow the pace in one scene, and a battle may rage in the next, as in *Henry IV.*

- **Character development.** What motivates the characters? Power? Greed? Love? What? Do they change? How?

- **Unveiling of the theme.** When does the theme become apparent? What is implied about the human condition? How would you state the theme?

Genre	Length	Plot	Span	Characters	Narrator
1. *Short story*	1–40 pp.	compact	1 day– a week	few	yes
2. *Novel*	150– 850 pp.	complex	may be years	many	yes
3. *Play*	2–3 hours (to view)	varies	1 day– a month	varies	rarely

DIFFERENCES IN THREE GENRES

ELEMENTS OF LITERATURE

Despite obvious differences, short stories, novels, and plays have much in common. All three genres of literature usually consider some facet of the human condition. All have unity—a central idea and a pattern of development. And all can be analyzed according to seven basic elements: point of view, setting, plot, characters, symbolism, irony, and theme.

Point of View

The outlook or *point of view* from which a work is told influences the effect of the story, novel, or play. Point of view is revealed through the narrator's voice or the voices of the characters. That means that the narrator's voice is *not* the voice of the author. The narrator may be one of the characters or someone outside the work. When the story is presented through the eyes of *a* character, you gain an *inside* view. You have access to one person's thoughts and observations. F. Scott Fitzgerald's *The Great Gatsby* opens with the narrator reminiscing in first person (italicized):

In *my* younger and more vulnerable years *my* father gave *me* some advice that *I've* been turning over in *my* mind ever since.

"Whenever you feel like criticizing any one," he told *me,* "just remember that all the people in this world haven't had the advantages that you've had."

He didn't say any more, but *we've* always been unusually communicative in a reserved way, and *I* understood that he meant a great deal more than that. In consequence, *I'm* inclined to reserve all judgments, a habit that has opened up many curious natures to *me* and also made *me* the victim of not a few veteran bores.

See page H-3 for case of pronouns.

Note that a first-person narrator observes or participates in the action. A third-person narrator, however, is outside the action. Usually, a third-person narrator enters the mind of just one character. But a third-person narrator with *limited omniscience* enters the minds of several characters. Sometimes a third-person narrator is *omniscient,* or all-knowing. You might think of an omniscient narrator as standing on a hill, looking down into the lives and minds of the characters, seeing everything that goes on.

Gauging the accuracy and truthfulness of a narrator, particularly one who is a character, is not always simple. Like human beings, characters may misjudge, understate, overstate, or deceive.

Setting

The time, place, atmosphere, weather, and culture make up the *setting.* Included in setting are the objects and articles the characters have and use. Symbolism is often intermingled with setting to create a mood. For example, Thomas Hardy's novels take place on wild and stormy moors, which set the scene for passion and outbursts of temper. Savvy readers know that the storms are omens of stormy relationships or tragic events.

As you read, note the setting of each action and the implications. Consider the area, time of year, and weather, all of which create a mood. What objects are present? What family, social, political, or religious obligations or conditions exist? How do they influence the plot and characters?

Plot

The series of actions and events that occur in a narrative make up the *plot.* Broadly defined, plot includes not only physical action but also words and thoughts. Conflicts arise not only from circumstance but also from human motivation. The main character may face an opponent or an impediment to a goal. The *conflict* may involve another individual, a natural force, an animal, or fate. Or the character may experience an *internal conflict* over ethical or moral issues.

Plots may move straight ahead, twist and turn, or pause for a *flashback* to a scene that happened before the story opened. Suspense increases as the turmoil caused by the conflict rises to a *climax,* the high point of the action. The ending may reveal a discovery or a reversal in the main character's fate, resulting in misfortune or success. Or the ending may resolve a problem between two enemies, imply a theme, or foreshadow a future event.

Sometimes plots are structured as letters, diaries, or other "found" writings. In Daniel Keyes's *Flowers for Algernon*, the main character, a mentally handicapped man named Charley, is asked by his doctor to prepare progress reports during the course of an experimental treatment. Early entries begin on a rudimentary level in Charley's diary:

progris riport 2—martch 6

Dr. Strauss says I shud rite down what I think and evrey thing that happins to me from now on. I dont know why but he says its importint so they will see if they will use me. I hope they use me. Miss Kinnian says maybe they can make me smart. I want to be smart. My name is Charlie Gordon. I am 37 years old and 2 weeks ago was my birthday. I have nuthing more to rite now so I will close for today.

This early entry reveals not only Charley's low level of understanding and education but also his desire to learn. Although Charley is unable to explain what is happening, the phrase "use me" suggests to the alert reader that Dr. Strauss's purpose may not be in Charley's best interest. After surgery and intensive training, Charley's intelligence and learning escalate—revealed by later diary entries that are longer and more explicit. Toward the end, as Charley deteriorates, the concluding entries parallel his deterioration.

Foreshadowing   When authors use *foreshadowing* in a plot, they scatter clues that hint of events to come. In *Flowers for Algernon*, Algernon the mouse and Charley have the same operation. When Algernon's condition worsens, the alert reader suspects that Charley will suffer the same fate. The drastic changes in Algernon foreshadow the plot's irrevocable conclusion.

Characters

To seem realistic, characters are endowed with certain qualities and quirks. They may be portrayed as primarily good or evil, weak or strong, serious or fun-loving. Major characters are usually revealed indirectly through behavior whereas minor characters tend to be revealed directly through explanation. *Round characters* change and mature; they learn from events and circumstances. *Flat characters,* usually minor characters, do not change or grow. They may lack insight, remaining unaware and insensitive.

As you read, assess the characters. Do they seem true to life or stereotypic? Real people exhibit a blend of many traits. Do the characters act predictably or inconsistently? Are inconsistent acts explainable through motivation? Not every character needs to be well developed, but all need to have a reason for their existence.

Symbolism

A *symbol* may be a name, person, place, object, action, or situation that represents something else. In other words, a symbol has a significant meaning beyond the literal meaning. For example, if a character named Cain lives in the small town of Eden, there is probably an idyllic meaning attached to the locale, and other related clues may appear.

Public symbols are widely known and understood, such as our national flag, various commercial logos, and many religious symbols. Water is universally regarded as a symbol both of purification and of life. A bubbling fountain may represent youth and optimism. A stagnant pond may symbolize contamination or ebbing of life. The condition of water may also symbolize the status of a relationship: Lovers may meet by a placid lake, a river with rapids, or aboard ship on a storm-tossed sea. Or there may be *private symbols,* limited to the one work. When you think something might be a symbol, place a question mark beside it. Or if you understand the symbol, make a note.

Irony

Irony exists when something is inconsistent with what is apparent or believed and what is real. Irony consists of a discrepancy between expectations and reality. Sarcasm is a form of *verbal irony;* a character says one thing but means another. Using *dramatic irony,* a writer reveals to readers something that the characters do not know, which creates suspense. *Situational irony* refers to an event that is contrary to what is expected (often painfully so). The unexpected event may be a wry twist of the plot, as often found in the stories of Edgar Allan Poe or the films of Alfred Hitchcock. Sometimes the villain or central character is faced with an unanticipated and deserved dilemma of his or her own making.

Writers often use irony to suggest human fallibility—vanity, unwise judgment, and other limitations that keep us from recognizing the truth around us. Such susceptibility to error is at its most extreme in *cosmic irony,* or irony of fate. Cosmic irony is prevalent in Greek tragedies and other writings; the gods or destiny seem to control events so as to test and frustrate the protagonist.

Theme

The main idea or message embodied in a work of literature is called the *theme.* Some works have more than one theme. Theme reflects a universal belief about human life or the human condition. Theme may concern good or evil, love or hate, modesty or pride, beliefs or values.

More often than not, theme is implicit. Theme can be implied through a series of events, actions, or dialogue. Theme may be revealed as an observation, insight, doctrine, or general principle by a character or the narrator. For example, a devout character might murmur, "Evil has its own reward," meaning "Evil will be punished, sooner or later." In much modern literature, themes are complex and cannot be reduced to a simple moral or proverb. Theme is the common thread that unifies the other elements of literature; theme establishes order and coherence.

Figurative Language and Literary Devices

A figure of speech has a special meaning and construction that deviates from standard use of the language. *Similes* and *metaphors* are figures of speech that are unusual comparisons. Similes contain *like* or *as;* metaphors do not (for extensive examples, see the index). *Personification,* another common figure of speech, is the giving of human attributes to an object, abstraction, or animal. For example, the animals in George Orwell's *Animal Farm* represent people.

Special effects can be achieved with words by using *onomatopoeia, alliteration,* and *assonance.* These literary devices can emphasize and smooth phrases, as well as enhance the sound of words. All three devices are explained in chapter 23, since they are so often incorporated into poetry (see the analysis of a poem on pages 331–33).

To prepare for a paper in response to a literary work, you might mark the pages as you read, making notes in the margins. Or if you do not own the book, use a pack of file cards or large Post-its. Write a key phrase and page number across the top of the card or Post-it. Insert the note card so that it protrudes from the top of the book. Or stick your Post-it notes on pages as tabs. To start, consider these questions:

1. **Does anything seem *odd?*** If so, note with a question mark.

2. **Does the title contain a clue?** Is there a hint in the title?

3. **Is anything repeated or similar?** Watch for repetition and echoes of ideas. Note relationships and links to the central idea.

4. **Do you notice any symbolism?** Consider the setting and objects mentioned.

5. **What might the names mean?** Look up the origin and meaning of *names* of people, trains, ships, or other objects. Names often tie into the theme. If you can't find a book on names at the library, buy a paperback such as *10,000 Baby Names,* by Bruce Lansky.

6. **What motivates the main character?** What is the character seeking? Wealth? Power? Fame? Love? What? Jot down clues to motivation as you read.

7. **Do you notice any objects or anything else that might act as a symbol?** Look closely at the names of characters and places. Are there any other clues?

8. **Examine the dialogue.** What does it reveal about a character?

9. **Consider point of view.** Who is the narrator? How is the story told?

10. **Consider the ending.** Does it seem satisfactory and complete? How does the ending fit with the title and the opening?

READING AND TAKING NOTES ON A LITERARY WORK

PREPARING AN ANALYSIS OF LITERATURE

When your instructor assigns a paper of analysis, sometimes called a "paper of explication," select a topic that interests you, one that you understand. You can discuss point of view, setting, plot, characterization, symbolism, irony, theme, or a combination. You might compare and contrast two characters in one work, or compare the central characters of two works. Or you might discuss a combination of elements. An analytical paper comments on the form as well as the content of the work. You interpret meaning and estimate the significance of what happens.

To achieve a valid interpretation, look at events, actions, and clues—a chain of evidence upon which to base your thesis. Your discussion of the elements should fit the total context. The best interpretations consider the entire work and offer an explanation of passages that may seem contradictory or inconsistent. You might begin by examining the element(s) you selected as a topic. How does it influence the work? As you write, observe three precautions:

1. **Avoid giving the impression that there is only one valid interpretation of a work.** Shun phrases such as "obviously" and "it is evident that." Use tentative words to leave the interpretation open to other possibilities.

2. **Analyze the work objectively.** Veto any inclination to give harsh criticism or sweet adoration. Be fair.

3. **Don't speculate about an author's intent.** A work may have a significance that the author was unaware of while writing, so don't attempt to mind-read. Instead, discuss the total effect. Describe the impression that is created. Supply reasons and examples.

TENTATIVE WORDS FOR INTERPRETING LITERATURE			
suggests	suggesting	implies
indicates	indicating	signals
possibly	apparently	foreshadows
probably	may	represents
not entirely	seems	appears
hints	connotes	gesture
seems	clue	sign

Writing about Point of View

A narrator may describe the story from inside or outside the action. The following example from a student paper focuses on the perspective of a lonely narrator who is outside the family circle and other groups, looking in. Gradually, the perspective of *The Grass Harp* changes, and the development of the central character, Collin, changes, too.

▶   *The Grass Harp*, by Truman Capote, is a beautifully written and sensitive account of a young boy, Collin, who becomes an orphan at age eleven. Collin goes to live with two aged cousins until he is eighteen. The novella chronicles the changes that occur in his life and the lives of people close to him. Written in first person with Collin as the narrator, the perspective of the book is cleverly done.

Collin is a shy boy who does not make friends easily and who remains on the outer fringes of most groups. He literally stays outside the action, a spectator most of the time. In the Talbo household, he lives with his cousins, Dolly and Verena, and the black maid, Catherine. Collin spends much of his time up in the attic, peering down through a knothole and cracks at the activities going on below. When the story opens, Collin is outside the action not only physically but also emotionally.

Collin is again a spectator when Riley Henderson, whom Collin greatly admires, confesses he is miserable. Riley would have killed himself if it were not for the responsibility of caring for his younger sisters. . . .

When Sister Ida invites the Judge and Dolly to go away with her, Collin feels left out, just as he has many times before; again he is on the outside of a circle, peering in. Again he is a spectator as he peers through a window at Riley, who is now his best friend and who is kissing a girl.

But later there are moments when Collin is accepted and moments when he is able to become an active participant. . . .

To start your prewriting notes on point of view, answer the questions in the checklist below after you complete your reading.

CHECKLIST   QUESTIONS FOR ANALYZING POINT OF VIEW

1.   Who is telling the story?

2.   Is the voice of the narrator consistent, or does it change? If it changes, how?

3.   How reliable is the narrator?

4.   Should the narrator be taken literally? Or is the piece a satire, tall tale, legend, myth, fable, or parable?

5.   Where is the narrator? Inside or outside the action? How does this perspective influence the plot, character, or theme?

Writing about Setting

To write about setting, specify the chief features of the place and time (era). Look for changes and contrasts in setting and wonder about their meaning. For example, if you were writing about *The Old Man and the Sea,* by Ernest Hemingway, you might examine how setting isolates the main character. You could explain how the old man copes with isolation and achieves a qualified success. Although you would also refer to plot, character, and symbolism, the focus would be on setting. Now let's take a look at how Hemingway sets the scene, introduces the main character, and prepares for the dramatic action of the novel all in one paragraph:

He was an old man who fished alone in a skiff in the Gulf Stream, and he had gone eighty-four days now without taking a fish. In the first forty days a boy had been with him. But after forty days without a fish the boy's parents had told him that the man was now definitely and finally *salao*, which is the worst form of unlucky, and the boy had gone at their orders in another boat which caught three good fish the first week. It made the boy sad to see the old man come in each day with his skiff empty and he always went down to help him carry either the coiled lines or the gaff and harpoon and the sail that was furled around the mast. The sail was patched with flour sacks and, furled, it looked like the flag of permanent defeat.

After you have taken notes on setting, you might reread them and write a quick draft, commenting on cause and effect and emphasizing your main idea. This exercise will spur thinking and should yield an overview of your forthcoming paper.

EXAMPLE OF A QUICK DRAFT

▶   Hemingway's *The Old Man and the Sea* begins in a poor fishing village off the Gulf Stream. There superstition influences the thought and behavior of many residents, but not the old man. The belief in *salao,* or bad luck, has isolated him. Because he has had bad luck in fishing, going eighty-four days without a good fish, he is shunned. The old man has even been separated from his former companion, the boy.

Alone on his skiff, the old man sits with his tattered flag and patched sail, which seem to be symbols—the sail "looked like a flag of permanent defeat." Two similarities between the boat and the old man stand out: both are old and both appear dysfunctional. Yet these appearances are deceiving. Despite the isolation and hardships imposed by weather, sea, and sharks, both endure. The old man continues his quest for a huge fish. Determined to succeed at any cost, he will not accept defeat.

Notes:

1. Need to discuss changes in setting at sea and effects on old man and the skiff.

2. Are sharks part of the setting? Not characters; must be setting.

3. Describe condition of the skiff, big fish, and old man when he returns to the harbor.

4. Is anything ironic?

5. What else should be mentioned?

CHECKLIST   QUESTIONS FOR ANALYZING SETTING

1. What in the setting is particularly significant? Features of the landscape? Time of year? Weather? What?

2. Do any parts of the setting seem to be symbolic?

3. How does setting contribute to the tone or mood?

4. Does the setting change? How does this influence the plot and the characters?

5. Do you notice any foreshadowing?

Writing about Plot

An analysis of plot is usually combined with one or more of the other elements of literature. The examples that follow are from an analysis of a novel. The student writer discusses plot, character, and theme. The title alludes to a nursery rhyme character, as explained in the opening sentence. The ending also hints at the analogy.

Men, Chicks, and Eggshells

Introduction

Willie Stark, the main character of *All the King's Men,* by Robert Penn Warren, is the Humpty Dumpty who sits on top of the wall, the governorship of Louisiana. Here he reigns in his own anthropocentric world until he falls. The book has an epic quality in plot, character, and theme.

Willie is a farm boy with little education, but one who works hard and long to become a lawyer and achieve admittance to the bar. He believes in God, in honor, and in goodness. And at first he believes what people tell him. But Sadie Burke wises him up. He forsakes orange soda pop and a wholesome view of the world to embrace Scotch whiskey, a realistic view, and Sadie (as well as other mistresses). *[A major section of the paper, which appears later, emphasizes character, although plot is mentioned throughout the paper. In the conclusion the student writer reacts to the novel, giving her response to plot and character.]*

Conclusion

All the King's Men, like a mighty river, snatches up the reader and thunders to the inexorable finish. When released, the reader is purged and saddened by the tragic mess which some characters have made of their lives, yet gladdened by the few who retain integrity and develop responsibility.

Rereading your notes and prewriting will help you trace the development of the plot. Look for cause and effect. Consider character flaws, impulses, values, goals, issues, or coincidences that influence the outcome. The checklist below will assist you.

CHECKLIST   QUESTIONS FOR ANALYZING PLOT

1.   What is the major conflict, dilemma, or problem?

2.   How does the main character cope?

3.   What aspects of the plot create tension?

4.   Where does the climax occur? What is the high point of the action?

5.   Does the chief character lose or triumph? Why or why not?

Writing about Character

Analyzing character takes time and thought. Consider whether or not the character seems realistic. Start with the external events of existence and go to internal qualities. To discover personality traits, notice how the character treats other people. How does he or she speak and act? Modestly or arrogantly? Kindly or rudely? Thoughtfully or impulsively? What motivates the character? For example, Willie Stark seeks political power, but attaining that power has a hidden price, an undesirable consequence.

Willie Stark is a complex character, a curious blend of good and evil, with Nietzsche-like overtones. As Stark gains power, he becomes a superman whose reign is based on *argumentum ad hominem,* blackmail, and the premise that all men have erred. Yet Stark has a curious code of honor: he never frames anybody. He believes framing is unnecessary; all he does is dig deeply until he finds something.

Although Stark manipulates people and abuses power, he does work for the ultimate good of the people as he conceives it. He provides social services and allocates funds for a lavish hospital, which will be free to the poor.

Stark has an unusual philosophy: "Goodness. . . . You got to make it. . . . And you got to make it out of badness. . . . Because there isn't anything else to make it out of" (257). Although this idea is reminiscent of Romans 8:28 ("And we know that all things work together for good to them that love God, to them who are the called according to *His* purpose"), there is an essential difference that illustrates this character: Stark is a pragmatist who acts independently; he does not rely on his creator for direction.

To discuss character, make an assertion or claim about the character's role or personality. Then support this thesis with adequate examples and proof. You might examine how the character functions in the story. Is he the hero? Is she the heroine? Or does the character act as a *foil* or contrast for a major character? The questions in the checklist will help you to continue your analysis and start prewriting.

CHECKLIST   QUESTIONS FOR ANALYZING CHARACTER

1. What is significant about the character's history, home, or appearance?

2. How does the character achieve desires or goals? What values are revealed here?

3. What do you notice about the characters and their relationships with each other? Do they change?

4. What similarities and differences do you see in characters?

5. Do the characters seem convincing and realistic? Why or why not?

Writing about Symbols

Finding a symbol can lead the reader to look beneath a surface meaning for a deeper abstract meaning. The names of characters and places are often symbolic: they represent some aspect of plot, characterization, or theme. In *Jane Eyre,* the mansion of Edward Rochester, Thornfield, is the site of much trouble and pain. Besides the obvious meaning (field of thorns), Rochester's mad first wife, who is imprisoned on the top floor, is a thorn in his life.

You may recall another symbol Charlotte Brontë used in this novel—the giant horse chestnut tree, which stood in the orchard at Thornfield for many years. Near this tree Edward proposed marriage to Jane without telling her he already had a wife. After Jane accepted his proposal, a storm arose and the huge tree "writhed and groaned." That night the tree, which symbolized Edward, was struck by lightning and split, *foreshadowing* the impending tragedy.

A paper on symbolism alone could be difficult and inappropriate for some works. Unless you are adept at interpreting symbols, you may want to include other elements. To start thinking about possible symbols in a work, consider the questions below.

CHECKLIST   **QUESTIONS FOR INTERPRETING SYMBOLS**

1. What features, objects, or persons might be symbols?

2. Where and how do they appear?

3. Do any of the symbols change? How?

4. Are there any connections between symbols? If so, what are they?

5. Are the symbols universal or individual? How are they related to the theme of the work?

Writing about Irony

If irony is a significant part of a story, you may want to analyze and categorize the types of irony embedded in the work. In Jane Austen's *Pride and Prejudice,* for example, verbal irony and situational irony appear throughout the novel. Verbal irony is habitual for the narrator as well as for Elizabeth Bennet and her father. The novel opens with the narrator speaking:

> It is a truth universally acknowledged that a single man in possession of a good fortune must be in want of a wife.
> However little known the feelings or views of such a man may be on his first entering a neighbourhood, this truth is so well fixed in the minds of the surrounding families, that he is considered as the rightful property of some one or other of their daughters.

Later Mr. Bennet, who assumes the role of an ironic spectator, says, "For what do we live, but to make sport for our neighbors, and laugh at them in our turn?" Elizabeth, like her father, categorizes people into the simple and the complex, finding amusement in the follies of the simple. Situational irony appears in minor incidents such as Lydia repeating much of her mother's behavior. The major example of irony evolves around Elizabeth, who begins by detesting Mr. Darcy but who finally loves and marries him.

Hemingway uses cosmic irony in *The Old Man and the Sea.* Even though the old man succeeds in catching the great fish and in taking it home, fate extracts an exorbitant price for success: not only do the sharks eat all the flesh off his prize, but the old man dies soon after.

If you should decide to write about irony, the prewriting checklist will help you begin.

CHECKLIST   QUESTIONS FOR DETECTING IRONY

1.   Does the reader or a character know something that another does not?

2.   Do any of the characters say the opposite of what they mean?

3.   Are there any inconsistencies between expectations and outcomes in the plot that create irony?

4.   Does fate or cosmic irony play a role in the plot? Do you notice any quirks or twists?

5.   How does irony influence the work? What is the effect?

Writing about Theme

Theme is a continuing thread, the central meaning that winds through a work. A theme contains an observation about human life or the conditions that prevail. Usually, the theme is implicit and unstated, but you may find a theme directly stated, perhaps tucked into an obscure turn of the plot. In *All the King's Men*, an explicit statement of the theme reposes in a journal entry of a man long deceased:

> . . . the world is like an enormous spider web and if you touch it, however lightly, . . . the vibration ripples to the remotest perimeter and the drowsy spider feels the tingle . . . springs out to fling the gossamer coils about you . . . then injects the black, numbing poison under your hide. It does not matter whether you meant to brush the web of things. . . . what happens always happens. (188)

Briefly summarized, the theme is that even small unintentional acts and events can have consequences that reverberate, setting up a chain of cause and effect in our lives and the lives of others. (Willie Stark and others touch the web of circumstance.)

To write about theme, consider that it results from other elements. Look for a series of events and ideas that seem to be connected. Are there sets of circumstances that seem significant? What do they say about human life or values? Also keep in mind that there is not just one way to set forth a theme; readers' statements of theme from the same work will vary. Try writing several one-sentence versions of what seems to you to be the message of the work. Although theme is sometimes difficult to state, you can start your prewriting notes by answering the questions in the checklist.

CHECKLIST   QUESTIONS FOR FINDING CLUES TO THEME

1.   Does a set of related events, decisions, behavior, or symbols seem noteworthy? What might they mean?

2.   What do characters feel strongly about? What is important to them?

3. What values are revealed by their responses?

4. What happens that strengthens or weakens human character? Could a universal statement be made about this?

5. What other aspects of plot and character challenge, entertain, or disgust readers? What do all these aspects seem to say about human life?

Revising

Accuracy, reasonableness, and fairness are key qualities to aim for in revising the draft of an analytical paper. Scrutinize your draft and add tentative words, qualifying phrases, and textual evidence to support claims and inferences. The following checklist will help you to avoid going out on the proverbial limb.

CHECKLIST   **QUESTIONS FOR REVISING A LITERARY ANALYSIS**

1. Is the thesis of my analysis clear? What elements will be discussed in the paper?

2. Is there enough evidence to support my thesis?

3. Are my main points clearly related to the thesis?

4. Is the discussion organized in a clear, logical order?

5. How familiar will the audience be with the work? How much do I need to explain?

6. How does the tone of the analysis sound? Is it serious? Is it overly critical or overly favorable?

7. Do I include at least one significant example (preferably more) to support each inference?

8. Are examples labeled correctly? (To check, see "Elements of Literature," near the beginning of this chapter.)

9. Has each inference been identified by a qualifier such as *indicates, suggests,* or another tentative term?

10. Do I explain how elements contribute to meaning?

11. Might I have overlooked any symbols or irony?

12. Have I identified the theme of the work?

STUDENT PAPER: LITERARY ANALYSIS

The writer of the next paper had difficulty in limiting her topic because Updike's story has such splendid unity. Each element is tightly linked to another. She wanted to focus on symbolism but found that impossible to discuss without mentioning plot and character. And since much of the symbolism is ambiguous, she selected only the clearest symbols.

Breaking Up Is Hard to Do

John Updike's short story "Still of Some Use" focuses on one day in the lives of a divorced couple and their children. The plot is simple, but the characterization and symbols are complex. Foster, his former wife, and their two grown sons are cleaning out the attic of the vacant house they once shared. The older son's girlfriend is also helping. Near the end, the former wife's friend Ted arrives. The story is revealed through Foster's eyes, although the omniscient narrator occasionally interjects a helpful comment.

To glimpse the conflicting emotions of the characters, the reader must peel back layers of symbolism, double meanings, and other clues. Implicit is an analogy between the contents of the attic and the former marriage: both are obsolete—the last tangible remnants of their lives together are being hauled to the dump. The characters' responses to this event vary. The older son seems unmoved, but the younger son, Tommy, is visibly upset. Although the older son and his girlfriend notice, neither seems empathetic. He remarks that Tommy has been "mooning over old stuff." She says Tommy is "very sensitive."

But the boys' mother is concerned and asks Foster to "talk to Tommy." She adds, "This is harder on him than he shows." Although Foster has kept a tight rein on his emotions, his inner conflict becomes evident when, "in a kind of agony," he shouts, "What shall we do with all these games?"

When his sons respond, "Trash 'em" and "Toss 'em," Foster is stunned. He stares at the "sad wealth of abandoned playthings" and remembers how "their lives had touched these tokens and counters once." He wishes they had played with them more often. Foster's former wife, too, seems reluctant to discard the games, asking, "Would Goodwill want them?"

Nor does she seem altogether happy about severing the marriage ties. Small clues hint at her emotional conflict. When Foster asks how she can bear to leave the house, she seems to reply a bit too quickly and flippantly to be convincing, saying, "Oh, it's fun once you get into it. Off with the old, on with the new." This response sounds defiant. She seems to still care for Foster. For instance, when he sits staring out the attic window, she asks, "What's the matter?" After listening a moment, she says, "You better stop now; it's making you too sad." Later she shares her drink with Foster—a gesture of intimacy.

There is little doubt about how Foster feels about the divorce. When he and his former wife are alone in the attic, regret overwhelms him. He looks at her, and the "attic tremble[s] slightly." Later he seems almost desperate as he begs, "Give me one sip." Only minutes before he had refused a drink. Does he want only to press his lips where hers have been?

Clearly, Foster is reluctant to part with the past. He wonders: What if they had "avoided divorce"? Then all the games would have stayed in the attic, their "sorrow [imperfections] unexposed." This passage suggests Foster would have preferred to remain in a marriage with his imperfections unexposed (to him).

So what does the reader actually learn about the breakup of the marriage? Not much, although the use of symbols is lavish. The most vivid is the image of games plummeting from the upstairs window to the truck bed: they "exploded," scattering "laughing children," "curious little faces," "hieroglyphs . . . whose code was lost." Like the games, the marriage undoubtedly started out with high expectations, but somehow the code to an enduring relationship was lost (or never found). Finally, the marriage "exploded" in divorce, scattering children and parents. Now the house is empty and the stove disconnected—just as the marriage has been abandoned and the family relationships disconnected.

The games, "aping the strategies of the stock market, of crime detection, of real estate speculation, of international diplomacy and war," seem to represent elements that marred the marriage. But the connection remains hazy and unclear. Had Foster speculated and lost family funds? What else happened? "War" seems to symbolize discord in the marriage.

The word *token* appears several times, suggesting Foster's minimal participation in the family. There are other hints he may have spent little time interacting with other family members: he says "he had not played enough with these games," and "now no one wanted to play." Yet he had spent many hours building a bookcase "so not a nailhead marred its smoothness." Did he devote more attention to objects than to family relationships? Was he an introvert who liked to go off alone? A stronger hint is that Foster never mentions his former wife's or his older son's names. This omission suggests that his relationships with them were not close.

In contrast, Ted is a "radiant brute," an extrovert, full of vitality and confidence, friendly even to Foster. Ted seems to prize time with his own children, visiting them instead of helping with the attic. He is charming and complimentary to Foster. Unlike Foster, Ted takes the initiative. Already he seems to have made himself a member of the family group: he gives fatherly advice, "Don't dawdle till the dump closes" and wipes away "a smudge of dirt along her [Mrs. Foster's] jaw." He even thanks Foster for helping clean the Foster attic, which seems unusual.

Foster realizes his former wife and Ted are now a "couple." Like the "cardboard spacemen" in the discarded games, Foster seems to feel he is a cardboard man, taking up space in a house no longer his. He feels he's "on the wrong square." He feels discarded—of no use as a husband or father. But as he is leaving, Tommy asks him to ride along to the dump. Foster declines, then asks, "This depresses you?"

Tommy admits, "Kind of," and adds, "It's changed since you left. They have all these new rules." Although Tommy is apparently talking about the dump, his face is clouded as if he's about to cry. His words seem to mirror a double meaning: Ted and his mother have new rules, and Tommy misses his father.

Foster senses these undercurrents, for suddenly he changes his mind and his mood. He jokes, "You win. I'll come along. I'll protect you." Foster seems pleased at the request—as if he is "still of some use."

The human desire to be needed and to be useful is a major theme in Updike's complex and disturbing story. Closely allied is the theme that divorce is not the perfect solution in such a situation. And even under amicable circumstances, divorce is never easy.

—Mae Mattix

- "Jumper Down," Don Shea, page 712
- "Scheherazade," Charles Baxter, page 714
- "The Story of an Hour," Kate Chopin, page 718
- "Still of Some Use," John Updike, page 721

FOR YOUR REFERENCE
Short Stories in the Reader

TEN IDEAS FOR PAPERS
OF LITERARY ANALYSIS

1   Discuss the characterization and plot of "Story of an Hour."

2   Discuss the plot and irony in "Story of an Hour."

3   Discuss the influence of setting on plot and character in "Scheherazade."

4   Discuss the title and symbolism of "Scheherazade."

5   Compare the reality of "Scheherazade" with the fantasy.

6   Compare and contrast Foster and his former wife in "Still of Some Use."

7   Is there hope and a chance for reconciliation in "Still of Some Use"?
Provide reasons and examples for your position.

8   Discuss the plot and characterization of "Jumper Down."

9   Compare two short stories with similar themes.

10   Analyze the symbolism and theme of a work.

Reading and Responding to Poetry

> The poet is the stained glass window that transmits sunlight just as ordinary windows do, but colors it as it passes through.
>
> —Robert Hillyer, *In Pursuit of Poetry*

Poetry has taken a backseat in an age of electronic gadgets and cyberspace. We whiz from our homes to our jobs to other places in a whirlwind of activity. At night we tap away at a computer keyboard or collapse in front of the tube. If we read, it's often the headline news or the comics or self-help books, which poet Tess Gallagher calls "hamburger stands of the soul." Gone are the leisurely evenings and Sunday afternoons spent reading and staring into a wood-burning fire. Now there just doesn't seem to be time to read poetry and ponder tendrils of meaning.

Yet poetry can help us discover a hidden dimension of ourselves. Poetry can connect us more closely to nature and to the human race. In reading a poem, we can peer through a new window on our existence, savoring beauty taken for granted, sharing the warmth of unselfish love or the frigid chill left by death. Poetry acts as a link to the past by recapturing the pleasures and the pains of an earlier age. A poem can reach into the future, kindling desires, fueling dreams—providing the spark that transforms a wish into reality. A poem can fill the present with delight, appreciation, and anticipation. Poetry can yield contentment and acceptance of things we cannot change.

Here the purpose of reading poetry is *not* to classify dozens of literary devices or to analyze meter or to hunt for a message. *The purpose is to enter a poem, to experience it, to look at its parts, and to marvel at its artistry.* Despite careful analysis, any such knowledge is always incomplete. We can never comprehend all there is to know about a work of art—not that all poems are art. But if we approach each one as if it were, then we are more apt to give it a fair hearing.

HOW CAN A READER GET HOLD OF A POEM?

Great poetry has an essence that is elusive. Unlike expository writing, which is primarily concerned with fact and explanation, poetry is primarily feeling. With a few words poets often sketch scenes or wisps of ideas, leaving the reader to fill in the rest. These poets tend to show rather than tell. Great poems do not have excess words. Often the more passionate their feelings, the simpler their statements. Consider the first verse of one of Emily Dickinson's most famous poems:

> Success is counted sweetest
> By those who ne'er succeed.
> To comprehend a nectar
> Requires sorest need.

In the opening *couplet* (a set of two successive lines), the poet poses a *paradox* (a strange but true statement). The third and fourth lines restate the same idea in different words. Every word counts; every word is in perfect alignment and tension. The poet has said just enough in a unique and thoughtful way, balancing expectation with surprise.

When readers are required to analyze a poem, they often begin with the question "What does the poem mean?" In the title of his famous textbook, John Ciardi suggests a more effective starting point: "*How* does a poem mean?" For the meaning of a poem is derived not only from its words but also from its structure. Ciardi also suggests that to study a poem, the reader adopt a playful attitude—for much poetry, like dance, is "a performance" to be appreciated for the pleasure it brings. Ciardi believes the "best any analysis can do is to prepare the reader to enter the poem more perceptively."

To experience joy in comprehending a poem, we need a sense of curiosity, of wonder, and of play. For poets often frolic with words, pairing them in unexpected ways. A sense of play permeates the next poem. To appreciate the structure and sound, read it aloud.

On the Vanity of Earthly Greatness
by Arthur Guiterman

The tusks that clashed in mighty brawls
Of mastodons, are billiard balls.

The sword of Charlemagne the Just
Is ferric oxide, known as rust.

The grizzly bear whose potent hug
Was feared by all, is now a rug.

Great Caesar's bust is on the shelf,
And I don't feel so well myself.

Notice that the poem is composed of four rhyming couplets. Listen to the pace of the words, their slowness or quickness. The first line of each couplet tends to be slow and ponderous whereas the second is quick, especially the last phrase. Hear the sound and movement of certain words: "tusks that clashed," "billiard balls," and "grizzly bear whose potent hug." Note that other words suggest a lack of motion: "rust," "now a rug," and "bust is on the shelf." Each couplet contains surprises not only in sound but also in meaning.

QUESTIONS FOR DISCUSSION

1. Where does the biggest surprise occur?
2. What is the effect of the last line?
3. Does the poem seem to have a purpose other than to provoke amusement?
4. What do you notice about the title that is very different from the poem?
5. How would you state the main idea of Guiterman's poem?

The next poem, by Carl Sandburg, is more explicit and quite different in tone. Yet despite the macabre images, there is a spirit of sly playfulness, revealed in the grim irony and choice of narrator.

Grass

Pile the bodies high at Austerlitz and Waterloo.
Shovel them under and let me work—
        I am the grass; I cover all.

And pile them high at Gettysburg
And pile them high at Ypres and Verdun.
Shovel them under and let me work.
Two years, ten years, and passengers ask the conductor:
        What place is this?
        Where are we now?

        I am the grass.
        Let me work.

QUESTIONS FOR DISCUSSION

1. What has happened at all the places Sandburg names?
2. Who is the narrator? What is the "work"?
3. What is the significance of the passengers' questions to the conductor? What is the irony here?
4. How is "Grass" similar to "On the Vanity of Earthly Greatness"?
5. How do the treatments of the topic differ?

You may feel frustrated as you try to interpret the layers of meaning and glimpse the core of an apparently simple poem. But if you approach a poem as a work of art with form, sound, movement, and meaning and if you examine its parts with care, then you will begin to see its fusion and unity. Then you will be better prepared to appreciate its artistry.

READING NARRATIVE POEMS

Narrative poems are like miniature stories. They begin with a place and a situation. Often the scene is set very simply with a sparseness of detail. Characters are briefly introduced, and the action begins. The movement is usually from specific to general. At the end, concrete details or symbols often hint of a greater meaning, a *universal truth.*

See chapter 22.

The length of a narrative poem may vary from an anecdote such as Countée Cullen's "Incident" to a very long ballad such as "The Rime of the Ancient Mariner." Cullen was born in Louisville, Kentucky, in 1903. By 1925 he had become the most renowned black writer in the United States. Cullen completed theological study at Morgan State College in Baltimore. There he was a Methodist pastor for two years. Then he moved to New York City, where he formed a storefront mission and became politically active. His poem "Incident" deserves several readings.

Incident
by Countée Cullen

Once riding in old Baltimore,
   Heart-filled, head-filled with glee,
I saw a Baltimorean
   Keep looking straight at me.

Now I was eight and very small,
   And he was no whit bigger,
And so I smiled, but he poked out
   His tongue, and called me, "Nigger."

I saw the whole of Baltimore
   From May until December;
Of all the things that happened there
   That's all that I remember.

QUESTIONS TO ANALYZE "INCIDENT"

1. Vocabulary: *glee, incident.* (Also see *incidental.*)
2. How would you describe the tone of verse one?

3. What line in verse one conveys strong feeling?

4. Where does Cullen pair expectation with surprise? What is the effect?

5. Comment on the movement of the poem. (*Hint:* Examine the changes in tone from verse to verse.)

6. Ordinarily, a rollicking rhyme structure is not used in a serious poem. Why does it work well here?

7. Is this a child's poem? Why or why not?

As you examine this poem, keep in mind that understatement provides a wellspring of power for English poetry. *Understatement,* however, requires the reader to look beneath the surface of a poem to glimpse its essence. To assist in detecting understatement, keep a dictionary handy. Look up any unfamiliar words or any that might have more than one meaning. Consider all meanings of a word; poets often select ambiguous words that create layers of meanings. Also consider the historical period and the cultural norms that existed then.

READING LYRIC POEMS

Originally, lyric poems were sung by the Greeks to the accompaniment of a lyre, a stringed instrument. Lyric poetry, which includes most short poems, covers a broad array of subjects and forms. Rather than telling a story as narrative poetry does, lyric poetry expresses a state of mind, revealing thought and feeling. Since there is no plot, word choice and imagery must be powerful in a lyric poem.

Special Effects with Words

Poets select words not only for meaning but also for sound, movement, and color. All four aspects are inseparable. *Alliteration* (repeated consonant sounds), *assonance* (repeated vowel sounds), and rhyme are the most common devices of sound. Another device is *onomatopoeia,* whereby the sound of the word mimics its denotation. Listen to *hum, buzz,* and *crack* as you say them. These words sound like the actions they represent. Onomatopoeia supplies vitality to any poem.

Action verbs also give vitality to poetry, enhancing the image and varying the pace. Words may skip or skitter, slink or slither, sprint or stroll across a page. Let's pause for a moment and consider the verb pairs in the previous sentence. First, visualize the difference in movement between *skip* and *skitter.* A child might skip down a sidewalk, but an autumn leave skitters across a lawn, blown by the wind in quick irregular spurts.

Next listen to the sounds of the verb pairs. Notice the repetition of *sli* in *slink* and *slither,* which adds smoothness to their sound. Similarly, *ski* is repeated in *skip* and *skitter.* But the third pair sets up a little surprise. Instead of exact repetition at the beginning of the words, the *t* sound comes at a different place in each word: *sprint, stroll.* Finally, listen to the pace. The first word in each verb pair quickens the pace whereas the second slows it. For example, *sprint* with its short *i* is much quicker to say than *stroll* with the long *o* and *ll* sounds.

When you consider adjectives such as *red* and *ruby* or *green* and *emerald*, you note contrasts in color as well as sound and pace. The eye easily detects that red and green offer an array of shades whereas *ruby* and *emerald* are each a specific shade. As you listen to the sounds, you can hear the quickness of *red* and *green*. *Ruby* and *emerald* sound slower and richer.

Imagery in Lyric Poems

Our cave-dwelling ancestors drew primitive sketches to represent activities and events in their lives. Similarly, poets sketch images with words to represent significant occurrences, ideas, and emotions. In a poem with a single image, all words contribute. *Haiku*, an ancient Japanese form of lyric verse, always focus on a single image. The form generally consists of three lines of seventeen sylla-bles, based on a metaphor. Implicit in the image is a comparison. Typical haiku describe nature or the seasons, much like the following examples:

The Barley Field	**The Barley Field**
by Joso	*by Sora*
Bent down by the rain,	Up the barley rows,
the ripe barley makes this	stitching, stitching them together
such a narrow lane!	a butterfly goes.

If you have seen wheat or oats growing in a field, then you can easily visu-alize a field of barley, which also grows in bearded, willowy stalks. To compare the two poems, jot down differences in the spaces below, beginning with con-crete details. Then ask: How do the details influence the effect of each poem?

	(Joso)	(Sora)
Angle of stalks	_____	_____
Width of rows	_____	_____
Image (metaphor)	_____	_____
Punctuation	_____	_____
Connotations	_____	_____
	_____	_____
Repetition	_____	_____
Literary devices	_____	_____
	_____	_____
Tone	_____	_____

Poems with more than one image lack the splendid unity of poems with a single image. Yet multiple images can be skillfully unified by a central theme. All connotative meanings must, as Ciardi points out, "combine the overtone themes of the words and the images into a single unity."

Emily Dickinson (1830–1886) became famous for her lyric poems after her death. She was educated at Amherst Academy and Mount Holyoke Seminary. Her innovative style, characterized by whimsical daring and nimble skill, became a strong influence on twentieth-century poets. Yet Emily Dickinson was practically unknown during her lifetime; only a few of her poems were published in a local newspaper. The following poem is characteristic of her style:

[I never hear the word]
by Emily Dickinson

I never hear the word "escape"
Without a quicker blood,
A sudden expectation,
A flying attitude!

I never hear of prisons broad
By soldiers battered down,
But I tug childish at my bars
Only to fail again!

(c. 1859, 1891)

QUESTIONS TO ANALYZE "I NEVER HEAR THE WORD"

1. To what does "quicker blood" refer? (*Hint:* Today we would use a similar word and "pulse," rather than "blood.")
2. How would you describe the feeling in verse one?
3. Can you find the *slant rhyme* (imperfect rhyme) in verse one?
4. What other literary devices do you see?
5. Verse one introduces the idea of escape. Verse two contains the central idea of the poem. How would you state the theme of the poem?

More than a century later, an anonymous poet chose a similar theme but wrote a very different poem:

INCEPTION

Last night I dreamed
     my budding self
     flexed against
     its acorn walls
     and
     hurtled into light.

QUESTIONS TO ANALYZE "INCEPTION"

1. What does "budding self" convey to you?
2. Describe the imagery evoked by "flexed" and "hurtled."
3. Do you see a connection between "acorn walls" and "light"?
4. How is the title connected to the poem? (See a dictionary.)
5. How does this poem differ from Dickinson's?
6. What does the poem mean to you?

Although a spirit of play is less apparent in the poetry of Archibald MacLeish, still it is there. MacLeish won the Pulitzer Prize for poetry in both 1933 and 1953. He was not only a distinguished poet but also an author and statesman, working for UNESCO and other organizations. Born in Glencoe, Illinois, MacLeish graduated from Yale University and obtained a law degree from Harvard, where he became a professor. His most famous poem, "Ars Poetica" (Latin for *poetics,* the theory of writing poetry), written in 1926, contains a series of images. These involve sight, sound (or the lack of it), movement, and touch as well as meaning. Think about the texture of the images. What qualities do they have in common?

Ars Poetica
by Archibald MacLeish

A poem should be palpable and mute
As a globed fruit,

Dumb
As old medallions to the thumb,

Silent as the sleeve-worn stone
Of casement ledges where the moss has grown—

A poem should be wordless
As the flight of birds.

*

A poem should be motionless in time
As the moon climbs,

Leaving, as the moon releases
Twig by twig the night-entangled trees,

Leaving, as the moon behind the winter leaves,
Memory by memory the mind—

A poem should be motionless in time
As the moon climbs

*

A poem should be equal to:
Not true.

For all the history of grief
An empty doorway and a maple leaf.

For love
The leaning grasses and the two lights above the sea—

A poem should not mean
But be

QUESTIONS TO ANALYZE "ARS POETICA"

1. Vocabulary: *palpable, mute, medallion, casement, be* ("to have life or reality")
2. Why is *palpable* an excellent word for this poem? (Consider the medical meaning of the word as well as the old Latin.)

3. Consider the sound and imagery of "globed fruit," "sleeve-worn stone," "moon climbs," and "poem." What do you notice?

4. What do you notice about the pace of the pair of lines below?
   A poem should be wordless
   As the flight of birds.

5. What words convey the idea of silence?

6. The final line has no period. What is the effect? (*Clues:* What does a period do? What idea is conveyed through "motionless in time" and "history" that is similar to ending without a period?)

7. What else do you notice?

8. Each couplet specifies a quality that a poem should have. What are the qualities?

9. The final verse summarizes the meaning of the poem. How would you paraphrase it?

PREPARING AN ANALYSIS OF A POEM

As you browse through poems, choose one you like that offers possibilities for serious discussion. A fairly short poem is usually preferable if it has depth of thought. You may find different versions of the poem or possibly different titles. For example, one of William Wordsworth's poems has been widely printed under two titles: "Daffodils" or "I wandered lonely as a cloud." (Sometimes brackets are placed around the title of a poem to indicate it was originally untitled.)

1. *Copy the poem, enlarging it, but leaving 1½-inch margins.* Use the copy to make notes and gain an overview.

2. *Read biographical sketches.* Gaining insight into the author's background and the spirit of the times is often helpful in understanding the work. Encyclopedias, some poetry books, and the Internet offer brief biographies.

3. *Hold off on interpretation.* Going into a poem with preset ideas can close the mind. Withhold judgment; be open to newness.

4. *Look up unfamiliar words.* Read all definitions listed for a word. Poets often select words with double or triple meanings to enrich a poem. Jot definitions near the example if possible.

5. *Examine the words.* What is the level of language? Is dialect, jargon, or special terminology used? What does this usage imply?

6. *Listen to the feeling.* How does the voice of the narrator sound? From what point of view is the voice speaking? Listen to the nuances of the words. What emotion do you sense?

TIPS FOR ANALYZING A POEM

continued

**TIPS FOR
ANALYZING
A POEM**
(continued)

7. *Listen for devices of sound and movement.* Do you notice rhyme? Alliteration? Assonance? Any other device? How does the rhythm (pattern of sound) of the poem reinforce the meaning?

8. *Look for figurative language.* Do similes, metaphors, personification, symbolism, or other devices contribute to an image?

9. *Notice punctuation.* Poetry, like prose, is punctuated for a reason. Consider the effect of punctuation—or the lack of it.

10. *Keep the context of the poem in mind while looking at its parts.* Try to discover how each part is linked to the whole.

11. *Consider possible meanings.* Read the poem aloud. What does the imagery suggest? What do the words say? Might there be more than one interpretation? If so, which one fits best and why? Review your notes.

12. *What is the total effect of the poem?* What is your response to it?

Developing Your Analysis

Do a little research on the poet. After that, reread the poem silently. Then read it aloud and listen to the sound and movement. Who is speaking? Watch for clues to how the speaker feels about the subject. If the poem has rhyme, is there a pattern to the rhyme? Next, count the number of syllables in each line and write them at the side to determine how the lines compare. Do any have the same number of syllables? Is there a pattern to the arrangement of the lines?

After that, study the definitions and connotations of key words to see how they contribute to the meaning. Write the definitions and connotations near each word. Next, look for similes, metaphors, analogies, personification, symbols—or any other device that links one part of the poem with another. (For more about figurative language, see chapter 22.) Jot brief notes as you go. Write any questions you have at the bottom of the page or on the reverse side. You may find the answers later, or you might discuss the questions with someone else. By the time you have finished, you should have accumulated a page of notes to serve as raw material for a rough draft. (See "Critical Reading," chapter 21.)

Finally, reread the poem aloud to reassemble the parts in your mind and focus on the effect of the entire work. As you do, chances are that you will begin to see how the parts fuse into a central image or theme.

Organizing the Paper

Although there are many aspects to poetry, first-year college students are usually not expected to cover all them. Often an analytical paper on a poem is only one or two pages long. If your instructor allows a choice, select major elements that interest you. Then explain your impression of the way various elements contribute to the unity and meaning of the poem.

1. Identify the poem as narrative or lyric. If a special type, specify.

2. Follow the order of the poem as nearly as possible.

3. Explain how the word choice, symbolism, or other elements contribute to the overall effect of the poem.

4. Cite examples of elements.

5. State your perception of the central idea.

6. Describe your response to the poem.

GUIDELINES: ORGANIZING AND DEVELOPING A POETIC ANALYSIS

If the poem is short, include the entire text in your paper. If over half a page, attach a copy to your paper unless the poem is in your textbook. To quote less than four lines, use quotation marks and indicate each line break between two or more lines by a slash mark: "I never hear the word 'escape' / Without a quicker blood" (Note: One space is placed before and after each slash.) If you quote four lines or more of poetry, indent and treat as a long direct quotation (with no quotation marks).

Revising an Analysis of a Poem

Even though your paper of analysis is only a page or two, check the organization and revise carefully. The following questions will help you revise your draft. Select the items that pertain to your subject.

CHECKLIST   REVISING AN ANALYSIS OF A POEM

1. Do I have a clear thesis?

2. Do I follow a logical order?

3. Have I discussed the central image (or series of images)?

4. Are any symbols present? Have I explained how they contribute?

5. Have I discussed the devices of sound in the poem?

6. Are there any similes, metaphors, or personification not yet discussed?

7. Have I pointed out connections between related ideas?

8. Have I considered how the poem appears on the page? How many stanzas there are? Their length and any other significant aspects?

9. Have I interpreted the central idea of the poem?

STUDENT PAPER: ANALYSIS OF A POEM

The following example shows one way to organize an analytical paper. A poem of this length usually appears on a separate page, before the analysis. Wordsworth's poem was written about 1800 in the British Lake District. In the spring when the lake floods today, the blooming daffodils stand in water.

[I wandered lonely as a cloud]
by William Wordsworth

I wandered lonely as a cloud
That floats on high o'er vales and hills,
When all at once I saw a crowd,
A host of golden daffodils;
Beside the lake, beneath the trees
Fluttering and dancing in the breeze.

Continuous as the stars that shine
And twinkle on the milky way,
They stretched in never-ending line
Along the margin of a bay:
Ten thousand saw I at a glance,
Tossing their heads in sprightly dance.

The waves beside them danced; but they
Outdid the sparkling waves in glee;
A poet could not but be gay
In such a jocund company;
I gazed—and gazed—but little thought
What wealth the show to me had brought:

For oft, when on my couch I lie
In vacant or in pensive mood,
They flash upon that inward eye
Which is the bliss of solitude;
And then my heart with pleasure fills,
And dances with the daffodils.

Form and Meaning in "I wandered lonely as a cloud"

Every time I read William Wordsworth's poem "I wandered lonely as a cloud," it is a source of pleasure. The dazzling beauty of the daffodils is one that any reader can readily conceive and enjoy. But this lyric poem is much more than a vivid description with contrasts of sight and sound. The poem is alive with motion.

In the first line the narrator compares himself to the cloud that "floats on high." The tone of this line and the next differs greatly from that of other lines. The narrator's loneliness is juxtaposed to the happy sight of a "host of golden daffodils. . . . Tossing their heads in sprightly dance."

Light radiates throughout the poem in the words *golden, stars, shine, twinkle, milky way, sparkling waves,* and *flash.* Alliteration in *stars, shine, stretched, saw, sprightly* and in *Ten thousand . . . Tossing* focuses on this glorious sight.

Assonance contributes not only to the unity of the poem but also to the sound, varying the pace. The repetition of the long *o* in *lonely, floats, o'er,* and other examples slows the lines and suggests aloneness. The long *a* in *gazed* and its repetition reflect the narrator's reluctance to leave. In contrast is the short, quick *e,* in "Beside the lake, beneath the trees."

Personification and movement are major features of the poem. The daffodils toss their heads, dance, and laugh with *glee.* Movements of dance are conveyed by the words. *Fluttering* suggests short spurts of movement; *dancing,*

a smooth glide. The rhyme scheme and the length of lines mimic the dance of
the daffodils. Although the end rhyme is exact, the pattern of rhyming varies
in the third stanza. No stanza has the same pattern, although some have the
same number of syllables per line. These lines suggest the movement of dancers to music.

If there is a theme to the poem, it might be stated as "Beauty can nourish
the spirit" or "Drink in every drop of beauty and store it to cheer the soul."

—**Elizabeth D.**

PRACTICE

IDEAS FOR WRITING

1. React to the two haiku entitled "The Barley Field." Which do you prefer? Why? Write a short essay giving your response.

2. Analyze Emily Dickinson's poem "I never hear the word."

3. Analyze another poem in this chapter and explain how some elements contribute to meaning.

4. Read and analyze another poem of your choice.

5. Research the life of your favorite poet and select one poem that reveals his or her philosophy. Write a short paper that summarizes his or her life and philosophy. Relate the poem to the philosophy.

The Student
Survival Guide

Would you like to improve your study habits? Accomplish more and raise your grades? The Student Survival Guide will help you with these concerns and more. You'll learn how to prepare well for exams and to take them effectively. Chapter 25, "Making Oral Presentations," will help you conquer stage fright and speak well. Chapter 26, "Effective Employment Writing," shows how to improve your résumé, cover letters, and letters of appreciation.

Start now to take advantage of these opportunities. The skills you develop will aid you not only in your college classes but also in your career.

WRITING EXERCISE

1. Have you ever felt overwhelmed in a course? Dissatisfied with an exam grade? Write a paragraph describing the problem and a way you might avoid it.
2. What grades would you like to receive in your courses? Write a paragraph setting forth your goals and a practical plan to achieve them.

FENDING OFF THE WOLVES

The wolf of failure trails students who procrastinate and shirk the task of preparing well for exams. The wolf of fear stalks those who evade speech courses and avoid giving oral presentations. The wolf of poverty pursues those who seek jobs with little understanding of how to format résumés, cover letters, and electronic messages.

The Student Survival Guide will help you elude these wolves. Chapter 24 shows how to prepare effectively for both objective and essay exams. The section on time management shows *how to achieve more in less time.* Chapter 25 is a mini-manual, complete with instructions for preparing, practicing, and delivering professional oral presentations. Included, too, are tips for using audiovisuals, improving vocal variety, and building confidence. These skills can enhance your performance not only in college classes but also in job interviews.

Chapter 26 shows the latest résumé styles, eye-catching cover letters, and letters of appreciation. It will help you focus on the needs of employers as you update your résumé. You can learn, step-by-step, how to research your career field, avoid common pitfalls, write a service-oriented job objective, and prepare effective employment documents. Included, too, are guidelines for writing e-mail, electronic and scannable résumés, and a sheet of employment references. If you are not looking for a job just now, you can save the book for future reference.

The most important step—whether preparing for an exam, a presentation, or job hunt—is to exert the necessary effort. Then you will be well on the road to success.

Preparing for Exams

> Procrastination is like a credit card; it's a lot of fun until you get the bill.
>
> —Christopher Parker

Many students procrastinate instead of preparing for exams. They wait until the night before and drink soda or coffee by the quart to stay awake while they study. The next day they are so exhausted they can barely keep their eyes open, much less focus their scattered thoughts to write complete essay answers. Pulling an all-nighter is not a good way to study for an exam—paced learning is more effective than cramming.

To do well on any exam, you need to prepare well throughout the term and get a good night's sleep beforehand. The journal *Nature* (9 Oct. 2003) reports that researchers at the University of Chicago and Harvard Medical School, in separate studies, found that a full night's sleep improves recall. Researchers believe that "sleep can rescue memories in a biological process of storing and consolidating them deep in the brain's complex circuitry."

TIME MANAGEMENT

The practical solution to the problem of procrastination is effective time management. By scheduling your time and studying regularly, you can increase your retention and decrease your stress. The rule of thumb for college study is "two hours out of class for every hour in class." This means that if you are taking sixteen hours of classes per week, you study thirty-two hours per week. Allotting this much time for study requires skillful planning.

If finding thirty-two hours or so a week to study seems impossible, don't despair. There are 168 hours in a week and many practical ways to become more efficient. The first step is simple—just *resolve early* in the term to manage your time wisely and to improve your study habits. The second step is to take control of your time by setting priorities and making a schedule.

PEANUTS reprinted by permission of United Feature Syndicate, Inc.

Setting Priorities, Scheduling, and Implementing

Three keys to efficient scheduling are identifying your priorities early in the term, making a workable schedule, and disciplining yourself to follow it. Even though you might prefer to hang out with friends, go to a concert, or build a new sundeck, put study time first. To start managing your time effectively, you might follow this procedure:

- **Make a list of the activities you must do.** Include adequate daily study time. Postpone less urgent items, such as painting, shopping, and extra cleaning.

- **Rate essential activities in order of priority.** Mark high-priority items, such as deadlines for projects, papers, and exams, as **HP**. Include essential personal activities, such as doctor or dental appointments. Mark medium priorities as MP.

- **Mark a *monthly* calendar.** One big monthly calendar allows you to quickly check each day and spot possible conflicts early. If two high-priority items conflict, reschedule one or complete a paper or project early. Shuffle MP items around high priorities.

- **Make a *weekly* calendar.** This way you can develop an efficient routine. Mark your class hours, study times, work hours, and other high-priority items. Leave a little flextime in case of an emergency.

- **Make a daily to-do list the night before a high-pressure day.** Carry the day's list with you. As you complete an item, cross it off. If something is left undone, place it on the next day's list.

Setting priorities and following a schedule will help you develop a "can-do" attitude and self-confidence. Then you can enjoy the satisfaction that flows from being in control of your time.

1. **Study during your *prime time*.** Are you a night owl or a lark? When are you most alert and able to retain what you read? Is one hour of study in the early morning more effective for you than two hours late at night? Or is night your best time?

2. **Make *double use* of time.** Study at odd moments—on breaks at work, during lunch, and while waiting for appointments. You might listen to taped class notes as you drive. Or while a car-pool buddy drives, hit the books. What else might you do?

3. **Obtain help, especially during exam week.** A study buddy can ask questions and help review major concepts. If you are responsible for a family, is there someone who might assist while you study? Might you trade child care with a friend?

4. **Forgo leisure *temporarily*.** Say no to television, films, and computer games. Placing a high priority on learning and disciplining yourself will help you not only to achieve your college and career goals but also to develop constructive habits that can last a lifetime.

FOUR TIME-SAVERS

READING, NOTE-TAKING, AND REVIEW

To better understand the lesson, always read assignments *before* going to class. This prior study will allow you to participate and increase your efficiency in taking good class notes. (Some instructors include participation as part of your grade.) As you think and write, try to *associate* new learning with what you already know. Jot down your associations in parentheses. Creating a connection will help you retain the information over time.

Ten Ways to Improve Retention

Keep in mind that not everyone learns the same way. To discover which memory aids work well for you, try all ten of them:

1. **Keep a small notebook just for assignments, deadlines, and "to-do's."** After completing each assignment, cross it off. Jot down words you need to look up and questions you want to ask in the next class.

2. **Condense and reword class notes.** Summarizing in your own words will enable you to recall material more easily than memorizing word for word.

3. **Develop your own code.** Since it is impossible to write down every word in a lecture, abbreviate some words and leave blanks. After class, fill them in. For example, b/c = because, i/t = into, w/o = without, b/t = between, c/ptr = computer.

4. **Keep a page of key terms.** For every course, start a page of key terms. Write out a definition for each one. Add to the list regularly and review.

5. **Make flash cards.** For difficult terms, make flash cards, using file cards and colored markers. Print the term on one side in large letters and the definition on the other. Then ask someone to flash the cards and quiz you.

6. **Create acronyms.** To memorize a short list, arrange the items to create an acronym. For example, if you have four skills to learn—*restatement/paraphrasing, summarizing, responding to nonverbal cues, responding to feelings*—memorize the first letter of each word: *RSRR.*

7. **Break large chunks into parts.** To memorize quantities of material, look for a way to break it into manageable parts or categories. Adding capitalized headings to your class notes and numbering points will clarify. (Look at this chapter.)

8. **Color-code lists.** Break lists of several items into two columns. Then color the section numbers, such as 1–3 blue, 4–6 green, 7–9 yellow, and 10 orange. (Not all people are sensitive to color, but color-coding helps many.)

9. **Review and practice.** Think "see and say." Look at an item, then look away. Repeat the item aloud. *Hearing it will help to anchor the meaning in your memory.*

10. **Quiz and test yourself.** Type a list of questions you might be asked. The next day, print it out and answer the questions. Check your answers with the textbook.

Reviewing for Final Exams

If you study regularly throughout the term, attend classes, and take good notes (perhaps typing them each evening), then a week of review for final exams should be enough. A strategy to study effectively can help you organize your review.

A STRATEGY FOR EFFECTIVE STUDY

- **Plan the review.** First, scan the table of contents in your textbook. That gives an *overview* of the material. Note the headings and subheadings of chapters. Second, *mark HP (for high priority) by sections that need extensive review.* That way you can study the most difficult sections first and spend more time on them.

- **Think and question.** Think about major ideas and how they are related. *Turn your textbook headings and subheadings into questions* and try to answer orally. Then scan the section for the answer. This tactic will force you to examine and summarize ideas in your own words.

- **Highlight your notes.** Highlight main points. In some courses you will need to consider major events, changes, causes, influences, and trends. How have they affected the culture? What results or consequences have occurred?

- **Make a time line, a diagram, or another visual.** This will help you retain certain information. Some students type an outline of very difficult material. That device condenses and saves time in reviewing.

- **Review quizzes and handouts.** Look up answers to quiz questions missed and write them on the quiz. Review any handouts.

- **Encourage yourself.** Visualize completing the exam successfully. Refuse to succumb to negative thoughts and the "what if" syndrome ("What if I can't remember? What if I fail?") Negative thinking is a dead end. It sabotages your time and disrupts your focus. Reward yourself with brief breaks.

Predicting Exam Questions

Attending class regularly, particularly before exams, is essential. Many instructors share study hints and sample questions. Have pen poised, ready to record even casual remarks an instructor makes. Listen for hints disguised as joking, for example, a laughing comment such as "Memorize all the headings!" Translated, this usually means to study the major ideas of the textbook.

Or an instructor may smile and say, "Just remember *everything* I've covered in the lectures!" This means you can depend heavily on your class notes—if they are complete. If not, try to secure a good copy from someone else. Beware, however, of letting your own notes out of your sight unless you have them on a computer disk in a safe place. There is the danger of notes not being returned or of being lost or stolen.

Some instructors prepare a short study guide. Others volunteer only the time of the exam and vague suggestions for study. In either case, feel free to ask reasonable questions: Will the exam be on paper or computer? Will dictionaries, spelling checkers, or thesauruses be allowed? Will the exam contain only essay questions or a combination of multiple choice and short answers?

Before the Exam

To perform at your best, eat lightly but avoid meal skipping on exam day. Not eating can lower blood sugar, causing fatigue and inability to concentrate. Daily exercise, even walking a few blocks, contributes to a sense of well-being and helps to control test anxiety. Deep breathing and drinking cold water can also help you feel more alert and less anxious. Rested and energized, you will be able to think more clearly.

Avoid bringing coffee, soft drinks, or food to the exam. If you are nervous or someone bumps you, drinks may spill. Crumbs and smears stick to exams. Food wrappings can distract other students who are trying to concentrate.

Arrive about five minutes early with all your supplies on exam day. If you arrive too early, you may find yourself listening to someone wail about the upcoming exam. Take two pens (one may run dry), plenty of paper (the instructor may not supply it), a dictionary, and anything else you may need. If the exam is on a computer with a spelling checker, some supplies may seem unnecessary but still may be useful.

Check the chalkboard for messages. Sometimes an exam is moved to another room or even another building. Yet some students may sit and chat, not thinking to glance at the board. As a result, they lose time for completing the exam.

THREE KINDS OF EXAMS

College exams may include essay, fill in the blank, true or false, matching, short answer, or others. Three kinds are discussed here: open book, multiple-choice, and essay exams. All require adequate preparation.

Open Book Exams

Be forewarned that a question about open book exams may evoke laughter. To the uninitiated, an open book exam sounds as if it would not require much study. But the truth is that you have to prepare just as much or more! Although textbooks are permitted during an open book exam, the odds are stacked against your having time to use them.

Open book exams are so long that if you spend time searching for answers, finishing the exam is doubtful. Once, while taking one, I saw three students come in with textbooks loaded with colored slips of paper. During the exam they rapidly flipped pages, hunting for answers. None of the three completed the exam. There is no substitute for well-planned study and review.

Multiple-Choice Exams

To prepare for a multiple-choice exam, you need to memorize much specific data. Scan your class notes and quizzes. Highlight statistics, dates, events, names of important people, inventions, processes, procedures, or other vital facts, depending on the course and what the instructor has emphasized. In literature courses, pay strict attention to titles, names of authors, and dates, as well as names of characters, setting, plot, and theme.

Then type a list of these items or make a summary sheet to review. As you study the sheet, read each item, then look away and repeat it out loud to reinforce retention.

BEFORE THE TEST

1. **Take notes every class and date each entry.** Jot down all hints and tips teachers give. Type your notes after class, adding explanations as needed. Review.

2. **Study diagrams and figures in the textbook.** Don't overlook anything.

3. **Review old quizzes and exams.** Look up the correct answers for items missed.

DURING THE TEST

4. **Read directions twice.** Highlight the key terms, if permitted. Follow directions *exactly.* Answer only the number of parts required. Carelessness costs points.

5. **Determine whether or not to guess at answers.** On most tests there is no penalty for guessing. For some standardized tests, you may be ahead to leave an item blank if you do not know the answer.

6. **Cover possible answers with your hand. Read the question and think the answer.** Select the item that is closest to your answer.

7. **Read all the questions about an excerpt from literature before you read the excerpt.** Then reread and answer each question.

8. **Don't waste time looking for a pattern to answers.** Invariably, answers are lettered (a, b, c, d, or e) randomly.

9. **On timed tests, work fast.** If you have extra time, go back and look over just the items you are unsure of.

10. **Do not change an answer unless you are absolutely sure it is wrong.** Research has shown that a first answer is more likely to be correct than a second answer when the test taker is unsure.

TIPS FOR TAKING MULTIPLE-CHOICE EXAMS

Essay Exams

Most essay exams have several questions that require a paragraph or more to answer completely. Other exams have just one question that calls for a long essay. Regardless, you will need to memorize certain facts, details, and definitions, as well as understand key concepts. Essay exams often require that you understand cause and effect, organize, analyze, and comment. You may also be asked to make a claim and supply evidence to support it. The next section presents an overview of essay questions, definitions of certain verbs, key phrases, and a strategy for drafting complete essay answers, as well as other help.

A STRATEGY FOR MANAGING TIME DURING ESSAY EXAMS

1. **Preview the test**. Scan the entire test. If you have a choice of questions, mark the ones you will answer. *Do not spend time on extra questions that earn no credit.*

2. **Plan your time according to the worth of questions**. If all questions are weighted equally, allot equal time. If a question is worth more than others, spend more time there.

3. **Start with the easiest question**. Answering one completely will boost your confidence.

4. **When stalled, move on, or take a quick break**. Breathe deeply. Sip water. You may think of an answer.

5. **Keep your exam until the last possible moment**. Do not leave early. Instead, go back and check your answers. If you see any omissions or think of significant details, add them.

6. **If time is running out, outline your answers**. It is better to earn partial points than leave a question blank and earn none.

WRITING COMPLETE ESSAY EXAM ANSWERS

Before writing an exam answer, read the entire question. Thirty seconds spent considering the question can make the difference between an incomplete answer and a complete one. Two major causes of low grades on essay exams are that students misread or omit parts of questions. Hurrying through instructions is a path to disaster. To understand what is required, read *every* word carefully. Then follow directions.

Understanding the Question

To answer essay questions completely, you need to know the precise meanings of certain verbs. These words contain clues to the writing strategy that will best organize an essay answer. Listed in the box below are definitions of verbs frequently found on essay exams.

Exam questions may be broad or narrowly focused. Broad questions allow leeway in answering. They may ask you to *trace* or *state* influences, developments, or history. Such questions require listing a series of significant events or changes in *chronological* order, then explaining their evolution and effects. Or you may be asked to *analyze, discuss, explain, comment on,* or *account for* influences, changes, or trends:

Account for: to explain, as a cause and its effect; to justify

Analyze: to examine the parts of and determine their connections

Clarify: to explain; to present details, reasons, or examples

Defend, justify, support: to give reasons for; to offer evidence

Define: to give the meaning; to describe basic characteristics

Discuss: to examine and consider; to present details and reasons

Evaluate: to examine advantages and disadvantages; to rate or judge

Explain: to make clear; to define or offer reasons

Identify: to define; to give the characteristics of

Trace: to track or explain in chronological order

DEFINITIONS OF COMMON VERBS IN ESSAY QUESTIONS

- Trace the development of computers from the first practical model up to the present.
- Analyze the influence of World War II on women's lives from 1941 to 1950.

Narrowly focused questions are more specific. They may ask you to *identify, cite, compare, contrast, list, argue, defend, justify, support, evaluate,* and so on. These questions may be stated in one sentence or in more than one:

- Discuss the roller-coaster performance of the Dow Jones Index in 2008 and cite the chief causes of its wide fluctuations.
- Contrast Walter Mitty's real life with his secret life. Give two major reasons why he feels the need to escape from reality.

Instructors expect you to cite significant points, supply adequate support, and explain connections clearly. Omit trivial details. Clear, concise answers are better than long rambling padded ones. Strive for quality, not quantity.

Key Phrases	Writing Strategies
• Trace, give the history of	*Narration*
• Provide details, describe	*Description*
• Explain, list, provide examples of	*Illustration*
• Discuss or analyze the parts of	*Classification*
• Analyze, explain how, show how	*Process analysis*
• Discuss advantages/disadvantages	*Comparison-contrast*
• Show similarities/differences	*Comparison-contrast*
• Account for, analyze the results of	*Cause-effect*
• Discuss or explain reasons for	*Cause-effect*
• Identify, clarify, explain the term	*Definition*
• Defend, evaluate, justify, support	*Argument-persuasion*

WRITING STRATEGIES SUGGESTED BY KEY PHRASES

Writing Paragraph Essays

To begin an essay paragraph, write a clear topic sentence. Then draft support sentences, keeping in mind the *basic pattern of claim and evidence.* In other words, every detail and example in the paragraph should support the claim of the topic sentence. Use complete sentences. Fragments can lead to confusion and a loss of points. At the end of your answer, leave a few lines in case you think of more to add later.

When you are faced with writing several exam answers, focus on one question at a time. If you should think of information for another question before you finish the first, jot down the idea and put it aside. The precautions that follow will also help you write complete essay answers.

PRECAUTIONS FOR WRITING COMPLETE ESSAY ANSWERS

1. **Heed directions.** Listen to oral instructions. During the exam, check the board for any corrections or changes to the exam. Read each exam question *twice.*

2. **Highlight or underline key terms.** If you are permitted to write on an exam, mark special terms.

3. **Number the parts of multifaceted questions.** Be sure that no part is omitted.

4. **Check off numbers of parts after you answer each one.**

5. **When finished, check the answers you are least sure of.** If you think of more information, add it. Then proofread.

SAMPLE PARAGRAPH ESSAY

The three-part essay question below calls for definition, contrast, and division. The one-paragraph answer opens with a definition before the topic sentence. The support sentences follow.

Question: Define *information interview.* How does it differ from an employment interview? State three specific advantages of this interview.

Definition
Contrast
Topic Sentence

Support

Example

Summary

Answer: An information interview is a meeting with an employer for the direct purpose of gaining information about a career field, not to get a job. The information interview has three distinct advantages. It provides firsthand information about a position you hope to be working in some day. It allows you an inside look at a company to see whether or not you would enjoy working there. It allows access to employers whom you might not be able to contact otherwise. You may even be asked to bring your résumé or to come in for an employment interview. In fact, that is what happened to me last week. Tomorrow I start my new job as a medical transcriptionist. The information interview is truly an excellent technique for uncovering the "hidden jobs" that are never advertised.

Writing Long Exam Essays

Instead of several paragraph essays, you may be asked to write an in-class paper, either in longhand or on a computer. As soon as you are clear about what the essay question requires, start a tiny scratch outline, possibly in the margin or on the back of a paper exam. Then identify your main points and number them. This start will help you focus your thoughts. If writing by hand, place your first draft in the exam booklet, if given one; rarely is there time to recopy.

Always state your thesis early and cite examples to support main points. Questions about literature usually ask you to analyze elements of fiction such as theme, plot, or character. They may also ask about symbolism, irony, or other literary devices (see chapters 22 and 23). Some essay questions call for a *reaction*. A well-written reaction goes a step further than analysis. You include your opinion—based on examples from the text you are given or have read previously. If asked to react to a reading, respond to the main *idea* and add a well-reasoned comment (see chapter 21).

- "A Strategy for Critical Reading and Prewriting," page 291
- "Writing a Paper of Reaction or Essay Exam Answers," page 293
- "Reading and Taking Notes on a Literary Work," page 309
- "A Tale of Four Learners," Bernice McCarthy, page 622

FOR YOUR REFERENCE
Study Aids
for Literature

PRACTICE

NOTETAKING IN CLASS

Would you like a preview of the contents of the midterm and final exams? By taking careful notes every day in class, beginning on the first day, you can create a summary of the course work. Instructors generally cover most major points of lessons in class or point them out in the textbook. Taking notes will also force you to pay close attention and increase your retention. Allot a section in a notebook, then follow this brief outline every day as you take notes:

Date:

Assignment: (Topic and page numbers)

Points (Number them 1, 2, 3, and so on, for clarity)

Before the exam, reread your notes carefully. Some students like to type them, which can also aid retention.

MAKE YOUR OWN STUDY QUESTIONS

To master the suggested study techniques for essay exams, make up your own study questions. Base them on the headings in this chapter. Leave spaces for your answers. After you have finished, check your answers with the text to see that you have included all significant points.

DRAFT AN ESSAY EXAM ANSWER

Sample Exam Question: Identify the chief obstacles you face when preparing for an essay exam. Which suggestions in this chapter might you adopt to alleviate these concerns and improve your study habits? Write a well-developed paragraph, citing specific details and reasons for your answer. You might also construct a plan for effective study.

Making Oral Presentations

In a survey of 480 companies, the National Association of Colleges and Employers asked what qualities were considered most important when hiring. The most frequent response was

> You gain strength, courage, and confidence by every experience in which you really stop to look fear in the face. . . . You must do the thing you think you cannot do.
>
> —Eleanor Roosevelt

"communication skills." Employers want applicants who can write well and speak effectively. To help meet this need, more and more colleges and universities are incorporating speaking skills, including oral presentations, into courses across the curriculum.

But many students quake at the thought of standing before a group and making a presentation.

WHETHER SPEAKING TO SIX OR TO SIXTY . . .

If your heart does a rapid tango and your face pales at the thought of giving an oral presentation, you will be glad to know that these responses are common and surmountable. And the fundamentals of speaking are easy to learn. In fact, many students discover they are better speakers than writers.

Whether facing six coworkers or sixty participants at a training seminar, you can learn to speak with confidence. The first key is to get your fear under control. By giving yourself a pep talk and applying the many guidelines in this chapter, you can ease the task of giving an oral presentation. The second key is to practice enough but not too much. We'll talk more about this point later.

The third key is to think of the audience as friends with whom you will share some interesting information. If you are enthusiastic, they will sit up and listen. Finally, the chances are good that your college classmates will be an empathic audience because they will be presenting, too. They are apt to encourage you by listening attentively, providing the kind of support they will want when they are speaking. Now are you ready to start?

HOW DO WRITING AND SPEAKING DIFFER?

If you are asked to present a paper orally to the class, rest assured that you have already accomplished a big chunk of the work. With a little tweaking, you can adapt the paper for presentation to a live audience. To start, you need to consider how your role as writer changes to that of speaker. For both rhetorical situations, the purpose and the topic remain the same, but three other factors—occasion, audience, and voice—change dramatically.

Writing and Speaking: Comparing Two Types of Rhetorical Situations

See chapter 1.

Three basic elements differ in the rhetorical situations of writing and speaking: the occasion, audience, and voice. These differences influence how an effective presenter prepares and how an audience receives the message.

OCCASION	PURPOSE	TOPIC	AUDIENCE	VOICE
• Writing	Same	Same	• Readers *see* words	*Writer's* voice
• Speaking	Same	Same	• Listeners *see* actions, *hear* words	*Speaker's* voice

In a paper the content, punctuation, and spelling are important. *In an oral presentation, however, the content and delivery are important.* Thus this chapter contains an overview of revising a paper for presentation as well as guidance for delivering the presentation. You will see examples of purpose statements, thesis statements, introductions, conclusions, and a student speech. Specific tips for preparing notes and audiovisuals; practicing; and improving eye contact, articulation, and vocal variety are also provided.

Presenting versus Reading

Any effective presentation requires that the speaker exude the energy, enthusiasm, and vocal variety found in animated conversation. Eye contact, facial expression, gestures, and tone of voice can make words come alive. A compelling speaker can make a message vibrant and persuasive in a way that differs radically from the mechanical reading of the same message.

Yet students who lack training in oral communication are often unsure of what is expected. Some assume they can just stand up and read their paper aloud, *little realizing that eye contact is an essential part of an effective presentation.* A scientist made that same mistake at a Society of Technical Communication conference in Chicago. After five minutes of his droning, people began to leave. As he continued in a monotone, head bowed with no eye contact, more and more left. By the end of the hour, two-thirds of the audience had gone.

By applying the guidelines in this chapter, you will be spared the embarrassment this man must have endured. As you gain experience in presenting, you will appear more confident and knowledgeable during job interviews. If asked to introduce yourself, report on a team project, give a sales presentation, or summarize a research paper or project, you will be able to smile, control the butterflies, and do a creditable job.

FOUR TYPES OF ORAL PRESENTATIONS

A speaker can choose from four types of oral presentations: *manuscript, memorized, extemporaneous,* and *impromptu.* Successful reading of a manuscript takes skill, training, and charisma. Memorized presentations are hazardous because they often lack spontaneity. Then too, nervousness can cause forgetfulness.

The most effective type of prepared presentation is extemporaneous. The secret of success for this type of presentation is sufficient preparation and speaking in a *conversational* manner. Although the presenter may glance at notes, the tone is informal and friendly. An impromptu speech is a spur-of-the-moment talk, given without more than a few moments of preparation. For example, you speak impromptu when introducing yourself to the class, when escorting visitors around your workplace, or when filling in for a master of ceremonies who is late or unexpectedly unable to attend an event. As you develop skill in speaking extemporaneously, your ease in impromptu speaking will increase.

PREPARING A
PAPER FOR ORAL
PRESENTATION

If you are asked to present a paper orally, don't panic! No radical changes are required. Here is an overview of the necessary steps. Tips and examples appear later in the chapter.

1. **Mark up your paper as you simplify and condense.** Most papers, especially research-based papers, will need to be simplified and condensed. Working on a printed copy of your paper, highlight the thesis, and sharpen it further (see "Define the Purpose" on page 358). Highlight statistics and brief anecdotes that lend support for your main point. Delete minor details and less relevant examples. Put brackets around extended discussions or complicated points, and jot summaries in the margins. Watch for an unusual fact or arresting quotation. Divide long sentences into shorter ones.

2. **Perk up your introduction.** To gain listeners' attention, you might start with an engaging quotation or example related to your topic. Then link the topic to the listeners. Emphasize the ways they can use the information.

3. **Include transition to your main points.** Prepare a link from your thesis to each main point, using numerical or embedded transition according to your purpose (see pages 83 and 150).

4. **Plan an effective and memorable conclusion.** Summarize the main idea, and then give your audience something extra to think about. You might add a bit of wisdom, a provocative thought, or a look to the future.

5. **Prepare an outline.** Using note cards, sheets of paper, or the notes pages tool of presentation software, work from your marked-up paper and written plans to prepare notes. Outline your main points and significant subpoints.

6. **Prepare audiovisuals.** People like to see as well as hear. If you are talking about coaching Little League baseball, wear your official shirt and bring a ball and bat. If you have access to PowerPoint or another presentation software program, you may want to use it to support your thesis (see chapter 20).

7. **Time the presentation.** Pause slightly between sentences. If allowed four to six minutes, aim for five. The extra minute will give you time to pause for emphasis (or laughs). If needed, cut or condense points.

8. **Practice but do not overpractice.** Practice enough times so that you're comfortable but not so many that you memorize every word. Your presentation should seem fresh and spontaneous.

9. **Revise troublesome phrases.** Mark any words that cause stumbling. Use a thesaurus to find synonyms, so you can recast and shorten awkward or confusing sentences. Find words you can use comfortably and pronounce easily.

10. **Check arrangements and arrive early.** Have your notes and audiovisuals in order. Test all equipment to make sure it's hooked up and working properly. Good preparation will ease your mind.

PLANNING AN EXTEMPORANEOUS PRESENTATION

The first step toward an effective extemporaneous presentation is to analyze the rhetorical situation. The setting may impose limitations that can be circumvented, but if the topic is inappropriate for the occasion and the audience, the presentation has little chance for success.

Preview the Setting

To begin planning any presentation, find out where it will be held and the nature of the space. How large is the room? How will the seating be arranged? Is there a lectern for notes? Will you be using a microphone? Can projectors or any other necessary equipment be reserved? Is an Internet connection available? Are electrical outlets near the lectern, or are extension cords available? Is the lighting satisfactory?

The closer you can be to the audience, the more intimate and informal the setting. A semicircle is ideal because it allows you to establish eye contact with everyone. For very large audiences, a center aisle is desirable so that you can actually walk into the audience and involve individuals, particularly if there is a question-and-answer session.

If you will be using a microphone, try to practice at least a few minutes beforehand. Familiarizing yourself with the room and the equipment will not only diminish the fear of the unknown but also allow you to plan around any deficiencies and tailor the presentation to the setting.

Assess the Audience

Before definitely settling on a topic, consider the attitudes, beliefs, and values of the people to whom you will speak. Find out as much as you can about their demographics—age range, gender, ethnicity, occupation, education, or other relevant cultural factors. Then estimate how the audience will be likely to react to your topic. To analyze the audience, you might start with the familiar pattern of *who, what, why, where, when,* and *how:*

- Who will be attending? How many? (All men? All women? Mixed group?)
- What special interests or concerns do they have? (Consider age, education, and culture.)
- Why will I be making the presentation? (What do they expect and want?)
- How much will most listeners *likely know* about the topic?
- How do they *feel* about the topic? (Is the topic charged with emotion?)
- When will the presentation occur? How will the time of day, current events, or an upcoming holiday affect the rhetorical situation?

The answers to these questions will guide you in planning your approach—your thinking about how to stimulate listeners' interest. If you lack a topic or decide to switch to another, see "Ten Ideas for Oral Presentations" at the end of the chapter.

MURPHY'S LAW IN ACTION

Skipping audience analysis can invoke Murphy's law: "If anything can go wrong, it will." One student, who skipped this step, asked in a strong confident voice, "How many of you smoke? How many have tried to quit?" Only two of twenty-five classmates raised their hands. When the presenter realized that almost all of her audience were non-smokers, her face paled and her voice wavered. Her enthusiasm fled. The response of the audience was polite but lukewarm. With an audience of smokers, the how-to-quit-smoking presentation had the potential to earn an A, but it earned a C.

Consider the Occasion

When and why a presentation is given influences the length, approach to the topic, and organization. In the classroom, oral presentations will be much shorter than those generally given at work, for clients or prospective customers, or in the community. For a class you might give a one- to three-minute practice speech or a lab report. A graded presentation might run from four to eight minutes, depending on the time available and the size of the class. The purpose and audience will influence how you shape and organize the material for the presentation.

Define the Purpose

The *general* purpose of an oral presentation may be to inform, to persuade, to inspire, to dedicate, to celebrate, to entertain, to express appreciation, or a combination of these. The general purpose indicates the type of presentation. The *specific purpose statement* has three parts: purpose, topic, and desired result. Once you define your specific purpose, you can write a clear thesis statement reflecting that purpose. The thesis statement is the central idea you want to convey.

SPECIFIC PURPOSE STATEMENTS

- [purpose]   [topic]
  The purpose is to *inform* the audience about *common spiders* and
  [desired result]
  show how to determine friend from foe.

- [purpose]   [topic]
  The purpose is to *persuade* the audience that since *most spiders are*
  [desired result]
  harmless and beneficial, they should not be killed.

THESIS STATEMENTS

- Common spiders are harmless and easily distinguished from several poisonous varieties. (informative)
- Let's spare the beneficial and harmless spiders around our homes. (persuasive)

Notice that the examples above illustrate how the same subject can be approached in different ways, according to your general purpose. Before starting your outline or notes, write a specific purpose statement. It will clarify your intent and help you stay on track. Your thesis can be written later.

Select an Appropriate Topic

For a successful classroom presentation, the topic should be suitable for both you and the audience. Never speak on a subject that causes you to feel uneasy; discomfort blunts enthusiasm and dulls a presentation. Select a topic you can discuss rationally without excessive emotion—one that offers an opportunity for listeners to learn as well as to enjoy. Opinions about issues such as gun control, abortion, religion, and politics tend to be deeply ingrained and highly charged. There is little chance of changing anyone's mind; in fact, a shouting match may erupt and distract from your presentation.

Chances are that if you have already prepared a paper for another class, and it has been graded, then the topic is suitable for an oral presentation. If in doubt, ask your instructor. The following tips will help you to adapt the paper or select an entirely new topic.

Get Off the Beaten Path   Topics that have been highly publicized tend to make boring presentations. For example, most people already know quite a bit about illegal drugs, guns, and AIDS. Unless you can provide additional information that is fresh and interesting, the audience will be unlikely to listen closely. You may need to research your topic further (see chapter R-2).

Sometimes you can freshen an old topic by researching the latest discoveries, such as advances in medicine. Or if you decide to look for another topic, you might share an area of personal expertise that would interest the audience, such as Web site design, genealogical research, or building a musical instrument.

Link the Topic to the Audience   During the introduction, effective presenters establish a link between the audience and the topic. To include listeners, use personal pronouns *(you, your, we, us)*. State an advantage, benefit, or reason for them to listen. To search for a connection, you might ask yourself:

- Why should the audience listen to me?
- What benefit can they derive? (Learn, improve, enjoy, or what?)

- How can I make them eager to listen? (Start with the unusual or amusing.)

Role-Play   You might ask the class to assume a role. A bank manager wanted to practice a presentation she would be giving at work. Before the presentation, she asked the class to pretend they were managers of local branch banks who were attending a training seminar. This role-playing heightened their interest, and their attentive feedback enabled her to give an excellent presentation.

FINDING A LINK TO THE AUDIENCE

A student who collected antique glass wanted to share his hobby but doubted that the men in the audience would be interested. When he sought help in finding a link, his instructor asked, "What are men generally interested in?"

The student thought a moment, smiled, and replied, "Money?"

"Right! You could present antique glass not only as fun but also as an investment. Have you ever made a profit this way?"

"Yes, just last week," he replied. "I was driving through a village and spotted a general store. On a dusty bargain table I found a lovely old glass bowl that was hand signed. It cost just $5, but a catalog lists it for $100!" That anecdote became the opening for his presentation.

Audience Analysis: Make a Brief Written Plan

Writing down a plan or an overview of the rhetorical situation for your presentation will help to clarify the steps of preparation. In fact, your instructor may require that a plan be handed in. Below is a sample format for such a plan or overview.

PRESENTATION PLAN/RHETORICAL SITUATION OVERVIEW

1. General purpose: to _____
   Specific purpose: to _____

2. Demographics of audience:
   Estimated age range: _____ to _____ Gender: _____
   Relevant cultural factors: _____

3. What will most listeners be apt to know about the topic? _____

4. What else can you tell them? _____

5. How do they *feel* about the topic? _____
   Any touchy aspects? If so, what? _____

6. What are the implications of your audience analysis for this presentation?
   _____

7. *If* you use an argument format, how will you establish common ground? (See chapter 19.)

_____

8. What audiovisual will you use? _____ When and how will you use it? _____

9. What factors influence your credibility? _____

10. What will be your biggest challenge? Why? _____

_____

CREDIBILITY, ORGANIZATION, AND DEVELOPMENT

The aim of an extemporaneous presentation is to talk *with* an audience in a forthright manner, not *at* them. This requires showing respect for their integrity, intelligence, and values. To gain the trust of the audience and establish credibility, you need to show regard for accuracy, for ethics, and for the listeners. A knowledgeable presenter who is poised, prepared, and considerate will earn respect. Preparation includes not only collecting reliable information, planning, organizing, and practicing but also giving attention to other factors that influence credibility.

Considering Credibility

Your *credibility* (estimate of trustworthiness by the audience) is based upon the quality of the information you present and the way you present it. To gain trust and respect, you need to sound as if you know and believe what you say. That means you collect reliable information, identify sources, and radiate sincerity. See chapter R-4.

Your credibility emanates not only from thorough preparation and reliable information but also from professional demeanor and energy level. A clear confident voice, proper pronunciation, and correct grammar promote respect. Appropriate attire and a neat appearance also contribute to credibility. Look professional, not flashy. To feel tip-top and maintain your energy level, get a full night's rest and eat breakfast. To decrease anxiety, do some form of exercise.

Organizing an Informative Presentation

Clarity, logical reasoning, and flexibility are the chief factors to keep in mind as you organize an oral presentation. Depending upon the rhetorical situation, an informative presentation can be organized in various ways. For example, to explain a training procedure, use chronological order just as you would in a process paper. See chapter 11.

If you are explaining something by giving three reasons, characteristics, or other categories, you could arrange them according to importance. To describe the layout and features of a historical park, you could use spatial order or a combination of orders. As you practice a presentation, revise the order as needed. See "The Seven Basic Orders," chapter 4.

Organizing a Persuasive Presentation

A low-key argument is generally more effective than direct confrontation. The wise presenter downplays disagreement by starting with a neutral overview of an issue. A wise strategy is to follow with a point that both sides agree on. This *common ground* sets the stage for discussion. Next, state the points of the opposition *fairly* before presenting your proposition (see pages 258–59).

Treating an issue as a problem to be resolved will establish an air of objectivity and fairness. Try to find a common goal. Use the pronoun *we* whenever possible: "*We* all want Children's Services to keep on serving needy children in Hardin County. The question is, How do *we* continue services after the present operating levy expires?" This attitude will foster respect for the other side and keep tempers banked. To elicit cooperation, *ask* questions such as "What are the alternatives?" "What are the advantages and disadvantages of each alternative?" "What is the best overall solution?"

To shape an effective argument, determine the *area of resistance* and find a way around it. Why does the other side reject a proposal? Often the area of resistance is cost. You might point out "The operating levy on the ballot is a renewal. It will not increase your taxes." List the benefits and conclude with a summation such as "Anything worthwhile is going to cost money. Let's not be penny-wise and pound foolish. Let's plan for the future."

Considering Ethics, Logic, and Emotion

See chapter 19.

An important factor in any presentation is the blending of logic, ethics, and emotion. Yet there is no quick formula. First of all, appeals should be ethical. Second, most classroom presentations will require that logic predominate and emotion remain subordinate. Emotion should be subtle and suitable, used to reinforce the central point. The emphasis should be on facts, data, details, reasons, and examples.

Choosing the Right Words

When considering words, select a level of formality that is appropriate for the topic and the audience. This guideline rules out nonstandard English for classroom presentations. Informal Standard English is generally suitable for these presentations. Contractions will lend a conversational tone. If you need a technical term that the audience may not know, define it and perhaps give a brief
See chapter 2.
example.

Sometimes you can make a presentation come alive with a vivid comparison—a simile, metaphor, or analogy. John F. Kennedy, in his inaugural address on January 20, 1961, used striking imagery. The excerpt that follows contains two metaphors:

> To our *sister republics* south of the border, we offer a special pledge: to convert our good words into good deeds—in a new alliance for progress—to assist free men and free governments in casting off the *chains of poverty*.

Shy away from buzzwords, slang, and clichés that may not be understood by some generations or ethnic groups. Avoid stereotypes and any language that might offend.

Improving Transition

To track the main idea, listeners need guide words even more than readers do. When there is a shift in meaning, place a transitional word or phrase at the head of the sentence. For example, *"But* the proponents believe that . . ."* If you use chronological order or an order of importance, begin with numerical transition (*first, second, third*). For other situations involving time, you can insert transitions of time: *fifty years ago, today,* or *in the future.* If you speak of different places, begin with phrases such as *in Europe* or *at Madiera Beach.* (For lists of transitions, see the index.)

OPTIONS FOR INTRODUCTIONS AND CONCLUSIONS

Unless you plan carefully, the closing of your presentation may be the only part that an audience remembers. Unless you hook their attention early, some may daydream for the entire presentation. The attention of others may fade in and out like a weak radio signal. A successful introduction has three key ingredients:

1. **Attention-getter.** It must relate to the topic.
2. **Topic.** State the topic and the thesis unless there is a logical reason for delaying the thesis (see page 254).
3. **Relevance.** Link the topic to the audience. Whet their curiosity and interest.

Introductions

An attention-getter hooks listeners and stimulates interest, perhaps through a reference to the occasion, an anecdote or example, unfamiliar facts or fragments of history, a startling statistic or opinion, an intriguing question, an apt quotation, or original humor—something that happened to you.

Refer to the Occasion   Does the day of the presentation have historical significance? Is the occasion special for the audience or just for you? A reference to the occasion can provide an effective entry into the main idea. On September 7, 1953, George Meany, president of the American Federation of Labor, broadcast a message to our nation. He began by defining the day:

> Labor Day is the one national holiday which does not commemorate famous heroes or historic events. It is dedicated to the millions of men and women who work for wages, the people who have built America's towns and cities, the skilled and unskilled laborers who are responsible, in large measure, for the miracle of American industrial progress. As the representative of

nine million of these working men and women, it is my purpose to report to you on the issues which are of supreme importance on this Labor Day.

Offer an Anecdote or Example   A personal story that illustrates the main point allows you to ease into the topic. For example, if your purpose was to inspire and pay tribute, you might begin, "My uncle would have scoffed if someone had said he had great courage. He would have replied, 'I just did what needed to be done.'" Then the story or example would follow.

Provide an Unfamiliar Fact or Bit of History   Little-known information about a famous person, event, or place can provide an interesting opening. For example, an article from the *Wall Street Journal* (16 Oct. 1998) could serve as an opening for a persuasive presentation:

> Our Congressional Cemetery, 191 years old and located near Capitol Hill, has sunk into obscurity and decay. In fact, this cemetery—where John Philip Sousa, Mathew Brady, and other noted persons lie—was cited in 1997 as "one of the nation's 11 most endangered historic places." That fall volunteers worked for two days cutting shrubbery and sprucing up the grounds. Retired FBI agents placed a bench and fence on J. Edgar Hoover's plot, but major improvements are needed.

Give a Surprising Statistic or Opinion   To capture attention, begin with an unexpected fact or statement. This opening is handy if the topic is familiar to the audience. To interest them, you need something different, a fresh angle or an unusual comment to make them sit up and listen. Consider the following example:

> When my great-grandmother traveled from Pennsylvania to Ohio in a covered wagon in the 1800s, the family had to buy safe drinking water along the way. A typhoid epidemic was raging and people were dying. Today many of us are faced with polluted drinking water on a lesser scale, and we may not even know it. Arsenic is a naturally occurring element in our soil that flows into well water and reservoirs.

Ask a Question   Asking a *rhetorical question,* one you will answer in the presentation, can stimulate curiosity about the topic. For instance, if you were going to talk on beekeeping, you might ask, "Did you know that worker bees have to put the queen on a diet before she can fly and start a new hive? Normally, she is too heavy. They have to keep her from eating until she is light enough to fly."

Or you might ask a question and take an answer from the audience. If you take individual responses, limit them to three. Call on people who are unlikely to toss in a joke or hog the stage. The safest way is to ask a direct question of the entire audience, one that requires a brief yes or no, such as "How many of you have bought a lovely house plant only to have it die within a short time?" Then raise your own hand to indicate a show of hands.

Find an Apt Quotation   The right quotation at the beginning can lend a professional touch. In the first line of your introduction, repeat a key word or phrase from the quotation. This repetition will provide a direct lead to the main idea. If you cannot create a link, find a quotation that is relevant.

Use Humor   Using humor is like lighting a fire—you need to know what you are doing, or you may be burned. Know your audience and be professional. Keep in mind that what is funny in one culture may seem rude or inappropriate in another. Avoid ethnic, sexist, and off-color jokes or any other kind that might cause embarrassment or hurt. Original humor is best, especially brisk one-liners that bring you quickly to the main idea. All jokes should be clearly related to the topic. Keep anecdotes short. A long-winded tale can create a top-heavy presentation.

If you direct good-natured humor toward someone, choose a close friend or the head of the company—a self-confident person who will not take offense. Or better yet, tell jokes on yourself. The audience will love it, and it will keep you humble.

Inappropriate humor can blast a speaker's credibility. If you intend to use humor in a presentation, appraise it carefully, and follow these guidelines:

1. **Be original and relevant.** Relate humor closely to the main idea.
2. **Use humor like salt—sparingly.** Keep jokes and stories brief.
3. **Be kind.** Avoid remarks that might offend individuals or groups.
4. **Practice your timing.** If people do not laugh, go right on.
5. **Practice your punch line.** Pause before the punch line. Then say it clearly. Do not rush. Emphasize the important words.

GUIDELINES FOR USING HUMOR

Conclusions

In a serious presentation, the conclusion has two prime functions: to summarize and to provide closure. For most informative and persuasive presentations, the ending should *restate the main idea*. As you restate the thesis, allude to the importance of the topic to the audience. Be concise. Three guidelines can help you avoid common problems:

- Do not end abruptly.
- Do not introduce new points.
- Do not ramble.

To devise an effective closing, think about the impression you want to leave. What do you want listeners to remember? Six common endings are listed here. They can be combined in various ways, depending upon the presentation.

Summarize   For emphasis in a serious presentation, remind listeners of the thesis, either directly or by allusion. When you repeat the main idea, listeners are more apt to remember it. Or summarize your main points if appropriate. To spice up a summary ending, combine it with another type of closing.

End with a Quotation   A relevant quotation can provide a thoughtful conclusion. Do not quote an entire poem—use only a few lines that apply to the central idea of the presentation. If you began with a quotation, do not end with another. Chances are the two will conflict and detract from the presentation.

Loop to the Introduction   Allude to the opening in some way for closure. If you began with a rhetorical question, you might answer it briefly in the conclusion. If you began with a quotation, you might repeat a key phrase. Or if you began with a story, you might quickly finish it as Paul Harvey does in "the rest of the story."

Pose a Challenge or Question   A challenge or provocative question can motivate an audience. This ending is often used to persuade. For example, a presentation that reports the progress on a volunteer playground project might end with appreciation, a summary, and a question (note the emotional appeal):

> We appreciate your generosity. You have opened your pocketbooks and lent your hands. The job is almost complete. Will you come once more to help rake the site and spread mulch this Saturday or Sunday? Seeing the delight on the children's faces when they can use this playground will make you glad you did.

Call for Action   A persuasive presentation requires a restatement of the proposition. Often a call for action is also included to motivate the audience. For example, "Tonight set your alarm ten minutes early. Then stop by the voting booth on your way to class or to work. You owe it to yourself and your country."

Refer to the Future   Mentioning the future can lend an optimistic note. In "I Have a Dream," Martin Luther King combined three techniques in his ending: he summarized the main idea, alluded to the future, and quoted from an old song. Note, too, the use of *we* to unite listeners:

> When we let freedom ring, when we let it ring from every village and every hamlet, from every state and every city, we will be able to speed up that day when all of God's children, black men and white men, Jews and Gentiles, Protestants and Catholics, will be able to join hands and sing in the words of the old Negro spiritual, "Free at last! Free at last! Thank God almighty, we are free at last!"

PREPARING NOTES

By preparing careful notes, you can build your confidence and enhance your presentation. True, some experienced speakers manage without notes, but most carry them as insurance. Even professional presenters are not immune to sudden memory loss. One strode up to the lectern without his notes, confident because he had practiced well. But when he looked out over a sea of five hundred faces, his mind went blank. While the audience waited, he walked back to his chair and picked up the notes. That was a humbling experience.

By now you should be convinced that notes are essential, even if your instructor does not require them. The one remaining question is whether to put the notes on file cards or paper.

Using Note Cards

For short presentations, such as those you give in class, note cards are practical and easy to use. Wind from an air conditioner or an overhead projector will not disturb them. Before the presentation, lay out the cards in order. Six large file cards will usually fit neatly in two rows on the lectern. Although six may seem like quite a few, that is better than crowding words on two or three. *You need to be able to scan your notes quickly without touching or bending over to read them.*

Note cards should be legible from three feet away so that you can glance at them unobtrusively. That will allow you to appear more informal and at ease.

1. **Use large 5- by 8-inch cards.** For easy reading, avoid crowding.
2. **Number the cards in the upper right corner.** Avoid mixups.
3. **Use an outline format.** Leave white space to add key phrases later.
4. **Print neatly with black ink in large letters.** Use broad strokes.
5. **Use numbers or bullets to list points.** Enhance visibility.
6. **Use only one side of each card.** Turning cards over diverts attention.
7. **Highlight.** Using a yellow marker, highlight statistics and any trouble spots. (You'll find those as you practice.)

TIPS FOR MAKING NOTE CARDS

Using Sheets of Paper

For long presentations, some speakers type their notes in an oversize font on 8- by 11-inch sheets of white paper. During the presentation they maintain eye contact and talk while sliding a used sheet to the left. (Picking up the sheets or turning them over is unnecessary and distracting.) One disadvantage of this method is that it takes considerable practice to do well. Another is that the sheets are easily disturbed by a puff of air and flutter to the floor.

If you decide to use this method, type your outline and double space. Follow the tips for preparing note cards. Number the sheets in the upper right corner and check the order carefully. Practice several times until you can use them smoothly. Before you begin speaking, place them in a neat pile on the *left* side of the lectern. As you finish using each page, *slide it to the other side of the lectern while looking at your audience.* (If you are using presentation software, the program will include options for preparing notes.)

PRACTICING A PRESENTATION

Planning and practice are essential for an effective presentation. Attending to equipment at the last minute and dropping or misplacing items can give the impression of carelessness and incompetence. Careful preparation will boost your confidence and help fend off mishaps.

Practice your presentation several times, using your note cards and audiovisuals, but do not overpractice, or it may sound memorized. To lend a natural conversational tone, you might imagine you are talking to friends. *Act as if you feel calm, even if you don't.* If you have the opportunity to videotape a practice session, do so. Then you can critique your eye contact, posture, gestures, vocal variety, and use of notes and audiovisuals.

Using Audiovisuals

Chances are that you will have a software program such as PowerPoint at your disposal for use in a classroom presentation. Or you might use an overhead projector, a flip chart, or other visual. If you use tapes or videos, keep the clips short—a minute or less for a five- to seven-minute speech. (A chalkboard is not recommended because it lacks novelty and requires turning your back while the audience waits.) On the job you might use virtual meeting software, which allows remote participants on broadband networks to hear and see the speaker and the presentation materials.

Plan how and when to use audiovisuals so that the audience does not have to wait. Can you set up and adjust PowerPoint, the VCR, or tape players before class? How will you prop up the antique doll? Can you get an easel so that the poster will not flop over? Other questions to consider are when to bring out objects and how long to leave them out.

As you speak, *look at the audience, not the visuals.* When using an overhead projector, use a pencil to point on the transparency. When slides or other visuals are projected on a screen behind you, use a longer object to point to areas of the screen. That way you can glance at it and look at the audience, not the screen. If you are describing an unfamiliar object or craft, such as punched tin, bring it out early. If the object will not distract, leave it out the entire time. Or some objects are more effective shown only at the end.

One student, who had won several trophies showing her horse, did not want to appear to be bragging, so she decided to display just one trophy. First she described the fun of displaying the horse in the ring; then she explained the unglamorous work behind the scenes. At the end she held up a large trophy and said, "But all the hard work was worthwhile, for I won first prize!" By then she had charmed the audience, and they were glad her efforts had been rewarded.

1. **Predict the effect of the visual and test it.** *Run unusual ideas past your instructor.* Use nothing that violates campus policies, such as guns, snakes, fire crackers, volatile liquids, or anything else that might pose a threat to the audience.

2. **Limit the number of visuals and keep them fairly simple.** Otherwise, you may feel like a juggler with too many balls in the air.

3. **If you have several statistics or other complex items, prepare a handout to pass out before you begin.** Do not interrupt your presentation to pass material. Less relevant information can be left near the door to be picked up afterward.

4. **Limit tapes and videos to one minute in a five- to seven-minute presentation.**

5. **Check to see that visuals are clear to persons seated in the back row.** If you are discussing a small object, show an enlargement.

6. **Retain the element of surprise!** To stimulate interest, keep the AV hidden until you use it. (Cover items before bringing them in. Reverse posters until you are ready to show them.)

Note: For tips on creating visuals, see chapter 20.

GUIDELINES FOR PLANNING AUDIOVISUALS

Revising Note Cards

As you practice your presentation, highlight key points on your notes with a colored marker. If you quote someone, highlight it. If certain terms are difficult to recall, print them in red. Reword any phrases or sentences that cause stumbling. Write the revision on your note card. Star the spots where audiovisuals will come. On the final card or page, write out the last sentence as a safety blanket. If your notes become messy from revision, recopy them as necessary for easy reading.

Improving Eye Contact, Posture, and Gestures

Before you ever open your lips, you send silent messages that enhance or diminish your credibility. Your eye contact, posture, and gestures greatly affect your presentation. Do you look at the audience—or do you stare at a point on the back wall? Do you stand erect or slumped? Do you have notes in hand ready to lay out, or do you fumble through a briefcase, backpack, or handbag?

Eye Contact   Smile and establish eye contact immediately before you say a word. During the presentation, look at one person for several seconds before moving on. Look at various people in different parts of the room, not just the front row. Avoid eye dart. You may *glance* at your note cards from time to time, but do not linger. Their purpose is merely to remind you of the next idea.

Gestures   Like your words, your gestures should appear spontaneous and natural. You might rest one hand on the lectern, but do not clutch it with both hands. The purpose of a lectern is to hold notes, not to lean on or hide behind. Once in a while you may want to walk out from behind the lectern, but beware of purposeless movement and repetitive gestures. Consider, too, that some gestures may have negative or humorous connotations. Three common stances have been identified as detrimental for speakers:

- **Fig leaf.** Avoid standing with hands clasped in front.
- **Parade rest.** Avoid standing with hands clasped behind the back like a general reviewing the troops.
- **Closed mind.** Avoid crossed arms on the chest. This posture may suggest coldness and a reluctance to admit new information.

While you speak, let you arms hang loosely at your sides so that you can use them naturally. Avoid nervous habits that dispel the illusion of spontaneity and distract. Common habits include scratching the nose, twisting long hair or beard, fidgeting with earrings, jingling coins, taking glasses on and off, or waving a note card around.

Improving Vocal Variety

The human voice is an instrument that conveys distinctive speech sounds that vary in volume, rate, and pitch. When we are relaxed and happy, the sounds are more pleasing than when we are tired or upset. Fear, anxiety, and anger tighten the vocal cords, producing a higher, thinner pitch than normal. With practice you can gain greater control of your voice. Volume and rate are easier to control than pitch, but all can be improved to some extent. Taping an entire presentation allows you not only to time it but also to hear how you sound.

Volume   A presenter's voice should be loud enough to be heard by everyone in the room, unless a microphone is available. To project your voice to the back row, you need plenty of air in the lungs. Shallow breathing interferes with vocal variety and quality. Try varying your volume according to the effect you wish to create. Emphasize important words. Be careful that your voice does not trail off at the ends of sentences, making them inaudible.

Rate   "Mallspeak" or immature speech patterns may be a concern for some readers. In "Taking Aim at Student Incoherence" (*Chronicle of Higher Education* 26 Mar. 1999), Alison Schneider cites this sample, delivered breathlessly: "Okay. Today I'm going to be talking to you guys about malaria." During the presentation the student fidgeted and giggled, ending with "So, in conclusion, I'd just like to say, malaria, you know, is the most prevalent of all tropical diseases." Speaking too fast, fidgeting, and giggling may be due to nervousness or feelings of inadequacy, intensified by habit. If you have any of these concerns, give yourself a little pep talk. Reassure yourself that these minutes are yours and you have an interesting topic to share. The audience is alert and waiting. You don't have to race to the finish line. Don't be afraid to pause at the right places, including a slight pause after periods. Pausing after an important point gives emphasis and allows the audience time to absorb the idea. Knowing that it is all right to pause naturally may help you delete unintentional fillers such as *uh, um, okay,* or *you know.*

Articulation Practice and pausing can alleviate slurring (running words together) or other problems in articulation. The lips, the tongue, and the teeth form speech sounds—they articulate the words. At the same time, the mouth has to open wide enough to let the words out or mumbling occurs. And *it must be empty*—chewing gum, candy, or cough drops interfere with clear delivery.

Common concerns are slurring and addition of or omission of syllables. Tape yourself and then check a dictionary for problem words. Listed here are common mispronunciations and the correct pronunciations:

INCORRECT	CORRECT
acrost	a-cross'
fishin'	fish'ing
gonna	go'ing to
pitchur	pic'ture
wanna	want to

Pitch *Pitch* refers to the lowness or highness of the voice. We all have a natural pitch that varies according to our emotions and health. Other factors also influence pitch. For example, if we ask a question, our voice goes up at the end of the sentence. At the end of a declarative sentence, the voice goes down. Most speakers, when relaxed, vary their pitch naturally. Those who speak in a monotone can add expression to their words through vocal exercise and practice (see the exercises at the end of the chapter).

GIVING A PRESENTATION

Enthusiasm and *sincerity* are two keys to an effective presentation. Enthusiastic speakers know and care about their topics. They vary their volume, rate, and pitch just as they would in casual conversation. Chances are that if you like your topic and prepare well, your enthusiasm will radiate from your face and your voice. And if you truly believe what you are saying, your sincerity will be apparent.

Arrive Early

Go early to the room where you will speak. Erase the board if necessary. Check to see that the equipment you need is in working order. (One mortified student forgot to plug in the VCR.) If you are supposed to sign equipment out some-where else, go get it.

Take a Deep Breath . . .

When introduced, take a deep breath and approach the lectern. Put down your notes or, if you're using note cards, lay them out in sequence. Then look out over the audience and smile. Chances are that some people will smile back. If you come across as a friendly person, listeners will be more apt to give you their un-divided attention. For some topics, smiling may be inappropriate.

On the job or in a community setting, extend an appropriate greeting, such as "Good Morning" or "Welcome." You may want to thank someone who has assisted or the group for inviting you. In the classroom these little courtesies are not expected.

Don't Apologize Unnecessarily

Even if you feel unprepared, rushed, or nervous, don't apologize or toss in un-necessary comments. Just ignore your feelings and begin with your planned opening. Once you get past that and the audience responds, speaking will be-come easier. If you should mispronounce a word, just correct yourself and go on. Avoid weak, *ineffective* remarks such as these:

- Uh, I guess I'm a little nervous.
- I didn't have as much time to prepare as I would have liked.
- I regret I am not an expert on this topic (false modesty).

Adapt to the Audience and Unexpected Events

Watching the audience will take your mind off yourself. Are they listening at-tentively? Or do they slump in their seats, gaze at the ceiling, or fidget? To re-gain lost attention, you can move out from behind the lectern, use more ges-tures, increase volume, or lower your voice to a whisper.

Handle unexpected incidents with poise. If a transparency falls, let it lie un-less you need it. If the bulb in an overhead projector burns out, flip the switch for the spare bulb. If there is none, continue anyway. If computer equipment malfunctions, take a moment to resolve the problem. If the problem can't be fixed within a few moments, go on without the audiovisual. Seldom is there cause to interrupt a presentation. In the unlikely event of a power outage, sonic boom, or storm alert, stop and wait. Then when you resume the presentation, you might toss in a quick joke about the interruption. The audience will admire your calm, professional demeanor and ability to function under duress.

End Purposefully and Gracefully

The last few words of a presentation tend to linger in the minds of the audience. Once in a while, an inexperienced presenter will skid to an abrupt stop with "That's it" or "that's all." Some go to the other extreme—tacking on afterthoughts, irrelevant jokes, or stories. Such tactics throw a presentation off balance and weaken its impact. Know when to stop.

Be Prepared for Questions

After a class presentation, there may not be time for questions. For presentations at work or in the community, however, question-and-answer sessions are often expected. In these cases, you should be prepared to say, "Are there any questions?"

Listen carefully to the entire question before answering. Maintain eye contact. If the question is unclear, ask for a restatement. Or you might paraphrase: "In other words, you are asking if . . . ?" Wait for a response. This tactic will allow you a little time to think. If you don't know the answer, you might reply, "That's an excellent question. I'd like to do a little research before responding. Can I get back to you?" Then ask for a phone number or an e-mail address.

STUDENT SAMPLE: A PERSUASIVE PRESENTATION

Carol Witzel gave the following presentation extemporaneously. She had outlined it on note cards but wrote out the draft later, when requested.

Give It More Respect!

Do you know what the hottest part of your body is? Do you know what part is the most dangerous if it becomes infected? The answer to both questions is your mouth, specifically your gums and teeth. Are you surprised? Like Rodney Dangerfield, your mouth and its contents get little respect. After you hear of my unfortunate experience, you should accord this part of your body much, much more respect.

During a regular checkup two years ago, my physician said that he did not like the looks of my gums and that I should have a dentist take a look at them. Immediately, I made an appointment with my regular dentist. I told him my mouth had a metallic taste, and my teeth seemed to hurt often. During the exam the dentist told me not to worry, everything was fine. He did not bother to take x-rays.

One year passed and the symptoms worsened. By then my gums were bleeding every time that I brushed my teeth. When I opened my mouth in cold air, my face and teeth hurt. Finally, I decided it was time to consult a different dentist. The second dentist did a quick exam—the results were dismal. Several teeth had advanced decay. Worst of all, my gums were in an advanced stage of periodontal disease or gingivitis. Gingivitis is inflammation and infection of the gingiva or gums. There are five stages of the disease, and I was in stage four.

What I needed was minor surgery on the gums to clear away the infection. Then he put in seven crowns to correct the problems with decayed teeth. After that came bridgework, which involved three additional crowns and two pontics (false teeth). The bridge was made to cover the loss of two teeth due to poor care. Correcting all these problems cost nearly $7,000.

Today you cannot tell my natural teeth from the crowns or bridgework. My teeth no longer hurt when I drink hot or cold liquids. I can actually breathe through my mouth without severe pain emitting from teeth to all points on my face.

Now you are probably wondering how you can prevent some of the problems I've experienced. The first step is to have regular dental checkups with a responsible dentist. Second, take good daily care of your teeth and mouth by brushing and flossing. Third, watch for any of these five symptoms:

1. **Bleeding in the mouth.** Have it checked just as you would if some other part of your body was bleeding regularly.
2. **A metallic taste.** If you already have fillings, this could mean you have decay under the filling, and the old filling is leaking.
3. **Extreme sensitivity** to hot and cold temperatures.
4. **Chronic bad breath.**
5. **Chronic tiredness, headaches, or white spots on the gums** could indicate infection. Those who use tobacco should watch these signs closely because of the risk of cancer in the mouth.

If your dentist does not stress good gum care, maybe you should consider finding another dentist. Just remember that your mouth is the gateway to your body. To have good health, respect and maintain your mouth, gums, and teeth. You will be glad you did!

QUESTIONS FOR DISCUSSION

1. How does Carol involve the audience in her opening?
2. What common order does she use to present information?
3. What signpost transitions indicate this order?
4. Can you find the transitional sentence that she uses to go from talking about herself to explaining about good dental care?
5. What do you notice about her ending?
6. React to the title of her speech.
7. How would you rate Carol's credibility? Why?

PRACTICE

EXERCISE: Articulation

To improve your articulation, say the alphabet aloud. Exaggerate each letter and say it distinctly. Listen and think about the position of your tongue and lips. They must be in the right position for a letter to be clear. To form an *l*, the tip of the tongue touches the roof of the mouth, and the mouth opens slightly. The *r* sound rumbles deep in the throat as the tongue is held up slightly and the mouth curls down, slightly open.

If dropping of *g*'s is a problem for you, practice words ending with *-ing* and think about the position of your tongue and mouth as you say them correctly, emphasizing *-ing*. As you attain greater self-awareness, your vocal variety will improve.

EXERCISE: Volume, Rate, Pitch

To improve vocal variety, you might read aloud to a child. To relax the vocal cords, exaggerate the sounds and have fun. *Goldilocks and the Three Bears* provides excellent practice, allowing the reader to assume different voices. Baby Bear's words tumble out in a high squeaky pitch. Mother Bear articulates clearly at a moderate rate in a medium-pitched voice. Papa Bear speaks in a slow, deep-pitched voice that rumbles with authority. (If the child can read, she can take Goldilocks's part. A boy might prefer a role in *The Three Little Pigs*.)

UNGRADED PRESENTATIONS

The chief purpose of an ungraded presentation is to alleviate speech fright. A one- or two-minute practice speech can use the basic claim-and-evidence order (opinion and support). For example, you might disagree with a news item, magazine article, political decision, or movie review. Give reasons. Close with a complete sentence, such as "See *Clint Rides Again* only if you want to be bored stiff." Or you might use one of the ideas below or one of your own.

1. Funny, exciting, or embarrassing moment
2. An incident: how your spouse proposed, prank at summer camp, et cetera
3. Anecdote: a lost pet, special birthday, or disastrous first date
4. Your first job, first car, or first day at school
5. A scary experience

TEN IDEAS FOR ORAL PRESENTATIONS

INFORMATIVE TOPICS

1 Present a research-based paper or project to the class (condense and simplify).

2 Practice a presentation you will be giving at work or elsewhere.

3 Present tips for doing or improving something.

4 Describe your job and three things you have learned.

5 Describe your hobby. (Bring objects in stages of completion.)

PERSUASIVE TOPICS

6 Research a local issue and take a position.

7 Take your pet to be neutered.

8 How to prevent fires in your home.

9 Make out a living will.

10 Be an organ donor.

Effective Employment Writing

First impressions are power-ful. During an interview you will be evaluated on how well you might fit the posi-tion. Beforehand, gather as much information as possi-ble online and from anyone

> Your expression, your handshake, your dress, your résumé can make you a success or failure in seconds.
>
> —Mark Mehler, Principal at CareerXroads, Kendall Park, New Jersey

you know within the company so that you can better estimate expectations for applicants. Select footwear, apparel, and accessories that fit the com-pany image; avoid trendy styles. Smile, respond with a firm handshake and direct eye contact. Radiate confidence, goodwill, and enthusiasm. Carry a copy of your résumé, protected in a large envelope.

CHALLENGING INTERVIEW QUESTIONS

Perhaps the most daunting questions in an employment interview are "Will you tell me about yourself?" and "Why do you want to work for us?" Be prepared for both. Give a brief summary of your education, training, and work history. Specify special projects completed and accomplishments that relate to the position. Avoid unrelated personal information. Refer to the company's reputation and other information you've learned while researching the company. Ask questions about job duties but wait for the interviewer to mention salary. If not mentioned then, near the end of the interview, ask a tactful question such as "What is the usual salary for this position?"

I. WRITING AN EFFECTIVE RÉSUMÉ

Your résumé can be the ticket to obtaining an interview. The aim is to fit your qualifications to the desired position. Keep in mind that employers look for applicants who are not only skilled and accurate but also reliable and trustworthy. Good character is a quality that employers invariably seek when hiring. In fact, integrity has become a hidden agenda for employers.

VITAL QUESTIONS TO CONSIDER

Do Employers Usually Check Résumés and References?

www.mhhe.com/dietsch
For online advice on writing in work settings, go to: Writing>Résumés/Writing at Work

Before hiring, most employers check résumés and references carefully. Flagrant abuses of truth on résumés have become common as more applicants fudge dates, magnify accomplishments, pad job duties, and invent college degrees. As employers scan résumés, they watch for anything that might indicate falsity, exaggeration, or carelessness. As they check references, they query former employers about the applicant's actual length of employment, position, awards, promotions, and other items. To ensure accuracy, allot plenty of time for preparing your résumé.

Is One Résumé Enough?

Most job seekers will need a *printed résumé* for mailing and faxing. If they apply to large companies that screen résumés with software, a *scannable résumé* will also be requested. Since many companies ask for an *e-mail résumé*, a third version may be necessary. Compiling different versions of a résumé is not as complicated as you might think, for all three have the same basic content. Only the format varies. Below are three basic guidelines for compiling an effective résumé:

- Focus the résumé toward the needs of the employer.
- Present all qualifications honestly and accurately.
- Proofread the résumé carefully several times before using. All spelling and punctuation must be correct.

You may also be questioned closely about other items on your résumé. Answer confidently. Be willing to take nicotine and drug tests, as well as psychological, math, or other competency tests. For many jobs, fingerprinting is required.

TEN REASONS RÉSUMÉS ARE DISCARDED

As you assemble personal data for your résumé, double-check all dates and consider the relevance of each item. Include only accurate information that is linked to your job objective. Here are ten common reasons résumés are discarded:

1. **Omission of keywords.** For the initial screening, many large companies use software that scans for keywords related to the position. Include them.
2. **Lack of focus.** Irrelevant information and lack of a job objective can cause an employer to wonder if the applicant is knowledgeable.
3. **Problems in format.** A résumé should be clear and easily scanned in twenty seconds or less. A summary of qualifications or "profile" should appear after the job objective. Avoid fancy fonts, crowding, and lengthy paragraphs. For most applicants, one or two pages is enough.
4. **Skimpy listing of skills and experience.** Be succinct but specific. Start each listing with an active verb and include your accomplishments.
5. **Few or no dates.** When dates are missing, the employer wonders what the applicant is trying to hide.
6. **Job hopping.** A series of short-term jobs may cause employers to wonder why you left and if you will do the same again. A functional résumé can de-emphasize this concern.
7. **Listing health problems.** One woman with an MBA and an impressive work history listed "2006–2007 Recovery from cancer. Cured." After receiving no calls, she removed the item and inserted "Personal obligations." Legally, *only disabilities that hinder your productivity* must be disclosed, not medical history. Before hiring, such disabilities must be revealed, but do not refer to them on your résumé.
8. **Discrepancies.** One woman accidentally misstated her college graduation date by one year. Her résumé, targeted for an accounting position, was weeded out.
9. **Not following employer's directions.** Include requested information such as licensure, bonding, or immigration status. Some employers request a cover letter be e-mailed *before* a résumé.

10. **Spelling and grammatical errors.** Employers consider such errors inexcusable. Most positions for college graduates require accuracy and writing competency.

TWO POPULAR STYLES OF RÉSUMÉS

An excellent résumé is more than a work history; *it states what you can do to benefit the employer.* The résumé should reveal how you performed in the workplace or in the community if you did volunteer work. If you have a dual major or work experience in two areas and wish to apply for two different jobs, then you will need two different résumés, each focused on just one position.

Two current résumé styles are the chronological and the functional. Actually, both are hybrids of their forerunners of a few years ago. Acute differences between the two styles have blurred: Now both invariably contain a job objective, a summary of qualifications, and a listing of accomplishments and skills, as well as work experience and education with dates.

The chief differences are that the chronological style emphasizes employment and skills gained on each job whereas the functional style emphasizes a mix of skills gained from work, education, and leisure. Both styles are quite flexible, and examples of each style vary widely. Still the basic principles for writing résumés apply, regardless of whether they are faxed, scanned, or e-mailed.

The Chronological Résumé

If you have worked in just one career field, progressed upward, and acquired the skills for your targeted position, then the chronological style is the best choice for you. The *chronological* style emphasizes solid qualifications and achievement on the job over several years. This style usually highlights work experience, setting forth what the applicant has accomplished (in reverse chronological order).

If you have a gap in employment, that does not necessarily raise a red flag, for layoffs have become routine at all ranks. If you have taken a job with less pay after such a gap, be prepared to supply a valid reason during an interview (family illness or similar one). If you are switching career fields or have been fired (never mention on a résumé), then the functional résumé is definitely the better choice.

The Functional Résumé

The *functional* résumé style emphasizes skills and abilities—not when, where, or how you obtained them. When new college graduates have minimal work experience, they can fill out their résumé with groups of skills learned in classes, during internships, or from volunteer projects. Older students who are switching career fields can de-emphasize the disparity between their work experience and job objective by listing relevant achievements before their work history. Dates of work experience and education are listed in reverse chronological order.

A series of short-term jobs and gaps in employment receive less emphasis on a functional résumé (more help on this point a little later). The flexibility of the functional style makes it the best choice for most young students or others with little or no work experience in their chosen field.

RESEARCH AND PREWRITING FOR A RÉSUMÉ

The purpose of any résumé is to obtain an interview. To succeed, you need to package your qualifications in the most appealing way possible without deviating from the truth. Writing an effective résumé requires knowledge, skill, effort, and accuracy. You need to have a general knowledge of your career field, know what employers want, have certain skills, and present yourself well. From your résumé and during interviews, prospective employers will be trying to predict how you will fit in with the company and how well you will perform.

The first step to a successful résumé is preliminary research of your career field. You need background knowledge of possible positions, job duties, working conditions, and the correct terminology to use. New jobs are being created constantly, and new words are born every day.

Tips for an Employment Search

During a preliminary career search, you should gain an overview of your field, employment opportunities, correct job titles, and possible keywords to include on a résumé. If your search is unfocused, you can fritter away hours. A good place to start is company Web sites in your field. There you can find information about employers and possible job openings. Some social networking Web sites, such as Facebook and MySpace, also carry such information.

Special databases that provide profiles of careers on state and national levels are available at campus libraries. A computerized index can assist in locating career articles in journals and magazines. A reference librarian can help you focus your search. The Career Resources Directory, which soon follows, also lists print, online, and database resources that should be helpful.

Identifying Employers' Needs

The more you know about the qualifications that employers seek, the better you can tailor your résumé to fit a company's specific needs. Read newspaper help-wanted ads, but also visit Web sites of employers and read their job descriptions, even if they want more skills than you have. They can help you gain command of the correct terminology to use. Print out any ads that interest you. Underline keywords relating to the job you would like.

PRINT SOURCES (To locate, ask the reference librarian.)

- *Encyclopedia of Careers and Vocational Guidance.* 13th ed. Ferguson Publishing Company, 2005. This five-volume set reviews 93 career fields and nearly 700 careers. The first volume includes finding a job, choosing a career, and networking.
- *Occupational Outlook Handbook.* 2006–2007 ed. US Department of Labor, Bulletin 2570. Includes job requirements, duties, salaries, and outlook.
- *O'Net Dictionary of Occupational Titles.* 4th ed. by Michael Farr and Lawrence Shatkin. JIST Works, 2007. Source: US Department of Labor.
- **Specialized Encyclopedias.** Ask if there are any in your field. They include job descriptions, licensing, salaries, and employment outlook.
- *VGM Opportunities Series.* VGM Career Books, 2001–2007. Covers a wide range of careers from culinary to veterinary medicine.

INTERNET RESOURCES

DIRECTORY 1:
PRINT AND ONLINE CAREER RESOURCES

The Web sites listed below provide free, up-to-date help with minimal sales promotion. (Most browsers will fill in http://.)

- **Career Onestop.** Free job and résumé postings. Explore wages, job trends, skills, abilities, et cetera. <www.careeronestop.org>
- *Occupational Outlook Handbook.* 2006–2007 ed. Printer-friendly version in HTML. <www.bls.gov/oco/home.htm>
- **O Net.** Online version of the *U.S. Dictionary of Occupational Titles,* the *Directory of Occupational Titles,* and the *Occupational Job Outlook.*

ONLINE DATABASES

Some libraries allow you to access these databases from your home computer, using your library card number. Ask the reference librarian.

- *EBSCOhost.* Offers articles and abstracts of periodicals from a range of disciplines. The *Vocational & Career Collection* provides the text of 400 trade- and industry-related periodicals.
- *Encyclopedia of Careers and Vocational Guidance.* Online version of the printed five-volume set (see above).

Note: Directory 2, "Online Employment Writing Resources," also lists sites that provide other career information (see page 399).

It also helps to understand problems that employers commonly face but rarely discuss with applicants: theft, security of data, low productivity, and lawsuits, to name a few. Such items compose an invisible agenda that directs the appraisal of résumés and applicants. If you can adroitly show on your résumé how a company can benefit from hiring you, the targeted job may well be yours. As you research, watch for answers to the following questions:

1. What are the main duties of the position?
2. Which skills, qualities, and habits do potential employers seek?
3. Which keywords recur in help-wanted ads?
4. Which kind of position is likely to be most appropriate for you?
5. What is likely to be the employer's chief concern? (Read your local newspapers carefully for news of businesses and other employers.)
6. How can I help to provide a solution for that concern?

Identifying Qualifications

A giant first step toward compiling an effective résumé is identifying *transferable skills*, skills that can be applied on another job. A *skill* is an art, trade, or craft honed by extensive practice. Thinking tasks require mental abilities such as problem solving, decision making, designing, and the like. After identifying your skills and abilities, devise ways to attest to your positive personal qualities and desirable work habits. Keep in mind that you need *concrete evidence* to back up these claims.

Transferable skills become the heart of your résumé. To identify skills, examine your experience in the workplace, in college, and during leisure hours. Take a sheet of paper and write three headings—"Work Skills," "Academic Skills," and "Leisure Skills"—and brainstorm. Jot down your work duties and the skills required. Consider both paid and unpaid jobs; include military service, internships, and volunteer work. Under "Academic Skills," list training and skills obtained during your education. Then list any skills developed during leisure hours that pertain to the job.

Workplace Skills   Your workplace skills include many abilities and responsibilities. Some may have been listed in your job description when you were hired, but others may have been added later. To prod your memory, you might ask yourself these questions:

- **What problems have I helped to solve or alleviate?** Include cost control, procedural changes, security, troubleshooting, or others.
- **What tasks can I perform effectively?** Include purchasing, data entry, network installations, software applications, Web site design.
- **What equipment can I operate, maintain, or repair?** Include everything from oscilloscopes to cash registers to backhoes.
- **What systems, layouts, or operations have I designed or executed?**
- **Have I ever inventoried, audited, or researched?** Include online research, lab or legal research, conducting surveys, and interviewing.

- **What writing did I do on the job?** Minutes or e-mails? Letters or newsletters? Procedures or manuals? Reports or proposals? Patient charts? Others?

- **What oral communication skills have I developed?** Have I conducted meetings? Given presentations? Taught or trained? Screened applicants? Greeted clients? Handled complaints?

- **What tasks have required interpersonal skill?** Handling difficult clients or patients? Negotiating? Making collections? Resolving problems?

- **What have I done that demonstrated responsibility?** Supervised or managed? Reorganized a department? Expanded? Resolved disputes? Budgeted? (State amount if large.) Hired? Scheduled? Coordinated projects?

- **How have I contributed to the success of projects and operations?** Decreased costs? Increased profits? Improved client or community relations?

- **Did I receive training in the military or in special courses on the job?**

- **Do I have any special licenses or certifications? Bonding? Security clearance?**

Academic Skills   Think of your college courses as training, but do *not* list courses. Look for *skills* you have acquired—that's what employers want to know. Consider, too, any skills developed from internships, clinics, or other educational outside work. You might start by asking yourself questions such as these:

- **What equipment have I learned to operate? Repair? Maintain?**

- **What procedures have I performed?** Medical, legal, accounting, insurance billing, or others?

- **How have I used management skills?** What projects have I completed? Include work with campus organizations, fund-raising, event planning, tutoring, counseling, case work, and other projects.

- **What oral communication skills and interpersonal skills have I honed?** Giving presentations? Listening? Questioning? Applying business etiquette training? Do I speak a second language?

- **What research and writing skills have I demonstrated?** Include research papers, business report writing, independent study projects, published work in campus newspapers or magazines, and the like.

- **What other specialized training do I have?** Include skills such as "build prototypes," "diagnose electrical failures," CPR or EMT training, or other special knowledge in your field.

Personal Skills   During leisure hours you may have acquired planning, leadership, financial, teaching, or other skills that are relevant to the position you seek. Consider activities in high school, college, or community organizations as well as hobbies.

- **What projects have I completed for my family and home?** You might list compiling a family genealogy, remodeling a kitchen, or building a patio. Then try to link the skill to the job objective. (All these tasks require planning and organizational skills.)
- **What community projects have I participated in?** Planning? Managing a scout troop? Coaching a team? Assisting in a day care center? Counseling on a hotline? Judging contests? Writing a newsletter? Organizing?
- **Have I developed special skills?** Photography, music, drawing, designing, writing, quilting, cooking, woodworking, or others?
- **Do I have other knowledge derived from adult education courses, seminars, workshops, or conferences?**

Revising Skill Lists

Compiling a detailed skills list will require more than one session. Time is needed to mull over your experience. When revising your lists, watch for vague fluff phrases, commonly found in résumés. Replace general terms such as "communication skills," "team player," "organizational skills," and "interpersonal skills" with active verbs, specific words, and examples. Avoid trite, unsubstantiated claims such as "work well with people," "honest," and "hard-working."

Adding Action Verbs   Accurate, positive verbs can make skills attractive, parallel, and convincing. "Managed fifteen employees" indicates a skill; "excellent manager" is a claim without evidence. Skills are written in the past tense if you no longer have that job.

calculate	establish	maintain	record	**ACTION VERBS FOR RÉSUMÉS**
compute	expand	operate	refine	
conduct	implement	organize	reorganize	
coordinate	increase	originate	repair	
create	initiate	plan	research	
decrease (costs)	innovate	prepare	schedule	
develop	install	produce	support	

Adding Specific Examples   Give specific examples that show not only experience but also indicate sound work habits. Employers look for reliability, confidentiality, congeniality, and flexibility. However, you won't claim these directly on your résumé. Instead, you might list items that indicate these qualities, such as these examples:

- Met all deadlines for reports and projects
- Collected cash receipts and made bank deposits
- Entrusted with keys to open and close business
- Maintained and monitored confidential client files
- Received two promotions within one year
- Acted as supervisor during boss's two-month leave
- Never missed a day's work in five years

DRAFTING A RÉSUMÉ

The major parts of a résumé are *job objective, summary, accomplishments, skills, work experience,* and *education.* The job objective always comes first and the summary second, but other major parts follow in most- to least-important order, according to the applicant's qualifications. In other words, you organize these sections to your best advantage, using either the chronological or functional résumé style. Major sections containing dates are arranged in *reverse chronological order.* Thus the most recent date is listed first. Minor information, if any, follows.

A few experts suggest omitting the objective. But job objectives are generally regarded as essential in order to focus the résumé and save the employer's time. Few are going to spend time trying to figure out which position the applicant wants.

The Service-Oriented Job Objective

As you look at résumé samples, notice that good job objectives focus on just one career field. They also focus on the needs of the employer, not those of the applicant. Notice, too, that they contain carefully worded fragments. A service-oriented job objective acts as a thesis statement with three parts:

- Job title with reference number, if there is one
- Type of business, industry, or institution (optional, especially when applying for a position with a reference number)
- Major skill areas of the applicant that can interest the employer

Career consultants warn against stating "entry level," lest you end up in a dead-end job. Shy away from underselling yourself. To prewrite your objective, quiz yourself and jot down your answers:

1. How can I show that I am well qualified for the position?
2. What two or three qualities are especially needed for this job?
3. What major skills do employers seek for this position?
4. Do my qualifications fit the objective? (If not, look for another job.)
5. Is the terminology correct for the field? Have I included keywords?

A service-oriented objective identifies the position and states how you can benefit the employer:

SERVICE-ORIENTED OBJECTIVES

- Pediatric nursing position #2023. Skilled in postsurgical and terminal care; experienced in working with children.
- Accounting position requiring proficiency in medical terminology, insurance billing, legal applications, and customer relations.
- Office manager. Skilled in major software applications, written communication, problem solving, and conflict resolution.
- Medical laboratory technician in a clinic or hospital seeking reliability, interpersonal skills, and superior accuracy.

A Summary of Qualifications

A job profile or *summary of qualifications* is a concise listing of your most important accomplishments and abilities that relate to the job objective. The summary and job objective may be the only sections that catch an employer's eye and rescue a résumé from oblivion. To fill just one position, employers may screen hundreds of résumés, spending twenty seconds or less on each one.

Make your summary easy to read by using bullets to list three to five accomplishments that relate to your job objective. Precede the summary by a brief statement of educational qualifications. Volunteer projects as well as actual work experience may be listed. In the example below, the new graduate has held various part-time jobs but has no paid teaching experience. Because her publications are not mentioned elsewhere, she puts the dates here in the summary.

Summary of Qualifications

BA in English education. Certified to teach English and speech. Recently graduated summa cum laude. Enthusiastic and dedicated to stimulating children to learn.

- Tutored dyslexic high school student who had been failing.
- Two years' experience teaching high school religious classes weekly.
- Won first prize in National Arts and Letters short story contest, 2008.
- Published five poems in little magazines in the past year.
- Active member of Toastmasters International. Made three presentations locally, using PowerPoint.

The next example summarizes the qualifications of an older student who has paid work experience in his chosen field and is still working at the same place while continuing his education. His job objective focuses on a supervisory position in the accounting department of a magazine subscription service. For emphasis, his most noteworthy achievements are placed first and last in the list:

▶ **Profile**

Five years' accounting experience in retail store. Associate Degree, 3.6 GPA. Accounting major, business management minor. Auditor internship with Deloitte & Touche. Continuing course work toward a BS degree.

- Promoted to supervisor in one year. Oversee two assistants.
- Proficient in Windows XP, Quicken, TurboTax, and other related software.
- Prepare payroll and tax forms, maintain records, compile sales reports.
- Practice computer security precautions. No data loss due to viruses in five years.
- Made cost analysis and recommended cost-cutting procedure that saved the company $10,500 in just three months.

WRITING A SUMMARY OF QUALIFICATIONS

To write a summary for your résumé, scan your skills lists. Select the most impressive achievements that relate to the position you want. The following questions should help you prewrite and revise:

- What is the employers' greatest need for this position?
- What evidence can I present to show that I am well qualified to fill that need?
- Does the summary correlate closely with my job objective?
- Might I find an instructor or trusted co-worker to critique my job objective and summary?
- Have I revised sufficiently so that the summary presents my chief credentials in the best possible way?

Grouping Skills and Citing Accomplishments

If you are fortunate enough to have work experience in your career field and are compiling a chronological résumé, list those work skills underneath the name of the employer. If the functional format is better for you, then revise and regroup your prewritten skills:

1. Sort skills and group according to the needs of potential employers.
2. Arrange the skills in neat columns under the group headings. Place the most important details at the beginning of each column.
3. Begin each skill entry with an appropriate action verb.

Employers seek people who can cut costs, solve problems, and perform quality work. To identify potential accomplishments, search your skills lists for superior work, especially in regard to finances or saving of resources, personnel, or time. Then *add a second part that provides specific data*. This addition can sometimes expand a skill to an accomplishment:

- *Skill:* Decreased costs
  Add: 20% through selective bulk buying.
- *Skill:* Generated sales
  Add: of $950,000 during the past year.
- *Skill:* Upgraded outdated inventory system,
  Add: cutting storage time by one-half.

To fill out a list of accomplishments, you may also include honors, awards, and other distinctions you've received. Yana Parker suggests writing PAR (Problem-Action-Results) statements in *24 Hot Tips on Résumé Writing*. (Her Web site is listed in Directory 2, page 399.) PAR statements can be included under accomplishments.

For example, the manager of mail services revised her résumé and applied for a similar position elsewhere when her department was outsourced. She labeled her accomplishments a "Record of Productivity," which she placed after her job objective:

Record of Productivity

- Streamlined entire mail services operation for corporate headquarters of _____, Inc. This changeover included reorganizing job duties of all mail room personnel, developing new procedures, and reorganizing the physical layout for greater efficiency.
- Despite a 25% increase in mail flow, maintained quality service with no additional personnel. Increased number of in-house mail services for employees.
- Wrote and justified proposal for $80,000 for new equipment through equivalent savings in one year's time.
- As benefits approver at _____, maintained 97% accuracy and production criteria.
- At _____ Corporation, changed all accounts receivable functions from manual to computerized system.

Education

When listing higher education on your résumé, provide names of institutions (and addresses of lesser known ones). Include dates, degrees, and major(s). Also state your minor concentration if relevant. Specify grade point average (GPA) if B+ or more. GPA is usually stated in decimals such as "3.35/4.0," the second figure indicating the scale. If the GPA of your major is higher, you can cite it: "Major GPA 3.6/4.0."

List teaching certificates, nursing licensure, and other professional certification with education. For young applicants with little experience, a high school degree can be included if space allows. You might also list items such as "Took college preparatory courses," "Wrote for school newspaper," "Trained in debate." You can list high school honors here, too. (Do not note a GED.)

Work Experience

Experience in your targeted field should be emphasized on your résumé by allotting it more space than for other jobs. If you have had steady employment, include the employers' names and dates with months (Jan. 2006–present). State job title(s) and promotions, if any. For example: "Hired as crew member. In six months, promoted to assistant manager." After that you can list work skills. Include minor job experience because it indicates a desire to work and familiarity with the work world. If you have served in the military, place that under work experience. State term of service, branch, and rank upon leaving. Include training or travel relevant to your job objective.

Gaps in Work Experience

If you have gaps in your employment due to layoffs or downsizing, time off for parenting or other family obligations, or another valid reason, list the item with dates. State what you were doing. For seasonal items, preface the date with the season, as in the following individual examples:

- 2007–Present. Maternity leave and full-time parenting.
- 2006–2007. Layoff. Temporary work: Compiled tax forms for H & R Block, taught computer classes at Franklin Vocational High School, and started home business.
- Spring 2005–Summer 2006. Travel and full-time study.

A Series of Short-Term Jobs

If have held a succession of minor jobs, unrelated to your job objective, perhaps with gaps in employment, provide a short summary with a *range of dates*. Preface with one or two sentences *stating qualities you have developed and skills you have learned* from these jobs:

> **Summary of Work Experience**
>
> During college years have held part-time employment that has developed initiative, accuracy, and flexibility. Have learned to budget, schedule, catalog books, find answers to research questions, service cars, make minor repairs, and provide courteous customer service.
>
> 2005–2008 **Library Assistant/Service Station Attendant:** BGSU main campus, Herbie's Marathon Station
>
> 2003–2004 **Server:** McMann's Restaurant, Burger Boy, Dolly's Coffee Shop

Other Information on a Résumé

If you have extra space on your résumé, use it for minor, but relevant, information. Do not mention firings, demotions, ethnicity, handicaps, age, or medical disabilities on a résumé. Possible items to include are as follows:

- **Honors or awards.** If not listed elsewhere, group honors such as "Employee of the Month," "Top Salesperson of the Year," civic awards, dean's list, and other distinctions under "Honors."

- **Memberships.** Memberships in professional organizations related to your job objective imply commitment to a career. Do *not* list lodges, religious affiliations, or any membership that might arouse prejudice.

- **Activities and interests.** Optional. Include only those that are related to your job objective.

- **Salary.** Do not mention unless requested; then simply state "Negotiable" or "Open." Otherwise, you may price yourself out of a job or be hired at a low rate. (Research the salaries in your field and locale.)

- **References.** Place "References upon request" last. Optional.

- **How far back should I go on work experience?** To avoid age discrimination, list only your last three jobs or the last ten years. That is usually enough unless you have earlier work in your targeted field. Label that section as "Relevant Work Experience."

- **Should any work experience ever be omitted?** Employment of one month or less can be omitted.

- **How can I make a job title sound better?** Retitle jobs such as dishwasher, cleaning lady, yard man, and bartender. For example: kitchen assistant, housekeeper, greenskeeper, and server. Avoid overstating the position, however.

- **What if I have no work experience?** Your best bet may be to head for the campus placement service or an employment agency to ask about temporary or part-time work in your targeted field, if possible.

FREQUENTLY ASKED QUESTIONS ABOUT WORK EXPERIENCE

ORGANIZING RÉSUMÉS

The job objective is the first item on any résumé after your name, home address, telephone number, and personal e-mail address. (Do not give your work number or e-mail address at work.) Next is the summary of qualifications. Arrange work experience, education, and skills in most- to least-important order, according to the format you choose.

Organizing a Chronological Résumé

After the job objective and summary, the next major part of a chronological résumé is usually a *reverse chronological listing* of work experience. Skills and

ANTHONY R. ROGERS   (303) 222-3333   arogers@service.net
3945 East Front Street
Denver, CO 80200

Objective: Assistant systems manager position requiring experience in
managing information systems, network communications, and
problem solving

SUMMARY OF QUALIFICATIONS

Five years' experience using computers in various capacities, plus management
experience. Soon to graduate with Bachelor of Science degree, *cum laude*. Majors:
Database Management and Network Administration.

- Microsoft Certified Systems Engineer
- Program in Oracle, SQL, C++, and Visual Basic
- Use Microsoft Office XP and Open Systems Traverse accounting
  software with e-commerce
- Customized software for company and client needs
- Won the *Wall Street Journal* award for student achievement
- Designed systems and created documentation

Experience

	PROTECH ELECTRONICS, INC., Denver, Colorado
April 2006	Promoted to Administrative Assistant to the President
to	- Perform financial analyses
present	- Assist in interviewing and hiring

- Assist in pricing and purchasing
- Track and report inventory
- Provide support for sales representatives
- Train employees
- Write brochures and design training literature
- Write proposals, business letters, and reports
- Make informative and persuasive presentations
- Provided support for end users
- Handled complaints and worked out compromises
- Performed user setup and maintenance on NT Server
- Detected and solved problems in software
- Improved computer security systems

FIGURE 26.1 Chronological résumé.

achievements, including promotions, are listed under each employer. But for
a teaching, a nursing, or another position that requires a certain degree and
certification or licensure, *education* can come second. The general rule for both
chronological and functional résumés is to place the most important major section
first and the least important last. (For an example of a chronological résumé,
see fig. 26.1.)

Anthony R. Rogers   3945 East Front Street   2

July 2001
to
March 2006

XYZ ELECTRONICS COMPANY, Denver, Colorado
Hired as a sales representative. Promoted to sales manager after
one year.

- Supervised five employees
- Hired, dismissed, and trained personnel
- Sold, installed, and provided support for systems/software
- Made minor repairs on PC desktop computers
- Revised performance evaluation procedure
- Assisted potential users in defining system needs
- Answered application and support questions for customers
- Designed local area networks
- Designed customer survey, compiled results, and wrote report
- Created motivational plan that led to increased sales of 20%

May 1999
to
June 2001

WENDY'S, Denver, Colorado
Hired as customer service representative. Promoted to assistant
manager after six months.

- Supervised six employees
- Kept sales records
- Ordered supplies
- Worked late shifts
- Balanced cash register
- Made bank deposits
- Opened and closed store

Education   **OLYMPIA UNIVERSITY,** Denver, Colorado

June 2008   Bachelor of Science, GPA 3.67/4.0
              Majors: Database Management and Network Administration
Member   Small Business Association

References upon request

FIGURE 26.1 Chronological résumé. (continued)

Organizing a Functional Résumé

The functional résumé style is quite flexible, suitable for anyone who lacks the
qualifications needed for the chronological style. If you are close to graduation
and have little work experience, you can emphasize your academic achievement
by using the following order: *job objective, summary, education,* and *work experience*

MELANIE A. ROBERTS
612 Greenlawn Drive
Marion, Ohio 43302
(614) 555-0755
maroberts@service.net

OBJECTIVE: Paralegal position with employer who seeks superior dedication, accuracy, and skill in paralegal duties, computer applications, and communications.

PROFILE

Recent graduate with Associate of Applied Business Degree, major in Paralegal Studies, GPA 3.7/4.0. Paralegal internship with Smith and Jones, Attorneys at Law. Apply basic accounting principles. Have notary public commission. Experienced in quality control.

- **Paralegal Experience:** Researched legal problems. Prepared and filed probate documents. Updated office filing system. Performed title searches. Proofread property descriptions and witnessed real estate closings. Wrote letters and contacted clients. Prepared corporation sales reports of securities.

- **Paralegal Training:** Investigated legal problems. Drafted contracts, complaints, and responses. Wrote and executed wills according to Ohio law. Prepared partnership agreements. Implemented debt collection practices. Applied problems in tort law and criminal law.

- **Computer Skills:** Use LEXIS, Access, Excel, Windows XP, TurboTax

- **Communication Skills:** Give quality oral presentations. Research and write arguments, essays, and reports. Trained in questioning and active listening. Surveyed opportunities for paralegals. Wrote for campus newspaper.

EDUCATION: Marion Technical College, Marion, Ohio, Associate Degree, June 2008. Dean's List. Served on student advisory board.

EARLY EXPERIENCE

2000–2006	Quality Control Inspector (promotion). A.O. Smith, Upper Sandusky, Ohio. Supervised 10 workers. Trained employees. Supplied parts.
1996–1999	Maintenance Supervisor/Receptionist. American Legion, Club 162; Howard Swink Advertising Agency, Marion, Ohio.

References upon request

FIGURE 26.2 Functional résumé, no paid experience in desired field.

(with skills listed), as shown in figure 26.2. Degreed applicants who are switching career fields might also use this order, particularly if their educational record matches well with the new career field. Or education might be included in the summary.

If you will be competing with applicants who have higher degrees than you and if you have some work in your targeted field, you can use a different arrangement: *job objective, summary, work experience* (listing skills), and *education*. College students who are *not* close to graduation but who have some work experience in their chosen field can use this same order.

MARK FOCUSES HIS FUNCTIONAL RÉSUMÉ

Mark, a young graduate with a bachelor's degree but little work experience, saw an ad for an administrative assistant that sounded interesting. The employer was seeking someone with three strengths: initiative, computer skills, and writing skills. Since Mark was strong in all three areas, he emphasized these categories in his summary of qualifications for his functional résumé:

PROFILE
Recent BA degree in Communications. Maintained a GPA of 3.6/4.0 while working twenty hours weekly.

- **Initiative:** Awarded full tuition scholarship for high school GPA of 4.0/4.0. Arose at 3 a.m. for disk jockey job for one year in college. Worked till midnight weekends at Burger King for two years.
- **Computer Skills:** Proficient in Word, Excel, PowerPoint, QuickBooks, and other software. At Champion Tile installed and maintained operating system, antivirus, and application software; entered data; compiled sales reports; and generated checks.
- **Writing Skills:** Wrote business letters, reports, research papers, and critiques of essays. Published two op-ed columns in a local paper.

Mark's effort won an interview and a job offer. He had tailored his summary of qualifications to the employer's specific needs.

Scannable Résumés

Sometimes human eyes never see a résumé. If your résumé will be scanned, prepare a scannable version that will keep it from being tossed out. Streamline your printed-style résumé. Keep margins rather narrow and do not center anything. (Length is seldom a concern as long as items are relevant.) Use a clear size 12 font such as Arial, Courier, or Verdana. *The general rule is "the plainer, the better."* That means no fancy fonts, bullets, italics, underlining, parentheses, brackets, graphics—anything that might end up as gibberish. Then place a keyword summary of your qualifications at the top of page 1.

Keyword Summary   Read ads and job boards to find the skills and abilities employers seek for different jobs. Then match these words with your qualifications and copy them into your keyword summary. The more matches you can provide, the more the scanner will select and the better your chances of having your résumé read. (Use hyphens in place of bullets to set off items.)

Editing and Printing   After you finish a scannable version of your résumé, run a spelling check and proofread it again. Then save it as an ASCII file. Name the file *resume.txt*. Use any text editor (such as Appletext, MS Word, or Notepad) to edit the resume.txt file to resemble your original résumé. Print your scannable résumé, using a high-resolution laser printer. Do not bend or fold the résumé. Place it in a large manila envelope to protect it.

E-Mail Résumés

If you have a choice between submitting an e-mail résumé and sending a scannable résumé by regular mail, take e-mail. Scanning managers of GTE and other companies prefer e-mail résumés because there is less chance for error when storing them in a database. In fact, many ads specify "a plain text document sent in the body of your [e-mail] message." This means the résumé is not sent as an attachment. Attached files can be cumbersome to download and print out.

An e-mail résumé does not need a keyword summary. Streamline the résumé as you would for a scannable version—taking out underlining, parentheses, brackets, graphics, bullets, centering, or anything that might become illegible. Run a spelling check and proofread thoroughly. Save the résumé as a text file (see "Scannable Résumés," on page 393). In this plain form, the résumé can be copied, pasted into e-mail, and read by unknown software. *Precaution:* Before e-mailing the résumé, insert a cover letter into the message first. Employers prefer to see the cover letter beforehand.

FORMATTING A PRINTED RÉSUMÉ

Since your printed résumé is your ambassador, an immaculate appearance is imperative. Purchase high-quality 20-pound bond paper. Buy enough so that you have matching paper for cover and follow-up letters. White is best for résumés that will be duplicated or scanned. Otherwise, ivory is suitable. Employers tend to dislike unusual colors and extravagant layouts. You can vary the format by using capital letters, boldface, or underlining for headings. You can lead into each skill entry with a bullet (oversized dot), followed by one space.

To give a picture-frame look, use the same-size margins all around. Triple-space between sections, if possible, and double-space between subsections. You can center major headings or locate them at the side or mix the two arrangements. Work with your résumé until you have an effective layout that enhances your qualifications.

Never send pale or smudged copies of your résumé to an interviewer. Avoid script and difficult-to-read fonts. Select a popular font that is neat and clear; use a laser printer if possible. For students, a résumé of one or two pages is adequate. Yet expectations for acceptable résumés vary among employers, particularly government agencies. If your résumé is to work efficiently for you, determine what each employer expects and do your best to meet those expectations.

REVISING, EDITING, AND PROOFREADING A RÉSUMÉ

Chances are that a superficial résumé, hastily compiled, will not yield interviews. Employers assume a résumé reflects the intellect, competency, and attitude of the applicant. Take time to revise as much as necessary so that your résumé will outclass the competition and earn you the opportunities you deserve.

Checking Layout and Order

Layout does make a difference. Consider the order of items in columns. The first and last positions carry the most emphasis; the middle spot has the least emphasis. The *white* space throughout the résumé, not just the margins, influences appearance, readability, and credibility. Neat, aligned columns provide a balanced look. A crowded résumé is more difficult to read than a well-spaced one. For ease in reading, place dates on the left except when you want to de-emphasize them.

If your résumé runs more than one page, place your name and a page number at the top of the second page (you can reduce the font two sizes for that line). This precaution will prevent loss or confusion when the interviewer compares applicants' qualifications. (Never staple a résumé.) Revise your layout until you attain an appropriate order and look. The following checklist can help in editing your résumé.

CHECKLIST   **REVISING LAYOUT, ORDER, AND EMPHASIS**

1. Is the layout well-balanced, attractive, and easy to read?
   Is every column aligned? Is there enough white space?

2. Are dates accurate? Arranged in reverse chronological order?

3. Does each skill start with an action verb?

4. Are all major sections well-developed, positive, and accurate?

5. Are minor sections relevant? If not, discard.

Adjusting Length of Printed Résumés

"How long should a résumé be?" is a common question with no definite answer. Although many employers prefer one-page résumés for *entry-level* employees, this preference does not rule out longer résumés for applicants with extensive qualifications. Two-page résumés are increasingly common for newly graduated applicants. If you plan a second page, have at least half a page. A fraction of a page may appear to be due to poor planning.

When expanding your résumé to fill a second page, be careful not to indulge in puffery. Wordiness and irrelevant details will detract from your purpose. A concise one-page résumé is far better than a puffed two-page one. The following options should help you to find more material and adapt the format, if you need a second page:

WAYS TO EXPAND A RÉSUMÉ

1. **Review the suggestions for identifying skills to find more.** Also consider adding more minor categories if relevant.
2. **Add white space.** Have you triple-spaced between sections? Have you centered your heading? A centered heading takes more space than one aligned on the left with items beside it. (See figs. 26.1 and 26.2.)
3. **Expand the margins a bit,** keeping the same size all around.
4. **If you are not working, you can supply the addresses and telephone numbers of previous employers.** If working, reserve this information for a sheet of references.
5. **Expand a summary of minor work experience.** The names of employers could be added.

Or on the other hand, if you must cut the length of your résumé, start with the first suggestion below. Then go down the list just as far as needed; don't toss out good material unnecessarily. To adjust the length, you have several options:

WAYS TO CUT THE LENGTH OF A RÉSUMÉ

1. **Omit minor items.** Personal activities must relate to the job.
2. **Group similar skills on one line.** This technique is simple and quick.
3. **Place company name in bold with address in plain type on the same line.**
4. **Summarize unrelated work experience.** Beware of cutting too much; work experience of any kind can be an asset.
5. **Reduce the font one size.** You might use size 11 instead of size 12 font.
6. **Last resort.** Narrow the margins a bit or double-space between sections.

Eagle-Eyed Proofreading

You know and I know that errors can creep into a draft for a multitude of reasons, but that does not excuse them in an employer's eyes. When you are fresh and alert, proofread your finished résumé several times. Otherwise, you are unlikely to nab every error. Although a spell checker can catch misspellings, it cannot monitor usage. An eagle eye is needed to detect inappropriate words.

CHECKLIST EDITING AND PROOFREADING A RÉSUMÉ

1. Are all dates accurate?

2. Are months as well as years specified for work experience?

3. Is there any duplication of skills? (If so, cut.)

4. Is every word positive or neutral?

5. Is every word spelled and hyphenated correctly?

6. Are punctuation and capitalization consistent and correct?

ONLINE SECURITY GUIDELINES

The World Privacy Forum, a nonprofit organization based in California, advises online users to read the privacy policy of Web sites carefully. Know who can share your information. They provide the following guidelines for online security:

- **Ensure that your résumé can be deleted.** If not, do not post it.
- **Get an e-mail address just for an online résumé.** Post only this e-mail address. Then cancel it later.
- **Reveal no private information.** Do not include numbers on debit or credit cards, bank accounts, or Social Security. Use your initials or just your first name. Omit your last name, address, and telephone number for an online résumé.

Identity Thieves at Work and Other Dangers

Although it is possible to post your e-mail résumé online, think twice before you do. Identity thieves visit these sites, hoping to gain personal data. Some may pretend to be recruiters and send an e-mail with an attachment, offering a job and asking for marital status, driver's license, and financial information. Do not open the attachment or give any private information by e-mail or by phone. Never send money.

Ads on job boards may be outdated or phony, aimed at obtaining personal information. If you spot spelling or grammar errors or odd wording, that is a tipoff the ad is fake. If you have the slightest doubt, do not respond. If you are working, avoid "blind" ads unless you know that they do not belong to your employer. If you should decide to post your résumé, obtain an e-mail address for that purpose only. (You may be bombarded with spam and can quickly cancel.) To avoid overexposure, post your résumé, on just one or two boards at a time.

The best way to find a job online is to visit the Web sites of employers. To determine whether a site is genuine, check the company information carefully. You can verify that the company exists by searching the *Better Business Bureau Web site* or<Lookstoogoodtobetrue.com>, a Web site run jointly by a federal law-enforcement and industry task force. If possible, set up a personal interview at the employer's site.

Video Clips for Résumés

The purpose of a video clip that accompanies a résumé is to introduce the applicant and gain an interview. Some tech-savvy job searchers are creating their own brief clips; others hire an agency. Producing a video clip to act as a job search tool is not as simple as it sounds. For applicants who lack a sense of purpose, expertise, or confidence before a camera, creation of a video clip is fraught with peril. The clip is not an occasion to show proficiency in leisure activities or do anything else that might distract.

If you decide to add a video clip to your job package, the following guidelines will be helpful:

1. **Focus on the purpose of the video.** Create questions an employer might ask. Answer, looking straight into the camera. If someone else asks the questions, then look at him or her. Omit jokes and irrelevant personal details.

2. **Regard the video as an interview.** Consider your appearance. Look professional and neat. Do you need a haircut? Where should the photo occur? What kind of chair will you use? (Not a recliner)

3. **Limit the video.** Three minutes is a good length. Do not include background music, posters, or other distractions.

4. **Practice so that you are comfortable before the camera.** Do not memorize answers exactly. You want the clip to resemble a conversation. (For tips on oral presentations, see chapter 25.)

5. **Critique the video.** Ask older friends to give you feedback. Listen to criticism and seek to improve this job-search tool.

6. **Create a new Web site to post the video. Then send a link to prospective employers.** That method limits access to the site.

The Web sites listed below provide free, up-to-date help with minimal sales promotion. View sample job objectives, résumés, letters, career guides, and more. (Most browsers will fill in http://.)

- **Best Sample Résumés.** Samples and tips <www .bestsampleresume.com>
- **The Damn Good Résumé.** Yana Parker's "Hot Tips for Résumés" and other advice <www.damngood.com/jobseekers/links.html>
- **JobStar Central.** Public library career resources <www.jobstar.org>
- **The Riley Guide.** Résumés, letters, jobs and more <www .rileyguide.com>
- **The Résumé Guide.** Over sixty résumé samples <www .susanireland.com>

DIRECTORY 2: ONLINE EMPLOYMENT RESOURCES

II. WRITING ELECTRONIC MESSAGES AND LETTERS

An effective cover letter and a sincere letter of appreciation can help you win the job you want. The subtle aspects of your written voice reveal your attitude— influencing whether or not you will be considered for the position. Well-organized content; a neat format; and correct grammar, punctuation, and spelling convey an air of professionalism. When corresponding with potential employers whether through e-mail or regular mail, always take the time to produce your best work.

If you are working, keep your job hunting secret; or you may be fired. Do not confide in coworkers. Never use a company phone or computer to make employment contacts. Many employers use software to monitor employee Internet usage and e-mail.

GHOSTS OF ELECTRONIC MESSAGES

Hasty electronic messages may come back to haunt you. Although writing e-mail may seem intimate and personal, it is like speaking on a cell phone in public. E-mail can be passed around or tacked to a bulletin board for anyone to read. Beware of what you write on blogs and social networking sites too. More and more employers are browsing sites such as Friendster, Facebook, and YouTube to check out applicants. Descriptions of bar scenes, sexual preferences, politics, and other personal details or photos can nix an interview.

Whether you send an instant message (IM), e-mail via your office computer, or other electronic message, your employer or a government agency may read it. Even if you quickly erase the message, its ghost may linger. Google's instant messages are saved automatically unless users disable them by going "off the record." Other search engines offer software to log onto IM conversations, which are not safe even though disguised by code names. E-mail is saved on the service provider's computer and can be subpoenaed by the government.

WRITING EFFECTIVE E-MAIL

Before sending an e-mail, consider the rhetorical situation. Is e-mail a suitable way to convey the message? Or does the situation require privacy? Would a letter, telephone call, or face-to-face conversation be more appropriate and effective? When e-mail is significant, give it the same care you would a business letter. Before sending, put the e-mail into a document and run a spelling check. It is far better to take a few minutes to be cautious and complete than to regret a hasty message later. The following guidelines can save you time, alleviate concern, and improve the tone of your messages.

**GUIDELINES FOR
E-MAIL MESSAGES**

1. **Keep e-mail short and focused.** Include a subject line. If you have two detailed topics to discuss, send two messages.

2. **Be friendly and courteous.**
   - To avoid abruptness, start with the person's name, a greeting, or salutation.
   - When appropriate, start with "Thank you for."
   - When making a request, use a question mark and include "please."
   - Avoid using all capital letters, which can give the impression of shouting.

3. **Place the important item first unless it is negative.** Deliver good news first. Build up to bad news and place it in a middle paragraph to de-emphasize.

4. **After you make your point, close.** Don't ramble on. End on a positive note, even if you say no more than "So long" "or "Take care." For a professional tone, use "Regards," Best wishes," "Sincerely," or other suitable closing.

5. **Reread each e-mail carefully before sending.** A hasty message may not say what you intend or carry the desired tone.

6. **Keep all office communications focused on business matters.** E-mail and instant messages to coworkers can become overly casual.

7. **If you use the "Reply" feature, check the message string.** Scroll down. Old messages to other people can accumulate and cause embarrassment.

8. **Double check the name of the recipient.** Did the right name come up from the address book? Is the salutation correct?

9. **Don't send e-mail when very tired.** Avoid writing when exhausted. The message will not be your best and may not say what you intend.

10. **Wait twenty-four hours before replying to an irritating message.** Consider whether the message merits a reply. Silence may be the best, and safest, response. If you reply, choose your words carefully. Read the message aloud to hear how it sounds.

TEN COMMON MISTAKES IN LETTERS

Employers often draw inferences from incidentals, even careless, illegible signatures. Regardless of the position you apply for, take extra pains to sign application forms and letters neatly. Employers may also cite a dozen or more other pet peeves, including these ten common mistakes in cover letters:

1. **Inappropriate salutations.** "Dear Sir," "Dear Madam," "To Whom It May Concern," and similar phrases are outdated. If possible, include a name and a job title. (Call and ask the receptionist who the human resource director is. If the name is unusual, ask how it is spelled.)

2. **Form letters.** Fill-in-the-blank letters or those copied from books or the Internet create a poor impression. Be original and tailor the message to the recipient.

3. **Grammatical errors.** Spelling errors, incorrect usage, unnecessary capitals, and unwieldy sentence structure also create a poor impression.

4. **Handwritten letters.** Short thank-you notes may be handwritten if neat and legible. Cover letters should be typed and spaced well.

5. **Hard-to-read format.** Omit clutter, graphics, and fancy fonts. Use a size 12 easy-to-read font. Use a balanced format with plenty of white space.

6. **Omissions.** Omitted signature, phone number, date, salutation, or résumé gives the impression of carelessness. Omissions may cause the letter to be discarded.

7. **Overuse of I.** Too many *I*'s can create a negative image. Instead, focus on the recipient and what you can do for the company. (See page 49.)

8. **Trite phrases.** Avoid wording such as "please find the attached résumé," "enclosed please find. . . . ," "I'm excited about. . . . ," "yours truly," "yours sincerely," and similar outworn phrases.

9. **Abbreviations.** Avoid unnecessary abbreviations such as "St.," "Ave.," "Jan.," "Wed.," and others. Write out words.

10. **Long sentences and paragraphs.** Limit most sentences to fifteen words or less. Limit paragraphs to five lines or so.

WRITING AN EFFECTIVE COVER LETTER FOR A RÉSUMÉ

When hundreds of people vie for a single position, a résumé cover letter may be the only document in a job packet that an interviewer reads. If the letter contains even a whiff of incompetence or dishonesty, the résumé may be tossed aside unread. Regardless of whether a résumé is mailed, faxed, e-mailed, or delivered in person, a cover letter is usually expected.

As you write your cover letter, keep in mind that the primary purpose is to motivate the interviewer to read your résumé. Express interest in the position, present an overview of your credentials, and make a courteous request for an interview. The tone of a well-written cover letter is professional and confident, never desperate, half-hearted, or arrogant. A confident letter may spark confidence in its reader—exactly the effect you wish to achieve. Like other business letters, cover letters have three basic parts: introduction, body, and closing.

Effective Introductions

A pet peeve of interviewers is triteness in cover letters. Imagine having to read dozens of letters that begin: "I saw your ad in . . ." or some other predictable phrase. To make a cover letter stand out, hook the reader's interest with your very first words. Select them judiciously: the wrong words may steer you into a low-paying position. If you have experience in your desired field, shy away from "entry-level" or "trainee." These words peg you as having minimal skills and lacking experience. For inexperienced applicants, however, an entry-level position in your chosen field affords an opportunity to gain practical knowledge and skill.

To get up-to-date information about employers' needs, clip job descriptions from newspapers and visit employers' Web sites. Underline the skills and abilities required for positions you would like. After that, draft an introduction that suggests how your training and experience meet those needs. Be sure that your description truly reflects your qualifications.

When applying for a specific position, give the exact job title and number (if there is one) in the introduction of your cover letter. To create a distinctive opening that will work for you, adapt one of the four basic openings for cover letters.

The Name Opening   You are fortunate, indeed, if you can begin with the name of a person the employer knows, one who has referred you or who will recommend you. A referral can open doors that might otherwise remain closed. If you learn of an available position from an executive or from someone else the employer respects, seize the opportunity! After you receive permission, state the name of the person making the referral. Then mention the position and give the main areas of your qualifications:

- Jason Kelly, systems manager of Syntech, spoke of an opening in your company for a junior accountant. He recommended I apply, for he is familiar with my accounting background and computer experience.
- Cynthia Hines, vice president of Hines' Advertising, has suggested I apply for the position of copywriter at your firm. The requirements she mentioned match my training and experience in advertising.

The Creative Opening   To find just the right detail for an unusual opening, search your résumé and memory. Watch local papers for news items about potential employers, possibly the arrival of a new business or the expansion of a local company. Then match your experience, activities, and talent so as to spark the interest of an interviewer:

- After Bantram and Bowman move to the new downtown location, they may need more personnel. If so, please consider my legal training and work experience, which should qualify me for a paralegal position.

- Perseverance does pay off. After five years of attending night classes, working as a restaurant manager, and providing for a family, I am graduating *magna cum laude* with a BS degree in restaurant management. Would these qualifications plus confirmed workaholic tendencies equip me for the position of manager of your hotel's dining room?

The Summary Opening   Although traditional, the summary opening can be quite workable when your strongest qualifications are linked to the desired position. You might give two or three main points taken from the headings of your résumé. But be sure the points are clearly connected to the current needs of potential employers. In the following summary openings, notice that the focus is upon *how the applicant can serve the employer:*

- Training in social work, an internship in student admissions, and a bachelor's degree in psychology should help me fulfill the responsibilities of Human Services Coordinator for Blinhard University.

- My management skills in nursing have been honed by supervision of nursing personnel, development of nursing policies and procedures, and preparation of six-figure budgets. This background, along with a recently acquired MSN degree, should qualify me for Director of Nursing at Memorial Hospital.

Employment consultants often advise clients to distinguish between "requirements" and "preferences" when applying for a job. If you don't have quite all the "preferences," apply anyway. Then shape your cover letter and interview responses to show that you fit the job:

1. **Secure the name of the interviewer or department head.** You may want to send your job package to each one. Check the company Web site or call the company for names. If unable to secure one, send to "Human Resources Director." Then "Dear Director" can serve as your salutation.

2. **Write in a confident, courteous tone.** Select your words with care (see chapter 8).

3. **Individualize the letter.** Avoid trite phrases and examples from books. Be original.

(continued)

DEVELOPING AN EFFECTIVE COVER LETTER

DEVELOPING
AN EFFECTIVE
COVER LETTER
(continued)

4. **Type an individualized letter for each company.** Form letters without an inside name and address are inappropriate and ineffective.

5. **Point out transferable skills.** Don't expect an employer to infer how your skills will fit the job. Your cover letter should state how these skills can be applied.

6. **Show prized qualities.** To *imply* flexibility, intellectual curiosity, and high energy level, share examples from your experience. For many positions, these three qualities have distinct advantages.

7. **Write with enthusiasm.** Your cover letter should try to convince the company that you are a good fit for the job, even if you are not an exact fit. *Note:* Never say "Although my skills don't exactly match" or "Although I am unqualified" (or inexperienced).

8. **Sign each letter neatly in *black* ink to match the type.** Never leave a letter unsigned. Employers tend to view the omission as carelessness and a disregard for detail.

The Question Opening   An original question opening can serve as an attention-getter if it is fresh, appealing, and relevant. But some personnel directors warn that question openings are overused and often filled with clichés. One interviewer even went so far as to say he tossed letters with stereotypic questions into the wastebasket unread.

Whatever opening you use, avoid any hint of overconfidence or presumption. Note that the sample introductions here use phrases such as "*should* qualify me for the position" rather than "*will* qualify me." At the same time, an opening that seems doubtful or anxious is not likely to open many doors. Striking the proper balance can be tricky. Thoughtful applicants evaluate and revise their openings carefully, using their own words and avoiding threadbare phrases.

The Body of the Letter

The body of a cover letter explains the qualifications mentioned in the introduction. When you develop these points, retain the order set forth in your opening. After summarizing the highlights from the résumé, conclude the body with an *indirect* reference to the résumé.

Reference to the Résumé   A direct reference, such as "Please see the enclosed résumé," is awkward. An indirect reference, is worked smoothly into a sentence in a dependent clause or phrase. The indirect references below are italicized:

- For five years I have provided customer service and gained significant insights. For me, the customer is really number one. Supervision of eight employees has also offered opportunities to polish my interpersonal skills, *as indicated on the enclosed résumé.*

- On June 12, 2008, I will graduate *summa cum laude* from Buckeye University with a bachelor of arts degree in education. There I concentrated in English, specifically the teaching of high school literature and composition. In my senior year, I won first prize in the National Arts and Letters contest involving five area colleges. Seven poems have been published in little magazines, *as explained in the enclosed résumé.*

How to Handle the Salary Question

Before you respond to an ad or contact an employer, research the salaries in your job field. Know the salary range in your locale. Although an ad may request "desired salary" or "salary history," you are not obligated to give a specific answer. In a cover letter, you might give an expected salary range, such as "$26,000 to $29,000" or "upper 20s." But before you do, consider that your answer may jeopardize your chances of being hired. The risk is twofold: If your figure is too high, employers may conclude you are overqualified or overpriced; if too low, they may think you underqualified.

In a telephone conversation, you might say that salary is "open" or sidestep questions about salary history until the interview. In the conclusion of a cover letter, you can postpone your answer tactfully:

- At your convenience, may I set up an interview to discuss my qualifications, including expected salary [or salary history, if requested]? My telephone number is (000) 555-6721, and I'm available after 6:30 p.m. Or if you prefer, send an e-mail to the address above.

Sooner or later, you will confront the question of salary. Rather than be unprepared, begin to research salaries in your field. Then you'll know what you can expect locally, statewide, or nationally. Information about salary ranges can be gained from libraries, friends, employment agencies, information interviews, and temporary employment.

Effective Conclusions

The end of a cover letter is rather like a goodbye. As such, it should be brief, cordial, and courteous. Courtesy is integral to good business relations, yet many applicants fail to include courtesy words in cover letters. Instead, they border on arrogance without realizing it, sounding presumptuous or overly forceful. One applicant concluded with "I will be in town Tuesday and will stop by . . . ," presuming that he would be welcomed. Others thank in advance, assuming they will gain an interview, unaware that busy interviewers may take offense.

You can transform a demand into a polite request with just a few courtesy words and a question mark:

- Demand: "E-mail me at . . ."
- Polite request: "Will you please e-mail me at . . . ?"

A question with a question mark is more polite than a statement. A question is a request whereas a statement often sounds like a demand. You can set an appropriate tone in your letters by using questions with courtesy words such as *may, please, appreciate, appreciation,* and *your convenience.* Let consideration shine through your words as in the following examples:

- May I make an appointment at your convenience to further explain how I can benefit your company? Please e-mail <amy301@service.net> or call (611) 555-2121 Monday through Thursday from 4:30 to 8:30 p.m.
- If you think there might be a place for me in your firm, will you please e-mail <Brad42@service.net> or leave a message at (402) 555-2626?

CHECKLIST   EFFECTIVE CONCLUSIONS

1. Is there a courteous request for an interview?

2. Are a home telephone number and e-mail address included? (Do not give a work number or company e-mail address.)

3. Are the hours stated when you can be reached at home?

Referrals and Other Considerations

Before replying to an ad, consider whether you know someone at the company. If so, contact the person, summarize any recently acquired skills, and ask for a recommendation. If you haven't seen the person for years, try to make a personal contact to refresh his or her memory. A referral will boost your chances of obtaining an interview. (See "The Name Opening" examples on page 402.)

A job search may require dozens of mailings and many interviews before the right position is found. The wisest course may be to write two basic cover letters and see which elicits more responses. Each time you contact a potential employer, customize the basic letter with the current date and correct inside address and salutation as well as any other suitable changes. A cover letter should be limited to one uncrowded page with "picture frame" margins and plenty of white space. Before mailing, proofread carefully, and check to see the letter is signed in black ink. When contacting several employers, be sure each letter is correctly addressed, signed, and placed inside the right envelope.

E-Mail Cover Letters   If an employer requests an e-mail résumé, then prepare a cover letter for e-mail, too. You can take your printed cover letter and save another version as a plain text document (explained in "Scannable Résumés" and "E-mail Résumés"). Then e-mail the cover letter before the résumé, preferably in the same message.

Revising a Cover Letter

Rarely is an excellent cover letter dashed off in a few minutes. Chances are that you will need several drafts before the letter reflects your best work. Revising requires examining, editing, and proofreading the drafts several times. Gaining an interview may hinge upon how effective your cover letter is—for if it is ineffective, your résumé may go unread.

CHECKLIST **REVISING A COVER LETTER**

1. Does the introduction focus on the employer's needs? Set up the main points?

2. Are qualifications linked to job requirements?

3. Does each paragraph center on one main idea?

4. Is the résumé referred to indirectly at the end of the *body?*

5. Is an interview *requested* in the closing?

6. Are a phone number and e-mail address included? A time to call?

7. Is the tone polite and confident without sounding overly confident?

FORMAT FOR A BUSINESS LETTER

All business letters contain similar parts, but their positioning differs slightly. Letters typed with letterheads often follow the *block format* (fig. 26.3) with the date and all other typed elements aligned at the left margin. The *modified block format* (shown in fig. 26.4) is most common for letters that are *not* typed on letterhead stationery. Then the typed signature may be followed by a line of type indicating the writer's business title. A business title accords respect.

MODIFIED BLOCK FORM

- **Heading.** Place your own address and the date on three lines in the top right corner.

- **Inside address.** Type the recipient's name and address—just as they appear on the envelope—several spaces below the heading at the left-hand margin.

- **Salutation:** Use a business title. The salutation falls two spaces below the heading, also at the left margin. In a business letter, the salutation is always followed by a colon.

- **Body.** Single-space the paragraphs. Double-space between paragraphs. Indentation is optional.

- **Complimentary close.** Double-space after the body and type "Sincerely," "Regards," "Best regards," or other suitable closing. Align the closing, followed by a comma, with the heading.

- **Signature.** Leave four lines after the complimentary close for the hand-written signature. Below this four-line space, type the signature.

325 Cedar Lane
Anywhere, USA 00000
May 1, 2008

Tara Chase, Manager
Tara's Tall and Short Shop
332 State Street
Smalltown, USA 00000

Dear Manager Chase:

As an amateur artist, I have developed a keen eye for detail, line, and color, as well
as an interest in people. These qualities along with my academic training and work
experience should qualify me for the position of assistant manager of Tara's Tall and
Short Shop.

Recently graduated from Washington State College, I have an Associate of Applied
Business degree with a major in business management. I received training not only in
small business management but also in business law, business ethics, accounting, and
data processing. My training in interpersonal communication included active listening,
questioning, and nonverbal communication.

For four years at Derrick's Designer Shop, I served customers, designed window displays, assisted in shop security, balanced the cash drawer, opened and closed the store,
and made bank deposits. Whenever the owner was away, I managed the shop, super-
vising eight employees. Other experience is explained on the enclosed résumé.

May I have an appointment to discuss my qualifications? Please send an e-mail
to <smbaker505@service.net> or phone (000) 555-1212 on Monday, Tuesday, or
Thursdays from 4:30 to 8 p.m.

Sincerely,

Sabrina M. Baker

Sabrina M. Baker

FIGURE 26.3 Cover letter with creative opening. (Block format)

PACKAGING JOB-SEARCH DOCUMENTS

A positive first impression is important not only for applicants but also for their
job-search packet. Chances are the applicant will never meet the interviewer unless
the documents in the packet are immaculate. Erasures, strikeovers, and smudges
are unacceptable. The résumé, cover letter, and other items should be perfectly
printed by a laser printer (if possible) or a high-quality inkjet printer, preferably on
white 20-pound bond paper. White paper transfers more clearly than colored when
duplicated or scanned or faxed. Use a clear, conventional type style. Italics or unusual fonts are difficult for a scanner to read.

331 Patterson Avenue
Wintoska, Oregon 47000
March 27, 2008

Craig Withers, Office Manager
Baywood and Goldberg
1221 North Main Street
Wintoska, Oregon 47000

Dear Manager Withers:

When an old and respected law firm like Baywood and Goldberg advertises for a junior accountant, I am interested. My three years' work experience and my training in accounting and information systems should enable me to perform successfully for you.

As the only accountant for a local hardware store, I assume many responsibilities, including writing a proposal that won a federally funded low-interest loan. During my first year, I streamlined bookkeeping operations, converting from QuickBooks to Microsoft Management System Headquarters. Currently, I am responsible for accounts receivable and accounts payable, insurance payments, and payroll. Quarterly, I write reports and file tax returns.

On June 10, 2008, I will graduate from Franklin University with a bachelor's degree in accounting. There I have received training not only in cost and corporate accounting but also in finance and business law. Since my minor is in data processing, I have experience with a wide range of microcomputers and accounting software, as explained on the enclosed résumé.

At your convenience, I would like to set up an appointment to discuss how I can serve your firm. Salary is open. Will you please call (000) 555-4689 between 5:30 and 9:00 p.m. Monday through Wednesday or weekends? Or if you prefer, e-mail <jasmith@service.net>.

Sincerely,

Jon Alan Smith

Jon Alan Smith

**FIGURE 26.4 Cover letter with summary opening.
(Modified block format with indented paragraphs)**

When finally satisfied with the quality of your résumé and cover letter, place them inside an 8½- by 11-inch manila envelope, unfolded. This precaution will protect against weather, wrinkling, fingerprints, or dropping. If you are employed, do *not* enclose a sheet of references, lest your employer be contacted prematurely. One applicant made this unfortunate mistake, only to find he had no job with either firm. The interviewer had telephoned the employer immediately, and the man was fired upon his return an hour later.

If unemployed, you can enclose references along with the résumé and cover letter; yet this is unnecessary, since most employers wait until after an interview to run a reference check. If you enclose letters of recommendation, do *not* send the originals, which could disappear into an employer's file. When an employer wants a grade transcript, order one and arrange to have it mailed directly to the company. Because oversized envelopes require extra postage, you can conserve by using standard envelopes for mailings to companies that seem less desirable.

PROVIDING A LIST OF REFERENCES

When you walk into an interview with an up-to-date, well-organized sheet of references, you have a definite advantage. This preparation not only boosts your confidence but also indicates to the interviewer your ability to plan ahead and organize. Yet relatively few job seekers are aware of the full significance of this important job-search tool, nor do they think to add *financial* references to the usual list of former employers, teachers, and the like. However, financial references are significant. From the employer's point of view, someone who is financially stable seems more likely to be trustworthy and reliable.

GUIDELINES: COMPILING A LIST OF REFERENCES

1. **Request permission before using names.** With teachers and others you have not seen for many years, try to meet in person to make sure you are remembered. Otherwise, telephone. If you must write, enclose a stamped, self-addressed envelope and politely request an early reply. (Employers expect to be contacted; it is unnecessary to ask for their permission.)

2. **Be sure the person is willing to give you a reference.** If you sense reluctance or a lack of enthusiasm, ask someone else. A lukewarm response can do harm.

3. **Provide employment references.** From your last two positions, list supervisors. If you know employees at the company to which you are applying who would give favorable references, include their names, too.

4. **Provide other references.** Include coworkers, teachers, coaches, scout leaders, or anyone else who can attest to your good qualities— except relatives and the clergy. For financial references, list banks, charge accounts, or paid-up loans.

5. **Indicate in parenthesis your relationship to the reference.**

6. **Organize the list of references in most- to least-important order.** Put employers first, character references second, and financial references third.

7. **Include your full name, address, telephone number, and e-mail address.** Place this information at the top of the sheet in a centered heading like the one on a résumé.

8. **If working, take precautions.** Across the top, before the heading with your name, type in capital letters: "PLEASE DO NOT CONTACT MY CURRENT EMPLOYER UNTIL THE FINAL STAGES OF INTERVIEWING." If using a résumé service, ask that neither your résumé nor your reference list be sent to your present employer.

WRITING A LETTER OF APPRECIATION

Several applicants had interviewed for the position of Financial Aid Director at Marion Technical College, but the search committee could not agree. Then a letter of appreciation for the interview arrived from Andrew Harper, who was the only applicant to send a thank-you. The committee reevaluated his credentials and called him for a second interview. Andy got the job. That one brief letter tipped the scales in his favor. Why? What is significant about a letter of appreciation?

First, a letter of appreciation reveals a sincere interest in a position. Since most applicants interview for several positions and seldom send follow-up notes, an employer does not know whether or not they are genuinely interested. Second, a thank-you conveys a message, implying the sender is considerate and appreciative. It also suggests motivation, perseverance, and a positive attitude. Third, the letter indicates good human relations skills. (See fig. 26.5 for an example.)

1122 Valley Road
Clearview, Washington 98222
February 6, 2008

Dr. Margaret Berman
Mad River Medical Association
1555 Main Street
Wenatchee, Washington 98555

Dear Dr. Berman:

Thank you for the opportunity to discuss the possibility of working at Mad River Medical Association. I enjoyed meeting with you and your staff; the friendly atmosphere and organization impressed me. After interviewing with you, I am even more eager to become a part of your medical team.

Once my program at Marion Technical College is complete on March 19, 2008, I will be available for employment. If accepted for the position of medical secretary, I am prepared to put all my efforts into achieving the goals set by your practice and to serving your patients accordingly. My 4.0/4.0 GPA attests to my concern for quality work.

If you should need any further information concerning my credentials, please contact me at (000) 555-1111 any time convenient for you or e-mail <tmcraig632@ service.net>.

Sincerely,

Trena M. Craig

Trena M. Craig

FIGURE 26.5 Letter of appreciation.

Interviewers advise restating your strongest qualifications in your thank-you letter. That may move your résumé up near the top of the heap.

There is no standard format for a letter of appreciation, but *timing* and *tone* are important. Mail your letter the day of the interview or the next day. But keep your priorities straight: accuracy and appropriateness are more important than same-day mailing. Read the letter aloud to gauge the tone. Edit and proofread several times. Be sure the tone mirrors enthusiasm, not the image of a forlorn applicant sitting by a silent telephone. Avoid phrases such as "I eagerly look forward to hearing from you," or "If you are interested please call me," or "I'll be waiting to hear from you."

To draft a successful letter of appreciation quickly, follow the outline below, including any of the six parts that are relevant to your situation.

OUTLINE: LETTER OF APPRECIATION

1. Thank you
2. I'm interested
3. I enjoyed . . . (or was impressed by . . .)
4. I'm available (give date)
5. Restate your strongest qualifications.
6. If you need more information (give telephone number, time to call, and e-mail address).

WORKPLACE CASE STUDY

CONNECT THE DOTS

During an interview, Valerie L. was asked if she had any grant-writing experience. She replied, "No, but I have had considerable experience writing letters, reports, and other documents. I would be glad to learn."

After the interview, Valerie went to the library, where she looked at sample grants. She realized that they were similar to the proposals that she had written at her previous job. In her letter of appreciation, she mentioned going to the library, the similarity between grants and proposals, as well as her proposal-writing experience.

As a result, she was hired.

Moral: Connect the dots of your experience to the job you apply for. Do not assume the interviewer will make the connections.

WRITING A LETTER OF ACCEPTANCE

Often employers notify successful applicants by telephone. If you should be called, be sure the terms of the job offer are clear before accepting. Acceptance over the telephone is an oral contract. During the call jot down the terms of the offer and ask for written confirmation to ensure there is no misunderstanding.

Dear Ms. Hendricks:

Thank you for the job offer. The staff nurse position, evening shift, on the surgical floor will be challenging and interesting since it offers numerous opportunities to learn. The salary of $_____ per hour with $_____ on weekends is more than acceptable.

On June 12, I will arrive early to fill out the insurance forms, receive instructions, and begin.

I am looking forward to working with you and the other members of the staff at Belvedere General Hospital.

Cordially,

Jonathan Jones

FIGURE 26.6 Abbreviated letter of acceptance.

If you are unsure or if you have other offers pending, you can ask for one to three days to decide. Competitive offers will enhance your desirability.

After making a decision, call in your acceptance and send a letter accepting the job offer and the terms (see fig. 26.6). Specify the primary provisions of the offer and keep a copy. This letter not only protects the employer but also protects you by forestalling misunderstanding or friction later.

The following outline will help you organize a letter accepting a job offer.

OUTLINE: LETTER OF ACCEPTANCE

1. Thank-you or another expression of appreciation
2. Acceptance of the offer (sound pleased)
3. Main points of the job offer
4. Date and time to begin work
5. Courtesy closing

WRITING A LETTER OF REFUSAL

Never let the door slam on a job offer. Courtesy is important even in a refusal, for some day you may wish to reapply at the company. A refusal should be made promptly so that the company can continue the search. The refusal can be made over the telephone, but unless you are adept at speaking off the cuff, it is wiser to mail a decision, if possible.

Begin by tactfully expressing appreciation for the offer. But avoid an overly enthusiastic tone that might mislead the reader into thinking the call or letter is an acceptance. Provide a general reason for the refusal, without mentioning anything that might seem negative about the company or the offer. Close with a positive comment (see fig. 26.7).

Dear Ms. Plymale:

Thank you for the informative tour of Tucker & Taylor's downtown facility and for the attractive offer of the junior accounting position.

I have, however, accepted another offer that is more consistent with my career goals.

Your time, consideration, and courtesy are appreciated.

Sincerely,

Raphael Perez

Raphael Perez

FIGURE 26.7 Abbreviated letter of refusal.

OUTLINE: REFUSAL OF A JOB OFFER

1. Expression of appreciation for the job offer
2. Brief refusal
3. General reason for the refusal (optional)
4. Courtesy closing

PRACTICE

COLLABORATIVE EXERCISE: Revising Skills Lists

Directions: Working with a partner, check each other's drafts of skills. Questioning your partner will help each of you to find more transferable skills and an action verb for each skill.

1. Is the item a claim or a skill?

    Note: A skill tells what one can *do:* "type 60 wpm" and "monitored cash drawer" are skills. But "work well with others" and "honest" are vague claims. Instead, cite specific duties that point to a skill or an ability.

    Example of an interpersonal skill: "Resolved customer complaints."

2. Does each item begin with an action verb?

3. What else did you do that required accuracy, responsibility, communication skill, tact, problem solving, or trustworthiness?

4. How can that task be reworded for your skills list?

5. Is there anything else that you did at work, in class, or during leisure hours that might be transferable?

COLLABORATIVE EXERCISE: Revising a Job Objective

Directions: Using the criteria below, critique the job objectives of your group members. Place a question mark after any word or phrase that does not sound appropriate. Make suggestions.

1. Is the objective limited to *one* position or area?

2. Does the objective focus on service to an employer?

3. Is the objective written in third person?

4. Is the objective written as a fragment, not a sentence?

5. Are the skills in the objective the same as those in the skill headings?

6. Is the wording correct and appropriate?

BOOK II: THE RESEARCH WRITING GUIDE

Planning Research and Preventing Plagiarism

> Learning without thought is labour lost; thought without learning is perilous.
>
> —Confucius (6th century BC), *Analects*, 2.15, trans. James Legge

Professionals in business, law, engineering, medicine, and other fields gather, digest, and condense large quantities of information during the course of their workdays. In the workplace you may observe sites and situations, interview prospective employees, or survey a group to gather opinions. You may analyze annual reports, budgets, government documents, court cases, medical journals, or other records. In the Information Age, work often requires research.

In your college classes, you gather information for research papers and reports. A research project can help you acquire a wide range of career skills. It can afford opportunities to develop the ability to

- Plan and schedule your time
- Observe, interview, and survey
- Locate information in the library or on the Internet
- Provide proper documentation for sources
- Summarize, paraphrase, and quote
- Analyze and evaluate
- Meet deadlines

PRIMARY AND SECONDARY RESEARCH

You can collect information in either of two general ways—primary research or secondary research. Or you can combine the two. Collecting data firsthand is called *primary research* or *field research.* You become the researcher and go to a *primary source,* one that has not been filtered through the eyes of another researcher. Whether you observe a class, interview someone, or survey a population sample, you go out in the "field" and conduct primary research. You may make careful notes, describing what happens and your perceptions. Or you may construct a questionnaire, administer it, and tabulate the responses. The data you collect becomes the basis of your report or paper.

Secondary research is the collecting of information that has passed through someone else's hands. You may find it in a library or on the Internet. When you use *secondary sources,* someone else has conducted the research and recorded the original data. Usually, this information has been published and printed. These two methods of research can be combined.

www.mhhe.com/dietsch

For a wealth of online research resources, visit: Research

See "Caterpillar Afternoon," p. 561.

See chapter R-2.

BASIC GUIDELINES FOR RESEARCH

1. For research to be reliable, the researcher must be accurate and objective in presenting findings and interpreting results.
2. Sources must be clearly identified.
3. Primary sources are preferable to secondary sources.
4. Both primary and secondary research require *documentation*, a listing of the source, the date, the author, and other related data. Omission of documentation can result in plagiarism.

See chapter R-4.

A basic concept to remember throughout your project is that for research to be reliable, the researcher must be accurate and objective in presenting findings and in interpreting results.

The Path to Objectivity

There are three sides to every story—yours, mine, and all that lie between.

—Jody Kern

Recently a National Public Radio panel discussed whether or not a reporter has the right to include opinion in a news report of an overseas conflict. The question was this: Should he give only the facts or should he put himself into the story as well? Traditionally, reporting and other research have constituted a quest for truth, a search for facts, not an opportunity to express a personal view.

Researchers are still expected to step back from their own beliefs and emotions—to be as objective and unbiased as possible. To maintain professional integrity and reliability, they must be observant and open to new information. They must be competent and honest, able to identify and describe data accurately, and able to understand what is occurring. They must be willing to question their own perceptions, for optical illusions and misperception can occur.

To check for bias, researchers need to be keenly aware that observation, description, interpretation, and writing are *separate* stages of primary research (see fig R-1.1). Distortion can occur at any stage. To ensure accuracy, researchers check their perceptions, word choice, interpretation, and final draft carefully.

Objectivity Requires Checking Each Stage of Research

Observe   Describe   Interpret   Write

FIGURE R-1.1 Path to objective research.

Fact or Idea?

See chapter 3.

Questioning the words you use to describe what you observe and making careful interpretations (inferences) can lead to objective writing. This doubting will help you differentiate fact from idea, which is not always easy. *Fact* is information generally accepted as real or true. But not all so-called facts are true. An *established fact* has been verified by substantial support/evidence. Some facts can be quickly verified through the five senses. Other facts are established through laboratory tests, control groups, and other measures.

In *The Modern Researcher,* fourth edition, Jacques Barzun defines an *idea* as "an image, inference, or suggestion that goes beyond the data [facts] nameable in conventional terms." This definition can guide you when the boundary between fact and idea blurs. Ask yourself if the information is entirely fact or if opinion has been injected. Is the information accepted by experts in the field as true or is it still in the realm of theory and unproven? Barzun explains, "An idea leads us on. . . . [It] suggests doubts and possibilities."

To test your alertness, consider the two sentences below. Which one is strictly fact? Which one mixes an idea with fact?

John F. Kennedy, a great president, was assassinated in 1963.

President John F. Kennedy was assassinated on November 22, 1963.

The first sentence contains the idea of greatness, which is a matter of opinion. Every word in the second sentence is factual.

As you record data, do not mix ideas with concrete facts. Ideas belong to a later stage when you make inferences and derive a conclusion. Taking three precautions will help you attain objectivity:

1. **Describe your observations with neutral and concrete words.** Avoid emotionally charged words that carry hidden meanings, associations, or opinions.

2. **Select tentative words when making interpretations and inferences.** Examples: *indicate, suggest, may, seem, appear, trend, apparently, evidently, probably, possibly, hint, imply, signal,* or *clue.* Keep in mind that the *image* you perceive may be incomplete or distorted, depending on your vantage point and your knowledge.

3. **Check interpretations and inferences.** Do they seem logical and reasonable, based on the observable facts? Do the inferences account for all the loose ends? Or are there conflicting data? If so, any doubts or questions should be noted and discussed.

GUIDELINES FOR OBJECTIVITY

SCHEDULING RESEARCH TASKS

Procrastination may be tempting when the deadline for a research report or paper seems distant—perhaps a month or more away. Yet don't be lulled into complacency by believing you can draft a questionnaire or find all the resources you need in an hour or two. Such misconceptions can lead to anxiety and even panic as your deadline looms.

Regardless of whether you do primary or secondary research, your project will require considerable time. If you interview, you will need to set up appointments, construct a list of questions, tabulate responses, and write a report (chapter R-5). For secondary research, you need to locate materials on the Internet or in the library (chapter R-2). Reading, analyzing, and writing will require much time.

A flexible schedule, tailored to your needs, can alleviate anxiety and increase efficiency. The first step is to list the tasks. The second is to estimate the time required for each task. Writing a paper based on either primary or secondary research will require drafting, revising, editing, and proofreading. If possible, allow a little leeway here and there.

TENTATIVE FIVE-WEEK SCHEDULE FOR SECONDARY RESEARCH

	Days Needed	Date to Complete
1. Select a topic. Locate materials. Do preliminary reading. Start note cards and source cards.	2–3	_____
2. Limit topic, read, and write a controlling question.	2	_____
3. Read. Start a scratch outline.	3	_____
4. As you read, continue making note and source cards.	3	_____
5. Revise outline. Write thesis and start draft.	3	_____
6. Reread notes. Refine outline. Finish first draft.	6	_____
7. Return unneeded materials. Get more if needed.	1	_____
8. Read. Revise draft. Print out.	4	_____
9. Revise draft. Check order and format. Print.	3	_____
10. Alphabetize source cards. Type list of works cited.	1	_____
11. Revise, edit, and proofread several times.	3	_____
12. *Tentative deadline:* Proof again. Print final copy.	1	_____
Final deadline: Submit research paper.		_____

As a safeguard, plan research tasks so that your final draft can be completed a day or two early. That way you can revise, edit, and proofread thoroughly. And if a minor emergency should occur, you will not have to worry about the deadline.

DETERMINING THE PURPOSE

The first step to any research project is to determine the purpose. Will your general purpose be to inform, to investigate a problem, or to persuade? All three kinds of papers require substantial reading, summary, paraphrase, quotation, and documentation of sources. As a result, the tone of research papers tends to be formal and less personal than papers based on experience.

Informative Research Papers

An *informative research paper* explores what is actually known about a topic and presents it in an objective manner. The paper ends with a logical conclusion, drawn from the research. The researcher boils down a wide range of information into a balanced summary, incorporating results of reputable studies and quoting opinion of authorities in the field, then points out the relevance to the reader.

You not only summarize and quote but also define, compare results, and paraphrase. You define terms not generally known and compare professional opinions. You report on areas of consensus or disagreement among experts. *You think about what the research means, how it can be applied, and what questions remain for future research.*

Research papers often require more than one kind of order. For example, you might use chronological order to summarize the onset of a disease and its symptoms, then use classification to list methods of treatment.

Problem-Solving Research Papers

Many topics for research papers center on problems. For example, you might investigate a business, medical, ethical, legal, social, or environmental problem. The problem might involve your campus, your community, your workplace, or a group to which you belong. You may do primary (field) or secondary research or a combination of both.

See chapter 18 .

Like an informative paper, a *problem-solving paper* reports existing data and expert opinion. But it goes a step further: you evaluate the alternatives for solving or alleviating the problem. A *recommendation* may also be included. If your paper is based on secondary research, the recommendation is based on the majority opinion of experts in the field. If you conduct primary research yourself and if you are the expert, then you make the recommendation. A problem-solving paper often combines chronological order with description and classification.

Argument Research Papers

An *argument paper* briefly summarizes a controversy and argues for a point of view, belief, or course of action. In other words, you take a stand and support it with facts, reasons, and examples. An argument may open with a chronological summary, then use illustration and classification to organize the supporting details. The tone of the argument depends upon the purpose, the topic, and the audience.

See chapter 19 .

SELECTING AN APPROPRIATE TOPIC

Your research topic should be provocative, worthwhile, and challenging. This project should offer you the opportunity to learn and to draw a conclusion. Avoid a rehash of a topic you covered in high school or one well covered in a single source. As you mull over choices, consider three important questions:

www.mhhe.com/dietsch

For more information on choosing a topic, go to:
Writing>Thesis/Central Idea

- **Can you find a topic that stirs your curiosity?** For example, if several of your family members have the same health problem, you might investigate the cause, effects, and current methods of treatment.

- **Can you find information that is unfamiliar to most readers?** Avoid familiar topics such as drinking and driving, abortion, or the death penalty, which have been widely publicized.

- **Can you locate conclusive support: data, studies, and expert opinion from several reliable sources?** A single source is not enough. (Ask your instructor how many sources are required.)

To determine whether or not a topic is feasible, do a *preliminary search* of possible sources. Can you secure enough suitable information within a few days? If a topic is quite new or old, you may find few sources.

WHERE TO FIND POSSIBLE TOPICS   Look for a topic that you would like to know more about. What items have been in the news lately? You can also find ideas for topics in weekly news magazines such as *Time, Newsweek,* and *U.S. News and World Report.* The suggestions at the end of this chapter may also stimulate ideas.

COLLECTING SOURCE INFORMATION

Whether you go to the library, go online, or do field research, you need to know what source information to collect. You also need to understand exactly what plagiarism is and the necessity of printing out any page you intend to summarize, paraphrase, or cite. (Chapters R-2, R-3, and R-4 provide detailed instructions.) Gathering source data as you research provides the following advantages:

- **Saves time.** You don't have to retrace the original source. Instead, you can quickly scan printouts, select quotations, and double-check for accuracy.
- **Prevents unintentional plagiarism and worry.** *Avoids risky shortcuts.*
- **Enhances credibility.** Readers feel they can trust someone who supports a claim with adequate documentation.
- **Provides evidence.** If there should be any questions from an instructor, you have proof that you researched the sources for your paper.

PREVENTING PLAGIARISM

Legally, you may use small parts of copyrighted works (less than 10 percent of the entire work) for research if the author does not prohibit such use and if you document clearly and completely. That means you identify the author and source, as well as enclose short quotations (four lines or less) in quotation marks. Indent long quotations. Omission of this vital documentation results in *plagiarism.* (See chapter R-3 for a complete explanation and examples.)

Why take unnecessary risks? Penalties for plagiarism in colleges and universities range from a failing grade to suspension.

Research often takes longer than anticipated, so start early. Collect complete source information as you go. If in doubt, see the source entries in chapter R-4. When making source cards or notes, follow these guidelines:

THREE STEPS TO PREVENT PLAGIARISM

1. **Note or print out all source information.** Identify the author's name, title and subtitle (if one) of the work, publisher, date of publication, pages of the selection, and volume number, if given. (See pages 478–500 for MLA style or pages 500–513 for APA style.)

2. **Use quotation marks.** Enclose copied material in quotation marks.

3. **Safeguard your list of sources (entries).** You will need this information when you write your paper and later when you prepare a works cited list or a reference list for the end page of your research report or paper. (See page 472.)

A Note of Encouragement

Beginning a research project can be daunting. You can make your project satisfying and challenging by choosing a topic that interests you and pushes you to learn beyond what you already know. You can ease the pressure of the assignment by drafting a schedule early and by adjusting the schedule to your needs.

PRACTICE

DRAFTING A SCHEDULE

Directions: If your assignment calls for field research, read chapter R-5, "Observation, Interviews, and Surveys," before drafting your schedule. For other research, read chapter R-2, "Locating Reliable Electronic and Print Resources."

1. Prewrite: List all the tasks you will need to complete your research project.

2. Draft: Copy your tasks in the order they will be done. At the bottom of the sheet, write *deadline*, followed by the date due.

3. If your instructor has included checkpoints, include those dates.

4. Determine the number of days until your deadline. Now allot a few days to each task, making sure you do not run over the total number of days. Include a *tentative deadline* to allow for an emergency.

5. Check to see that your estimates are realistic. Revise as needed. (See page 422.)

Locating Reliable Electronic and Print Resources

An open mind is an asset for research. To be open does not mean you accept everything you see in print. It just means you are willing to consider new information and dissenting views rather than hastily rejecting anything that seems strange or different. In other words, you review a claim before you evaluate it. You examine the evidence and appraise it impartially, yet question any point that seems doubtful.

> To be conscious that you are ignorant of the facts is a great step to knowledge.
>
> —Benjamin Disraeli (1845)

427

The principal goal of research is to obtain an objective assessment of the facts—to discover the unvarnished truth. For a research paper, you also need to narrow your topic and consult a range of reliable sources.

NARROWING THE TOPIC

Limiting a broad topic for a research paper can be frustrating. You may wonder how much can be covered in a 1,500- to 2,000-word paper (or whatever was assigned). To find the main points of your topic quickly, read overviews in encyclopedias, abstracts, or digests, either online or in the library.

How to Begin

To limit a topic, you could type the subject into a search engine and scan the first few pages of Web listings. For example, starting with "ethanol," you might limit to "ethanol as a fuel." Sometimes a link will yield a table of contents that lists categories such as "technology," "environment," "research and criticisms," each with subcategories. If you narrow the topic to "technology," you might find three subtopics:

1. Ethanol-based engines
2. Ethanol fuel mixtures
3. Fuel economy

Another way to limit a subject is to consult print sources in a library, using the *Library of Congress Subject Headings* (LCSH). This multivolume book is usually located adjacent to the reference section. In the LCSH under the subject headings for books, you can find subheadings to use in your search of the library's online central catalog.

Drafting a Controlling Question

Writing a *controlling question* will help you focus your topic and narrow it further, if needed. For example, you might ask, "What are the advantages and disadvantages of ethanol as a fuel?" Here are other examples:

- Which home security systems are most effective in deterring burglars?
- How effective is solar energy for heating new homes?
- What should parents look for when selecting day care?

A controlling question can establish the direction of your paper and save time in writing. As you examine materials, you can list possible main points and start a scratch outline.

WORKPLACE CASE STUDY

FLORA LIMITS A VERY BROAD TOPIC

During preliminary reading on rain forests, Flora Kyle found that several rain forests exist around the world. She limited her topic to Amazon rain forests, but still she found too much information for the assignment of a 1,500–1,700-word paper. Feeling overwhelmed, she consulted her instructor, who suggested asking: How does deforestation of the Amazon rain forests affect residents of the United States? Then Flora was able to restate the question, limit her focus to three main reasons, and begin an outline:

SCRATCH OUTLINE

Controlling Question: Why should U.S. citizens be concerned about deforestation of the Amazon rain forest?

1.   Habitat of many plants and animals destroyed
2.   Spread of disease from fleas and mites that leave the deforested area
3.   Effect on the ozone layer by greenhouse gases produced by burning in the rain forest
4.   Worldwide climate changes

I. FINDING RELIABLE RESOURCES ON THE INTERNET

By being selective, you can access a wide range of reliable references on the Internet without charge. These include dictionaries, encyclopedias, thesauruses, recent periodicals, biographies, and classic fiction with expired copyrights. But there are limitations, as well as the ever-present problem of unsafe sites. Back issues of periodicals in online archives generally require a fee and a credit card number. Online technical manuals and many other materials require a fee or a subscription. (For free, reliable information, see the directory on pages 435–436.)

Accessing Subscription Databases without Charge

Students and patrons can obtain reliable information from a campus or public library's paid subscription database at no charge. Usually, you can access these databases at home with your student ID as the password or by using your library card number. For example, Ohio State University students can use the online "Net Library" subscription database to access a wide range of books, made available by publishers.

At public libraries patrons can access extensive paid subscription databases. Your local library may have the following online resources, as well as others:

- **eLibrary** Popular magazines, scholarly journals, newspapers, TV and radio transcripts, photos, maps, and other materials are available.
- **EBSCOhost** Articles and abstracts of periodicals from a range of disciplines are offered.
- **Annals of American History Online** Entries from 1493 to the present include speeches, essays, biographies, and editorials.
- **Biographies Plus Illustrated** Literary criticism can be accessed from an author's biography.
- **Literature Online** Poetry, drama, and fiction.
- **Enciclopedia Universal en Español** Includes photos, maps, et cetera.

Avoid Plagiarizing

If you stumble onto Web sites where research papers can be downloaded, beware. Some sites post a warning about *plagiarism*; others do not. Still, some errant students submit these papers in college classes, which is foolish. They not only rob themselves of an opportunity to learn but also run a high risk of detection and punishment. Plagiarism can result in failing a course, suspension, or rejection of an application to graduate school. If tempted, consider six salient points:

1. **Free student papers on the Internet tend to be mediocre.** They are replete with errors in content, sentence structure, spelling, and grammar.
2. **Such papers tend to be poorly documented, listing few sources.** For example, one paper, "Evolution vs. Creationism," merely compares the content of two Web sites. Such methods constitute shoddy research.
3. **Few students have the writing proficiency of professionals.** If you buy a professionally written paper, the differences in writing style are likely to be detected by experienced instructors.
4. **Instructors can easily check a paper with those on Web sites.** All they have to do is type a distinctive sentence or phrase into a search engine. It can quickly find the original paper when copied. Other resources to check papers for plagiarism are also available.
5. **To be safe, insert quotation marks around all copied material in your notes immediately.** This way you can avoid borrowing the author's words unintentionally. Later you can integrate the material into your draft by quoting, summarizing, or paraphrasing. (See chapter R-3.)

6. **Gather all data required for source entries as you print out.** (Keep chapter R-4 handy as you go online.) Include extra information such as volume, issue, and page numbers and other data required for Web sites. (See the *home page*.)

EVALUATING WEB SITES

Reliability and quality are prime concerns for researchers. As you know, anyone who can construct a Web page or type a blog can post almost anything—accurate or inaccurate, legitimate or fraudulent. As you browse the net, keep an eye out for doubtful information, disclaimers, errors, and scams.

BEWARE OF FREEBIES!

Web sites frequently offer free songs or other gifts that include adware or result in spam. But greater dangers exist that can evade security software. While browsing online, an instructor came across the offer of a free syllabus. The site seemed reliable with an ".edu" (indicating a university). She clicked and her screen went black. Yet after rebooting, the computer worked.

Suspicious, she checked her files and found a "Trojan horse" hiding in the systems folder. Even though she tried to destroy it, the thing was invulnerable. Evidently, the spyware was there to siphon private information. To be safe, she wiped the hard drive and reinstalled all applications and documents. Her next purchase was an antivirus package, which she now updates regularly.

A week later, a friend who has security software downloaded a free cookie recipe. Her screen went black and her PC froze, too. Unable to fix the problem, she hired a technician, who repaired the damage.

Moral: If offered an online freebie from an unknown site, think twice before accepting.

WORKPLACE CASE STUDY

Clues to Sponsors of Web Sites

When visiting a Web site, look on the home page for the sponsor. Sponsorship can give clues to the reliability of posted information. The suffix, or extension, at the end of the URL is a clue to the sponsor and type of site; private sites have a *tilde* (~), which indicates a personal page. For example, if a tilde is part of the extension .edu, the tilde usually indicates the page of a faculty member or a graduate student.

Domain Names and Extensions

Look for traditional sources to use in your research. The domain name and extension of a URL also yield clues to the kind of source, as in <www.mhhe.com>. This URL is the address of a private company, McGraw-Hill. In the United States *.com* is used by commercial enterprises; *.edu* is used by colleges and universities; *.gov* by government agencies; *.mil* by the military; *.net* by some Internet service providers; and *.org* by nonprofit groups. The air-transport industry uses *aero;* businesses, *biz;* cooperatives, *coop;* museums, *museum;* and individuals, *name. Pro* is used by accountants, lawyers, physicians, or other professionals. *Info* indicates unrestricted use.

You can also find information about sponsors at links such as "About This Page" and "About Us." If there is no such link, try cutting the URL down to the domain name, using just the information before the first single slash.

CRITERIA FOR EVALUATING WEB SITES

PURPOSE
- What is the purpose of the site?
- Does the site advocate a point of view, policy, product, or action?
- Does the site charge a fee or solicit donations?

EXPERTISE
- Has the author been trained in this field?
- Is the author a member of an academic or professional organization?
- Has the document or site been reviewed by a peer or noted by a respected publication in print?
- Has the author published in print or only in electronic format?
- If the material is from a secondary source, are citations included for the original source?

OBJECTIVITY
- Does the language sound professional and fair?
- Does the site contain informational advertisements, testimonials, or other commercial interests?
- If research was conducted, who paid for it? (Be wary of studies paid for by the author or sponsor.)

TIMELINESS
- When was the site established?
- When was the material posted? Updated?
- Are there dead links on the page?

(continued)

ACCURACY

- Are sources of information properly cited?
- Are there bibliographic links to check against library holdings?
- Are spelling and grammar standard usage?

COVERAGE

- Is the material comprehensive, covering the main aspects of the topic?
- Does it give enough specific details to serve your purpose?
- Are references, bibliographies, or links included to access other current information on the topic? (Before deciding, check out the links to other pages.)

RESPONSIBILITY

- Is there a way to contact the author?
- Does the Web site list a Webmaster or a way to supply feedback?

CRITERIA FOR EVALUATING WEB SITES *(continued)*

EVALUATING THE RELIABILITY OF INTERNET RESOURCES

Researchers need to scrutinize Web sites not only to see if they are safe but also to evaluate the quality and suitability of the materials. Are they accurate, expert, objective, timely, comprehensive, and responsible? Are they written on an appropriate level? The six guidelines that follow will help you evaluate the reliability of resources.

Check for a Monitor   Web sites of reputable companies, institutions, organizations, and government agencies are generally monitored for accuracy. For example, some medical Web sites are screened by physicians. The Encyclopaedia Britannica site is vetted by editors. In Wikipedia, however, anyone can change entries and post information. In some cases, fraudulent credentials have been attached.

Watch for Credentials   Look for the qualifications of the author. What else has he or she written? You may be able to check by typing "bio of" and the name into a search engine. Reputable medical advice is available from physicians who publish the full text of articles related to their specialty. They provide their names, cities, states, and credentials at the top of the articles they publish. To check the credentials of physicians, go to <www.ama-assn.org>. This site lists their education, residencies, and specialties.

Examine Source Data   Is documentation provided for quotations? Is the copyright permission for use listed for reprinted information? Have medicines been approved by the FDA? Are side effects stated? If a study was done, who conducted it? Who paid for it? Companies that hire researchers may slant results to confirm their products.

Listen to the Tone   How does the writer's voice sound? Are various theories, policies, methods, or other ideas discussed objectively? Or does the author seem bent on pushing an ideological or political agenda? Be suspicious if the document is filled with negativity or sensationalism. Watch out for special interests, such as info-ads and testimonials.

Notice Dates   Is the information up-to-date? Look for dates on Web pages. Most reliable Web pages specify a date at the start or end. Lack of dates on a Web site and in the text of an article casts doubt on reliability and timeliness.

Examine the Research Method   How and where was the study or experiment conducted? By whom? What were the characteristics of the study group? Size? Was the sample representative of the general population? If an experiment was controlled in a laboratory, have other qualified personnel been able to replicate the experiment? Have other researchers obtained similar results?

Evaluate the Coverage   Look for a statement of purpose. What is the intent of the Web site? How detailed is the material? Does it seem factual? If a topic or treatment is controversial, is the article fair and well balanced, citing risks as well as advantages? Is the material written on a suitable level, or is it too technical? Has the purpose been fulfilled? Is the coverage comparable to that gained from scholarly sources in a library?

CHECKLIST   EVALUATING ELECTRONIC AND PRINT RESOURCES

1. **For whom is the site aimed?** Adults? Youth? Children? Is it written in plain English or does it contain numerous technical terms?

2. **When and how was the data collected?** Is it relevant? Valid? Scientific and technological data tend to change rapidly. Not all early sources are outdated; some are classics.

3. **What is the author's professional status?** Look for a brief biography in the introduction of a book or article.

4. **How credible is the publication?** To assess the credibility of a nontechnical book, consult *Book Review Digest*. For reviews of technical works, see *Technical Book Review Digest*. Match the copyright date of the book with the volume of the digest. You can also check the next volume after that date.

5. **If a topic is controversial, do sources examine various points of view?** A balance of viewpoints is necessary to give comprehensive coverage. Does the tone seem impartial or biased?

6. **Are enough sources available to give comprehensive coverage?** A few articles, even well-detailed ones, are inadequate for a research paper. To understand the thinking in a field and find adequate coverage, you need numerous sources with a variety of viewpoints.

PRESERVING ONLINE SOURCE INFORMATION

When you find a relevant and reliable article on the Internet, print it out immediately to ensure that you have all the information you need. If you wait, it may be gone when you return. Keep in mind these two points:

- **Obtain as much data about each source as possible.** You will need it later to construct a works cited entry or reference list for each source.

- **Save Internet source documents until your paper is returned.** Your instructor may ask to see your sources before a grade is placed on a paper. If you cannot provide evidence of your research, this lack may lead to embarrassing questions.

DIRECTORY OF RELIABLE WEB SITES

General Reference Web Sites

- **Librarian's Index to the Internet** This directory lists 7,000 sites relating to the arts, education, law, medicine, sports, and other subjects <www.lii.org/>.
- **Libraryspot Resources** Links to encyclopedias and a wide range of topics at other sites <www.libraryspot.com/encyclopedias.htm>.
- **National Archives** <www.archives.gov/index.html>.
- **The World Wide Web Virtual Library** <www.vlib.org/Overview.html>.
- **US government agencies** Access these agencies by either going directly to their individual sites or by going through <www.gpoaccess.gov>.

Literature and Media Web Sites

- **Bibliomania** Browse the complete texts of literary classics, reference books, novels, short stories, drama, poetry, biographies, science texts, and other works <www.bibliomania.com/>.
- **Famous quotations** Three excellent sites are <www.quotationspage.com>, <www.quoteland.com>, and <www.bartleby.com/100/>.
- **MagPortal.com** A categorized index of links to the latest magazine articles available on the Web <www.magportal.com>.
- **Your Dictionary** Multilingual dictionaries, thesaurus, grammars, research, and more are available <www.your dictionary.com>.

(continued)

Medical Web Sites

- **National Cancer Institute** Provides information on types, topics, clinical trials, NCI Drug Dictionary, and free booklets <http://www.cancer.gov>.
- *New England Journal of Medicine* offers a partial text or an entire text of some articles <www.nejm.org>.
- **US National Library of Medicine** World's largest medical library <www.nlm.nih.gov/>.

Career Web Sites: See pages 380 and 399.

II. LIBRARY RESOURCES ON THE PREMISES

Many libraries provide full-text articles and books, both online and print, as well as digitized resources such as videos and images. Libraries often provide a map of the facility and a brochure describing available services; look for these near the main entrance or at the information desk. In the periodical room or area, you'll find recent copies of magazines, journals, and newspapers. Computers, serving different functions, are located in various areas.

Libraries have four excellent sources for beginning a search of print sources: general references, a central catalog, indexes, and bibliographies. These materials are generally arranged by subject and may have special locations. If you don't find what you need, inquire at the reference desk.

FINDING YOUR WAY AROUND THE LIBRARY

Preliminary Reading: General References

Brief reading in some general references will provide a quick overview of your topic and help you limit it. If the subject is not new, begin with short selections from dictionaries, encyclopedias, or abstracts. Many encyclopedias give not only an overview but also a bibliography for locating additional sources. Many libraries subscribe to both general and specialized encyclopedias online and provide access to patrons in addition to having print copies on the premises.

Online Library Catalog

After you have gained an overview, it is time to seek detailed material to flesh out your topic. The *online library catalog* allows you to use a computer terminal to locate most of the holdings housed on the premises, as well as those in other library locations. You can search by subject, author, title, or keyword. Most systems indicate the call number or shelf location of a book, availability, and date of return—if it has been borrowed.

Indexes and Abstracts

You can locate articles in periodicals by consulting online databases or indexes in the library on CDs or computer terminals. Articles are listed alphabetically according to subject; specific titles, authors, and publications are given. Magazines, newspapers, pamphlets, government publications, maps, pictures, records, tapes, films, and videos are also included. Many specialized databases and indexes list sources of information for science and technology, art, business, nursing, medicine, drama, education, and other areas.

Abstracts not only list subject headings but also summarize key information in a highly condensed form. For example, you might consult *Psychological Abstracts* (1927 to present) or *Historical Abstracts* (1955 to present).

Government Publications

A broad array of government publications are available online, so you might prefer to visit <www.gpoaccess.gov> first. If you do not find what you want, then search *Monthly Catalog of United States Publications* and *American Statistics Index* or the *Public Affairs Information Service* (PAIS) (1915 to present), which carries subject listings of material by public and private agencies. These materials are cataloged according to a different system. Ask a reference librarian to help you.

Bibliographies

These publications are similar to catalogs and indexes, but they may be more comprehensive. *Books in Print* lists every book in print in the United States, giving authors, titles, and subject area. *Paperbound Books in Print* is valuable in locating sources on recent topics. *The Bibliographic Index* is helpful for locating subjects you cannot find in other indexes. Other sources may also use the *Library of Congress Subject Headings* as a guide.

FINDING PRINT SOURCES ON THE PREMISES

The most recent periodicals are usually displayed on shelves in a reading area. They are arranged alphabetically according to title, left to right. The shelves, on which the latest copies rest, generally lift up. Underneath are recent copies. Older periodicals may be shelved in the stacks by title and date or by subject, title, and date.

To use materials that are stored on site, print out your selections from the online library catalog and take to the stacks. The *stacks* are the rows of shelves where less recent periodicals and books are stored. To find the correct row, look up at the outside ends of the stacks. There the subject listing or the range of call letters for each row is found. Books are shelved in numerical order by call numbers as well as alphabetical order by the author's last name. Nonfiction and fiction are stored in separate areas.

PREVIEWING AND SAMPLING SOURCES

A brief preview in the library will avoid lugging home irrelevant materials. Check the copyright date and skim introductory pages to discover the author's credentials and what the periodical or book covers. Then read a page here and there to sample the depth and tone. To obtain a variety of viewpoints, look for materials by several authors. Although they may all cite classic research, their interpretations may differ somewhat.

> **CHECKLIST   PREVIEWING SOURCES**
>
> 1. **Is the material current or outdated?** Some fields need frequent updating. Material should be current and appropriate for the field.
>
> 2. **Is the material relevant?** Scan the table of contents, preface, and index. Read the chapter titles, a few paragraphs here and there, as well as sub-headings. Consider your purpose and audience.
>
> 3. **Is the treatment of the topic evenhanded?** Differing viewpoints should be recognized and treated with respect. Consider the tone of each source.
>
> 4. **Is there solid support for the conclusions reached?** Watch for inconsistencies. Are any fallacies apparent?
>
> 5. **Is the source primary or secondary?** Try to obtain information from primary sources whenever possible.

See chapter 16.

See chapter R-1.

ACCESSING LIBRARY NETWORKS TO BORROW MATERIALS

To locate materials at other campuses and libraries, you can use a computer connected to a regional network. These networks allow you to borrow materials through an interlibrary loan system. OCLC, an international online network, makes difficult-to-obtain materials available at <www.oclc.org/support/documentation/default.htm>. The library catalog for OCLC is located at <www.worldcat.org>.

Once you begin gathering potential sources for your research paper, you will need a working bibliography to organize them.

COMPILING A WORKING BIBLIOGRAPHY

A *working bibliography* is a list of possible sources to consult. When you go to the library, you may want to take a pack of 3- by 5-inch index cards so that you can start a bibliography, which may be required by some instructors. Cards work well because you can easily sort and alphabetize them. These source cards or your printout will help you find materials and start an outline.

At this point, you may want to turn to chapter R-4, which shows how to document sources required for research. You may follow the MLA or APA guidelines, depending on the course and the instructor. You might mark that chapter with a paper clip so that you can quickly refer to it while making your working bibliography.

How to Begin

To keep track of your sources, copy all information for each source onto one card, using only one side. Copy or print out the call numbers from the online library catalog onto the upper right corner of the source card. Underneath that, copy other pertinent data such as author, title, editor (if one), year of publication, publisher, city, and state. Making a working bibliography will give you a head start on your works cited or reference list.

After you select your reference materials, check your source cards to be sure all items are accurate and complete. For computerized listings, printouts will suffice temporarily, but make sure you get all needed information, *including site address (URL) and access date.*

MAKING SOURCE NOTES

1. For *books*, you need:
   a. Full name(s) of author(s)
   b. Full title (including subtitle, if any)
   c. Editor(s) or translator(s)
   d. Total volumes and specific volume number(s) you will use
   e. City of publication (if unfamiliar, also include state), name of publisher, and date of publication

2. For *periodicals*, you need:
   a. Full name(s) of author(s)
   b. Full title of article (including subtitle, if any)
   c. Name of periodical
   d. Full date of periodical (for academic journals also include the volume and issue number, if listed)
   e. Inclusive page numbers (including section letters for newspapers)

3. For *special sources, such as nonprint material and online sources,* you need to jot down various items as shown in chapter R-4. Note that entries for a subscription database and CD-ROMs differ from those for Web sites.

PRACTICE

PRELIMINARY LIBRARY SEARCH

Directions: To become familiar with your campus library and start a working bibliography for your research paper, search the following sources.

1. *Find your subject in the Library of Congress Subject Headings.* What headings could you use in your search?
2. *Electronic Database.* Type in a subject to research in periodicals. Select sources that might be useful. Print out a list.
3. *Online Library Catalog.* Select three books that might be useful. Print out (or copy) the bibliographic data.
4. *Encyclopedia.* Check an encyclopedia to find basic information. In three sentences, summarize the most important points. If a topic is not listed, try an almanac, atlas, or yearbook.
5. Find an online abstract relevant to your search. Print the abstract, adding source data, if needed.
6. List four sources not listed on this quiz that you might consult. Specify the general area of the library where the material is located.

TEN IDEAS FOR RESEARCH

1. What career opportunities will you be qualified for after graduation? Discuss the advantages and disadvantages of two or three.

2. Investigate potential employers you might apply to after graduation. Discuss three or fewer. Cite advantages and disadvantages of each one. Or compare two.

3. How well do hybrid autos perform?

4. What side effects do artificial sweeteners or some other substance have?

5. How have prohibitions on smoking affected smokers in the USA?

6. How practical is solar energy in home construction?

7. Causes and prevention of burnout in nurses (or anyone else)

8. Pollution of the oceans (or another element of our environment)

9. Effects of sleep deprivation

10. What risks do maternal alcohol and drug use pose to unborn children?

Writing a Research Paper Using Sources

Both primary and secondary research require a thorough, objective consideration of established facts before a conclusion is reached. When doing any research, be open to new evidence even if it conflicts with what you believe. Withhold judgment until you have examined all the available facts, noted inferences, and labeled theories. Otherwise, severe mistakes may occur.

> I have lived in this world just long enough to look carefully the second time into things that I am the most certain of the first time.
>
> —Josh Billings (1818–1885)
> (Henry Wheeler Shaw)

See chapter R-1.

See "The Logical Appeal," chapter 19.

WORKPLACE CASE STUDY

TRACKING THE TRUTH

As an employee was leaving a plant, security guards stopped him to search his brief-case. They found a $35 telephone. Assuming he had stolen the phone, the company fired him. Notices were placed on eleven bulletin boards and the electronic mail system, saying the phone was company property and the employee had violated work rule number 12 about theft. The employee filed suit against the company for libel.

At the trial a coworker testified to going with the defendant to a mall where he had purchased the phone. The defendant explained that his company phone had been damaged by a flood. He had lost the sales slip for the new phone and his former boss had said to just keep the phone. After the firing, the man had applied for a hundred jobs, but was rejected each time it was learned why he had been fired. The jury awarded the defendant $1.3 million in damages.

Moral: Keep an open mind as you examine the facts.

WHEN IS A LIST OF SOURCES REQUIRED?

A paper based on secondary research always requires a list of the sources consulted, both printed and electronic. If you are doing field research, you may or may not need a list of sources, depending upon how you obtain your information. A paper based on personal observation or a survey alone does not require a list of sources (see chapter R-5).

But if you conduct interviews, you need to list each interviewee's name, the place of the interview, and the date. (For telephone interviews, the place is omitted.) When primary research and secondary research are combined, the different source entries can be integrated into one list. Then follow the MLA style guidelines for a works cited list on page 479 (or a reference list, following the APA style). Chapter R-4 explains and shows model entries for both the MLA and APA documentation styles.

TIPS FOR COMPILING A LIST OF SOURCES

- **Start making source cards early.** Note the author, publication, volume, date, page numbers, URL, or other required information.
- **To make entries, find the correct model in chapter R-4.** Check the order and punctuation of each entry you construct.
- **Make a source entry for each quotation and parenthetical citation in your paper.**
- **Alphabetize source cards before typing your list of sources.** This saves time.
- **Double-space entries when typing your list of sources.** Do not indent the first line. Indent all succeeding lines.

CRITICAL READING

Research reading implies a search of existing information, not just one or two books or a few articles. By reading widely, you can gain not only a comprehensive view of your topic but also an awareness of the latest discoveries in a field. As new knowledge is discovered, previous knowledge may become dated. You need to be alert and critical; question any information that conflicts with what you know or have heard. To discover the prevailing view in a field, consult several sources. Note conflicting views so that you can discuss the disagreement in your paper.

Examining Dates and Credentials

Consider the credentials of the writer or researcher of each resource you use. To find this background information, check the home page of a Web site or the preface, introduction, and any footnotes of printed materials. As you read the material, examine the dates of surveys, studies, and other research. (See chapter R-2 for guidelines.) Also notice the language used to discuss research findings and conclusions.

Using Tentative Words to Discuss Findings and Theories

A research paper requires more precise word choice than does a less formal paper. As you read reputable accounts of polls, experiments, and studies, notice the tentative, or provisional, words that qualify discussions of results. These *uncertain* words indicate that evidence is *not* conclusive even though a growing body of research may indicate a conclusion or theory is probably true. Let's look at how the journal *Science* uses tentative words (italicized here) to discuss results of several studies about the cause of perfect pitch:

> A research team from Düsseldorf, Germany, *may* have located the physical basis of one exceptional form of mental performance: perfect pitch—the ability to identify any musical note without comparison to a reference note. . . .
>
> A team led by neurologists Gottfried Schlaug and Helmuth Steinmetz of Düsseldorf's Heinrich Heine University *reports* that the planum temporale, a region of the brain cortex that processes sound signals, is far larger on the left side than on the right in professional musicians—and especially in those who have perfect pitch.

Overstatement undermines the credibility of research. Yet beginning writers sometimes assume that because a study or experiment *suggests* that something is true, it is, indeed, true. By the time they summarize their research notes, they have catapulted theory into the realm of fact. Often one word, *prove,* is what launches this assault upon truth. To discuss uncertain research findings competently, qualify your statements with tentative words. Use accurate terminology, as shown on the following page.

TENTATIVE WORDS COMMONLY USED IN RESEARCH

Verbs	Nouns	Phrases
indicates	indication	probable cause
found	findings	possible influence
may	possibility	apparently is
reported	report	is often a sign of
suggest	suggestion	could indicate
influence	tendency	suggests that
theorize	theory	may affect
imply	implication	can produce
seems	symptoms	
appears	trend	

Reading Research and Taking Notes Effectively

Research reading covers numerous pages, details, and statistics that will need to be condensed when you write your paper. To summarize, paraphrase, and quote well, you need to understand the material. By dividing your reading and notetaking into three stages—prereading, rereading, and prewriting—you can save time (see "A Strategy for Critical Reading," chapter 21).

FOUR BASIC STEPS TO AVOID PLAGIARIZING

Careless use of an author's work and omission of source data can result in unintentional plagiarism. The penalties for this offense can be severe, and the chances of detection are great. Take care in gathering all source information. When you start drafting, be sure you understand what material is common knowledge.

1. Restate Common Knowledge   Factual information that is familiar to the general public is considered common knowledge. For example, it is commonly known that orange juice is high in vitamin C, that Thomas A. Edison perfected the incandescent lightbulb, and that Alfred Hitchcock directed suspense films. So if you come across such facts in your research and use them, you will not be expected to cite the source—unless you decide to quote the source. *If you copy an author's words, you need to enclose them in quotation marks and cite the source.* In your early efforts at research, it is best to cite the source of any information you were unaware of before your reading.

2. Acknowledge Everything Else Practically all other information gathered in research requires documentation. Here is a list of ten types of information to watch for so that you can cite all required sources:

- Historical information not commonly known
- A writer's direct observation or reporting
- Statistics
- Surveys and opinion poll results. Give the researcher, date, place, size of sample, and any other pertinent information in the text of the paper, if possible.
- Research findings and interpretations. Give names of researchers, sponsors, date, place, and any other relevant data.
- Expert opinion, estimates, predictions, or theories. Identify the person who originated the theory, if possible.
- Artistic interpretations or criticisms
- Tables, charts, graphs, and other visuals
- Footnote from printed material
- Any statement that is subject to debate

3. Cite Research Findings, Professional Opinions, and Conclusions When doing secondary research and writing an *informative* research paper, you summarize the findings and cite the opinions of authorities in the field. You offer a logical interpretation of the evidence, citing the words of experts as support. You do not interject your own personal opinion. If you will be writing a *persuasive* paper or a paper of *argument,* check with your instructor, who may have other guidelines. (Also see chapter 19.)

As you start your research reading, the following questions should be helpful in selecting information for your paper and in interpreting it:

- What are the findings?
- What are the implications of the findings?
- What points do most authorities in the field agree on?
- Why do some authorities disagree?
- What does it all mean?

4. Practice Plagiarism Prevention As you take notes, either in the margins of photocopies or on note cards, insert quotation marks around any material you intend to copy into your paper or report. *Then transfer the quotation marks as you copy the material into your paper.* Use ellipsis to indicate omissions and shorten long quotations. If a quotation runs five lines or more, omit the quotation marks and *indent* the passage. *Include the necessary documentation in parentheses.* (See "Block Quotations," page 456.) Your Handbook also provides examples of quotations, ellipsis, and brackets. (See the Handbook Directory, page 728.)

SUMMARIZING, PARAPHRASING, AND QUOTING

As you summarize, paraphrase, and quote, take care to preserve the meaning of each original passage. Distinguish fact from opinion. Transcribe numbers and other figures correctly. With thought and care, you can avoid four common problems in student research papers:

- Omitting significant information
- Pulling ideas out of context
- Using too many quotations or too few quotations
- Inadequately documenting sources

An informative freshman research paper is usually expected to consist mainly of summary. Paraphrase appears at times, and short direct quotations are sprinkled at appropriate intervals. One or more long direct quotations may be used, depending on the assignment and the material. An example of an informative research paper appears at the end of this chapter. To see a researched argument, turn to chapter 19.

Writing a Summary

A well-written summary is clear, concise, and informative, often condensed 50 to 75 percent. It restates the main ideas of the original piece in the same order but omits lesser details. Brief quotations are sometimes included. The following example shows the first two paragraphs of a column and a summary.

Original

Executive Warms to His New Role: The Climate Fixer
by Matt Moffett

Manicoré, Brazil—Deep in the rain forest, Johan Eliasch, the Swedish-born executive who revived sports-equipment Head BV, was inspecting his latest turnaround project. Peering under a wooden trellis, he examined hundreds of tiny seedlings that will be planted on land he now owns. Trees act as a kind of sponge for carbon dioxide, the most prevalent of the gases contributing to global warming.

In 2005, Mr. Eliasch bought titles to about 400,000 acres here, an area twice the size of New York City, He shut down a timber-cutting operation and plywood plant, and planted trees, motivated, he says, by what he considers slow progress in tackling climate change. "Things needed to be stirred up a bit," he says. (*Wall Street Journal,* 7 April 2007)

Summary

In the rain forest of Brazil, Johan Eliasch, a Swedish CEO, examined his many little trees that will be transplanted to deter global warming. Two years ago, he purchased approximately 400,000 acres, closed a "timber-cutting operation and plywood plant," and began setting out trees. But numerous Brazilians resent his purchase and project. They claim he and other outsiders have "designs on their natural resources," which have resulted in unemployment for citizens (Moffett 1-A).

Notice that the name of the reporter is not mentioned in the summary. Therefore, his last name appears in parentheses with the page number. This source note links back to an entry in the works cited or reference list of a research paper, where his complete name, the newspaper, and date appear.

See chapter R-4 for example.

To summarize your research findings, condense and present them in your own words. Try to simplify the passage so that it is not too technical or too complex for readers. Take care not to change the meaning. Retain the original order. To start, you might copy the relevant topic sentences in order, then use synonyms to reword them. If you need some of the original words for a good reason, recopy those that are necessary. Try to *vary your sentence structure from the original.* (For help, see chapter 7.)

Replacing Major Words with Synonyms

To summarize and paraphrase, you replace the original *major words* (specific nouns, verbs, adjectives, adverbs, and gerunds) with synonyms that mean the same. But do not use another form of the same root word. For example, if a writer uses *give,* then you cannot use *giving* or *gift.* A thesaurus will help you find synonyms to replace an author's major words. If you have the slightest doubt about the accuracy of synonyms, check in a dictionary to ensure they have the same meaning as the original words. Not all synonyms have exactly the same meaning.

Using Generic Nouns and Minor Words

Generic nouns have no accurate synonym (tree, cat, dog, freezer). Be careful though. Don't assume that a word is generic; use a thesaurus and a dictionary. For example, Kleenex is not generic; *facial tissue* is generic. *Car* may seem generic, but it has accurate synonyms: *auto* and *automobile.* According to the kind of vehicle, you might substitute *jalopy, SUV, sedan, Toyota Camry,* or another suitable word.

If needed, minor words from the original can be reused without adding quotation marks. But try to vary your wording whenever possible. Still, do not create awkwardness or confusion just to avoid reusing a minor word. *Minor words* include the three articles (*a, an, the*), prepositions, conjunctions, relative pronouns, and some other pronouns. (To review the parts of speech, see the Handbook Directory, page 728.)

To summarize and paraphrase, you need to be able to distinguish major words from minor words. Listed below are examples of each to help you avert unintentional plagiarism:

REPLACE MAJOR WORDS:

- **Specific nouns**
  boulder, mansion, edge, way, logic, photo

- **Adjectives**
  huge, fragile, dewy, quick, tiny, sad, happy

MINOR WORDS (can be reused):

- *Prepositions*
  on, over, under, for, off, in, into, of, beneath, after

- *Conjunctions*
  but, and, either, for, or because, yet, when, until

(continued)

AVOIDING PLAGIARISM: USING MAJOR WORDS AND MINOR WORDS

AVOIDING PLAGIARISM: USING MAJOR WORDS AND MINOR WORDS
(continued)

- **Verbs**
  hit, strolled, jogged, is, was lapped, ate, smile, slept, saw
- **Adverbs**
  very, quite, also, too, surely, where, fast, lately, certainly
- **Gerunds** (verbal nouns)
  steering, soaring, sunbathing
  (See page H-18)

- *Relative Pronouns*
  who, whom, which, whose, that, whomever, whoever
- *Other Pronouns*
  she, he, it, her, his, its, they, them, their, theirs
- *Articles*
  a, an, the

A Summary and the Original   In the summary that follows, notice that the author is identified in the first sentence. Synonyms replace major words. Generic nouns such as *horse, musical pitch,* and *alphabet* are reused because they have no close synonyms. At the end, only the page number of the original source is placed in parentheses *before* the period because the author's name is stated earlier. A source note is a link back to the related works cited entry that appears on the final page of a research paper.

Summary

Mark L. Knapp tells an amazing story of a horse owned by Herr von Osten of Germany in the early 1900s. His owner taught Hans to do arithmetic, drummed out with a front hoof. Then von Osten began showing the horse in public, where Hans computed the total of persons with spectacles and did other tricks. He appeared to have learned the alphabet, for he could rap out a response to most queries. Many people were convinced Hans knew German well. In fact, he appeared brighter than many people (1).

Original

Herr von Osten purchased a horse in Berlin, Germany, in 1900. When von Osten began training his horse, Hans, to count by tapping his front hoof, he had no idea that Hans was soon to become one of the most celebrated horses in history. Hans was a rapid learner and soon progressed from counting to addition, multiplication, division, subtraction, and eventually the solution of problems involving factors and fractions. As if this were not enough, von Osten exhibited Hans to public audiences where he counted the number in the audience or simply the number of people wearing eyeglasses. Still responding only with taps, Hans could tell time, use a calendar, display an ability to recall musical pitch, and perform numerous other seemingly fantastic feats. After von Osten taught Hans an alphabet which could be coded into hoof beats, the horse could answer virtually any question—oral or written. It seemed that Hans, a common horse, had complete comprehension of the German language, the ability to produce the equivalent of words and numerals, and an intelligence beyond that of many human beings.

—Mark L. Knapp, *Nonverbal Communication in Human Interaction*

Example of Plagiarism   In the following example, major words were copied needlessly. Quotation marks around the copied words were omitted. Instead of synonyms, *variations* of major words were used. For instance, Knapp writes "began training," and the example uses "trained," which uses the same root word. And there is no source note at the end. The plagiarized portions are italicized.

Plagiarized Summary

According to Mark L. Knapp, in 1900 in Berlin, Germany, Herr von Osten *purchased* a horse. *When von Osten trained* the horse to *count* by rapping his hoof, he did not know that Hans would *become one* of the most famous horses *in history*. Hans was a *rapid learner* and *soon* could do arithmetic and other tricks. *After von Osten taught Hans a coded* alphabet, *it seemed that* Hans, a horse, understood German well and knew more than many people *[source note needed here]*.

Paraphrasing

A *paraphrase* is a restatement that is not condensed or is just slightly condensed. To paraphrase, you use synonyms to replace the major words of the original passage without shortening it appreciably. A few brief quotations may be included. A paraphrase may be one sentence or a paragraph or more. Paraphrasing is used to emphasize significant points or to clarify a difficult passage. It should not be overused, for awkwardness and wordiness can result. Paraphrasing requires the same precautions as those for summarizing to avoid plagiarism.

A Paraphrase with Brief Quotations

To explain how animals understand nonverbal signals, Mark L. Knapp tells a strange story. In 1900 Herr von Osten of Berlin, Germany, bought a horse. While teaching the horse, Hans, to rap out numbers with a fore hoof, von Osten did not suspect that the animal would ever become famous. But Hans learned so fast that he soon went from simple calculation to addition, multiplication, division, and subtraction. Before long Hans could answer "problems involving factors and fractions." When von Osten showed Hans in public, the horse could tally the persons present and those wearing spectacles. He could rap out the time of day, read a calendar, remember musical pitch, and do other tricks. When von Osten drilled the horse in the alphabet, rapped out with a hoof, Hans responded to almost any query. He appeared not only to understand German well but also to know more than many people (1).

In the source note above, only the page is given because the author is identified earlier.

1. **Read and reread the entire original carefully.** Take notes or mark the original, underlining topic sentences and key points. (For help, see "A Strategy for Critical Reading," chapter 21.) 2. **Rewrite and restate.** In your own words, restate the chief ideas from topic sentences and key points, using accurate synonyms. *(continued)*

GUIDELINES: WRITING SUMMARIES AND PARAPHRASES

**GUIDELINES:
WRITING
SUMMARIES AND
PARAPHRASES**
(continued)

3. **Retain the order of the original.** Changes in order may distort the meaning.

4. **Check your draft with the original.** Have you included all significant points? Have you restated appropriately, or have you unwittingly copied material that should be paraphrased or quoted?

5. **Enclose all copied material in quotation marks.** Then use a thesaurus and a dictionary to help you paraphrase and summarize. If a few sentences are too technical, quote them directly.

6. **For a summary reduce material by 50 percent or more.** Restate major points. Combine and condense related ideas. Omit examples and minor details.

7. **Cite sources, pages, and dates.** Check to see that you have adequate documentation. (See chapter R-4 for documenting print and Internet sources.)

8. **Read the summary or paraphrase aloud.** Is it clear? Has all important information been included? You might also ask someone else to read it for clarity.

Reasons for Using Quotations

Quotation is a respected practice that is used by educators, researchers, and other writers. Appropriate quotation in a research paper indicates responsible writing. Use quotations for a purpose. Keep most quotations brief, according to your assignment and the difficulty of the material. Below are five reasons that you might include quotations (*The Writer*, January 2001).

1. **To present technical words for which there is no accurate paraphrase.** Quoting the exact words prevents misunderstanding. In "Selling Your Work Online," Emily Vander Veer points out a new term:

   Stephen King single-handedly catapulted the term "e-publishing" into the mainstream last March when over half a million readers logged onto their computer and downloaded electronic copies of his novella *Riding the Bullet.*

2. **To allay any doubt about the accuracy of a surprising statement or evidence.** By giving the exact words, you avert the reader's suspicion. In "Take the Reader Along," Martha Sutro quotes a paradoxical truism to illustrate the risks that authors take in pitching their work to editors:

   Throughout the process, I remembered a helpful adage: "You have to increase your rate of failure in order to increase your rate of success." You have to be willing to put yourself out there.

3. **To capture the flavor of the original.** Paraphrase will often not do justice to a passage that is vivid and unusual. Aly Colón opens "Avoid the Pitfalls of Plagiarism" by quoting a distinctive phrase:

Plagiarism is the "unoriginal sin," writes writing coach Roy Peter Clark, a senior scholar at the Poynter Institute, in an article first published in the March 1983 issue of *Washington Journalism Review.* And it seems to be a very common sin.

4. **To avoid an awkward or wordy paraphrase.** Do not abuse this privilege, however. Keep such quotations brief. Here Colón quotes a list of criteria rather than attempting to paraphrase. Because the material is identified and indented, no quotation marks are required. It is treated as a long quotation:

   • Was there intent? Did the writer intend to pass the work off as his or her own?

   • If there was no intent, then did the writer's work habits and methods lead to unintended replication?

5. **To enhance your credibility as a writer.** By including quotations appropriately, you demonstrate professionalism.

Making Changes in Quotations

Your readers expect that what you enclose in quotation marks will be the *exact words* of the original source. Sometimes that requires a set of double and single quotation marks. Other quotations may be too lengthy or detailed for your purpose. In that case you may be able to shorten the quotation by omitting unnecessary words and replacing them with an ellipsis. Other quotations may be unclear and need a word added (or changed) in brackets.

Quotation within a Quotation   Short quotations (four lines or less) are enclosed by a set of double quotation marks (" "). If a quotation occurs within the quotation, change the double quotation marks of the original to single marks (' '). Then enclose the entire quoted selection in double quotation marks. The page number follows in parentheses.

> In *Strictly Speaking* Edwin Newman writes: "Most conversation these days is as pleasing to the ear as a Flash-Frozen Dinner is to the palate, consisting largely of 'You've got to be kidding,' 'It's a bad scene,' 'How does that grab you?' 'Just for openers'" (16).

Ellipsis   An *ellipsis* is a set of three spaced dots used to replace insignificant or irrelevant material. When you omit words and use ellipses, take care that the meaning does not change. You can use an ellipsis at the beginning, middle, or end of a sentence. The result should still be a complete sentence. If the ellipsis comes at the end of a sentence or if you omit more than an entire sentence, *then the period makes a fourth dot.* Place a space before each of the dots. When a parenthetical reference comes after an ellipsis at the end of a sentence, place the fourth dot after the parenthesis.

See page H-36.

> In "Out of Jamestown," *Smithsonian,* April 2007, the Chesapeake Bay in Captain John Smith's time (1607) is compared to its condition now: "When

Smith arrived, there were only 50,000 to 100,000 people . . . living along the bay's shores. Today, the population of the watershed is more than 16 million . . ." (T. Smith 51).

Using Brackets and Changing Tense   If you need to add something to a quotation for clarity or logic, you can insert the explanatory words within brackets [ ]. In the paragraph below, the name of the bay was added for clarity.

"Today the [Chesapeake] Bay is being loved to death. Its current ills—clouded water, depleted fish stocks, oxygen-poor 'dead zones'—stem from development. . . . Yet each year 170,000 new residents arrive" (T. Smith 55).

When the verb tense of a quotation differs from the text of your paper, you can resolve this inconsistency by substituting another tense in brackets. In the example below, the original was written in the present tense. For the sake of logic, two changes to the past tense (in brackets) replace the original wording.

Farley Mowat describes the clothes of the Ihalmiut, a tribe that became extinct in the 1950s, as "two suits of fur, worn one over the other. . . . The inner suit [was] worn with the hair of the hides facing inward and touching the skin while the outer suit [had] its hair turned out to the weather" (422).

Once in a while, you may find an error in grammar or spelling in one of your sources. To indicate that you are reproducing the original error rather than creating one of your own, you may insert the Latin word *sic* ("thus") in brackets after the error, as shown after this grammatical mishap:

An example of the radical nature of the organization is this advice from a pamphlet it published: "Thieves should be punished by having there [*sic*] hands cut off."

Keep in mind, however, that some words have two or more correct spellings. It is always a good idea to check two dictionaries to be sure a word is actually misspelled or misused.

MAKING A WORKING OUTLINE

www.mhhe.com/dietsch

For online outlining help, check out: Writing>Outlines

Once you have completed the bulk of your research and note-taking, you can use your note cards to start a working outline. A simple way to start is to classify your note cards. Sort through the cards according to subject and place related items in piles. Then examine each pile and label it with a category under which all items will fit. After that, organize the categories into a possible order. If you become puzzled, ask yourself questions as you draft your outline.

1. **What is the purpose of the paper?** How can I make the purpose clear?

2. **What are the main points of my research?** List them.

3. **What thesis can serve as an umbrella for all the main points?** Do I have irrelevant material? Do I need to narrow the topic?

4. **Is chronological order visible anywhere?** Are there historical items to place in chronological order? Might they make an interesting introduction, or should they come later? Will the overall order be chronological or just the introduction?

5. **How should the body of the paper be organized?** Should main points be arranged according to importance? Or should they go from concrete to abstract? Or would some other order, possibly problem solving, work best?

6. **How has the research been interpreted?** What does it indicate?

7. **Does the material seem comprehensive?** Are there significant gaps? Do I need more information to be complete?

QUESTIONS FOR DEVELOPING A THESIS AND AN OUTLINE

When you are comfortable with a tentative order, number your note cards and copy the categories and subcategories into outline form. Leave spaces for adding items. By the end of the writing process, your working outline will have become a formal outline, ready for submission along with your paper, if required. (An example of an outline submitted with a student paper appears near the end of this chapter.)

DRAFTING A RESEARCH PAPER

As you begin to draft, keep in mind that your working outline is subject to change. In the course of getting your thoughts on paper, you may make slight changes or even find a different organization emerging. If so, take the time to rethink your working outline before continuing to draft.

Drafting a Thesis and Introduction

The sooner you can state a clear thesis, the sooner you can begin to organize and draft your research paper. If uncertain, reexamine your controlling question and rewrite it as a thesis statement. Or you might draft the introduction by speculating about the future and giving a brief history of the topic before stating the thesis, as Wilma Dunnington does.

www.mhhe.com/dietsch

Want online help with your introductions? Go to:
Writing>Introductions

The Personal Genome Project

Probably few readers can imagine a time when genetic profiles would be used as a basis for marriage or divorce, a time when genetic testing would

Summary of possible effects

be required by employers to screen applicants. It is easier to envision a world where children "diagnosed with cystic fibrosis would be spared their fate by a gene transplant," a world where cancers would be revealed and treated before a single cancer cell could grow (Bishop and Waldholz 22). These are the "threats and promises" of what could be the "most ambitious scientific research project ever undertaken" (22).

Definition

Paraphrase with quotation

The Human Genome Project, completed in 2000, was the first to list all of the genes in the human body. The overriding goal of the project was to "conquer genetic disease" (Tortora and Anagnostakos 953). Marwick points out that a gene is occasionally injured, resulting in "abnormal features or with disorders." Sometimes an embryo will not grow; other times children are born with defects. Some conditions caused by a damaged gene may not be apparent until a person becomes aged (3247).

Goals and thesis

Now Harvard University has begun a "Personal Genome Project" to decode DNA letters throughout human genomes to determine DNA influences, including an individual's risk of contacting various diseases. But there is a downside to such knowledge (Regalado A-1).

Another way to begin an introduction is with a definition of a special term, followed by a brief history and explanation. Note, too, that Kathy Rummer includes a statement of purpose:

Dr. Nightingale: Nurse Practitioners in Primary Medical Care

The role of the nurse practitioner has evolved over several decades in response to a shortage of physicians and physician's assistants, escalating costs, and a shortage of affordable health care. A nurse practitioner (NP) is a registered nurse who has completed an "accredited two-year program of study and clinical practice," earned a master's degree in nursing, and passed a national exam ("Nurse Practitioners" 4). In California, for example, NPs are certified to provide basic medical care, prenatal care, and family planning assistance. They must pass a course in pharmacology and work for six months in an internship, receiving intense supervised training, before they can write prescriptions ("Need a" 4).

Definition

Example

History

The nurse practitioner program has evolved as a result of the short supply of physician's assistants (PAs). In 1965 the physician's assistant program was created to relieve the shortage of physicians. Using a physician's assistant for routine medical care freed physicians to concentrate on more complex medical problems (Sidel and Sidel 203, 204). But for some reason the program attracted relatively few medical students. In 1970 the American Medical Association asked the American Nurses Association (ANA) to supply nurses to be trained as physician's assistants. Instead of complying with the request, the ANA created its own alternative to the physician's assistant—the nurse practitioner (Sidel and Sidel 204).

Purpose

The intent of the American Nurses Association was that this new health care professional's "training and philosophy [would reflect] nursing and not medicine" (Sidel and Sidel 204). Dock and Stewart point out that this philosophy is based on the "Nightingale concept" of nursing in which there is "neither independence nor subordination but interdependence and cooperation." According to the Nightingale philosophy, nursing is not a "subcaste of medicine." A nurse is not a "handmaid," but a "helpmate and partner" (367).

For other kinds of openings, see chapter 4.

Using Signal Phrases to Integrate Quotations into the Text

Every quotation you use requires transition to weave it into your text. Usually, a *signal* phrase precedes the quotation. This introductory phrase signals the reader that a direct quotation will be presented. To keep your signal phrases strong and responsible, give the full name of the researcher, team, organization, study, or poll whenever possible. To identify a person, give degrees, position, or other credentials. The examples below illustrate signal phrases for introducing quotations:

- According to Dr. Sheila S. Smith, a psychologist at Blake University,
- A study by an Ohio State University medical team found "...."
- In March 2008, the American Medical Association reported:
- James A. Bell, a scientist at Jones Laboratories of New York City, stated:
- In *American Indian Myths and Legends,* the Blackfoot Indians relate a tale about "The Orphan Boy and the Elk Dog," from which this excerpt is taken.

More examples of signal phrases can be viewed in student examples throughout the chapter as well as in the research paper at the end of the chapter.

Weak Phrases   Some popular magazines and newspapers omit vital source information. Instead, they substitute vague transitional phrases and the word *it.* All of the following examples are evasive and *inappropriate* for research papers and reports:

A study revealed . . .	(What study? Who conducted the study?)
Experts/researchers/ authorities say . . .	(Who? All?)
It is believed . . .	(Who believes?)
It is estimated . . .	(Who estimated?)
It is predicted . . .	(Who predicted?)
"In my opinion" or "I feel"	(So what?)

The verb in a signal phrase should indicate the intent of the writer or speaker. Usually the verb is in the present tense unless the context requires the past tense *(found, reported, stated).* The reference list of verbs below are all in the present tense:

admits	concedes	discloses	holds	observes	**VERBS IN**
agrees	concludes	disputes	highlights	refuses	**SIGNAL PHRASES**
argues	concurs	emphasizes	insists	refutes	
believes	denies	finds	maintains	reveals	
claims	disagrees	grants	notes	stresses	

Using Short and Long Quotations   Short quotations of four lines (three for poetry) or fewer require quotation marks when used in the text of a paper. Short quotations are useful to identify special terms or to include vivid words and difficult-to-paraphrase segments. Both short and long quotations require special transitions (signal phrases) to link them to the text.

A long quotation, or *block quotation,* has five lines (four for poetry) or more. For a research paper (MLA style), double-space and indent block quotations *ten* spaces on the left margin; none on the right. Do *not* use quotation marks for a block quotation because the indention and parenthetical citation alert the reader that the material has been borrowed. Careful writers use long quotations for a valid reason; overuse signals a hastily written paper. In the example below notice that (1) the source and author are identified in the text of the paper *before* the long quotation, (2) a *colon* is placed after the verb, (3) the period appears one space *before* the citation.

In *The Managerial Woman,* management consultants Margaret Hennig and Anne Jardim state:

> Studies of women who enroll in continuing college education programs show that many of the women who fail in these programs . . . have never discussed their goals with their husbands. The husbands never really understood why their wives had gone back to school, and the wives on their own had attempted to maintain the same level of housework they had been accustomed to. (212)

Inserting Explanatory Notes

Once in a great while you may have material that is useful in discussing your subject but that seems to interrupt the text. In such cases you have the option of including the information in an explanatory note. To do so, insert a superscript numeral at an appropriate point in your text. Then you can place the note either at the bottom of the same page or on a separate page, headed "Note" or "Notes." Begin the note with a matching superscript number (see "Content Notes" on page 483).

Writing a Conclusion

www.mhhe.com/dietsch
For more coverage of conclusions, check out: Writing>Conclusions

The conclusion of a research paper may be longer than those of the other papers you have been writing. A graceful ending of three to five (or more) sentences is usually expected. Although new information is not introduced in the conclusion, a writer may leave the reader with a new thought. A brief summary or reference to the future may be appropriate. Peggy Bean combines these three techniques in her closing:

> Although the fetal alcohol syndrome is a tragic disorder, it is also a preventable one. Therefore, it is important that the general public become aware of the risks alcohol poses to the developing fetus, especially to the fetus of a chronic alcoholic. Once families know the cause of this disorder, they can assist the alcoholic mother-to-be in securing professional help.

Bonnie L. Rice ends her research paper with a reference to the future and to what a reader might do to help in a similar situation:

> Efforts toward education, intervention, and prevention of adolescent suicide are being made. They must continue and expand. But can the individual do something to help? Yes, the greatest problem for the unhappy adolescent is isolation from close relationships; one person can be that caring friend who is missing from someone's lonely life.

Sometimes beginning writers tack on a quotation at the end without transition. Although the quotation may be appropriate, the gap between the body and the quotation halts the smooth flow of thought. To link a quotation to a conclusion, use a transitional segment, as italicized in the following example:

> *Child abuse is an ancient problem, but it is an occurrence that concerns us all, a problem that needs to be solved. For as James Agee wrote,* "In every child who is born, under no matter what circumstances, and of no matter what parents, the potentiality of the human race is born again; and in him, too once more, and of each of us, our terrific responsibility towards human life. . . ."

REVISING, EDITING, AND FORMATTING

When you finish the rough draft of your research paper, heave a sigh of relief, and take a break if possible. If not, perhaps you might alphabetize the entry cards for your works-cited list and start typing that or do some other related chore. Before you start to revise your paper, however, you need to gain distance so that you can come back and examine it objectively.

Revising

Persistence, time, and care are the keys to successful revision and proofreading.   See chapter 5.
Yet you may be so preoccupied with content that order, documentation, and mechanics receive low priority. Several revisions spaced over several days will catch more errors than one intensive session the night before a deadline. The checklist below will prove helpful in assisting a tired brain to focus during this all-important stage.

CHECKLIST   REVISING SOURCE-BASED PAPERS

1. Compare your outline and paper. Is the order the same? Is it sound?

2. Now read the paper aloud. Is the introduction interesting and complete?

3. Are the main ideas clear?

4. Is there sufficient transition? Is each quotation linked to the text?

5. Are there too many direct quotations? Should some be paraphrased or summarized instead?

6. Could the order of details within paragraphs be improved?

7. Is the conclusion logical and complete?

Checking Documentation

Every source you use in your research paper must be acknowledged according to a standard documentation style. Two of the most common—Modern Language Association (MLA) style and American Psychological Association (APA) style—are described in detail in chapter R-4. Both use parenthetical citations within the text that are keyed to a complete bibliographical list.

In the course of drafting and revising, even the most conscientious writer may omit, misplace, or lose a text citation while rearranging sentences or paragraphs. If a problem occurs, don't panic! Remember you have your earlier drafts and note cards. Also check to see that every paragraph in your research paper has at least one text citation unless there is a reason for not including one. Remember, too, that if you split a paragraph you will probably have to make another citation.

CHECKLIST   USING PARENTHETICAL CITATIONS

1. Is there a citation for every source used?

2. Does every parenthetical citation for a printed source include a page number (except for single-page sources and entire works)?

3. Is the name of the author/researcher/group included either in the parenthetical citation or in an introductory phrase?

4. If there is more than one source by the same author, does a short form of the title appear in parenthetical citations?

Editing and Proofreading

www.mhhe.com/dietsch

You can find a wealth of editing resources at: Editing

To catch errors in a research paper, proofread when you are alert. Go over your paper several times—one sitting is seldom enough. For example, watch to see that you have the correct spelling of prefixes, as in words beginning with *per-* and *pre-*. To attain the high grades that most students desire, revise and proofread several times. If you follow the editing guidelines outlined in chapter 5 and provide the necessary effort, your paper should be a success.

Using an Appropriate Format

Some instructors may give few or no instructions for formatting a research paper; others may give precise instructions. Most expect good-quality white, 8½-by 11-inch paper. A title (cover) page may or may not be required. Some instructors like the title page format commonly used in the workplace (see the research paper at the end of this chapter). The APA style requires a title page, but the MLA does not. Both styles require that you double-space the entire manuscript, including quotations and list of sources. Some instructors also prefer that you staple or use a paper clip rather than a binder to keep pages together.

Margins and Indentation   Standard specifications for research papers call for one-inch margins (top, bottom, and sides). Pages numbers are placed one-half inch from the top right and flush with the right margin. Indent the first line of paragraphs one-half inch (5 spaces on a typewriter). For long quotations, the MLA style indents one inch (10 spaces) from the left margin. The APA style, however, indents long quotations one-half inch (5 spaces).

MLA-Style Heading, Title, and Page Numbering   If you decide not to have a title page, the MLA style advises starting the first page of the manuscript with

Bellows 1

Susan N. Bellows

Professor Raintree

English Composition 112

May 15, 2008

New Sources of Antibiotics from Land and Sea

Many of the wonder drugs of former decades are losing their effectiveness as bacteria acquire immunity to certain antibiotics. Thus there is a never-ending search for new medicines to replace older ones that have become obsolete.

FIGURE R-3.1 Format for page 1 of a research paper, MLA style.

your name, your instructor's name, the course number, and the date on consecutive lines one inch from the top left margin. Next, center the title. Capitalize the first and last words and major words of the title. Do not italicize any words unless you mention a book title or use a foreign phrase or other wording that requires italicizing. (Never italicize your own title.) Page numbers, in the upper right corner, are preceded by the writer's last name, as shown on page 459.

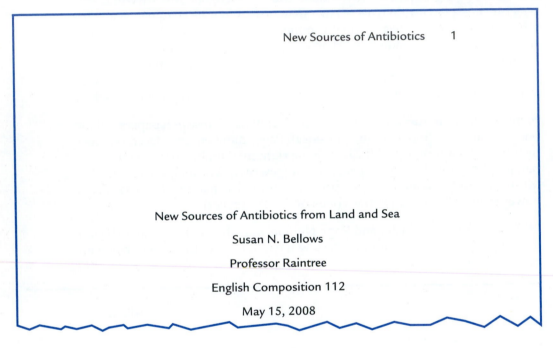

New Sources of Antibiotics   1

New Sources of Antibiotics from Land and Sea

Susan N. Bellows

Professor Raintree

English Composition 112

May 15, 2008

FIGURE R-3.2 Format for a title page, APA style.

APA-Style Heading, Title, and Page Numbering   The APA style requires a title page with a "running head" (abbreviated title) of the first two or three words of the title, the full title, and the byline. The full title should summarize the main idea of the manuscript briefly and simply. The byline contains the writer's name and the institutional affiliation (college, university, or other site). In the byline use no extra words such as *by* or *from*. The preferred form of an author's name is first name, middle initial, and last name.

First, type the running head (the first two or three words of the title) and the page number one-half inch from the top right margin in upper and lowercase. Skip down about one-third of the page and type the full title, centered, in lowercase with capitals (if needed, on two lines. double-spaced). Double-space, then center the writer's name. Double-space again and center the name of the institution, as shown above.

Page numbers in APA style are preceded by the running head from the title page on succeeding pages. This means that the first two or three words are taken from the title. Note that the page number appears five spaces after the head.

SAMPLE STUDENT RESEARCH PAPER: MLA STYLE

A complete student research paper using the Modern Language Association style follows; the title page is optional. The outline appears before the paper by Lois J. Gordon. For specific guidelines regarding the parenthetical citations in this paper, see chapter R-4.

www.mhhe.com/dietsch

To read another student essay in MLA format, check out:
Research>Sample Research Papers>Sample Paper in MLA Style

Workers' Compensation: The Employee's Insurance Policy

by

Lois J. Gordon

CM 110 Research Writing

Professor Leslie Weichenthal

April 10, 2007

Gordon 1

Workers' Compensation: The Employee's Insurance Policy

<u>Thesis:</u> Over the years so many workers' compensation laws have been passed that volumes of information have accumulated, much of it written in legalese. Discerning what is directly relevant to an injured employee is an overwhelming task. And since laws differ so much from state to state, this paper is limited to an overview of workers' compensation in the United States, common problems in resolving claims, and basic suggestions for filing a claim.

I. Brief history of workers' compensation in the United States

II. Overview of workers' compensation

III. Common problems in resolving claims

    A. Prevalence of conditions causing musculoskeletal disorders and implementation of ergonomic rules. Explanation of ergonomics.

    B. Determining whether or not an injury is work-related

    C. Employers, even when negligent, may contest claims.

    D. Genetic testing

IV. Procedure for filing a claim, time limits, and liability

V. Suggestions for filing a claim

Gordon 2

Workers' Compensation: The Employee's Insurance Policy

Before workers' compensation programs came into effect, injured employees had no recourse except to sue for coverage of their medical bills and lost wages. This chore was not only extremely difficult but also unpleasant because of possible retaliation from the employer. Then too, coworkers were often hesitant to testify on behalf of the employee. Awards hinged upon the expertise of the lawyers involved, not actual losses. Cases could take years to settle while legal costs accumulated for the injured employee (Williams 4).

In 1908 President Theodore Roosevelt proposed that workmen's compensation be applied to all workers (Williams 43). In 1912 an amendment to the Constitution of the United States established Workmen's Compensation, which was changed to Workers' Compensation on January 17, 1977. The 1912 amendment required employers to provide insurance for work-related diseases, injuries, or death caused by mental, physical, and emotional factors. No longer would employees be required to prove that their employers intentionally harmed them (Swisher 283). But this amendment does not cover all categories of workers. For example, migrant or seasonal farm workers may or may not be covered according to the state and the employer ("Texas" 1). Some states make other exceptions.

Now, nearly a century after Roosevelt's recommendation, the United States has fifty-three workers' compensation systems in various stages of development with assorted rules and provisions. Two

Gordon 3

federal programs cover federal employees and longshore workers.
There are fifty state programs and another system that covers Washington, DC, because workers' compensation is a form of insurance
regulated by the state in which the company is located (Williams 43).

    Over the years so many laws relating to workers' compensation
have been passed that volumes of information have accumulated,
much of it written in legalese. Discerning what is directly relevant to
an injured employee is an overwhelming task. And since these laws
differ so much from state to state, this paper is limited to an overview
of workers' compensation, common problems in resolving claims,
and basic suggestions for filing a claim.

    A short, convenient description of workers' compensation is
that it is an employee's insurance policy. An explicit definition of this
term is provided by William R. Tracey:

> Workers' compensation—Statutes passed by all
> states designed to protect workers from the hazards and
> consequences of accidents, injuries, illnesses, and death
> to themselves and their families as a result of their em-
> ployment. Benefits are paid to workers suffering job-
> related physical, mental, or emotional accidents, injuries,
> disabilities, or disfigurement or who aggravate preexisting
> physical or mental conditions at work. In addition to
> death payments, they typically include weekly payments,
> based on earnings and size of family, medical and

Summary (margin annotation)

Topic narrowed: Thesis sentence (margin annotation)

Author's name precedes the quotation (margin annotation)

Block quotation indented 10 spaces—no quotation marks (margin annotation)

Extended definition of workers' compensation (margin annotation)

Quotation is double-spaced (margin annotation)

Gordon 4

hospital bills, scheduled loss (amputation, loss of use, or

loss of a bodily function), payments for scarring, rehabili-

tation, retraining, settlements, travel expenses, and attor-

ney fees paid to the employee or his or her surviving

spouse or children. Businesses must either have adequate

funds to pay claims or carry appropriate workers' com-

pensation insurance coverage. The laws also provide some

protection to employers against excessive liability. (375)

Employees who are injured on the job or disabled from work-

related mental or emotional illnesses or diseases are eligible for work-

ers' compensation benefits, according to state regulations, the em-

ployee's wages, and the severity of the disability. Financial benefits

may be awarded in a lump sum or a weekly check. Other common

benefits include medical treatment, prosthetics, rehabilitation, living

expenses, job retraining, funeral expenses, and death benefits for de-

pendents. In Ohio, "employees using alcohol or illicit drugs" are not

eligible for benefits ("Ohio").

United States federal regulations override state laws whenever

there is a contradiction in rules. The Occupational and Safety Health

Act (OSHA) was passed to protect workers' safety and health while

in the workplace, regardless of the state. OSHA laws regulate private

employers that conduct business in interstate traffic. The federal gov-

ernment has also established health and safety laws for its own agen-

cies. To guarantee that regulations are being followed, the secretary

---

Period precedes page of block quotation

Summary: Eligibility and benefits explained

Summary: Role of federal government explained

Gordon 5

of labor has the authority to inspect workplaces, investigate com-

plaints, and make decisions about needed laws. A citation may be

given to employers who violate regulations. Fines may be imposed;

the amount varies according to duration and type of violations

("OSHA Facts").

Problems have long existed in workers' compensations systems

in the United States. In 1970 a national commission was set up to

evaluate all fifty-three systems (Williams 43). The commission discov-

ered many deficiencies and recommended that every state be required

to meet nineteen essential standards by July 1, 1975. Several states

still have some standards to be met (Williams 44).

Summary: Deficiencies in state systems and recommendations cited

One of the major health problems of employees is a group of

conditions classified as musculoskeletal disorders. According to the

United States Bureau of Standards, musculoskeletal disorders trace-

able to the workplace are responsible for "a third of the occupational

illnesses reported." These conditions range from carpal tunnel syn-

drome to back and neck injuries (Pramik 1). In response to this find-

ing, President Clinton's administration enacted regulations on ergo-

nomics that would require "companies to implement comprehensive

programs to protect their workers from repetitive-motion injuries" by

May 2001("Bush"). Almost two dozen states had begun making rules

to meet the deadline when Congress repealed the legislation in March

200l. The reasoning was that implementing the programs would be

so expensive that it would work an undue hardship on employers.

Summary: Explanation of a major health problem

Summary: Progress to date

Gordon 6

Three states—North Carolina, California, and Washington—had already enacted the ergonomics regulations ("Ergonomics").

Definition of ergonomics includes direct quotation

Ergonomics includes everything from office furniture to the "walk through the parking lot to the relationships among coworkers." Adjustable chair seats and backs, improved keyboards, a track ball instead of a mouse, antiglare screens, glasses to reduce eyestrain, and other features can alleviate strain and stress. Some companies furnish recreation rooms, weight rooms, and jogging tracks (Pramik H4).

Cites examples

Problems in resolving workers' compensation claims often arise when a determination is needed to prove an injury or disease is work-related. This decision is particularly difficult in cases where the employee uses a home computer or other appliance that may lead to musculoskeletal disorders. In such cases, a physician often considers the number of hours spent on each appliance and arrives at a split estimate. The decision becomes more complicated when employers

Explanation of how decisions are made on claims

urge the employee to see a company doctor. Although the law may state that an injured employee can see his or her own physician, employees may believe that this is their only choice. Even if they know better, they may feel pressured to see the company physician. Sometimes an injured employee sees several doctors who may disagree. Some states, like New York, require that an "impartial specialist" be appointed ("Rules" 1). Other states identify specific criteria to classify the degree of incapacitation.

Gordon 7

Even when negligence seems clear-cut, an employer may dispute the claim for fear the employee will seek a large settlement. For
example, an employee stepped into a puddle on a sunken sidewalk on
company property. Ice lay beneath the water, causing her feet to fly
out from under her. She suffered a mild concussion. The company
contested, claiming the accident was "an act of God." The agency
settled in her favor, finding that the walk constituted a hazard and
should have been repaired. She asked only for payment of medical
costs, which was awarded ("Anonymous"). In other cases, of course,
employees often do receive large awards.

Yet another complication in the resolution of workers' compensation claims is DNA testing. In February 2001, the United States
Equal Employment Opportunity Commission called for a stop to
genetic testing of employees by the Burlington Northern Santa Fe
Railroad. The commission's lawsuit, filed in the US District Court
in Sioux City, Iowa, said a "nationwide policy of requiring employees who have submitted claims of work-related carpal-tunnel syndrome . . . to provide blood samples for DNA tests" infringes on
rights to privacy and freedom from discrimination (Chen). The next
day the company halted the tests (Machalaba).

The general procedure for filing a claim for workers' compensation is similar throughout the United States, although time limits and
requirements vary. Complete documentation must accompany each
claim. For example, any of the following may be required: A wage

Marginal annotations:

Interview to supple-
ment research

Quotation

Court decision on
DNA testing cited

Ellipsis to indicate
omission in
quotation

Procedure for filing
a claim explained

Gordon 8

schedule, pay stubs, a W-2 tax form, hospital records, physician's statement, treatment and itemized costs, parking receipts, cancelled checks or receipts, "an affadavit from the claimant or claimant's attorney attesting to exact mileage," marriage license, "birth certificates for each child under 18," death certificate, and any itemized bills, depending on the nature of the claim ("Massachusetts").

To obtain specific information about workers' compensation laws in a state of residence or employment, visit WorkersCompensation.com or another Web site written in plain English. (Government sites often contain legalese.) Some employers furnish such information. Some basic suggestions for filing a claim, based on this research and my experience, are presented here:

1. When an accident or illness occurs, record the exact time, conditions, cause, and names of any eyewitnesses. Photograph the accident scene if possible.

2. Secure medical treatment. If an on-site specialist sees you, secure a second opinion from your own physician.

3. Report the accident or illness to the employer as soon as possible.

4. Do not sign a waiver or take a quick settlement until the extent of injury is known. Some injuries may not become apparent until weeks later.

5. Fill out all necessary forms neatly and completely. Be polite and cooperative in follow-up meetings.

Gordon 9

6. If necessary, secure the services of a competent attorney. If
   the state pays the fees, this step will have to be preapproved
   by the court.

Finally, an injured employee who is well-informed and proactive
will have a better chance of resolving a claim fairly with a minimum
of stress than the one who leaves everything to the employer and to
chance.

Cites a benefit of being well informed

Gordon 10

Works Cited

Entry for interview

Anonymous. Personal interview. 28 Mar. 2007.

"Bush Could Move to Wipe Out Clinton's Final Actions." <u>Wall Street</u>

<u>Journal</u> 19 Jan. 2001, Midwest ed.: A16.

Entry for newspaper article

Chen, Kathy. "U.S. Seeks to Halt Employee DNA Tests." <u>Wall Street</u>

<u>Journal</u> 12 Feb. 2001, Midwest ed.: B2.

"Ergonomics Rules Still Alive in Many States." <u>Wall Street Journal</u>

14 Mar. 2001: B15.

Machalaba, Daniel. "Burlington Northern Ceases Its Genetic Test-

ing." <u>Wall Street Journal</u> 13 Feb. 2001, Midwest ed.: B10.

"Massachusetts." Workers' Compensation Legal Library. n.d. 3 Apr.

Entry for online article

2007 <http://www.workerscompensation.com/

massachusetts.php>.

Entry for online article with no date

"Ohio." Workers' Compensation Legal Library. n.d. 3 Apr. 2007

<http://www.workerscompensation.com/workers-comp-

research.php>.

Entry for US government online article

"OSHA Facts." US Dept. of Labor, Occupational Safety and Health

Administration. 2004. 1 Apr. 2007 <http://www.osha.gov/as/

opa/oshafacts.html>.

Pramik, Mike. "Health Risks Also Found in Modern Workplaces."

<u>Columbus Dispatch</u> 3 Sept. 2000: H1, H4.

Gordon 11

"The Rules of New York: Workers' Compensation Subchapter A,

 part 303." WorkersCompensation.com, n.d. 3 Apr. 2007

 <http://www.workerscompensation.com/new_york.php>.

"Texas Workers' Compensation Commission Rules."

 WorkersCompensation.com, n.d. 4 Apr. 2007 <http://

 www.workerscompensation.com/texas.php>.

Tracey, William R. The Human Resources Glossary: A Complete Desk

 Reference for HR [Human Resource] Professionals. New York:

 American Management, 1991.

Williams, C. Arthur, Jr. An International Comparison of Workers'

 Compensation. Boston: Kluwer, 1991.

Entry for state government online article

Entry for book with one author

PRACTICE

TRANSITIONAL PHRASES TO INTRODUCE QUOTATIONS

Directions: For the following items, write a transitional phrase to introduce the quotation. For help, see "Using Signal Phrases to Integrate Quotations into the Text," page 455. (*Source for this exercise:* Siebert, Al. *The Survivor Personality.* New York: Berkley, 1996, page 64.)

1. Quotation: "The most direct access to the subconscious mind is through dreams. When we fall asleep, our rational, logical thinking relaxes."

2. Quotation: "Our dreams contain information about what is happening in our lives, our bodies, and the world around us."

WRITING A SUMMARY

Directions: Write a summary following the guidelines in "Summarizing, Paraphrasing, and Quoting," pages 446–450. Your tasks are as listed:

1. Find a one- or two-page article (three pages if much space is taken by pictures) in a popular magazine. Or if you prefer, select a short article from a journal to be used for your research paper.

2. Duplicate the article on a copier. This copy will be turned in to the instructor along with the summary.

3. Reread the article. Underline each topic sentence and essential supporting data. Number each topic sentence for convenience in writing your summary.

4. To begin your summary, write an introductory sentence that gives the author's name and the source. (See "Using Signal Phrases to Integrate Quotations into the Text," page 455.)

5. Make one entry for a works cited list. Place at the bottom of your paper.

6. Staple the copy of the article to your completed summary.

Supplying Documentation: MLA and APA Styles

Careful documentation is a hallmark of professionalism. In the workplace, you need accurate and complete information not only to write checks and invoices but also to record daily business and legal transactions. Problems in safety, personnel, and other areas must be investigated and noted. Medical treatments, lab tests, and drug dosages must be logged. All these records constitute proof in case of complaints, disputes, or audits.

> Every [person] has a right to [an] opinion, but no [one] has a right to be wrong in . . . facts.
>
> —Bernard Baruch

In college classes you are required to supply documentation for all citations in speeches, reports, and papers, including those from dictionaries and encyclopedias.

WHAT PRECISELY IS DOCUMENTATION?

When a speaker or writer uses someone else's work and provides source information, this process is known as *documentation.* You give credit to the author and provide other data that allows listeners or readers to check facts and search further. For reports and papers, always state the author, title, place and date of publication. Volume numbers and other information may be needed for certain source entries. Entries for the Internet also vary. To scan the different MLA entries, turn to the directory on page 478. For APA entries, see the directory on page 500.

HOW EASILY IS PLAGIARISM DETECTED?

Whether intentional or unintentional, plagiarism is risky and impractical for the following reasons:

1. **Experienced instructors usually detect plagiarism.** When plagiarized material from professional writers is added to most undergraduate writing, the patchwork additions are readily apparent to the practiced eye.

2. **Papers that have been borrowed or purchased from Web sites can be easily tracked.** And coincidences do occur. One professor, who was not suspicious, tells of awarding a history paper a B until another student submitted its duplicate. Both papers had been purchased at the same site.

3. **Search engines can quickly take instructors to plagiarized portions of online material.** If you can find it, so can your instructor.

WHICH DOCUMENTATION STYLE IS APPROPRIATE?

Documentation styles vary according to disciplines. For courses in the humanities, including freshman composition, the Modern Language Association (MLA) style is widely recommended. For the social and behavioral sciences, the American Psychological Association (APA) style is generally used. Models for citations and entries for both styles appear in this chapter. For more detailed information, see the *MLA Handbook for Writers of Research Papers,* sixth edition, 2003, by Joseph Gibaldi or the *Publication Manual of the American Psychological Association,* fifth edition, 2001. For online APA examples, visit <www.apastyle.org>.

FREQUENTLY ASKED QUESTIONS: SOURCE INFORMATION

1. Where are the date and place of publication found?

   Answer: Near the beginning of the book, usually on the back of the title page.

2. What if there is more than one publication date?

   Answer: Take the latest one.

3. What if more than one city of publication is given?

   Answer: Cite the first one.

4. What if the book has been published by two companies?

   Answer: List both publishers in the order given.

5. What if no date, place, page, or publisher is given?

   Answer: Use *n.d.* to mean "no date," *n.pag.* for "no page." Use *n.p.* for "no publisher" or "no place."

6. What if a model for an entry is not shown?

   Answer: Construct a model similar to the one most like it.

7. What title is used for the source page?

   Answer: If MLA style is used, the page is called "Works Cited." The APA style has a page called "References."

8. Are Internet entries the same as those for printed sources?

   Answer: No. Construct an example according to the Internet models.

9. What extra information do Internet entries require?

   Answer: Web publication date (if available), date of access, URL (Web address), and other data may be required.

10. Which style of documentation should be used on the job?

    Answer: Follow the firm's guidelines. If none, use either the MLA or APA style.

For classes in other disciplines, your instructor may ask you to use some other citation style, such as that of the *Chicago Manual of Style* (CMS), often used in business, history, and other sciences. The Council of Biology Editors (CBE) style is used in the life sciences and explained in *Scientific Style and Format: The CBE Manual for Authors, Editors, and Publishers.* The Institute of Electrical and Electronic Engineers (IEEE) style is used in computer science and other fields.

MLA STYLE OF DOCUMENTATION

www.mhhe.com/dietsch

To read a student essay written in MLA style, visit:
Research>Sample
Research Papers>Sample
Paper in MLA Style

The MLA has endorsed a style of documentation that has been widely adopted for research in the humanities. The MLA style requires brief source references within the text of a research paper. The paper concludes with a list of sources, entitled "Works Cited." For abbreviations to use in parenthetical citations, see pages H-43 and 460.

CHAPTER R-4 MLA STYLE DIRECTORY

Parenthetical Citations: MLA Style

Source information placed within parentheses is called *parenthetical citation*. You will be using these citations throughout your research paper. For easy reading, keep citations brief. When feasible, insert the author's name into the text of your paper so that you can limit citations to just a page number (in parentheses). Key or match each of your citations to a source entry at the end of your paper. Several citations may refer to the same entry.

You may have used an earlier method of documentation that varied somewhat from the updated MLA style. As you construct MLA parenthetical citations to use in the text of your paper, keep these three guidelines in mind:

- If the source is from more than one page, cite the full range of pages (19–23).
- Use a parenthetical citation *each time* a source is cited. Some paragraphs may need several citations for different sources. Rarely will you have a paragraph without a citation.
- Optional: Cite one or more works within a paragraph in one parenthetical reference, using semicolons between citations: (Bernstein 17; Zinsser 59). If the citations are long and distracting, use a content note (see page 483).

One Author When you identify the author in your text, put only the page number in parentheses. When you do not mention the author's name, include the author's last name inside the parentheses, before the page number. Do *not* separate with a comma (see example 2).

- Theodore Bernstein, assistant managing editor of the New York Times

  for seven years, points out that the word bandit "has a flavor of heroism."

  Bernstein advises: "Avoid any suggestion of glorifying outlaws" (17).

- One editor has advised against the use of the word bandit because its

  "flavor of heroism" has the effect "of glorifying outlaws" (Bernstein 17).

Work Cited

Bernstein, Theodore M. Watch Your Language. Great Neck, NY: Channel

  Press, 1958.

Two or More Works by the Same Author To make citations for two or more works by the same author, place a comma after the author's name, followed by a condensed title and the page reference: (Barrett, "Claw" 123) (Barrett, "Sickness" 103).

Works Cited

Barrett, Deirdre. "The Claw of the Panther: Dreams and the Body." The

  Committee of Sleep. New York: Crown, 2001.

---. "Mourning Sickness." The Pregnant Man. New York: Random House,

  1998.

Two or More Authors For works with two or more authors, include all last names; spell out *and:*

- Four "aims of argument" are identified: "inquiry, convincing, persuasion,

  and negotiation" (Crusius and Channell 8).

- Some researchers recommend "rapid-fire questioning" during survey inter-

  views (Kinsey, Pomeroy, and Martin 54).

For four or more authors, include only the first author's last name and the Latin abbreviation *et al.* ("and others"): (Klein et al. 53).

Works by Two Authors with the Same Last Name   When two authors have the same last name, give their full names in the text (preferred usage) with just the page number in each citation. If names are not given in the text, then include the first initial in the parenthetical citation: (G. Mueller 24), (A. Mueller 36).

Entire Work   When citing an *entire* work, not a specific page, state only the author's name in the text and, if helpful, the title. Be sure the source is on your works cited list.

> H. W. Fowler's <u>Modern English Usage</u> reflects his spartan life. Fowler believed
>
> in simplicity not only in living but also in writing a sentence. Clarity had top
>
> priority.

One-Page Articles   It is not necessary to include the page number when referring to an article that is a page or less long:

> Anthropologist Roy Grinker, who has studied autism in cultures around the
>
> world, believes that "Autism is probably many different highly variable disor-
>
> ders caused by multiple genes interacting in complicated ways."

Note that in the example below, only the volume number is cited:

> Work Cited
>
> Arthur Allen. "Interview with Roy Richard Grinker." <u>Smithsonian</u> Apr. 2007:
>
>   38.

Source with No Author Given   For unsigned works, shorten long titles. Begin with the word by which the work is alphabetized in works cited: ("Visa").

> Work Cited
>
> "Visa Rush Begins for Skilled Workers." <u>Wall Street Journal</u>, 29 Mar. 2007,
>
>   Midwest ed.: A4.

Corporate Author   Although a work by a group or an agency can be cited in parentheses, the preferred usage is to include the name in the text:

> Nuveen Investments' 2007 January semiannual report stated: "While munici-
>
> pal issuance in Michigan during this six-month period was basically the same
>
> as that of the same period a year earlier, Ohio saw a 57% increase in supply
>
> for this period, compared with a 14% increase nationwide."

Work Cited

Nuveen Investments Municipal Bond Funds. Semiannual report January 31,

    2007. Chicago: Nuveen Investments, 2007.

Indirect Source When possible, use an original source rather than a second-hand one that quotes the original. If you are unable to obtain the original source and must use a secondary source, place *qtd. in* ("quoted in") before the citation for the secondary source.

Ralph Waldo Emerson said: "Our best thoughts come from others" (qtd. in

Cohen 9).

Work Cited

Cohen, Herb. You Can Negotiate Anything. New York: Bantam, 1980.

Quotations by Two or More Authors in One Sentence Follow each quotation with a separate parenthetical citation:

Zinsser says, "The most important sentence in any article is the first one" (59),

and Bernstein suggests the writer "ask . . . what it is he is writing about" to

find the focus for that sentence (75).

Two or More Sources in One Citation If you cite information from two or more sources, include identifying information for each source in your parenthetical citation, separated by semicolons.

All seem to agree that good writing is hard work (Bernstein 44; Trimble 54;

Zinsser 33).

Work of More than One Volume If your works-cited list includes more than one volume of a multivolume work, include the volume number, separated from the page number by a colon and a space: (Nicolson and Trautman 3: 25).

Literary Works Because classic prose works may appear in different editions, include chapter (ch.), book (bk.), and part (pt.) in addition to page numbers. Place extra information after the page with a semicolon and a space between:

In The Republic, Plato has Socrates ask: "What do you consider to be the

greatest blessing which you have reaped from your wealth?" (221; bk. 1)

▶   Work Cited

Plato. "The Republic." Five Great Dialogues. Trans. B. Jowett. Ed. Louise

     Ropes Loomis. Roslyn, NY: Classics Club-Black, 1942.

To cite classic verse plays, poems, and other works, leave out page numbers. Instead, give the division—canto, act, scene, book, part—and the line(s). Separate
numbers by periods. For example, (*Waste Land* 1.35) refers to canto 1, line 35;
(*Electra* 1.60) refers to scene 1, line 60. Note that the word *line* is spelled out in
citations:

▶
   • Dickinson ends her poem "Success Is Counted Sweetest" with a paradox:

     "The distant strains of triumph / Break, agonized and clear." (lines 11-12).

   • Romeo and Juliet provides one of Shakespeare's most quoted lines: "But

     soft! What light through yonder window breaks?" (2.2.2).

Nonprint Sources   Works taken from a Web site are cited just like printed
works. If Internet sources are not marked with page numbers, paragraph or section numbers may be included. If so, include those numbers, preceded by the
proper abbreviation (*par.* or *sec.*).

    If a nonprint source (interview, television program, compact disc, CD-
ROM, or other) lacks page numbers, you can omit a parenthetical citation if you
state the author's name in the text. A works-cited entry is still needed. If the author's or performer's name is not stated in the text, place it in a parenthetical citation: (Enya). For sound recordings, italicize the medium before the manufacturer's name: *Audiocassette.* If the medium is a compact disc, omit it in the
works-cited entry:

▶   Work Cited

Enya. Paint the Sky with Stars. Warner, 1996.

Long Quotations   Quotations of five lines or more are set off, indented ten
spaces. After the final punctuation, type one space, then the parenthetical
citation.

▶
   Charles C. Moskos summarizes the argument well:

          The principal argument raised against linking national service and

          federal educational aid is that it would have a regressive effect. . . .

          Students from wealthy families who do not need aid would be un-

> affected, while poor students would have to enter national service
>
> in order to get aid. (380)

Punctuation   For short quotations within the text, place a period or other punctuation *after* the parenthetical citation. For long block quotations, set off from the text, place the period and a space *before* the parenthetical citation.

Using Notes with MLA Parenthetical Citations

Content notes and bibliographic notes can be used along with parenthetical citations to provide more information. To insert a note, place a superscript arabic number at a suitable place in the text. Then at the bottom of the same page, place a matching number before the note. Keep the notes short and informative. Content notes and bibliographic notes can be mingled and numbered in sequence.

Content Notes   When a secondary source is cited, a content note can provide complete publication data on the original source. Or a necessary explanation may be included as in the example below:

> Several months ago when obesity specialist Dr. Frank Greenway from
>
> UCLA revealed that a thigh reduction cream really worked, several news ac-
>
> counts incorrectly reported reductions of as much as 1½ inches. The fact was
>
> that the most a woman's thighs shrunk was 1½ *centimeters* or approximately
>
> ½ inch. Furthermore, the safety of the cream has been questioned.[1]

Note

> [1]Several news sources have pointed out this misstatement.

Bibliographic Notes   To provide evaluative comments on sources or for references having several citations, use notes.

> The Wall Street Journal and many other newspapers carried articles
>
> about the resignation of David Howard, head of the District Office of Public
>
> Advocate, Washington, DC, over his use of a standard word that sounded
>
> like a taboo term.[1]

Note

> [1]For a sample of articles taken from editorial pages, see Dooling and
>
> Parker.

Works Cited

Dooling, Richard. "What a Niggling Offense! Oops, We Mean . . ." Wall Street

Journal 29 Jan. 1999, Midwest ed.: A14.

Parker, Kathleen. "Must We Be So Niggling about Words?" Marion Star

[Marion, OH] 7 Feb. 1999: A6.

PREPARING A LIST OF WORKS CITED: MLA STYLE

Use these general guidelines for the format of your works cited page:

1. Type *Works Cited,* centered, at the top of the page.
2. Alphabetize entries according to the last name of the author. When an author's name is not known, alphabetize by the first word in the title except for *a, an,* or *the.*
3. Double-space the entire listing of works cited.
4. Do not indent the first line of an entry. Indent *five* spaces (or one-half inch) for succeeding lines of the entry. This style of indention is called a "hanging indention."
5. Place a period after each subdivision of an entry and at the end of each entry.
6. *A, An,* or *The:* Retain as the first word in a book title. Omit in periodical titles (*Washington Post* not *The Washington Post*).
7. Underline the title of works such as books, magazines, newspapers, plays, paintings, and others. (See "Italics," page H-35.)
8. Place quotation marks around titles of short works that appear in longer works, such as articles, chapters, stories, poems, and songs.
9. Cite inclusive page numbers (121–28) for specific essays, articles, short stories, and so forth that appear in a book or periodical.
10. Number the works cited pages using arabic numerals, just as the other pages of the paper.

1. SAMPLE MLA ENTRIES: BOOKS AND OTHER NONPERIODICAL PUBLICATIONS

Include the author's name as it is printed on the title page. In the works-cited entry, reverse the name and place a comma between the last and first part: Bickford, Scott, Jr. Except for Jr. and roman numerals that are part of a name, leave out titles, affiliations, and degrees.

Underline the titles and subtitles of books. Separate the title and subtitle with a *colon* unless the main title ends with a question mark, an exclamation point, or a dash. An underline can be typed as a solid line under all the words in a title or name even when it contains a colon. Do *not* underline the period at the end of a title.

Specify the city of publication, publisher, and year of publication (or copyright date if publication date isn't listed). If the city is well-known, you can omit the state, country, or province if there is no chance of confusion.

1.1. A Book by One Author

The last name of a single author comes first.

> Cameron, Julia. Mozart's Ghost. New York: St. Martin's, 2008. ◀

1.2. Two or More Books by One Author

List the name once in the first entry (alphabetically by title). For the second entry, type three hyphens and a period instead of the name.

> Mayer, Martin. The Judges. New York: St. Martin's, 2006. ◀
>
> ---. The Banker's: The Next Generation. New York: Truman Talley/Dutton,
>
>   1997.

1.3. A Book by Two or Three Authors

When there are two or three authors, reverse only the first name. Spell out *and*. When citing the title for a research paper, capitalize the first and last words and all significant words. Do not reproduce special capitalization or case of all letters.

> Woodall, Trinny, and Susannah Constantine. Take on America: What Your ◀
>
>   Clothes Say About You. New York: Harper Collins, 2006.

1.4. A Book by Four or More Authors

For a book with four or more authors, you may include only the first author and add *et al.* ("and others"), or you may state all the authors in the order given on the title page.

> Burrows, Thomas D., et al. Video Production: Disciplines and Techniques. ◀
>
>   New York: McGraw, 2000.

1.5. Corporate Author: A Book by a Group

> Images Publishing Group. 100 More of the World's Best Houses. ◀
>
>   Victoria, Australia: Images Publishing, 2008.

1.6. Second or Later Edition of a Book

Specify any edition other than the first by number (2nd ed., 3rd ed.), by name (Rev. ed.), or by year (2008 ed.) after the book title (see 1.12). Or if the name of an editor, compiler, or translator follows, place the edition after the name (see 1.14).

▶ Musciano, Chuck, and Bill Kennedy. HTML & XHTML: The Definitive Guide.

6th ed. Sebastopol, CA: O'Reilly, 2006.

1.7. A Work in a Compilation, an Anthology, or a Collection

Enclose in quotation marks the title of an essay, a short story, a poem, or another work collected in a book. The book title and editor(s) follow. State the inclusive page numbers for the specific piece at the end of the entry. If you are citing a previously published scholarly article, insert *Rpt. in* ("Reprinted in"), the title of the collection, and the new publication data.

▶ Glaspell, Susan. "A Jury of Her Peers." The Best Short Stories of the Century. Eds.

John Updike and Katrina Kenison. New York: Houghton, 2000. 18-37.

RECOMMENDED ABBREVIATIONS FOR MLA WORKS CITED ENTRIES

PUBLISHERS' NAMES

Shorten the names of publishers, omitting *Inc., Company,* and so forth, and using only the first name when there is more than one name. *University Press* is shortened to *UP* (or *U of . . . P*). In some cases, initials are used. Some examples follow:

Appleton-Century-Crofts	Appleton
Beacon Press, Inc.	Beacon
Cambridge University Press	Cambridge UP
Henry Holt and Company	Henry Holt
Holt, Rinehart and Winston	Holt
New American Library	NAL
University of Chicago Press	U of Chicago P

STATES

Use state abbreviations without periods: NY, OH, CA.

GOVERNMENT PUBLICATIONS

Use the following abbreviations:

Congressional Record	Cong. Rec.
Government Printing Office	GPO
House of Representatives Report	H. Rept.
House of Representatives Document	H. Doc.
Library of Congress	LC
Senate Resolution	S. Res.
Senate Document	S. Doc.

1.8. A Book by an Anonymous Author

Go Ask Alice. New York: Prentice, 1971.

1.9. A Book with an Editor or Editors, No Author Listed

Parkyn, Neil, ed. The Seventy Wonders of the Modern World. New York:

Thames-Hudson, 2002.

1.10. A Book with an Author and an Editor

Monagan, David. Journey into the Heart. Medical ed. David O. Williams. New

York: Gotham, 2007.

1.11. A Book in Volumes

When using just one volume of a multivolume work, give that volume number before the place of publication (*Vol.* is capitalized).

Shakespeare, William. "Cymbeline." The Tragedies of Shakespeare.

Ed. Warren Chappell. Vol. 2. New York: Random, 1944.

When using two or more volumes of a work, include the total number of volumes after the title (vol. is not capitalized).

Nicolson, Nigel, and Joanne Trautmann, eds. The Letters of Virginia Woolf.

5 vols. New York: Harcourt, 1977.

1.12. An Article or Definition from a Reference Book

The place and publisher can be omitted for encyclopedias, dictionaries, and other well-known reference books. Page numbers can also be omitted if the entries are alphabetical. If the entry is signed, lead with the author's name.

"Civil Disobedience." Merriam-Webster's Collegiate Dictionary, Rev. ed.

Springfield, MA: Merriam-Webster, 2006.

1.13. An Introduction, Preface, Foreword, or Afterword

Start with the author and title (if any) of the introduction, preface, foreword, or afterword, enclosing the title in quotation marks. Then state the part, using a capital letter but no underlining or quotation marks (Preface). If the book is by a different writer, place *By* before his or her full name. Place inclusive page numbers at the end. In the example here, the preface has no title and only one page.

▶ Perlmutter, David. Foreword. <u>Younger You: Unlock the Hidden Power of Your</u>

    <u>Brain and Feel 15 Years Younger.</u> By Eric R. Braverman. New York:

    McGraw, 2007. vii-viii.

1.14. A Translation or Edited Edition

▶ Melograni, Piero. <u>Mozart.</u> Trans. Lydia G. Cochrane. Chicago: U of Chicago P,

    2007.

1.15. A Pamphlet

Treat a pamphlet as a book, even if very short. A corporate author is listed below:

▶ US Dept. of Justice. <u>ATE Records: A Quick Reference on How Long You</u>

    <u>Should Keep Your Records.</u> Washington: GPO, 2004.

1.16. Government Publications

When the writer is known, see 1.15. When the writer is unknown, list the government agency as author (see 1.15). If two or more works are issued by the same agency, place three hyphens in place of the author's name (---). Repeat if the works are by the same agency (---. ---.). Most congressional documents require the number and session of Congress, the house (S or HR), and the kind and number of publication (S. Res. 19, H. Res. 49). The *Congressional Record,* however, requires just the date and page.

▶ United States. Health Care Financing Administration. <u>Medicare & You 2008</u>.

    Washington: GPO, 2008.

  ---. Dept. of Justice. <u>FBI National Academy Directory of Graduates 2004</u>

    Edition. Quantico,VA.: FBI Academy, 2004.

1.17. Sacred Writings

The article, chapter, or "book" (as in books of the Bible) is placed before the verses (if applicable). The title of the entire work follows. (Titles of sacred writing are not underlined or enclosed with quotations marks.) If the work has more than one version, the abbreviation for the version is placed last.

▶ Proverbs 22:1. Bible. KJV.

  Genesis 1:3. Torah.

2. SAMPLE MLA ENTRIES: ARTICLES

Periodicals comprise journals, magazines, newspapers, newsletters, and similar publications. Scholarly journals, which are often published quarterly, are not aimed at a general audience. Since these articles often describe original research and give professional opinion, they are valuable sources for research papers. As you consult periodicals, collect the following information.

1. Name of author, editor, compiler, or translator (if given)
2. Full title of article (enclose with quotation marks)
3. Name of source (underline or italicize title of periodical)
4. Series (if given)
5. Volume number (journals only)
6. Issue number (Number 2) or month or season before year (Spring 2005)
7. Journals with continuous paging: Omit issue numbers, months, or seasons.
8. Publication date
9. Edition (if given)
10. Inclusive page numbers of the article

As you construct entries for periodicals, the following guidelines will be helpful:

- Omit the introductory word *a, an,* or *the* from names of periodicals: *American Scholar* not *The American Scholar.*

- For a daily periodical, put the day before the month and year with no intervening punctuation (17 June 2005).

- If the article is from a source that is not a periodical, identify the type of article, such as *Letter* or *Editorial.* Reviews have a special format (see 2.7).

2.1. Journal Article with Continuous Paging

Many scholarly journals use continuous paging, starting in January and continuing throughout the year. Include only the volume number and year, not the issue or month. Give the range of pages.

Bobrow, Bentley J. "Minimally Interrupted Cardiac Resuscitation." Journal of

the American Medical Association 299 (2008): 1158-1165.

2.2. Journal Article with Each Issue Paged Separately

Include issue numbers for journals that do *not* number pages continuously. After the volume number, place a period and the issue number together with no space: 10.3 (indicating volume 10, issue 3).

▶ Carr, Jeffrey. "Some Essentials for Succeeding in Technical Writing." The

Writer 121.3 (2008): 13.

2.3. Article from a Daily Newspaper

When a newspaper has different editions, specify the edition between the date and the page. If the article runs beyond one page, use a plus sign to indicate that it continues.

▶ Reddy, Sudeep. "Bernanke's Fate May Hang on Economy." Wall Street Journal

14 Feb. 2008, Midwest ed.: A6.

2.4. Article from a Monthly Magazine

Include the cover date. Abbreviate all months except May, June, and July. If the paging of an article is interrupted, write only the first page and a plus sign. Otherwise, hyphenate the range of page numbers.

▶ Mitani, Sam. "Mitsubishi Lancer vs. Subaru Impreza WRXSTI." Road & Track

Mar. 2008: 40-49.

2.5. Article from a Weekly Newspaper or Weekly Magazine

▶ Romano, Andrew. "He's One of Us Now." Newsweek 18 Feb. 2008: 38-41.

2.6. An Anonymous Article

When the author of an article is unstated, begin with the title and alphabetize by the first significant word in the title.

▶ "Wild Things." Smithsonian. Apr. 2007: 38.

2.7. Review

▶ Holmes, Martha Stoddard. Rev. of The Fasting Girl: A True Victorian Medical

Mystery, by Michelle Stacy. New England Journal of Medicine 348

(2003): 870-71.

2.8. Abstract and a Review

The citation for the book appears before the citation for the abstract and review. The periodical carrying the abstract and review is placed last. If the abstract has no review, omit *Rev. by.*

> Sunstein, Cass R., and Martha C. Nussbaum. Animal Rights. Oxford, UK:
>
> Oxford U.P. 2004. Rev. by B. R. Myers, Atlantic Monthly 296.2 (2005):
>
> 134, 136-9.

2.9. An Editorial

When citing a signed editorial, start with the author's name, then the title. Next write *Editorial* (not underlined or italicized). When the editorial is unsigned, start with the title.

> Novak, Robert D. "Obama's Bradley Effect?" Editorial. Washington Post
>
> 11 Feb. 2008: A13.

2.10. A Letter to the Editor

> Hara, Genki, "Try Textbook Swaps to Cut Costs of College." Letter.
>
> USA Today 15 Feb. 2008: A 10.

2.11. Newsletter Article

> Laidlaw, Bill. "Perspective." Ohio Historical Society Newsletter 42 (Mar.-Apr.
>
> 2007): 1.

3. SAMPLE MLA ENTRIES: MISCELLANEOUS PRINT AND NONPRINT SOURCES

For broadcast, film, and recorded sources involving various personnel, begin the entry with the name or title that is the primary subject of emphasis in your paper, as shown below:

- "Live from Carnegie Hall." 4 episodes. Christopher O'Riley. From the Top.

  PBS. WOSU-TV, Columbus, OH. 15 April, 12 noon and 12:30 p.m., 22

  April, 29 April 2007.

- Yo-Yo Ma. "Live from Carnegie Hall." Episode 1. From the Top. PBS.

  WOSU-TV, Columbus, OH. 15 April 2007.

3.1. Television or Radio Programs

The items in a works cited entry for a television or radio program generally follow the order below. (Omit any items that are not relevant, but include relevant items such as performers, director, conductor, or number of episodes.)

1. Episode or segment title (Enclose in quotation marks. If there are two or more episodes, state the total.)
2. Author's name (in reverse order if it begins the entry)
3. Program title (underline)
4. Series title
5. Network (for example, CNN)
6. Local call letters and city (for example, WMAQ, Chicago)
7. Date of broadcast

▶ "The Godfather of Pops." Saturday at the Pops. Host and prod. Boyce Lancaster. WOSU-FM, Columbus, OH. 31 Mar. 2007.

Kiss Me Kate. By Sam and Bella Spewak. Music and lyrics by Cole Porter. Perf. Nancy Anderson and Michael Berresse. Broadway performance. Great Performances. PBS. WOSU-TV, Columbus, OH. 26 Feb. 2003.

Schama, Simon. "The Body of the Queen." 5 episodes. A History of Britain. Narr. Simon Schama. The History Channel. CNBC, Columbus, OH. 29 Oct. 2001.

If a transcript is available online, provide the information:

▶ Shaw, Bernard. "Clinton's Boom Era Not as Turbulent as LBJ's." Program segment. Inside Politics. CNN. 29 June 1999. Transcript. 1 July 1999 <http://www.cnn.com/TRANSCRIPTS/9906/29/ip.06.html>.

For sound recordings of television or radio programs, see 3.2. For a videotape of a performance, see 3.3. For interviews conducted on television or radio, see 3.4.

3.2. Sound Recordings

If the recording is on compact disc, omit the medium. Specify audiocassette tape or LP. Include manufacturer and date. The name you place first depends on whom you want to emphasize—composer, conductor, or performer. Insert a comma between the manufacturer and the date.

▶ Beach Boys. The Greatest Hits: The Beach Boys. Capitol, 1999.

Strauss, Edvard. "The Merry Widow Waltz." Viennese Favorites. L.P. Cond.

Arthur Fiedler. Boston Pops Orchestra. Audiocassette. RCA Victrola,

1983.

3.3. Film or Video Recording

Include all pertinent information in an order that reflects your emphasis. For video recordings, include the original date of release as well as the date the recording was released.

a.   A Film, Video Recording, or Performance

Enchanted April. Dir. Mike Newell. Perf. Miranda Richardson, Josie Lawrence,

Polly Walker, and Joan Plowright. Screenwriter Peter Barnes. Warner

Brothers, 1992.

If material is not a film, specify the medium. Some materials may include an original release date, perhaps in another form. For example, some laser discs contain films in IMAX. If material has an original release date, include that date before the medium.

b.   Videocassette, DVD, Laser Disc, Slide Program, or Filmstrip

My Fellow Americans. Dir. Peter Segal. Perf. Jack Lemmon, James Garner, Dan

Aykroyd, John Heard, Wilford Brimley, and Lauren Bacall. 1996. Video-

cassette. Warner Home Video, 2000.

Freedom Writers. Dir. Richard La Gravenese. Perf. Hilary Swank, Scott Glenn,

Imelda Staunton, and Patrick Dempsey. DVD. Paramount Home Enter-

tainment. 2007.

3.4. Interviews

Published interviews are treated as excerpts from anthologies and periodi-cals. Broadcast interviews are treated as television or radio programs. Personal and telephone interviews are listed as such. In all cases list the name of the per-son interviewed first.

MacLeish, Archibald. "Archibald MacLeish." Interview with Benjamin

De Mott. Writers at Work: The Paris Review Interviews 5. Ed. George

Plimpton. New York: Penguin, 1988. 23-48.

Rivers, Brittany. Personal interview. 2 Feb. 2008.

Witzel, Carol. Telephone interview. 3 Jan. 2008.

3.5. Map or Chart

If the author of a map or chart is unknown, list as you would an anonymous book (1.8) and identify as map or chart. If it appears in a book or periodical, cite that source. The map listed below was drawn by Captain John Smith. It was first published in 1612 and later in the May 2007 issue of *Smithsonian* magazine on page 52. (For online maps and charts see 4.11.)

> ▶ Smith, John. The Virginian Sea. Map. London, Eng.: n.p., 1612. Smithsonian
>
> May 2007: 52.

3.6. Comic Strip or Cartoon

> ▶ Schulz, Charles. "Peanuts." Comic strip. Marion Star [Marion OH] 10 Apr.
>
> 2007: B7.

3.7. Legal References

For papers requiring several legal citations, see the most recent edition of *The Blue Book: A Uniform System of Citation* (Cambridge: Harvard Law Rev. Assn.). A usual rule is to neither underline nor enclose in quotation marks any titles of laws, acts, or similar documents in the text or in the list of works cited. Works of this sort are generally cited by sections. The year is included when it is significant.

- 14 US Code. Sec. 77a. 1964
- US Const. Art. 2, sec. 1.

4. SAMPLE MLA ENTRIES: ELECTRONIC SOURCES

Entries for electronic sources begin with the author's name and title of the document, followed by print publication information (if any), electronic publication information, and access information. There is no punctuation between the access date and the URL. Place a period after the URL. For details about the components of an electronic source entry in MLA documentation style, see the guidelines on page 495.

4.1. An Entire Internet Site, Scholarly Project, Professional or Personal Site

Cite what is given of the following: Title of site or project (underlined), editor's name (preceded by "Ed."), and electronic publication information. That includes the version number (if given and not part of the title), publication date or latest update, sponsor's name, date of access, and URL.

a. Entire Internet Site or Scholarly Project

> ▶ CNN.com. 2008. Cable News Network. 18 Mar. 2008 <http://www.cnn.com/>.

Encyclopaedia Britannica Online. 2008. Encyclopaedia Britannica. 18 Mar.

2008 <http://www.britannica.com>.

Victorian Women Writers Project. Ed. Perry Willett. 24 Apr. 2008. Indiana U.

14 Mar. 2008 <http://www.indiana.edu/~letrs/vwwp/>.

When online material carries a printed source and date, cite that first, according to the MLA guidelines for books and periodicals (see 1.1 to 2.11 in the preceding discussion) before electronic information. All the information below may not be available in every situation.

1. **Author(s).** Reverse the name of the first (or only) author so that it can be alphabetized. If an editor is listed instead of an author, place *ed.* after the name (see 1.9).

2. **Title of an article, poem, short story, or similar item in a scholarly project, database, or periodical.** Enclose the title with quotation marks.

3. **Book title.** Underline both main title and subtitle.

4. **Editor, compiler, or translator.** If there is one, place *Ed., Comp., or Trans.* before the name (see 1.10 and 1.14).

5. **Edition, version, volume, or issue.** If a version number is included in the title, do not repeat. For a journal include volume, issue, or any other number needed (see 2.1, 2.2, and 4.4).

6. **Title of a scholarly project, database, periodical, or professional or personal Web site.** Underline. If there is no title, write a description such as *Search page* or *Home page* (see 4.1.b).

7. **Other publication information.** Give publisher's name, place of publication, copyright date, and any other identification.

8. **Medium of publication.** If the source is on a CD-ROM, diskette, tape, DVD, or similar source, state the medium (see 4.13–4.15).

9. **Dates of information.** Include the dates of posting, electronic publication, and most recent update, if there is one.

10. **Article or work from a subscription service.** Identify the service, subscriber (often a library), and place of subscriber (see 4.12).

11. **Online posting or forum.** Supply name of list or forum (see 4.9).

12. **Range or number of pages, paragraphs, or sections.** Include if the material is numbered.

13. **Sponsor of the Web site.** Identify the individual, institution, organization, or agency sponsoring or associated with the Web site.

14. **Date of access.** Place the date you obtained the material right before the URL.

15. **URL of the source.** Place in angle brackets (< >), followed by a period. If the URL is long and complex, cite the search page URL. For a subscription service, use the home page URL. Or give the keyword of the service, preceded by *Keyword,* or give the sequence of links after the URL: *Path* and a semicolon (see 4.7).

MLA STYLE: DOCUMENTING ELECTRONIC SOURCES

b. *Professional Site or Personal Site*

First give the name of the person who created the site (if given) and the title of the site (underline). If there is no title, use a description such as *Home page* (no underlining). Next give the date of the last update, or, in the case of a course home page, give the dates of the course. Follow with the sponsor of the site (if applicable), date of access, and URL.

> Microsoft® Corporation. PressPass - Information for Journalists. 2008.
>
> 16 Mar. 2008 <http://www.microsoft.com/presspass/exec/billg/
>
> default.mspx>.
>
> Dietsch, Terry. Cycling Ohio Rail-Trails & Bikeways. 14 August 2001. 1 May
>
> 2007 <http://home.earthlink.net/~bikeohio/celina.html>.

4.2. An Entire Online Book

The book below was originally published in 1878. In 1892 Harper published an edition. This information is placed in parentheses because it was not given online. Print information is optional if not provided online.

> James, Henry. Daisy Miller. [1878]. [New York: Harper, 1892]. 16 Mar. 2008
>
> <http://www.gutenberg.org/etext/208>.

4.3. A Poem, Short Story, or Other Short Work within a Book

The first example, a poem, lists the publication data of the original print version, which was on the Web site. The second example, a short story, is available online with no information about the author; the first date there is the date of posting.

> Frost, Robert. "Mending Wall." Boston: North, 1915. 16 Mar. 2008 <http://
>
> www.bartleby.com/verse>.
>
> Poe, Edgar Allan. "The Cask of Amontillado." East of the Web. May 1999.
>
> 16 Mar. 2008 <http://www.short-stories.co.uk/>.

4.4. Online Article in a Scholarly Journal

The online article below was printed in *American Psychologist*, volume 63, issue 2 February/March 2008. The Web site was accessed March 16, 2008.

Borckardt, Jeffrey J., et al. "Clinical Practice Is Natural Laboratory for Psychotherapy Research: A Guide to Case-based Time-series Analyses."
American Psychologist 63.2 (2008): 77-95. 16 Mar. 2008 <http://
www.content.apa.org/journals>.

4.5. Online Article in a Newspaper

Andrews, Edmund L. "Federal Reserve Cuts Key Rate by 0.75 Percent." New
York Times 18 Mar. 2008. 18 Mar 2008 <http://www.nytimes.com/>.

4.6. Online Article in a Magazine

Bai, Matt. "What's the Real Racial Divide?" New York Times Magazine 18
Mar. 2008. 18 Mar 2008 <http://www.nytimes.com/pages/magazine/>.

4.7. Online Abstract (showing a sequence of links)

The example below shows a sequence of links after the URL.

Dahl, Ronald E. and Mona El-Sheikh. "Considering Sleep in a Family Context."
Journal of Family Psychology 21.1 (Mar. 2007): 1-3. Abstract 16 Mar.
2008 <http://www.content.apa.org/journals> Path: Table of contents:
abstract.

4.8. Online Article from a Newsletter

Eastman, Dick. "Footnote.com Adds Millions of Historical Newspapers to Its
Collection." Eastman's Online Genealogy Newsletter. 14 Mar. 2008
<http://blog.eogn.com>.

4.9. Posting to a Discussion Group

Osheroff, J. A. "Computers in Medicine." Editorial and invitation to respond
by e-mail. 2007. American College of Physicians–American Society of
Internal Medicine. 1 May 2007 <http://www.acponline.org/computer/
sgim_edit.htm>.

4.10. E-Mail Communication

▶ Dietsch, Betty M. "Reviewers." E-mail to Josh Feldman. 20 May 2007.

4.11. Map or Chart

For a map or chart, list print information first, including the name of the publisher and the date. Insert the appropriate label (Map or Chart), the title of the Web site, date of access, and URL.

▶ "New Hampshire." National Geographic Society, 1998. Map. Infoplease.com.

15 Mar. 2008 <http://print.infoplease.com/atlas/state/

newhampshire.html>.

4.12. A Work from a Library or Personal Subscription Service

To cite material found through an online subscription service, follow the guidelines for citing print and online works. Then add the other required information, as shown here.

a. A Work from a Library Subscription Service

Give the print or online information first. Add the name of the database underlined, the name of the service, name of the library (city and state abbreviation, if needed), and date of access. Include the URL of the home page of the service.

▶ Fill, Kaye Middleton, et al. "Has Alcohol Been Proven to Be Protective Against

Coronary Heart Disease?" Addiction Research & Theory 15.1 (2007):

35-46. Sociological Collection. EBSCO. Marion Public Lib., Marion, OH.

15 Mar. 2008 <http://search.ebscohost.com>.

"Industry News." Sci-Tech. Online 31.2 (2007): 8-8. MasterFILE Premier.

EBSCO. Marion Public Lib., Marion, OH. 15 Mar. 2008

<http://search.ebscohost.com>.

b. A Work from a Personal Subscription Service

For print sources, give only the data the service provides. Include the date of the material or the copyright date (if known) or the date of the Web site. List the name of the service provider (such as Earthlink). If you used a keyword to retrieve material, add *Keyword*, followed by a colon, and the term used. No URL is necessary.

▶ "Croquet." Compton's Encyclopedia, 6th ed. 2007. Netlink. 18 Mar. 2008.

Keyword: Compton's.

TIP
Some online subscription databases, such as EBSCO HOST, offer formatting options for printing out source data (MLA, APA, or other styles). But you still need to check punctuation, capitalization, and other formatting details with your style guidelines. Titles are often printed in lowercase, and underlining may not be visible. Other data also may be required.

4.13. Publication on CD-ROM, Diskette, Microfilm, or Microfiche

Cite the print information first. Then add other available publication data: the medium; edition, release, or version; place of publication; name of publisher or vendor; and date of publication.

a. Periodical Published on CD-ROM

Some newspapers, magazines, journals, and other periodicals can be accessed from databases. Usually source information is provided at the beginning of the file.

> Hansen, Robert W. "Stigma, Conflict, and the Approval of AIDS Drugs."
>
> Journal of Drugs (Winter 1995): 129-39. CD-ROM. UMI-ProQuest,
>
> 1995.

b. Nonperiodical Publication on CD-ROM or Diskette

Many nonperiodical databases are published only once with no revisions or updates. Cite nonperiodical CD-ROMs the way you would cite a book but include the publication medium as well as the place, publisher, and date of publication.

> 1880 United States Census and National Index. CD-ROM. Salt Lake City:
>
> Intellectual Reserve, 2001.
>
> Bird, Alan. "TimeOut." Quickspell. Diskette. San Diego: Beagle Bros., 1987.

c. Updated Nonperiodical Publication on CD-ROM or Diskette

> McAfee Internet Security Suite. CD-ROM. McAfee.com Corporation. Sunny-
>
> vale, CA: McAfee.com Corp, 2007.

d. *Microfilm or Microfiche*

▶ <u>Death Certificate Index: Years 1900–1910</u>. Microfilm. Ohio Department of

Health. Columbus, Ohio. Ohio Historical Society. n.d.

4.14. A Work in More than One Publication Medium

Some stores offer bundles of software in one package. Follow the directions for a nonperiodical CD-ROM (see 4.11a) and list the media in the package, the place, the publisher, and the copyright date.

▶ Newman, John J. "Ohio." <u>Uncle, We Are Ready! Registering America's Men</u>

<u>1917-1918</u>. CD-ROM and book. North Salt Lake, UT: Heritage Quest,

2001.

4.15. Other Electronic Sources

To document online sources that are not mentioned here, find a similar model and follow the general guidelines for citing print and electronic sources. Construct your entry appropriately, making changes as needed. For example, you may need to add a label such as *interview* or *photo* (no quotation marks or underlining).

APA STYLE OF DOCUMENTATION

For research papers about the social sciences, many instructors prefer the American Psychological Association style of documentation. The explanations and examples shown here follow the guidelines in the *Publication Manual of the American Psychological Association,* fifth edition, 2001 and the *APA Style Guide to Electronic References,* 2007.

CHAPTER R-4 APA STYLE DIRECTORY

Parenthetical Citations: APA Style

The APA style keys reference citations in a text to a list of sources. In parentheses, include the author's last name, the year of publication, the abbreviation for page (*p.* or *pp.* for pages), and the page number. Use ampersands (&) instead of *and.* Abbreviate *chapter* as *chap.* and *section* as *sec.* For quotations, always cite page numbers (Raines, p. 132).

Single Author   The author's name is usually mentioned in the text, followed by parentheses containing the year of publication and page. (Omit suffixes, such as *Jr.*) If the entire work is cited, no page numbers are needed. If the author is not listed in the text, include the author's last name in the parenthetical citation.

- Theodore Bernstein (1958) points out that the word *bandit* "has a flavor of heroism."

- Research shows that experienced writers seem to have much stronger revision habits than do student writers (Sommers, 2004).

Two or More Authors   Arrange the names alphabetically. Cite the year just once in the paragraph. Citations vary, depending upon the number of authors:

- These findings have been labeled "ridiculous, perhaps fraudulent" (Alberti & King, 2008). (Cite two authors every time.)

- Moss, Rivers, and Wang (2007) claim . . . Moss et al. reported . . . (Cite three to five authors once. Use just the first one after that, followed by *et al.,* not italicized.)

- Chadry et al. (2008) found that . . . (Six or more authors)

Two or More Works by the Same Author   Distinguish different works by one author by their dates. For multiple references in the same year by one author, add *a, b,* or *c* in lowercase letters: 2008a, 2008b, and so forth.

Works by Two Authors with the Same Last Name   Distinguish by using initials: "C. A. Neff (2007) and J. Neff (2005) also found. . . ."

Source with No Author Name Given   For unsigned sources, use an abbreviated version of the title. Place article titles in quotation marks, and underline or italicize book and pamphlet titles: ("Timber Wolves," 2005), (*Recycling,* 2008).

Groups as Authors   In general, give the name of the group in full each time you cite it. If the name is long, abbreviate it in subsequent citations.

- First reference: (American Association of Retired People [AARP], 2008)

- Later references: (AARP, 2008)

Secondary Source   If you are citing an author quoted by another author, precede the secondary source with the phrase *as cited in.* Always give page numbers for quotations.

▶   Jameson's findings (as cited in Baure & Dinks, 2006, p. 124)

Two or More Sources in One Citation   List alphabetically by authors' last names, separated by semicolons: (Adams, 2005; Coates & Tan, 2004; Martiniu, 2004). If citations include two works by the same author, list the dates chronologically, separated by commas: (Wiggins 2007, 2005).

Personal Communications   E-mail, personal interviews, letters, and the like are cited only in the text, not on the reference list.

▶   According to the hospital's chief administrator, the procedure is no longer

performed there (J. A. Wells, personal communication, March 15,

2008).

Long Quotations   Quotations of forty words or more are double-spaced and set off, indented five spaces. The parenthetical citation is placed one space after the final punctuation.

▶   Moskos (2000) summarizes the argument well:

The principal argument raised against linking national service and

federal educational aid is that it would have a regressive effect. . . .

Students from wealthy families who do not need aid would be un-

affected, while poor students would have to enter national service

in order to get aid. (p. 380)

**PREPARING A
REFERENCE LIST:
APA STYLE**

Preparing a reference list is tricky, so keep the models and general guidelines below handy. Double check the order of entries, punctuation, capitalization, parentheses, and brackets in each entry. All references cited in the text, except personal communication, belong in the reference list. Here are general guidelines for the format:

- Type *Reference List,* centered, at the top of the page.
- Double-space entries.
- Alphabetize entries according to authors' last names or, when no author is listed, the first major word of the title. Use initials and the surname. Include Jr. or II after an author's name when applicable in reference entries (not citations).

(continued)

- After the author's name, enclose the date of publication (year, month, day) in parentheses, followed by a period.
- Do not indent the first line of each entry. Indent subsequent lines five spaces (hanging indention).
- Italicize the titles of periodicals, volume numbers, and book titles. If your keyboard does not italicize, underline.
- Place nonroutine information that is necessary to identify and recover a source in brackets after the article title.
- Use arabic numerals for volume (e.g., 4, not IV). Retain roman numerals that are part of a title.

PREPARING A REFERENCE LIST: APA STYLE *(continued)*

A. APA ENTRIES: PERIODICALS

Since entries for periodicals vary, check each item carefully after you type it. Compare it with the model in the textbook. Then proofread again when you are fresh. The guidelines below will help you type your entries correctly:

> **www.mhhe.com/dietsch**
> Bibliomaker can create APA entries. Find it at: Research>Bibliomaker

- Include *The* in the name of a periodical: *The New York Times.*
- Italicize the full name of the journal or magazine and the volume number (omit *Vol.*). Do not italicize issue numbers: *Book Review Digest, 97*(6).
- Capitalize just the first word of an article title and of a subtitle. Capitalize all proper nouns.
- Do not enclose article titles in quotation marks.
- Omit *p.* or *pp.* for references to journal and magazine articles.
- To list pages of newspapers, abbreviate as *p.* or *pp.* (p. B23).
- Place the range of pages at the end of the entry (352–357).
- Use an ampersand (&) instead of *and* when listing two or more authors.
- Spell out months.

1. Journal Article with One Author, Each Issue Paged Separately

Place issue numbers in parentheses after the volume number with no space between: *37*(3). Follow with a comma and the range of pages.

> Carr, J. (2008). Some essentials for succeeding in technical writing. *The Writer*
>
> *121*(3), 13.

2. Journal Article with Two to Six Authors, Continuous Paging

Omit issue numbers for journals with continuous paging. When citing the range of pages, include each full number. State all the authors up to and including six.

For more than six authors, cite six, then *et al.* (not italicized), set off by a comma.

▷ Halonen, J., Halonen, P., Järvinem, O., Taskinem, P., Auvinem, T., Tarkka, M.,

et al. (2007). Corticosteriods for the prevention of atrial fibrillation after

cardiac surgery: A randomized controlled trial. *Journal of the American*

Medical Association, 297, 1562–1567.

3. Magazine Article

▷ Mitani, S. (2008, March). Mitsubishi Lancer vs. Subaru Impreza WRX STI.

Road & Track, 40–49.

4. An Unsigned Article in a Magazine

"Wild Things." (2007, April). *Smithsonian,* 38.

5. Newsletter Article

For works with no author, alphabetize by the first significant word. Separate the volume number and the page number in that order with a comma.

▷ Laidlaw, B. (2007, March-April). Perspective. *Ohio Historical Society Newsletter,*

42, 1.

6. Daily Newspaper Article Continued to Other Pages

▷ Frank, R. (2008, February 14). Debt crisis hits a dynasty. *The Wall Street*

Journal, Midwest ed., pp. A1, A14.

7. Editorial

After the article title, place nonroutine information necessary for identification in brackets.

▷ Novak, R. (2008, February 11). Obama's Bradley effect? [Editorial].

The Washington Post, p. A13.

8. Letter to the Editor

▷ Hora, G. (2008, February 15). Try textbook swaps to cut costs of college.

[Letter to the Editor]. *USA Today,* p. A10.

9. Abstract and Review from a Secondary Source (print periodical)

In scholarly research cite primary sources when possible. If an abstract has no review, omit *Review by.*

> Sunstein, C. R., & Nussbaum, M. C. (2004). *Animal rights.* Oxford, UK: Oxford
>
> U. P. Review by B. R. Myers (2005) in *Atlantic Monthly, 296*(2), pp.134,
>
> 136–9.

B. APA ENTRIES: BOOKS, BROCHURES, AND GOVERNMENT PUBLICATIONS

Entries for books include author, date, title, place of publication (city and state), and publisher. Use all the surnames in a publishing company (Simon & Schuster, not just Simon), but don't include *Publishing Company, Inc.,* or other non-essential words. Retain *Books* and *Press.*

- Capitalize just the first word of the title and of the subtitle, as well as proper nouns.
- Use initials and the surname.
- If a book has more than six authors, cite just six, followed by *et al.* (see A.2).
- Spell out names of associations and university presses: National Audubon Society, Oxford University Press.
- Do not invert the names of editors not in the author position. Identify the editor by (Ed.) after the surname.
- Italicize book titles (or underline if you lack that function).
- Do not enclose article or chapter titles in quotation marks.

10. A Book by One Author

> Cameron, J. (2008). *Mozart's ghost.* New York: St. Martin's Press.

11. Two or More Books by One Author

Books by the same author are listed according to date, from least to most recent. The author's name is repeated in each subsequent entry.

> Mayer, M. (1997). *The bankers: The next generation.* New York: Truman Talley
>
> Books/Dutton.
>
> Mayer, M. (2006). *The judges.* New York: St. Martin's Press.

12. A Book by Two or More Authors

▶ Woodall, T., & Constantine, S. (2006). *Take on America: What your clothes say about you.* New York: HarperCollins.

13. Book by a Group Author

▶ Images Publishing Group. (2008). *100 more of the world's best houses.* Victoria, Australia: Images Publishing Group.

14. A Book by an Unknown Author

▶ *Go ask Alice.* (1971). New York: Prentice-Hall.

15. Book, Revised or Later Edition

▶ Musciano, C., & Kennedy, B. (2006). *HTML & XHTML: The definitive guide* (6th ed.). Sebastopol, CA: O'Reilly.

16. A Book with an Author and an Editor or Translator

▶ Monagan, D. (2007). *Journey into the heart.* David O. Williams (Ed.). New York: Gotham Books.

Melograni, P. (2007). *Mozart.* Lydia G. Cochrane (Trans.). Chicago: University of Chicago Press.

17. Article or Chapter in a Book

Cite the inclusive pages of the article or chapter in parentheses after the book title.

▶ Ryan, T. (2001). Such a thing as destiny. In *The prize winner of Defiance, Ohio* (pp. 283–289). New York: Simon & Schuster.

18. A Work in an Anthology

If you consult one book of a multivolume set, capitalize the volume number (Vol. 5) and place it after the volume title without parentheses. (See example 22.) The example below is for a single-volume anthology:

▶ Glaspell, S. (2000). A jury of her peers. In J. Updike & K. Kenison (Eds.), *The best short stories of the century* (pp. 18–37). New York: Houghton Mifflin.

19. Published Interview

Begin with the name of the person interviewed and the date of the interview, then the title (if any), and the identifying information in brackets. Place source information according to the guidelines for books (or periodicals if the interview was published in a periodical).

MacLeish, A. (1974, Summer). Archibald MacLeish. [Interview with Benjamin

De Mott]. In G. Plimpton (Ed.) (1988), *Writers at work: The Paris review*

interviews 5 (pp. 23–48). New York: Penguin.

20. Review

Dickison, S. (2004, February). An entertaining primer for beginning writers

[Review of the book *The pen commandments: A guide for the beginning*

writer]. *The Writer, 45.*

21. Dictionary or Encyclopedia

If a major reference work has a large editorial board, you may cite only the name of the executive editor and follow it with "et al." as in the first example.

A Single Volume with Several Editors

Civil disobedience. (2006). Mish, F. C., et al. (Eds.). *Merriam-Webster's colle-*

giate dictionary (rev. ed.). Springfield, MA: Merriam-Webster.

Entry in an Encyclopedia, No Author Given

The Civil War. (1995). In *Encyclopedia Americana* (Vol. 6, pp. 782–819). Dan-

bury, CT: Grolier.

22. Chapter in a Volume in a Series

Moore, W. E. (1969). Social structure and behavior. In G. Lindzey & E. Aron-

son (Eds.), *The handbook of social psychology: Vol. 4. Group psychology and*

phenomena of interaction (2nd ed.). Reading, MA: Addison-Wesley.

23. Brochure, Corporate Author

Start with the name of the corporation or organization; then give the date and title. Identify the publication in brackets. List the place and publisher. If the publisher is the same as the author, write "Author" after the place.

US Dept. of Justice. (2004). *ATE records: A quick reference on how long you should keep*

your records. [Brochure]. Washington: U.S. Government Printing Office.

24. Government Publications with a Group Author

▶ Health Care Financing Administration. (2008). *Medicare & you 2008*.

Washington, DC: U.S. Government Printing Office.

U.S. Department of Justice. (2004). *FBI National Academy directory of*

graduates 2004 edition. Quantico, VA: Federal Bureau of Investigation

Academy.

C. APA ENTRIES: AUDIOVISUAL MEDIA

For broadcast, film, and recorded sources, enclose in *parentheses* the role of the contributing personnel and the date. Place the medium [Motion picture], [Television broadcast] or other in *brackets.*

25. Motion Pictures, VCRs, and DVDs

Indicate the specific medium in brackets [Motion picture], [VCR], or [DVD]. Include the country and producing organization, if available.

▶ Newel, M. (Director), & Barnes, P. (Screenwriter). (1992). *Enchanted April*

[Motion picture]. United States: Warner Brothers.

La Gravenese, R. (Director/Screenwriter). (2007). *Freedom Writers* [DVD].

United States: Paramount Home Entertainment.

26. Television and Radio Broadcasts

Using brackets, identify the broadcast: [Television broadcast]. If you cite one episode of a series, use [Television series episode].

▶ O'Riley, C. (Classical pianist/ Producer). (2007, April 15). Live from Carnegie

Hall. [Television series episode]. *From the top*. Columbus, OH: WOSU-TV.

Lancaster. B. (Host & Producer). (2007, March 31). The godfather of pops.

[Radio series episode]. On *Saturday at the pops*. Columbus, OH: WOSU-

FM.

27. Music and Audio Recordings

When referring to specific lyrics or compositions, begin with the lyricist/composer, followed by the original copyright date. Then provide recording information, including the date if different from the copyright date. Or if appropriate, begin with the performer, conductor, or title. For nonmusical recordings, start with the original writer's name (if provided) or with the title. Include the medium and the number in brackets.

> Blitzstein, M. (1941). In the clear [Recorded by D. Upshaw]. On *I wish it so*
>
> > [CD]. New York: Elektra Entertainment. (1994).
>
> *Official audio guide to Quicken.* (1992). [Cassette Recording No. IQU4.00M-1-A].
>
> > San Jose, CA: Personal Training Systems.

D. APA ENTRIES: ELECTRONIC MEDIA

The general guideline for a reference entry to electronic media is to attach a *retrieval statement* that gives enough information to locate the online source. A retrieval statement usually cites the date the material was obtained and the Web address of the source or the name of the database. Because the content of some Web sites is updated or changed, the date of retrieval can be significant.

To make a retrieval statement, follow these guidelines:

- List the print source (if any) *before* the online data. (See examples 1–24.)

- When page numbers are not given or if the online format differs from the print version, add a retrieval statement with the date and URL.

- Place *Retrieved*, the date, and *from* before the URL.
  Exception: If the URL directs you to information about obtaining the material (not the actual material), then state "Available from" in place of "Retrieved from." (See example 38.)

- If the name of the publisher is unclear from the URL, database, or other reference data, place the sponsor or publisher's name followed by a colon before the URL.

- Split URLs only after a slash [/] or before a period within the URL. Do not use angle brackets or add a period.

- **Databases:** For all databases, including CD-ROMs and software, provide the name of the database and the date. If you access the database online, provide a URL that links to the main search page (see example 34). If there is an item or access number, place it at the end of the entry in parentheses.

- *Exception:* If an article has a DOI, no retrieval statement is needed. Instead, simply copy the DOI of the article and place at the end of the reference (see examples 28 and 29).

USING A DOI INSTEAD OF A RETRIEVAL STATEMENT

Some scholarly articles are assigned a Digital Object Identifier (DOI), which you cite in your reference list. No retrieval statement is necessary. A DOI is a long alphanumeric string that identifies a document and helps to locate it on the Internet. DOI's vary in appearance, including punctuation. For accuracy, copy and paste this long string of numbers (and possibly letters).

Using a DOI can save time and effort. You simply type the DOI into a search engine, which brings up a link to the correct page. The DOI usually appears on the first page of an article, but a DOI may be hidden under a button. For help in finding a hidden DOI, see page 2 of the online instructions at <http://www.apastyle.org/elecmedia.html>.

Periodicals on the Internet

28. Article in a Journal with a DOI Assigned

▶   Wolfe, C. R., & Britt, M. A. (2008, February). The locus of the my side bias in

written argumentation. *Thinking & Reasoning 14*(1), 1–27.

doi: 10.1080/13546780701527674

29. Article in a Journal with a DOI Assigned with a Special Ending

The APA Style Guide of Electronic References (page 7) shows a different sort of DOI. The volume, issue, and page number (separated by periods) appear at the end of the DOI.

▶   Stultz, J. (2006). Integrating exposure therapy and analytic therapy in trauma

treatment. *American Journal of Orthopsychiatry, 76*(4), 482–488. doi:

10.1037/0002-9432.76.4.482

30. Article in a Journal with No DOI Assigned

▶   Borckardt, J. J., et al. (2008, February/March). Clinical practice is natural lab-

oratory for psychotherapy research: A guide to case-based time-series

analyses. *American Psychologist, 63*(2), 77–95. Retrieved March 16, 2008,

from http://www.apa.org./journals

31. Article in a Magazine, No Page Numbers

▶   Takeuchi, L. C. (2007, March 22). Defending jerks at work. *Time*. Retrieved

March 25, 2007, from http://www.time.com

32. Daily Newspaper Article, No Page Number

Cowell, A. (2008, March 15). Heathrow opens new terminal. *New York Times*. Retrieved March 15, 2008, from http://www.nytimes.com

33. Article in an Internet-only Newsletter, No Page Numbers

Eastman, D. (2008). Footnote.com adds millions of historical newspapers to its collection. *Eastman's Online Genealogy Newsletter*. Retrieved March 14, 2008, from http://blog.eogn.com

34. Abstract, No Page Numbers

Bishop, J. A., Haiyong, L., & Meng, Q. (2007). Are Chinese smokers sensitive to price? *China Economic Review,18*(2). Abstract retrieved March 13, 2008, from http://web.ebscohost.com

Nonperiodical Documents on the Internet

35. Entire Book, Section, or Chapter

A section of a book is cited below. The book was originally published in 1878. The online source is based on Harper's 1892 edition.

James, H. (1892). Part 1. *Daisy Miller*. Retrieved March 13, 2008, from http://www.gutenberg.org./etext/208

36. Online Anthology (Poem)

Frost, R. (n.d.). Mending wall. Boston: North (1915). Retrieved March 15, 2008, from http://www.bartleby.com/verse

37. Collection of Short Stories

Poe, E. A. (n.d.). The cask of Amontillado. *East of the Web*. Retrieved March 14, 2008, from http://www.short-stories.co.uk/

38. Document Available on University Program or Department Web Site

Nesbit, E. (1922). Many voices. In P. Willett (Ed.), *Victorian women writers project*. Available from http://www.indiana.edu/~letrs/wwwp/html

39. Online Encyclopedia, No Volume or Page Number

▶ Tooley, M. (2008). The problem of evil. In E. N. Zalta (Ed.). *The Stanford encyclopedia of philosophy*. Retrieved March 17, 2008, from http://plato .stanford.edu

40. Online Encyclopedia, No Author, Editor, Volume, or Page Number Given

▶ Wild rice. (2001). In *The Columbia encyclopedia* (6th ed.). Columbia University Press. Retrieved March 14, 2008, from http://www.bartleby.com/65/

41. Online Dictionary

▶ Racon. (n.d.) In Merriam-Webster's online dictionary. Retrieved March 16, 2008, from http://www.m-w.co/dictionary/

42. Professional or Personal Site

▶ *PressPass—Information for journalists*. (2008). Microsoft® Corporation. Retrieved March 16, 2008, from http://www.microsoft.com/presspass/exec/billg/ default.mspx

Dietsch, Terry. (2001, August 18). *Cycling Ohio rail-trails & bikeways*. Retrieved May 1, 2007, from http:/home.earthlink.net/~bikeohio/ celina.html

43. Message Posted to an Online Forum or Discussion Group

▶ Osheroff, J. A. (2007). Computers in medicine. [Editorial and invitation to re-spond by e-mail.] 2007. American College of Physicians-American Society of Internal Medicine. Message posted to http://www.acponline.org/ computer/sgim_edit.htm

44. E-mail (Included Only in Citations)

Online correspondence between individuals is not included in the reference list or a research paper. E-mail is cited as *personal communication* in the text of your paper only. List the initials of the sender and the exact date.

▶ (C. M. Smith, personal communication, March 18, 2008)

45. Map or Chart

For a map or chart, list print information first, including the date and publisher. Identify as [Map] or [Chart]. Give the title of the Web site, date of access, and URL.

> New Hampshire. (1998). National Geographic Society. [Map].
>
> > Infoplease.com. Retrieved March 14, 2008, from http://print
> >
> > .infoplease.com/atlas/state/newhampshire.html

46. Material from a Library or Other Subscription Service

To cite a work found through an online library or other subscription service, include the author's name, the title of the work, and publication information about the printed version (if given). In the retrieval statement, include the name of the database, the name of the service, the date of access, and the URL of the service's home page.

> Fill, Kaye Middleton, et al. (2007). Has alcohol been proven to be protective
>
> > against coronary heart disease? *Addiction Research & Theory 15*(1),
> >
> > 35–46. Retrieved March 15, 2008, from *Sociological Collection,*
> >
> > EBSCOhost at http://search.ebscohost.com

Nonperiodical Publications on CD-ROMs

Cite nonperiodical CD-ROMs the way you would cite a book title and author. Include the publisher and disc or item number (if there is one).

47. CD-ROMs

The example below refers to one disc of a set of CD-ROMs that are available at many public libraries. Because the sets are stored on the premises, there is no URL. Still, there is a retrieval statement naming the database.

> *1880 United States census and national index.* (2001). Retrieved March 13, 2008,
>
> > from Family Search Family History Resource File [CD-ROM]. Salt Lake
> >
> > City, UT: Intellectual Reserve.

48. Computer Software and Computer Programs

> *McAfee Internet Security Suite.* (2007). [Computer software]. Sunnyvale, CA:
>
> > McAfee.com Corporation.

PRACTICE

RECOGNIZING ITEMS THAT NEED TO BE DOCUMENTED

Directions: Go to a library or use some of your own materials to create examples of entries for an MLA-style list of works cited or an APA-style reference list. Follow the textbook models carefully, checking format and punctuation.

1. Book by two or three authors
2. Book with an editor or editors
3. A work in an anthology by several authors
4. Book with several volumes
5. Article from a daily newspaper
6. Article from a monthly magazine
7. Article from a journal with continuous paging
8. Videotape or DVD
9. One author quoting another author
10. Internet source: published newspaper, magazine, or journal article
11. Internet source: article from a professional Web site

Observation, Interviews, and Surveys

> A prudent question is one-half of wisdom.
>
> —Francis Bacon (1561–1626)

To determine which fads are in and which are out, market research firms observe street wear of urban and suburban teens and conduct focus groups. The researchers ask questions, listen, and videotape every word and gesture. From these observations and interviews, they predict new teen trends in products from fast food to jeans. Corporate clients use the reports to shape commercials and products to teen tastes. Observation, interviews, and surveys are three methods of field research.

OBSERVATION

Observation can be done in other ways. In "Caterpillar Afternoon," Sue Hubbell, a naturalist, tells how she chanced upon a queer object, which appeared to be a snakeskin, lying on a dirt road. But when she knelt down, she found it was a mass of small white, hairless caterpillars that exhibited unusual behavior, especially when disturbed. Quite curious, she examined them and later searched through her library until she found a book that mentioned experiments with pine processionaries by a nineteenth-century entomologist. Later in an interview with another naturalist, Hubbell learned that such a sight was quite rare. Thus she combined primary and secondary research. (Hubbell's narrative is located on page 561.)

Observational research involves methodically watching a specimen, activity, interaction, or phenomenon and recording data. Observation can be done up close through the five senses or through cameras, tape recorders, X-ray machines, microscopes, radar, and other devices. The main advantage of observation is that the observer sees the subject firsthand. And if strict standards are maintained, findings can be quite reliable. The main disadvantage is that observation is limited to subjects verifiable through the senses. Observation is not a reliable method for testing attitudes or motives.

Selecting a Site

To accurately assess specimens, situations, or behavior, you need a certain amount of expertise. For instance, if enrolled in certain education courses, you might observe a class of schoolchildren. You could categorize their interactions with the teacher and each other, comment on patterns observed, and relate them to a course. Or as a student who has taken several college courses, you might observe the instructional styles of several professors who teach the same course and rate their effectiveness. This would require more than your opinion; you would need to survey other students, too. Then you could compare responses.

Or you might observe the instructional styles of one instructor who teaches in two areas, perhaps composition and speech. The findings for the two areas might vary considerably. The disparity might be due to greater competency in one area; attitude of the instructor and of the students toward the subject; potential to use audiovisuals, small groups, and humor; or other factors. Obtaining other students' opinions would make the research more valid.

Other projects for observation might be much simpler. You might watch various TV networks, perhaps ABC, CBS, and CNN, to see how each covers the same stories. Or you might watch several TV programs to classify and count actions that indicate courtesy as opposed to rudeness. Or you might play arcade games and categorize acts of violence and how they are treated. Is there fighting, blood, or killing? How much? Are gory scenes shown close up? How do characters respond to gore? How do the children/youth who play the games respond? Do the games seem to have redeeming value? If so, how would you rate them on a scale of one to ten?

Preparing to Observe

Some research requires obtaining permission and making appointments. If you would like to tape your observation, this privilege will require permission, which should be secured well in advance. Inquire as to when you should arrive and where you should sit so as to be unobtrusive.

Be prepared. Remember to take an extra pen and a note pad of convenient size. Devise a system to take notes, perhaps abbreviating, so that you can watch as much as possible. If you will be taping, check your supply of blank tapes and fresh batteries. Have the recorder working and ready to go with the flick of a switch. (Observing more than once will yield information to compare and to verify impressions.)

Keeping a Log

A detailed log of research data and results is essential. After you leave the site, rewrite and expand your notes as soon as possible. (The ability to recall falls off after one hour.) Flesh out the notes with precise details and examples of what happened. Your objective at this point is to record the facts, describing exactly what you saw and heard. Tell what occurred, under what conditions, the exact time of day, who was present, and other vital information. If an interaction occurred, describe it and the precise words said. Do not inject opinion.

Use quotation marks to enclose a comment or remark you include. Note nonverbal communication: gestures, frowns, smiles, touching, vocal intonations, and other nonverbal cues. Hold off on analysis and interpretation until you have the facts down on paper and have time to consider their meaning. To be as comprehensive and objective as possible, you need to look at the entire episode, not isolated fragments. The checklist below can help you expand your notes.

CHECKLIST   MAINTAINING OBJECTIVITY

1. Observation

    ☐ What do I see?

    ☐ What do I hear?

    ☐ What do I smell?

    ☐ What do I taste?

    ☐ What do I perceive by touch?

    ☐ Is anything else significant?

2. Description
   - ☐ What are the physical features?
   - ☐ What behavior is observable?
   - ☐ What interactions are occurring?
   - ☐ Would someone else agree?
   - ☐ Are the words neutral?

3. Interpretation
   - ☐ What might it mean?
   - ☐ What else might it mean?
   - ☐ Are the inferences logical?
   - ☐ Are the inferences unbiased?
   - ☐ Do inferences account for all events/behavior?

4. Writing
   - ☐ Is the description neutral?
   - ☐ Is the interpretation logical?
   - ☐ Does the conclusion flow logically from observable data?
   - ☐ Is the conclusion fair?

Later you can analyze and look for links—common threads and patterns of behavior. If you observed more than once, did similar or dissimilar interactions occur on different days? Describe your overall impression each time. Date each observation as to the hour. In some cases, morning or afternoon can make a difference in activities and behavior.

INTERVIEWS

An interview is sometimes defined as a conversation with a purpose. Employers conduct interviews to hire, appraise, debrief, and fire employees. Computer sales reps interview clients to ascertain system needs. Journalists interview, seeking news and feature stories. Police officers interview witnesses and interrogate suspects. Lawyers interview clients to establish a defense. As a part of your field research, you might interview to learn more about a community problem, the history of your city, the underground railroad, or another topic.

Types of Interviews

Telephone interviews allow you to contact more people than face-to-face interviews do. But usually you gain less information since most people are less inclined to volunteer details to a faceless, unknown caller. Successful telephone interviews require lessening interviewees' suspicion and gaining their trust. Telephoning, however, may be a quick alternative when face-to-face interviews are canceled and you lack time to schedule more.

Talking face-to-face takes longer than telephoning but yields more information. Face-to-face interviews require planning and persistence. You have to call ahead, request appointments, and then travel. If an appointment is suddenly canceled, you may need to reschedule or find an alternative. Yet face-to-face interviews are worth the extra effort because you gain more details and make contacts that may prove beneficial.

Informational Interviewing   Informational interviews allow you to research family history, a product, or other topics. For a college research project, you might obtain preemployment information about your career field. If you do, keep in mind that informational interviews are not a job search although they may lead to a position later. An employer is apt to be kindly disposed to someone who is motivated to conduct preemployment research and to prepare a list of well-crafted questions. For example, you could ask about skills needed for a position, training offered, responsibilities, starting salary range, travel, chances for advancement, and related questions.

Before going to any interview, consider your choice of apparel carefully. If you are interviewing an elderly relative in her home, casual dress is appropriate. But if you are doing a preemployment interview, dress just as if you were applying for a job. Before you leave, convey your appreciation to the interviewee.

Unstructured versus Structured Interviews   *Unstructured* interviews are casual with no set format. They may elicit information that would not surface in a structured interview, but they are time-consuming and difficult to compare if you are doing a series. In an unstructured interview, interviewer and interviewee often contribute equally to the conversation. Yet authorities on interviewing recommend a 30 to 70 percent ratio with the interviewer doing the least talking, according to Charles J. Stewart and William B. Cash, Jr., in *Interviewing: Principles and Practices*. The interviewer's prime task is to listen.

The *structured* interview is based upon a list of prepared questions that is used for every interview. This approach not only saves time but also ensures coverage of all planned questions. A set of questions also provides a clear base for comparison.

Types of Questions

Well before your interviews start, read all you can on the subject to be discussed. You need to know enough to prepare a list of quality questions that will yield the information you seek. Using a format similar to that of a questionnaire will ease tabulation. Provide checklists for answers to allow comparison of responses.

Leave an extra space after each question for comments. Include some open questions to elicit unanticipated information.

Open questions are broad and unlimited. Their flexibility allows the interviewee to answer in several ways—for example, "Can you tell me about the duties of a bank teller?" Open questions may begin with phrases such as *what happened, how do you see this,* or *what experience have you. . . .* Often they are used at the beginning of interviews to decrease tension.

Closed questions limit an interviewee's response; they are more specific. For example, "What does a bank teller do when the day's accounts do not balance?" or "After one year what are the promotional opportunities for a teller?" These questions are so limited they have only one answer. Degrees of openness vary, as shown in the following examples:

OPEN: What types of crime have occurred in this neighborhood?

LESS OPEN: What types of vandalism have occurred in this neighborhood this year?

CLOSED: Have you had any vandalism on your property this year?

Avoid a series of closed questions that might cause defensiveness and cut off the flow of information. If questions about sensitive topics are necessary, ask them near the end of the interview. Be discreet. For example, if you ask about income or age, have the respondent indicate a range rather than a specific figure.

GUIDELINES FOR INTERVIEWING

1. **Call for an appointment.** Give full name and college or university. State the purpose of the call. Use courtesy words. (Reduces suspicion of unknown callers.)

2. **Arrive a few minutes early** to catch your breath and relax a bit.

3. **Shake hands.** A woman should extend her hand first so that the other person knows she is comfortable shaking hands.

4. **Do not sit until invited.**

5. **Politely decline an offer of a beverage.** Don't chance a spill.

6. **Have a typed list of questions handy.** Leave spaces to jot brief notes. Bring a clipboard or tablet for support. (Never use a corner of the person's desk.)

7. **Do not stay over the appointed time.** Ask important questions first.

8. **Thank the interviewee before you leave.**

9. **Write up your notes soon after the interview.** Expand. Include the date, place, and name of the interviewee. Use quotation marks to enclose exact words.

10. **Write a thank-you note to the interviewee.** Although this last tip is optional, it may be wise to cultivate some contacts for future reference. (See chapter 26.)

Leading questions indicate an expected answer. They yield little information and lead to dead ends. In the examples below, the tip-off word is italicized:

- Do you *dislike* filling out all those government forms?
- Do you *enjoy* flying to consulting sites?
- This seems like a progressive company. *Would you agree?*

Make several copies of your set of questions so that you have a clean sheet for each interview. During the interview, briefly note replies. Expand your notes soon afterward. With permission, you may tape-record. Be wary of promising copies of the results unless you have the time and resources to duplicate, mail, or deliver.

SURVEYS

Professional opinion polls and surveys are taken often. News organizations may survey a president's popularity monthly; a magazine may survey readers' preferences; manufacturers may offer free coupons to entice you to reveal personal information. A survey requires a questionnaire, skillfully designed to yield the desired information. For your research project, you might conduct a student survey on campus. You would need good questions to elicit responses that reveal views and attitudes about a concern, a problem, an issue, or another topic. After you obtain the sample responses, you tabulate and interpret the results of the research.

Planning a Survey

In 1995, shortly after the Internet was opened to commercial activity, Jeanne Dietsch designed and conducted the first e-commerce market research study. The purpose of that study was "to determine whether any companies were actually making money online." Ms. Dietsch, founder of ActivMedia Research and CEO of ActivMedia Robotics, Inc., offers valuable advice for students: "Have a *specific* and *significant purpose* in mind as you draft questions. A major problem with many questionnaires is haphazard questions that yield trivial information."

Another major problem with some surveys is that the samples are neither random or representative. For example, over the years Alfred Kinsey has been widely criticized for his statistical sampling. The *Wall Street Journal* (31 Mar. 1993) reported that "about 25% of Kinsey's 5300 male subjects were former or present prisoners . . ." Yet Kinsey claimed that the results of the survey were representative of the general population. Ten years later, criticism of Kinsey's methods was still newsworthy. Robert Stacy McCain of the *Washington Times* (8 Sept. 2003) wrote: "The Kinsey Reports have been criticized for methodological flaws . . . [one] sample included hundreds of prison inmates. Those criticisms intensified after the admission by Kinsey Institute officials that the reports' information about children's sexual behavior was based on 'research' by sex offenders."

Representative and Random Samples

A *representative* sample is a group that is typical of the general population in age, gender, education, socioeconomic status, and other significant characteristics. The size of a sample should be statistically significant. This means that a reasonable number of instances should be examined before any inference is made—the larger the sample, the better. Ten percent of the population is considered ideal, but few professional surveys have that much. *Still, the typicality of the sample is more important than size.* For example, to be typical, a campus survey would include students of both genders, various age ranges and ethnic groups, all programs, and day and evening classes. In other words, the sample should represent the mix of the campus population.

A sample is *random* if all members of the population have equal chances of being chosen. If not, the results do not reflect the opinion of the larger population, only the group sampled. Random sampling is not simple. Even if you were to select every thousandth name in a telephone directory, you would omit the poor, those too ill to answer, and others who do not have telephones. To obtain a random sample, consider the place, the day, the time, and any other factors that influence randomness. The checklist below will help you plan.

CHECKLIST   PLANNING A SURVEY

1. **Have a significant purpose.** Find an interesting project that will supply meaningful information.

2. **Determine how the survey can be representative and random.** How large will the survey be? (Check with your instructor.) Where and how will you conduct it?

3. **How much time will the survey take?** Consider that you will need to design a questionnaire, duplicate, administer, tabulate, and interpret in addition to writing. If you have to do research to pose questions, that takes time, too.

4. **How much will paper and copying cost?** If you research a topic for a business, supplies might be furnished. One student received $100 for conducting a customer survey for a barber shop.

5. **Will there be an additional cost for distribution?** Some students have been dismayed to find they spent over $50 for copies, envelopes, stamps, and gas for distributing and picking up questionnaires.

Constructing a Questionnaire

After you determine the topic, a group to sample, and a method of distribution, draft a set of questions. They should be appropriate for the topic, the situation, and the audience. Try to limit your questions to one page for easy answering.

1. Phrase questions clearly in *neutral* words. Be specific.
2. Ask for information that is easily recalled.
3. Keep questions *short.*
4. Ask only *one* question to a sentence.
5. Provide spaces, checklists, and multiple choices for *ease in answering.*
6. Plan *equal* ranges: 1–10; 11–20; 21–30. *Error: 1–10; 10–20; 20–30*
7. Use scale items (with a key) to circle for opinion:

    SA   A   N   D   SD

    SA = strongly agree, A = agree, N = neutral, D = disagree, SD = strongly disagree
8. Arrange questions in a *logical order.*
9. Place *sensitive* questions (age, salary, and so forth) near the end. Word them carefully using ranges.
10. Place any open-ended questions at the end for additional comments.
11. Limit questionnaire to one page if possible. (People dislike filling out long forms.)
12. If space allows, add a one-line thank-you.

GUIDELINES FOR CONSTRUCTING QUESTIONNAIRES

Next, write a brief set of *directions* for the questionnaire. Test the directions and questions to see whether or not they are clear and suitable. For some topics, you might seek feedback from half a dozen classmates, or you may need the expertise of an instructor or someone in the field. (See Figure R-5.1.)

Dear Student,

　　Help!!! Will you please take five minutes of your valuable time to assist a fellow student? I have to conduct a survey and write a report. Will you please complete this short questionnaire and drop it in the box labeled "Survey" in the student lounge by [date]?

　　　　　　　　　　　　　　Thanks loads,
　　　　　　　　　　　　　　[Your name]

FIGURE R-5.1 Sample cover note for a student questionnaire.

Distributing Questionnaires

Mailing questionnaires is time-consuming and expensive. You need not only a cover letter but also a stamped, self-addressed envelope unless you plan to pick up the questionnaires. Another disadvantage is that mailed questionnaires usually have a low rate of return. Although dropping off and picking up takes time, the rate of return rises considerably. Handing out a questionnaire in a store, for return later, is apt to be unsuccessful. Instead, you might have customers write on a clipboard while you wait. One student set up a card table and chairs near the front of her parents' clothing store.

For a campus survey, you might select students at random in the student lounge, but you would need to spend equal time in the library and other places where students go. Otherwise, you would be unable to obtain a cross section. Or you might ask some instructors to distribute the questionnaire at the end of certain classes. If all students at your college are required to take freshman English, you might get a representative sample there. If you use that method, you will need a brief note to enlist cooperation and to direct respondents to an easily found box in the same building. (See fig. R-5.1.)

WORKPLACE CASE STUDY

NATHAN SURVEYS DRESS CODES FOR BANK EMPLOYEES

Nathan is majoring in business management. For his research project, he surveyed local bank managers to determine policies on attire.

Survey of Clothing Worn by Local Bank Employees

Directions: Please check *all* answers that apply to your bank.

1. Does the bank have a dress code?
   - ☐ Dress code written in handbook or elsewhere.
   - ☐ Unwritten dress code/guidelines given orally to employees.
   - ☐ No dress code. Employees wear what they like.
2. Indicate all suitable attire for employees Monday through Thursday:
   - ☐ suit
   - ☐ shirt/sweater, pants
   - ☐ jeans
   - ☐ jacket & slacks
   - ☐ women wear skirts
   - ☐ no expectations
3. If you have casual Fridays, please indicate all suitable attire for Friday:
   - ☐ jacket & slacks
   - ☐ shorts, miniskirts
   - ☐ shirt/sweater, jeans
   - ☐ T-shirt/sweatshirt
4. What is the bank's policy on jewelry and tattoos?
   - ☐ small earrings permitted
   - ☐ no nose, tongue, or eyebrow piercing
   - ☐ two-per-ear limit
   - ☐ no visible tattoos

continued

5. Does the bank provide financial assistance to encourage professional attire?

☐ gift certificate   ☐ other _____
                                                            (please explain)

☐ clothing bonus   ☐ no assistance

6. If an employee wears unsuitable attire, does the bank take action?

☐ sends home without pay   ☐ gives warning

☐ sends home to change   ☐ other _____
                                                            (please explain)

7. If an employee persists in wearing unsuitable attire, does the bank take action?

☐ may fire   ☐ warns of possible firing

☐ places on probation   ☐ other _____
                                                            (please explain)

8. Please indicate the approximate number of employees at this facility. (Do not count branch banks.)

☐ 101 or more   ☐ 61–80   ☐ 21–40
☐ 81–100   ☐ 41–60   ☐ 20 or fewer

9. Estimate the number of employees who have been notified of unsuitable attire in the past year:

☐ 21 or more   ☐ 11–15   ☐ 1–5
☐ 16–20   ☐ 6–10   ☐ none

10. Is your bank contemplating a change in the current policy on employee attire?

☐ yes   *Comment:* _____
☐ no   _____

Thank you for your courtesy and cooperation.

WORKPLACE CASE STUDY

Drawing Conclusions from a Survey and Interviews

After you tabulate the results of your survey, you draw a logical conclusion based on the findings. This step requires interpreting the results: What do they mean and what are the implications? Then you make a reasonable generalization and possibly a prediction or recommendation, depending upon the rhetorical situation.

Let's assume Nathan's survey revealed that each of the ten banks had 21 to 40 employees. Six banks had written policies governing attire. Each bank's manager estimated five or fewer instances of improper attire in the past year. Warnings had been effective; no one was discharged.

But four banks had no policy. In follow-up interviews with the managers of these banks, Nathan learned that some employees repeatedly wore beach sandals, sheer blouses, visible tattoos, ponytails, or unusual haircuts. They were warned; this policy worked for a while. Three managers estimated a dozen instances of improper dress had occurred; one manager estimated two dozen instances. Nathan concludes that written policies are more effective than unwritten policies.

MAKING AN OUTLINE

Next, Nathan makes a working outline for his report. He follows a basic report format and lists the tabulation of each question in the original order:

   I. **Introduction:** Purpose and scope of the project (list of 12 banks)

  II. **Method of research:** Survey of six banks and interviews with six other bank managers

 III. **Body of report**

      A. Summary of results of survey (results converted to percentages)

      B. Additional findings obtained through six interviews

 IV. **Conclusion:** Enforced policies with warnings and penalties do work.

  V. **Recommendation:** Banks lacking a written policy on proper work attire should appoint a committee composed of bank officials and employees to write one. The policy should consider not only clothing and shoes but also jewelry, visible tattoos, body piercings, hairstyles, and hair colors.

To see student examples of a primary research paper and a report, turn to the end of this chapter. The section that follows will help you organize and interpret findings for your paper or report.

WRITING A PRIMARY RESEARCH PAPER OR REPORT

Whether you write a research paper or report, be sure you understand the assignment. Then examine your materials carefully. Do you have everything you need? If you made notes, have they been rewritten and amplified in your log so that you have all the data in front of you? If you used a set of questions, have they been tabulated? (For quick counting, use a blank copy of the questionnaire.)

If you did background reading, have you made a source card for each work (see chapter R-2)? Is a list of works cited required (chapter R-4), or can you state sources and dates in the text (see "Using Signal Phrases to Integrate Quotations into the Text," chapter R-3).

Organizing and Interpreting Findings

Before starting to draft, consider what the findings of your research mean. Jot down your interpretation in a sentence or two. This prewriting exercise will help you focus on your thesis, the main idea of the research. Raw data is not sufficient to present in a paper or report. You not only summarize and explain the findings but also draw a conclusion. Then the reader who is unfamiliar with the subject will understand the purpose of the project and the meaning of the results.

Observation   If you observe a site or subjects, you might classify the examples from your log. Classification can help you organize by importance, such as *minor to major* or *mild to severe,* or in another way. For example, if you observe traffic at an intersection several times (for the purpose of proving that a stoplight is needed), you might begin by classifying your observations by the type of safety infraction. Then you could organize the categories according to severity of the consequences. Which infractions led to near misses? Which ones led to accidents? What was the extent of damages and injuries? Was a citation issued? Anything else?

If you observed animals or people, you might classify by physical characteristics, behavior, personality, or other traits that are relevant. For example, in a study of twins, physical characteristics and DNA results would be significant whereas for some other studies, these would be insignificant. What similarities and differences might you see? What categories of behavior would you note? Isolation? Positive interactions with others? Antisocial behavior? What else?

Next, look for patterns, trends, or tendencies. What links and connections can you spot? What do these seem to indicate? What logical inferences can you make? What is your overall impression?

Interviews and Surveys   After you add the responses to each question, convert the total into a percentage. Divide each total by the number of returned questionnaires. For example, if an item received 60 *yeses* out of 80 returns, divide 60 by 80, which equals 75 percent. (Divide the smaller number by the larger one.) Next consider whether a majority is large or small. Or is opinion almost evenly split? Look for attitudes, patterns, trends. Think about implications. What reasonable inferences can you derive from this data? What can you reasonably conclude? How will you state your findings in *tentative* terms, without overstating?

For example, two of the nation's top family scholars, Cynthia Harper at the University of California and Sara McLanahan at Princeton, conducted a longitudinal study, which was reported in the *Wall Street Journal* in December 1998. Using a large national database, Harper and McLanahan analyzed family breakdown and compared theories about "root causes" of crime. They found that "boys raised outside of intact marriages are, *on average,* more than twice as *likely* as other boys to end up jailed, even after controlling for other demographic factors. Each year spent without a dad in the home increases the *odds* of future incarceration by *about* 5%." (The tentative words are italicized here. For a list of tentative terms, see chapter R-3.)

To simplify drafting of your report, make a working outline, based on classification or whatever organizational strategy you select. If you used a questionnaire, you may want to follow the order set up there. (An example of an outline appears with the student report later in this chapter.)

How Research Papers and Research Reports Differ

Research papers and reports differ considerably in format. The chief difference is that a research paper does not have internal headings. A research report is usually divided into three sections or more, each preceded by a heading.

The introduction of a research paper states the purpose and often gives an overview of the research. The methodology may be placed there, in a preface, in a content note at the bottom of a page, or at the end of the paper. The methodology tells what was observed, who was interviewed, or who was surveyed. For a survey the date, demographics, and size of the sample should also be provided. (For several interviews, your instructor may require a list of sources at the end of the report. See chapter R-4 for MLA or APA style.)

The first section of a report, often called the "Purpose and Scope," states the purpose and tells why the research was conducted. This section also sets forth the range (coverage of the topic) of the research and may include the methodology. Or it may be placed in a separate section. Regardless of where this essential information is placed, it should be specific. State how the observation was made and under what conditions. For an interview or survey, tell how it was conducted, the number of questionnaires given out, and the rate of return.

The body of the research paper contains the findings and the discussion. There data and examples are presented; data is interpreted; patterns and trends are described. For a report, this material is also placed in the body, but in one section or more. The section may be entitled "Results of the Survey" or another suitable heading.

The conclusion of an informative research paper is a short summary of the results, the chief idea. The conclusion of a problem-solving paper recommends an alternative. In an argument, the conclusion restates the proposition. The final section of a report is often entitled "Conclusion" or "Recommendations." *Conclusion* implies a summary. *Recommendations* are suggestions for action. In student research reports, recommendations are usually those of professionals, such as physicians, engineers, or environmentalists.

A research paper may not be quite as concise as a report. A paper may spend more time explaining data, including definitions and examples, and may include several direct quotations—significant responses to open-ended questions. The following paper and report show two of many ways to organize and format. The structure you use will vary, depending on the assignment, the topic, and the method(s) of research.

STUDENT PAPER BASED ON OBSERVATION

Janet Burks, a volunteer playground supervisor at her children's school, observed the situation described here. She used a problem-solving strategy to organize her paper.

Playground Supervision

There was an old woman who lived in a shoe;
She had so many children she didn't know what to do.
                    —MOTHER GOOSE

www.mhhe.com/dietsch
You can find other examples of student writing at:
Writing>Writing Samples

The old lady living in a shoe and a volunteer playground supervisor have a similar problem. Both have so many children they do not know what to do. Although Mother Goose does not tell readers how many children the old woman had, the number was certainly fewer than the 120 or so children for whom the playground supervisor is responsible.

What, specifically, can be done to solve this problem? Apparently, there are three possible solutions: soliciting additional volunteers, decreasing the number of children released for recess at any one time, or presenting a tax levy to pay the salaries for full-time supervisors. But any possible solution would be governed by two major constraints: cost and feasibility.

Presently, volunteers come to the playground to supervise during the hour-long midday recess (which includes lunch time). The supervisor's responsibility is to circulate among the children and either to help them or to maintain discipline. The job is physically, emotionally, and mentally draining because the supervisor's tasks vary all the way from tying a kindergartner's shoe to helping a child who has fallen off the slide to resolving disputes. During this vigil, children may approach the volunteer frequently with problems, complaints, or accident reports. The supervisor cannot be everywhere at once. Children can be hurt before he or she even knows about a fight.

A complication arises when the supervisor must handle an extreme disciplinary situation. He or she is not allowed to administer discipline, but instead escorts unruly (and often unwilling) children to the principal's office. While the supervisor is attending to one child, 119 or so are outside without supervision.

As the volunteer program has continued, more people have been quitting because of difficulties they confront. This factor has made the playground problem even worse. One proposal is to solicit the help of more volunteers. Having more would provide two supervisors each day. Then the child-to-supervisor ratio of 120 to 1 would decrease to 60 to 1. Although this proposal has the advantage of being inexpensive, it also has the disadvantage of being unlikely. Most parents are not volunteering to help (many work) and probably will not volunteer in the future.

A second proposal is to decrease the number of children released for recess at any one time. This proposal would involve shortening the midday recess to thirty minutes and staggering recess times. Only two classes (of the usual five) would be on the playground at once, cutting the number of children to supervise to approximately 40 per session. The others would return to their rooms for quiet play with teacher supervision. But the children would probably object, and teachers would not want to assume additional duties.

The third proposal would be to present a tax levy to pay the salaries of full-time supervisors. The rate per hour would be much less than the rate required to pay teachers to supervise the playground during their lunch break. At the same time, the rate would be high enough to attract people to the job. Full-time volunteers sometimes do not come. Then, too, full-time supervisors would have standard rules, which the volunteers do not have. The main disadvantage is voter reluctance to approve higher taxes.

The writer's recommendation is a combination of the first and third proposals. First, information concerning the problem could be distributed to parents. They would know that if enough volunteers were not found, then a tax levy would be necessary. The levy would provide the necessary funds for employing full-time supervisors.

Although the old lady in the shoe did not know what to do, let it not be said that the same is true of Sycamore's parents and teachers. Let us solve this problem together.

In the student report that follows, notice that there are two sections in the body, entitled "Background Reading and Reactions" and "Self-Evaluation: Progress toward Objectives." These headings reflect the nature of the assignment and of the research.

STUDENT REPORT BASED ON READING AND OBSERVATION

The following report by Lisa White, a nursing student, was written for an oral communications class. The project required reading one book or more, applying principles learned in class and through reading to the student's personal or work life, and keeping a log. In their reports, students were to react to their reading, citing the most helpful ideas. Then they were to present and explain their findings as well as to evaluate progress toward their objectives. Before the project, they received an outline with suggested headings for formatting the report. (See Figure R-5.3.)

No list of references was required although sources were to be provided. Lisa supplied her source information in the text of the report.

NONVERBAL COMMUNICATION WITH GERIATRIC PATIENTS

Prepared for Betty M. Dietsch, Prof.
CM 116 Oral Communications
Individual Goals Project

Prepared by Lisa White
February 28, 2002

FIGURE R-5.2 Sample cover page of a student report.

Outline of the Report

I. Purpose and Scope
II. Methods of Research
III. Background Reading and Reactions
   A. *How to Win Friends and Influence People*, by Dale Carnegie
   B. *Nonverbal Communication with Patients*, by Marion Nesbitt Blondis
   C. *How to Stop Worrying and Start Living*, by Dale Carnegie
   D. *How to Manage Conflict*, by William Hendricks
IV. Self-Evaluation: Progress toward Objectives
   A. Appraisal of Progress
   B. Examples of Progress
V. Conclusion

FIGURE R-5.3 Sample outline of a student report.

NONVERBAL COMMUNICATION WITH GERIATRIC PATIENTS

I. Purpose and Scope

Lake View Center (a pseudonym) is a geriatric care facility. The patients range from those needing postsurgical care to those needing care for Alzheimer's disease. As a nurse's aide, I daily encounter numerous situations that are taxing mentally, physically, and emotionally. Yet I lack the training to cope with them as I would like. I want to learn more about the importance of nonverbal communication and how to apply it to geriatric nursing. To become more skilled in interacting with patients and staff, I set the following objectives for this project:

1. To learn how to use nonverbal communication to enhance interactions with patients

2. To learn how to accept criticism

3. To develop ways to control anger

II. Methods of Research

Four library books supplied information on nonverbal communication. Most helpful were the specific suggestions that I could apply on the job. For three weeks (January 31 to February 19), I tried out the suggestions and kept a log. Every day after work, I recorded at least one incident, telling what happened, how I felt, how the other person reacted and seemed to feel. Then I stated what I had learned. As the days passed, I began to rate my progress. The log has twenty entries.

III. Background Reading and Reactions

A. *How to Win Friends and Influence People,* Dale Carnegie, 1981 (1964).

In this early book, Carnegie offers some fundamental techniques for dealing with people. The first is to remember that the deepest urge in human nature is the desire to be important. Sometimes we forget that other people besides us need to feel important. The second technique is to remember that everyone wants to be appreciated in one way or another. We can remember to thank people in small ways by words or by a quick note.

A third way to develop the best in another person is through encouragement. We all need to be encouraged, to know that we are heading in the right direction. Most helpful was Carnegie's reminder that other people need to feel important, too. I tend to get so wrapped up in trying to get everything done that I forget to try to help people feel valued, especially my patients.

B. *Nonverbal Communication with Patients,* Marion Nesbitt Blondis, 1977.

Blondis makes many excellent points about geriatric nursing. Her first suggestion is that when pausing to talk, one should speak patients' names, stand very close, look directly at them, and touch them lightly on the hand or arm. This sends a nonverbal message of "I am not too busy for you. You are important. I do care."

A second excellent point is that some elderly patients may not understand verbal communication due to hearing loss or mental impairment. But they are apt to note and understand nonverbal cues. Yet even when they understand, there is often a cultural gap of fifty or sixty years separating them from their young nurses. A word I say in one way may not be understood in the same context.

Third, patients will be more likely to judge us kindly when our nonverbal behavior is cheerful and effective. And it often seems that when one person is cheerful, the other person responds likewise. Fourth, Blondis warns that we should not confuse a patient's having a problem with the patient's being a problem. For example, some of the patients I take care of have been diagnosed as "hostile," "confused," or "senile." In reality, they may simply be unable to communicate verbally. Nevertheless, they still have thoughts and feelings.

C. *How to Stop Worrying and Start Living,* Dale Carnegie, 1984 (1970).

In his book, Carnegie explains several ways to accept and deal with criticism. The first is to remember that when we are "kicked" and criticized, it is often done because it gives the kicker a feeling of importance. Some people seem to derive satisfaction out of denouncing others who are better educated or more successful than they are. They are envious or jealous.

A second way to alleviate the sting of criticism is to remember that unjust criticism may be a compliment in disguise. We may just need to search for the motive behind it. If we keep that idea in mind, we will be less apt to worry so much about what some people say. A third suggestion is to just do the best we know how and can do when criticized unjustly—to retain dignity.

A fourth way is to keep a log of the foolish things we do and criticize ourselves for. After that, we can ask someone we respect and trust for unbiased, helpful, constructive criticism. I think this is a great idea because it helps us to improve.

D. *How to Manage Conflict,* William Hendricks, 1989.

Hendricks shares some practical tips on how to reduce and control anger through conflict management. His first suggestion is to have tolerance for diversity among people. We need to understand that other people's thoughts and ideas about issues may not reflect the same views we have. The second suggestion is to learn how to properly focus our anger on issues, not people.

This concept is difficult to apply, at least for me. I find that venting my anger on people is much easier than focusing on the issue.

Third, Hendricks points out that repressing anger will eventually lead to an explosion. Basically what he is saying is that we need to find a healthy way to handle anger. A good way, I think, is through exercise, cleaning, making crafts, or talking to a friend. This book has been very helpful because I have a quick temper.

IV. Self-Evaluation: Progress toward Objectives
A. Appraisal of Progress

Objective 1. I wanted to learn how to use nonverbal communication effectively on the job. Now when I talk to my patients, I look them in the face and smile. I speak in a cheerful tone. I also touch them on the hand to show I am not too busy for them and that I truly care. I have learned how powerful nonverbal cues can be.

Objective 2. I am learning to handle criticism in a calm, logical way. First, I assess the remark or comment to determine whether it is unjust or constructive criticism. If unjust, I take it as someone just being jealous or envious. If it is constructive criticism, I use it to improve myself and what I am doing. This procedure helps me to avoid taking offense.

Objective 3. I have been trying to focus my anger on the issue and not the person. I have also started activities to vent my emotion in a healthy manner. As soon as I get home after work, I exercise. Or if I am so angry, I cannot wait until I get home, I clean out the patients' closets. Talking to coworkers who have been in the same or a similar situation also helps.

B. Examples of Progress

Before I started this project, I used to become upset, worry, and sometimes cry. Now I do not let anybody's unjust criticism bother me. For example, a nurse at work was criticizing what I wear. I took it as her opinion and did not become upset. In fact, I used the "sponge" method, taught in class. I told her that she was probably right and that I probably could dress differently.

Another day a nurse criticized me because I was having trouble taking patients off the bedpan and keeping their beds dry. As a result, they were angry and complaining. I asked her if she would show me how she did it. She explained and then showed me. As a result of her constructive criticism and instruction, I learned to do the chore better and patients stopped complaining.

My log contains many other examples of progress, but two are especially significant. One evening a patient began yelling at me for not putting her to bed when she wanted. I tried using nonverbal communication in order to make her feel more important. It worked! I looked her in the eye while smiling and touching her hand. I explained it would be some time before I could put her to bed, but I would come back as soon as I could. Suddenly, she smiled and said that would be fine. Ever since then she has not given me any more problems.

The most trying incident occurred when I was trying to put a patient to bed. She slapped my face, scratched my arms, and bit me. I felt like screaming and hitting her back, but did not. Instead, I walked up and down the halls until I cooled down a bit. Then I went back and cleaned out her closet. (I cleaned out a lot of closets before the project was finished.)

V. Conclusion

This project has given me the opportunity to learn more about an important part of communication and to improve my work habits. My supervisor noticed the improvement and commended me. I told her about the communication project, and she seemed quite interested. Although I am well pleased with my success, I plan to continue the project. I want to learn more about nonverbal communication and continue to gain skill in accepting criticism.

TEN IDEAS FOR OBSERVATION, INTERVIEWING, AND SURVEYS

OBSERVATION

1   Observe a neighborhood problem such as litter control. Discuss possible alternatives and recommend action to alleviate the problem.

2   Observe a crossing that needs a stoplight. Count the cars that pass through at peak times. Describe reckless driving. What else? You might send the report to the editor of a local newspaper.

3   Observe a family communication problem. What is happening? What alternatives might alleviate the problem?

4   Preschool television: Time? Purpose? Themes? Hosts? Graphics? Value? Observe children viewing and record their responses, verbal and nonverbal.

INTERVIEWING

5   Jobs and salaries available locally in your career field. Will you need more training to qualify?

6   Qualities and training employers look for in _____ (your field).

7   Tour day-care centers: Interview personnel and observe. Which would be the best emotionally and educationally for your child?

8   Interview an elderly relative. Ask about his or her youth, parents, and grandparents. Record and analyze the anecdotes for your family history.

SURVEYS

9   Conduct a campus survey on the need for more litter control, parking lot surveillance at night, or another concern.

10 Survey to determine major concerns of a community: More police/deputies? Repair of schools? New schools? Street repair? Vandalism? What?

A READER FOR WRITERS

THE READER

THE READINGS BY THEME

THE READINGS
BY THEME

STRATEGIES FOR INSIGHTFUL READING

As you contemplate and discuss these essays and short stories, you will learn much about critical thinking, reading, and writing. You can sharpen your analytical and evaluative skills, which are valuable not only in the classroom but also in the workplace. Whether you prefer nonfiction or fiction, you can learn much about writing strategies by observing the work of professional writers and understanding the difference between purpose and intent.

How Do the Writer's Purpose and Intent Differ?

The writer's purpose in essays is usually *stated* directly in a thesis or purpose statement. A thesis statement makes the purpose clear, whether to inform, entertain, define, or persuade. Often there are dual purposes, although just one may be stated. When the purpose is stated, then it is possible to evaluate whether or not the writer has achieved it. In fiction the writer's purpose is rarely stated in the work itself.

Even though a writer may state a purpose, the reader can't be absolutely sure of the writer's intent. The reader must be alert to irony and satire, as in Jonathan Swift's "A Modest Proposal" (page 289). Then, too, the writer may be reluctant to share the actual intent. The finished piece may contain a hidden agenda or words that have different meanings for different readers. Or *the result may be different from what the writer intended.* It is not unusual for authors of fiction to admit they were unaware of certain symbols or themes in their work until someone else pointed them out. In *The Writer* (Nov. 1937), Wallace Stegner explains:

> I have found writing to be the most amazingly unpredictable exercise man can engage in. Characters are forever developing sinister neurotic tendencies under one's hands. Originally planned minor incidents expand and lengthen until they swallow up what was designed as the main action. Finished stories have a habit of meaning something different from, and frequently better than, the meaning one intended.

So What Can You Learn?

Sound critical reading does not second guess an author's intent. All we can logically evaluate in any work is the result—what a writer has achieved. Chapter 21 has tips to improve your reading comprehension, analysis, and note-taking in "A Strategy for Critical Reading and Prewriting." Chapter 22 provides a strategy for reading, analyzing, and evaluating fiction. Chapter 23 discusses literary devices and strategies you can use in your college and business writing. All will help you gain more from your reading and give you more options to use in writing.

Writing Narratives

<table>
<tr><td>SOUND AND FURY</td><td>DAN GREENBURG</td></tr>
</table>

A sense of humor percolates through most of Dan Greenburg's novels, plays, magazine articles, and children's books. He has written for the New Yorker, Esquire, Ms., Time, Newsweek, Life, New York, Cosmopolitan, Playboy, New York Times Book Review, *and* Vanity Fair. *His books for adults include* How to Be a Jewish Mother *(1993),* How to Avoid Love and Marriage *(1985),* How to Make Yourself Miserable *(1976), and others. Inspired by his young son, Greenburg has written over three dozen children's books with such intriguing titles as* Never Trust a Cat Who Wears Earrings *(1997) and* It's Itchcraft *(2003). In this essay he describes an incendiary incident that was deflected with adroit words.*

1   We carry around a lot of free-floating anger. What we do with it is what fascinates me.

My friend Lee Frank is a stand-up comedian who works regularly in New York comedy clubs. Not long ago I accompanied him to one of these places, where he was to be the late-night emcee and where I myself had once done a stand-up act in a gentler era.

The crowd that night was a typical weekend bunch—enthusiastic, hostile and drunk. A large contingent of inebriated young men from Long Island had decided that a comedian named Rusty who was currently on stage was the greatest thing since pop-top cans and began chanting his name after almost everything he said: "Rus-TEE! Rus-TEE!"

My friend Lee knew he had a tough act to follow.

5   Indeed, the moment Lee walked on stage, the inebriated young men from Long Island began chanting "Rus-TEE! Rus-TEE!" and didn't give him a chance. Poor Lee, the flop sweat running into his eyes, tried every trick he knew to win them over, and finally gave up.

When he left the stage I joined him at the bar in the back of the club to commiserate.

"You did the best you could," I told him.

"I don't know," he said, "I could have handled it better."

"How?"

"I don't know," he said.

As we spoke, the young men who'd given him such a tough time trickled into the bar area. One of them spotted Lee and observed to a companion that Lee might want to do something about their heckling.

Lee thought he heard the companion reply, "I'm down," a casual acknowledgment that he was willing to have a fistfight. Lee repeated their remarks to me and indicated that he, too, was "down."

Though slight of frame, Lee is a black belt in Tae Kwon Do, has had skirmishes with three-card monte con men in Times Square, and once even captured a robber-rapist. I am also slight of frame but have had no training in martial arts. I did have one fistfight in my adult life (with a movie producer), but as Lee's best friend, I assumed that I was "down" as well.

Considering that there were more than a dozen of them and only two of us, the period of time that might elapse between our being "down" and our being down seemed exceedingly brief.

The young man who'd made the remark drifted toward Lee.

The eyes of everyone in the bar shifted slightly and locked onto the two men like heat-seeking missiles. Fight-or-flight adrenaline and testosterone spurted into dozens of male cardiovascular systems. Safeties snapped off figurative weapons. Red warning lights lit up dozens of DEFCON systems; warheads were armed and aimed. In a moment this bar area might very well resemble a saloon in a B grade western.

"How ya doing?" said Lee, his voice flat as unleavened bread, trying to make up his mind whether to be friendly or hostile.

"Okay," said the guy, a pleasant-looking, clean-cut kid in his mid-20s.

I was fascinated by what was going on between the two of them, each feeling the other out in a neutral, unemotional, slightly bemused manner. I saw no hostility here, no xenophobic loathing, just two young males jockeying for position, going through the motions, doing the dance, willing to engage at the slightest provocation. I had seen my cat do this many times when a stranger strayed onto his turf.

And then I had a sudden flash of clarity: These guys could either rip each other's heads off now or they could share a beer, and both options would be equally acceptable to them.

I'd felt close to critical mass on many occasions myself. But here, feeling outside the action, I could see clearly that it had to do with the enormous reservoir of rage that we men carry around with us, rage that seethes just under the surface and is ready to be tapped in an instant, with or without just provocation.

"What're you in town for?" asked Lee casually.

The guy was watching Lee carefully, making minuscule adjustments on his sensing and triggering equipment.

"It's my birthday," said the guy.

25   Lee mulled over this information for a moment, still considering all his options. Then he made his decision.

"Happy birthday," said Lee finally, sticking out his hand.

The guy studied Lee's hand a moment. Then, deciding the gesture was sincere, he took the hand and shook it.

"Thanks," he said, and walked back to his buddies.

REFLECTING AND INTERPRETING

1. What do you notice about Greenburg's opening?

2. In narratives, we speak of "rising action" and "falling action." When does the action start to rise?

3. Note the change in structure and tone in paragraph 13. How does it differ from paragraphs 3 to 12?

4. How does the narrator think the fistfight will turn out? How long does he think it will last? Why?

5. What do you notice about paragraphs 18 and 19? Why are they significant?

6. Describe the emotions that hover beneath the surface of the conversation. How does the narrator explain them?

7. At what point does the action start to fall? Why?

8. How important are nonverbal signals in this episode? Why?

9. Which sentence serves as a transition to leap from this one episode to a universal statement about humankind?

10. Examine Greenburg's title. Do you think it appropriately reflects the point of the story? Why or why not?

A WRITER'S RESPONSE

1. Have you or any of your friends been the unwitting victim of such a hostile confrontation? If so, describe it.

2. Have you ever been able to turn a difficult situation to your advantage by using calming words and friendly signals? If so, how did you do it?

MOMMA'S ENCOUNTER   MAYA ANGELOU

This African-American poet, editor, essayist, songwriter, actress, and television producer speaks five languages. Born Marguerite Johnson in 1928, she lived most of her childhood with her grandmother, who ran a store in Stamps, Arkansas. Although she dropped out of school at age sixteen and got a job, she graduated from Mission High School in 1945. Later, while performing at a San Francisco night club, she chose the name of Maya Angelou. From 1961 to 1965 she lived in Africa, where she worked at the University of Ghana for a time. Later she wrote for the *African Review*, the *Ghanaian Times*, and the Ghanaian Broadcasting Company. Her five autobiographies describe her varied experiences. Her volumes of poetry include *Just Give Me a Cool Drink of Water 'Fore I Die'* (1971) and *And Still I Rise* (1978). In 1993 she delivered her poem "On the Pulse of Morning" at the inauguration of President William Clinton. The essay below is taken from *I Know Why the Caged Bird Sings* (1970).

"Thou shall not be dirty" and "Thou shall not be impudent" were the two commandments of Grandmother Henderson upon which hung our total salvation.

Each night in the bitterest winter we were forced to wash faces, arms, necks, legs and feet before going to bed. She used to add, with a smirk that unprofane people can't control when venturing into profanity, "and wash as far as possible, then wash possible."

We would go to the well and wash in the ice-cold, clear water, grease our legs with the equally cold stiff Vaseline, then tiptoe into the house. We wiped the dust from our toes and settled down for schoolwork, cornbread, clabbered milk, prayers and bed, always in that order. Momma was famous for pulling the quilts off after we had fallen asleep to examine our feet. If they weren't clean enough for her, she took the switch (she kept one behind the bedroom door for emergencies) and woke up the offender with a few aptly placed burning reminders.

The area around the well at night was dark and slick, and boys told about how snakes love water, so that anyone who had to draw water at night and then stand there alone and wash knew that moccasins and rattlers, puff adders and boa constrictors were winding their way to the well and would arrive just as the person washing got soap in her eyes. But Momma convinced us that not only was cleanliness next to Godliness, dirtiness was the inventor of misery.

The impudent child was detested by God and a shame to its parents and could bring destruction to its house and line. All adults had to be addressed as Mister, Missus, Miss, Auntie, Cousin, Unk, Uncle, Buhbah, Sister, Brother and a thousand other appellations indicating familial relationship and the lowliness of the addressor.

Everyone I knew respected these customary laws, except for the powhitetrash children.

Some families of powhitetrash lived on Momma's farm land behind the school. Sometimes a gaggle of them came to the Store, filling the whole room, chasing out the air and even changing the well-known scents. The children crawled over the shelves and into the potato and onion bins, twanging all the time in their sharp voices like cigarbox guitars. They took liberties in my Store that I would never dare. Since Momma told us that the less you say to whitefolks (or even powhitetrash) the better, Bailey and I would stand, solemn, quiet, in the displaced air. But if one of the playful apparitions got close to us, I pinched it. Partly out of angry frustration and partly because I didn't believe in its flesh reality.

They called my uncle by his first name and ordered him around the Store. He, to my crying shame, obeyed them in his limping dip-straight-dip fashion.

My grandmother, too followed their orders, except that she didn't seem to be servile because she anticipated their needs.

10   "Here's sugar, Miz Potter, and here's baking powder. You didn't buy soda last month, you'll probably be needing some."

Momma always directed her statements to the adults, but sometimes, Oh painful sometimes, the grimy, snotty-nosed girls would answer her.

"Naw, Annie . . ."—to Momma? Who owned the land they lived on? Who forgot more than they would ever learn? If there was any justice in the world, God should strike them dumb at once!—"Just give us some extry sody crackers, and some more mackerel."

At least they never looked in her face, or I never caught them doing so. Nobody with a smidgen of training, not even the worst roustabout, would look right in a grown person's face. It meant the person was trying to take the words out before they were formed. The dirty little children didn't do that, but they threw their orders around the Store like lashes from a cat-o'-nine tails.

When I was around ten years old, those scruffy children caused me the most painful and confusing experience I had ever had with my grandmother.

15   One summer morning, after I had swept the dirt yard of leaves, spearmintgum wrappers and Vienna-sausage labels, I raked the yellow-red dirt, and made half-moons carefully, so that the design stood out clearly and mask-like. I put the rake behind the Store and came through the back of the house to find Grandmother on the front porch in her big, wide white apron. The apron was so stiff by virtue of the starch that it could have stood alone. Momma was admiring the yard, so I joined her. It truly looked like a flat red-head that had been raked with a big-toothed comb. Momma didn't say anything but I knew she liked it. She looked over toward the school principal's house and to the right at Mr. McElroy's. She was hoping one of those community pillars would see the design before the day's business wiped it out. Then she looked upward to the school. My head had swung with hers, so at just about the same time we saw a troop of the powhitetrash kids marching over the hill and down by the side of the school.

I looked to Momma for direction. She did an excellent job of sagging from her waist down, but from the waist up she seemed to be pulling for the top of the oak tree across the road. Then she began to moan a hymn. Maybe not to moan, but the tune was so slow and the meter so strange that she could have been moaning. She didn't look at me again. When the children reached halfway down the hill, halfway to the Store, she said without turning, "Sister, go on inside."

I wanted to beg her, "Momma, don't wait for them. Come on inside with me. If they come in the Store, you go to the bedroom and let me wait on them. They only frighten me if you're around. Alone I know how to handle them." But of course I couldn't say anything, so I went in and stood behind the screen door.

Before the girls got to the porch I heard their laughter crackling and popping like pine logs in a cooking stove. I suppose my lifelong paranoia was born in those cold, molasses-slow minutes. They came finally to stand on the ground in front of Momma. At first they pretended seriousness. Then one of them wrapped her right arm in the crook of her left, pushed out her mouth and started to hum. I realized that she was aping my grandmother. Another said, "Naw, Helen, you ain't standing like her. This here's it." Then she lifted her chest, folded her arms and mocked that strange carriage that was Annie Henderson. Another laughed, "Naw, you can't do it. You mouth ain't pooched out enough. It's like this."

I thought about the rifle behind the door, but I knew I'd never be able to hold it straight, and the .410, our sawed-off shotgun, which stayed loaded and was fired every New Year's night, was locked in the trunk and Uncle Willie had the key on his chain. Through the fly-specked screen-door, I could see that the arms of Momma's apron jiggled from the vibrations of her humming. But her knees seemed to have locked as if they would never bend again.

She sang on. No louder than before, but no softer either. No slower or [20] faster.

The dirt of the girls' cotton dresses continued on their legs, feet, arms and faces to make them all of a piece. Their greasy uncolored hair hung down, uncombed, with a grim finality. I knelt to see them better, to remember them for all time. The tears that had slipped down my dress left unsurprising dark spots, and made the front yard blurry and even more unreal. The world had taken a deep breath and was having doubts about continuing to revolve.

The girls had tired of mocking Momma and turned to other means of agitation. One crossed her eyes, stuck her thumbs in both sides of her mouth and said, "Look here, Annie." Grandmother hummed on and the apron strings trembled. I wanted to throw a handful of black pepper in their faces, to throw lye on them, to scream that they were dirty, scummy peckerwoods, but I knew I was as clearly imprisoned behind the scene as the actors outside were confined to their roles.

One of the smaller girls did a kind of puppet dance while her fellow clowns laughed at her. But the tall one, who was almost a woman, said something very quietly, which I couldn't hear. They all moved backward from the porch, still watching Momma. For an awful second I thought they were going to throw a rock at Momma, who seemed (except for the apron strings) to have turned into stone herself. But the big girl turned her back, bent down and put her hands flat on the ground—she didn't pick up anything. She simply shifted her weight and did a hand stand.

Her dirty bare feet and long legs went straight for the sky. Her dress fell down around her shoulders, and she had on no drawers. The slick pubic hair made a brown triangle where her legs came together. She hung in the vacuum of that lifeless morning for only a few seconds, then wavered and tumbled. The other girls clapped her on the back and slapped their hands.

25 Momma changed her song to "Bread of Heaven, bread of Heaven, feed me till I want no more."

I found that I was praying too. How long could Momma hold out? What new indignity would they think of to subject her to? Would I be able to stay out of it? What would Momma really like me to do?

Then they were moving out of the yard, on their way to town. They bobbed their heads and shook their slack behinds and turned, one at a time:

"Bye, Annie."

"Bye, Annie."

30 "Bye, Annie."

Momma never turned her head or unfolded her arms, but she stopped singing and said, " 'Bye, Miz Helen, 'bye, Miz Ruth, 'bye, Miz Eloise."

I burst. A firecracker July-the-Fourth burst. How could Momma call them Miz? The mean nasty things. Why couldn't she have come inside the sweet, cool store when we saw them breasting the hill? What did she prove? And then if they were dirty, mean and impudent, why did Momma have to call them Miz?

She stood another whole song through and then opened the screen door to look down on me crying in rage. She looked until I looked up. Her face was a brown moon that shone on me. She was beautiful. Something had happened out there, which I couldn't completely understand, but I could see that she was happy. Then she bent down and touched me as mothers of the church "lay hands on the sick and afflicted" and I quieted.

"Go wash your face, Sister." And she went behind the candy counter and hummed, "Glory, glory, hallelujah, when I lay my burden down."

35 I threw the well water on my face and used the weekday handkerchief to blow my nose. Whatever the contest had been out front, I knew Momma had won.

I took the rake back to the front yard. The smudged footprints were easy to erase. I worked for a long time on my new design and laid the rake behind the wash pot. When I came back in the Store, I took Momma's hand and we both walked outside to look at the pattern.

It was a large heart with lots of hearts growing smaller inside, and piercing from the outside rim to the smallest heart was an arrow. Momma said, "Sister, that's right pretty." Then she turned back to the Store and resumed, "Glory, glory, hallelujah, when I lay my burden down."

REFLECTING AND INTERPRETING

1. What impression of Grandmother Henderson do you gain from the first sentence?

2. How does Maya's rearing differ from that of the "powhitetrash" children?

3. What clue in paragraph 16 reveals that Momma senses what is to come?

4. What do you learn about Maya in paragraph 17? Why can't she say anything?

5. What is the significance of the dialogue in paragraphs 28–31?

6. When does the action start to rise? Where does the climax occur?

7. How does Momma feel after the encounter? What nonverbal signals reveal her emotions?

8. What effect does the first-person point of view, rather than third person, have upon the narrative?

9. How might the final design in the yard be interpreted?

10. How would you state the point of or lesson to be gained from this narrative?

A WRITER'S RESPONSE

Compare and contrast "Momma's Encounter" with "Sound and Fury." How do they differ in tone? In the resolution of the problem?

THE ART OF ACKNOWLEDGEMENT   JEAN HOUSTON

Life is like a roller coaster that can take us from the depths of despair to the apex of joy—if we can just hang on. Clinging precariously, some hardy souls survive alone; others derive strength from the support of a family member, friend, or teacher. In this excerpt from *The Possible Human* (1982), Jean Houston, social scientist, describes the visiting professor who enabled her to surmount a devastating experience during her college years. This tale reminds us that we all have the ability to give a priceless gift to help others. Houston is the author of *A Mythic Life* (1996), *The Search for the Beloved* (1997), *The Passion of ISIS and OSIRIS* (1998), *A Passion for the Possible* (1998), *Jump Time* (2000), and *Mystical Dogs: Animals as Guides to Our Inner Life* (2005). Houston is the coauthor of numerous books and other publications.

I was eighteen years old and I was the golden girl. A junior in college, 1 I was president of the college drama society, a member of the student senate, winner of two off-Broadway critics' awards for acting and directing, director of the class play, and had just turned down an offer to train for the next Olympics (fencing). In class my mind raced and dazzled, spinning off facile but "wowing" analogies to the kudos of teachers and classmates. Socially, I was on top of the heap. My advice was sought, my phone rang constantly, and it seemed that nothing could stop me.

I was the envy of all my friends and I was in a state of galloping chutzpah.

The old Greek tragedies warn us that when hubris rises, nemesis falls. I was no exception to this ancient rule. My universe crashed with great suddenness. It began when three members of my immediate family died. Then a friend whom I loved very much died suddenly of a burst appendix while camping alone in the woods. The scenery of the off-Broadway production fell on my head and I was left almost blind for the next four months. My friends and I parted from each other, they out of embarrassment and I because I didn't think I was worthy. My marks went from being rather good to a D-plus average.

I had so lost confidence in my abilities that I couldn't concentrate on anything or see the connections between things. My memory was a shambles, and within a few months I was placed on probation. All my offices were taken away; public elections were called to fill them. I was asked into the advisor's office and told that I would have to leave the college at the end of the spring term since, clearly, I didn't have the "necessary intelligence to do academic work." When I protested that I had had the "necessary intelligence" during my freshman and sophomore years, I was assured with a sympathetic smile that intellectual decline such as this often happened to young women when "they became interested in other things; it's a matter of hormones, my dear."

5　　Where once I had been vocal and high-spirited in the classroom, I now huddled in my oversized camel's-hair coat in the back of classes, trying to be as nonexistent as possible. At lunch I would lock myself in the green room of the college theater, scene of my former triumphs, eating a sandwich in despondent isolation. Every day brought its defeat and disacknowledgments, and after my previous career I was too proud to ask for help. I felt like Job and called out to God, "Where are the boils?" since that was about all I was missing.

These Jobian fulminations led me to take one last course. It was taught by a young Swiss professor of religion, Dr. Jacob Taubes, and was supposed to be a study of selected books of the Old Testament. It turned out to be largely a discussion of the dialectic between St. Paul and Nietzsche.

Taubes was the most brilliant and exciting teacher I had ever experienced, displaying European academic wizardry such as I had never known. Hegel, gnosticism, structuralism, phenomenology, and the intellectual passions of the Sorbonne cracked the ice of my self-noughting and I began to raise a tentative hand from my huddle in the back of the room and ask an occasional hesitant question.

Dr. Taubes would answer with great intensity, and soon I found myself asking more questions. One day I was making my way across campus to the bus, when I heard Dr. Taubes addressing me:

"Miss Houston, let me walk with you. You know, you have a most interesting mind."

10　　"Me? I have a *mind?*"

"Yes, your questions are luminous. Now what do you think is the nature of the transvaluation of values in Paul and Nietzsche?"

I felt my mind fall into its usual painful dullness and stammered, "I d-don't know."

"Of course you do!" he insisted. "You couldn't ask the kinds of questions you do without having an unusual grasp of these issues. Now please, once again, what do you think of the transvaluation of values in Paul and Nietzsche? It is important for my reflections that I have your reactions."

"Well," I said, waking up, "if you put it that way, I think . . ."

I was off and running and haven't shut up since.   **15**

Dr. Taubes continued to walk me to the bus throughout that term, always challenging me with intellectually vigorous questions. He attended to me. I existed for him in the "realest" of senses, and because I existed for him I began to exist for myself. Within several weeks my eyesight came back, my spirit bloomed, and I became a fairly serious student, whereas before I had been, at best, a bright show-off.

What I acquired from this whole experience was a tragic sense of life, which balanced my previous enthusiasms. I remain deeply grateful for the attention shown me by Dr. Taubes. He acknowledged me when I most needed it. I was empowered in the midst of personal erosion, and my life has been very different for it. I swore to myself then that whenever I came across someone "going under" or in the throes of disacknowledgment, I would try to reach and acknowledge that person as I had been acknowledged.

I would go so far as to say that the greatest of human potentials is the potential of each one of us to empower and acknowledge the other. We all do this throughout our lives, but rarely do we appreciate the power of the empowering that we give to others. To be acknowledged by another, especially during times of confusion, loss, disorientation, disheartenment, is to be given time and place in the sunshine and is, in the metaphor of psychological reality, the solar stimulus for transformation.

The process of healing and growth is immensely quickened when the sun of another's belief is freely given. This gift can be as simple as "Hot Dog Thou Art!" Or it can be as total as "I know you. You are God in hiding." Or it can be a look that goes straight to the soul and charges it with meaning.

I have been fortunate to have known several of those the world deems   **20** "saints": Teilhard de Chardin, Mother Teresa of Calcutta, Clemie, an old black woman in Mississippi. To be looked at by these people is to be gifted with the look that engenders. You feel yourself primed at the depths by such seeing. Something so tremendous and yet so subtle wakes up inside that you are able to release the defeats and denigrations of years. If I were to describe it further, I would have to speak of unconditional love joined to a whimsical regarding of you as the cluttered house that hides the holy one.

Saints, you say, but the miracle is that anybody can do it for anybody! Our greatest genius may be the ability to prime the healing and evolutionary circuits of one another.

It is an art form that has yet to be learned, for it is based on something never before fully recognized—deep psychological reciprocity, the art and science of mutual transformation. And all the gurus and masters, all the prophets, profs, and professionals, can do little for us compared to what we could do for each other if we would but be present to the fullness of each other. For there is no answer to anyone's anguished cry of "Why am I here, why am I at all?" except the reply, "Because I am here, because I am."

REFLECTING AND INTERPRETING

1. Notice the title. *Acknowledgement* is not commonly used in this way. What word would you use instead?

2. In the second paragraph, Houston says she was in a state of "galloping chutzpah." What does she mean?

3. Houston says, "I felt like Job and called out to God, 'Where are the boils?'" (See Job 2:1–10.) What do Houston's comparison and question reveal?

4. In the third paragraph, there is a sudden change in tone. What does Houston mean when she refers to hubris? Does this passage remind you of an old saying? (See Proverbs 16:18.) How does this proverb apply to Houston?

5. What do you think she means when she says, "I existed for him in the 'realest' of senses, and because I existed for him I began to exist for myself"? How does Dr. Taubes's attention affect Houston?

6. Houston says, "I acquired . . . a tragic sense of life, which balanced my previous enthusiasms" (paragraph 17). Can you explain this idea in your own words?

7. How would you describe Houston's attitude as she looks back on this troubling experience? Does she retain a sense of humor? Find examples to support your claim.

8. Notice Houston's alternating of colloquialisms with literary allusions. For example, what is the effect of "wowing" and "on top of the heap" in one paragraph and "hubris" and "nemesis" in another?

9. Note how she contrasts the "before and after" at several points. What is the effect of these contrasts as opposed to a simple chronological narrative?

10. Comment on Houston's last statement, which seems puzzling and somewhat contradictory to the ideas expressed in the essay.

A WRITER'S RESPONSE

Have you ever undergone a distressing experience and been helped by someone? Or perhaps you have been able to "prime the healing and evolutionary circuits" of someone. Describe what happened in an essay.

ASSEMBLY LINE ADVENTURE   LESLEY HAZELTON

Lesley Hazelton graduated from Manchester University (England) in 1966 with a BA Honors in psychology. She moved to Jerusalem, where she resided for thirteen years and earned an MA in psychology at Hebrew University. In 1979 she moved to the United States, becoming a citizen in 1994. She has worked as a reporter, teacher, counselor, reviewer, columnist, and contributing editor of *Harper's*, *Lear's*, and *Self*. Her writing has been published in numerous magazines, newspapers, and anthologies. Her many books include *Israeli Women: The Reality Behind the Myths* (1978), *In Defense of Depression* (1984), *Jezebel: The Untold Story of the Bible's Harlot Queen* (2007), and *Driving to Detroit: An Automotive Odyssey* (1998), from which the following excerpt is taken.

I'd toured many auto plants before, and physically this was not much 1 different. That is, it was an assault on the senses: an enclosed, windowless world of harsh artificial light and hard concrete floors ringing with the discordant cacophony of industrial production. Metal rang on metal. Stamping presses clanked, power tools whined, pulleys groaned, hoists clanged, welding robots whooshed, sparks crackled, lasers beeped, compressed air hissed, bolts banged into place, trolleys rumbled down the aisles, and all the while, conveyor belts carrying cars in one stage or another of production, from bare metal frames to fully painted bodies, clattered and clanketed beside us and behind us and even over our heads.

At five in the afternoon, I started work, joining three other workers stationed around a huge rotating machine. Our job was to feed a robot.

Officially, we were preparing dashboard molds for foam injection. In fact, we were simply loading and unloading the machine for the robot, which injected the foam and then wiped its own nozzle as though it were wiping its nose—one of those infuriatingly human gestures that make you think, "Cute," and then hate yourself for having thought it.

This was one of the simplest tasks on the whole assembly line. Squirt some filler release into a hole. Lift a light plastic mold and place it on a protruding lip of the machine. Bang a board with your knee to drop three locks to hold the mold in place. Check the locks. Push a black button to bring the lip down into the right position for the next guy. Wait for the machine to rotate and present you with a new lip. And that was it. A ten-second job to be repeated ad infinitum.

Two hours later, I moved from one of the simplest jobs on the line to one 5 of the most complicated: assembling the whole instrument panel. Steering wheel, indicator and wiper wands, gauges, dashboard line, the lot.

Audrey, the woman whose task it was to teach me this job, had a tough challenge ahead of her.

I guessed she was in her mid-thirties. Despite a mass of long brown curly hair, she had a boyish way to her, maybe because of the leather builder's apron she was wearing, its pockets so full of connectors and screws and bolts that it took me a while to realize she was six months pregnant.

"Is this your first?" I asked.

She burst out laughing. "Honey, I'm forty-three years old. And a grandmother. I married again not long ago, and"—she spread her arms wide and stared at her belly—"just look what happened. This sure is the last thing I ever expected."

"How long will you go on working?" 10

She laughed again. "Do you know how much kids cost? I'm staying right here till the day I pop."

She hadn't stopped working for a moment as we talked. She couldn't. The line was rolling, and it was either keep up or bring everything to a halt. We were standing *on* the line, a wide conveyor belt rumbling past an array of shelves piled high with parts, and beneath an overhead rack dangling power tools and bins of screws. On the line with us, every six feet or so, was a workstand holding an empty dashboard shell, placed upside down on the stand so that it was easy to work on. Audrey's job was to make it into a complete instrument panel.

For the first few moments, standing on the moving belt was almost childishly fun. The world was reversed: you stood still and it went past you. Your mind knew it was you moving, not the world, but your senses told you otherwise. And all the time, the belt vibrated gently underfoot; if it weren't for the noise, it might even have been pleasantly sexy.

"Watch your head," Audrey said, and I ducked as a power wrench came dangling past my right ear. Followed by another. And yet another. Even though I reminded myself that it was me moving, not them, every time I looked up they seemed to be aiming for my brains with a certain in-
15 exorable malevolence.

I spent the first half-hour watching Audrey and figuring out how to stay out of the way. So far as I could make out, she had a total of some fifty separate procedures to complete in a logic-defying sequence of about three minutes. Each step had to be performed in perfect timing, so that the right parts and tools were at hand exactly when she needed them. And to add to the pressure, this job was what they called a "show-stopper."

Farther on down the line, the completed instrument panel would be lowered into the "smile joint"—a large lazy U going from side to side of the car's frame. If it didn't fit, the line would stop, and the whole plant would start running behind. "You can't go back and do it again," Audrey said. "You got to do it perfect the first time."

I knew I'd never be able to do this job. Yet Audrey seemed convinced that I was educable. She talked each movement out loud as she worked, with me following her around like a pet dog. Somehow, she convinced me to do a bit here and a bit there, until within an hour, I had the beginning of it down pat:

Walk six stands down the line, past other team members at different stages of the job, and read the manifest hanging on the dashboard shell. Pick up different parts from the shelves alongside the line, depending on whether this is to be a sedan or a wagon, an automatic or a manual shift. Jam a leather sheath over the sharp metal edge to the side of the module. Ease the parts into place. Snap-connect electrical wires: gray to the right, blue to the middle, white to the left.

So far so good. I was feeling quite proud of myself. Trouble was, this
20 was only the beginning of the beginning.

The rest began to blur: Snap-connect a black fastener, then a yellow one. Don't delay. If you go too slow, the line will take you past the parts you need, and you'll have to start running back and forth for them. Pick up the steering shaft from a shelf and ease its thirty-pound weight down through the center of the module. Arrange the wires to run over the top of the shaft. Slip on and snap a green fastener . . .

Or were those last two steps the other way round? "Here," said Audrey, redoing my work.

Okay, now pick up two bronze-colored bolts and screws, two black bolts, a circular piece, and two silver bolts from those big bins alongside the line. Insert the silver bolts. Fine. Place the bronze-colored ones in one place, the black ones in another. Great. Pull down a power wrench from the overhead line . . .

I grabbed for it and missed. It began to recede from me. I stretched and yanked it down just in time to tighten the bolts. I had no idea of what I was bolting to what, or why. Neither, it turned out, did Audrey.

Right, you've got those bolts nice and tight. Now pick different bronze-colored bolts from another bin. No, not alongside the line—right here, hanging overhead. Fine. Insert them and tighten them by hand for now. What about the wrench? Not there yet, that comes soon. First, thread the electrical wires through the back of the module and out through this flap, then loop them over and under the shaft like so, and then . . . 25

Then what? I couldn't remember. And I was only a third of the way through the job.

"Don't worry," said Audrey. "It takes most people four days to learn this job. You're doing real good."

That was sweet of her, but it didn't feel real good to me. My attention strayed for a moment, I lost a beat, and suddenly the power tools and screw bins were bearing down on me way before I was ready for them. I worked as fast as I could, one eye on my hands, the other on the dangling wrench going past. I swore, lunged for it, and yanked at the cord as though if I pulled hard enough I could pull back the whole line and slow things down to my pace. I remembered Charlie Chaplin's desperation in *Modern Times,* and suddenly there was nothing remotely funny about it. I dropped a bolt, reached for the wrong wrench, and watched pathetically as Audrey stepped in and put everything to rights. I hadn't felt quite this incompetent since I was a kid trying to thread a sewing machine at school. I never did master that.

Every time I thought I had the hang of it all, another two steps somehow reversed themselves in my mind, or one slipped out of existence altogether. My ears were ringing, my mind was reeling, and my hands had never felt clumsier. I began to fumble the screws, inserting them at an angle so that they wouldn't tighten properly and had to be taken out and inserted anew. Audrey was working as hard as I was by now; we stood shoulder to shoulder, me fouling things up, her fixing them.

And suddenly it was ten o'clock, and there was a half-hour break for lunch. Ten at night, that is. By now, I was squinting to stop from seeing double. I was convinced that if I could just work through to the end of the shift, I'd get this job down pat. But as the line came to a halt and everything stopped moving, some remote part of my brain managed to signal a weak but just decipherable message that the pressure was getting to me. It was time to call it quits before I damaged a car, or myself, or worse still, some-
30 body else.

"Don't you want some lunch before you go?" said Audrey. But I was too exhausted to even look at food. I needed fresh air. And solitude. And silence. I made my excuses, stuffed my yellow Kevlar gloves into my pocket as a memento, got lost twice trying to find the way out, and finally emerged into the parking lot.

Never had a parking lot seemed so beautiful: so quiet, so peaceful, so serene. Even the buzzing yellow of the sodium vapor lights seemed soothing. Behind me, the plant hummed gently, its skylights glowing into the night. Midshift, I was the only person out here, and I had a flash of guilt mixed with giddy freedom, the kind that comes from playing hooky.

I found the truck, climbed in, made to start it up. Then stopped, hand in midair, and sat staring at the instrument panel. Something was wrong. I took a moment to figure it out: I'd spent the past few hours working on upside-down instrument panels, and now I was seeing this one the right way up.

I reached out and examined it for its component parts, thinking of the man or the woman who'd put it together, and appreciating the way it had been done. This thing I usually took so for granted that I'd never before paid a moment's attention to it, was now an astounding piece of man-made—woman-made—complexity.

I started the truck and drove slowly out of the lot, wondering how long I'd keep this awareness that cars are not merely machines, but things put together by human beings, products of real men and real women doing the kind of work that would drive most people crazy. Not long enough, for sure.

REFLECTING AND INTERPRETING

1. Describe the tone and expectations the title sets up.
2. What do you notice about most of the verbs in paragraph 1? What impression do they create?
3. Consider the sentence structure of paragraph 4. How does the sentence structure reflect the nature of the job?
4. What is your impression of Audrey?
5. Why is her job called a "show-stopper"?
6. Describe the difference in Audrey's attitude toward teaching the job and the author's attitude in learning the job.

7. How would you describe Audrey's work ethic?

8. See paragraphs 20, 21, 23, 28, and 30. What kinds of problems did the author experience?

9. Reread the first three lines of the author's background. Do you see any reason she might have difficulty performing this complex job on the automotive assembly line?

10. How would you describe the author's work ethic? Should the fact that she worked just one-half of a shift influence your opinion? Why or why not?

A WRITER'S RESPONSE

1. Have you ever worked at a job you did not like? How long did you work there? Explain your impressions in a paragraph or two.

2. Have you ever worked at a summer job or any other that you enjoyed? What features made the job enjoyable? Describe your experience there.

Describing for a Purpose

THE BARRIO   ROBERT RAMIREZ

Robert Ramirez, born in 1949, graduated from the University of Texas–Pan American. He has a varied work history: freshman composition instructor, reporter, photographer, salesman, fund-raiser, and CBS anchor man. The following essay, formerly titled "The Woolen Serape" and published in *Pain and Promise: The Chicano Today*, provides a sense of community that exists in this "refuge from . . . the Anglo world."

1   The train, its metal wheels squealing as they spin along the silvery tracks, rolls slower now. Through the gaps between the cars blinks a streetlamp, and this pulsing light on a barrio streetcorner beats slower, like a weary heartbeat, until the train shudders to a halt, the light goes out, and the barrio is deep asleep.

Throughout Aztlán (the Nahuatl term meaning "land to the north"), trains grumble along the edges of a sleeping people. From Lower California, through the blistering Southwest, down the Rio Grande to the muddy Gulf, the darkness and mystery of dreams engulf communities fenced off by railroads, canals, and expressways. Paradoxical communities, isolated from the rest of the town by concrete columned monuments of progress, and yet stranded in the past. They are surrounded by change. It eludes their reach, in their own backyards, and the people, unable and unwilling to see the future, or even touch the present, perpetuate the past.

Leaning from the expressway or jolting across the tracks, one enters a different physical world permeated by a different attitude. The physical dimensions are impressive. It is a large section of town which extends for fifteen blocks north and south along the tracks, and then advances east-ward, thinning into nothingness beyond the city limits. Within the invisi-ble (yet sensible) walls of the barrio are many, many people living in too few houses. The homes, however, are much more numerous than on the outside.

Members of the barrio describe the entire area as their home. It is a home, but it is more than this. The barrio is a refuge from the harshness and the coldness of the Anglo world. It is a forced refuge. The leprous peo-ple are isolated from the rest of the community and contained in their sec-tion of town. The stoical pariahs of the barrio accept their fate, and from the angry seeds of rejection grow the flowers of closeness between out-casts, not the thorns of bitterness and the mad desire to flee. There is no want to escape, for the feeling of the barrio is known only to its inhabitants, and the material needs of life can also be found here.

The *tortillería* [tortilla factory] fires up its machinery three times a day, 5 producing steaming, round, flat slices of barrio bread. In the winter, the warmth of the tortilla factory is a wool *sarape* [blanket] in the chilly morning hours, but in the summer, it unbearably toasts every noontime customer.

The *panadería* [bakery] sends its sweet messenger aroma down the dimly lit street, announcing the arrival of fresh, hot sugary *pan dulce* [sweet rolls].

The small corner grocery serves the meal-to-meal needs of customers, and the owner, a part of the neighborhood, willingly gives credit to people unable to pay cash for foodstuffs.

The barbershop is a living room with hydraulic chairs, radio, and tele-vision, where old friends meet and speak of life as their salted hair falls aimlessly about them.

The pool hall is a junior level country club where *'chucos* [young men], strangers in their own land, get together to shoot pool and tap, while vet-erans, unaware of the cracking, popping balls on the green felt, compla-cently play dominoes beneath rudely hung *Playboy* foldouts.

The *cantina* [canteen or snackbar] is the night spot of the barrio. It is 10 the country club and the den where the rites of puberty are enacted. Here the young become men. It is in the taverns that a young dude shows his *machismo* through the quantity of beer he can hold, the stories of *rucas* [women] he has had, and his willingness and ability to defend his image against hardened and scarred old lions.

No, there is no frantic wish to flee. It would be absurd to leave the fa-miliar and nervously step into the strange and cold Anglo community when the needs of the Chicano can be met in the barrio.

The barrio is closeness. From the family living unit, familial relation-ships stretch out to immediate neighbors, down the block, around the cor-ner, and to all parts of the barrio. The feeling of family, a rare and treasur-able sentiment, pervades and accounts for the inability of the people to leave. The barrio is this attitude manifested on the countenances of the people, on the faces of their homes, and in the gaiety of their gardens.

The color-splashed homes arrest your eyes, arouse your curiosity, and make you wonder what life scenes are being played out in them. The flimsy, brightly colored, wood-frame houses ignore no neon-brilliant color. Houses trimmed in orange, chartreuse, lime-green, yellow, and mixtures of these and other hues beckon the beholder to reflect on the peculiarity of each home. Passing through this land is refreshing like Brubeck, not narcoticizing like revolting rows of similar houses, which neither offend nor please.

In the evenings, the porches and front yards are occupied with men calmly talking over the noise of children playing baseball in the unpaved extension of the living room, while the women cook supper or gossip with female neighbors as they water the *jardines* [gardens]. The gardens mutely echo the expressive verses of the colorful houses. The denseness of multicolored plants and trees gives the house the appearance of an oasis or a tropical island hideaway, sheltered from the rest of the world.

15   Fences are common in the barrio, but they are fences and not the walls of the Anglo community. On the western side of town, the high wooden fences between houses are thick, impenetrable walls, built to keep the neighbors at bay. In the barrio, the fences may be rusty, wire contraptions or thick green shrubs. In either case you can see through them and feel no sense of intrusion when you cross them.

Many lower-income families of the barrio manage to maintain a comfortable standard of living through the communal action of family members who contribute their wages to the head of the family. Economic need creates interdependence and closeness. Small bare-footed boys sell papers on cool, dark Sunday mornings, deny themselves pleasantries, and give their earnings to *mamá.* The older the child, the greater the responsibility to help the head of the household provide for the rest of the family.

There are those, too, who for a number of reasons have not achieved a relative sense of financial security. Perhaps it results from too many children too soon, but it is the homes of these people and their situation that numbs rather than charms. Their houses, aged and bent, oozing children, are fissures in the horn of plenty. Their wooden homes may have brick-pattern asbestos tile on the outer walls, but the tile is not convincing.

Unable to pay city taxes or incapable of influencing the city to live up to its duty to serve all the citizens, the poorer barrio families remain trapped in the nineteenth century and survive as best they can. The backyards have well-worn paths to the outhouses, which sit near the alley. Running water is considered a luxury in some parts of the barrio. Decent drainage is usually unknown, and when it rains, the water stands for days, an incubator of health hazards and an avoidable nuisance. Streets, costly to pave, remain rough, rocky trails. Tires do not last long, and the constant rattling and shaking grind away a car's life and spread dust through screen windows.

The houses and their *jardines,* the jollity of the people in an adverse world, the brightly feathered alarm clock pecking away at supper and cautiously eyeing the children playing nearby, produce a mystifying sensation at finding the noble savage alive in the twentieth century. It is easy to look at the positive qualities of life in the barrio, and look at them with a distantly envious feeling. One wishes to experience the feelings of the barrio and not the hardships. Remembering the illness, the hunger, the feeling of time running out on you, the walls, both real and imagined, reflecting on living in the past, one finds his envy becoming more elusive, until it has vanished altogether.

Back now beyond the tracks, the train creaks and groans, the cars jostle each other down the track, and as the light begins its pulsing, the barrio, with all its meanings, greets a new dawn with yawns and restless stretchings. **20**

REFLECTING AND INTERPRETING

1. What do you notice about paragraph 1? Describe the effect created by the concrete images.

2. What literary devices do you see in paragraph 1?

3. How does paragraph 2 differ from paragraph 1? (Hint: Think about the perspective.)

4. How has the physical location and the dense housing affected the people of the barrio?

5. Which paragraphs remind you of a former era in the Anglo world?

6. What is *machismo*?

7. In what way do fences become a symbol in this essay (paragraph 15)? Do you think this generalization is accurate or overstated?

8. How do low-income families of the barrios survive? How would you describe their work ethic?

9. Describe the conflict the author experiences in viewing the barrio.

10. What device links the final paragraph to the opening paragraph?

A WRITER'S RESPONSE

How has the place you were born and raised influenced your perspective? Have you lived in another place that has had a significant influence on your life? Write an essay describing the effect of a place on you. Give examples.

CATERPILLAR AFTERNOON   SUE HUBBELL

Sue Hubbell is a naturalist, a commercial beekeeper, who lives in the Ozark Mountains. She is the author of numerous books, including *A Book of Bees* (1988), *On This Hilltop* (1991), *Far-Flung Hubbell: Essays from the American Road* (1997), *Waiting for Aphrodite* (2000), *Shrinking the Cat* (2001), and *From Here to There and Back Again* (2005). One day as Hubbell was walking down a dusty country road, she spied what appeared to be a snakeskin lying in the road. Curious, she bent down and saw, instead, a strange procession of maggoty-like caterpillars. This essay, "Caterpillar Afternoon," from *A Country Year* (1999), illustrates one way primary and secondary research can be combined.

1   A year ago, on an afternoon late in springtime, I was walking on the dirt road that cuts across the field to the beehives. I noticed a light-colored, brownish dappled something-or-other stretched across the roadway ahead of me, and decided that it was a snakeskin. I often find them, crumpled husks shed by snakes as they grow. They are fragile and delicate, perfect but empty replicas of the snakes that once inhabited them. I started to turn it over with the toe of my boot, but stopped suddenly, toe in air, for the flecked, crumpled-looking empty snakeskin was moving.

It gave me quite a start and I was amused at my own reaction, remembering that Ronald Firbank wrote somewhere that the essence of evil was the ordinary become unnatural, the stone in the garden path that suddenly begins to move.

I squatted down to see what queer thing I had here, and found that my supposed snake skin was a mass of maggoty-like caterpillars, each one no more than half an inch long. They were hairless, with creamy white smooth skin, black heads and brown stripes along their backs. They were piled thickly in the center, with fewer caterpillars at the head and rear end of the line, which was perhaps eighteen inches long. They moved slowly, each caterpillar in smooth synchrony with its fellows, so that a wave of motion undulated down the entire length of the line.

They seemed so intensely social that I wondered what they would do on their own. I gently picked up half a dozen or so, and isolated them a few inches from the column. Their smooth, easy movements changed to frantic, rapid ones, and they wriggled along the ground quickly until they rejoined the group. They certainly were good followers. How did they ever decide where to go? The single caterpillar in the lead twisted the forepart of his body from side to side as though taking his bearings; he appeared to be the only one in the lot capable of going in a new direction, of making a decision to avoid a tuft of grass here, of turning there. Was he some special, super-caterpillar? I removed him from the lead position and put him off to the side, where he became as frantic as had the others, wriggling to rejoin the group somewhere in the middle, where he was soon lost to view, having turned into just another follower. At the head, the next caterpillar in line had simply assumed leadership duties and was bending his body from side to side, making the decision about the direction the column was to take. I removed three leaders in a row with the same result: each time, the next caterpillar in line made an instant switch from loyal and will-less follower to leader.

5   What were they doing? Were they looking for food? If so, what kind? What manner of creature were they? The beework that I had set out to do could wait no longer, so I went back to the hives. When I returned along the road, the caterpillars, if that is what they were, had disappeared.

Back in my cabin, none of the books on my shelves were much help explaining what I had seen, except one by Henri Fabre, the nineteenth-century French entomologist who had conducted one of his famous experiments with pine processionaries, one of the Thaumatopoeidae. Fabre's caterpillars were *Thaumatopoea processionea*, "the wonder maker that parades"; eventually they become rather undistinguished-looking moths.

The pine processionaries are a European species, but their behavior was similar to that of my caterpillars, although not identical. Pine processionaries travel to feed in single file, not massed and bunched, but they do touch head to rear and have only one leader at a time. Fabre found them so sheeplike that he wondered what they would do if he could somehow manage to make them leaderless. In a brilliant experiment, he arranged them on the upper rim of a large vase a yard and a half in circumference, and waited until the head end of the procession joined the tail end, so that the entire group was without a leader. All were followers. For seven days, the caterpillars paraded around the rim of the vase in a circle. Their pace slowed after a while, for they were weary and had not been able to feed, but they continued to circle, each caterpillar unquestioningly taking his direction from the rear of the one in front, until they dropped from exhaustion. However, even Fabre never discovered what it was that could turn one caterpillar into a leader as soon as he was at the head of the line.

It was not until several months later, when I was talking to Asher, that I was able to find out anything about the caterpillars I had found in the roadway. He said that I probably had seen one species or another of sawfly larvae. They are gregarious, he told me, and some are whitish with brown stripes. Sure identification could only be made by counting the pairs of their prolegs, and of course I had not known enough to look at them that closely. Asher said that they were a rare sight and that I would probably never see them again, but if I did I should gather up a few and put them in a solution of 70 percent alcohol; then he would help me identify them. He had read about Fabre's experiment too, but knew nothing more about their behavior.

He added, "If you ever find out what makes processionary caterpillars prosesh, please enlighten me. Maybe it's the same thing that makes people drive in Sunday traffic or watch TV or vote Republican."

It is springtime again. I would like to count the caterpillars' prolegs and am prepared to pickle a few to satisfy my curiosity, but mostly I should just like to watch them again. This time I should let the beework go. I should like to know where these caterpillars go, and what it is they are looking for. I wonder if I could divide them up into several small columns that would move along independently, side by side. I have more questions about them than when I first saw them.

This spring I often walk along, eyes to the ground, looking for them. There may have been nobler quests—white whales and Holy Grails—and although the Ahabs and Percivals of my acquaintance are some of my most entertaining friends, I am cut of other stuff and amuse myself in other ways. The search for what may or may not be sawfly larvae seems quite a good one this springtime.

REFLECTING AND INTERPRETING

1. What two strategies of exposition does Hubbell use to explain her research?
2. Note the distinctive way that Hubbell describes the caterpillars. What device does she use in the third sentence?
3. What was unusual about the physical appearance of the caterpillars?
4. What spur-of-the-moment experiments did Hubbell conduct? How did the individual caterpillars react?
5. What paragraph presents the questions that Hubbell wants to research?
6. What transition shifts the reader to the next scene, where Hubbell continues her research?
7. How and when did Hubbell gain more specific information about the kind of caterpillars she had seen? By what name are they tagged?
8. What had Henri Fabre discovered in the nineteenth century about a similar caterpillar?
9. What experiment does Hubbell plan to do if she ever finds more of these strange caterpillars?
10. Do you see any similarities between the behavior of the caterpillars and some people? What kinds of events can cause people to suddenly become leaders?

A WRITER'S RESPONSE

1. Have you ever been thrust into a circumstance where you suddenly had to assume a leadership role? If so, write an essay describing your experience.
2. *Small Groups:* Have you ever seen something that appeared to be something else at first? What does this reveal about the process of perception? Can you list a few precautions to promote objectivity? (After the group is finished, turn to "Checklist: Maintaining Objectivity" on pages 517–18.)

DAWN WATCH   JOHN CIARDI

A renowned poet, essayist, and translator, John Ciardi (1916–86) wrote over fifty books. He received the Prix de Rome of the American Academy of Arts and Letters, the Harriet Monroe Memorial Award, and the NCTE Award for Children's Poetry. He first published a book of poems entitled *Homeward to America* (1940). Two years later he enlisted in the Army Air Force and served with distinction as an aerial tail gunner during World War II. He taught at Harvard and Rutgers; spent twenty years as poetry editor for the *Saturday Review* magazine; wrote children's books, poetry textbooks, and others; and translated *The Divine Com-*

edy and other classic works. Some of his well-known works are *Mid-Century American Poets* (1950), *How Does a Poem Mean* (1959), *Selected Poems* (1984), *Saipan: The War Diary of John Ciardi* (1988), *The Birds of Pompeii* (1988), and *The Selected Letters of John Ciardi* (1991), some of which were published posthumously. In this essay from *Manner of Speaking* (1972), Ciardi praises a magical time of day.

Unless a man is up for the dawn and for the half hour or so of first light, 1
he has missed the best of the day.

The traffic has just started, not yet a roar and a stink. One car at a time goes by, the tires humming almost like the sound of a brook a half mile down in the crease of a mountain I know—a sound that carries not because it is loud but because everything else is still.

It isn't exactly a mist that hangs in the thickets but more nearly the ghost of a mist—a phenomenon like side vision. Look hard and it isn't there, but glance without focusing and something registers, an exhalation that will be gone three minutes after the sun comes over the treetops.

The lawns shine with a dew not exactly dew. There is a rabbit bobbing about on the lawn and then freezing. If it were truly a dew, his tracks would shine black on the grass, and he leaves no visible track. Yet, there is something on the grass that makes it glow a depth of green it will not show again all day. Or is that something in the dawn air?

Our cardinals know what time it is. They drop pure tones from the hem- 5
lock tops. The gang of grackles that makes a slum of the pin oak also knows the time but can only grate at it. They sound like a convention of broken universal joints grating uphill. The grackles creak and squeak, and the cardinals form tones that only occasionally sound through the noise. I scatter sunflower seeds by the birdbaths for the cardinals and hope the grackles won't find them.

My neighbor's tomcat comes across the lawn, probably on his way home from passion, or only acting as if he had had a big night. I suspect him of being one of those poolroom braggarts who can't get next to a girl but who likes to let on that he is a hot stud. This one is too can-fed and too lazy to hunt for anything. Here he comes now, ignoring the rabbit. And there he goes.

As soon as he has hopped the fence, I let my dog out. The dog charges the rabbit, watches it jump the fence, shakes himself in a self-satisfied way, then trots dutifully into the thicket for his morning service, stopping to sniff everything on the way back.

There is an old mountain laurel on the island of the driveway turn-around. From somewhere on the wind a white morning-glory rooted next to it and has climbed it. Now the laurel is woven full of white bells tinged pink by the first rays through the not quite mist. Only in earliest morning can they be seen. Come out two hours from now and there will be no morning-glories.

Dawn, too, is the hour of a weed I know only as day flower—a bright blue button that closes in full sunlight. I have weeded bales of it out of my flower beds, its one daytime virtue being the shallowness of its root system that allows it to be pulled out effortlessly in great handfuls. Yet, now it shines. Had it a few more hours of such shining in its cycle, I would cultivate it as a ground cover, but dawn is its one hour, and a garden is for whole days.

10   There is another blue morning weed whose name I do not know. This one grows from a bulb to pulpy stems and a bedraggled daytime sprawl. Only a shovel will dig it out. Try weeding it by hand and the stems will break off to be replaced by new ones and to sprawl over the chosen plants in the flower bed. Yet, now and for another hour it outshines its betters, its flowers about the size of a quarter and paler than those of the day flower but somehow more brilliant, perhaps because of the contrast of its paler foliage.

And now the sun is slanting in full. It is bright enough to make the leaves of the Japanese red maple seem a transparent red bronze when the tree is between me and the light. There must be others, but this is the only tree I know whose leaves let the sun through in this way—except, that is, when the fall colors start. Aspen leaves, when they first yellow and before they dry, are transparent in this way. I tell myself it must have something to do with the red-yellow range of the spectrum. Green takes sunlight and holds it, but red and yellow let it through.

The damned crabgrass is wrestling with the zinnias, and I stop to weed it out. The stuff weaves too close to the zinnias to make the iron claw usable. And it won't do to pull at the stalks. Crabgrass (at least in a mulched bed) can be weeded only with dirty fingers. Thumb and forefinger have to pincer into the dirt and grab the root-center. Weeding, of course, is an illusion of hope. Pulling out the root only stirs the soil and brings new crabgrass seeds into germinating position. Take a walk around the block and a new clump will have sprouted by the time you get back. But I am not ready to walk around the block. I fill a small basket with the plucked clumps, and for the instant I look at them, the zinnias are weedless.

Don't look back. I dump the weeds in the thicket where they will be smothered by the grass clippings I will pile on at the next cutting. On the way back I see the cardinals come down for the sunflower seeds, and the jays join them, and then the grackles start ganging in, gatecrashing the buffet and clattering all over it. The dog stops chewing his rawhide and makes a dash into the puddle of birds, which splashes away from him.

I hear a brake-squeak I have been waiting for and know the paper has arrived. As usual, the news turns out to be another disaster count. The function of the wire services is to bring us tragedies faster than we can pity. In the end we shall all be inured, numb, and ready for emotionless programming. I sit on the patio and read until the sun grows too bright on the page. The cardinals have stopped singing, and the grackles have flown off. It's the end of birdsong again.

Then suddenly—better than song for its instant—a hummingbird the **15** color of green crushed velvet hovers in the throat of my favorite lily, a lovely high-bloomer I got the bulbs for but not the name. The lily is a crest of white horns with red dots and red velvet tongues along the insides of the petals and with an odor that drowns the patio. The hummingbird darts in and out of each horn in turn, then hovers an instant, and disappears.

Even without the sun, I have had enough of the paper. I'll take that hummingbird as my news for this dawn. It is over now. I smoke one more cigarette too many and decide that, if I go to bed now, no one in the family need know I have stayed up for it again. Why do they insist on shaking their heads when they find me still up for breakfast, after having scribbled through the dark hours? They always do. They seem compelled to express pity for an old loony who can't find his own way to bed. Why won't they understand that this is the one hour of any day that must not be missed, as it is the one hour I couldn't imagine getting up for, though I can still get to it by staying up? It makes sense to me. There comes a time when the windows lighten and the twittering starts. I look up and know it's time to leave the papers in their mess. I could slip quietly into bed and avoid the family's headshakes, but this stroll-around first hour is too good to miss. Even my dog, still sniffing and circling, knows what hour this is.

Come on, boy. It's time to go in. The rabbit won't come back till tomorrow, and the birds have work to do. The dawn's over. It's time to call it a day.

REFLECTING AND INTERPRETING

1. Ciardi's essay has an argumentative edge that is apparent in his thesis statement. Where is it?

2. What is the dominant impression of "Dawn Watch"?

3. Can you find similes?

4. Can you find an example of personification?

5. Throughout the essay, Ciardi's carefully chosen words create sensory descriptions that convey an essence of the scene. How many types of appeals to the senses can you find?

6. What is the primary order used to organize details?

7. Ciardi alternates subjectivity with objectivity at times in his description. Can you find examples of each?

8. Instead of presenting only beautiful images of the morning, Ciardi pairs negative images with positive ones and presents other unusual contrasts. What are the effects?

9. Does Ciardi make his reversed schedule seem logical? Has he supplied enough support for his claim to be convincing? Give reasons for your answer.

10. Describe the voice of the writer. Where does he seem to be poking fun at himself?

A WRITER'S RESPONSE

1. Whether you agree or disagree with Ciardi's belief that early morning is the best time of all may depend upon whether you are a "lark" or "night owl." What time of day or night do you like best? Why?

2. List favorite spots where you can be alone. Focus on one and freewrite about the atmosphere there, incorporating as many sights, sounds, and other sensory images as possible. Next add a chronological structure, similar to Ciardi's, describing the "events" of a typical visit from beginning to end. How does the passing of time affect what happens there? What time of day is best? Rewrite your draft into a revised essay.

INTERVIEW FROM *WORKING*   STUDS TERKEL

Louis "Studs" Terkel, born in 1912, obtained a law degree from the University of Chicago in 1934 but never practiced law. Instead, he became a radio broadcaster and an award-winning author. He has written more than a dozen books, including ten oral histories, based on interviews with ordinary people. One, *The Good War* [WWII] earned the 1985 Pulitzer Prize. In *Working* (1972), Terkel asks people from many occupations "what they do all day and how they feel about what they do." In this interview Delores Dante reveals a strong commitment to the work ethic.

Dolores Dante

1   She has been a waitress in the same restaurant for twenty-three years. Many of its patrons are credit card carriers on an expense account—conventioneers, politicians, labor leaders, agency people. Her hours are from 5:00 p.m. to 2:00 a.m. six days a week. She arrives earlier "to get things ready, the silverware, the butter. When people come in and ask for you, you would like to be in a position to handle them all, because that means more money for you.

"I became a waitress because I needed money fast and you don't get it in an office. My husband and I broke up and he left me with debts and three children. My baby was six months. The fast buck, your tips.

I have to be a waitress. How else can I learn about people? How else does the world come to me? I can't go to everyone. So they have to come to me. Everyone wants to eat, everyone has hunger. And I serve them. If they've had a bad day, I nurse them, cajole them. Maybe with coffee I give them a little philosophy. They have cocktails, I give them political science.

I'll say things that bug me. If they manufacture soap, I say what I think about pollution. If it's automobiles, I say what I think about them. If I pour water I'll say, "Would you like your quota of mercury today?" If I serve cream, I say, "Here is your substitute. I think you're drinking plastic." I just can't keep quiet. I have an opinion on every single subject there is. In the beginning it was theology, and my bosses didn't like it. Now I am a political and my bosses don't like it. I speak *sotto voce.* But if I get heated, then I don't give a damn. I speak like an Italian speaks. I can't be servile. I give service. There is a difference.

I'm called by my first name. I like my name. I hate to be called Miss. **5** Even when I serve a lady, a strange woman, I will not say madam. I hate ma'am. I always say milady. In the American language there is no word to address a woman, to indicate whether she's married or unmarried. So I say milady. And sometimes I playfully say to the man milord.

It would be very tiring if I had to say, "Would you like a cocktail?" and say that over and over. So I come out different for my own enjoyment. I would say, "What's exciting at the bar that I can offer?" I can't say, "Do you want coffee?" Maybe I'll say, "Are you in the mood for coffee?" Or, "The coffee sounds exciting." Just rephrase it enough to make it interesting for me. That would make them take an interest. It becomes theatrical and I feel like Mata Hari and it intoxicates me.

People imagine a waitress couldn't possibly think or have any kind of aspiration other than to serve food. When somebody says to me, "You're great, how come you're *just* a waitress?" *Just* a waitress. I'd say, "Why, don't you think you deserve to be served by me?" It's implying that he's not worthy, not that I'm not worthy. It makes me irate. I don't feel lowly at all. I myself feel sure. I don't want to change the job. I love it.

Tips? I feel like Carmen. It's like a gypsy holding out a tambourine and they throw the coin. (Laughs.) If you like people, you're not thinking of the tips. I never count my money at night. I always wait till morning. If I thought about my tips I'd be uptight. I never look at a tip. You pick it up fast. I would do my bookkeeping in the morning. It would be very dull for me to know I was making so much and no more. I do like challenge. And it isn't de-meaning, not for me.

There might be occasions when the customers might intend to make it demeaning—the man about town, the conventioneer. When the time comes to pay the check, he would do little things, "How much should I give you?" He might make an issue about it. I did say to one, "Don't play God with me. Do what you want." Then it really didn't matter whether I got a tip or not. I would spit it out, my resentment—that he dares make me feel I'm operating only for a tip.

He'd ask for his check. Maybe he's going to sign it. He'd take a very long **10** time and he'd make me stand there, "Let's see now, what do you think I ought to give you?" He would not let go of that moment. And you knew it. You know he meant to demean you. He's holding the change in his hand, or if he'd sign, he'd flourish the pen and wait. These are the times I really get angry. I'm not reticent. Something would come out. Then I really didn't care.

There are conventioneers, who leave their lovely wives or their bad wives. They approach you and say, "Are there any hot spots?" "Where can I find girls?" It is, of course, first directed at you. I don't mean that as a com-pliment, 'cause all they're looking for is females. They're not looking for companionship or conversation. I am quite adept at understanding this. I think I'm interesting enough that someone may just want to talk to me. But I would philosophize that way. After all, what is left after you talk? The hours have gone by and I could be home resting or reading or studying guitar, which I do on occasion. I would say, "What are you going to offer me? Drinks?" And I'd point to the bar, "I have it all here." He'd look blank and then I'd say, "A man? If I need a man, wouldn't you think I'd have one of my own? Must I wait for you?"

Life doesn't frighten me any more. There are only two things that relegate us—the bathroom and the grave. Either I'm gonna have to go to the bathroom now or I'm gonna die now. I go to the bathroom.

And I don't have a high opinion of bosses. The more popular you are, the more the boss holds it over your head. You're bringing them business, but he knows you're getting good tips and you won't leave. You have to worry not to overplay it, because the boss becomes resentful and he uses this as a club over your head.

If you become too good a waitress, there's jealousy. They don't come in and say, "Where's the boss?" They'll ask for Dolores. It doesn't make a hit. That makes it rough. Sometimes you say, Aw hell, why am I trying so hard? I did get an ulcer. Maybe the things I kept to myself were twisting me.

15   It's not the customers, never the customers. It's injustice. My dad came from Italy and I think of his broken English—*injoost.* He hated injustice. If you hate injustice for the world, you hate more than anything injustice toward you. Loyalty is never appreciated, particularly if you're the type who doesn't like small talk and are not the type who makes reports on your fellow worker. The boss wants to find out what is going on surreptitiously. In our society today you have informers everywhere. They've informed on cooks, on coworkers. "Oh, someone wasted this." They would say I'm talking to all the customers. "I saw her carry such-and-such out. See if she wrote that on her check." "The salad looked like it was a double salad." I don't give anything away. I just give myself. Informers will manufacture things in order to make their job worthwhile. They're not sure of themselves as workers. There's always someone who wants your station, who would be pretender to the crown. In life there is always someone who wants somebody's job.

I'd get intoxicated with giving service. People would ask for me and I didn't have enough tables. Some of the girls are standing and don't have customers. There is resentment. I feel self-conscious. I feel a sense of guilt. It cramps my style. I would like to say to the customer, "Go to so-and-so." But you can't do that, because you feel a sense of loyalty. So you would rush, get to your customers quickly. Some don't care to drink and still they wait for you. That's a compliment.

There is plenty of tension. If the cook isn't good, you fight to see that the customers get what you know they like. You have to use diplomacy with cooks, who are always dangerous. (Laughs.) They're madmen. (Laughs.) You have to be their friend. They better like you. And your bartender better like you too, because he may do something to the drink. If your bartender doesn't like you, your cook doesn't like you, your boss doesn't like you, the other girls don't like you, you're in trouble.

And there will be customers who are hypochondriacs, who feel they can't eat, and I coax them. Then I hope I can get it just the right way from the cook. I may mix the salad myself, just the way they want it.

Maybe there's a party of ten. Big shots, and they'd say, "Dolores, I have special clients, do your best tonight." You just hope you have the right cook behind the broiler. You really want to pleasure your guests. He's selling something, he wants things right, too. You're giving your all. How does the steak look? If you cut his steak, you look at it surreptitiously. How's it going?

Carrying dishes is a problem. We do have accidents. I spilled a tray 20 once with steaks for seven on it. It was a big, gigantic T-bone, all sliced. But when that tray fell, I went with it, and never made a sound, dish and all (softly) never made a sound. It took about an hour and a half to cook that steak. How would I explain this thing? That steak was salvaged. (Laughs.)

Some don't care. When the plate is down you can hear the sound. I try not to have that sound. I want my hands to be right when I serve. I pick up a glass, I want it to be just right. I get to be almost Oriental in the serving. I like it to look nice all the way. To be a waitress, it's an art. I feel like a ballerina, too. I have to go between those tables, between those chairs . . . Maybe that's the reason I always stayed slim. It is a certain way I can go through a chair no one else can do. I do it with an air. If I drop a fork, there is a certain way I pick it up. I know they can see how delicately I do it. I'm on stage.

I tell everyone I'm a waitress and I'm proud. If a nurse gives service, I say, "You're a professional." Whatever you do, be professional. I always compliment people.

I like to have my station looking nice. I like to see there's enough ash trays when they're having their coffee and cigarettes. I don't like ash trays so loaded that people are not enjoying the moment. It offends me. I don't do it because I think that's gonna make a better tip. It offends me as a person.

People say, "No one does good work any more." I don't believe it. You know who's saying that? The man at the top, who says the people beneath him are not doing a good job. He's the one who always said, "You're nothing." The housewife who has all the money, she believed housework was demeaning, 'cause she hired someone else to do it. If it weren't so demeaning, why didn't *she* do it? So anyone who did her housework was a person to be demeaned. The maid who did all the housework said, "Well hell, if this is the way you feel about it, I won't do your housework. You tell me I'm no good, I'm nobody. Well, maybe I'll go out and be somebody." They're only mad because they can't find someone to do it now. The fault is not in the people who did the—quote—lowly work.

Just a waitress. At the end of the night I feel drained. I think a lot of 25 waitresses become alcoholics because of that. In most cases, a waiter or a waitress doesn't eat. They handle food, they don't have time. You'll pick at something in the kitchen, maybe a piece of bread. You'll have a cracker, a little bit of soup. You go back and take a teaspoonful of something. Then maybe sit down afterwards and have a drink, maybe three, four, five. And bartenders, too, most of them are alcoholics. They'd go out in a group. There are after-hour places. You've got to go release your tension. So they go out before they go to bed. Some of them stay out all night.

It's tiring, it's nerve-racking. We don't ever sit down. We're on stage and the bosses are watching. If you get the wrong shoes and you get the wrong stitch in that shoe, that does bother you. Your feet hurt, your body aches. If you come out in anger at things that were done to you, it would only make you feel cheapened. Really I've been keeping it to myself. But of late, I'm beginning to spew it out. It's almost as though I sensed my body and soul had had quite enough.

It builds and builds and builds in your guts. Near crying. I can think about it . . . (She cries softly.) 'Cause you're tired. When the night is done, you're tired. You've had so much, there's so much going . . . You had to get it done. The dread that something wouldn't be right, because you want to please. You hope everyone is satisfied. The night's done, you've done your act. The curtains close.

The next morning is pleasant again. I take out my budget book, write down how much I made, what my bills are. I'm managing. I won't give up this job as long as I'm able to do it. I feel out of contact if I just sit at home. At work they all consider me a kook. (Laughs.) That's okay. No matter where I'd be, I would make a rough road for me. It's just me, and I can't keep still. It hurts, and what hurts has to come out.

REFLECTING AND INTERPRETING

1. In paragraphs 1 through 7 what do you learn about Dolores's attitude?

2. In paragraph 4 she mentions *sotto voce*. What does she mean? What does the use of this phrase reveal about her?

3. Dolores refuses to use the term *madam*, preferring *milady* to address a customer. How do the connotations of the two words differ? (You may use a dictionary.)

4. How do some male customers show power when giving a tip? How does Dolores react?

5. Describe the tension or friction that exists with other employees. How does she handle it?

6. At one point Dolores says she feels "like Carmen" and later "like a ballerina." What duties might lead to these feelings?

7. Dolores says, "We are on stage and the bosses are watching." What might she mean?

8. When a customer demeans her, she shows resentment. But later she says, "If you come out in anger at things that were done to you, it would only make you feel cheapened." How do you account for the differing points of view? Is she talking about something else at the end?

9. Comment on "At work they all consider me a kook."

10. Define "work ethic." How does Dolores reveal her commitment to the work ethic?

A WRITER'S RESPONSE

1. How does Dolores Dante deal with the stereotype of "just a waitress"? How does she make her job interesting? How would you describe her ability to size up customers and coworkers? What are the secrets of her success? Write a description of Dolores as seen through your eyes.

2. Write an essay about your job, paid or unpaid. What do you do and how do you feel about it?

Explaining a Process

FAST TRACK TO PERFECTION — IAN DUNBAR

Veterinarian, animal behaviorist, and dog trainer, Ian Dunbar has attained international renown. A graduate of the Royal Veterinary College (London University), he completed his doctorate at the University of California in Berkeley. He is a columnist, the host of the British television show *Dogs with Dunbar,* and the founder of several dog-training organizations. Dr. Dunbar has given more than 750 seminars and workshops around the globe. He has made over a dozen videos and written numerous books, including *Doctor Dunbar's Good Little Dog Book* and a set of behavior booklets on dog-owner concerns. His *How to Teach a New Dog Old Tricks* and *Sirius Puppy Training* won Best Book and Best Video awards. His dog-friendly training method is based upon "six crucial developmental deadlines." He advocates "off-leash socialization" classes, "lure/reward," and games training for puppies and dogs. In this essay Dr. Dunbar explains how to encourage good habits while training puppies.

1   Puppies mature at an astounding rate. Don't let yours fall behind on the developmental curve. Nearly everything a puppy needs to learn must be taught in 12 weeks—between the ages of 2 and 5 months. You can buy yourself time by knowing what and how to teach the puppy before you bring it home. Go to puppy classes, read behavior and training books, watch instructional videos and consult your veterinarian. Then raise your puppy perfectly by meeting these six training deadlines.

Deadline 1: Before You Bring Home a Puppy

Your puppy should be accustomed to a domestic environment before you bring it home—at around 8 weeks of age. Make sure it has been raised indoors and in close contact with people. It should be prepared for the clamor of everyday life—the noise of the vacuum cleaner, the hoopla surrounding sports programs on the television, children crying, adults arguing. Early exposure—before the pup's eyes and ears have fully opened—allows the puppy to gradually assimilate sights and sounds that otherwise might frighten.

The window for socializing begins to close by the time the pup turns 3 months of age, and its most impressionable learning period starts to fade by its fifth month.

Deadline 2: Puppy's First Day at Home

Misbehavior is the most common reason dogs end up in shelters. This is especially sad because owners can prevent most behavior problems. For instance, if you avoid leaving the pup unsupervised, it won't chew furniture and belongings or soil your house; while teeny accidents do little damage in themselves, they may set a precedent for habits in months to come.

When you cannot watch your pup, confine it to a crate or a puppy-proofed room, which should contain:

- a comfortable bed.
- a bowl of fresh water.
- a doggie toilet placed away from the bed and which simulates the outdoors. Lay down a sheet of linoleum and cover it with a disposable plastic sheet. Next lay newspaper or something absorbent. Top the three layers with dirt or sod to teach the pup to relieve itself on grass (or concrete slabs for city pups that relieve themselves curbside).
- Hollow chew toys with kibble inside to reward your puppy for chewing toys rather than furniture. During its first few weeks at home, a marvelous training ploy is to serve your puppy's food only in chew toys. After it's a chew toy-aholic—and has not had a chewing mishap for at least three months—begin to serve its dinner in a bowl.

At least every hour, release your puppy from its crate, quickly leash it and hurry it to its outdoor toilet area. Stand still and give the pup three minutes to produce. When it does, lavishly praise and offer *three* extra special treats. Freeze-dried liver treats work well because dogs love their strong smell.

If your puppy eliminates, it may be allowed supervised exploration of the house. If it does not eliminate, lead it back to its crate or puppy-proof room and try again in half an hour.

Keep up the once an hour schedule until your pup is at least 3 months old to make certain it never eliminates indoors. After 3 months of age pups start to develop the bladder control necessary for longer waits between potty breaks, but you must still be vigilant. One mistake can set a bad precedent.

Always reward your puppy for using its outdoors toilet area, but wait until it has completed its shots before taking it to public property; otherwise it can pick up other dogs' diseases. A pup must not walk or sniff where other dogs have been until it has developed sufficient immunity (between 3 and 4 months old).

Deadline 3: Puppy at 3 Months

10   By 3 months your pup must master socialization and basic manners. Pups that do not will have a hard time picking up these skills later in life. Unfortunately, the risk of disease means dog-to-dog socialization must wait. Meanwhile, teach your pup to be people-friendly.

As a general rule, your pup should socialize with at least 100 people before it is 3 months old. This is easier than it sounds. Invite eight friends over each Sunday to watch sports on the television. Each Monday invite eight different friends to watch *Ally McBeal* and *Dateline.* Catch up on outstanding social obligations by inviting family, friends and neighbors to weekly puppy parties. On another night, invite some neighborhood children. Socializing a puppy is great because it does wonders for *your* social life.

Show your guests how to hand feed the puppy's kibble to encourage and reward it for coming, sitting and lying down. Ask your puppy to come. Praise profusely as it approaches and offer a piece of kibble when it arrives. Back up, then do it again—and again and again. Then say "Puppy, Sit" and slowly move a piece of kibble from in front of the puppy's nose to between its eyes. As the puppy raises its nose to sniff, it will lower its rear and sit. If the puppy jumps up, you're holding the food too high. When your puppy sits, say "Good dog" and offer the kibble. Now say "Puppy, Down" and lower a piece of kibble from in front of the puppy's nose to between its forepaws. As the puppy lowers its head to follow the food, it will usually lie down. If your puppy stands, hide the kibble in your palm until it lies down. Then say "Good dog" and offer the food. Coach your guests until each can get the puppy to come, sit and lie down three times for a piece of kibble.

When a puppy approaches promptly and happily, it is a sign the dog is people-friendly. Sitting and lying down on request indicates respect for the person issuing instructions. If your puppy is regularly hand-fed by guests, it will learn to enjoy people's company.

Deadline 4: Puppy at 4½ Months

Seemingly overnight, puppies become adolescents. Enroll in a training class before yours is 14 weeks old—that is, before it starts to test your limits. A professional will teach it to stop nipping and other behavior no-no's, as well as temper its hyper-turbo energy.

15   Most puppies can start classes at 3 months. Classrooms are generally safe places; the puppies are vaccinated, the floors regularly sterilized. I advise delaying walks in public places until your puppy is 4 months old because of the risk of disease.

Puppy classes develop canine social savvy through play with other puppies in a controlled setting. Most classes are family-oriented, offering pups opportunities to socialize with all sorts of people—men, women and children. The number of behaviors your pup learns in its first training lesson will amaze you. Shy and fearful pups gain confidence. Bullies tone it down and become gentle. All dogs learn to come, sit and lie down when requested and listen to their owners and ignore distractions.

Deadline 5: Puppy at 5 Months

Take your dog everywhere—errands around town, car trips to visit friends, picnics in the park and especially to explore the neighborhood. And bring a little bag of kibble. Give a couple of pieces to each stranger who wants to meet your dog. Ask each person to offer the kibble only after your pup sits to say hello.

At this point, you may come to believe the canine weight-pulling record exceeds 10,000 pounds. Your dog also may begin to ignore you. A few tips:

- **Make your dog walk for its dinner.** With kibble in hand, stand still and wait for the dog to sit. Ignore everything else your dog does; it will sit eventually. When it does, say "Good dog," offer the kibble, take one giant step forward, stand still and wait for your dog to sit again. Repeat this until your dog sits each time you stop. Now take two giant steps before your stop. Then three steps, five, eight, 10, 20, and so on. *Voilà,* your dog walks calmly and attentively by your side and sits each time you stop.

- **Take a few time-outs on each walk.** Sit down, relax and allow the dog to settle down and watch the world go by. If your pup is not the sit-still type, take along a treat-stuffed chew toy as an incentive.

- **Never take your dog's sound temperament for granted.** Outdoors can be scary and offer the occasional surprise. Give your dog a piece of kibble every time a big truck, noisy motorcycle or child on a skateboard whizzes by and your dog doesn't overreact.

- **Don't make a habit of letting your dog off-leash to run and play with other dogs;** your dog may eventually refuse to come when called. Instead, take your dog's dinner to the park and, throughout its play session, call your dog every minute or so and have it sit for a couple of pieces of kibble. It will soon get the idea and its enthusiastic response will be the talk of the park.

Deadline 6: Now and Forever

Continue walking your dog at least once a day and take it to a dog park several times a week. Find different walks and dog parks to meet a variety of dogs and people. If your dog always sees the same people and dogs, it may regress socially and become intolerant of strangers.

Now enjoy life with your good-natured, well-mannered companion. Give your dog a special bone—Good dog!—and yourself a pat on the back—Good owner!

20

REFLECTING AND INTERPRETING

1. Consider the second sentence. What is its purpose?
2. What is the first step that Dr. Dunbar advocates?
3. What does he mean by the "window of socializing"? When is this?
4. What does he believe about puppy misbehavior?
5. What procedure should you follow to train the puppy in elimination?
6. Why does Dunbar recommend that your dog meet many other people and dogs?
7. What two incentives does Dunbar stress to promote good puppy behavior?
8. At one point he compares puppies to adolescents. Why? What do they need?
9. Consider his ending. How would you rate it? Why?
10. After reading this article, would you adopt a puppy? Why or why not?

A WRITER'S RESPONSE

1. Write an essay giving directions, perhaps for training a horse, a farm dog to herd, or a helping dog for the handicapped. Or if you have had success in training a cat or another animal, you might write about that.
2. Describe a pet that you have owned. Give examples.

WRITE YOUR OWN SUCCESS STORY   CAROL CARTER

Coasting through high school, seldom studying, seventeen-year-old Carol Carter was yanked from a career disaster by a conversation with her brother. This vivid essay from *Majoring in the Rest of Your Life: Career Secrets for College Students* (1999) relates how she suddenly changed direction, "determined to learn all she could." Since graduating from the University of Arizona, Carter has also written *Student Planner* (1998) and *Keys to Success* (2000). She has coauthored and collaborated on more than a dozen other books designed to help students increase their effectiveness.

1   Who am I to talk to high school graduates and college freshmen about planning? As a high school student in Tucson, Arizona, I never planned. I just coasted along letting things happen to me. Sure, I was spontaneous. I spent weeknights talking on the phone and studied only when I felt like it— i.e., seldom. On weekends my friends and I roamed shopping malls and partied in the mountains. The typical irresponsible high school student.

And then BOOM. The ax fell. The ax was not some accident, scandal, or divine intervention. It was simply a conversation with my older brother Craig during the first week of my senior year in high school. Our talk changed the course of my life.

At seventeen, I was intimidated by my four older brothers. I saw them as bright, motivated, and respected achievers—the opposite of me. Whenever one of them asked me about what I was doing or thinking, I'd answer with a one-liner and hope he'd soon leave me alone.

This conversation with Craig was different. He didn't give up after five minutes despite my curt, vague responses.

"Carol, what are you interested in?"   5

"I dunno."

"What do you think about all day?"

"I dunno."

"What do you want to do with your life?"

"I'll just let things happen."   10

Craig persisted. His voice grew indignant. He criticized me for talking on the phone, for spending too much time at pep rallies and rock concerts, for not studying, for not challenging myself. He pointed out that I hadn't read an unassigned book in three years. He asked if I intended to approach college the way I'd approached high school—as one continuous party. If so, he warned, I'd better start thinking of a career flipping burgers at the local hamburger stand because no respectable employer would ever take me seriously. He asked me if that was what I wanted to do with my life. He cautioned that out of laziness and lack of planning I would limit my options so narrowly that I would never be able to get a real job. I had wasted three years of high school, he said. College was a new start, since employers and graduate schools seldom check as far back as high school for records. So he advised me to quit making excuses, decide what I wanted and plan how to achieve it. My only limitations would be self-imposed.

Craig then left my room—sermon completed. I didn't speak to him before he flew back to New York that afternoon to finish his senior year at Columbia. I hated him for interfering in my life. He made me dissatisfied with myself. I was scared he was right. For the first time, I realized that "typical" was not necessarily what I wanted to be.

The next day, still outraged but determined to do something, I went to the library and checked out six classics: *Pride and Prejudice* by Jane Austen; *The Great Gatsby* by F. Scott Fitzgerald; *A Farewell to Arms* and *For Whom the Bell Tolls* by Ernest Hemingway; *A Portrait of the Artist as a Young Man* by James Joyce; and *Sister Carrie* by Theodore Dreiser. Then I wrote down in a notebook a few goals that I wanted to accomplish. They all seemed boldly unattainable: earn straight A's (previously I had made B's and C's), study every week including one weekend night, keep reading classics on my own. If I couldn't make it in my senior year of high school, why should I waste time and money in college? I'd beat fate to the door and begin my career at the hamburger stand directly.

Three weeks later I got a letter from Craig. He knew how angry I was with him. He told me our conversation wasn't easy for him either but if he hadn't cared, he wouldn't have bothered to say anything. He was right. I needed that sermon. If I didn't come to terms with my problems, I could never have moved from making excuses to making things happen.

15   I worked hard and got results. The second semester of my senior year I made all A's (except for a B in physics). I finished the six classics and others as well. I started reading newspapers and magazines. I had to move the *Vogue* on my nightstand to make room for *Time, Harper's,* and *Fortune.* I found that I could set goals and attain them, and I started to realize that I wasn't so different from my brothers after all.

To my utter astonishment, I discovered that for the first time I enjoyed learning. My world seemed to open up just because I knew more about different kinds of people, ways of thinking and ways of interpreting what I had previously assumed to be black-and-white. (If you are a shy person, joining a club and getting to know—and actually like—a few people whom you originally perceived as unfriendly or uninteresting may astonish you as much as my newfound appreciation for learning astonished me.)

The summer before college, I thought about what I wanted to do with my life, but couldn't decide on a direction. I had no notion of what I wanted to major in. What to do . . . what to do?

I turned to Craig, a phone call away in New York City. He told me not to worry in my first year of college about what I wanted to do. The main priority: learn as much as I could. College, he told me, was my golden opportunity to investigate all kinds of things—biology, psychology, accounting, philosophy. He told me I'd become good at writing and critical thinking techniques—skills that would help me learn any job after graduation. And though I could continue to expand my educational horizons throughout life, college was the best opportunity to expose myself to the greatest minds and movements of our civilization.

Craig also warned me that being a scholar, though important, wouldn't be enough. (He had just graduated from Columbia as a Phi Beta Kappa, but since he hadn't gained any real-world experience in college, it took him several months to find his first job.) To maximize options upon graduation, I would have to do three things:

1. Learn as much as possible from classes, books, professors, and other people

2. Participate in extracurricular activities

3. Get REAL-WORLD experience by working part-time and landing summer internships

20   If I did these three things reasonably well, Craig assured me, I could choose from a number of career opportunities at the end of my senior year. And even if I only did two of the three full-force and one half-speed, I'd be in good shape. The effort in each area, and a modest outcome, was an attainable goal. That way I could balance my college experience and open options for the future.

Craig advised me that I should look ahead and develop a plan of action for each of my four years of college. He told me that foresight—the ability to consider the bigger picture beyond short-term challenges and intermittent goals—is invaluable in most jobs; it distinguishes outstanding people from the rest of the pack. . . . Most important, you'll learn that everyone— including YOU—has his or her own set of skills, abilities, passions and talents to tap. Finding the career and lifestyle that allows you to cultivate and nurture them is one of the most important success secrets.

So Take Action!

A good way to start is to assess your shortcomings and strengths. As I've already told you, one of my shortcomings in high school was not learning all I could from my classes and teachers. Your shortcoming may have been that you focused entirely on your studies without developing many outside interests. Someone else may feel that he concentrated so much on an outside activity—such as training for a particular sport—that he had no time for studies or friends. What was your major shortcoming in high school?

Now think about three things:

1. What pleased you in high school?

2. What could you have done better?

3. What do you want to improve upon in the future?

Identifying these areas will help you strike a good balance during college. Once you get in the habit of analyzing past experiences, you will have a clearer notion of what you do and don't want in the future. That's important. 25

As a high school senior, a college freshman, or a college senior, the next thing you must do is decide to take action. Don't worry if you don't know what you want to do. Just commit yourself to the process. If you do, you'll eventually find out which careers might be best for you and how you could best prepare for them.

RECAP: The priorities

1. Gain knowledge

2. Participate in activities

3. Get REAL-WORLD experience

Making It Happen

"Luck is the residue of design," said Branch Rickey, known as the baseball mahatma for his strategic methods for playing and organizing baseball. He developed the farm system on which the minor leagues were formed. His PLANS OF ACTION took a handful of disjointed teams in faraway cities and banded them into an organization which has left its mark on American culture.

Nothing happens magically. If you want to be a success, you are going to have to take personal responsibility for your life. Why do some graduates get twenty job offers and others receive none?

30   While successful people may appear lucky, they, in fact, illustrate the maxim that "luck favors the prepared mind."

Joe Cirulli agrees. He is the owner of the successful Gainesville Health and Fitness Center in Florida. Early on in his life, exercise was a priority, an essential part of his day. So he followed his interests and put his talents to work to start his own health club. While many other clubs have folded around him, he has experienced enormous success—his membership continues to grow, and he is able to keep his club filled with the best equipment and the most knowledgeable professionals.

When Joe was twenty, he worked as an assistant manager and a sales representative for a health club. One of his responsibilities was to train new sales representatives for the club. He worked hard to prepare them for their jobs only to have to compete with them once they were trained.

He remembers talking with the vice president of the company about his frustration. The vice president, a person Joe respected, advised him to keep on putting his best efforts into his work. "Right now you may not see the benefit of your hard work, but one day you will."

Joe followed his advice. Less than five years later his skill at training people in the health club industry paid off—he was able to put his expertise to work for his own health club. "Knowing how to motivate employees to do their best, to care about the quality of their work, and to care about our customers has had an enormous impact on the success of my own company."

35   Joe believes the secret to his success is giving 100 percent of himself in everything he does. "Success is the culmination of all your efforts. There are thousands of opportunities for people who give their all."

How do you arrange to have the most options when you leave college? Plan, develop foresight, and take charge of your life, and you will become one of the lucky ones. Most important, decide that you want to succed—and believe it.

Charles Garfield a clinical psychologist who has spent his career studying what motivates people to superior effort, says that the drive to excel comes primarily from within. Can "peak performances" be learned? Yes, says Garfield. High achievers are not extraordinarily gifted superhumans. What they have in common is the ability to cultivate what the German writer Johann Wolfgang von Goethe termed "the genius, power, and magic" that exists in all of us. These doers increase the odds in their favor through simple techniques which anyone can cultivate:

1. Envision a mission

2. Be result-oriented

3. Tap your internal resources

4. Enlist team spirit

5. Treat setbacks as stepping stones

First Things First

The first thing to keep in mind when planning: accept the world the way it is. Your plans should be based on a realistic assessment of how things are, not some starry-eyed vision of how they should be. You can dream, but there's a happy medium between cold reality and pie in the sky. That's why you must be open to opportunity. Indeed, you must create it. Although you can't change the hand you were dealt, you can play it as wisely as possible.

So start today. Start now.

The more questions you ask now, the better prepared you'll be in four   40
years. You don't want to be stuck in a boring job or wondering why you can't find work.

Are you going to make mistakes? I hope so, unless you're not of the human species. Making mistakes is the process by which we learn. And whenever we're disappointed by the outcome, we have to maintain a positive attitude, log the information, and keep going. The key is to learn from mistakes without letting them slow us down.

REFLECTING AND INTERPRETING

1. What rhetorical strategy does Carter use in the first sentence? What is the effect?

2. How did Carol's careless attitude in high school affect her self-image?

3. What three main points did Craig make in his criticism?

4. How did Carol react to her brother's advice? Why? What did she do the next day?

5. What three things did Carol discover about herself?

6. When Craig pointed out that high grades alone were not enough to land a job, what three actions did he recommend?

7. What four actions does Carol recommend readers take to "have the most options when you leave college"?

8. Does the author seem convincing? Why or why not?

9. What type of support does she provide other than personal experience?

10. What is appealing about her writing style?

A WRITER'S RESPONSE

What is the most significant point that you derived from this essay? Did you learn anything that can help you be more successful in college? On the job? What do you plan to do differently to improve your grades and chances for success? Write an essay that responds to these questions and any other points Carter raises.

HOW TO GET OUT OF A LOCKED TRUNK   PHILIP WEISS

Weiss blends humor, suspense, and romance while explaining a process (in fact, several versions of it). In this clever piece, originally published in *Harper's* magazine and later in *The Best American Essays* (1993), Weiss begins with an investigation of one process of escape and uses it as a metaphor to reflect on another. He has written for *The New York Times Magazine*, *The New York Observer*, *Jewish World Review*, and other publications. Weiss is the author of *Religion & Art* (1964), *Modes of Being* (1968), *Art Deco Environment* (1976), *Cock-A-Doodle-Doo* (1995), and *American Taboo: A Murder in the Peace Corps* (2005).

1   On a hot Sunday last summer my friend Tony and I drove my rental car, a '91 Buick, from St. Paul to the small town of Waconia, Minnesota, forty miles southwest. We each had a project. Waconia is Tony's boyhood home, and his sister had recently given him a panoramic postcard of Lake Waconia as seen from a high point in the town early in the century. He wanted to duplicate the photograph's vantage point, then hang the two pictures together in his house in Frogtown. I was hoping to see Tony's father, Emmett, a retired mechanic, in order to settle a question that had been nagging me: Is it possible to get out of a locked car trunk?

We tried to call ahead to Emmett twice, but he wasn't home. Tony thought he was probably golfing but that there was a good chance he'd be back by the time we got there. So we set out.

I parked the Buick, which was a silver sedan with a red interior, by the graveyard near where Tony thought the picture had been taken. He took his picture and I wandered among the headstones, reading the epitaphs. One of them was chillingly anti-individualist. It said, "Not to do my will, but thine."

Trunk lockings had been on my mind for a few weeks. It seemed to me that the fear of being locked in a car trunk had a particular hold on the American imagination. Trunk lockings occur in many movies and books—from *Goodfellas* to *Thelma and Louise* to *Humboldt's Gift.* And while the highbrow national newspapers generally shy away from trunk lockings, the attention they receive in local papers suggests a widespread anxiety surrounding the subject. In an afternoon at the New York Public Library I found numerous stories about trunk lockings. A Los Angeles man is discovered, bloodshot, banging the trunk of his white Eldorado following a night and a day trapped inside; he says his captors went on joyrides and picked up women. A forty-eight-year-old Houston doctor is forced into her trunk at a bank ATM and then the car is abandoned, parked near the Astrodome. A New Orleans woman tells police she gave birth in a trunk while being abducted to Texas. Tests undermine her story, the police drop the investigation. But so what if it's a fantasy? That only shows the idea's hold on us.

Every culture comes up with tests of a person's ability to get out of a 5 sticky situation. The English plant mazes. Tropical resorts market those straw finger-grabbers that tighten their grip the harder you pull on them, and Viennese intellectuals gave us the concept of childhood sexuality— figure it out, or remain neurotic for life.

At least you could puzzle your way out of those predicaments. When they slam the trunk, though, you're helpless unless someone finds you. You would think that such a common worry should have a ready fix, and that the secret of getting out of a locked trunk is something we should all know about.

I phoned experts but they were very discouraging.

"You cannot get out. If you got a pair of pliers and bat's eyes, yes. But you have to have a lot of knowledge of the lock," said James Foote at Automotive Locksmiths in New York City.

Jim Frens, whom I reached at the technical section of *Car and Driver* in Detroit, told me the magazine had not dealt with this question. But he echoed the opinion of experts elsewhere when he said that the best hope for escape would be to try and kick out the panel between the trunk and the backseat. That angle didn't seem worth pursuing. What if your enemies were in the car, crumpling beer cans and laughing at your fate? It didn't make sense to join them.

The people who deal with rules on auto design were uncomfortable 10 with my scenarios. Debra Barclay of the Center for Auto Safety, an organization founded by Ralph Nader, had certainly heard of cases, but she was not aware of any regulations on the matter. "Now, if there was a defect involved—" she said, her voice trailing off, implying that trunk locking was all phobia. This must be one of the few issues on which she and the auto industry agree. Ann Carlson of the Motor Vehicle Manufacturing Association became alarmed at the thought that I was going to play up a non-problem: "In reality this very rarely happens. As you say, in the movies it's a wonderful plot device," she said. "But in reality apparently this is not that frequent an occurrence. So they have not designed that feature into vehicles in a specific way."

When we got to Emmett's one-story house it was full of people. Tony's sister, Carol, was on the floor with her two small children. Her husband, Charlie, had one eye on the golf tournament on TV, and Emmett was at the kitchen counter, trimming fat from meat for lunch. I have known Emmett for fifteen years. He looked better than ever. In his retirement he had sharply changed his diet and lost a lot of weight. He had on shorts. His legs were tanned and muscular. As always, his manner was humorous, if opaque.

Tony told his family my news: I was getting married in three weeks. Charlie wanted to know where my fiancée was. Back East, getting everything ready. A big-time hatter was fitting her for a new hat.

Emmett sat on the couch, watching me. "Do you want my advice?"

"Sure."

15   He just grinned. A gold tooth glinted. Carol and Charlie pressed him to yield his wisdom.

Finally he said, "Once you get to be thirty, you make your own mistakes."

He got out several cans of beer, and then I brought up what was on my mind.

Emmett nodded and took off his glasses, then cleaned them and put them back on.

We went out to his car, a Mercury Grand Marquis, and Emmett opened the trunk. His golf clubs were sitting on top of the spare tire in a green golf bag. Next to them was a toolbox and what he called his "burglar tools," a set of elbowed rods with red plastic handles he used to open door locks when people locked their keys inside.

20   Tony and Charlie stood watching. Charlie is a banker in Minneapolis. He enjoys gizmos and is extremely practical. I would describe him as un-flappable. That's a word I always wanted to apply to myself, but my fian-cée had recently informed me that I am high-strung. Though that surprised me, I didn't quarrel with her.

For a while we studied the latch assembly. The lock closed in much the same way that a lobster might clamp on to a pencil. The claw portion, the jaws of the lock, was mounted inside the trunk lid. When you shut the lid, the jaws locked on to the bend of a U-shaped piece of metal mounted on the body of the car. Emmett said my best bet would be to unscrew the bolts. That way the U-shaped piece would come loose and the lock's jaws would swing up with it still in their grasp.

"But you'd need a wrench," he said.

It was already getting too technical. Emmett had an air of endless pa-tience, but I felt defeated. I could only imagine bloodied fingers, cracked teeth. I had hoped for a simple trick.

Charlie stepped forward. He reached out and squeezed the lock's jaw. They clicked shut in the air, bound together by heavy springs. Charlie now prodded the upper part of the left-hand jaw, the thicker part. With a rough flick of his thumb, he was able to force the jaws to snap open. Great.

25   Unfortunately, the jaws were mounted behind a steel plate the size of your palm in such a way that while they were accessible to us, standing outside the car, had we been inside the trunk the plate would be in our way, blocking the jaws.

This time Emmett saw the way out. He fingered a hole in the plate. It was no bigger than the tip of your little finger. But the hole was close enough to the latch itself that it might be possible to angle something through the hole from inside the trunk and nudge the jaws apart. We tried with one of my keys. The lock jumped open.

It was time for a full-dress test. Emmett swung the clubs out of the trunk, and I set my can of Schmidt's on the rear bumper and climbed in. Everyone gathered around, and Emmett lowered the trunk on me, then pressed it shut with his meaty hands. Total darkness. I couldn't hear the people outside. I thought I was going to panic. But the big trunk felt comfortable. I was pressed against a sort of black carpet that softened the angles against my back.

I could almost stretch out in the trunk, and it seemed to me I could make them sweat if I took my time. Even Emmett, that sphinx, would give way to curiosity. Once I was out he'd ask how it had been and I'd just grin. There were some things you could only learn by doing.

It took a while to find the hole. I slipped the key in and angled it to one side. The trunk gasped open.

Emmett motioned the others away, then levered me out with his big 30 right forearm. Though I'd only been inside for a minute, I was disoriented—as much as anything because someone had moved my beer while I was gone, setting it down on the cement floor of the garage. It was just a little thing, but I could not be entirely sure I had gotten my own beer back.

Charlie was now raring to try other cars. We examined the latch on his Toyota, which was entirely shielded to the trunk occupant (i.e., no hole in the plate), and on the neighbor's Honda (ditto). But a 1991 Dodge Dynasty was doable. The trunk was tight, but its lock had a feature one of the mechanics I'd phoned described as a "tailpiece": a finger-like extension of the lock mechanism itself that stuck out a half inch into the trunk cavity: simply by twisting the tailpiece I could free the lock. I was even faster on a 1984 Subaru that had a little lever device on the latch.

We went out to my rental on Oak Street. The Skylark was in direct sun and the trunk was hot to the touch, but when we got it open we could see that its latch plate had a perfect hole, a square in which the edge of the lock's jaw appeared like a face in a window.

The trunk was shallow and hot. Emmett had to push my knees down before he could close the lid. This one was a little suffocating. I imagined being trapped for hours, and even before he had got it closed I regretted the decision with a slightly nauseous feeling. I thought of Edgar Allan Poe's live burials, and then about something my fiancée had said more than a year and a half before. I had been on her case to get married. She was divorced, and at every opportunity I would reissue my proposal—even during a commercial. She'd interrupted one of these chirps to tell me, in a cold, throaty voice, that she had no intention of ever going through another divorce: "This time, it's death out." I'd carried those words around like a lump of wet clay.

As it happened, the Skylark trunk was the easiest of all. The hole was right where it was supposed to be. The trunk popped open, and I felt great satisfaction that we'd been able to figure out a rule that seemed to apply about 60 percent of the time. If we publicized our success, it might get the attention it deserved. All trunks would be fitted with such a hole. Kids would learn about it in school. The grip of the fear would relax. Before long a successful trunk-locking scene would date a movie like a fedora dates one today.

35   When I got back East I was caught up in wedding preparations. I live in New York, and the wedding was to take place in Philadelphia. We set up camp there with five days to go. A friend had lent my fiancée her BMW, and we drove it south with all our things. I unloaded the car in my parents' driveway. The last thing I pulled out of the trunk was my fiancée's hat in its heavy cardboard shipping box. She'd warned me I was not allowed to look. The lid was free but I didn't open it. I was willing to be surprised.

When the trunk was empty it occurred to me I might hop in and give it a try. First I looked over the mechanism. The jaws of the BMW's lock were shielded, but there seemed to be some kind of cable coming off it that you might be able to manipulate so as to cause the lock to open. The same cable that allowed the driver to open the trunk remotely . . .

I fingered it for a moment or two but decided I didn't need to test out the theory.

REFLECTING AND INTERPRETING

1. Where is the thesis statement located?
2. Do you see any foreshadowing? (Hint: Why is the epitaph included?)
3. In paragraph 5 there is a hint that the essay may be about more than finding a way out of a locked trunk. Where is the hint?
4. Where does the first step of the process begin? How does the author succeed in opening the trunk of the Mercury Grand Marquis?
5. How many car trunks do they examine? How many is the author successful in escaping?
6. Climbing out of the trunk, he was "disoriented . . . someone had moved my beer. . . ." What does this incident suggest about his personality?
7. Examine paragraph 33. What conclusion do you draw from the inclusion of the three very different examples in one paragraph?
8. What might escape from a car trunk symbolize to the narrator?
9. In Philadelphia, he decided he "didn't need to test out the theory" on the BMW his fiancée had borrowed. What are the implications of this decision?
10. By the end of the story, do you see any change in Weiss? If so, what?

A WRITER'S RESPONSE

1. Freewrite about physical states that mimic social or emotional entrapment.
2. *Small Groups:* The steps of the trunk-opening process are intermingled with the narrative. What are the six steps?

HOW DO YOU KNOW IT'S GOOD?   MARYA MANNES

What makes writing, art, music, or theater good? One popular approach denies the existence of any valid criteria to measure the quality of a work. This approach claims that decisions about value are merely a matter of personal taste. But Marya Mannes disagreed, saying there are standards to determine value. She said that the prime function of art is "to create order out of chaos—again, not the order of neatness or rigidity or convention or artifice, but the order of clarity. . . ." There is room for "incredible diversity of forms" within a universal pattern and rhythm. Mannes (1904–90) was born into a family of prominent musicians and chemists. She was a columnist, editor, and television commentator for PBS. She wrote two novels, *Message from a Stranger* (1948) and *They* (1968), as well as an autobiography, *Out of My Time* (1971). Best known was her collection of essays, *But Will It Sell?* (1964), in which "How Do You Know It's Good?" was first published.

Suppose there were no critics to tell us how to react to a picture, a play, or a new composition of music. Suppose we wandered innocent as the dawn into an art exhibition of unsigned paintings. By what standards, by what values would we decide whether they were good or bad, talented or untalented, successes or failures? How can we ever know that what we think is right? 1

For the last fifteen or twenty years the fashion in criticism or appreciation of the arts has been to deny the existence of any valid criteria and to make the words "good" or "bad" irrelevant, immaterial, and inapplicable. There is no such thing, we are told, as a set of standards, first acquired through experience and knowledge and later imposed on the subject under discussion. This has been a popular approach, for it relieves the critic of the responsibility of judgment and the public of the necessity of knowledge. It pleases those resentful of disciplines, it flatters the empty-minded by calling them open-minded, it comforts the confused. Under the banner of democracy and the kind of equality which our forefathers did *not* mean, it says, in effect, "Who are you to tell us what is good or bad?" This is the same cry used so long and so effectively by the producers of mass media who insist that it is the public, not they, who decides what it wants to hear and see, and that for a critic to say that *this* program is bad and this program is good is purely a reflection of personal taste. Nobody recently has expressed this philosophy more succinctly than Dr. Frank Stanton, the highly intelligent president of CBS television. At a hearing before the Federal Communications Commission, this phrase escaped him under questioning: "One man's mediocrity is another man's good program."

There is no better way of saying "No values are absolute." There is another important aspect to this philosophy of *laissez faire:* It is the fear, in all observers of all forms of art, of guessing wrong. This fear is well come by, for who has not heard of the contemporary outcries against artists who later were called great? Every age has its arbiters who do not grow with their times, who cannot tell evolution from revolution or the difference between frivolous faddism, amateurish experimentation, and profound and necessary change. Who wants to be caught *flagrante delicto* with an error of judgment as serious as this? It is far safer, and certainly easier, to look at a picture or a play or a poem and to say "This is hard to understand, but it may be good," or simply to welcome it as a new form. The word "new"— in our country especially—has magical connotations. What is new must be good; what is old is probably bad, and if a critic can describe the new in language that nobody can understand, he's safer still. If he has mastered the art of saying nothing with exquisite complexity, nobody can quote him later as saying anything.

But all these, I maintain, are forms of abdication from the responsibility of judgment. In creating, the artist commits himself; in appreciating, you have a commitment of your own. For after all, it is the audience which makes the arts. A climate of appreciation is essential to its flowering, and the higher the expectations of the public, the better the performance of the artist. Conversely, only a public ill-served by its critics could have accepted as art and literature so much in these last years that has been neither. If anything goes, everything goes; and at the bottom of the junkpile lie the discarded standards, too.

5   But what are these standards? How do you get them? How do you know they're the right ones? How can you make a clear pattern out of so many intangibles, including that greatest one, the very private I?

Well for one thing, it's fairly obvious that the more you read and see and hear, the more equipped you'll be to practice that art of association which is at the basis of all understanding and judgment. The more you live and the more you look, the more aware you are of a consistent pattern— as universal as the stars, as the tides, as breathing, as night and day— underlying everything. I would call this pattern and this rhythm an order. Not order—an order. Within it exists an incredible diversity of forms. Without it lies chaos. I would further call this order—this incredible diversity held within one pattern—health. And I would call chaos—the wild cells of destruction—sickness. It is in the end up to you to distinguish between the diversity that is health and the chaos that is sickness, and you can't do this without a process of association that can link a bar of Mozart with the corner of a Vermeer painting, or a Stravinsky score with a Picasso abstraction; or that can relate an aggressive act with a Franz Kline painting and a fit of coughing with a John Cage composition.

There is no accident in the fact that certain expressions of art live for all time and that others die with the moment, and although you may not always define the reasons, you can ask the questions. What does an artist say that is timeless; how does he say it? How much is fashion, how much is merely reflection? Why is Sir Walter Scott so hard to read now, and Jane Austen not? Why is baroque right for one age and too effulgent for another?

Can a standard of craftsmanship apply to art of all ages, or does each have its own, and different, definitions? You may have been aware, inadvertently, that craftsmanship has become a dirty word these years because, again, it implies standard—something done well or done badly. The result of this convenient avoidance is a plenitude of actors who can't project their voices, singers who can't phrase their songs, poets who can't communicate emotion, and writers who have no vocabulary—not to speak of painters who can't draw. The dogma now is that craftsmanship gets in the way of expression. You can do better if you don't know *how* you do it, let alone *what* you're doing.

I think it is time you helped reverse this trend by trying to rediscover craft: the command of the chosen instrument, whether it is a brush, a word, or a voice. When you begin to detect the difference between freedom and sloppiness, between serious experimentation and ego-therapy, between skill and slickness, between strength and violence, you are on your way to separating the sheep from the goats, a form of segregation denied us for quite a while. All you need to restore it is a small bundle of standards and a Geiger counter that detects fraud, and we might begin our tour of the arts in an area where both are urgently needed: contemporary painting.

I don't know what's worse: to have to look at acres of bad art to find 10 the little good, or to read what the critics say about it all. In no other field of expression has so much double-talk flourished, so much confusion prevailed, and so much nonsense been circulated: further evidence of the close interdependence between the arts and the critical climate they inhabit. It will be my pleasure to share with you some of this double-talk so typical of our times.

Item one: preface for a catalogue of an abstract painter:

"Time-bound meditation experiencing a life; sincere with plastic piety at the threshold of hallowed arcana; a striving for pure ideation giving shape to inner drive; formalized patterns where neural balances reach a fiction." End of quote. Know what this artist paints like now?

Item two: a review in the *Art News:*

". . . a weird and disparate assortment of material, but the monstrosity which bloomed into his most recent cancer of aggregations is present in some form everywhere. . . ." Then, later, "A gluttony of things and processes terminated by a glorious constipation."

Item three, same magazine, review of an artist who welds automobile 15 fragments into abstract shapes:

"Each fragment . . . is made an extreme of human exasperation, torn at and fought all the way, and has its rightness of form as if by accident. *Any technique that requires order or discipline would just be the human ego.* No, these must be egoless, uncontrolled, undesigned and different enough to give you a bang—fifty miles an hour around a telephone pole. . . ."

"Any technique that requires order or discipline would just be the human ego." What does he mean—"just be"? What are they really talking about? Is this journalism? Is it criticism? Or is it that other convenient abdication from standards of performance and judgment practiced by so many artists and critics that they, like certain writers who deal only in sickness and depravity, "reflect the chaos about them . . ."? Again, whose chaos? Whose depravity?

I had always thought that the prime function of art was to create order *out* of chaos—again, not the order of neatness or rigidity or convention or artifice, but the order of clarity by which one will and one vision could draw the essential truth out of apparent confusion. I still do. It is not enough to use parts of a car to convey the brutality of the machine. This is as slavishly representative, and just as easy, as arranging dried flowers under glass to convey nature.

Speaking of which, i.e., the use of real materials (burlap, old gloves, bottletops) in lieu of pigment, this is what one critic had to say about an exhibition of Assemblage at the Museum of Modern Art last year:

20   Spotted throughout the show are indisputable works of art, accounting for a quarter or even half of the total display. But the remainder are works of non-art, anti-art, and art substitutes that are the aesthetic counterparts of the social deficiencies that land people in the clink on charges of vagrancy. These aesthetic bankrupts . . . have no legitimate ideological roof over their heads and not the price of a square intellectual meal, much less a spiritual sandwich, in their pockets.

I quote these words of John Canaday of *The New York Times* as an example of the kind of criticism which puts responsibility to an intelligent public above popularity with an intellectual coterie. Canaday has the courage to say what he thinks and the capacity to say it clearly: two qualities notably absent from his profession.

Next to art, I would say that appreciation and evaluation in the field of music is the most difficult. For it is rarely possible to judge a new composition at one hearing only. What seems confusing or fragmented at first might well become clear and organic a third time. Or it might not. The only salvation here for the listener is, again, an instinct born of experience and association which allows him to separate intent from accident, design from experimentation, and pretense from conviction. Much of contemporary music is, like its sister art, merely a reflection of the composer's own fragmentation: an absorption in self and symbols at the expense of communication with others. The artist, in short, says to the public: If you don't understand this, it's because you're dumb. I maintain that you are not. You may have to go part way or even halfway to meet the artist, but if you must go the whole way, it's his fault, not yours. Hold fast to that. And remember it too when you read new poetry, that estranged sister of music.

A multitude of causes, unknown to former times, are now acting with a combined force to blunt the discriminating powers of the mind, and, unfitting it for all voluntary exertion, to reduce it to a state of almost savage torpor. The most effective of these causes are the great national events which are daily taking place and the increasing accumulation of men in cities, where the uniformity of their occupations produces a craving for extraordinary incident, which the rapid communication of intelligence hourly gratifies. To this tendency of life and manners, the literature and theatrical exhibitions of the country have conformed themselves.

This startingly applicable comment was written in the year 1800 by William Wordsworth in the preface to his "Lyrical Ballads"; and it has been cited by Edwin Muir in his recently published book, *The Estate of Poetry.* Muir states that poetry's effective range and influence have diminished alarmingly in the modern world. He believes in the inherent and indestructible qualities of the human mind and the great and permanent objects that act upon it, and suggests that the audience will increase when "poetry loses what obscurity is left in it by attempting greater themes, for great themes have to be stated clearly." If you keep that firmly in mind and resist, in Muir's words, "the vast dissemination of secondary objects that isolate us from the natural world," you have gone a long way toward equipping yourself for the examination of any work of art.

When you come to theatre, in this extremely hasty tour of the arts, you can approach it on two different levels. You can bring to it anticipation and innocence, giving yourself up, as it were, to the life on the stage and reacting to it emotionally, if the play is good, or listlessly, if the play is boring; a part of the audience organism that expresses its favor by silence or laughter and its disfavor by coughing and rustling. Or you can bring to it certain critical faculties that may heighten, rather than diminish, your enjoyment.

You can ask yourselves whether the actors are truly in their parts or merely projecting themselves; whether the scenery helps or hurts the mood; whether the playwright is honest with himself, the characters, and you. Somewhere along the line you can learn to distinguish between the true creative act and the false arbitrary gesture; between fresh observation and stale cliché; between the avant-garde play that is pretentious drivel and the avant-garde play that finds new ways to say old truths.

Purpose and craftsmanship—end and means—these are the keys to your judgment in all the arts. What is this painter trying to say when he slashed a broad band of black across a white canvas and lets the edges dribble down? Is it a statement of violence? Is it a self-portrait? If it is *one* of these, has he made you believe it? Or is this a gesture of the ego or a form of therapy? If it shocks you, what does it shock you into?

And what of this tight little painting of bright flowers in a vase? Is the painter saying anything new about flowers? Is it different from a million other canvases of flowers? Has it any life, any meaning, beyond its statement? Is there any pleasure in its forms or texture? The question is not whether a thing is abstract or representational, whether it is "modern" or conventional. The question, inexorably, is whether it is good. And this is a decision which only you, on the basis of instinct, experience, and association, can make for yourself. It takes independence and courage. It involves, moreover, the risk of wrong decision and the humility, after the passage of

25

time, of recognizing it as such. As we grow and change and learn, our attitudes can change too, and what we once thought obscure or "difficult" can later emerge as coherent and illuminating. Entrenched prejudices, obdurate opinions are as sterile as no opinions at all.

Yet standards there are, timeless as the universe itself. And when you have committed yourself to them, you have acquired a passport to that elusive but immutable realm of truth. Keep it with you in the forest of bewilderment. And never be afraid to speak up.

REFLECTING AND INTERPRETING

1. Where is the thesis statement located?
2. Mannes says a denial of the existence of criteria to evaluate the arts has been popular for several reasons. What are they?
3. What is the general fear of observers of all forms of art? Yet what danger lies in accepting a critic's verdict of "exquisite complexity" without evaluation?
4. Mannes says that appreciation is necessary for the arts to flower. How do the expectations of the public influence art? Are there any other factors that Mannes does not mention?
5. What two basic criteria can be used to judge any piece of art? (Hint: See paragraphs 6 and 7.)
6. What does Mannes mean when she says, "The dogma now is that craftsmanship gets in the way of expression."
7. How does Mannes define *craft*? She says that an audience needs to be able to distinguish what from what?
8. Mannes gives a final piece of advice. What is it?
9. Mannes suggests we ask, "What does an artist say that is timeless; how does he say it?" Using these guidelines, how would you explain Jane Austen's popularity?
10. What four steps does Mannes suggest the reader take to acquire the standards needed to distinguish good art from bad art?

SMALL GROUP DISCUSSION

With your group explore the criteria you use to rate a film as good or bad—one that you would or would not recommend to friends. Have a recorder jot down the proceedings and tabulate the votes for each criterion. After the discussion, the recorder should read the results.

Selecting
Effective Examples

FRUITFUL QUESTIONS

JAMES SOLLISCH

A freelance writer and literary critic, James Sollisch is also a commentator for National Public Radio. He has published in various periodicals, including the *Journal of Financial Planning, U.S.A Today*, and the *Chicago Tribune*. The following essay was first published in *The Chicago Tribune Magazine*. In "Fruitful Questions" Sollisch explains how his young children used synthesis, an upper-level thinking skill, to create different answers to the question "What Doesn't Belong?" They thought about the three objects from different perspectives and devised different answers, all correct.

The other night at the dinner table, my three kids—ages 9, 6 and 4— took time out from their food fight to teach me about paradigm shifts, and limitations of linear thinking and how to refocus parameters.

Here's how it happened: We were playing our own oral version of the Sesame Street game, "What Doesn't Belong?," where kids look at three pictures and choose the one that doesn't fit. I said, "OK, what doesn't belong, an orange, a tomato or a strawberry?"

The oldest didn't take more than a second to deliver his smug answer: "Tomato because the other two are fruits." I agreed that this was the right answer despite the fact that some purists insist a tomato is a fruit. To those of us forced as kids to eat them in salads, tomatoes will always be vegetables. I was about to think up another set of three when my 4-year-old said, "The right answer is strawberry because the other two are round and a strawberry isn't." How could I argue with that?

Then my 6-year-old said, "It's the orange because the other two are red." Not to be outdone by his younger siblings, the 9-year-old said, "It could also be the orange because the other two grow on vines."

5   The middle one took this as a direct challenge. "It could be the strawberry because it's the only one you put on ice cream."

Something was definitely happening here. It was messier than a food fight and much more important than whether a tomato is a fruit or vegetable. My kids were doing what Copernicus did when he placed the sun at the center of the universe, readjusting the centuries-old paradigm of an Earth-centered system. They were doing what Reuben Mattus did when he renamed his Bronx ice cream Haagen-Dazs and raised the price without changing the product. They were doing what Edward Jenner did when he discovered a vaccination for smallpox by abandoning his quest for a cure.

Instead of studying people who were sick with smallpox, he began to study people who were exposed to it but never got sick. He found that they'd all contracted a similar but milder disease, cow pox, which vaccinated them against the deadly smallpox.

They were refocusing the parameters. They were redefining the problems. They were reframing the questions. In short, they were doing what every scientist who's ever made an important discovery throughout history has done, according to Thomas Kuhn, in his book, "The Structure of Scientific Revolutions": They were shifting old paradigms.

But if this had been a workbook exercise in school, every kid who didn't circle tomato would have been marked wrong. Every kid who framed the question differently than "Which is not a fruit?" would have been wrong. Maybe that explains why so many of the world's most brilliant scientists and inventors were failures in school, the most notable being Albert Einstein, who was perhaps this century's most potent paradigm-shifter.

10   This is not meant to be a critique of schools. Lord knows, that's easy enough to do. This is, instead, a reminder that there are real limits to the value of information. I bring this up because we seem to be at a point in the evolution of our society where everyone is clamoring for more technology, for instant access to ever-growing bodies of information.

Students must be on-line. Your home must be digitally connected to the World Wide Web. Businesses must be able to download volumes of data instantaneously. But unless we shift our paradigms and refocus our parameters, the super information highway will lead us nowhere.

We are not now, nor have we recently been suffering from a lack of information. Think how much more information we have than Copernicus had four centuries ago. And he didn't do anything less Earth-shattering (pun intended) than completely change the way the universe was viewed. He didn't do it by uncovering more information—he did it by looking differently at information everyone else already had looked at. Edward Jenner didn't invent preventive medicine by accumulating information; he did it by reframing the question.

What we need as we begin to downshift onto the information highway is not more information but new ways of looking at it. We need to discover, as my kids did, that there is more than one right answer, there is more than one right question and there is more than one way to look at a body of information. We need to remember that when you have only a hammer, you tend to see every problem as a nail.

REFLECTING AND INTERPRETING

1. How would you condense and restate the first sentence in your own words? (Use a dictionary and two sentences if needed. Omit unnecessary details.)

2. Consider the answers of the three children. Which one gave the typical answer?

3. How might you explain the fact that the four-year-old and the six-year-old came up with creative answers before the nine-year-old did? (Hint: What happens as we grow older?)

4. What occurred after the two younger children responded with unusual answers and their father voiced no disagreement?

5. Consider the smallpox example. What did Edward Jenner do that led to success?

6. What were Copernicus, Jenner, Mattus, and the author's children doing in their thinking?

7. This incident points out a problem that sometimes arises on multiple-choice exams. What is it?

8. In paragraphs 10 and 11, Sollisch points out a danger in our technological society. What is it?

9. What tendency in human nature can limit problem solving and discoveries?

10. What have you learned from reading this essay?

A WRITER'S RESPONSE

Write a paragraph summarizing what you have learned about creative thinking. What conditions encourage creative thinkers? What often happens in the classroom when teachers expect and reward conventional answers? How might you be more creative? (If you quote phrases from the essay, enclose them with quotation marks. For help, see "Using and Formatting Quotations" in chapter R-3.)

ROAD RAGE

JASON VEST
WARREN COHEN
MIKE THARP

Have you ever been crowded onto a shoulder of the road, insulted, or assaulted by an angry driver? If so, you were a victim of "road rage," an ever-increasing phenomenon that sometimes results in fatalities. Vest, Cohen, and Tharp researched this problem for *U.S. News & World Report* and reported their findings in an article, first published June 2, 1997. Jason Vest is a Washington DC-based reporter for *The Nation.* He has also written for the *Washington Post, Miami New Times, Boston Phoenix, U.S. News & World Report, Village Voice, Atlantic Monthly,* and others. He also covered the Eritrea-Ethiopia border war. Warren Cohen is a journalist who has written for *U.S. News & World Report, Common Cause, Rolling Stone, Fortune, New Republic, Washington Monthly, Pittsburgh Post-Gazette, Washington City Paper,* and others. Mike Tharp is a communications professor at California State Fullerton. A former reporter for *U.S. News & World Report,* Tharp has worked in Japan and served as president of the Foreign Correspondents' Club there. He also covered Somalia and the Gulf War.

1   Some of the incidents are so ludicrous you can't help but laugh—albeit nervously. There was the case in Salt Lake City, where 75-year-old J. C. King—peeved that 41-year-old Larry Remm Jr. honked at him for blocking traffic—followed Remm when he pulled off the road, hurled his prescription bottle at him, and then, in a display of geriatric resolve, smashed Remm's knees with his '92 Mercury. In tony Potomac, Md., Robin Ficker—an attorney and ex-state legislator—knocked the glasses off a pregnant woman after she had the temerity to ask him why he bumped her Jeep with his.

Other incidents lack even the element of black humor. In Colorado Springs, 55-year-old Vern Smalley persuaded a 17-year-old boy who had been tailgating him to pull over; Smalley decided that, rather than merely scold the lad, he would shoot him. (And he did. Fatally—after the youth had threatened him.) And last year, on Virginia's George Washington Parkway, a dispute over a lane change was settled with a high-speed duel that ended when both drivers lost control and crossed the center line, killing two innocent motorists.

Anyone who spent the Memorial Day weekend on the road probably won't be too surprised to learn the results of a major study to be released this week by the American Automobile Association. The rate of "aggressive driving" incidents—defined as events in which an angry or impatient driver tries to kill or injure another driver after a traffic dispute—has risen by 51 percent since 1990. In those cases studied, 37 percent of offenders used "firearms" against other drivers, an additional 28 percent used other weapons, and 35 percent used their cars.

Fear of (and participation in) aggressive driving has grown so much that in a poll last year residents of Maryland, Washington, D.C. and Virginia listed it as a bigger concern than drunk driving. The Maryland highway department is running a campaign called "The End of the Road for Aggressive Drivers," which, among other things, flashes anti-road-rage messages on electronic billboards on the interstates. Delaware, Pennsylvania, and New Jersey have initiated special highway patrols targeting aggressive drivers. A small but busy community of therapists and scholars has arisen to study the phenomenon and counsel drivers on how to cope. And several members of Congress are now trying to figure out ways to legislate away road rage.

5   Lest one get unduly alarmed, it helps to put the AAA study's numbers in context: Approximately 250,000 people have been killed in traffic since 1990. While the U.S. Department of Transportation estimates that two-thirds of fatalities are at least partially caused by aggressive driving, the

AAA study found only 218 that could be directly attributable to enraged drivers. Of the more than 20 million motorists injured, the survey identified 12,610 injuries attributable to aggressive driving. While the study is the first American attempt to quantify aggressive driving, it is not rigorously scientific. The authors drew on reports from 30 newspapers—supplemented by insurance claims and police reports from 16 cities—involving 10,037 occurrences. Moreover, the overall trendlines for car accidents have continued downward for several decades, thanks in part to increases in the drinking age and improvements in car technology like high-mounted brake lights.

But researchers believe there is a growing trend of simple aggressive behavior—road rage—in which a driver reacts angrily to other drivers. Cutting them off, tailgating, giving the finger, waving a fist—experts believe these forms of nonviolent fury are increasing. "Aggressive driving is now the most common way of driving," says Sandra Ball-Rokeach, who codirects the Media and Injury Prevention Program at the University of Southern California. "It's not just a few crazies—it's a subculture of driving."

In focus groups set up by her organization, two-thirds of drivers said they reacted to frustrating situations aggressively. Almost half admitted to deliberately braking suddenly, pulling close to the other car, or taking some other potentially dangerous step. Another third said they retaliated with a hostile gesture. Drivers show great creativity in devising hostile responses. Doug Erber of Los Angeles keeps his windshield-wiper-fluid tank full. If someone tailgates, he turns on the wipers, sending fluid over his roof onto the car behind him. "It works better than hitting the brakes," he says, "and you can act totally innocent."

Mad Max

While the AAA authors note there is a profile of the lethally inclined aggressive driver—"relatively young, poorly educated males who have criminal records, histories of violence, and drug or alcohol problems"—road-rage scholars (and regular drivers) believe other groups are equally represented in the less violent forms of aggressive driving. To some, it's tempting to look at this as a psychologically mysterious Jekyll-and-Hyde phenomenon; for others, it's simply attributable to "jerk drivers." In reality, there's a confluence of emotional and demographic factors that changes the average citizen from mere motorist to Mad Max.

First, it isn't just your imagination that traffic is getting worse. Since 1987, the number of miles of roads has increased just 1 percent while the miles *driven* have shot up by 35 percent. According to a recent Federal Highway Administration study of 50 metropolitan areas, almost 70 percent of urban freeways today—as opposed to 55 percent in 1983—are clogged during rush hour. The study notes that congestion is likely to spread to currently unspoiled locations. Forty percent of the currently gridlock-free Milwaukee County highway system, for example, is predicted to be jammed up more than five hours a day by the year 2000. A study by the Texas Transportation

Institute last year found that commuters in one-third of the largest cities spent well over 40 hours a year in traffic jams.

10   Part of the problem is that jobs have shifted from cities to suburbs. Communities designed as residential suburbs with narrow roads have grown into "edge cities," with bustling commercial traffic. Suburb-to-suburb commutes now account for 44 percent of all metropolitan traffic versus 20 percent for suburb-to-downtown travel. Demographer and *Edge City* author Joel Garreau says workers breaking for lunch are essentially causing a third rush hour. He notes that in Tysons Corner, Va., it takes an average of four traffic signal cycles to get through a typical intersection at lunchtime. And because most mass transit systems are of a spoke-and-hub design, centering on cities and branching out to suburbs, they're not really useful in getting from point A to point B in an edge city or from one edge city to another. Not surprisingly, fewer people are relying on mass transit and more on cars. In 1969, 82.7 percent drove to work; in 1990, 91.4 percent did. Despite the fact that the Washington, D.C., area has an exemplary commuter subway system, it accounts for only 2 percent of all trips made.

Demographic changes have helped put more drivers on the road. Until the 1970s, the percentage of women driving was relatively low, and many families had only one car. But women entered the work force and bought cars, something developers and highway planners hadn't foreseen. From 1969 to 1990 the number of women licensed to drive increased 84 percent. Between 1970 and 1987, the number of cars on the road more than doubled. In the past decade, the number of cars grew faster (17 percent) than the number of people (10 percent). Even carpooling is down despite HOV lanes and other preferential devices. The cumulative effect, says University of Hawaii traffic psychology professor Leon James, is a sort of sensory overload. "There are simply more cars—and more behaviors—to deal with," says James.

As if the United States couldn't produce enough home-grown lousy drivers, it seems to be importing them as well. Experts believe that many immigrants come from countries that have bad roads and aggressive styles. It's not just drivers from Third World countries, though. British drivers are considered among the safest in Europe, yet recent surveys show that nearly 90 percent of British motorists have experienced threats or abuse from other drivers. Of Brits who drive for a living, about 21 percent report having been run off the road. In Australia, one study estimates that about half of all traffic accidents there may be due to road rage. "There are different cultures of driving all over the world—quite clearly, if we mix new cultures in the melting pot, what we get is a culture clash on the roadway," says John Palmer, a professor in the Health Education and Safety Department at Minnesota's St. Cloud University.

The peak moment for aggressive driving comes not during impenetrable gridlocks but just before, when traffic density is high but cars are still moving briskly. That's when cutting someone off or forcing someone out of a lane can make the difference (or so it seems) between being on time and being late, according to Palmer.

Unfortunately, roads are getting more congested just as Americans feel even more pressed for time. "People get on a time line for their car trips," says Palmer. "When they perceive that someone is impeding their progress or invading their agenda, they respond with what they consider to be 'instructive' behavior, which might be as simple as flashing their lights to something more combative."

Suburban Assault Vehicles

This, uh, "instruction" has become more common, Palmer and others 15 speculate, in part because of modern automotive design. With hyper-adjustable seats, soundproof interiors, CD players, and cellular phones, cars are virtually comfortable enough to live in. Students of traffic can't help but wonder if the popularity of pickup trucks and sport utility vehicles has contributed to the problem. Sales have approximately doubled since 1990. These big metal shells loom over everything else, fueling feelings of power and drawing out a driver's more primal instincts. "A lot of the anecdotal evidence about aggressive driving incidents tends to involve people driving sport utility vehicles," says Julie Rochman of the Insurance Institute for Highway Safety. "When people get these larger, heavier vehicles, they feel more invulnerable." While Chrysler spokesman Chris Preuss discounts the notion of suburban assault vehicles being behind the aggressive-driving phenomenon, he does say women feel more secure in the jumbo-size vehicles.

In much of life, people feel they don't have full control of their destiny. But a car—unlike, say, a career or a spouse—responds reliably to one's wish. In automobiles, we have an increased (but false) sense of invincibility. Other drivers become dehumanized, mere appendages to a competing machine. "You have the illusion you're alone and master, dislocated from other drivers," says Hawaii's James.

Los Angeles psychologist Arnold Nerenberg describes how one of his recent patients got into an angry road confrontation with another motorist. "They pulled off the road and started running toward each other to fight, but then they recognized each other as neighbors," he says. "When it's just somebody else in a car, it's more two-dimensional; the other person's identity boils down to, 'You're someone who did something bad to me.'"

How can aggressive driving be minimized? Some believe that better driver's education might help. Driver's ed was a high school staple by the 1950s, thanks to federal highway dollars given to states. But a 1978 government study in De Kalb County, Ga., found no reduction in crashes or traffic violations by students who took a driver's ed course compared with those who didn't. Rather than use these results to design better driver's ed programs, the feds essentially gave up on them and diverted money to seat belt and anti-drunk-driving programs. Today, only 40 percent of new drivers complete a formal training course, which may be one reason 20 percent to 35 percent of applicants fail their initial driving test.

The Inner Driver

But governments are looking anew at the value of driver's education. In April, Michigan passed sweeping rules that grant levels of privilege depending on one's age and driving record. States with similar systems, like California, Maryland, and Oregon, have seen teen accident rates drop.

20   Those who lose their licenses often have to return to traffic school. But some states have generous standards for these schools. To wit: California's theme schools. There, errant drivers can attend the "Humor's My Name, Traffic's My Game," school, in which a mock jury led by a stand-up comic decides who the worst drivers are; the "Traffic School for Chocoholics," which plies errant drivers with chocolate and ice cream; and the gay and lesbian "Pink Triangle Traffic School."

But the real key to reducing road rage probably lies deep within each of us. Professor James of the University of Hawaii suggests that instead of emphasizing defensive driving—which implies that the other driver is the enemy—we should focus on "supportive driving" or "driving with the aloha spirit." Of course that's hard to do if (a) someone has just cut you off at 60 mph or (b) you live in Los Angeles instead of Hawaii. Nerenberg, the Los Angeles psychologist, has published an 18-page booklet called "Overcoming Road Rage: The 10-Step Compassion Program." He recommends examining what sets off road rage and to "visualize overcoming it." Other tips: Imagine you might be seeing that person at a party soon. And remembering that other drivers "are people with feelings. Let us not humiliate them with our aggression." In the chapter titled, "Peace," he suggests, "Take a deep breath and just let it go." And if that doesn't work, the windshield-wiper trick is pretty clever.

REFLECTING AND INTERPRETING

1. Comment on the incidents described in the opening. Do you think such conflicts are common or isolated? Do they seem to occur more often in certain areas? If so, where?

2. How does the American Automobile Association define an "aggressive driving" incident?

3. When does the peak moment for aggressive driving occur?

4. What do the authors cite as major causes of the increase in aggressive driving?

5. Do the authors of the AAA research believe that aggressive drivers tend to have criminal records, histories of violence, or drug or alcohol problems?

6. What did the drivers in focus groups set up by the University of Southern California admit?

7. How does the type of vehicle seem to influence a driver's feelings and behavior?

8. Since 1987, the miles of roadway in the USA have increased by 1 percent, but the miles driven have increased 35 percent. What conclusions can you draw from these statistics?

9. What is the predominant rhetorical strategy used in this article?

10. How do the authors support their claims?

SMALL GROUP DISCUSSION

1. What tends to set off road rage? What can a driver do to forestall arousing his or her own impatience and irritating other drivers?

2. Discuss possible ways of self-preservation when risky on-the-road situations occur. How can you diffuse the wrath of a driver? What should you do if that person signals you to stop?

3. Have you ever witnessed an incident of road rage? If so, write an essay describing what happened. Is there a moral to the tale?

GOING FOR BROKE

MATEA GOLD
DAVID FERRELL

Staff writers for the *Los Angeles Times*, Matea Gold and David Ferrell have a variety of publications to their credit. Gold specializes in political reporting but has also written about food safety, Yiddish literature, and language. She wrote a "First Person" column for the *Times* and won Sacramento Press awards in 1994 and 1995. Ferrell was a finalist in 1996 for the Investigative Reporting and Editors Award. He has been a member of two news teams that won Pulitzer prizes. In 1998 his work was included in *Best American Sports Writing*. His black comedy baseball novel, *Screwball*, was published in 2003. The essay that follows is based upon data from a seven-month investigation of legalized gambling nationwide.

Rex Coile's life is a narrow box, so dark and confining he wonders how   1
he got trapped inside, whether he'll ever get out.

He never goes to the movies, never sees concerts, never lies on a sunny beach, never travels on vacation, never spends Christmas with his family. Instead, Rex shares floor space in cheap motels with other compulsive gamblers, comforting himself with delusional dreams of jackpots that will magically wipe away three decades of wreckage. He has lost his marriage, his home, his Cadillac, his clothes, his diamond ring. Not least of all, in the card clubs of Southern California, he has lost his pride.

Rex no longer feels sorry for himself, not after a 29-year losing streak that has left him scrounging for table scraps to feed his habit. Still, he agonizes over what he has become at 54 and what he might have been.

Articulate, intellectual, he talks about existential philosophy, the writings of Camus and Sartre. He was once an editor at Random House. His mind is so jampacked with tidbits about movies, television, baseball and history that card room regulars call him "Rex Trivia," a name he cherishes for the remnant of self-respect it gives him. "There's a lot of Rexes around these card rooms," he says in a whisper of resignation and sadness.

5   And their numbers are soaring as gambling explodes across America, from the mega-resorts of Las Vegas to the gaming parlors of Indian reservations, from the riverboats along the Mississippi to the corner mini-marts selling lottery tickets. With nearly every state in the union now sanctioning some form of legalized gambling to raise revenues, evidence is mounting that society is paying a steep price, one that some researchers say must be confronted, if not reversed.

Never before have bettors blown so much money—a whopping $50.9 billion last year—five times the amount lost in 1980. That's more than the public spent on movies, theme parks, recorded music and sporting events combined. A substantial share of those gambling losses—an estimated 30% to 40%—pours from the pockets and purses of chronic losers hooked on the adrenaline rush of risking their money, intoxicated by the fast action of gambling's incandescent world.

Studies place the total number of compulsive gamblers at about 4.4 million, about equal to the nation's ranks of hard-core drug addicts. Another 11 million, known as problem gamblers, teeter on the verge. Since 1990, the number of Gamblers Anonymous groups nationwide has doubled from about 600 to more than 1,200.

Compulsive gambling has been linked to child abuse, domestic violence, embezzlement, bogus insurance claims, bankruptcies, welfare fraud and a host of other social and criminal ills. The advent of Internet gambling could lure new legions into wagering beyond their means.

Every once in a while, a case is so egregious it makes headlines: A 10-day-old baby girl in South Carolina dies after being left for nearly seven hours in a hot car while her mother plays video poker. A suburban Chicago woman is so desperate for a bankroll to gamble that she allegedly suffocates her 7-week-old daughter 11 days after obtaining a $200,000 life-insurance policy on the baby.

10   But these tragedies that flash before the public eye are just lightning strokes of a roiling night storm. Far more often, compulsive gambling bends lives more subtly, less sensationally, over the course of years.

Gwen, one of the unseen masses trying to keep her head above water, sits on an easy chair in the living room of her worn Jefferson Park bungalow, watching the movie "Titanic" on an old TV. Her hair is uncombed and there are bags under her eyes. She puffs on a cigarette and shakes her foot nervously. On the screen, the great ship begins to founder.

"That's me," she says, tears rolling down her checks. "I'm sinking."

Gwen has just come off a three-day bender at the Hollywood Park Casino in Inglewood. She blew a paycheck, emptied out her new checking account, gambled right through her work shift. Driving home from the casino, she contemplated veering off the road, ending it all. "I just don't want to be here," she mumbles, watching Titanic's Rose and Jack struggling to hold on to a piece of driftwood in the freezing sea. "I just feel like I'm living a hopeless life. So hopeless."

She's written bad checks and maxed out her credit cards. One bank closed her checking account after she put too many fake deposit slips in the ATM to withdraw cash. She lies. She tells her boss she needs a salary advance because her son is in the hospital. Late on the rent, she parks a block from the house to duck the landlord. For the last eight years, this has been her life, one so empty of joy and options that the card clubs have become her only hope of filling the hole.

She thinks back to that night a few years ago when, desperate to recoup her gambling losses, she pilfered several thousand dollars from the safe of a restaurant where she was working. She just needed something to get herself started, she told herself. She'd pay it back with the winnings. She blew it all in one weekend. 15

Overwhelmed by guilt, she came clean with her manager. She was booked, fingerprinted and briefly thrown behind bars. "It was the worst experience of my life," she says.

Gwen now makes monthly $75 restitution payments to the restaurant as part of her court-ordered probation.

"I have hurt so many people with my gambling," says Gwen. "I have lost best friends. After all the pain I've caused everybody, the pain I caused myself, I still have the urge to gamble. I never know what I'm going to do. I'm so afraid. I'm really afraid."

Science has begun to uncover clues to compulsive gambling—genetic predispositions that involve chemical receptors in the brain, the same pleasure pathways implicated in drug and alcohol addiction. But no amount of knowledge, no amount of enlightenment, makes the illness any less confounding, any less destructive. What the gamblers cannot understand about themselves is also well beyond the comprehension of family members, who struggle for normality in a world of deceit and madness.

Money starts vanishing: $500 here, $200 there, $800 a couple of weeks later. Where is it? The answers come back vague, nonsensical. It's in the desk at work. A friend borrowed it. It got spent on family dinners, car repairs, loans to in-laws. Exasperated spouses play the sleuth, combing through pockets, wallets, purses, searching the car. Sometimes the incriminating evidence turns up—a racing form, lottery scratchers, a map to an Indian casino. Once the secret is uncovered, spouses usually fight the problem alone, bleeding inside, because the stories are too humiliating to share. 20

"Anybody who is living with a compulsive gambler is totally overwhelmed," says Tom Tucker, president of the California Council on Problem Gambling. "They're steeped in anger, resentment, depression, confusion. None of their personal efforts will ever stop a person from their [*sic*] addiction. And they don't really see any hope because compulsive gambling in general is such an under-recognized illness."

One Los Angeles woman, whose husband's gambling was tearing at her sanity, says she slept with her fists so tightly clenched that her nails sliced into her palms. She had fantasies of death—first her own, thinking he'd feel sorry for her and stop gambling. Later, she harbored thoughts of turning her rage on her husband. She imagined getting a gun, hiding in the closet and blasting him out of her life.

"The hurt was so bad I think I would have pulled the trigger," she says. "There were times the pain was so much I thought being in jail, or being in the electric chair, would be less than this."

Five years in Gam-Anon, the 12-step support group for family and friends of compulsive gamblers, has only begun to heal her. "I don't think I'm even halfway there," she says.

25   Too often, families of gambling addicts endure more than warped finances and wrecked psyches. They have come to fear for their physical safety.

Trena, a 42-year-old Whittier homemaker, is among them. Several months ago, after years of agony, she filed for divorce. Her husband, a manager in an industrial plant, was making decent money and took pride in his job. He had two good children and a nice home, an airy bungalow with hardwood floors and a white-brick fireplace. Inside him, though, was a fearsome need to fulfill some glossy vision.

Lottery keno became the rhythmic pulse of his life. For five years, Trena says, she awoke in an empty bed every weekend. Her husband would be gone by 5:30 or 6, joining other keno regulars at the neighborhood dough-nut shop, watching the numbers flash on an overhead monitor. He'd shuffle home hours later, refusing to divulge his losses.

Trena did what tens of thousands of spouses do: She struggled des-perately to pay the bills. She hid money in Cheerios boxes, books, couch cushions, under the doormat. She drew up household budgets—hundreds of them. They became her obsession. She drafted a new one almost every day, never able to get one to work.

Absurd dramas were played out. On paydays, when her husband's check was directly deposited into their account, they would race each other to the bank. Trena would go to one branch, he'd head to another. She would sit at the drive-up window, jamming her withdrawal slip in the pneu-matic tube the moment the bank opened. If she got the money, they could pay the utilities and keep the phone connected. If not, he'd be off to the races, the casinos or the doughnut shop.

30   Like a caged animal, she threw things—smashed a clock against the wall, broke the portable TV in the bedroom. She yelled, clawed and some-times just sank down and cried. Trena had no money for herself, for the im-portant personal things. She got nothing for her mom on Mother's Day.

Increasingly reclusive, she stopped returning calls. Chit-chatting with friends seemed a frivolous distraction when dealing with foreclosure no-tices, filing for bankruptcy or, worse, fending off her husband's angry de-mands for cash.

He would burst into the house shouting, "Give me my money!" Pacing, following her, tipping over plants, rifling through drawers, dumping them out to try to find it. "Don't you touch my money!"

Joining Gam-Anon, where Trena receives emotional support from the spouses of other gamblers, has helped her deal with her decade-long ordeal. She says she is not bitter and understands that compulsive gambling is an illness.

While her husband now lives with his parents, she remains in their home of 19 years, a place filled with memories as wistful as they are painful.

With drug or alcohol abusers, there is the hope of sobering up, an accomplishment in itself, no matter what problems may have accompanied their addictions. Compulsive gamblers often see no way to purge their urges when suffocating debts suggest only one answer: a hot streak. "They have nowhere to turn—they feel cornered," says Dr. Richard J. Rosenthal, a Beverly Hills psychiatrist who founded the California Council on Problem Gambling. "Very often they are motivated by their shame into more and more desperate attempts to avoid being found out." 35

David Phillips, a UC San Diego sociology professor, studied death records from 1982 to 1988—before legalized gambling exploded across America—and found that people in Las Vegas, Atlantic City and other gambling meccas showed significantly higher suicide rates than people in non-gambling cities.

Rex Trivia is not about to kill himself, but like most compulsive gamblers, he occasionally thinks about it. Looking at him, it's hard to imagine he once had a promising future as a smart young New York book editor. His pale eyes are expressionless, his hair yellowish and brittle. In his fifties, his health is failing: emphysema, three lung collapses, a bad aorta, rotting teeth.

His plunge has been so dizzying that at one point he agreed to aid another desperate gambler in a run of bank robberies—nine in all, throughout Los Angeles and Orange counties. When the FBI busted him in 1980, he had $50,000 in cash in a dresser drawer and $100,000 in traveler's checks in his refrigerator's vegetable crisper. Rex, who ended up doing a short stint in prison, hasn't seen that kind of money since.

At 11 P.M. on a Tuesday night, with a bankroll of $55—all he has—he is at a poker table in Gardena. With quick, nervous hands he stacks and unstacks his $1 chips. The stack dwindles. Down $30, he talks about leaving, getting some sleep. Midnight comes and goes. Rex starts winning. Three aces. Four threes. Chips pile up—$60, $70. "A shame to go when the cards are falling my way." He checks the time: "I'll go at 2. Win, lose or draw."

Fate, kismet, luck—the cards keep falling. At 2 A.M., Rex is up $97. He stands, leaves his chips on the table and goes out for a smoke. In the darkness at the edge of the parking lot, he loiters with other regulars, debating with himself whether to grab a bus and quit. 40

"I should go back in there and cash in and get out of here," he says. "That's what I should do."

A long pause. Crushing out his cigarette, Rex turns and heads back inside. He has made his decision.

"A few more hands."

REFLECTING AND INTERPRETING

1. Where is the thesis statement located?

2. Identify the two sentences that provide transition from the opening example to the thesis statement.

3. In paragraph six Gold and Ferrell provide a comparison to the statistic of $50.9 billion spent last year on gambling. What is the effect of the comparison?

4. Is compulsive gambling generally regarded as a bad habit or as an illness? Why?

5. Why is compulsive gambling a social and criminal problem rather than just a problem of individuals?

6. How did compulsive gambling affect death records near gambling meccas?

7. Consider the analogy in paragraphs 11 to 13. Is it apt? Why or why not?

8. What is the effect of including direct quotations such as those in paragraph 31?

9. Examine the opening example and its continuation at the ending. How does it function? What is the effect of the last sentence?

10. Consider the title. Have you ever heard that expression? Why is it ironic here?

A WRITER'S RESPONSE

1. Do you regard gambling as a harmless pastime? If so, defend your point of view.

2. Do you consider gambling to be a problem in your state? Why or why not?

REFUSE TO LIVE IN FEAR   DIANA BLETTER

Born in New York in 1957, Diana Bletter earned a degree in comparative literature from Cornell University. Working as a freelance writer, she published in *The Southampton Press*, *The Philadelphia Inquirer*, *Newsday*, and other periodicals. Her book *The Invisible Thread: A Portrait of Jewish American Women* (1989) was nominated for a Jewish national prize. In 1991 she, her husband, and their six young children moved to a small farming village in Israel, ten miles from the Mediterranean Sea. They never dreamed that their three sons would go off to war. Bletter says she "had naively assumed that by the time they were of army age, there would be peace in the Middle East" <www.beliefnet.com/story/199/story_19922_1.html>. In the essay here, Bletter describes how daily life in a small town has changed under the threat of terrorism.

For most of my life, I thought a shoe box was just a shoe box. Until the 1 afternoon I discovered that it could also be considered a lethal weapon.

This is what happened: I had just gone shopping for shoes—one of my favorite pastimes—in the small Mediterranean town of Nahariyya in northern Israel, where I've lived for the last five years. I sat down on a bench to change into my new purchase. I was so busy admiring my feet that I left the shoe box (with my old shoes) on the bench. Fifteen minutes later, I suddenly remembered it and turned back. When I approached the street, I saw crowds of people, barricades and at least five policemen.

"What happened?" I asked.

"Everyone's been evacuated. Someone reported a suspicious object on a bench down the street."

"Oh, no!" I shouted. "My shoes!"   5

Had I arrived even a few seconds later, a special bomb squad—complete with robot—would have imploded my shoe box to deactivate what could have been a bomb hidden inside. The policeman shook his finger at me. "This is the Middle East!" he said angrily. "You can't be careless like that!"

Reality Bites, Hard

Moving to Israel from America's tranquil suburbia has taught me about living with the threat of terrorism, something we Americans—after the bomb at Atlanta's Olympic Games and the explosion of TWA Flight 800—are finally being forced to think about on our own turf. The brutal fact of a terrorist attack is that it shatters the innocent peace of our days, the happy logic of our lives. It inalterably changes the way we live.

I can no longer daydream as I walk down a street—now I know that, to stay alive, I have to remain aware of who and what surrounds me. As my fiance always tells me, "Your eyes are your best friends!" and I use them to keep track of emergency exits, the closest windows, the nearest heavy object that could be used in self-defense.

I used to be a reflexive litter-grabber—in my hometown, I never hesitated to pick up a coffee cup from the sidewalk and toss it in a nearby garbage can. In Israel, I've learned not to touch litter and to stay away from garbage cans—on several occasions, bombs have been placed in them. If I see a knapsack, shopping bag or—yes—a shoe box left unattended, I now do three things: One, ask passersby if they forgot the package; two, get away from it as fast as I can; and three, report it to the police.

Necessary Inconveniences

Living in a country where terrorism is always a possibility means that at 10 every entrance to a public place, guards search every bag. I forgot this the first time I walked into Nahariyya's lone department store; a guard stopped me to look through my pocketbook. "How could I have shoplifted?" I asked. "I haven't set foot in the store." Then I remembered that in America, people worry about what someone might sneak *out* of a store; in Israel, people worry what weapons or bombs someone might sneak *in* to a store.

The first few days after a terrorist attack seem very quiet. Since all of Israel is only the size of New Jersey, everybody usually knows someone who was hurt or killed. The nation slips into mourning: People avoid going out, attending parties, sitting in cafés.

Gradually, though, daily life returns to normal. Israelis (and now, Americans) have to prove again and again to potential terrorists that we're not giving in to our fears. If we voluntarily restrict our movements and our lives, terrorists have vanquished us.

During the latest hostilities in Lebanon (whose border is about seven miles from Nahariyya), Samia Zina, my dear friend—and a Muslim Arab—dreamed about me, one of those vivid dreams that seems prophetic when you wake. She dreamed that the fighting had forced her to flee her home, and that I'd hidden her and her children in my house (and I certainly would have, had the nightmare been a reality). The next day, Samia popped by to tell me her dream and give me the two stuffed chickens she'd been moved to cook for me.

"Thank you," I said, astonished by the food and the dream. "But I know you would have hidden me, too."

15   Terrorists attempt to divide people by fear, but in our community they've brought so-called enemies together: Even Arabs and Jews watch out for each other in public places, knowing that terrorists target everyone. By resisting the temptation to become paranoid and isolated, by sticking up for one another, we remain undefeated.

REFLECTING AND INTERPRETING

1. What is the effect of beginning with this ordinary incident that was regarded as unordinary?

2. In paragraph 7 Bletter refers to events that happened several years ago. Does that make this article seem dated? Why or why not?

3. How has this incident affected Bletter's habits on the street?

4. What later example sharply illustrates a difference between life in the USA and life in Israel?

5. Can you explain why a dream might cause a friend to act as she did?

6. What benefit has resulted from the hostile attacks and terrorism?

7. Explain the final sentence of the essay.

8. The author uses first person in telling of her experiences in Israel. Would third person have been more or less effective? Why?

A WRITER'S RESPONSE

Have you ever feared for your life, possibly during an accident, a robbery, or other frightening experience? Have you lost a close friend or relative due to a tragic circumstance? Describe the event and how it affected you.

Classifying into Categories

HOW FIT ARE YOU?   KENNETH H. COOPER

Kenneth H. Cooper, MD, MPH became the director of the Aerospace Medical Laboratory in San Antonio, Texas, and consultant for the National Aeronautics Space Administration after thirteen years in the Navy. He developed his famous physical fitness tests and the Aerobics Point System for conditioning USA astronauts. His system is now used by the military, athletic teams, law enforcement, and many other organizations. Head of the Cooper Aerobics Center, he has his own radio and television programs. His latest book (of nearly twenty) is *Regaining the Power of Youth at Any Age* (2005). The excerpt below is from the second chapter of his first book, *Aerobics* (1968), which publicized a fitness program that has spread around the world.

I was visiting a colleague who was testing volunteers for a special project that would require men in the best possible condition. I passed three of the volunteers in the hall. Two had normal builds, but the third was definitely muscular.

"Which of the three do you think will get our recommendation?" my friend asked, tossing their medical records across the desk. I skimmed over the physiological data until I came to the slot where it asked, "Regular exercise?"

One wrote, candidly, "None."

The second, "Nothing regular. Just ride my bike to the base and back every day. About three miles one way."

The third, "Isometrics and weight lifting, one hour a day, five days a week." The muscular one!

I glanced back over each of the records. All pilots, all in their early 30s, none with any history of illness.

"Well?" asked my friend.

"I'd bet on the cyclist."

"Not the weight lifter?"

10   "Not if that's all he does."

My friend smiled. "I think you're right."

Next day he proved it. The three came back for their treadmill tests and the nonexerciser and the weight lifter were completely fatigued within the first five minutes. The cyclist was still going strong 10 minutes later, running uphill at a 6½ mph clip. He was recommended for the project. The other two weren't.

This story, when I use it in my lectures, always surprises people. The nonexerciser they can believe. The cyclist, maybe. But the weight lifter, or anyone who does strictly isometrics or calisthenics, they all *look* in such good condition!

In my business, looks are deceitful. Some exceptionally physically fit men tested in our laboratory were middle-aged types with slight builds, including an occasional one with a paunch. Some of the most unfit we've ever seen were husky young men with cardiac conditions.

15   If this shatters any illusions about slim waistlines and large biceps being the key to good health, I'm sorry. They're not a deterrent, but they're no guarantee either. They're mostly a byproduct. The real key is elsewhere.

Take those three volunteers. By ordinary standards, all three should have been accepted. None of them had any physical defects, or ever had any. Why the discrimination?

For special projects, the military services can afford to be discriminate. They can afford to classify the physically fit into their three classic categories and choose only the most fit.

The nonexerciser represents passive fitness. There's nothing wrong with him—not yet anyway—but there's nothing really right with him either. If he's lucky, he can coast like that for years. But, without any activity, his body is essentially deteriorating.

The weight lifter, or those who emphasize isometrics or calisthenics, represent muscular fitness. These types, who have the right motives but the wrong approach, are struck with the myth that muscular strength or agility means physical fitness. This is one of the great misconceptions in the field of exercise. The muscles that show—the skeletal muscles—are just one system in the body, and by no means the most important. If your exercise program is directed only at the skeletal muscles, you'll never achieve real physical fitness.

20   The cyclist, whether he knew it or not, had found one of the most basic means to overall fitness. . . . By riding three miles to work, six miles round trip, he was earning more than enough points to answer the question, "How much exercise?" and he proved it on the treadmill.

The cyclist represents the third, and best, kind of fitness, overall fitness. We call it endurance fitness, or working capacity, the ability to do prolonged work without undue fatigue. It assumes the absence of any ailment, and it has little to do with pure muscular strength or agility. It has very much to do with the body's *overall* health, the health of the heart, the lungs, the entire cardiovascular system and the other organs, *as well as* the muscles.

REFLECTING AND INTERPRETING

1. Consider how a questioning title functions. What did you think of first after you read this title?
2. Do you think the anecdote is an effective opening for this article? Why?
3. Where is the thesis of this essay?
4. What three categories of fitness does Dr. Cooper use here?
5. What is "endurance fitness"?
6. How does "muscular fitness" differ from "endurance fitness"?
7. Why can't physical fitness be accurately judged by considering the age and build of a person?
8. How can a fitness routine improve academic performance? How can fitness help you in a job interview? To function effectively on the job?

A WRITER'S RESPONSE

Do you have a fitness routine? How might you improve it? If you lack such a routine, how might you begin? How would you benefit? Would you like to read a fitness book? Use the fitness center on campus? Or start a walking or cycling regimen? Write a paragraph setting forth your plan to increase your fitness.

WHERE DO WE STAND?   LISA DAVIS

Have you noticed any slight differences in behavior or conversational style among students of varying cultures on your campus? In this essay, first published in *Health* magazine, Lisa Davis discusses how different spatial needs and eye contact can cause hasty judgments and misunderstanding. Davis graduated with a BA in psychology from the University of California and an MS in education and psychology from California State University. She served as editor of *Health* magazine and as advisor to the San Joaquin Family Preservation and Family Support Program. She received awards from the Sierra Health Foundation (1995), City of Manteca (1995), and University of California (1992), as well as an Excellence award (1998). Davis has published *Journeys Within: Source Book of Guided Meditations* (1997) and articles in the *Los Angeles Times, Science News, Discover, More, Reader's Digest,* and *O,* the Oprah magazine.

Call it the dance of the jet set, the diplomat's tango: A man from the Middle East, say, falls into conversation with an American, becomes animated, takes a step forward. The American makes a slight postural adjustment, 1 shifts his feet, edges backward. A little more talk and the Arab advances; a little more talk and the American retreats.

"By the end of the cocktail party," says Middle East expert Peter Bechtold of the State Department's Foreign Service Institute, "you have an American in each corner of the room, because that's as far as they can back up."

What do you do when an amiable chat leaves one person feeling vaguely bullied, the other unaccountably chilled? Things would be simpler if these jetsetters were speaking different languages—they'd just get themselves a translator. But the problem's a little tougher, because they're using different languages of space.

Everyone who's ever felt cramped in a crowd knows that the skin is not the body's only boundary. We each wear a zone of privacy like a hoop skirt, inviting others in or keeping them out with body language—by how closely we approach, the angle at which we face them, the speed with which we break a gaze. It's a subtle code, but one we use and interpret easily, indeed automatically, having absorbed the vocabulary from infancy.

5   At least, we *assume* we're reading it right. But from culture to culture, from group to group within a single country, even between the sexes, the language of space has distinctive accents, confusing umlauts. That leaves a lot of room for misinterpretations, and the stakes have gotten higher as business has become increasingly international and populations multicultural. So a new breed of consultants has appeared in the last few years, interpreting for globe-trotters of all nationalities the meaning and use of personal space.

For instance, says international business consultant Sondra Snowdon, Saudi Arabians like to conduct business discussions from within spitting distance—literally. They bathe in each other's breath as part of building the relationship. "Americans back up," says Snowdon, "but they're harming their chances of winning the contracts." In seminars, Snowdon discusses the close quarters common in Middle Eastern conversations and has her students practice talking with each other at very chummy distances.

Still, her clients had better be careful where they take their shrunken "space bubble," because cultures are idiosyncratic in their spatial needs. Japanese subways bring people about as close together as humanly possible, for instance, yet even a handshake can be offensively physical in a Japanese office. And, says researcher and writer Mildred Reed Hall, Americans can even make their business counterparts in Japan uncomfortable with the kind of direct eye contact that's normal here.

"Not only do most Japanese businessmen not look at you, they keep their eyes down," Hall says. "We look at people for hours, and they feel like they're under a searchlight."

The study of personal space got under way in the early 1950s, when anthropologist Edward Hall described a sort of cultural continuum of personal space. (Hall has frequently collaborated with his wife, Mildred.) According to Hall, on the "high-contact" side of the continuum—in Mediterranean and South American societies, for example—social conversations include much eye contact, touching and smiling, typically while standing at a distance of about a foot. On the other end of the scale, say in Northern European cultures, a lingering gaze may feel invasive, manipulative or disrespectful; a social chat takes place at a remove of about 2½ feet.

In the middle-of-the-road United States, people usually stand about **10** 18 inches apart for this sort of conversation—unless we want to win foreign friends and influence people, in which case, research shows, we'd better adjust our posture. In one study, when British graduate students were trained to adopt Arab patterns of behavior (facing their partners straight on, with lots of eye contact and smiling), Middle Eastern exchange students found them more likable and trustworthy than typical British students.

In contrast, the misuse of space can call whole personalities into suspicion: When researchers seated pairs of women for conversation, those forced to talk at an uncomfortably large distance were more likely to describe their partners as cold and rejecting.

Don't snuggle up too fast, though. Men in that study were more irritated by their partners when they were forced to talk at close range. Spatially speaking, it seems men and women are subtly foreign to each other. No matter whether a society operates at arm's length or cheek-to-jowl, the women look at each other more and stand a bit closer than do the men.

Anthropologist Hall suggests that a culture's use of space is evidence of a reliance on one sense over another: Middle Easterners get much of their information through their senses of smell and touch, he says, which require a close approach; Americans rely primarily on visual information, backing up in order to see an intelligible picture.

Conversational distances also tend to reflect the standard greeting distance in each culture, says State Department expert Bechtold. Americans shake hands, and then talk at arm's length. Arabs do a Hollywood-style, cheek-to-cheek social kiss, and their conversation is similarly up close and personal. And, at a distance great enough to keep heads from knocking together—about two feet—the Japanese bow and talk to each other. On the other hand, the need for more or less space may reflect something of a cultural temperament. "There's no word for privacy in Arab cultures," says Bechtold. "They think it means loneliness."

Whatever their origin, spatial styles are very real. In fact, even those **15** who set out to transgress find it uncomfortable to intrude on the space of strangers, says psychologist John Aiello at Rutgers University. "I've had students say, 'Boy, that was the hardest thing I ever had to do—to stand six inches away when I was asking those questions.'"

Luckily, given coaching and time, it seems to get easier to acculturate to foreign habits of contact. Says Bechtold, "You often see men holding hands in the Middle East and walking down the street together. It's just that they're concerned and don't want you to cross the street unescorted, but I've had American pilots come in here and say, 'I don't want some SOB holding my hand.' Then I see them there, holding the hand of a Saudi."

"Personal space isn't so hard for people to learn," Bechtold adds. "What is really much harder is the business of dinner being served at midnight."

REFLECTING AND INTERPRETING

1. How does Davis classify people in this essay?

2. What divisions of conversational distances are discussed?

3. What is unusual about the way the first example is given? Describe the tone.

4. How does Davis establish credibility in the second paragraph and again later?

5. What function does paragraph 3 serve?

6. Davis makes unusual comparisons. Identify the literary devices in "a zone of privacy like a hoop skirt" and "bathe in each other's breath."

7. How do the personal space needs of Americans and those of Middle Eastern people generally differ? What American habits make Japanese uncomfortable?

8. Who studied the use of personal space in the 1950s? At what average distance do Americans converse? How does this distance vary with gender?

9. What danger exists in nonverbal communication?

10. How do greetings and other habits influence personal space? How does this vary from culture to culture? Is it difficult to learn about this topic? To adapt?

A WRITER'S RESPONSE

In your future career, will it be beneficial for you to be keenly aware of cultural diversity? Why or why not? Write an essay explaining your point of view.

THE MYTH OF THE LATIN WOMAN: I JUST MET A GIRL NAMED MARIA
JUDITH ORTIZ COFER

At age four Judith Ortiz Cofer came with her family to the United States from Puerto Rico. Now a professor of English at the University of Georgia, Cofer has written a dazzling array of books, short stories, essays, and poetry. Her writings have garnered numerous awards, including the Anisfield Wolf Book Award for *The Latin Deli: Prose and Poetry* (1993), the PEN/Martha Albrand Special Citation in nonfiction for *Silent Dancing* (1995), Best Book of the Year 1995–96 for *An Island Like You: Stories of the Barrio*, and the Paterson Book Prize for *The Year of Our Revolution: New and Selected Stories and Poems* (1998). Her work has been published in the *Kenyon Review, Southern Review, Georgia Review,* and *Glamour,* as well as numerous anthologies and textbooks. This essay, taken from *The Latin Deli,* explores the stereotypes often appended to Latinas.

On a bus trip to London from Oxford University where I was earning 1
some graduate credits one summer, a young man, obviously fresh from a
pub, spotted me and as if struck by inspiration went down on his knees in
the aisle. With both hands over his heart he broke into an Irish tenor's ren-
dition of "Maria" from *West Side Story.* My politely amused fellow passengers gave his lovely voice the round of gentle applause it deserved.
Though I was not quite as amused, I managed my version of an English
smile: no show of teeth, no extreme contortions of the facial muscles—I
was at this time of my life practicing reserve and cool. Oh, that British control, how I coveted it. But Maria had followed me to London, reminding me
of a prime fact of my life: you can leave the Island, master the English language, and travel as far as you can, but if you are a Latina, especially one
like me who so obviously belongs to Rita Moreno's gene pool, the Island
travels with you.

This is sometimes a very good thing—it may win you that extra minute
of someone's attention. But with some people, the same thing can make
you an island—not so much a tropical paradise as an Alcatraz, a place nobody wants to visit. As a Puerto Rican girl growing up in the United States
and wanting like most children to "belong," I resented the stereotype that
my Hispanic appearance called forth from many people I met.

Our family lived in a large urban center in New Jersey during the sixties, where life was designed as a microcosm of my parents' casas on the
island. We spoke in Spanish, we ate Puerto Rican food bought at the
bodega, and we practiced strict Catholicism complete with Saturday con-
fession and Sunday mass at a church where our parents were accommo-
dated into a one-hour Spanish mass slot, performed by a Chinese priest
trained as a missionary for Latin America.

As a girl I was kept under strict surveillance, since virtue and modesty
were, by cultural equation, the same as family honor. As a teenager I was
instructed on how to behave as a proper señorita. But it was a conflicting
message girls got, since the Puerto Rican mothers also encouraged their
daughters to look and act like women and to dress in clothes our Anglo
friends and their mothers found too "mature" for our age. It was, and is,
cultural, yet I often felt humiliated when I appeared at an American friend's
party wearing a dress more suitable to a semiformal than to a playroom
birthday celebration. At Puerto Rican festivities, neither the music nor the
colors we wore could be too loud. I still experience a vague sense of let-
down when I'm invited to a "party" and it turns out to be a marathon conversation in hushed tones rather than a fiesta with salsa, laughter, and
dancing—the kind of celebration I remember from my childhood.

I remember Career Day in our high school, when teachers told us to 5
come dressed as if for a job interview. It quickly became obvious that to the
barrio girls, "dressing up" sometimes meant wearing ornate jewelry and
clothing that would be more appropriate (by mainstream standards) for
the company Christmas party than as daily office attire. That morning I had
agonized in front of my closet, trying to figure out what a "career girl"

would wear. . . . I knew how to dress for school: at the Catholic school I attended we all wore uniforms; I knew how to dress for Sunday mass, and I knew what dresses to wear for parties at my relatives' homes. Though I do not recall the precise details of my Career Day outfit, it must have been a composite of the above choices. But I remember a comment my friend (an Italian-American) made in later years that coalesced my impressions of that day. She said that at the business school she was attending the Puerto Rican girls always stood out for wearing "everything at once." She meant, of course, too much jewelry, too many accessories. On that day at school, we were simply made the negative models by the nuns who were themselves not credible fashion experts to any of us. But it was painfully obvious to me that to the others, in their tailored skirts and silk blouses, we must have seemed "hopeless" and "vulgar." Though I now know that most adolescents feel out of step much of the time, I also know that for the Puerto Rican girls of my generation that sense was intensified. The way our teachers and classmates looked at us that day in school was just a taste of the culture clash that awaited us in the real world, where prospective employers and men on the street would often misinterpret our tight skirts and jingling bracelets as a come-on.

Mixed cultural signals have perpetuated certain stereotypes—for example, that of the Hispanic woman as the "Hot Tamale" or sexual firebrand. It is a one-dimensional view that the media have found easy to promote. In their special vocabulary, advertisers have designated "sizzling" and "smoldering" as the adjectives of choice for describing not only the foods but also the women of Latin America. From conversations in my house, I recall hearing about the harassment that Puerto Rican women endured in factories where the "boss men" talked to them as if sexual innuendo was all they understood and, worse, often gave them the choice of submitting to advances or being fired.

It is custom, however, not chromosomes, that leads us to choose scarlet over pale pink. As young girls, we were influenced in our decisions about clothes and colors by the women—older sisters and mothers who had grown up on a tropical island where the natural environment was a riot of primary colors, where showing your skin was one way to keep cool as well as to look sexy. Most important of all, on the island, women perhaps felt freer to dress and move more provocatively, since, in most cases, they were protected by the traditions, mores, and laws of a Spanish/Catholic system of morality and machismo whose main rule was: *You may look at my sister, but if you touch her I will kill you.* The extended family and church structure could provide a young woman with a circle of safety in her small pueblo on the island; if a man "wronged" a girl, everyone would close in to save her family honor.

This is what I have gleaned from my discussion as an adult with older Puerto Rican women. They have told me about dressing in their best party clothes on Saturday nights and going to the town's plaza to promenade with their girlfriends in front of the boys they liked. The males were thus given an opportunity to admire the women and to express their admiration in the form of *piropos:* erotically charged street poems they composed on the spot. I have been subjected to a few piropos while visiting the Island, and they can be outrageous, although custom dictates that they must never cross into obscenity. This ritual, as I understand it, also entails a show of studied indifference on the woman's part; if she is "decent," she must not acknowledge the man's impassioned words. So I do understand how things can be lost in translation. When a Puerto Rican girl dressed in her idea of what is attractive meets a man from the mainstream culture who has been trained to react to certain types of clothing as a sexual signal, a clash is likely to take place. The line I first heard based on this aspect of the myth happened when the boy who took me to my first formal dance leaned over to plant a sloppy overeager kiss painfully on my mouth, and when I didn't respond with sufficient passion said in a resentful tone: "I thought you Latin girls were supposed to mature early"—my first instance of being thought of as a fruit or vegetable—I was supposed to *ripen,* not just grow into womanhood like other girls.

It is surprising to some of my professional friends that some people, including those who should know better, still put others "in their place." Though rarer, these incidents are still commonplace in my life. It happened to me most recently during a stay at a very classy metropolitan hotel favored by young professional couples for their weddings. Late one evening after the theater, as I walked toward my room with my new colleague (a woman with whom I was coordinating an arts program), a middle-aged man in a tuxedo, a young girl in satin and lace on his arm, stepped directly into our path. With his champagne glass extended toward me, he exclaimed, "Evita!"

Our way blocked, my companion and I listened as the man half-recited, 10 half-bellowed "Don't Cry for Me, Argentina." When he finished, the young girl said: "How about a round of applause for my daddy?" We complied, hoping this would bring the silly spectacle to a close. I was becoming aware that our little group was attracting the attention of the other guests. "Daddy" must have perceived this too, and he once more barred the way as we tried to walk past him. He began to shout-sing a ditty to the tune of "La Bamba"—except the lyrics were about a girl named María whose exploits all rhymed with her name and gonorrhea. The girl kept saying "Oh Daddy" and looking at me with pleading eyes. She wanted me to laugh along with the others. My companion and I stood silently waiting for the man to end his offensive song. When he finished, I looked not at him but at his daughter. I advised her calmly never to ask her father what he had done in the army. Then I walked between them and to my room. My friend complimented me on my cool handling of the situation. I confessed to her that I really had wanted to push the jerk into the swimming pool. I knew that this same man—probably a corporate executive, well educated, even worldly by most standards—would not have been likely to regale a white woman with a dirty song in public. He would perhaps have checked his impulse by assuming that she could be somebody's wife or mother, or at least *somebody* who might take offense. But to him, I was just an Evita or a María: merely a character in his cartoon-populated universe.

Because of my education and my proficiency with the English language, I have acquired many mechanisms for dealing with the anger I experience. This was not true for my parents, nor is it true for the many Latin women working at menial jobs who must put up with stereotypes about our ethnic group such as: "They make good domestics." This is another facet of the myth of the Latin woman in the United States. Its origin is simple to deduce. Work as domestics, waitressing, and factory jobs are all that's available to women with little English and few skills. The myth of the Hispanic menial has been sustained by the same media phenomenon that made "Mammy" from *Gone with the Wind* America's idea of the black woman for generations; María, the housemaid or counter girl, is now indelibly etched into the national psyche. The big and the little screens have presented us with the picture of the funny Hispanic maid, mispronouncing words and cooking up a spicy storm in a shiny California kitchen.

This media-engendered image of the Latina in the United States has been documented by feminist Hispanic scholars, who claim that such portrayals are partially responsible for the denial of opportunities for upward mobility among Latinas in the professions. I have a Chicana friend working on a Ph.D. in philosophy at a major university. She says her doctor still shakes his head in puzzled amazement at all the "big words" she uses. Since I do not wear my diplomas around my neck for all to see, I too have on occasion been sent to that "kitchen," where some think I obviously belong.

One such incident that has stayed with me, though I recognize it as a minor offense, happened on the day of my first public poetry reading. It took place in Miami in a boat-restaurant where we were having lunch before the event. I was nervous and excited as I walked in with my notebook in my hand. An older woman motioned me to her table. Thinking (foolish me) that she wanted me to autograph a copy of my brand new slender volume of verse, I went over. She ordered a cup of coffee from me, assuming that I was the waitress. Easy enough to mistake my poems for menus, I suppose, I know that it wasn't an intentional act of cruelty, yet of all the good things that happened that day, I remember that scene most clearly, because it reminded me of what I had to overcome before anyone would take me seriously. In retrospect I understand that my anger gave my reading fire, that I have almost always taken doubts in my abilities as a challenge—and that the result is, most times, a feeling of satisfaction at having won a convert when I see the cold, appraising eyes warm to my words, the body language change, the smile that indicates that I have opened some avenue for communication. That day I read to that woman and her lowered eyes told me that she was embarrassed at her little faux pas, and when I willed her to look up at me, it was my victory, and she graciously allowed me to punish her with my full attention. We shook hands at the end of the reading, and I never saw her again. She has probably forgotten the whole thing but maybe not.

Yet I am one of the lucky ones. My parents made it possible for me to acquire a stronger footing in the mainstream culture by giving me the chance at an education. And books and art have saved me from the harsher forms of ethnic and racial prejudice that many of my Hispanic *compañeras* have had to endure. I travel a lot around the United States, reading from my books of poetry and my novel, and the reception I most often receive is one of positive interest by people who want to know more about my culture. There are, however, thousands of Latinas without the privilege of an education or the entrée into society that I have. For them life is a struggle against the misconceptions perpetuated by the myth of the Latina. . . . We cannot change this situation by legislating the way people look at us. The transformation, as I see it, has to occur at a much more individual level. My personal goal in my public life is to try to replace the old pervasive stereotypes and myths about Latinas with a much more interesting set of realities. Every time I give a reading, I hope the stories I tell, the dreams and fears I examine in my work, can achieve some universal truth which will get my audience past the particulars of my skin color, my accent, or my clothes.

I once wrote a poem in which I called us Latinas "God's brown daugh-   15
ters." This poem is really a prayer of sorts, offered upward, but also, through the human-to-human channel of art, outward. It is a prayer for communication, and for respect. In it, Latin women pray "in Spanish to an Anglo God / with a Jewish heritage," and they are "fervently hoping / that if not omnipotent, / at least He be bilingual."

REFLECTING AND INTERPRETING

1. Does the opening anecdote influence your feeling toward the narrator? If so, how?

2. Where is the thesis statement?

3. Did Cofer's parents help her to blend in with her American peers? Cite examples.

4. What assumption did the teachers make about Career Day that caused problems for the Puerto Rican girls? What should the teachers have done?

5. Explain the "circle of safety" that existed for women in Puerto Rico. What underlying premise protected women there?

6. What are the stereotypic classifications that Cofer has been subjected to?

7. How has Cofer channeled her anger? Cite an example.

8. Does the anecdote in paragraph 13 seem incomplete? What else would you like to know?

9. Why does Cofer say she is "one of the lucky ones"? What is her personal goal?

10. Examine the title. How do "myth" and "Maria" work together?

A WRITER'S RESPONSE

1. Have you ever been stereotyped? How did you react?

2. In the past decade, have expectations for appearance in job interviews changed? If so, how?

A TALE OF FOUR LEARNERS   BERNICE MCCARTHY

After earning a doctorate in education and learning theory from Northwestern University, Bernice McCarthy has become a leading expert on learning styles. To make learning more effective, she devised the 4MAT™ System, which has been adopted by numerous schools and organizations internationally. She has given countless workshops and presentations at universities, the Smithsonian, the U.S. Navy War College, and other institutions of learning. She has written five books on learning, including coauthoring *4MAT: 8 Steps to Designing and Delivering Effective Training*. Here she classifies learning according to the 4MAT System.

1   A young man at a midwestern middle school said of his social studies teacher, "She doesn't label us, and she helps us do all kinds of things." That student expressed very simply my evolving understanding of style since I created the 4MAT System in 1979. The way one perceives reality and reacts to it forms a pattern over time. This pattern comes to dominate the way one integrates ideas, skills, and information about people and the way one adapts knowledge and forms meaning.

But to learn successfully, a student also needs expertise in other learning styles; together these styles form a natural cycle of learning. That middle school teacher apparently honored the unique style that each student brought to her classroom, while helping each one do some stretching and master all the ways of learning.

Following are true stories about four types of learners. They illustrate how students with different learning styles experience school and why we must create opportunities for diverse learning experiences for every child.

Linda was in 6th grade when she hit the wall in math. She had loved school up until then. Her teachers and classmates agreed that her poetry was quite good, and her poems often appeared in local publications. But math was a problem. She couldn't connect it to anything—she simply could not see the patterns. Her teachers were not pleased with her and she longed to please them.

5   Linda went on to college, and when she was a junior, a new professor arrived on campus. The day before Linda's statistics class began, she met

him in the hallway. He said, "Oh, you're Linda; I've been reading your poetry. You are going to do very well in statistics."

She looked at him in amazement. "How can you say that? I have such difficulty in all my math classes."

He smiled and answered, "I can tell from your poetry that you understand symmetry. Statistics is about symmetry. As a matter of fact, statistics is the poetry of math." Linda went on to earn an A in that class. Her professor had connected statistics to her life and showed her the patterns (McCarthy 1996).

Linda is a Type 1 learner—the highly imaginative student who favors feeling and reflecting. These learners

- are at home with their feelings, people-oriented, outstanding observers of people, great listeners and nurturers, and committed to making the world a better place.

- prefer to learn by talking about experiences; listening and watching quietly, then responding to others and discussing ideas; asking questions; brainstorming; and examining relationships. They work well in groups or teams but also enjoy reading quietly. 10

- experience difficulty with long verbal explanations, with giving oral presentations, and with memorizing large chunks of abstract information. They dislike confusion or conflict, environments where mistakes are openly criticized, or where they cannot discuss their perceptions.

- have a cognitive style that puts perception before judgment, subjective knowledge before objective facts, and reflection before action. They prefer to make decisions based on feeling, are visual/auditory/kinesthetic, and experiential before conceptual.

As a Type 1 learner, Linda needed to connect math to her real life, to know why it was useful as a way of thinking and a way of formulating problems and solutions. She also needed her teachers to believe in her and to spend time with and nurture her.

Marcus was in 1st grade, and he loved school. Everything he longed for was present there—the teacher's loving interest, the thrill of deciphering the symbols that meant things, the things he could touch and feel, the addition problems that the teacher wrote on the chalkboard. He could always see the answers. His excitement was like that of the basketball player who knows that if he can just get his hands on the ball, he can sink it. Each question became an exciting foray into even more questions. And as his reading improved rapidly, he could not get enough of books. He welcomed the words and ideas of each new writer. He felt confident; he knew he belonged (McCarthy 1996).

Marcus is a Type 2 learner—the analytic student who favors reflecting 15 and thinking. These learners

- have a knowledge-oriented style; are outstanding at conceptualizing material; analyze and classify their experiences and organize ideas; are highly organized and at home with details and data; are good at step-by-step tasks; are fascinated with structure; believe in their ability to understand; and are committed to making the world more lucid.

- prefer to learn through lectures and objective explanations, by working independently and systematically, and by reading and exchanging ideas.

- experience difficulty in noisy, high-activity environments, ambiguous situations, and working in groups. They also have trouble with open-ended assignments, as well as with presentations, role-playing, and nonsequential instructions. They have difficulty talking about feelings as well.

- have a cognitive style that is objective thinking, reflection before action, impersonal, auditory/visual/kinesthetic, conceptual over experiential. They tend to make judgments first, then support them with their perceptions.

20   As a Type 2 learner, Marcus found school an absolute joy. Testing, so frightening to Linda, was a tonic for him, a chance to prove he could do it. Because he was naturally verbal and school is mostly a verbal challenge, he was—and continues to be—successful.

When Jimmy was in 2nd grade he did not like to read, and that made school difficult. He did enjoy having others read to him, and his younger brother, a 1st grader, read him stories every night. Jimmy did excel in math and art. He loved to work alone on projects and never wanted help. When he was asked to illustrate a story or build something to depict a math concept, he approached the task excitedly. He was happiest when he could solve a problem by creating a three-dimensional solution.

Unfortunately, Jimmy had a rigid teacher whose timing was always different from his own. Jimmy either finished too fast or took too long when he got really interested in a project. Once his teacher said in exasperation, "I didn't say you had to do your best work, Jimmy, just get it done!" When Jimmy's family bought a new VCR, they read the directions aloud to figure out how it worked. Jimmy stepped up and simply made it work. His reading problem continued into 3rd grade when he caught up with the others, but he never let it get him down—he was simply too busy doing other kinds of things (McCarthy 1996).

Jimmy is a Type 3 learner—the common-sense learner who favors thinking and doing. These learners

- are great problem solvers and are drawn to how things work. They are at home with tasks and deadlines, are productive and committed to making the world work better, and they believe in their ability to get the job done. They are also active and need opportunities to move around.

25 - prefer to learn through active problem solving; step-by-step procedures; touching, manipulating, and constructing; demonstrations; experimentation and tinkering; and competition.

- experience difficulty when reading is the primary means of learning and whenever they cannot physically test what they are told. They have trouble with verbal complexity, paradoxes or unclear choices, subtle relationships, and open-ended academic tasks. They also have difficulty expressing feelings.

- have a cognitive style that features objective thinking and facts over ideas, action before reflection, and judgment before perception. Their style is impersonal and kinesthetic/auditory/visual.

As a Type 3 learner, Jimmy needed to work things out in his own way, to create unique solutions to problems, and, most of all, to show what he learned by doing something concrete with it. His verbal skills did not kick in until well into the 3rd grade. Although this is not unusual with highly spatial learners, teachers treated it as an aberration. School was simply too regimented and too verbal for Jimmy. What saved him was his focus on his own learning.

When Leah was a high school freshman, she liked her new friends and some of her teachers. But she had a fierce need to learn, and school was not nearly exciting enough for her. She found so much of it deadening—memorizing endless facts that were totally irrelevant to her life. Leah had a wonderful spontaneity, and when it took hold of her, she focused so intensely that time became meaningless. Her teachers came to regard this spontaneity as a liability that was taking her away from the things she needed to know.

At first Leah persevered. Instead of preparing a juvenile justice report[30] based on her social studies text, she asked to be allowed to go to juvenile court and see for herself, and then present her findings in a skit. Her teachers seldom agreed to her proposals, and after a while Leah stopped trying. She had natural leadership talent, which she expressed through her extracurricular activities—the one part of school she came to love. She graduated, but has believed ever since then that real learning does not happen in school (McCarthy 1996).

Leah is a Type 4 learner—the dynamic learner who favors creating and acting. These learners

- are proud of their subjectivity, at home with ambiguity and change, and great risk takers and entrepreneurs. They act to extend and enrich their experiences and to challenge the boundaries of their worlds for the sake of growth and renewal, and they believe in their ability to influence what happens. They initiate learning by looking for unique aspects of the information to learn and they sustain learning through trial and error.

- prefer to learn by self-discovery, talking, convincing others, looking for creative solutions to problems, and engaging in free flights of ideas. They also like to work independently and tackle open-ended academic tasks with lots of options, paradox, or subtle relationships. Their interpersonal skills are good.

35 • experience difficulty with rigid routines when they are not allowed to question. They also have trouble with visual complexity, methodical tasks, time management, and absolutes.

• have a cognitive style that is perception first with slight attention to judgment, subjective, relational, action-oriented, kinesthetic/auditory/visual, and experiential over conceptual.

Leah found learning for school's sake incomprehensible. As in Jimmy's case, doing was crucial to her approach. She preferred interviewing over reading, going to court to see for herself, exploring instead of hearing how others see things.

In any classroom, Linda, Marcus, Jimmy, Leah, and their many shades and varieties sit before the teacher—challenging and waiting to be challenged. The frustrating question is: why are some learners honored in our schools and others ignored, discouraged, or even frowned upon? Why did Marcus fare so well, while Linda, Jimmy, and Leah struggled to be accepted?

In my definition of learning, the learner makes meaning by moving through a natural cycle—a movement from feeling to reflecting to thinking and, finally, to acting. This cycle results from the interplay of two separate dimensions—perceiving and processing (Kolb 1984).

40 In perceiving, we take in what happens to us by (1) feeling, as we grasp our experience, and then by (2) thinking, as we begin to separate ourselves from the experience and name and classify it. The resulting concepts become our way of interpreting our world (Kegan 1982).

We also process experiences in two ways: by (1) reflecting on them, and then by (2) acting on those reflections. We also try things; we tinker.

The places in this cycle that we find most comfortable—where we function with natural ease and grace—are our learning preferences or styles, the "spins" we put on learning.

Unfortunately, schools tend to honor only one aspect of perceiving—thinking. This is very tough on kids whose approach to learning is predominately feeling. Linda and Leah, like many other Type 1 and 4 learners—both male and female—are naturals on the feeling end of experience. Jimmy and Marcus, the Type 2 and 3 learners, favor the thinking end.

As with feeling and thinking, reflecting and acting need to be in balance. But our schools favor reflecting. Marcus excelled at that, while both Jimmy and Leah needed to act. The lack of hands-on learning created difficulties for both of them.

45 Even as I define styles in my work, I caution that we must be wary of labels. Over time, and with experience, practice, and encouragement, students become comfortable with learning styles that aren't naturally their own. Successful learners, in fact, develop multiple styles.

The 4MAT framework is designed to help students gain expertise in every learning style. We design lesson units as cycles built around core concepts, each of which incorporates experiencing (Type 1), conceptualizing (Type 2), applying (Type 3), and creating (Type 4). The styles answer the questions:

- Why do I need to know this? (the personal meaning of Type 1).
- What exactly is this content or skill? (the conceptual understanding of Type 2).
- How will I use this in my life (the real-life skills of Type 3).
- If I do use this, what possibilities will it create? (the unique adaptations of Type 4).

Had the teachers of Linda, Marcus, Jimmy, and Leah used the entire cycle of learning styles, including those areas in which each student needed to stretch, all four students would have acquired expertise in all facets of the cycle. They would have made personal connections to the learning, examined expert knowledge, used what they were learning to solve problems, and come up with new ways to apply the learning—both personally and in the world at large. (As it happened, the students learned to do these things on their own.)

In addressing the various learning styles, the 4MAT System also incorporates elements of brain research—in particular, the different ways that the right and left hemispheres of the cerebral cortex process information (Benson 1985, McCarthy 1981 and 1987, Sylvester 1995, Wittrock 1985). I call these contrasting mental operations the Left and Right Modes.

The Left Mode is analytical and knows those things we can describe **50** with precision. It examines cause and effect, breaks things down into parts and categorizes them, seeks and uses language and symbols, abstracts experience for comprehension, generates theory, and creates models. It is sequential and works in time.

The Right Mode knows more than it can tell, filling in gaps and imagining. It is intuitive. It senses feelings; forms images and mental combinations; and seeks and uses patterns, relationships, and connections. It manipulates form, distance, and space.

Excellence and higher-order thinking demand that we honor both sides of the brain, teaching interactively with hands-on, real-life, messy problem solving. Learners speak in words, signs, symbols, movement, and through music. The more voices students master, the more new learning they will do. Unfortunately, however, teachers persist in lecturing and using logical, sequential problem solving most of the time.

In assessing student performance, traditional methods work fairly well for Type 2 learners, who like to prove themselves, and Type 3 learners, who do well on tests in general. Traditional testing doesn't work as well for Types 1 and 4, however. Type 1 learners have difficulty in formal testing situations, especially when tests are timed and call for precise answers. Type 4 learners have trouble doing things by the book and with absolutes and rigid routines when they are not allowed to ask questions.

Further, students change roles as they move through the learning cycle. Tests that require students to recall facts obviously do not reflect the subtlety of these changes.

55   We need assessment tools that help us understand the whole person. We must assess the students' ability to picture the concept, to experiment with the idea, to combine skills in order to solve complex problems, to edit and refine their work, and to adapt and integrate learning. We need to know how students are connecting information to their own experiences, how they are blending expert knowledge with their own, and how creative they are. We also need some way of measuring how students reflect on material, conceptualize, and represent what they have learned through various kinds of performances.

Successful learning is a continuous, cyclical, lifelong process of differentiating and integrating these personal modes of adaptation. Teachers do not need to label learners according to their style; they need to help them work for balance and wholeness. Leah needs to learn the ways of Marcus; Jimmy needs Linda's ways. And all learners need encouragement to grow.

Learning is both reflective and active, verbal and nonverbal, concrete and abstract, head and heart. The teacher must use many instructional methods that are personally meaningful to each student. The more students can travel the cycle, the better they can move to higher-order thinking.

As a final note, what became of the students I described earlier? Linda directs the management division of a major human resources consulting firm. Marcus, a former professor of statistics at a prestigious university, is now president of a research firm. Jimmy will be a senior in high school this fall. He scored 100 percent on the Illinois State Math Achievement Test and achieved cum laude in the International Latin Exam. He also had his art portfolio favorably reviewed by the Art Institute of Chicago. And Leah? Leah is a pseudonym for the author of this article.

References

Benson, D. F. "Language in the Left Hemisphere." *The Dual Brain: Hemispheric Specialization in Humans.* Eds. D. F. Benson and E. Zaidel. New York: Guilford, 1985.

Kegan, R. *The Evolving Self: Problems and Process in Human Development.* Cambridge, MA: Harvard UP, 1982.

Kolb, D. A. *Experiential Learning: Experience as the Source of Learning and Development.* Englewood Cliffs, NJ: Prentice-Hall, 1984.

McCarthy, B. *The 4MAT System: Teaching to Learning Styles with Right/Left Mode Techniques.* Barrington, IL: Excel, Inc., 1981, 1987.

McCarthy, B. *About Learning.* Barrington, IL: Excel, Inc., 1996.

Sylvester, R. *A Celebration of Neurons: An Educator's Guide to the Human Brain.* Alexandria, VA: ASCD, 1995.

Wittrock, M. C. "Education and Recent Neuropsychological and Cognitive Research." *The Dual Brain: Hemispheric Specialization in Humans.* Eds. D. F. Benson and E. Zaidel. New York: Guilford, 1985.

REFLECTING AND INTERPRETING

1. Using your own words, restate the meaning of the final two sentences of paragraph 1.

2. Examine the anecdote about Linda. Why wasn't she able to do well in math after sixth grade? What factor is needed to make learning meaningful to Type 1 learners?

3. Which type of learner loves school and fits into our conventional school system easily? Why?

4. Which type of learner does not like to read but works well with hands and loves to solve problems? Why does this learner succeed in school?

5. Describe Leah, Type 4 learner, and explain why she often experienced dissatisfaction with school assignments.

6. What is McCarthy's goal in the 4MAT System? What does she say "successful learners develop"?

7. Reread the four questions in paragraph 47. Are all equally significant to you personally, or are you more concerned with one or two? Why?

8. The author alludes to brain research on dominance of one hemisphere over the other. What functions occur in the right hemisphere (mode)?

9. Based on your experience, do you agree or disagree with the author's conclusion in paragraph 52? Did methods of instruction vary much with different teachers?

10. How is this essay relevant to you? How can you use this learning?

A WRITER'S RESPONSE

1. What is your primary learning style? Which of the four students seem the most like you? Does any early school project or assignment stand out in your mind? Was it difficult or easy? Frustrating or fun? Write an essay describing your learning style and how it affected your attitude toward school.

2. Who was your best teacher? Why do you think he or she was effective? Think about the methods of instruction and learning materials used. Were challenging assignments made? How would you classify his or her learning style?

Comparison: Explaining Relationships

THAT LEAN AND HUNGRY LOOK [1]   SUZANNE BRITT

Suzanne Britt is an Assistant Professor at Meredith College, Raleigh, North Carolina. A prolific author, she has published numerous essays, articles, and poems in newspapers, magazines, and anthologies. She has also written several books, including *Show and Tell* (1983), *A Writer's Rhetoric* (1988), and *Images: A Centennial Journey* (1991). "That Lean and Hungry Look," a witty satire originally published in *Newsweek* (1978), has become somewhat of a classic.

1   Caesar was right. Thin people need watching. I've been watching them for most of my adult life, and I don't like what I see. When these narrow fellows[2] spring at me, I quiver to my toes. Thin people come in all personalities, most of them menacing. You've got your "together" thin person, your mechanical thin person, your condescending thin person, your tsk-tsk thin person, your efficiency-expert thin person. All of them are dangerous.

In the first place, thin people aren't fun. They don't know how to goof off, at least in the best, fat sense of the word. They've always got to be adoing. Give them a coffee break, and they'll jog around the block. Supply

---

[1] The title alludes to the words from Act I, Scene ii of Shakespeare's *Julius Caesar* spoken by the title character:

Let me have men about me that are fat;
Sleek-headed men and such as sleep o' nights;
Yond' Cassius has a lean and hungry look;
He thinks too much: such men are dangerous.

[2] "A narrow Fellow in the Grass" is the first line of an Emily Dickinson poem about snakes.

them with a quiet evening at home, and they'll fix the screen door and lick S&H green stamps. They say things like "there aren't enough hours in the day." Fat people never say that. Fat people think the day is too damn long already.

Thin people make me tired. They've got speedy little metabolisms that cause them to bustle briskly. They're forever rubbing their bony hands together and eyeing new problems to "tackle." I like to surround myself with sluggish, inert, easygoing fat people, the kind who believe that if you clean it up today, it'll just get dirty again tomorrow.

Some people say the business about the jolly fat person is a myth, that all of us chubbies are neurotic, sick, sad people. I disagree. Fat people may not be chortling all day long, but they're a hell of a lot nicer than the wizened and shriveled. Thin people turn surly, mean and hard at a young age because they never learn the value of a hot-fudge sundae for easing tension. Thin people don't like gooey soft things because they themselves are neither gooey nor soft. They are crunchy and dull, like carrots. They go straight to the heart of the matter while fat people let things stay all blurry and hazy and vague, the way things actually are. Thin people want to face the truth. Fat people know there is no truth. One of my thin friends is always staring at complex, unsolvable problems and saying, "The key thing is . . ." Fat people never say that. They know there isn't any such thing as the key thing about anything.

Thin people believe in logic. Fat people see all sides. The sides fat people see are rounded blobs, usually gray, always nebulous and truly not worth worrying about. But the thin person persists. "If you consume more calories than you burn," says one of my thin friends, "you will gain weight. It's that simple." Fat people always grin when they hear statements like that. They know better.   ₅

Fat people realize that life is illogical and unfair. They know very well that God is not in his heaven and all is not right with the world. If God was up there, fat people could have two doughnuts and a big orange drink anytime they wanted it.

Thin people have a long list of logical things they are always spouting off to me. They hold up one finger at a time as they reel off these things, so I won't lose track. They speak slowly as if to a young child. The list is long and full of holes. It contains tidbits like "get a grip on yourself," "cigarettes kill," "cholesterol clogs," "fit as a fiddle," "ducks in a row," "organize" and "sound fiscal management." Phrases like that.

They think these 2,000-point plans lead to happiness. Fat people know happiness is elusive at best and even if they could get the kind thin people talk about, they wouldn't want it. Wisely, fat people see that such programs are too dull, too hard, too off the mark. They are never better than a whole cheesecake.

Fat people know all about the mystery of life. They are the ones acquainted with the night, with luck, with fate, with playing it by ear. One thin person I know once suggested that we arrange all the parts of a jigsaw puzzle into groups according to size, shape and color. He figured this would cut the time needed to complete the puzzle at least by 50 per cent. I said I wouldn't do it. One, I like to muddle through. Two, what good would it do to finish early? Three, the jigsaw puzzle isn't the important thing. The important thing is the fun of four people (one thin person included) sitting around a card table, working a jigsaw puzzle. My thin friend had no use for my list. Instead of joining us, he went outside and mulched the boxwoods. The three remaining fat people finished the puzzle and made chocolate, double-fudged brownies to celebrate.

10   The main problem with thin people is they oppress. Their good intentions, bony torsos, tight ships, neat corners, cerebral machinations and pat solutions loom like dark clouds over the loose, comfortable, spread-out, soft world of the fat. Long after fat people have removed their coats and shoes and put their feet up on the coffee table, thin people are still sitting on the edge of the sofa, looking neat as a pin, discussing rutabagas. Fat people are heavily into fits of laughter, slapping their thighs and whooping it up, while thin people are still politely waiting for the punch line.

Thin people are downers. They like math and morality and reasoned evaluation of the limitations of human beings. They have their skinny little acts together. They expound, prognose, probe and prick.

Fat people are convivial. They will like you even if you're irregular and have acne. They will come up with a good reason why you never wrote the great American novel. They will cry in your beer with you. They will put your name in the pot. They will let you off the hook. Fat people will gab, giggle, guffaw, gallumph, gyrate and gossip. They are generous, giving and gallant. They are gluttonous and goodly and great. What you want when you're down is soft and jiggly, not muscled and stable. Fat people know this. Fat people have plenty of room. Fat people will take you in.

REFLECTING AND INTERPRETING

1. Notice the title. What do you expect in the essay?
2. What is the effect of the literary allusions?
3. How does the author categorize thin people?
4. What does she do in these claims that creates a humorous effect?
5. How accurate are Britt's generalizations about thin people?
6. Which literary device is used in "Thin people are . . . crunchy and dull like carrots"?
7. Examine paragraphs 7 and 9. What do you learn about the author from these examples?
8. Examine sentences 7, 8, and 9 of paragraph 12. Which literary device enhances the humor of the verbs and adjectives?

9. How does the structure of paragraphs 1 through 3 differ from that of paragraph 4? What happens in paragraphs 7 to 12?

10. How does the mixing of the block and alternate block patterns reflect the content of the essay?

A WRITER'S RESPONSE

What do you like about Britt's essay? What do you notice about her voice? Her similes and metaphors? What have you learned about using humor? How can you use some of these strategies and literary devices in your own writing? Write a paragraph.

THE STUBBORN TWIG: MY DOUBLE DOSE OF SCHOOLING

MONICA SONE

Born in Seattle in 1917, Monica Sone lived her first five years in "amoebic bliss" with her parents in an old hotel on the waterfront. At age six she was shocked to learn of her Japanese descent. In 1942, after World War II broke out, she and her family were forced to relocate to a prison camp in Idaho, along with other Japanese Americans. There they lived in drafty tar-paper barracks heated by coal-burning stoves. The 950-acre camp was guarded by barbed wire, watchtowers, armed guards, and dogs. In 1943 Monica Sone was allowed to leave to take a job in Chicago as a dental assistant. In 1953 she published *Nisei Daughter*, an autobiography. Later she became a clinical psychologist. This essay describes her reaction to attending both an American and a Japanese school when she was six years old.

The inevitable, dreaded first day at Nihon Gakko [Japanese school] arrived. Henry and I were dumped into a taxicab, screaming and kicking against the injustice of it all. When the cab stopped in front of a large, square gray-frame building, Mother pried us loose, though we clung to the cab door like barnacles. She half carried us up the hill. We kept up our horrendous shrieking and wailing, right to the school entrance. Then a man burst out of the door. His face seemed to have been carved out of granite and with turned-down mouth and nostrils flaring with disapproval, his black marble eyes crushed us into a quivering silence. This was Mr. Ohashi, the school principal, who had come out to investigate the abominable, un-Japanesey noise on the school premises. 1

Mother bowed deeply and murmured, "I place them in your hands."

He bowed stiffly to Mother, then fastened his eyes on Henry and me and again bowed slowly and deliberately. In our haste to return the bow, we nodded our heads. With icy disdain, he snapped, "That is not an *ojigi*." He bent forward with well-oiled precision. "Bow from the waist, like this."

I wondered, if Mr. Ohashi had the nerve to criticize us in front of Mother, what more he would do in her absence.

School was already in session and the hallway was empty and cold. Mr. Ohashi walked briskly ahead, opened a door, and Henry was whisked 5 inside with Mother. I caught a glimpse of little boys and girls sitting erect, their books held upright on the desks.

As I waited alone out in the hall, I felt a tingling sensation. This was the moment for escape. I would run and run and run. I would be lost for days so that when Father and Mother finally found me, they would be too happy ever to force me back to Nihon Gakko. But Mr. Ohashi was too cunning for me. He must have read my thoughts, for the door suddenly opened, and he and Mother came out. He bowed formally again, "*Sah,* this way," and stalked off.

My will completely dissolved, I followed as in a terrible nightmare. Mother took my hand and smiled warmly, "Don't look so sad, Ka-chan. You'll find it a lot of fun when you get used to it."

I was ushered into a brightly lighted room which seemed ten times as brilliant with the dazzling battery of shining black eyes turned in my direction. I was introduced to Yasuda-sensei, a full-faced woman with a large, ballooning figure. She wore a long, shapeless cotton print smock with streaks of chalk powder down the front. She spoke kindly to me, but with a kindness that one usually reserves for a dull-witted child. She enunciated slowly and loudly, "What is your name?"

I whispered, "Kazuko," hoping she would lower her voice. I felt that our conversation should not be carried on in such a blatant manner.

10   "*Kazuko-san desuka?*" she repeated loudly. "You may sit over there." She pointed to an empty seat in the rear and I walked down an endless aisle between rows of piercing black eyes.

"Kazuko-san, why don't you remove your hat and coat and hang them up behind you?"

A wave of tittering broke out. With burning face, I rose from my seat and struggled out of my coat.

When Mother followed Mr. Ohashi out of the room, my throat began to tighten and tears flooded up again. I did not notice that Yasuda-sensei was standing beside me. Ignoring my snuffling, she handed me a book, opened to the first page. I saw a blurred drawing of one huge, staring eye. Right above it was a black squiggly mark, resembling the arabic figure one with a bar across the middle. Yasuda-sensei was up in front again, reading aloud, "*Meh!*" That was "eye." As we turned the pages, there were pictures of a long, austere nose, its print reading "*hana,*" an ear was called "*mi-mi,*" and a wide anemic-looking mouth, "*ku-chi.*" Soon I was chanting at the top of my voice with the rest of the class, "*Meh! Hana! Mi-mi! Ku-chi!*"

Gradually I yielded to my double dose of schooling. Nihon Gakko was so different from grammar school I found myself switching my personality back and forth daily like a chameleon. At Bailey Gatzert School I was a jumping, screaming, roustabout Yankee, but at the stroke of three when the school bell rang and doors burst open everywhere, spewing out pupils like jelly beans from a broken bag, I suddenly became a modest, faltering, earnest little Japanese girl with a small, timid voice. I trudged down a steep hill and climbed up another steep hill to Nihon Gakko with other black-haired boys and girls. On the playground, we behaved cautiously. Whenever we spied a teacher within bowing distance, we hissed at each other to stop the game, put our feet neatly together, slid our hands down to our knees and bowed slowly and sanctimoniously. In just the proper, moderate tone, putting in every ounce of respect, we chanted, "*Konichi-wa, sensei.* Good day."

For an hour and a half each day, we were put through our paces. At the beginning of each class hour, Yasuda-sensei punched a little bell on her desk. We stood up by our seats, at strict attention. Another "ping!" We all bowed to her in unison while she returned the bow solemnly. With the third "ping!" we sat down together.

There was *yomi-kata* time when individual students were called upon to read the day's lesson, clear and loud. The first time I recited I stood and read with swelling pride the lesson which I had prepared the night before. I mouthed each word carefully and paused for the proper length of time at the end of each sentence. Suddenly Yasuda-sensei stopped me.

"Kazuko-san!"

I looked up at her confused, wondering what mistakes I had made.

"You are holding your book in one hand," she accused me. Indeed, I was. I did not see the need of using two hands to support a thin book which I could balance with two fingers.

"Use both hands!" she commanded me.

Then she peered at me. "And are you leaning against your desk?" Yes, I was slightly. "Stand up straight!"

"*Hai!* Yes, ma'am!"

I learned that I could stumble all around in my lessons without ruffling sensei's nerves, but it was a personal insult to her if I displayed sloppy posture. I must stand up like a soldier, hold the book high in the air with both hands, and keep my feet still.

We recited the Japanese alphabet aloud, fifty-one letters, over and over again. "Ah, ee, oo, eh, *OH!* Kah, kee, koo, key, *KOH!* Sah, shi, soo, seh, *SOH!*" We developed a catchy little rhythm, coming down hard on the last syllable of each line. We wound up the drill with an ear-shattering, triumphant, "Lah, lee, loo, leh, *Loh!* WAH, EE, OO, EH, OH! UN!"

Yasuda-sensei would look suspiciously at us. Our recital sounded a shade too hearty, a shade rhythmic. It lacked something . . . possibly restraint and respect.

During *kaki-kata* hour, I doubled up over my desk and painfully drew out the *kata-kanas,* simplified Japanese ideographs, similar to English block printing. With clenched teeth and perspiring hands, I accentuated and emphasized, delicately nuanced and tapered off lines and curves.

At five-thirty, Yasuda-sensei rang the bell on her desk again. "Ping!" We stood up. "Ping!" We bowed. "Ping!" We vanished from the room like magic, except for one row of students whose turn it was to do *otohban*, washing blackboards, sweeping the floor, and dusting the desks. Under sensei's vigilant eyes, the chore felt like a convict's hard labor.

As time went on, I began to suspect that there was much more to Nihon Gakko than learning the Japanese language. There was a driving spirit of strict discipline behind it all which reached out and weighed heavily upon each pupil's consciousness. That force emanated from the principal's office.

Before Mr. Ohashi came to America, he had been a zealous student of the Ogasawara Shiko Saho, a form of social conduct dreamed up by a Mr. Ogasawara. Mr. Ohashi himself had written a book on etiquette in Japan. He was the Oriental male counterpart of Emily Post. Thus Mr. Ohashi arrived in America with the perfect bow tucked under his waist and a facial expression cemented into perfect samurai control. He came with a smoldering ambition to pass on this knowledge to the tender Japanese saplings born on foreign soil. The school-teachers caught fire, too, and dedicated themselves to us with a vengeance. It was not enough to learn the language. We must talk and walk and sit and bow in the best Japanese tradition.

30 As far as I was concerned, Mr. Ohashi's superior standard boiled down to one thing. The model child is one with deep *rigor mortis* . . . no noise, no trouble, no back talk.

We understood too well what Mr. Ohashi wanted of us. He yearned and wished more than anything else that somehow he could mold all of us into Genji Yamadas. Genji was a classmate whom we detested thoroughly. He was born in Seattle, but his parents had sent him to Japan at an early age for a period of good, old-fashioned education. He returned home a stranger among us with stiff mannerisms and an arrogant attitude. Genji boasted that he could lick anyone, one husky fellow or ten little ones, and he did, time and time again. He was an expert at judo.

Genji was a handsome boy with huge, lustrous dark eyes, a noble patrician nose, jet crew-cut setting off a flawless, fair complexion, looking every bit the son of a samurai. He sat aloof at his desk and paid strict attention to sensei. He was the top student scholastically. He read fluently and perfectly. His handwriting was a beautiful picture of bold, masculine strokes and curves. What gnawed at us more than anything else was that he stood up as straight as a bamboo tree and never lost rigid control of his arms or legs. His bow was snappy and brisk and he always answered "*Hai!*" to everything that sensei said to him, ringing crisp and clear with respect. Every time Mr. Ohashi came into our room for a surprise visit to see if we were under control, he would stop at Genji's desk for a brief chat. Mr. Ohashi's eyes betrayed a glow of pride as he spoke to Genji, who sat up erect, eyes staring respectfully ahead. All we could make out of the conversation was Genji's sharp staccato barks, "*Hai! . . . Hai! . . . Hai!*"

This was the response sublime to Mr. Ohashi. It was real man to man talk. Whenever Mr. Ohashi approached us, we froze in our seats. Instead of snapping into attention like Genji, we wilted and sagged. Mr. Ohashi said we were more like "*konyaku,*" a colorless, gelatinous Japanese food. If a boy fidgeted too nervously under Mr. Ohashi's stare, a vivid red stain rose from the back of Mr. Ohashi's neck until it reached his temple and then there was a sharp explosion like the crack of a whip. "*Keo-tsuke!* Attention!" It made us all leap in our seats, each one of us feeling terribly guilty for being such an inadequate Japanese.

I asked Mother, "Why is Mr. Ohashi so angry all the time? He always looks as if he had just bitten into a green persimmon. I've never seen him smile."

Mother said, "I guess Mr. Ohashi is the old-fashioned schoolmaster. I know he's strict, but he means well. Your father and I received harsher discipline than that in Japan . . . not only from schoolteachers, but from our own parents." **35**

"Yes, I know, Mama." I leaned against her knees as she sat on the old leather davenport, mending our clothes. I thought Father and Mother were still wonderful, even if they had packed me off to Nihon Gakko. "Mrs. Matsui is so strict with her children, too: She thinks you spoil us." I giggled, and reassured her quickly, "But I don't think you spoil us at all."

Mrs. Matsui was ten years older than Mother, and had known Mother's father in Japan. Therefore she felt it was her duty to look after Mother's progress in this foreign country. Like a sharp-eyed hawk, she picked out Mother's weaknesses. . . . It was impossible for us to remember the endless little things we must not do in front of Mrs. Matsui. We must not laugh out loud and show our teeth, or chatter in front of guests, or interrupt adult conversation, or cross our knees while seated, or ask for a piece of candy, or squirm in our seats. . . .

Mr. Ohashi and Mrs. Matsui thought they could work on me and gradually mold me into an ideal Japanese *ojoh-san,* a refined young maiden who is quiet, pure in thought, polite, serene, and self-controlled. They made little headway, for I was too much the child of Skidrow. As far as I was concerned, Nihon Gakko was a total loss. I could not use my Japanese on the people at the hotel. Bowing was practical only at Nihon Gakko. If I were to bow to the hotel patrons, they would have laughed in my face. Therefore promptly at five-thirty every day, I shed Nihon Gakko and returned with relief to an environment which was the only real one to me. Life was too urgent, too exciting, too colorful for me to be sitting quietly in the parlor and contemplating a spray of chrysanthemums in a bowl as a cousin of mine might be doing in Osaka.

REFLECTING AND INTERPRETING

1. What impression do you gain of the two children from the opening paragraph?

2. What method of teaching was used in the Japanese school?

3. How did Kazuko's behavior differ at the two schools?

4. What seems to be the primary emphasis of the Japanese school? How did it affect Kazuko?

5. Why were some students required to stay after school?

6. What literary devices does the author use in paragraphs 14 and 23 to describe her behavior?

7. What goal other than teaching the Japanese language did the principal and teachers strive to attain?

8. To avoid having their mother criticized by a neighbor, what seven things must she and her brother not do?

9. What does Sone say about the effect of the Japanese school upon her?

10. How might the strict discipline of the Japanese school have helped Sone later in life? (Tip: Reread the introduction.)

A WRITER'S RESPONSE

1. Describe your first day of school. How did you feel at the beginning and end of the day?

2. Have you attended more than one school? If so, compare them and their influence on you.

MOTHER TONGUE   AMY TAN

Born and raised in California, Amy Tan (1952–) graduated from high school in Montreux, Switzerland. She earned a master's degree in linguistics from San Jose State University. For five years she served as a language development consultant and directed programs for young disabled children. Next she turned to freelance writing, including corporate communications for companies such as AT&T, IBM, and Pacific Bell. Her first novel *The Joy Luck Club* (1989), brought her international acclaim. Her other works include *The Kitchen God's Wife* (1991), *The Hundred Secret Senses* (1995), *The Bonesetter's Daughter* (2001), *The Opposite of Fate: A Book of Musings* (2003), *Saving Fish from Drowning* (2006), and two children's books—*The Moon Lady* (1992) and *The Chinese Siamese Cat* (1994). "Mother Tongue" was selected for *Best American Essays 1991*.

1   I am not a scholar of English or literature. I cannot give you much more than personal opinions on the English language and its variations in this country or others.

I am a writer. And by that definition, I am someone who has always loved language. I am fascinated by language in daily life. I spend a great deal of my time thinking about the power of language—the way it can evoke an emotion, a visual image, a complex idea, or a simple truth. Language is the tool of my trade. And I use them all—all the Englishes I grew up with.

Recently, I was made keenly aware of the different Englishes I do use. I was giving a talk to a large group of people, the same talk I had already given to half a dozen other groups. The nature of the talk was about my writing, my life, and my book, *The Joy Luck Club.* The talk was going along well enough, until I remembered one major difference that made the whole talk sound wrong. My mother was in the room. And it was perhaps the first time she had heard me give a lengthy speech, using the kind of English I have never used with her. I was saying things like, "The intersection of memory upon imagination" and "There is an aspect of my fiction that relates to thus-and-thus"—a speech filled with carefully wrought grammatical phrases, burdened, it suddenly seemed to me, with nominalized forms, past perfect tenses, conditional phrases, all the forms of standard English that I had learned in school and through books, the forms of English I did not use at home with my mother.

Just last week, I was walking down the street with my mother, and I again found myself conscious of the English I was using, the English I do use with her. We were talking about the price of new and used furniture and I heard myself saying this: "Not waste money that way." My husband was with us as well, and he didn't notice any switch in my English. And then I realized why. It's because over the twenty years we've been together I've often used that same kind of English with him, and sometimes he even uses it with me. It has become our language of intimacy, a different sort of English that relates to family talk, the language I grew up with.

So you'll have some idea of what this family talk I heard sounds like, I'll   5
quote what my mother said during a recent conversation which I videotaped and then transcribed. During this conversation, my mother was talking about a political gangster in Shanghai who had the same last name as her family's, Du, and how the gangster in his early years wanted to be adopted by her family, which was rich by comparison. Later, the gangster became more powerful, far richer than my mother's family, and one day showed up at my mother's wedding to pay his respects. Here's what she said in part:

"Du Yusong having business like fruit stand. Like off the street kind. He is Du like Du Zong—but not Tsung-ming Island people. The local people call putong, the river east side, he belong to that side local people. That man want to ask Du Zong father take him in like become own family. Du Zong father wasn't look down on him, but didn't take seriously, until that man big like become a mafia. Now important person, very hard to inviting him. Chinese way, came only to show respect, don't stay for dinner. Respect for making big celebration, he shows up. Mean gives lots of respect. Chinese custom. Chinese social life that way. If too important won't have to stay too long. He come to my wedding. I didn't see, I heard it. I gone to boy's side, they have YMCA dinner. Chinese age I was nineteen."

You should know that my mother's expressive command of English belies how much she actually understands. She reads the *Forbes* report, listens to *Wall Street Week,* converses daily with her stockbroker, reads all of Shirley MacLaine's books with ease—all kinds of things I can't begin to understand. Yet some of my friends tell me they understand 50 percent of what my mother says. Some say they understand 80 to 90 percent. Some say they understand none of it, as if she were speaking pure Chinese. But to me, my mother's English is perfectly clear, perfectly natural. It's my mother tongue. Her language, as I hear it, is vivid, direct, full of observation and imagery. That was the language that helped shape the way I saw things, expressed things, made sense of the world.

Lately, I've been giving more thought to the kind of English my mother speaks. Like others, I have described it to people as "broken" or "fractured" English. But I wince when I say that. It has always bothered me that I can think of no way to describe it other than "broken," as if it were damaged and needed to be fixed, as if it lacked a certain wholeness and soundness. I've heard other terms used, "limited English," for example. But they seem just as bad, as if everything is limited, including people's perceptions of the limited English speaker.

I know this for a fact, because when I was growing up, my mother's "limited" English limited *my* perception of her. I was ashamed of her English. I believed that her English reflected the quality of what she had to say. That is, because she expressed them imperfectly her thoughts were imperfect. And I had plenty of empirical evidence to support me: the fact that people in department stores, at banks, and at restaurants did not take her seriously, did not give her good service, pretended not to understand her, or even acted as if they did not hear her.

10   My mother has long realized the limitations of her English as well. When I was fifteen, she used to have me call people on the phone to pretend I was she. In this guise, I was forced to ask for information or even to complain and yell at people who had been rude to her. One time it was a call to her stockbroker in New York. She had cashed out her small portfolio and it just so happened we were going to go to New York the next week, our very first trip outside California. I had to get on the phone and say in an adolescent voice that was not very convincing, "This is Mrs. Tan."

And my mother was standing in the back whispering loudly, "Why he don't send me check, already two weeks late. So mad he lie to me, losing me money."

And then I said in perfect English, "Yes, I'm getting rather concerned. You had agreed to send the check two weeks ago, but it hasn't arrived."

Then she began to talk more loudly. "What he want, I come to New York tell him front of his boss, you cheating me?" And I was trying to calm her down, make her be quiet, while telling the stockbroker, "I can't tolerate any more excuses. If I don't receive the check immediately, I am going to have to speak to your manager when I'm in New York next week." And sure enough, the following week there we were in front of this astonished stockbroker, and I was sitting there redfaced and quiet, and my mother, the real Mrs. Tan, was shouting at his boss in her impeccable broken English.

We used a similar routine just five days ago, for a situation that was far less humorous. My mother had gone to the hospital for an appointment, to find out about a benign brain tumor a CAT scan had revealed a month ago. She said she had spoken very good English, her best English, no mistakes. Still, she said, the hospital did not apologize when they said they had lost the CAT scan and she had come for nothing. She said they did not seem to have any sympathy when she told them she was anxious to know the exact diagnosis, since her husband and son had both died of brain tumors. She said they would not give her any more information until the next time and she would have to make another appointment for that. So she said she would not leave until the doctor called her daughter. She wouldn't budge. And when the doctor finally called her daughter, me, who spoke in perfect English—lo and behold—we had assurances the CAT scan would be found, promise that a conference call on Monday would be held, and apologies for any suffering my mother had gone through for a most regrettable mistake.

I think my mother's English almost had an effect on limiting my possibilities in life as well. Sociologists and linguists probably will tell you that a person's developing language skills are more influenced by peers. But I do think that the language spoken in the family, especially in immigrant families which are more insular, plays a large role in shaping the language of the child. And I believe that it affected my results on achievement tests, IQ tests, and the SAT. While my English skills were never judged as poor, compared to math, English could not be considered my strong suit. In grade school I did moderately well, getting perhaps B's, sometimes B-pluses, in English and scoring perhaps in the sixtieth or seventieth percentile on achievement tests. But those scores were not good enough to override the opinion that my true abilities lay in math and science, because in those areas I achieved A's and scored in the ninetieth percentile or higher.

This was understandable. Math is precise; there is only one correct answer. Whereas, for me at least, the answers on English tests were always a judgment call, a matter of opinion and personal experience. Those tests were constructed around items like fill-in-the-blank sentence completion, such as, "Even though Tom was _____, Mary thought he was _____." And the correct answer always seemed to be the most bland combinations of thoughts, for example, "Even though Tom was shy, Mary thought he was charming," with the grammatical structure "even though" limiting the correct answer to some sort of semantic opposites, so you wouldn't get answers like, "Even though Tom was foolish, Mary thought he was ridiculous." Well, according to my mother, there were very few limitations as to what Tom could have been and what Mary might have thought of him. So I never did well on tests like that.

The same was true with word analogies, pairs of words in which you were supposed to find some sort of logical, semantic relationship—for example, "*Sunset* is to *nightfall* as _____ is to _____." And here you would be presented with a list of four possible pairs, one of which showed the same kind of relationship: *red* is to *stoplight, bus* is to *arrival, chills* is to

15

fever, yawn is to *boring.* Well, I could never think that way. I knew what the tests were asking, but I could not block out of my mind the images already created by the first pair, "*sunset* is to *nightfall*"—and I would see a burst of color against a darkening sky, the moon rising, the lowering of a curtain of stars. And all the other pairs of words—red, bus, stoplight, boring—just threw up a mass of confusing images, making it impossible for me to sort out something as logical as saying: "A sunset precedes nightfall" is the same as "a chill precedes a fever." The only way I would have gotten that answer right would have been to imagine an associative situation, for example, by being disobedient and staying out past sunset, catching a chill at night which turns into feverish pneumonia as punishment, which indeed did happen to me.

I have been thinking about all this lately, about my mother's English, about achievement tests. Because lately I've been asked, as a writer, why there are not more Asian Americans represented in American literature. Why are there few Asian Americans enrolled in creative writing programs? Why do so many Chinese students go into engineering? Well, these are broad sociological questions I can't begin to answer. But I have noticed in surveys—in fact, just last week—that Asian students, as a whole, always do significantly better on math achievement tests than in English. And this makes me think that there are other Asian-American students whose English spoken in the home might also be described as "broken" or "limited." And perhaps they also have teachers who are steering them away from writing and into math and science, which is what happened to me.

Fortunately, I happen to be rebellious in nature and enjoy the challenge of disproving assumptions made about me. I became an English major my first year in college, after being enrolled as pre-med. I started writing nonfiction as a freelancer the week after I was told by my former boss that writing was my worst skill and I should hone my talents toward account management.

20   But it wasn't until 1985 that I finally began to write fiction. And at first I wrote using what I thought to be wittily crafted sentences, sentences that would finally prove I had mastery over the English language. Here's an example from the first draft of a story that later made its way into *The Joy Luck Club,* but without this line: "That was my mental quandary in its nascent state." A terrible line, which I can hardly pronounce.

Fortunately, for reasons I won't get into today, I later decided I should envision a reader for the stories I would write. And the reader I decided upon was my mother, because these were stories about mothers. So with this reader in mind—and in fact she did read my early drafts—I began to write stories using all the Englishes I grew up with: the English I spoke to my mother, which for lack of a better term might be described as "simple"; the English she used with me, which for lack of a better term might be described as "broken"; my translation of her Chinese, which could certainly be described as "watered down"; and what I imagine to be her translation of her Chinese if she could speak in perfect English, her internal language, and for that I sought to preserve the essence, but neither an English nor a Chinese structure. I wanted to capture what language ability tests can never reveal: her intent, her passion, her imagery, the rhythms of her speech and the nature of her thoughts.

Apart from what any critic had to say about my writing, I knew I had succeeded where it counted when my mother finished reading my book and gave me her verdict: "So easy to read."

REFLECTING AND INTERPRETING

1. Note how the author opens the first two paragraphs. What parallel pattern does she use to precede the definition? ("I am not . . . I am.") What technique is this? (See Developing an Extended Definition, chapter 15.)

2. How does Amy Tan define *writer*?

3. How did her mother's English influence Amy?

4. Amy Tan and her husband sometimes use her "mother's tongue" to communicate when they are alone. Why?

5. Does Amy's mother's English reflect the depth of her understanding of the language? How do you know?

6. How did the public and hospital employees react to Mrs. Tan's broken English?

7. What does Amy Tan notice about math and English test scores of Asian students? How does this affect course scheduling in high schools?

8. How does Amy Tan react to disillusionment?

9. What advantages does Standard English have over broken English?

10. If this essay had been written in third person by a biographer, how would that change have affected the essay?

A WRITER'S RESPONSE

1. Have you ever turned disillusionment or failure into something positive? Write an essay describing how you achieved this feat.

2. *Small Groups:* How many tips for good writing can you glean from this essay?

FUN ETHIC VS. WORK ETHIC?   ROBERT J. SAMUELSON

A graduate of Harvard, Robert J. Samuelson writes for *Newsweek, The L. A. Times, The Washington Post*, and other publications. He has won numerous honors, including the Gerald Loeb Award for Best Commentary in 1986 and 1993, the 1993 John Hancock Award for Best Business and Financial Columnist, and the Consistently Outstanding Column on One Subject in 1987, 1992, 1993, and 1995. He has written two books, *Untruth: Why the Conventional Wisdom is (Almost Always) Wrong* and *The Good Life and Its Discontents:*

The American Dream and the Age of Entitlement 1945–1995. "Fun Ethic vs. Work Ethic" was first printed in *Newsweek* in 2001.

1   The transformation of labor since the creation of Labor Day a century ago tells, in many ways, the story of modern America. Paid labor was then all-consuming, generally backbreaking, done mainly by men, often dangerous and, of course, endless—that is, most men worked until they couldn't. In 1880, 58 percent of men 75 or older worked; the figure today is 8 percent. The factory workweek averaged about 60 hours, spread over six days. Sunday was a day of rest and prayer, but not really recreation.

Economic historian Stuart Bruchey has written: "By present standards the age of America's first Industrial Revolution must be regarded as callous in its relative indifference to the welfare and safety of workers. The unemployed worker was cast adrift. As a rule, there was no such thing as public relief, and private charity was either insufficient or offered only on demeaning terms. The risks of injury or death on the job were grievously high." From 1880 to 1900 about 35,000 workers died and 500,000 were injured annually in work accidents, he reports. This was in a work force between one ninth of today's (in 1880) and one fifth (in 1900).

It was the oppressive and precarious nature of employment that led the Knights of Labor to agitate in the early 1880s for an annual celebration that would honor the dignity of ordinary workers—a campaign that culminated with Congress's designating a national holiday in 1894. Since then, work has slowly become less demanding of our time and bodies. In 1998 there were 5,100 on-the-job deaths, a seventh of accidents outside the workplace. Although dangerous and degrading jobs remain, most of us trudge to offices, where the greatest threat is getting stuck in an elevator or, more seriously, developing a repetitive-stress injury. In factories, automation has reduced risks dramatically. Machines perform operations that once mangled hands and arms.

Similarly, a gradual explosion of leisure has completely changed how Americans think about their daily lives. It is no longer a simple rotation of work, sleep, eat. We now cram our days with TV, restaurants, shopping, soccer, PTA meetings and health clubs. Curiously, the poor may have benefited more from this than the wealthy, according to economist Dora Costa of the Massachusetts Institute of Technology. By her estimates, the lowest-paid 10 percent of workers in 1890 worked about two hours more a day than the richest 10 percent (11 hours versus 9 hours). A century later the best-paid 10 percent labored an hour more a day than the poorest-paid 10 percent (8.5 hours versus 7.5 hours).

5   Just what caused this reversal isn't clear. Perhaps the highest-paid workers and managers are also the most committed, passionate and besieged. Or they may feel pressured to stay longer to protect their positions. Whatever the explanation, work's burdens (if not benefits) have become more evenly distributed. And for everyone—including, now, the half of the work force who are women—expectations have broadened.

Jobs should not just improve our incomes, we think. Like candy and cars, they should also enhance psychic well-being. They should be gratifying and stimulating. Every Labor Day produces a pile of reports on the state of working America. Perhaps the most interesting this year comes from Karlyn Bowman of the American Enterprise Institute, who has assembled public-opinion data on recent worker attitudes. Pollsters reflect public tastes and therefore ask questions like whether we feel our jobs have "importance to society," allow us "to influence decisions made at work" or provide agreeable friends. A century ago, had polling existed, questions would have been cruder: "Do you expect to die on the job?" Or "Do you make enough to feed your family?" In 1888 a typical family spent 45 percent of its budget on food; the comparable figure today is about 14 percent.

In many respects, the polls show remarkable stability. For example, 45 percent of workers report being "very satisfied" and 44 percent "moderately satisfied" with their jobs, according to the National Opinion Research Center at the University of Chicago. In 1972 the results were similar (49 percent and 37 percent, respectively). When Americans detest their jobs, they tend to quit. But there are hints of change. One survey asks "whether work is the important thing—and the purpose of leisure time is to recharge people's batteries so they can do a better job or . . . leisure is the important thing—and the purpose of work is to make it [leisure] possible." In 1975, 48 percent of respondents rated work as "the important thing" versus 36 percent for leisure. By 2000 the numbers had reversed—43 percent chose leisure and 34 percent work.

"It's the movement from the work ethic to the fun ethic," says Thomas Riehle of Ipsos-Reid, a survey firm. But, as Riehle notes, the work ethic is not collapsing so much as the boundaries between work and leisure are blurring—a combination that often produces stress and confusion. According to a new Ipsos-Reid poll, about 43 percent of workers say they bring work home or are "on call"; similarly, 30 percent admit using the Internet or e-mail at work for play or personal matters. Companies are now routinely expected to help workers balance family and job demands. There is some success. One poll in Bowman's collection finds that 47 percent of workers rated their companies as "very accommodating" and 33 percent as "somewhat accommodating" in reconciling job and family pressures.

The late economist Herbert Stein once attributed America's progress to the fact that "100 million people got up every morning to do the best they could for themselves and their children." The figure today would be about 140 million, but the appraisal was equally true a century ago, when workers numbered 28 million. What has changed is that work has become less manual and more mental, less regimented and more collaborative, and—as an activity—less economic and more social. To Stein, freedom was the key. It allowed people to strive to earn the most for themselves and be the most productive for society. Although this remains true, we have amended freedom to include some fun.

REFLECTING AND INTERPRETING

1. How would you rate the effectiveness of the title on a scale of 1 to 10? Why?

2. How does Samuelson capture the reader's attention in paragraph 1?

3. In paragraph 2, he presents shocking statistics. Who is the source? How does he cite most of the information? How do the last two sentences of the paragraph differ? What does he do there? (For help, see "Summarizing, Paraphrasing, and Quoting" in chapter R-3.)

4. What is the chief cause of fewer deaths and injuries since the early days of the Industrial Revolution?

5. Can you find the irony in paragraph 4?

6. How have the expectations of workers toward their jobs changed in the past century? How has the meaning of jobs to workers changed?

7. How have attitudes toward leisure changed?

8. How does Thomas Riehle view the changes in labor?

9. In what ways has technology blurred the boundary between work and leisure?

10. Consider the various major factors that are influencing jobs at the present time. What changes do you foresee in the future? What seems likely to happen?

A WRITER'S RESPONSE

How would you define "work ethic" and "fun ethic"? Consider the questions raised in paragraph 6. If you work or have had a job, what job factors are most important to you? Write a paragraph setting forth your view of work.

Definition: An Introduction to Using Sources

IN PRAISE OF THE HUMBLE COMMA | PICO IYER

Born in England, Pico Iyer lived in California during his youth with his Indian parents. After attending Eton and Oxford, he became a world travel writer and moved to Japan. His writings have appeared in numerous publications, including *Time*, *Harper's*, *The New Yorker*, *The New York Times Magazine*, and *Sports Illustrated*. He is the author of nine books, of which the latest are *Sun After Dark* (2005), *Abandon* (2004), and *The Global Soul* (2001). In this essay he explains the functions of punctuation, particularly the comma.

The gods, they say, give breath, and they take it away. But the same 1 could be said—could it not?—of the humble comma. Add it to the present clause, and, of a sudden, the mind is, quite literally, given pause to think; take it out if you wish or forget it and the mind is deprived of a resting place. Yet still the comma gets no respect. It seems just a slip of a thing, a pedant's tick, a blip on the edge of our consciousness, a kind of printer's smudge almost. Small, we claim, is beautiful (especially in the age of the microchip). Yet what is so often used, and so rarely recalled, as the comma—unless it be breath itself?

Punctuation, one is taught, has a point: to keep up law and order. Punctuation marks are the road signs placed along the highway of our communication—to control speeds, provide directions, and prevent head-on collisions. A period has the unblinking finality of a red light; the comma is a flashing yellow light that asks us only to slow down; and the semicolon is a Stop sign that tells us to ease gradually to a halt, before gradually starting up again. By establishing the relations between words, punctuation establishes the relations between the people using words. That may be one reason why schoolteachers exalt it, and lovers defy it ("We love each other and belong to each other let's don't ever hurt each other Nicole let's don't ever hurt each other," wrote Gary Gilmore to his girlfriend). A comma, he must have known, "separates inseparables," in the clinching words of H.W. Fowler, King of English Usage.

Punctuation, then, is a civic prop, a pillar that holds society upright. (A run-on sentence, its phrases piling up without division, is as unsightly as a sink piled high with dirty dishes.) Small wonder, then, that punctuation was one of the first proprieties of the Victorian Age, the age of the corset, that the modernists threw off: the sexual revolution might be said to have begun when Joyce's Molly Bloom spilled out all her private thoughts in thirty-six pages of panting, unperioded, and officially censored prose; and another rebellion was surely marked when e. e. Cummings first committed "god" to the lower case.

Punctuation thus becomes the signature of cultures. The hot-blooded Spaniard seems to be revealed in the passion and urgency of his doubled exclamation points and question marks ("¡Caramba! ¿Quíen sabe?"), while the impassive Chinese traditionally added to his so-called inscrutability by omitting all directions from his ideograms. The anarchy and commotion of the sixties were given voice in the exploding exclamation marks, riotous capital letters, and Day-Glo italics of Tom Wolfe's spray-paint prose; and in Communist societies, where the State is absolute, the dignity—and divinity—of capital letters is reserved for Ministries, Subcommittees and Secretariats.

5   Yet punctuation is something more than a culture's birthmark; it scores the music in our minds, gets our thoughts moving to the rhythm of our hearts. Punctuation is the notation in the sheet music of our words, telling us when to rest, or when to raise our voices; it acknowledges that the meaning of our discourse, as of any symphonic composition, lies not in the units but in the pauses, the pacing, and the phrasing. Punctuation is the way one bats one's eyes, lowers one's voice, or blushes demurely. Punctuation adjusts the color and tone and volume till the feeling comes into perfect focus: not disgust exactly, but distaste; not lust, or like, but love.

Punctuation, in short, gives us the human voice, and all the meanings that lie between the words. "You aren't young, are you?" loses its innocence when it loses the question mark. Every child knows the menace of a dropped apostrophe (the parent's "Don't do that" shifting into the more slowly enunciated "Do not do that") and every believer the ignominy of having his faith reduced to "faith." Add an exclamation point to "To be or not to be . . ." and the gloomy Dane has all the resolve he needs; add a comma, and the noble sobriety of "God save the Queen" becomes a cry of desperation bordering on double sacrilege.

Sometimes, of course, our markings may be simply a matter of aesthetics. Popping in a comma can be like slipping on the necklace that gives an outfit quiet elegance, or like catching the sound of running water that complements, as it completes, the silence of a Japanese landscape. When V. S. Naipaul, in his latest novel, writes, "He was a middle-aged man, with glasses," the first comma can seem a little precious. Yet it gives the description a spin, as well as a subtlety, that it otherwise lacks, and it shows that the glasses are not part of the middle agedness, but something else.

Thus all these tiny scratches give us breadth and heft and depth. A world that has only periods is a world without inflections. It is a world without shade. It has a music without sharps and flats. It is a martial music. It has a jackboot rhythm. Words cannot bend and curve. A comma, by comparison, catches the gentle drift of the mind in thought, turning in on itself and back on itself, reversing, redoubling, and returning along the course of its own sweet river music; while the semicolon brings clauses and thoughts together with all the silent discretion of a hostess arranging guests around her dinner table.

Punctuation, then, is a matter of care. Care for words, yes, but also, and more important, for what the words imply. Only a lover notices the small things: the way the afternoon light catches the nape of a neck, or how a strand of hair slips out from behind an ear, or the way a finger curls around a cup. And no one scans a letter so closely as a lover, searching for the small print, straining to hear its nuances, its gasps, its sighs and hesitations, poring over the secret messages that lie in every cadence. The difference between "Jane (whom I adore)" and "Jane, whom I adore," and the difference between them both and "Jane—whom I adore," marks all the distance between ecstasy and heartache. "No iron can pierce the heart with such force as a period put at just the right place," in Isaac Babel's lovely words; a comma can let us hear a voice break, or a heart. Punctuation, in fact, is a labor of love. Which brings us back, in a way, to gods.

REFLECTING AND INTERPRETING

1. What kind of comparison does Iyer use in paragraph 1?
2. What is the function of punctuation? How do the general functions of the period, comma, and semicolon differ?
3. Discuss sentence 1 of paragraph 3. Consider how dialogue and its punctuation reflect the relationship between people speaking. What do you notice about the example?
4. Compare the use of punctuation in literature of the Victorian Age with that in some modern literature.
5. How does punctuation vary according to culture?
6. Give examples of how punctuation can change meaning.
7. What can the comma do that the semicolon cannot (paragraph 9)?
8. Consider the title. Would a reference to punctuation have been more fitting? Why or why not?

A WRITER'S RESPONSE

Summarize this essay in your own words in a paragraph or two. Explain the functions of the various marks of punctuation and how they differ. You might also discuss the author's tone and use of language. If you quote an example, place quotation marks around the copied portion.

ON BEING 17, BRIGHT, AND UNABLE TO READ

DAVID RAYMOND

Someone who has experienced a disability can give an insider's view, providing insights that increase an outsider's understanding in a way that a technical definition cannot. David Raymond was a junior in high school when his essay on dyslexia was published in the *New York Times*. Dyslexics think in pictures and experience problems in perceiving letters or numbers. Words may appear jumbled, upside down, backwards, or in other ways that hinder reading. Symptoms vary in range and intensity. Special programs are now available to help dyslexics.

1   One day a substitute teacher picked me to read aloud from the textbook. When I told her "No, thank you," she came unhinged. She thought I was acting smart, and told me so. I kept calm, and that got her madder and madder. We must have spent 10 minutes trying to solve the problem, and finally she got so red in the face I thought she'd blow up. She told me she'd see me after class.

Maybe someone like me was a new thing for that teacher. But she wasn't new to me. I've been through scenes like that all my life. You see, even though I'm 17 and a junior in high school, I can't read because I have dyslexia. I'm told I read "at a fourth-grade level," but from where I sit, that's not reading. You can't know what that means unless you've been there. It's not easy to tell how it feels when you can't read your homework assignments or the newspaper or a menu in a restaurant or even notes from your own friends.

My family began to suspect I was having problems almost from the first day I started school. My father says my early years in school were the worst years of his life. They weren't so good for me, either. As I look back on it now, I can't find the words to express how bad it really was. I wanted to die. I'd come home from school screaming, "I'm dumb. I'm dumb—I wish I were dead!"

I guess I couldn't read anything at all then—not even my own name—and they tell me I didn't talk as good as other kids. But what I remember about those days is that I couldn't throw a ball where it was supposed to go, I couldn't learn to swim, and I wouldn't learn to ride a bike, because no matter what anyone told me, I knew I'd fail.

5   Sometimes my teachers would try to be encouraging. When I couldn't read the words on the board they'd say, "Come on, David, you know that word." Only I didn't. And it was embarrassing. I just felt dumb. And dumb was how the kids treated me. They'd make fun of me every chance they

got, asking me to spell "cat" or something like that. Even if I knew how to spell it, I wouldn't; they'd only give me another word. Anyway, it was awful, because more than anything I wanted friends. On my birthday when I blew out the candles I didn't wish I could learn to read; what I wished for was that the kids would like me.

With the bad reports coming from school, and with me moaning about wanting to die and how everybody hated me, my parents began looking for help. That's when the testing started. The school tested me, the child-guidance center tested me, private psychiatrists tested me. Everybody knew something was wrong—especially me.

It didn't help much when they stuck a fancy name onto it. I couldn't pronounce it then—I was only in second grade—and I was ashamed to talk about it. Now it rolls off my tongue, because I've been living with it for a lot of years—dyslexia.

All through elementary school it wasn't easy. I was always having to do things that were "different," things the other kids didn't have to do. I had to go to a child psychiatrist, for instance.

One summer my family forced me to go to a camp for children with reading problems. I hated the idea, but the camp turned out pretty good, and I had a good time. I met a lot of kids who couldn't read and somehow that helped. The director of the camp said I had a higher I.Q. than 90 percent of the population. I didn't believe him.

About the worst thing I had to do in fifth and sixth grade was go to a 10 special education class in another school in our town. A bus picked me up, and I didn't like that at all. The bus also picked up emotionally disturbed kids and retarded kids. It was like going to a school for the retarded. I always worried that someone I knew would see me on that bus. It was a relief to go to the regular junior high school.

Life began to change a little for me then, because I began to feel better about myself. I found the teachers cared; they had meetings about me and I worked harder for them for a while. I began to work on the potter's wheel, making vases and pots that the teachers said were pretty good. Also, I got a letter for being on the track team. I could always run pretty fast.

At high school the teachers are good and everyone is trying to help me. I've gotten honors some marking periods and I've won a letter on the cross-country team. Next quarter I think the school might hold a show of my pottery. I've got some friends. But there are still some embarrassing times. For instance, every time there is writing in the class, I get up and go to the special education room. Kids ask me where I go all the time. Sometimes I say, "to Mars."

Homework is a real problem. During free periods in school I go into the special ed room and staff members read assignments to me. When I get home my mother reads to me. Sometimes she reads an assignment into a tape recorder, and then I go into my room and listen to it. If we have a novel or something like that to read, she reads it out loud to me. Then I sit down with her and we do the assignment. She'll write, while I talk my answers to her. Lately I've taken to dictating into a tape recorder, and then someone—my father, a private tutor or my mother—types up what I've dictated. Whatever homework I do takes someone else's time, too. That makes me feel bad.

We had a big meeting in school the other day—eight of us, four from the guidance department, my private tutor, my parents and me. The subject was me. I said I wanted to go to college, and they told me about colleges that have facilities and staff to handle people like me. That's nice to hear.

15   As for what happens after college, I don't know and I'm worried about that. How can I make a living if I can't read? Who will hire me? How will I fill out the application form? The only thing that gives me any courage is the fact that I've learned about well-known people who couldn't read or had other problems and still made it. Like Albert Einstein, who didn't talk until he was 4 and flunked math. Like Leonardo da Vinci, who everyone seems to think had dyslexia.

I've told this story because maybe some teacher will read it and go easy on a kid in the classroom who has what I've got. Or, maybe some parent will stop nagging his kid, and stop calling him lazy. Maybe he's not lazy or dumb. Maybe he just can't read and doesn't know what's wrong. Maybe he's scared, like I was.

REFLECTING AND INTERPRETING

1. Rather than calling on one person to read, what might the teacher have done?
2. At no point does the author give the technical definition of dyslexia. Should he? What is the effect of this omission?
3. What is dyslexia? Does it vary in how it affects people?
4. What experience was a turning point for David? How did it help?
5. What changes occurred in David's life during junior high school?
6. Why is he confident that he can graduate from college? What does he fear?
7. Why does he mention Albert Einstein and Leonardo da Vinci?
8. David includes many colloquialisms in the essay. How do "blow up" and "didn't talk as good as other kids" affect the tone?
9. What is the author's purpose in writing the essay?
10. What factor do you think is most influential in David's or anyone's success?

A WRITER'S RESPONSE

Have you had a long, difficult experience that makes you somewhat of an expert? Write an essay that gives an insider's view. If you haven't, perhaps a close family member has. How did the problem affect you and other family members?

THE HANDICAP OF DEFINITION   WILLIAM RASPBERRY

Born in a small town in Mississippi in 1935, William Raspberry knows firsthand about the various connotations that have been attached to his race. In this essay, taken from *Instilling Positive Images* (1982), he explores the ways *black* is used in regard to race and the meaning of *blackness*. At the end he issues a challenge to blacks and mainstream Americans to expect more from black youth, encourage them, and expand the definition of *black*. Raspberry worked his way through Indiana Central College as a reporter, photographer, and editor for the *Indianapolis Recorder*. After a two-year stint in the Army, he joined *The Washington Post*, where he writes a column, now syndicated in 225 newspapers. He has won Journalist of the Year (1965), a Citation of Merit in Journalism (1967), and the Pulitzer Prize for Distinguished Commentary (1994). Fifty of his favorite columns were published in *Looking Backward at Us* (1991). Raspberry has also served as a television commentator and taught journalism classes at Howard University.

I know all about bad schools, mean politicians, economic deprivation and racism. Still, it occurs to me that one of the heaviest burdens black Americans—and black children in particular—have to bear is the handicap of definition: the question of what it means to be black.

Let me explain quickly what I mean. If a basketball fan says that the Boston Celtics' Larry Bird plays "black," the fan intends it—and Bird probably accepts it—as a compliment. Tell pop singer Tom Jones he moves "black" and he might grin in appreciation. Say to Teena Marie or The Average White Band that they sound "black" and they'll thank you.

But name one pursuit, aside from athletics, entertainment or sexual performance in which a white practitioner will feel complimented to be told he does it "black." Tell a white broadcaster he talks "black," and he'll sign up for diction lessons. Tell a white reporter he writes "black," and he'll take a writing course. Tell a white lawyer he reasons "black" and he might sue you for slander.

What we have here is a tragically limited definition of blackness, and it isn't only white people who buy it.

Think of all the ways black children can put one another down with charges of "whiteness." For many of these children, hard study and hard work are "white." Trying to please a teacher might be criticized as acting "white." Speaking correct English is "white." Scrimping today in the interest of tomorrow's goals is "white." Educational toys and games are "white."

An incredible array of habits and attitudes that are conducive to success in business, in academia, in the non-entertainment professions are likely to be thought of as somehow "white." Even economic success, unless it involves such "black" undertakings as numbers banking, is defined as "white."

And the results are devastating. I wouldn't deny that blacks often are better entertainers and athletes. My point is the harm that comes from too narrow a definition of what is black.

One reason black youngsters tend to do better at basketball, for instance, is that they assume they can learn to do it well, and so they practice constantly to prove themselves right.

Wouldn't it be wonderful if we would infect black children with the notion that excellence in math is "black" rather than white, or possibly Chinese? Wouldn't it be of enormous value if we could create the myth that morality, strong families, determination, courage and love of learning are traits brought by slaves from Mother Africa and therefore quintessentially black?

10 There is no doubt in my mind that most black youngsters could develop their mathematical reasoning, their elocution and their attitudes the way they develop their jump shots and their dance steps: by the combination of sustained, enthusiastic practice and the unquestioned belief that they can do it.

In one sense, what I am talking about is the importance of developing positive ethnic traditions. Maybe Jews have an innate talent for communication; maybe the Chinese are born with a gift for mathematical reasoning; maybe blacks are naturally blessed with athletic grace. I doubt it. What is at work, I suspect, is assumption, inculcated early in their lives, that this is a thing our people do well.

Unfortunately, many of the things about which blacks make this assumption are things that do not contribute to their career success—except for that handful of the truly gifted who can make it as entertainers and athletes. And many of the things we concede to whites are the things that are essential to economic security.

So it is with a number of assumptions black youngsters make about what it is to be a "man": physical aggressiveness, sexual prowess, the refusal to submit to authority. The prisons are full of people who, by this perverted definition, are unmistakably men.

But the real problem is not so much that the things defined as "black" are negative. The problem is that the definition is much too narrow.

15 Somehow, we have to make our children understand that they are intelligent, competent people, capable of doing whatever they put their minds to and making it in the American mainstream, not just in a black subculture.

What we seem to be doing, instead, is raising up yet another generation of young blacks who will be failures—by definition.

REFLECTING AND INTERPRETING

1. Where is the transitional sentence that spans the chasm between the positive examples and the negative ones?

2. How does the construing of saving money, pleasing the teacher, having educational toys, and speaking correct English as "white" prove detrimental to blacks?

3. What reasons does Raspberry cite for blacks' success in basketball? Do you agree or disagree? Why?

4. What rhetorical strategy does Raspberry use in paragraph 9?

5. What image, in particular, is harmful for young black males?

6. Notice the three-word sentence "I doubt it" in paragraph 11. What is the effect?

7. See paragraph 15. In 1987 Raspberry pinpointed a crucial aspect of the problem: For most black children, the subculture is their world, meaning they do not see themselves as an integral part of a larger society. Do you think this perspective has changed since 1987? Since September 11, 2001? How?

8. How would you classify Raspberry's ending? (Hint: See "Writing an Effective Conclusion," chapter 4.)

9. How would you describe the writer's voice? How does the tone differ from that of many other black writers?

10. Raspberry says that "an incredible array of habits and attitudes are conductive to success in business, in academia, and in the nonentertainment professions." Can you specify some of these?

A WRITER'S RESPONSE

How does a person's attitude and behavior define his or her chances for success? Write an essay explaining these vital influences. Cite positive and negative examples as Raspberry does.

THE INSUFFICIENCY OF HONESTY   STEPHEN L. CARTER

The *New York Times* has termed Stephen L. Carter one of the foremost intellectuals in the USA. Born black in Washington, DC, in 1954, he first distinguished himself by earning a bachelor's degree from Stanford and a law degree from Yale (1979). After gaining experience as a law clerk for the United States Court of Appeals and later for Supreme Court Justice Thurgood Marshall, Carter joined the Yale faculty in 1982. He has taught constitutional law, contracts, law and religion, law and science, and legal ethics—framing debate on national issues ranging from the role of religion in politics to the influence of civility and integrity in everyday life. His nonfiction and fiction writings have been critically acclaimed. Best known are *Reflections of an Affirmative Action Baby* (1991), *The Culture of Disbelief: How American Law and Politics Trivialize Religious Devotion* (1993), *Civility: Manners, Morals, and the Etiquette of Democracy* (1998), *God's Name in Vain* (2000), *The Emperor of Ocean Park* (2002), and *New England White* (2007). In this essay Carter defines integrity, differentiating it from honesty.

A couple of years ago I began a university commencement address by 1 telling the audience that I was going to talk about integrity. The crowd broke into applause. Applause! Just because they had heard the word "integrity": that's how starved for it they were. They had no idea how I was using the word, or what I was going to say about integrity, or, indeed, whether I was for it or against it. But they knew they liked the idea of talking about it.

Very well, let us consider this word "integrity." Integrity is like the weather: everybody talks about it but nobody knows what to do about it. Integrity is that stuff that we always want more of. Some say that we need to return to the good old days when we had a lot more of it. Others say that we as a nation have never really had enough of it. Hardly anybody stops to explain exactly what we mean by it, or how we know it is a good thing, or why everybody needs to have the same amount of it. Indeed, the only trouble with integrity is that everybody who uses the word seems to mean something slightly different.

For instance, when I refer to integrity, do I mean simply "honesty"? The answer is no; although honesty is a virtue of importance, it is a different virtue from integrity. Let us, for simplicity, think of honesty as not lying; and let us further accept Sissela Bok's definition of a lie: "any intentionally deceptive message which is *stated*." Plainly, one cannot have integrity without being honest (although, as we shall see, the matter gets complicated), but one can certainly be honest and yet have little integrity.

When I refer to integrity, I have something very specific in mind. Integrity, as I will use the term, requires three steps: discerning what is right and what is wrong; acting on what you have discerned, even at personal cost; and saying openly that you are acting on your understanding of right and wrong. The first criterion captures the idea that integrity requires a degree of moral reflectiveness. The second brings in the ideal of a person of integrity as steadfast, a quality that includes keeping one's commitments. The third reminds us that a person of integrity can be trusted.

5   The first point to understand about the difference between honesty and integrity is that a person may be entirely honest without ever engaging in the hard work of discernment that integrity requires: she may tell us quite truthfully what she believes without ever taking the time to figure out whether what she believes is good and right and true. The problem may be as simple as someone's foolishly saying something that hurts a friend's feelings; a few moments of thought would have revealed the likelihood of the hurt and the lack of necessity for the comment. Or the problem may be more complex, as when a man who was raised from birth in a society that preaches racism states his belief in one race's inferiority as a fact, without ever really considering that perhaps this deeply held view is wrong. Certainly the racist is being honest—he is telling us what he actually thinks—but his honesty does not add up to integrity.

Telling Everything You Know

A wonderful epigram sometimes attributed to the filmmaker Sam Goldwyn goes like this: "The most important thing in acting is honesty;

once you learn to fake that, you're in." The point is that honesty can be something one *seems* to have. Without integrity, what passes for honesty often is nothing of the kind; it is fake honesty—or it is honest but irrelevant and perhaps even immoral.

Consider an example. A man who has been married for fifty years confesses to his wife on his deathbed that he was unfaithful thirty-five years earlier. The dishonesty was killing his spirit, he says. Now he has cleared his conscience and is able to die in peace.

The husband has been honest—sort of. He has certainly unburdened himself. And he has probably made his wife (soon to be his widow) quite miserable in the process, because even if she forgives him, she will not be able to remember him with quite the vivid image of love and loyalty that she had hoped for. Arranging his own emotional affairs to ease his transition to death, he has shifted to his wife the burden of confusion and pain, perhaps for the rest of her life. Moreover, he has attempted his honesty at the one time in his life when it carries no risk; acting in accordance with what you think is right and risking no loss in the process is a rather thin and unadmirable form of honesty.

Besides, even though the husband has been honest in a sense, he has now twice been unfaithful to his wife: once thirty-five years ago, when he had his affair, and again when, nearing death, he decided that his own peace of mind was more important than hers. In trying to be honest he has violated his marriage vow by acting toward his wife not with love but with naked and perhaps even cruel self-interest.

As my mother used to say, you don't have to tell people everything you 10 know. Lying and nondisclosure, as the law often recognizes, are not the same thing. Sometimes it is actually illegal to tell what you know, as, for example, in the disclosure of certain financial information by market insiders. Or it may be unethical, as when a lawyer reveals a confidence entrusted to her by a client. It may be simple bad manners, as in the case of a gratuitous comment to a colleague on his or her attire. And it may be subject to religious punishment, as when a Roman Catholic priest breaks the seal of the confessional—an offense that carries automatic excommunication.

In all the cases just mentioned, the problem with telling everything you know is that somebody else is harmed. Harm may not be the intention, but it is certainly the effect. Honesty is most laudable when we risk harm to ourselves; it becomes a good deal less so if we instead risk harm to others when there is no gain to anyone other than ourselves. Integrity may counsel keeping our secrets in order to spare the feelings of others. Sometimes, as in the example of the wayward husband, the reason we want to tell what we know is precisely to shift our pain onto somebody else—a course of action dictated less by integrity than by self-interest. Fortunately, integrity and self-interest often coincide, as when a politician of integrity is rewarded with our votes. But often they do not, and it is at those moments that our integrity is truly tested.

Error

Another reason that honesty alone is no substitute for integrity is that if forthrightness is not preceded by discernment, it may result in the expression of an incorrect moral judgment. In other words, I may be honest about what I believe, but if I have never tested my beliefs, I may be wrong. And here I mean "wrong" in a particular sense: the proposition in question is wrong if I would change my mind about it after hard moral reflection.

Consider this example. Having been taught all his life that women are not as smart as men, a manager gives the women on his staff less-challenging assignments than he gives the men. He does this, he believes, for their own benefit: he does not want them to fail, and he believes that they will if he gives them tougher assignments. Moreover, when one of the women on his staff does poor work, he does not berate her as harshly as he would a man, because he expects nothing more. And he claims to be acting with integrity because he is acting according to his own deepest beliefs.

The manager fails the most basic test of integrity. The question is not whether his actions are consistent with what he most deeply believes but whether he has done the hard work of discerning whether what he most deeply believes is right. The manager has not taken this harder step.

15   Moreover, even within the universe that the manager has constructed for himself, he is not acting with integrity. Although he is obviously wrong to think that the women on his staff are not as good as the men, even were he right, that would not justify applying different standards to their work. By so doing he betrays both his obligation to the institution that employs him and his duty as a manager to evaluate his employees.

The problem that the manager faces is an enormous one in our practical politics, where having the dialogue that makes democracy work can seem impossible because of our tendency to cling to our views even when we have not examined them. As Jean Bethke Elshtain has said, borrowing from John Courtney Murray, our politics are so fractured and contentious that we often cannot even reach *disagreement*. Our refusal to look closely at our own most cherished principles is surely a large part of the reason. Socrates thought the unexamined life not worth living. But the unhappy truth is that few of us actually have the time for constant reflection on our views—on public or private morality. Examine them we must, however, or we will never know whether we might be wrong.

None of this should be taken to mean that integrity as I have described it presupposes a single correct truth. If, for example, your integrity-guided search tells you that affirmative action is wrong, and my integrity-guided search tells me that affirmative action is right, we need not conclude that one of us lacks integrity. As it happens, I believe—both as a Christian and as a secular citizen who struggles toward moral understanding—that we *can* find true and sound answers to our moral questions. But I do not pretend to have found very many of them, nor is an exposition of them my purpose here.

It is the case not that there aren't any right answers but that, given human fallibility, we need to be careful in assuming that we have found them. However, today's political talk about how it is wrong for the government to impose one person's morality on somebody else is just mindless chatter. *Every* law imposes one person's morality on somebody else, because law has only two functions: to tell people to do what they would rather not or to forbid them to do what they would.

And if the surveys can be believed, there is far more moral agreement in America than we sometimes allow ourselves to think. One of the reasons that character education for young people makes so much sense to so many people is precisely that there seems to be a core set of moral understandings—we might call them the American Core—that most of us accept. Some of the virtues in this American Core are, one hopes, relatively noncontroversial. About 500 American communities have signed on to Michael Josephson's program to emphasize the "six pillars" of good character: trustworthiness, respect, responsibility, caring, fairness, and citizenship. These virtues might lead to a similarly noncontroversial set of political values: having an honest regard for ourselves and others, protecting freedom of thought and religious belief, and refusing to steal or murder.

Honesty and Competing Responsibilities

A further problem with too great an exaltation of honesty is that it may [20] allow us to escape responsibilities that morality bids us bear. If honesty is substituted for integrity, one might think that if I say I am not planning to fulfill a duty, I need not fulfill it. But it would be a peculiar morality indeed that granted us the right to avoid our moral responsibilities simply by stating our intention to ignore them. Integrity does not permit such an easy escape.

Consider an example. Before engaging in sex with a woman, her lover tells her that if she gets pregnant, it is her problem, not his. She says that she understands. In due course she does wind up pregnant. If we believe, as I hope we do, that the man would ordinarily have a moral responsibility toward both the child he will have helped to bring into the world and the child's mother, then his honest statement of what he intends does not spare him that responsibility.

This vision of responsibility assumes that not all moral obligations stem from consent or from a stated intention. The linking of obligations to promises is a rather modern and perhaps uniquely Western way of looking at life, and perhaps a luxury that only the well-to-do can afford. As Fred and Shulamit Korn (a philosopher and an anthropologist) have pointed out, "If one looks at ethnographic accounts of other societies, one finds that, while obligations everywhere play a crucial role in social life, promising is not preeminent among the sources of obligation and is not even mentioned by most anthropologists." The Korns have made a study of Tonga, where promises are virtually unknown but the social order is remarkably stable. If life without any promises seems extreme, we Americans sometimes go too far the other way, parsing not only our contracts but even our marriage vows in order to discover the absolute minimum obligation that we have to others as a result of our promises.

That some societies in the world have worked out evidently functional structures of obligation without the need for promise or consent does not tell us what *we* should do. But it serves as a reminder of the basic proposition that our existence in civil society creates a set of mutual responsibilities that philosophers used to capture in the fiction of the social contract. Nowadays, here in America, people seem to spend their time thinking of even cleverer ways to avoid their obligations, instead of doing what integrity commands and fulfilling them. And all too often honesty is their excuse.

REFLECTING AND INTERPRETING

1. In one sentence, summarize the gist of the first two paragraphs.
2. What simple definition of honesty does Carter put forth?
3. What three steps are essential to achieve integrity?
4. If a person omits step one, what is the risk?
5. Can a person be honest yet lack integrity? Explain.
6. Examine and summarize paragraph 10 in one sentence.
7. Carter cites two obligations that a manager must fulfill in order to have integrity. What are they?
8. Carter speaks of an "American Core" that has six values necessary for good character. What are they?
9. What "further problem" does he point out when honesty is honored too highly? Do you believe that honesty can be misused? How?
10. Consider the title of this essay. What is the effect?

A WRITER'S RESPONSE

1. Have you ever worked at a place where you knew fraud was occurring? What did you do? Now through hindsight, would you have followed the same course of action? Why or why not?
2. Select a quality such as reliability, faithfulness, or loyalty as a topic for an essay. Use examples to clarify and support your purpose.

Examining Cause and Effect

THE REBIRTH OF CIVILITY?   DANIEL HENNINGER

Earning a bachelor's degree from Georgetown University's School of Foreign Service, Daniel Henninger later hired on as a staff writer for the *National Observer* in 1971. Since then he has won wide recognition, including the Gerald Loeb Award (1985), Scripps Howard Foundation's Walker Stone Award (1998), and American Society of Newspaper Editors' Distinguished Writing Award (1995). He also shared in the *Wall Street Journal's* 2002 Pulitzer Prize for reporting on the September 11 attacks. In the following editorial, Henninger describes "A revolt against people who are behaving badly" (*Wall Street Journal*, 12 April 2007).

And so it came to pass in the year 2007 that a little platoon came forth 1 to say unto the world: Enough is enough.

Two leading citizens of the Web, Tim O'Reilly and Jimmy Wales, have proposed a "Bloggers Code of Conduct." The reason for this code is the phenomenon of people posting extremely nasty verbal comments about other people on Web sites devoted to political and social commentary. For Mr. O'Reilly, a publisher and activist for open Web standards, the last blogospheric straw involved a friend whose suggestion that it was OK to delete offensive comments from Web sites earned her a backlash of vitriol on several sites, with one posting a photo of her alongside a drawing of a noose.

It is appropriate that this line should be drawn in the ether of the World Wide Web, whose controlling ethos up to now has been that speech and expression should remain free, unfettered and—the totemic word that ends all argument—"democratic." As it developed, too many of the Web's democrats, for reasons that have provided much new work for clinical psychologists, tend to write in a vocabulary of rage and aggression.

Take politics. In the House of Representatives, Members by tradition address each other as the "gentleman" or "gentlewoman." These salutations often drip with irony but exist nonetheless to temper the bitterness beneath much political combat. The democrats around the Web regard any such modulating habits as hypocritical.

5   Unlike the fogies in politics or tradition-hampered media, they describe their opponents as what they believe they are: morons, idiots, fools, sellouts, traitors, liars (perhaps the most used word on the politicized Web), crooks and various other expressions that the touchingly termed "family" newspapers still won't print.

The admission of need for something called a Bloggers Code of Conduct is about more than just the Web. The deeper import of what may be happening here should be evident in Mr. O'Reilly's remark, which was the final sentence in a long New York Times article on the subject last Sunday: "Free speech is enhanced by civility."

It is difficult for me to imagine a more revolutionary sentence. One might call it "subversive."

"Free speech is enhanced by civility." The revolution comes at the end of that sentence. Free speech we know about. Civility we have forgotten. Ask Don Imus.

Subsets of civility would include courtesy, respect, politeness and deference. Civility is a public virtue. Like oil or wheat, it is a necessary social commodity that allows society to function.

That said, it would be overreaching to lay the blame for civility's fall on the World Wide Web. The erosion of our stores of civility occurred over the past 40 years, undermined by torrents of political rage and self-assertion.

10   In 1968, Abbie Hoffman, the Yippie saint and a founding father of anti-civility, wrote a book whose title alone still stands as the best summary of the new game: "Revolution for the Hell of It." The Web democrats, the public hecklers, the loudmouths are Abbie's children. They know it and are proud of it. No limits. Don't like it? Get over it. If you object, they will, like characters in a Dick Tracy cartoon, scream, "I demand my constitutional rights!"

With the Bloggers Code of Conduct comes the counterrevolution. Some excerpts:

From the Wiki site, put up by Jimmy Wales, co-founder of the remarkable and controversial Web-based encyclopedia, Wikipedia: "We take responsibility for our own words and reserve the right to restrict comments on our blog that do not conform to basic civility standards." This is a shift from an early precept of the Web known by the acronym YOYOW, or "you own your own words." In the world of YOYOW, one is responsible only to the drummer keeping the beat in one's head.

From Mr. O'Reilly's Web site: "If you know someone who is behaving badly, tell them so." Which is to say, we are surrounded now by people who have no clue that they are behaving badly, or don't believe that they are, or who argue that behaving badly is their "right." Are they wrong?

Psychologists commenting on the phenomenon of Web-based verbal abuse or aggressive public heckling often talk about society's expanded notions of personal entitlement and the failure of baby-boomer parents to set norms of behavior for their infallible children. We have ratified a lot of over-the-line behavior.

College administrators held the door open for four decades. The question at the center of oral arguments in the Supreme Court's "Bong Hits 4 Jesus" case last month was: Who runs the schools, the kids or the adults? People behaving badly have simply taken the norms their elders gave them to a logical ending point on the Web. On one level, the idea of a code of conduct for language on the Web marks the overdue restoration of adulthood in American life.

But there is a harder side to this tension. After news spread of the O'Reilly-Wales proposal, an (needless to say) angry battalion of bloggers counterattacked, crying "censorship." Now we're beyond the merely obnoxious culture of chin-dribble. Now we're talking politics and power. So the cry goes up: You can't tell us *how* to talk. That's "censorship." 15

The censorship claim is often made by political Web players who want to be "free" to use whatever means will achieve the end of driving their opponents over the cliff. Consider the Congressional Black Caucus. Its affiliation with Fox News to conduct presidential debates was fire-bombed recently on "progressive" Web sites. Example: "Guess it takes a whole lot of grease to fry CBC's chicken." Scared, the three major Democratic presidential candidates pulled out. Censorship? Try doublespeak. The strategy of deploying charged and hyper-aggressive language is now evident: First intimidate one's targets, then coerce them—into conformity or silence. And do it always under the banner of free speech and democracy.

There is no evident political coloration to the broader concern that's arisen about conduct on the Web. The anti-civility trolls are in restaurants, stadiums, theaters, planes, church, the airwaves, in dreams. This is merely a recognition that rules of the road can indeed enhance, not suppress, the flow of truly free expression and minimize the already ample frictions of daily life. Better late than never.

REFLECTING AND INTERPRETING

1. Who are Tim O'Reilly and Jimmy Wales? Why have they made headline news?

2. What has been the past "controlling ethos" of the World Wide Web in regard to free speech and expression?

3. What early custom still exists in the House of Representatives? What effect does this custom have?

4. How does the author define "subsets of civility"?

5. Henninger cites whose book as a summary of the turning point in the revolution in public behavior? What year was it published?

6. To what factor do some psychologists attribute the "verbal abuse or aggressive public heckling" that exists on the Web? Do you see any other possible causes?

7. Some bloggers have protested that the proposal of a "Bloggers Code of Conduct" is censorship. Why does this claim have reverberations beyond the Web?

8. What tactics have been used to silence those who back a proposal to limit "over-the-line" behavior?

9. Have you noticed any exhibitions of anti-civility behavior? If so, where?

10. Do you think a turning point has been reached in the anti-civility movement, as Henninger suggests? Why or why not?

A WRITER'S RESPONSE

Why is Tim O'Reilly's statement that "Free speech is enhanced by civility" revolutionary? Do you agree or disagree? Why?

WHY MARRIAGES FAIL   ANNE RICHARDSON ROIPHE

Born in New York City, Anne Roiphe graduated from Sarah Lawrence College with a BA degree. In the past four decades, she has published a dozen fiction and nonfiction books, as well as collaborated on several others. Her latest works include *If You Knew Me* (1995), *Lovingkindness* (1997), *Fruitful: Living the Contradictions: A Memoir of Modern Motherhood* (1997), *For Rabbit, with Love and Squalor: An American Read* (2000), and *1185 Park Avenue: A Memoir* (2000). Roiphe writes a column for the *New York Observer*. Her articles and reviews have appeared in *Vogue, Redbook, Glamour, Family Circle,* and *Working Woman*. In this essay, which first appeared in *Family Weekly* (27 Feb. 1983), she analyzes the factors that lead to divorce.

1   These days so many marriages end in divorce that our most sacred vows no longer ring with truth. "Happily ever after" and "Till death do us part" are expressions that seem on the way to becoming obsolete. Why has it becomes so hard for couples to stay together? What goes wrong? What has happened to us that close to one-half of all marriages are destined for the divorce courts? How could we have created a society in which 42 percent of our children will grow up in single parent homes? If statistics could only measure loneliness, regret, pain, loss of self-confidence and fear of the future, the numbers would be beyond quantifying.

Even though each broken marriage is unique, we can still find the common perils, the common causes for marital despair. Each marriage has crisis points and each marriage tests endurance, the capacity for both intimacy and change. Outside pressures such as job loss, illness, infertility, trouble with a child, care of aging parents and all the other plagues of life hit marriage the way hurricanes blast our shores. Some marriages survive these storms and others don't. Marriages fail, however, not simply because of the outside weather but because the inner climate becomes too hot or too cold, too turbulent or too stupefying.

When we look at how we choose our partners and what expectations exist at the tender beginnings of romance, some of the reasons for disaster become quite clear. We all select with unconscious accuracy a mate who will recreate with us the emotional patterns of our first homes. Dr. Carl A. Whitaker, a marital therapist and emeritus professor of psychiatry at the University of Wisconsin explains, "From early childhood on, each of us carried models for marriage, femininity, masculinity, motherhood, fatherhood and all the other family roles." Each of us falls in love with a mate who has qualities of our parents, who will help us rediscover both the psychological happiness and miseries of our past lives. We may think we have found a man unlike Dad, but then he turns to drink or drugs, or loses his job over and over again or sits silently in front of the T.V. just the way Dad did. A man may choose a woman who doesn't like kids just like his mother or who gambles away the family savings just like his mother. Or he may choose a slender wife who seems unlike his obese mother but then turns out to have other addictions that destroy their mutual happiness.

A man and a woman bring to their marriage bed a blended concoction of conscious and unconscious memories of their parents' lives together. The human way is to compulsively repeat and recreate the patterns of the past. Sigmund Freud so well described the unhappy design that many of us get trapped in: the unmet needs of childhood, the angry feelings left over from frustrations of long ago, the limits of trust and the recurrence of old fears. Once an individual senses this entrapment, there may follow a yearning to escape, and the result could be a broken, splintered marriage.

Of course people can overcome the habits and attitudes that devel-   5
oped in childhood. We all have hidden strengths and amazing capacities for growth and creative change. Change, however, requires work—observing your part in a rotten pattern, bringing difficulties out into the open—and work runs counter to the basic myth of marriage: "When I wed this person all my problems will be over. I will have achieved success and I will become the center of life for this other person and this person will be my center, and we will mean everything to each other forever." This myth, which every marriage relies on, is soon exposed. The coming of children, the pulls and tugs of their demands on affection and time, place a considerable strain on that basic myth of meaning everything to each other, of merging together and solving all of life's problems.

Concern and tension about money take each partner away from the other. Obligations to demanding parents or still-depended-upon parents create further strain. Couples today must also deal with all the cultural changes brought on in recent years by the women's movement and the sexual revolution. The altering of roles and the shifting of responsibilities have been extremely trying for many marriages.

These and other realities of life erode the visions of marital bliss the way sandstorms eat at rock and the ocean nibbles away at the dunes. Those euphoric, grand feelings that accompany romantic love are really self-delusions, self-hypnotic dreams that enable us to forge a relationship. Real life, failure at work, disappointments, exhaustion, bad smells, bad colds and hard times all puncture the dream and leave us stranded with our mate, with our childhood patterns pushing us this way and that, with our unfulfilled expectations.

The struggle to survive in marriage requires adaptability, flexibility, genuine love and kindness and an imagination strong enough to feel what the other is feeling. Many marriages fall apart because either partner can-not imagine what the other wants or cannot communicate what he or she needs or feels. Anger builds until it erupts into a volcanic burst that buries the marriage in ash.

It is not hard to see, therefore, how essential communication is for a good marriage. A man and a woman must be able to tell each other how they feel and why they feel the way they do; otherwise they will impose on each other roles and actions that lead to further unhappiness. In some cases, the communication patterns of childhood—of not talking, of talking too much, of not listening, of distrust and anger, of withdrawal—spill into the marriage and prevent a healthy exchange of thoughts and feelings. The answer is to set up new patterns of communication and intimacy.

10   At the same time, however, we must see each other as individuals. "To achieve a balance between separateness and closeness is one of the major psychological tasks of all human beings at every stage of life," says Dr. Stuart Bartle, a psychiatrist at the New York University Medical Center.

If we sense from our mate a need for too much intimacy, we tend to push him or her away, fearing that we may lose our identities in the merging of marriage. One partner may suffocate the other partner in a childlike dependency.

A good marriage means growing as a couple but also growing as indi-viduals. This isn't easy. Richard gives up his interest in carpentry because his wife, Helen, is jealous of the time he spends away from her. Karen quits her choir group because her husband dislikes the friends she makes there. Each pair clings to each other and are angry with each other as life closes in on them. This kind of marital balance is easily thrown as one or the other pulls away and divorce follows.

Sometimes people pretend that a new partner will solve the old prob-lems. Most often extramarital sex destroys a marriage because it allows an artificial split between the good and the bad—the good is projected on the new partner and the bad is dumped on the head of the old. Dishonesty, hid-ing and cheating create walls between men and women. Infidelity is just a symptom of trouble. It is a symbolic complaint, a weapon of revenge, as well as an unraveler of closeness. Infidelity is often that proverbial last straw that sinks that camel to the ground.

All right—marriage has always been difficult. Why then are we seeing so many divorces at this time? Yes, our modern social fabric is thin, and yes the permissiveness of society has created unrealistic expectations and thrown the family into chaos. But divorce is so common because people today are unwilling to exercise the self-discipline that marriage requires. They expect easy joy, like the entertainment on TV, the thrill of a good party.

Marriage takes some kind of sacrifice, not dreadful self-sacrifice of   15
the soul, but some level of compromise. Some of one's fantasies, some of one's legitimate desires have to be given up for the value of the marriage itself. "While all marital partners feel shackled at times, it is they who really choose to make the marital ties into confining chains or supporting bonds," says Dr. Whitaker. Marriage requires sexual, financial and emotional discipline. A man and a woman cannot follow every impulse, cannot allow themselves to stop growing or changing.

Divorce is not an evil act. Sometimes it provides salvation for people who have grown hopelessly apart or were frozen in patterns of pain or mutual unhappiness. Divorce can be, despite its initial devastation, like the first cut of the surgeon's knife, a step toward new health and a good life. One the other hand, if the partners can stay past the breaking up of the romantic myths into the development of real love and intimacy, they have achieved a work as amazing as the greatest cathedrals of the world. Marriages that do not fail but improve, that persist despite imperfections, are not only rare these days but offer a wondrous shelter in which the face of our mutual humanity can safely show itself.

REFLECTING AND INTERPRETING

1. Reread the first paragraph. What rhetorical strategy is used here? How does it function?

2. In paragraph 3, Roiphe cites expert opinion. Why?

3. Do you agree or disagree with Dr. Whitaker's theory? Why?

4. What is the basic marriage myth that Roiphe wrote about two decades ago? Do you think the myth still exists? Why or why not?

5. What five qualities does Roiphe identify that are essential for a marriage to endure? Can you think of any others?

6. What pretense does a partner often use to "solve old problems"? How effective is it? What are the risks? (Think about the opening sentence.)

7. What are some of the factors that have created more tension in marriages than those of a century ago?

8. Roiphe says that divorce is so common for one chief reason. What is it? What can couples do to evade divorce? Can you think of some ways that she does not name?

9. What is the basic question that couples must resolve in order for a marriage to succeed?

10. What advantages does a successful marriage offer a family? Consider effects on children, education, health, and others.

A WRITER'S RESPONSE

1. If you are married, analyze the growth that you have attained since your wedding vows. Write an essay analyzing the cause and effects. If you are single, describe the kind of marriage you would like to have some day. Then analyze the responsibilities you will need to assume and the changes you will need to make.

2. *Small Groups:* Roiphe points out that growth must take place for a marriage to succeed. What kind of growth does she mean? How do changes in perception and perspective figure in? Can you give some examples?

THE TEACHER WHO CHANGED MY LIFE   NICHOLAS GAGE

Running barefoot through minefields with his three sisters, Nicholas Gage left his Greek village to escape communist guerrillas. The children stayed in a refugee camp until their father, who lived in the United States, located them. When nine-year-old Nicholas Gage arrived in the United States, he did not expect to be placed in a class for the mentally retarded. Non-English speaking, he and his sisters learned English. Four years later Gage met a teacher who changed his life. He won a scholarship to Boston University and later attended Columbia's Graduate School of Journalism. He worked for the Associated Press, *Boston Herald Traveler, Wall Street Journal,* and *New York Times,* which sent him to Greece as a foreign correspondent. His book *Eleni* (1987), which relates his early experiences, was a best-seller and later produced as a film. He has written several other books, including *Hellas: A Portrait of Greece* (1987), *Greece: Land of Light* (1998), and *Greek Fire* (2001). The following excerpt is from *A Place for Us* (1990).

1   The person who set the course of my life in the new land I entered as a young war refugee—who, in fact, nearly dragged me onto the path that would bring all the blessings I've received in America—was a salty-tongued, no-nonsense schoolteacher named Marjorie Hurd. When I entered her classroom in 1953, I had been to six schools in five years, starting in the Greek village where I was born in 1939.

When I stepped off a ship in New York Harbor on a gray March day in 1949, I was an undersized 9-year-old in short pants who had lost his mother and was coming to live with the father he didn't know. My mother, Eleni Gatzoyiannis, had been imprisoned, tortured and shot by Communist guerrillas for sending me and three of my four sisters to freedom. She died so that her children could go to their father in the United States.

The portly, bald, well-dressed man who met me and my sisters seemed a foreign, authoritarian figure. I secretly resented him for not getting the whole family out of Greece early enough to save my mother. Ultimately, I would grow to love him and appreciate how he dealt with becoming a single parent at the age of 56, but at first our relationship was prickly, full of hostility.

As Father drove us to our new home—a tenement in Worcester, Mass.—and pointed out the huge brick building that would be our first school in America, I clutched my Greek notebooks from the refugee camp, hoping that my few years of schooling would impress my teachers in this cold, crowded country. They didn't. When my father led me and my 11-year-old sister to Greendale Elementary School, the grim-faced Yankee principal put the two of us in a class for the mentally retarded. There was no facility in those days for non-English-speaking children.

By the time I met Marjorie Hurd four years later, I had learned English, 5 been placed in a normal, graded class and had even been chosen for the college preparatory track in the Worcester public school system. I was 13 years old when our father moved us yet again, and I entered Chandler Junior High shortly after the beginning of seventh grade. I found myself surrounded by richer, smarter and better-dressed classmates who looked askance at my strange clothes and heavy accent. Shortly after I arrived, we were told to select a hobby to pursue during "club hour" on Fridays. The idea of hobbies and clubs made no sense to my immigrant ears, but I decided to follow the prettiest girl in my class—the blue-eyed daughter of the local Lutheran minister. She led me through the door marked "Newspaper Club" and into the presence of Miss Hurd, the newspaper adviser and English teacher who would become my mentor and my muse.

A formidable, solidly built woman with salt-and-pepper hair, a steely eye and a flat Boston accent, Miss Hurd had no patience with layabouts. "What are all you goof-offs doing here?" she bellowed at the would-be journalists. "This is the Newspaper Club! We're going to put out a *newspaper*. So if there's anybody in this room who doesn't like work, I suggest you go across to the Glee Club now, because you're going to work your tails off here!"

I was soon under Miss Hurd's spell. She did indeed teach us to put out a newspaper, skills I honed during my next 25 years as a journalist. Soon I asked the principal to transfer me to her English class as well. There, she drilled us on grammar until I finally began to understand the logic and structure of the English language. She assigned stories for us to read and discuss; not tales of heroes, like the Greek myths I knew, but stories of underdogs—poor people, even immigrants, who seemed ordinary until a crisis drove them to do something extraordinary. She also introduced us to the literary wealth of Greece—giving me a new perspective on my war-ravaged, impoverished homeland. I began to be proud of my origins.

One day, after discussing how writers should write about what they know, she assigned us to compose an essay from our own experience. Fixing me with a stern look, she added, "Nick, I want you to write about what happened to your family in Greece." I had been trying to put those painful memories behind me and left the assignment until the last moment. Then, on a warm spring afternoon, I sat in my room with a yellow pad and pencil and stared out the window at the buds on the trees. I wrote that the coming of spring always reminded me of the last time I said goodbye to my mother on a green and gold day in 1948.

I kept writing, one line after another, telling how the Communist guerrillas occupied our village, took our home and food, how my mother started planning our escape when she learned that the children were to be sent to re-education camps behind the Iron Curtain and how, at the last moment, she couldn't escape with us because the guerrillas sent her with a group of women to thresh wheat in a distant village. She promised she would try to get away on her own, she told me to be brave and hung a silver cross around my neck, and then she kissed me. I watched the line of women being led down into the ravine and up the other side, until they disappeared around the bend—my mother a tiny brown figure at the end who stopped for an instant to raise her hand in one last farewell.

10   I wrote about our nighttime escape down the mountain, across the minefields and into the lines of the Nationalist soldiers, who sent us to a refugee camp. It was there that we learned of our mother's execution. I felt very lucky to have come to America, I concluded, but every year, the coming of spring made me feel sad because it reminded me of the last time I saw my mother.

I handed in the essay, hoping never to see it again, but Miss Hurd had it published in the school paper. This mortified me at first, until I saw that my classmates reacted with sympathy and tact to my family's story. Without telling me, Miss Hurd also submitted the essay to a contest sponsored by the Freedoms Foundation at Valley Forge, Pa., and it won a medal. The Worcester paper wrote about the award and quoted my essay at length. My father, by then a "five-and-dime-store chef," as the paper described him, was ecstatic with pride, and the Worcester Greek community celebrated the honor to one of its own.

For the first time I began to understand the power of the written word. A secret ambition took root in me. One day, I vowed, I would go back to Greece, find out the details of my mother's death and write about her life, so her grandchildren would know of her courage. Perhaps I would even track down the men who killed her and write of their crimes. Fulfilling that ambition would take me 30 years.

Meanwhile, I followed the literary path that Miss Hurd had so forcefully set me on. After junior high, I became the editor of my school paper at Classical High School and got a part-time job at the Worcester *Telegram and Gazette.* Although my father could only give me $50 and encouragement toward a college education, I managed to finance four years at Boston University with scholarships and part-time jobs in journalism. During my last year of college, an article I wrote about a friend who had died in the Philippines—the first person to lose his life working for the Peace

Corps—led to my winning the Hearst Award for College Journalism. And the plaque was given to me in the White House by President John F. Kennedy.

For a refugee who had never seen a motorized vehicle or indoor plumbing until he was 9, this was an unimaginable honor. When the Worcester paper ran a picture of me standing next to President Kennedy, my father rushed out to buy a new suit in order to be properly dressed to receive the congratulations of the Worcester Greeks. He clipped out the photograph, had it laminated in plastic and carried it in his breast pocket for the rest of his life to show everyone he met. I found the much-worn photo in his pocket on the day he died 20 years later.

In our isolated Greek village, my mother had bribed a cousin to teach 15 her to read, for girls were not supposed to attend school beyond a certain age. She had always dreamed of her children receiving an education. She couldn't be there when I graduated from Boston University, but the person who came with my father and shared our joy was my former teacher, Marjorie Hurd. We celebrated not only my bachelor's degree but also the scholarships that paid my way to Columbia's Graduate School of Journalism. There, I met the woman who would eventually become my wife. At our wedding and at the baptisms of our three children, Marjorie Hurd was always there, dancing alongside the Greeks.

By then, she was Mrs. Rabidou, for she had married a widower when she was in her early 40s. That didn't distract her from her vocation of introducing young minds to English literature, however. She taught for a total of 41 years and continually would make a "project" of some balky student in whom she spied a spark of potential. Often these were students from the most troubled homes, yet she would alternately bully and charm each one with her own special brand of tough love until the spark caught fire. She retired in 1981 at the age of 62 but still avidly follows the lives and careers of former students while overseeing her adult stepchildren and driving her husband on camping trips to New Hampshire.

Miss Hurd was one of the first to call me on Dec. 10, 1987, when President Reagan, in his television address after the summit meeting with Gorbachev, told the nation that Eleni Gatzoyiannis' dying cry, "My children!" had helped inspire him to seek an arms agreement "for all the children of the world."

"I can't imagine a better monument for your mother," Miss Hurd said with an uncharacteristic catch in her voice.

Although a bad hip makes it impossible for her to join in the Greek dancing, Marjorie Hurd Rabidou is still an honored and enthusiastic guest at all family celebrations, including my 50th birthday picnic last summer, where the shish kebab was cooked on spits, clarinets and *bouzoukis* wailed, and costumed dancers led the guests in a serpentine line around our Colonial farmhouse, only 20 minutes from my first home in Worcester.

My sisters and I felt an aching void because my father was not there to 20 lead the line, balancing a glass of wine on his head while he danced, the way he did at every celebration during his 92 years. But Miss Hurd was there, surveying the scene with quiet satisfaction. Although my parents are gone, her presence was a consolation, because I owe her so much.

This is truly the land of opportunity, and I would have enjoyed its bounty even if I hadn't walked into Miss Hurd's classroom in 1953. But she was the one who directed my grief and pain into writing, and if it weren't for her I wouldn't have become an investigative reporter and foreign correspondent, recorded the story of my mother's life and death in *Eleni* and now my father's story in *A Place for Us,* which is also a testament to the country that took us in. She was the catalyst that sent me into journalism and indirectly caused all the good things that came after. But Miss Hurd would probably deny this emphatically.

A few years ago, I answered the telephone and heard my former teacher's voice telling me, in that won't-take-no-for-an-answer tone of hers, that she had decided I was to write and deliver the eulogy at her funeral. I agreed (she didn't leave me any choice), but that's one assignment I never want to do. I hope, Miss Hurd, that you'll accept this remembrance instead.

REFLECTING AND INTERPRETING

1. Where is Gage's thesis statement?

2. Although this essay is primarily about a teacher that Gage had the year he was thirteen, he talks about virtually his entire life. Why?

3. What order does Gage use to present the events of so many years? At times he uses what device to weave in past events? How does he accomplish these shifts so that readers can easily follow?

4. How did Miss Hurd (later Mrs. Rabidou) occasionally make a "project" of one of her students?

5. What are stories of "underdogs"? Can you think of one of our presidents who was an underdog?

6. What skills did Gage develop as a result of Miss Hurd's instruction? How did one of her assignments change his life?

7. Trace Miss Hurd's influence on Gage after he left her junior high class.

8. When Gage uses "salty-tongued, no-nonsense" to describe Miss Hurd, what do you think he means? What other glimpses of her personality do you gain from her interaction not only with Gage but also with other students?

9. An excerpt from Gage's book *Eleni* was quoted on national television. Who referred to it? What was the occasion? How did one of Miss Hurd's assignments change his life?

10. How would you describe Gage's attitude and the tone of the essay?

A WRITER'S RESPONSE

1. Have you ever changed schools and felt uncomfortable among students who seemed quite different? Describe the experience and how you ad-

justed. Was any particular person helpful in making you feel comfortable? Write an essay describing the experience and how it affected you.

2. Consider the people who have influenced your life. Write an essay identifying the incidents that were particularly significant to you. Explain why.

CUT	BOB GREENE

An award-winning journalist and *New York Times* bestselling author, Bob Greene was born in Columbus, Ohio, in 1947. Since graduating from Northwestern University in 1969, he has published in *Life, Esquire,* the *Chicago Sun-Times,* the *Tribune,* and the *New York Times.* Bob has also worked as a correspondent for ABC News *Nightline.* His most recent books include *Fraternity: A Journey in Search of Five Presidents* (2005), *Once Upon a Town: The Miracle of the North Platte Canteen* (2003), and *The Man Who Won the War* (2001). The essay here was originally printed in *Esquire* magazine.

I remember vividly the last time I cried. I was twelve years old, in the 1 seventh grade, and I had tried out for the junior high school basketball team. I walked into the gymnasium; there was a piece of paper tacked to the bulletin board.

It was a cut list. The seventh-grade coach had put it up on the board. The boys whose names were on the list were still on the team; they were welcome to keep coming to practices. The boys whose names were not on the list had been cut; their presence was no longer desired. My name was not on the list.

I had not known the cut was coming that day. I stood and stared at the list. The coach had not composed it with a great deal of subtlety; the names of the very best athletes were at the top of the sheet of paper, and the other members of the squad were listed in what appeared to be a descending order of talent. I kept looking at the bottom of the list, hoping against hope that my name would miraculously appear there if I looked hard enough.

I held myself together as I walked out of the gym and out of the school, but when I got home I began to sob. I couldn't stop. For the first time in my life, I had been told officially that I wasn't good enough. Athletics meant everything to boys that age; if you were on the team, even a substitute, it put you in the desirable group. If you weren't on the team, you might as well not be alive.

I had tried desperately in practice, but the coach never seemed to no- 5 tice. It didn't matter how hard I was willing to work; he didn't want me there. I knew that when I went to school the next morning I would have to face the boys who had not been cut—the boys whose names were on the list, who were still on the team, who had been judged worthy while I had been judged unworthy.

All these years later, I remember it as if I were still standing right there in the gym. And a curious thing has happened: in traveling around the country, I have found that an inordinately large proportion of successful men share that same memory—the memory of being cut from a sports team as a boy.

I don't know how the mind works in matters like this; I don't know what went on in my head following that day when I was cut. But I know that my ambition has been enormous ever since then; I know that for all of my life since that day, I have done more work than I had to be doing, taken more assignments than I had to be taking, put in more hours than I had to be spending. I don't know if all of that came from a determination never to allow myself to be cut again—never to allow someone to tell me that I'm not good enough again—but I know it's there. And apparently it's there in a lot of other men, too.

Bob Graham, thirty-six, is a partner with the Jenner & Block law firm in Chicago. "When I was sixteen, baseball was my whole life," he said. "I had gone to a relatively small high school, and I had been on the team. But then my family moved, and I was going to a much bigger high school. All during the winter months I told everyone that I was a ballplayer. When spring came, of course I went out for the team.

"The cut list went up. I did not make the team. Reading that cut list is one of the clearest things I have in my memory. I wanted not to believe it, but there it was.

10   "I went home and told my father about it. He suggested that maybe I should talk to the coach. So I did. I pleaded to be put back on the team. He said there was nothing he could do; he said he didn't have enough room.

"I know for a fact that it altered my perception of myself. My view of myself was knocked down; my self-esteem was lowered. I felt so embarrassed; my whole life up to that point had revolved around sports, and particularly around playing baseball. That was the group I wanted to be in—the guys on the baseball team. And I was told that I wasn't good enough to be one of them.

"I know now that it changed me. I found out, even though I couldn't articulate it at the time, that there would be times in my life when certain people would be in a position to say 'You're not good enough' to me. I did not want that to happen ever again.

"It seems obvious to me now that being cut was what started me in determining that my success would always be based on my own abilities, and not on someone else's perceptions. Since then I've always been something of an overachiever; when I came to the law firm I was very aggressive in trying to run my own cases right away, to be the lead lawyer in the cases with which I was involved. I made partner at thirty-one; I never wanted to be left behind.

"Looking back, maybe it shouldn't have been that important. It was only baseball. You pass that by. Here I am. That coach is probably still there, still a high school baseball coach, still cutting boys off the baseball team every year. I wonder how many hundreds of boys he's cut in his life?"

15   Maurice McGrath is senior vice-president of Genstar Mortgage Corporation, a mortgage banking firm in Glendale, California. "I'm forty-seven

years old, and I was fourteen when it happened to me, and I still feel something when I think about it," he said.

"I was in the eighth grade. I went to St. Philip's School in Pasadena. I went out for the baseball team, and one day at practice the coach came over to me. He was an Occidental College student who had been hired as the eighth-grade coach.

"He said, 'You're no good.' Those were his words. I asked him why he was saying that. He said, 'You can't hit the ball. I don't want you here.' I didn't know what to do, so I went over and sat off to the side, watching the others practice. The coach said I should leave the practice field. He said that I wasn't on the team, and that I didn't belong there anymore.

"I was outwardly stoic about it. I didn't want anyone to see how I felt. I didn't want to show that it hurt. But oh, did it hurt. All my friends played baseball after school every day. My best friend was the pitcher on the team. After I got whittled down by the coach, I would hear the other boys talking in class about what they were going to do at practice after school. I knew that I'd just have to go home.

"I guess you make your mind up never to allow yourself to be hurt like that again. In some way I must have been saying to myself, 'I'll play the game better.' Not the sports game, but anything I tried. I must have been saying, 'If I have to, I'll sit on the bench, but I'll be part of the team.'

"I try to make my own kids believe that, too. I try to tell them that they 20 should show that they're a little bit better than the rest. I tell them to think of themselves as better. Who cares what anyone else thinks? You know, I can almost hear that coach saying the words. 'You're no good.'"

Author Malcolm MacPherson (*The Blood of His Servants*), forty, lives in New York. "It happened to me in the ninth grade, at the Yalesville School in Yalesville, Connecticut," he said. "Both of my parents had just been killed in a car crash, and as you can imagine, it was a very difficult time in my life. I went out for the baseball team, and I did pretty well in practice.

"But in the first game I clutched. I was playing second base; the batter hit a pop-up, and I moved back to catch it. I can see it now. I felt dizzy as I looked up at the ball. It was like I was moving in slow motion, but the ball was going at regular speed. I couldn't get out of the way of my own feet. The ball dropped to the ground. I didn't catch it.

"The next day at practice, the coach read off the lineup. I wasn't on it. I was off the squad.

"I remember what I did: I walked. It was a cold spring afternoon, and the ground was wet, and I just walked. I was living with an aunt and uncle, and I didn't want to go home. I just wanted to walk forever.

"It drove my opinion of myself right into a tunnel. Right into a cave. 25 And when I came out of the cave, something inside of me wanted to make sure in one manner or another that I would never again be told I wasn't good enough.

"I will confess that my ambition, to this day, is out of control. It's like a fire. I think the fire would have pretty much stayed in control if I hadn't been cut from that team. But that got it going. You don't slice ambition two ways; it's either there or it isn't. Those of us who went through something like that always know that we have to catch the ball. We'd rather die than have the ball fall at our feet.

"Once that fire is started in us, it never gets extinguished, until we die or have heart attacks or something. Sometimes I wonder about the home-run hitters; the guys who never even had to worry about being cut. They may have gotten the applause and the attention back then, but I wonder if they ever got the fire. I doubt it. I think maybe you have to get kicked in the teeth to get the fire started.

"You can tell the effect of something like that by examining the trail you've left in your life, and tracing it backward. It's almost like being a junkie with a need for success. You get attention and applause and you like it, but you never quite trust it. Because you know that back then you were good enough if only they would have given you a chance. You don't trust what you achieve, because you're afraid that someone will take it away from you. You know that it can happen; it already did.

"So you try to show people how good you are. Maybe you don't go out and become Dan Rather; maybe you just end up owning the Pontiac dealership in your town. But it's your dealership, and you're the top man, and every day you're showing people that you're good enough."

30   Dan Rather, fifty-two, is anchor of the CBS *Evening News.* "When I was thirteen, I had rheumatic fever," he said. "I became extremely skinny and extremely weak, but I still went out for the seventh-grade baseball team at Alexander Hamilton Junior High School in Houston.

"The school was small enough that there was no cut as such; you were supposed to figure out that you weren't good enough, and quit. Game after game I sat at the end of the bench, hoping that maybe this was the time I would get in. The coach never even looked at me; I might as well have been invisible.

"I told my mother about it. Her advice was not to quit. So I went to practice every day, and I tried to do well so that the coach would be impressed. He never even knew I was there. At home in my room I would fantasize that there was a big game, and the three guys in front of me would all get hurt, and the coach would turn to me and put me in, and I would make the winning hit. But then there'd be another game, and the late innings would come, and if we were way ahead I'd keep hoping that this was the game when the coach would put me in. He never did.

"When you're that age, you're looking for someone to tell you you're okay. Your sense of self-esteem is just being formed. And what that experience that baseball season did was make me think that perhaps I wasn't okay.

"In the last game of the season something terrible happened. It was the last of the ninth inning, there were two outs, and there were two strikes on the batter. And the coach turned to me and told me to go out to right field.

"It was a totally humiliating thing for him to do. For him to put me in 35 for one pitch, the last pitch of the season, in front of all the other boys on the team . . . I stood out there for that one pitch, and I just wanted to sink into the ground and disappear. Looking back on it, it was an extremely un-kind thing for him to have done. That was nearly forty years ago, and I don't know why the memory should be so vivid now; I've never known if the coach was purposely making fun of me—and if he was, why a grown man would do that to a thirteen-year-old boy.

"I'm not a psychologist. I don't know if a man can point to one event in his life and say that that's the thing that made him the way he is. But when you're that age, and you're searching for your own identity, and all you want is to be told that you're all right . . . I wish I understood it better, but I know the feeling is still there."

REFLECTING AND INTERPRETING

1. The author opens by describing a childhood experience that has haunted him all his adult life. Why was this event so significant?

2. How has this experience influenced his work ethic?

3. What did Bob discover as he traveled around the United States?

4. How does the experience of Malcolm MacPherson differ from those of the other interviewees?

5. Consider the imagery in paragraphs 25 and 26. What literary devices do you notice?

6. Examine paragraph 29. What two functions does it perform? (What does the paragraph do?)

7. How did Dan Rather's experience differ from the others' experiences?

8. When Dan's dream came true and he was offered the chance to play ball, why did he view it as "terrible"? How might the coach have regarded it?

9. Greene describes "cuts" from ball teams. What other kinds of "cuts" occur in life?

10. Do you think these reactions to being "cut" are typical? Have any of the people whom you know well been able to gain strength from such an experience?

A WRITER'S RESPONSE

Have you ever endured a humiliating experience such as the author describes? Or perhaps you suffered a different sort of experience that has haunted you for years? How has it influenced your life? Write a paragraph describing the event and its effect on you.

Constructing
a Convincing Argument

LAST RITES FOR INDIAN DEAD SUZAN SHOWN HARJO

President and executive director of the Morning Star Foundation, Suzan Shown Harjo is also a founding trustee of the National Museum of the American Indian. She is a citizen of the Cheyenne and Arapaho tribes of Oklahoma. On July 25, 2000, she spoke to the U.S. Senate Committee on Indian Affairs, urging changes in the administration and implementation of the Native American Graves and Repatriation Act of 1990. In "Last Rites for Indian Dead," originally printed in the *Los Angeles Times* (16 Sept. 1989), Harjo provides an eye-opening perspective of practices and attitudes concerning Indian burials and relics. Since then illegal digging has multiplied—due to inadequate enforcement, loopholes in the law, collectors, galleries, trade shows, and international markets such as eBay.

1   What if museums, universities and government agencies could put your dead relatives on display or keep them in boxes to be cut up and otherwise studied? What if you believed that the spirits of the dead could not rest until their human remains were placed in a sacred area?

The ordinary American would say there ought to be a law—and there is, for ordinary Americans. The problem for American Indians is that there are too many laws of the kind that make us the archeological property of the United States and too few of the kind that protect us from such insults.

Some of my own Cheyenne relatives' skulls are in the Smithsonian Institution today, along with those of at least 4,500 other Indian people who were violated in the 1800s by the U.S. Army for an "Indian Crania Study." It wasn't enough that these unarmed Cheyenne people were mowed down by the cavalry at the infamous Sand Creek massacre; many were decapitated and their heads shipped to Washington as freight. (The Army Medical Museum's collection is now in the Smithsonian.) Some had been exhumed only hours after being buried. Imagine their grieving families' reaction on finding their loved ones disinterred and headless.

Some targets of the Army's study were killed in noncombat situations and beheaded immediately. The officer's account of the decapitation of the Apache chief Mangas Coloradas in 1863 shows the pseudoscientific nature of the exercise. "I weighed the brain and measured the skull," the good doctor wrote, "and found that while the skull was smaller, the brain was larger than that of Daniel Webster."

These journal accounts exist in excruciating detail, yet missing are any 5 records of overall comparisons, conclusions or final reports of the Army study. Since it is unlike the Army not to leave a paper trail, one must wonder about the motive for its collection.

The total Indian body count in the Smithsonian collection is more than 19,000 and it is not the largest in the country. It is not inconceivable that the 1.5 million of us living today are outnumbered by our dead stored in museums, educational institutions, federal agencies, state historical societies and private collections. The Indian people are further dehumanized by being exhibited alongside the mastodons and dinosaurs and other extinct creatures.

Where we have buried our dead in peace, more often than not the sites have been desecrated. For more than 200 years, relic-hunting has been a popular pursuit. Lately, the market in Indian artifacts has brought this abhorrent activity to a fever pitch in some areas. And when scavengers come upon Indian burial sites, everything found becomes fair game, including sacred burial offerings, teeth and skeletal remains.

One unusually well-publicized example of Indian grave desecration occurred two years ago in a western Kentucky field known as Slack Farm, the site of an Indian village five centuries ago. Ten men—one with a business card stating "Have Shovel, Will Travel"—paid the landowner $10,000 to lease digging rights between planting seasons. They dug extensively on the 40-acre farm, rummaging through an estimated 650 graves, collecting burial goods, tools and ceremonial items. Skeletons were strewn about like litter.

What motivates people to do something like this? Financial gain is the first answer. Indian relic-collecting has become a multimillion-dollar industry. The price tag on a bead necklace can easily top $1,000; rare pieces fetch tens of thousands.

And it is not just collectors of the macabre who pay for skeletal re- 10 mains. Scientists say that these deceased Indians are needed for research that someday could benefit the health and welfare of living Indians. But just how many dead Indians must they examine? Nineteen thousand?

There is doubt as to whether permanent curation of our dead really benefits Indians. Dr. Emery A. Johnson, former assistant Surgeon General, recently observed, "I am not aware of any current medical diagnostic or treatment procedure that has been derived from research on such skeletal remains. Nor am I aware of any during the 34 years that I have been involved in American Indian . . . health care."

Indian remains are still being collected for racial biological studies. While the intentions may be honorable, the ethics of using human remains this way without the full consent of relatives must be questioned.

Some relief for Indian people has come on the state level. Almost half of the states, including California, have passed laws protecting Indian burial sites and restricting the sale of Indian bones, burial offerings and other sacred items. Rep. Charles E. Bennett (D-Fla.) and Sen. John McCain (R-Ariz.) have introduced bills that are a good start in invoking the federal government's protection. However, no legislation has attacked the problem head-on by imposing stiff penalties at the marketplace, or by changing laws that make dead Indians the nation's property.

Some universities—notably Stanford, Nebraska, Minnesota and Seattle—have returned, or agreed to return, Indian human remains; it is fitting that institutions of higher education should lead the way.

15   Congress is now deciding what to do with the government's extensive collection of Indian human remains and associated funerary objects. The secretary of the Smithsonian, Robert McC. Adams, has been valiantly attempting to apply modern ethics to yesterday's excesses. This week, he announced that the Smithsonian would conduct an inventory and return all Indian skeletal remains that could be identified with specific tribes or living kin.

But there remains a reluctance generally among collectors of Indian remains to take action of a scope that would have a quantitative impact and a healing quality. If they will not act on their own—and it is highly unlikely that they will—then Congress must act.

The country must recognize that the bodies of dead American Indian people are not artifacts to be bought and sold as collector's items. It is not appropriate to store tens of thousands of our ancestors for possible future research. They are our family. They deserve to be returned to their sacred burial grounds and given a chance to rest.

The plunder of our people's graves has gone on too long. Let us rebury our dead and remove this shameful past from America's future.

_____

REFLECTING AND INTERPRETING

1. What two implicit questions does Harjo raise in paragraph 1?
2. What question does she raise about the purpose and results of the 1863 Army Medical Study?
3. What shared values does the writer assume we have in paragraph 6?
4. What motivates some people to desecrate graves?
5. Is the evidence that Harjo provides in paragraphs 6 to 12 strong enough to support her contention?

6. Which words and phrases reveal Harjo's indignation?

7. What have some states done to remedy this problem?

8. The 1990 Native American Graves Protection and Repatriation Act specifies a way for museums and federal agencies to restore Native American remains and cultural objects to descendants and related Indian tribes. What seems to be delaying this return?

9. How does Harjo conclude her argument?

10. Examine the structure of Harjo's argument. Considering that readers are mostly of other cultures, do you think the organization is effective? Why or why not?

A WRITER'S RESPONSE

Do you know of any archaeological digs in your state? Do you think archaeologists and students should be allowed access to digs that are not burial sites but contain only cultural items? (Such digging is legal on privately owned land when permission is obtained and ownership of findings agreed upon.) Why or why not? Write a short essay arguing for your position.

LOGGING IN GIANT SEQUOIA NATIONAL MONUMENT	SIERRA CLUB SEQUOIA TASK FORCE

In 1892 John Muir, renowned preservationist, founded the Sierra Club in San Francisco, California. The club now has hundreds of employees and hundreds of thousands of members who actively volunteer. The mission of the club is to

1. explore, enjoy, and protect the wild places of the earth;
2. practice and promote the responsible use of the earth's ecosystems and resources;
3. educate and enlist humanity to protect and restore the quality of the natural and human environment; and
4. use all lawful means to carry out these objectives.

An issue that has long concerned the Sierra Club and other environmental groups, as well as private citizens, is the logging of mature trees in U.S. national forests and monuments. In recent years this practice, which often violates current laws, has increased throughout the United States. The two online articles here describe logging in the Giant Sequoia National Monument and explain how the Sierra Club was able to halt it.

SEQUOIA NATIONAL MONUMENT BEING LOGGED TODAY!
August 3, 2005

The Sequoia Task Force of the Sierra Club is protesting the Forest Service's decision to allow commercial logging to go forward in a logging project that is today bulldozing huge swathes and removing ancient trees, many several centuries old, on ridgetops adjacent to five giant sequoia groves in the Giant Sequoia National Monument. This timber sale is called the Saddle Fuels Reduction Project and is all about removing big trees, not about fire control. This project will take more than 5 million board feet of big timber! We have asked for an immediate halt to this project!

The Giant Sequoia National Monument was created in April of 2000. The Proclamation's provisions was supposed to stop bulldozing, logging and exploitation of Monument lands. It called for restoration from a century of logging. However, the Proclamation did allow a few timber sales that had been approved prior to the creation of the Monument to be completed as a short term transition for the timber industry. The Secretary of Agriculture Dan Glickman, whose department included the Forest Service, announced that this logging was estimated to be completed within about two and a half years of the signing of the Proclamation.

At the time of the signing of the Proclamation, the Saddle Project contract termination date was March, 2004. That meant logging should have been completed by November of 2003 because of seasonal closure of the forest for winter. But, quietly in the backroom of the Forest Service, the contract deadline was changed giving the industry until 2005. Then the deadline was changed yet again so the industry now can log until 2006.

Why did this happen? A Forest Service press release implies that the timber industry had some hazard trees to remove but no documentation confirms any legal justification for these extensions. We note that our local McNally fire occurred long after the contract extensions were given.

5   Local activists have been investigating the logging site where trees have been falling this week and have found stumps well over 30 inches in diameter. Such trees here in the arid southern Sierra can be extremely old since there can be 10 or more annual growth rings to an inch on some sites. Logging these ancient trees means that it will be centuries before these areas will recover old growth characteristics and, meanwhile, species that depend on ancient unlogged forests will have no refuge. The Pacific fisher is making its last stand here in the southern Sierra; projects such as the Saddle could mean losing this valiant little creature forever.

We have found no compelling reasons for the Forest Service to have extended the contracts so that damage could continue in this new Monument. The Sierra Club has already taken the Forest Service to court for approving a Sequoia Monument Management Plan that perpetuates logging instead of restoration from logging; now we find the Forest Service helping the industry to continue and extend the old damaging pre-Monument logging projects. The only reasonable explanation is that the Forest Service is just as addicted to logging as the timber industry itself. The Forest Service cannot be allowed to continue to manage this National Monument with its emerald meadows, sparkling streams and over half the earth's groves of giant sequoia! We must turn over management of the Giant Sequoia National Monument to Sequoia National Park! They have a proven record of nurturing the resources in their care.

The Sierra Club cheered the creation of this Monument as the realization of John Muir's dream to have all Sequoias protected throughout their range. The Sierra Club will do its best to protect this magnificent National Monument. We will keep you posted on our next step!

We urge you to protest the implementation of the Saddle Project by writing letters to your Congressional representatives and to the Supervisor of Sequoia National Forest, 1500 West Grand Avenue, Porterville CA 93257.

GIANT SEQUOIA WINS COURT PROTECTION
August 22, 2006

San Francisco, CA—A federal judge today ruled that the Bush administration's controversial plan to allow commercial logging in Giant Sequoia National Monument Conservation is illegal. The Sierra Club and other conservation groups celebrated the decision and urged the Bush administration to restore and protect the Giant Sequoia National Monument with the same standard of care given to neighboring Sequoia National Park.

"The Forest Service's interest in harvesting timber has trampled the applicable environmental laws," wrote Judge Charles R. Breyer, writing for the United States District Court for Northern California, who also ruled that the "Monument Plan is decidedly incomprehensible." 10

In addition to ruling that the Forest Service's overall plan to allow commercial logging in Giant Sequoia Monument is illegal, Judge Breyer also invalidated several individual timber sales because of their impact on endangered wildlife.

"The Forest Service should be managing Giant Sequoia as a gift to future generations, not as a gift to the timber industry," said Bruce Hamilton, Sierra Club's Conservation Director. "Today's ruling only strengthens the case for transferring management of this magnificent Monument to neighboring Sequoia National Park, where it would be treated with the good stewardship it deserves."

Giant Sequoia National Monument boasts more than half of all the Sequoia redwoods in the world, with most of the remainder found in the adjacent National Park. The popularity and awe-inspiring beauty of the Sequoia forest and its wildlife led President Bill Clinton [to] permanently protect the forest as a National Monument under the Antiquities Act. Earlier, President George Bush Sr. had proclaimed the Sequoia groves off limits to commercial logging.

In 2005, the Bush administration officially reversed those policies by finalizing plans to allow what amounts to commercial logging in the Monument, even inside the prized Giant Sequoia groves. The administration's plan would have allowed 7.5 million board feet of timber to be removed annually from the Monument, enough to fill 1,500 logging trucks each year. This policy would have included logging of healthy trees of any species as big as 30 inches in diameter or more. Trees that size can be as much as 300 years old.

As a model for better management, the Sierra Club and others strongly urged the Bush administration to look to nearby Sequoia National Park, 15 where innovative conservation and fire prevention strategies have reinvigorated the Sequoia groves and made nearby communities safer. Unlike the Forest Service, which has proposed selling timber contracts to log healthy trees, the National Park Service effectively uses prescribed burning and thinning of smaller, more flammable trees and brush.

The complaint against the Forest Service was brought by the Sierra Club, Sierra Nevada Forest Protection Campaign, Earth Island Institute, Tule River Conservancy, Sequoia Forest Keeper, and Center for Biological Diversity, and in separate suit filed by the California Attorney General. The Sierra Club, Earthjustice and John Muir Project co-counselled the case.

"The plan proposed by the Forest Service ignores the clear recommendations of its own fire scientists that fire risk reduction is not about logging large trees," stated Craig Thomas, Director of the Sierra Nevada Forest Protection Campaign.

"The American people are looking to their government to protect these forests forever as a National Monument, not as a tree farm," stated Carla Cloer of the Tule River Conservancy. "Logging the Sequoia National Monument is just as unacceptable as selling the Statue of Liberty for scrap metal.

REFLECTING AND INTERPRETING

1. Why did the Proclamation allow a few timber sales?
2. When was the original termination date? What happened? Why?
3. Legally, loggers were allowed to cut which trees? What happened?
4. What action does this argument call for?
5. What 2006 judicial decision resulted from the Sierra Club's efforts?
6. What further action did the Sierra Club request in 2006?
7. Give three reasons for preserving the ancient trees in Giant Sequoia National Monument.
8. What analogy did Judge Breyer make?
9. Do you agree with Judge Breyer's analogy? Why or why not?
10. Does the Sierra Club use ethical, logical, or emotional appeals? Give examples. What is the effect of exclamation marks?

A WRITER'S RESPONSE

What environmental issue interests you the most? Describe the problem and give reasons for your concern.

HISTORICAL PERSPECTIVE OF THE WAL-MART CONTROVERSY

In 1945 Sam Walton purchased a Ben Franklin five-and-dime store in Newport, **10** Arkansas. By 2002 Wal-Mart had mushroomed into the largest corporation in the world. Consumers heartily welcomed Wal-Mart's expansion because of new jobs and low prices, but in recent years widespread doubt about the long-term effects of Wal-Mart's presence has arisen. Many areas in the USA have reported tax losses from abatements afforded Wal-Mart, yet their fire and police protection costs have risen. Many small businesses have closed because of an inability to compete, contributing to downtown decay. Nor can large chains that pay union wages compete with nonunionized Wal-Mart.

Hourly wages for Wal-Mart grocery store workers have changed little since 2004. Then the average hourly wage was $8.23, "compared to $10.35 for an average supermarket worker" (George Miller, Rep. 7th District, California, 16 Feb. 2004). Because many workers are allowed just a twenty-eight-hour week, they do not have health insurance. In many communities Wal-Mart's low wages have increased the demand for social services—free school lunches, housing, children's health insurance, and Medicaid.

Over the years Wal-Mart has had its share of lawsuits, including patent infringement, liability for accidents, unsafe parking lots, disability discrimination, sexism, hiring of illegal workers, child labor violations, and unpaid overtime. In 2002 in Portland, Oregon, a federal jury found that Wal-Mart had made employees work overtime without pay from 1994 to 1999. Since then, similar lawsuits have been filed in several states. In 2007 the Labor Department stated that "Wal-Mart Stores, Inc., will pay more than $33 million in back wages to thousands of workers . . . for paying too little in overtime" (*Wall Street Journal*, 26 Jan. 2007).

Documentary films such as "Wal-Mart: The High Cost of Low Price," shown at colleges and independent theaters, have fanned the anti–Wal-Mart furor. Now, as Wal-Mart seeks approval, coast to coast, to build supercenters, many communities are lobbying to keep out the discount chain. Yet some malls with vacancies are welcoming Wal-Mart. By late 2006, Wal-Mart had "26 stores attached to malls" and "18 more . . . adjacent to malls." Attracting many customers, Wal-Mart has helped to revitalize those malls (*Wall Street Journal*, 22 Nov. 2006).

The city council of Hartford, Connecticut, also sought Wal-Mart. They waived the city's living-wage ordinance. The two essays that follow give differing accounts of the Hartford controversy and opposing views of an unregulated Wal-Mart.

WAL-MART'S BIG CITY BLUES   DAN LEVINE

Based in Hartford, Connecticut, Dan Levine is a staff writer for the *New Haven Advocate*, an alternative weekly newspaper. Levine's stories have appeared in a variety of local and national outlets, including *In These Times, The Nation, Valley Advocate, Fairfield County Weekly*, and *Connecticut Law Tribune*. His journalism career began at the *Village Voice* in New York City. He writes on social and political issues—everything from deadbeat dads to Saddam Hussein's banning of labor unions. The following op-ed column was published in *The Nation* (8 Dec. 2003), soon after Hartford city officials suspended the city's living-wage ordinance to lure Wal-Mart there.

1   Having plundered America's countryside and suburbs for decades, Wal-Mart is now setting its sights on unfamiliar urban territory: a grassy lot in Hartford, Connecticut. But as the mega-corporation expands out of America's conservative strongholds, it must contend with a phenomenon it hasn't previously encountered—an opposition armed with a living-wage ordinance.

Forging a countermovement to the retailer's one-step-from-welfare wage policy, activists have successfully pushed living-wage ordinances in 110 cities and counties across the country since the mid-1990s, most often in Northern, urban areas—like Hartford—and in California. Typically those laws require companies seeking city contracts, property tax abatements or other public subsidies to pay their employees a living wage, which can come to several dollars above hourly minimum-wage rates.

Other big-box developers have made a mockery of similar guidelines. When politicians in St. Paul, Minnesota, granted Target Corporation a $6.3 million subsidy in 2001 to redevelop a downtown department store, the city council simply waived its own living-wage policy. But in Hartford, a coalition of progressive advocacy groups is determined not to let Wal-Mart secure the same sort of pass.

Wal-Mart has not sought a property tax break in Hartford, but the city's housing authority owns the meadow where the store will sit. And the living-wage ordinance covers real estate deals, according to the coalition, which includes the United Food and Commercial Workers Local 371, ACORN and the state Working Families Party, among other organizations. It is a natural campaign to launch, because the unions and community groups advancing living-wage ordinances are usually part of the same crowd that opposes construction of new Wal-Mart stores. Their task is a difficult one: convincing unfriendly city officials to make the mega-retailer abide by the law.

5   And the corporation did its groundwork in Hartford, lining up a segment of community leaders to support the development before the plans became public. So shifting focus from prohibition of a Wal-Mart store to regulation of its labor standards is a significant change in strategy for an anti-big-box campaign. It is a shift that acknowledges how hard it is to convince residents of a depressed city to oppose the lure of economic development.

"If it's a question of nothing versus Wal-Mart, that's sort of a losing battle for us. So the question is: Should Wal-Mart provide living-wage jobs and [affordable] health benefits, or not?" says Jon Green, director of the Working Families Party in Connecticut. "That's a different kind of question than, 'Should there be nothing, or should there be a massive retail development?' Politically, we think that's a better wedge for us."

Wal-Mart's vital statistics are remarkable. Annual sales ($244 billion) comparable to the gross domestic product of Austria. Plans to open a new Supercenter every two days. No unionized American workers.

The last bit is one of Wal-Mart's keys to profitability. By keeping wages close to subsistence level, the Arkansas-based retailer offers low prices that draw herds of gleeful shoppers away from the competition. Little wonder the company dispatches squads of unionbusters whenever its happy "associates" breathe the phrase "living wages."

But ubiquitous as it seems, Wal-Mart operated none of its Supercenters (giant structures that include grocery stores) in urban areas at the end of 2001. And more than half of those existing stores could be found in one region: the eleven states of the Old South, according to a study by Retail Forward, an industry analysis group. California had none. To maintain its fantastic growth rate, Wal-Mart is beginning to target territory that it had previously neglected.

In Hartford—an economically depressed city with a 73 percent Puerto Rican and African-American population—the retailer plans to break ground by the end of July on a 165,000 square-foot store; without a supermarket, at first, but with enough room to build one in the future. A massive effort to build forty Supercenters is under way in California. Key to the activists' success is explaining the hidden societal costs of allowing an unregulated Wal-Mart into town. Since workers don't make enough money to afford company health insurance, taxpayers end up footing the bill by subsidizing Medicaid coverage and other economic assistance. 10

Hartford's economic development chief says his office looked at the city's living-wage ordinance but decided it was moot. Why? Wal-Mart indicated their wages would be high enough to comply. As a backup, city lawyers argue that the ordinance doesn't apply to the corporation, because it only covers city land, not city housing authority land. Never mind that the city manager appoints the authority's entire board.

Living-wage campaigns are geared specifically toward companies like Wal-Mart. It would be devastating if activists who have already achieved victory in 110 localities let skittish politicians eviscerate their hard-won ordinances.

REFLECTING AND INTERPRETING

1. Examine the opening sentence. What do you learn about the writer?

2. What is a "living-wage ordinance"?

3. Levine does not use the classic argument opening. What does he do?

4. What is the pivotal question that the city leaders of Hartford had to decide?

5. Why was it so difficult to convince Hartford residents to oppose the development?

6. What is the key to Wal-Mart's profitability?

7. Does Levine acknowledge Wal-Mart's point of view? If so, where?

8. Is Hartford the only city with a living-wage ordinance that has caved in to Wal-Mart's demands? Have you heard of any areas that have refused to let Wal-Mart in?

9. What kind of ending does Levine use? How objective does the tone sound to you?

10. How would you rate the tone of his entire argument? Why?

A WRITER'S RESPONSE

Write a paragraph or an essay setting forth your position on the Wal-Mart controversy. Give specific reasons. Do you shop there? Why or why not?

THE WAR ON WAL-MART   STEVEN MALANGA

Presently a contributing editor of *City Journal* and a senior fellow at the Manhattan Institute, Steven Malanga writes articles and op-ed columns about intersection urban economies, business communities, and public policy. For seven years prior, he served as managing editor and executive editor of Crain's New York Business. In 1998 he cowrote "Tort-ured State," a series about trial lawyers in the state of New York that AABP cited as the "best investigative story of the year." Malanga has written articles for the *New York Post*, *New York Daily News*, *Newsday*, and other publications. This op-ed column was published in the *Wall Street Journal* (7 Apr. 2004) several months after Hartford City Council had decided to welcome Wal-Mart.

1   Here is a story you're unlikely to read in the spate of press attacks on Wal-Mart these days:

When Hartford, Conn., tore down a blighted housing project, city officials hatched an innovative redevelopment plan: Lure Wal-Mart to the site, entice other retailers with the promise of being near the discount giant, and then use the development's revenues to build new housing. After Wal-Mart agreed, city officials and residents celebrated the idea of better shopping, more jobs and new housing in one of America's poorest cities.

But then outsiders claiming to represent the local community began protesting the project. Astonished city leaders and residents quickly discovered the forces fueling the campaign: a Connecticut chapter of the United Food and Commercial Workers Union; and ACORN, the radical community group. Outraged residents denounced outside interference. "These people looked for every possible reason to stop a project that the community wants," says Jackie Fongemie, a resident.

Though Wal-Mart has encountered opposition for years from anti-sprawl activists or small-town merchants, the Hartford drama exemplifies a new form of opposition, a coordinated effort of the Left in which unions, activist groups like ACORN and the National Organization of Women, and even plaintiffs' attorneys work together in alliances. They are fighting the giant retailer in statehouses, city halls and courts.

More than just a skirmish over sites, theirs is an assault on a company 5 that embodies the productivity-driven, customer-oriented economy that emerged in the '90s, by opponents who argue that there is a hidden cost to business's increasing emphasis on low prices and high employee output. Opponents seek government or court edicts to force Wal-Mart and others like it to raise wages and offer workers more benefits, and they are rushing into battle just as the company expands to underserved urban communities, making the conflict a vital issue not just in Wal-Mart's traditional rural and suburban markets but, increasingly, in American cities.

Few would have imagined that when Sam Walton started Wal-Mart more than 40 years ago, he was hatching anything that would become so controversial. Though his first Wal-Marts, opened in the early '60s, were chaotic, with goods piled high on tables, the stores charged unparalleled low prices and crowds flocked to them. The company's success rested on "Mr. Sam's" formula of scouring the marketplace for the best prices and keeping a relentless rein on expenses. But the folksy country retailer, recognizing the importance of efficient systems, also led a technology revolution, installing computerized ordering and distribution that others quickly imitated. So efficient did the system become that Wal-Mart was soon selling goods in its stores even before it had to pay suppliers for them.

Pursuing this formula, Wal-Mart has led a productivity revolution in retailing which super-charged the American economy. Warren Buffett even declared that Wal-Mart—not Microsoft—has contributed more than any other business to the health of the economy.

Because non-union Wal-Mart represents the leading edge of this American business revolution, the left's crusade against it has emerged as a clash of worldviews, as unions and their allies try to convince the public that super-efficient operators like Wal-Mart lower workers' standard of living. The left has especially targeted Wal-Mart's push into grocery super centers, which have been pulverizing unionized grocery stores. In an age when supermarkets already operate on single-digit profit margins, Wal-Mart's entry into a market can still drive down grocery prices 15%.

A coalition of more than 30 unions and left-wing groups kicked off the campaign with a national day of protest in October 2002, urging shoppers to boycott the company as a "Merchant of Shame." The boycott got no results, but the coalition has more effectively waged legislative battles around the country. In California, the anti-Wal-Mart coalition has successfully lobbied more than a dozen cities and towns to pass ordinances to keep Wal-Mart out, while dozens of other such bills are in the legislative hopper.

The real issue in this battle is union wages. Unions argue that super- 10 markets in California pay store workers from $18 to $25 an hour (though Wal-Mart says those wages represent the high end of the union scale), while Wal-Mart pays its California store associates about $10 on average. The effect of Wal-Mart entering the market, union advocates say, would be a vast reduction in the wage pool. "While charging low prices obviously has some consumer benefits . . . these benefits come at a steep price for American workers," alleged a recent diatribe by California Democratic Congressman George Miller. Instead, union think tanks argue, Wal-Mart should be made to pay "sustainable" or "self-sufficiency" wages, a popular idea with the left, which holds that wages should be based on an area's cost of living. In many parts of California, liberal economists estimate, that means up to $38,000 a year for a worker supporting a spouse.

But the left's case ignores the greater benefit that an efficient operator like Wal-Mart brings to an entire economy by driving down prices and forcing other stores to perform better. A Wal-Mart-sponsored study, undertaken by the Los Angeles Economic Development Council, estimates that Wal-Mart's entry into the local market would save southern California shoppers $3.76 billion annually, or nearly $600 per household, creating up to 36,000 new jobs.

Despite opponents' charges, Wal-Mart has had little trouble recruiting workers, in part because the gap between its pay and union wages isn't as large as opponents claim, and because Wal-Mart is growing so rapidly that it attracts ambitious workers looking for a career. In particular, workers in minority communities traditionally friendly to the left's agenda have shocked opponents by welcoming Wal-Mart. Unions tried to stop the opening of the company's store in Crenshaw Plaza, Los Angeles, even unsuccessfully urging the Urban League not to work with Wal-Mart on a job-training program; but more than 10,000 locals applied to work at the store. "It's those who don't live in this community who did the most objecting to this store," says councilman Bernard Parks. "The community has clearly spoken, and it supports this store."

Though union-sponsored campaigns have meant little to consumers, the constant attacks are scoring in the elite media, whose members rarely go to Wal-Mart and can't understand the importance of the stores to middle-American shoppers. Once celebrated in the press for Sam Walton's folksy wisdom, Wal-Mart today is just as likely to be the subject of stories with headlines such as: "Is Wal-Mart Too Powerful?"—which advance the left's line that Wal-Mart's business model is undermining the buying power of the American worker. So striking have the attacks been that a Kansas City newspaper columnist recently suggested that the national press is "angry that average Americans don't share their perceptions of Wal-Mart as the bad guys."

Not surprisingly, the press downplays Wal-Mart's virtues: that it has never been accused of funny accounting; that it doesn't reward its executives with exorbitant salaries or perks; that not only do other executives call it the most admired company in America, but shopping surveys show it is the consumer's favorite store. But acclaim from common folk may not protect a company when elite opinion turns against it, influencing legislators, regulators and the courts. That's why Wal-Mart has become the chief private-sector target of trial lawyers, sued more than any other company, as the plaintiff's bar and its allies seek to achieve through litigation what activists struggle to accomplish in organizing drives. And every battle they win will cost the American consumer.

REFLECTING AND INTERPRETING

1. What type of opening does Malanga use? Does it arouse your interest?

2. Malanga does not follow the classic argument format. What do you notice about the structure of the third paragraph?

3. How does the account set forth in Malanga's third paragraph differ from Levine's? What vital information has Malanga omitted?

4. Where does Malanga summarize the opposing view?

5. Malanga contends that opponents have ignored what long-term benefit that a Wal-Mart store brings? How might opponents answer this point? (Tip: Refer to "Historical Perspective.")

6. He believes that Wal-Mart is a leader in a "clash of worldviews." Explain.

7. Malanga claims that the "elite media, whose members rarely go to Wal-Mart," are behind the "constant attacks." Examine the word choice and claim. Are most reporters highly paid? What do you make of this charge?

8. Examine the last paragraph. Does the press tend to report more bad news than good, or is this tendency limited only to reporting about Wal-Mart?

9. Examine the word choice and selected examples throughout the piece. Rate Malanga's objectivity on a scale of 1–10, with 10 being most objective.

10. What type of location will Wal-Mart occupy in Hartford? (Refer to Levine's and Malanga's descriptions.) How does this location differ from the typical Wal-Mart location? Is the difference significant? Why or why not?

A WRITER'S RESPONSE

Reread "Historical Perspective," then Levine's and Malanga's arguments. Which argument do you find more convincing? Why?

WHAT IS THE "PURSUIT OF HAPPINESS"?

HISTORICAL BACKGROUND

1 In 1776 Thomas Jefferson drafted the Declaration of Independence, which contains the momentous phrase: *"We hold these truths to be self-evident, that all men are created equal, that they are endowed by their Creator with certain unalienable Rights, that among these are Life, Liberty and the pursuit of Happiness.—"*

In 1789 Congress adopted the American Bill of Rights, which specifies basic rights and freedoms of all citizens. These amendments to the United States Constitution act as safeguards for our freedoms, but they do not mention the "pursuit of happiness." Yet this right is generally accepted as inborn and covered by the Bill of Rights. In the following arguments, two authors ask "What is the 'pursuit of happiness'?" and "Does the right to pursue happiness have limits?"

SUMMARY OF TWO ARGUMENTS

C. S. Lewis, an author of world renown, claims "We Have No 'Right to Happiness.'" In this essay he and "Clare" discuss an affair—Mr. A's getting a divorce to marry Mrs. B. and her divorcing to marry him—followed by his first wife's suicide. Mr. A., though shocked, defended his action with "A man has a right to happiness."

Clare agrees. Lewis analyzes her belief, knowing that Clare thinks Mr. A. "had not only a legal but also a moral right to act as he did." Lewis disagrees about the moral right to "sexual happiness" and explains why he thinks Mr. A's actions were wrong. Implicit is Lewis's belief in marital fidelity and upholding of the marriage contract. He presents a strong argument, based upon the deleterious effects that uncontrolled erotic passion and sexual permissiveness wreak upon society, as well as individuals. He points out that certain impulses must be curbed if [civilized] society is to endure.

5   In the other essay on the *pursuit of happiness*, Andrew Sullivan, a well-known political commentator, dissects this weighty phrase. He explores its meaning and implications—not from a moral/social perspective as Lewis does—but from a political perspective. Sullivan points out that in former centuries, tyrants and religious fanatics ruled with an iron hand. Personal freedom for ordinary citizens was greatly limited, and the idea of pursuing happiness was "revolutionary." Yet our early settlers uprooted the traditional authority of divine right and the church—replacing it with the United States Constitution.

Sullivan examines various meanings of the pursuit of happiness and whether or not it is connected to virtue. Then he looks at the effects of American culture and dominance around the globe, ending with an explanation of why the American pursuit of happiness is so repulsive to Muslim nations.

WHAT DOES "PURSUIT OF HAPPINESS" MEAN TO YOU?

Is happiness simply self-indulgence? Or a "sense of well-being"? What else might happiness be? Does true happiness require virtue and a recognition of responsibility? Regardless of whether you agree or disagree with the opinions of these authors, you will be challenged to think as you consider how the pursuit of happiness has affected our culture and that of other nations around the world.

WE HAVE NO "RIGHT TO HAPPINESS"　　　C. S. LEWIS

A writer of world renown, Clive Staples Lewis (1898–1963) taught literature courses at Oxford and Cambridge Universities. His work includes fiction, children's books, poetry, and numerous books and essays on Christianity. Some of his best-known works are *The Allegory of Love: A Study in Medieval Tradition* (1936), *The Screwtape Letters* (1942), *Mere Christianity* (1943), *Miracles: A Preliminary Study* (1947), and the seven *Chronicles of Narnia* (1950–56). In this essay Lewis raises questions of morality that are even more pertinent today than four decades ago: What exactly did the writers of the Declaration of Independence mean in the phrase "pursuit of happiness"? What are the limitations of this freedom in regard to individual behavior?

"After all," said Clare, "they had a right to happiness." 1

We were discussing something that once happened in our own neighborhood. Mr. A. had deserted Mrs. A. and got his divorce in order to marry Mrs. B., who had likewise got her divorce in order to marry Mr. A. And there was certainly no doubt that Mr. A. and Mrs. B. were very much in love with one another. If they continued to be in love, and if nothing went wrong with their health or their income, they might reasonably expect to be very happy.

It was equally clear that they were not happy with their old partners. Mrs. B. had adored her husband at the outset. But then he got smashed up in the war. It was thought he had lost his virility, and it was known that he had lost his job. Life with him was no longer what Mrs. B. had bargained for. Poor Mrs. A., too. She had lost her looks—and all her liveliness. It might be true, as some said, that she consumed herself by bearing his children and nursing him through the long illness that overshadowed their earlier married life.

You mustn't, by the way, imagine that A. was the sort of man who nonchalantly threw a wife away like the peel of an orange he'd sucked dry. Her suicide was a terrible shock to him. We all knew this, for he told us so himself. "But what could I do?" he said. "A man has a right to happiness. I had to take my one chance when it came."

I went away thinking about the concept of a "right to happiness." 5

At first this sounds to me as odd as a right to good luck. For I believe—whatever one school of moralists may say—that we depend for a very great deal of our happiness or misery on circumstances outside all human control. A right to happiness doesn't, for me, make much more sense than a right to be six feet tall, or to have a millionaire for your father, or to get good weather whenever you want to have a picnic.

I can understand a right as a freedom guaranteed me by the laws of the society I live in. Thus, I have a right to travel along the public roads because society gives me that freedom; that's what we mean by calling the roads "public." I can also understand a right as a claim guaranteed me by the laws, and correlative to an obligation on someone else's part. If I have a right to receive £100 from you, this is another way of saying that you have a duty to pay me £100. If the laws allow Mr. A. to desert his wife and seduce his neighbor's wife, then, by definition, Mr. A. has a legal right to do so, and we need bring in no talk about "happiness."

But of course that was not what Clare meant. She meant that he had not only a legal but a moral right to act as he did. In other words, Clare is—or would be if she thought it out—a classical moralist after the style of Thomas Aquinas, Grotius, Hooker and Locke. She believes that behind the laws of the state there is a Natural Law.

I agree with her. I hold this conception to be basic to all civilization. Without it, the actual laws of the state become an absolute, as in Hegel. They cannot be criticized because there is no norm against which they should be judged.

10   The ancestry of Clare's maxim, "They have a right to happiness," is august. In words that are cherished by all civilized men, but especially by Americans, it has been laid down that one of the rights of man is a right to "the pursuit of happiness." And now we get to the real point.

What did the writers of that august declaration mean?

It is quite certain what they did not mean. They did not mean that man was entitled to pursue happiness by any and every means—including, say, murder, rape, robbery, treason and fraud. No society could be built on such a basis.

They meant "to pursue happiness by all lawful means"; that is, by all means which the Law of Nature eternally sanctions and which the laws of the nation shall sanction.

Admittedly this seems at first to reduce their maxim to the tautology that men (in pursuit of happiness) have a right to do whatever they have a right to do. But tautologies, seen against their proper historical context, are not always barren tautologies. The declaration is primarily a denial of the political principles which long governed Europe: a challenge flung down to the Austrian and Russian empires, to England before the Reform Bills, to Bourbon France. It demands that whatever means of pursuing happiness are lawful for any should be lawful for all; that "man," not men of some particular caste, class, status or religion, should be free to use them. In a century when this is being unsaid by nation after nation and party after party, let us not call it a barren tautology.

15   But the question as to what means are "lawful"—what methods of pursuing happiness are either morally permissible by the Law of Nature or

should be declared legally permissible by the legislature of a particular nation—remains exactly where it did. And on that question I disagree with Clare. I don't think it is obvious that people have the unlimited "right to happiness" which she suggests.

For one thing, I believe that Clare, when she says "happiness," means simply and solely "sexual happiness." Partly because women like Clare never use the word "happiness" in any other sense. But also because I never heard Clare talk about the "right" to any other kind. She was rather leftist in her politics, and would have been scandalized if anyone had defended the actions of a ruthless man-eating tycoon on the ground that his happiness consisted in making money and he was pursuing his happiness. She was also a rabid teetotaler; I never heard her excuse an alcoholic because he was happy when he was drunk.

A good many of Clare's friends, and especially her female friends, often felt—I've heard them say so—that their own happiness would be perceptibly increased by boxing her ears. I very much doubt if this would have brought her theory of a right to happiness into play.

Clare, in fact, is doing what the whole western world seems to me to have been doing for the last forty-odd years. When I was a youngster, all the progressive people were saying, "Why all this prudery? Let us treat sex just as we treat all our other impulses." I was simple-minded enough to believe they meant what they said. I have since discovered that they meant exactly the opposite. They meant that sex was to be treated as no other impulse in our nature has ever been treated by civilized people. All the others, we admit, have to be bridled. Absolute obedience to your instinct for self-preservation is what we call cowardice; to your acquisitive impulse, avarice. Even sleep must be resisted if you're a sentry. But every unkindness and breach of faith seems to be condoned provided that the object aimed at is "four bare legs in a bed."

It is like having a morality in which stealing fruit is considered wrong—unless you steal nectarines.

And if you protest against this view you are usually met with chatter [20] about the legitimacy and beauty and sanctity of "sex" and accused of harboring some Puritan prejudice against it as something disreputable or shameful. I deny the charge. Foam-born Venus . . . golden Aphrodite . . . Our Lady of Cyprus . . . I never breathed a word against you. If I object to boys who steal my nectarines, must I be supposed to disapprove of nectarines in general? Or even of boys in general? It might, you know, be stealing that I disapproved of.

The real situation is skillfully concealed by saying that the question of Mr. A.'s "right" to desert his wife is one of "sexual morality." Robbing an orchard is not an offense against some special morality called "fruit morality." It is an offense against honesty. Mr. A.'s action is an offense against good faith (to solemn promises), against gratitude (toward one to whom he was deeply indebted) and against common humanity.

Our sexual impulses are thus being put in a position of preposterous privilege. The sexual motive is taken to condone all sorts of behavior which, if it had any other end in view, would be condemned as merciless, treacherous and unjust.

Now though I see no good reason for giving sex this privilege, I think I see a strong cause. It is this.

It is part of the nature of a strong erotic passion—as distinct from a transient fit of appetite—that it makes more towering promises than any other emotion. No doubt all our desires make promises, but not so impressively. To be in love involves the almost irresistible conviction that one will go on being in love until one dies, and that possession of the beloved will confer, not merely frequent ecstasies, but settled, fruitful, deep-rooted, lifelong happiness. Hence *all* seems to be at stake. If we miss this chance we shall have lived in vain. At the very thought of such a doom we sink into fathomless depths of self-pity.

25   Unfortunately these promises are found often to be quite untrue. Every experienced adult knows this to be so as regards all erotic passions (except the one he himself is feeling at the moment). We discount the world-without-end pretensions of our friends' amours easily enough. We know that such things sometimes last—and sometimes don't. And when they do last, this is not because they promised at the outset to do so. When two people achieve lasting happiness, this is not solely because they are great lovers but because they are also—I must put it crudely—good people; controlled, loyal, fairminded, mutually adaptable people.

If we establish a "right to (sexual) happiness" which supersedes all the ordinary rules of behavior, we do so not because of what our passion shows itself to be in experience but because of what it professes to be while we are in the grip of it. Hence, while the bad behavior is real and works miseries and degradations, the happiness which was the object of the behavior turns out again and again to be illusory. Everyone (except Mr. A. and Mrs. B.) knows that Mr. A. in a year or so may have the same reason for deserting his new wife as for deserting his old. He will feel again that all is at stake. He will see himself again as the great lover, and his pity for himself will exclude all pity for the woman.

Two further points remain.

One is this. A society in which conjugal infidelity is tolerated must always be in the long run a society adverse to women. Women, whatever a few male songs and satires may say to the contrary, are more naturally monogamous than men; it is a biological necessity. Where promiscuity prevails, they will therefore always be more often the victims than the culprits. Also, domestic happiness is more necessary to them than to us. And the quality by which they most easily hold a man, their beauty, decreases every year after they have come to maturity, but this does not happen to those qualities of personality—women don't really care twopence about our *looks*—by which we hold women. Thus in the ruthless war of promiscuity women are at a double disadvantage. They play for higher stakes and are also more likely to lose. I have no sympathy with moralists who frown at the increasing crudity of female provocativeness. These signs of desperate competition fill me with pity.

Secondly, though the "right to happiness" is chiefly claimed for the sexual impulse, it seems to me impossible that the matter should stay there. The fatal principle, once allowed in that department, must sooner or later seep through our whole lives. We thus advance toward a state of society in which not only each man but every impulse in each man claims *carte blanche.* And then, though our technological skill may help us survive a little longer, our civilization will have died at heart, and will—one dare not even add "unfortunately"—be swept away.

REFLECTING AND INTERPRETING

1. Examine paragraph 3. What irony do you see?

2. What implicit question is the central idea of this essay? (Look at the first sentence and the title.)

3. Can you find an example of negation, a technique of definition?

4. Is there a difference between a right to happiness and the right to pursue happiness? If so, what is it?

5. Clare believes that "behind the laws of the state there is a Natural Law." Does Lewis agree or disagree? Why?

6. In paragraph 10 Lewis begins to trace the history of Clare's belief and where it leads. What is the pivotal question on which he disagrees?

7. How does Lewis view the marriage vow?

8. What kind of happiness does Lewis believe Clare means? Why does this kind raise moral questions?

9. What does Lewis say is necessary for two people to achieve lasting happiness?

10. What six rhetorical patterns does Lewis combine to organize his complex argument?

A WRITER'S RESPONSE

Lewis says, "In the ruthless war of promiscuity, women are at a double disadvantage." Write an essay agreeing or disagreeing with his position. Cite facts and examples to support your claim.

THE PURSUIT OF HAPPINESS: FOUR REVOLUTIONARY WORDS
ANDREW SULLIVAN

Born in Great Britain in 1963, Andrew Sullivan earned a bachelor's degree at Oxford. At Harvard he earned a doctorate in political science (1990). A well-known political commentator, he has written for the *New York Times, Washington Post, New York Post, Daily Telegraph, Wall Street Journal, New York Times Magazine, Sunday Times* of London, and others. Editor of the *New Republic* from 1991 to 1996, he was named *AdWeek*'s Editor of the Year in 1996. Sullivan is the editor of three anthologies and the author of several books, including *Sound and Fury: The Making of the Punditocracy* (2000, 1992), which won the 1992

Orwell Award. In this essay he discusses the broad political implications of four words in the Declaration of Independence.

1   It's a small phrase when you think about it: "the pursuit of happiness." It's somewhat overshadowed in the Declaration of Independence by the weightier notions of "life" and "liberty." In today's mass culture, it even comes close to being banal. Who, after all, doesn't want to pursue happiness? But in its own day, the statement was perhaps the most radical political statement ever delivered. And when we try and fathom why it is that the United States still elicits such extreme hatred in some parts of the world, this phrase is as good a place to start as any.

2   Take the first part: pursuit. What America is based on is not the achievement of some goal, the capture of some trophy, or the triumph of success. It's about the process of seeking something. It's about incompletion, dissatisfaction, striving, imperfection. In the late eighteenth century, this was a statement in itself. In the Europe of the preceding centuries, armies had gone to war, human beings had been burned at stakes, monarchs had been dethroned, and countries torn apart because imperfection wasn't enough. From the Reformation to the Inquisition, religious fanatics had demanded that the state enforce holiness, truth and virtue. Those who resisted were exterminated. Moreover, the power and status of rulers derived from their own perfection. Kings and queens had artists portray them as demi-gods. Dissenters were not merely troublemakers, they were direct threats to the perfect order of the modern state. This was a political order in which everything had to be perfectly arranged—even down to the internal thoughts of individual consciences.

3   Enter the Americans. Suddenly the eternal, stable order of divine right and church authority was replaced by something far more exclusive, difficult, even intangible. Out of stability came the idea of pursuit. To an older way of thinking, the very idea is heretical. The pursuit of what? Where? By whom? Who authorized this? By whose permission are you off on some crazy venture of your own? Think of how contemporary Islamic fundamentalists must think of this. For them, the spiritual and intellectual life is not about pursuit; it's about submission. It's not about inquiry into the unknown. It's about struggle for the will of Allah. Since the result of this struggle is literally the difference between heaven and hell, there can be no doubt about what its content is, or the duty of everyone to engage in it. And since doubt can lead to error, and error can lead to damnation, it is also important that everyone within the community adhere to the same struggle—and extend the struggle in a fight against unbelievers.

4   Today, we find this religious extremism alien. But it was not alien to the American founders. The European Christians of the sixteenth and seventeenth centuries were not so different in their obsessiveness and intolerance from many Islamic fundamentalists today. And against that fundamentalist requirement for uniformity, the Founders of a completely new society countered with the notion of a random, chaotic, cacophonous pur-

suit of any number of different goals. No political authority would be able to lay down for all citizens what was necessary for salvation, or even for a good life. Citizens would have to figure out the meaning of their own lives, and search for that meaning until the day they died. There would be no certainty; no surety even of a destination. Pursuit was everything. And pursuit was understood as something close to adventure.

And then comes the even more radical part. The point of this pursuit 5 was happiness! Again, this seems almost banal to modern ears. But it was far from banal in the eighteenth century and it is far from banal when interpreted by the radical mullahs of political Islam. Here's the difference. Before the triumph of American democracy, governments and states and most philosophers viewed happiness as incidental to something else. For Christians, happiness was only achieved if you were truly virtuous. Happiness was the spiritual calm that followed an act of charity; the satisfied exhaustion after a day caring for others. For Aristotle, happiness was simply impossible without virtue. Happiness was an incidental experience while pursuing what was good and true. The idea of pursuing happiness for its own sake would have struck Aristotle as simple hedonism. The happiness someone feels drinking a cold beer on a hot day or bungee-jumping off a bridge was not a happiness he recognized. And for almost every pre-American society, other goals clearly had precedence over the subjective sense of well-being. Remember Cromwell's England? Or Robespierre's France? Or Stalin's Russia? They weren't exactly pleasure-fests. Again, in radical Islam today, American notions of happiness—choice, indulgence, whimsy, humor, leisure, art—always have to be subjected to moral inspection. Do these activities conform to religious law? Do they encourage or discourage virtuous behavior, without which happiness is impossible and meaningless? These are the questions human beings have always historically asked of the phenomenon we call happiness.

Not so in America. Here, happiness is an end in itself. Its content is up 6 to each of us. Some may believe, as American Muslims or Christians do, that happiness is still indeed only possible when allied to virtue. But just as importantly, others may not. And the important thing is that the government of the United States take no profound interest in how any of these people define their own happiness. All that matters is that no-one is coerced into a form of happiness he hasn't chosen for himself—by others or by the state. Think of this for a moment. What America means is that no-one can forcibly impose a form of happiness on anyone else—even if it means that some people are going to hell in a hand basket. Yes, there have been many exceptions to this over the years—and America has often seen religious revivals, spasms of cultural puritanism, cultural censorship, and so on. But the government has been barred from the deepest form of censorship—the appropriation of any single religion under the auspices of the state. You can call this all sorts of things. In my book, it's as good a definition of freedom as any. But to others—countless others—it seems a callous indifference to the fate of others' souls, even blasphemy and degeneracy. This view is held by some Christian fundamentalists at home. And it is surely held by Islamic fundamentalists abroad. We ignore this view at our peril.

7   There are, of course, many reasons why America evokes hostility across the globe. There are foreign policies; there are historical failings. There is resentment of American wealth and power. There is fear of the social dislocation inherent in globalization. But there is also something far deeper. What we have forgotten is how anomalous America is in the history of the world. Most other countries have acquired identity and culture through ancient inheritance, tribal loyalty, or religious homogeneity. Even a country very like the United States, Britain, still has a monarchy and an established church. If you told the average Brit that his government was designed to help him pursue "happiness," he'd laugh. Other developed countries, like Germany, have succumbed to the notion of race as a purifying and unifying element. Many others, like Pakistan or India, cling to a common religious identity to generate a modicum of political unity. In none of these countries is "happiness" even a political concept. And in none of these places is the pursuit of something in and of itself an admirable goal, let alone at the center of the meaning of the state and Constitution.

8   And when the society which has pioneered this corrosively exhilarating idea of happiness becomes the most powerful and wealthy country on earth, then the risks of backlash increase exponentially. In the late eighteenth century Europeans could scoff at banal American encomiums to happiness as an amusing experiment doomed to failure. At the beginning of the twenty-first century, with the products of such happiness—from McDonald's to Starbucks to MTV—saturating the globe, foreigners can afford no such condescension. Happiness is coming to them—and moral, theological certainty is departing. In response to this, they can go forward and nervously integrate—as countries like China, South Korea, and Russia are attempting. Or they can go back, far, far back to a world where such notions of happiness were as alien as visitors from outer space.

9   Far, far back is where some in the Middle East now want to go. The roots of Islamic fundamentalism go back centuries and bypass many more recent, and more open, strains of Islam. And we are foolish if we do not see the internal logic of this move. The fundamentalist Muslims are not crazy. They see that other cultures are slowly adapting to the meme of the pursuit of happiness—from Shanghai to Moscow, from Bombay to Buenos Aires. They see that they are next in line. But they also see that such a change would deeply alter their religion and its place in society. So they resist. They know that simply accommodating piece-meal to slow change will doom them. So they are pulling a radical move—a step far back into the past, allied with a militarist frenzy and rampant xenophobia to buttress it. This move is the belated response of an ancient religious impulse to the most-radical statement of the Enlightenment, which is why it is indeed of such world-historical importance. As I write I have no idea as to the conclusion of this new drama in world history—except that it will have

ramifications as large and as lasting as the end of the Cold War.

What power four little words still have. And what carnage they must still endure to survive.   10

REFLECTING AND INTERPRETING

1. Sullivan makes a claim and then supplies support. Where does the claim first appear? Where is his thesis statement?

2. He points out that in the United States the elusive concept of "pursuit of happiness" replaced what historical concept of authority?

3. What basic requirement of many Islamic fundamentalists does Sullivan mention?

4. What responsibility does the "pursuit of happiness" impose on individuals?

5. For Aristotle, Christians, and "American Muslims," what is an essential requirement for happiness?

6. What is Sullivan's point in paragraph 6? Does he agree or disagree with C. S. Lewis on this point?

7. What is the "deepest form of censorship" that our government forbids?

8. How does this definition of freedom appear to some countries?

9. Does Sullivan's essay provide insight into Muslim resistance to the USA's attempt to establish a democracy in Iraq? If so, how?

10. Look up *carnage* in the dictionary. What is Sullivan saying in his final sentence?

A WRITER'S RESPONSE

What is happiness? Write an essay defining your idea of happiness. Give examples. What conditions are needed for you to be happy?

SHOULD THE USA HAVE AN OFFICIAL LANGUAGE?

1   Although fifty-one countries have declared English to be their official language, the USA is not among them. In 1981 Senator S. I. Hayakawa introduced a constitutional amendment to designate English as the official tongue, but the bill failed. Since then similar legislation has been introduced, but not enacted. HR 997, the English Language Unity Act of 2007, is still pending.

In 2002 Congress repealed the Bilingual Education Act, requiring schools to teach immigrants in their native language. This law was widely viewed as impractical and ineffective because more than 300 languages are spoken in the United States. Many people, including parents, believe the immersion method is more effective.

Meanwhile, the USA has rapidly become bilingual. When you dial a switchboard or use a credit card, you often have a choice of English or Spanish. Conversations in Spanish are frequently heard in stores and streets; Mexican restaurants abound. Even crossword puzzles use Spanish words, such as *casa* (home). The influx of Hispanic immigrants has raised many questions, including these three common questions:

1. Should driver's licenses be printed in other languages when traffic signs are in English? (Just six states require a licensed driver to be able to speak and read English.)

2. Should multilingual ballots be used when most candidates campaign only in English?

3. Should immigrants seeking U.S. citizenship be required to read and understand English?

5   By fall 2007, thirty states had declared English as the official language for their government documents. (Hawaii and Louisiana have two official languages.) The primary purpose of one official language is not only to provide a strong incentive for immigrants to learn English but also to promote assimilation and preserve national unity. In addition, this policy promotes road and workplace safety as well as saves on printing, translation, and other production costs of state documents.

A recent Rasmussen poll revealed that 87 percent of voters believe that learning to read and speak "ordinary English" is "very important . . . with four out of five Hispanics agreeing." In fact, Mexico's TV network Azteca "is launching a 60-hour series of English classes on all its U.S. affiliates." Yet in 2006 the Equal Employment Opportunity Commission, a federal agency, sued more than 200 employers for having "English-only rules." Presently, House Speaker Nancy Pelosi is delaying a "$53 billion appropriations bill funding the FBI, NASA, and Justice Department solely to block an attached amendment passed by both the Senate and House" that would safeguard employers and charities from federal lawsuits over English-only rules (*Wall Street Journal*, 28 Nov. 2007, p. A23).

Clearly, the issue of an official language has far-reaching implications not only for immigrants but also for our nation. The following three authors present pros and cons of this issue.

THE OFFICIAL ENGLISH QUESTION

JAMES CRAWFORD

James Crawford is the Executive Director of the National Association for Bilingual Education and the former Washington editor of *Education Week*. He is the author of several books, including *History, Politics, Theory, and Practice* (1989), *At War with Diversity: U.S. Language Policy in an Age of Anxiety* (2000), and *Educating English Learners: Language Diversity in the Classroom*, 5th ed. (2004). Crawford has published countless arguments against English-only legislation, including "The Official English Question" printed here.

For more than 200 years, Americans have gotten by without declaring English our official language. This raises an obvious question: Why should we do so now? Why does English suddenly need "legal protection" in a federal Language of Government Act? English Only advocates respond:

- Language diversity is a recent phenomenon in the United States, which the Founders never had to cope with.

- Before the last couple of decades, Americans had never provided bilingual ballots, education, publications, and similar services at public expense.

- Native-language accommodations discourage immigrants from learning English.

- Plenty of other countries have designated official languages to manage diversity. Why not the USA?

Let's examine the factual basis of these claims.

First, some history. Congress had never even considered declaring English the nation's official language until 1981, when a constitutional English Language Amendment was introduced by the late Senator S. I. Hayakawa. The only previous official-language legislation dates back to 1923: a bill designating "American" the national tongue. Less a patriotic gesture than a put-down of literary Anglophiles, the idea proved especially popular with Irish Americans, who saw an attempt to insult the British Empire. The measure died in Congress without coming to a vote, but was adopted by the state of Illinois (where English was quietly rehabilitated in 1969).

Notwithstanding a persistent legend that German missed becoming our official language by a single vote, American English has never been in jeopardy. In 1795, the 3rd Congress did consider and reject a petition by German Americans in Virginia to translate all federal laws into their language. A tie vote in the House of Representatives appears to have been broken by Speaker Frederick A. C. Muhlenberg, a Pennsylvania German with budgetary concerns and assimilationist tendencies. Poor recordkeeping leaves much uncertainty about what role he may have played. But the Muhlenberg legend is certainly false: German was never seriously considered as an official language—despite a century of claims by the likes of Ripley's Believe-It-or-Not, the German-American Bund, and *Parade* magazine.

5   Americans have traditionally resisted language legislation, beginning in 1780, when John Adams proposed to establish an official Language Academy to set standards for English. This idea was rejected by the Continental Congress as an improper role for government and a threat to individual liberties. A century later President Teddy Roosevelt's attempt to "reform" English spelling met a similar fate. There was no English proficiency requirement to become naturalized as a U.S. citizen until 1906—the first major language restriction to be enacted at the federal level.

On the other hand, the Continental Congress saw nothing wrong with printing its Journals and other official documents in German and in French (hoping to win Québécois support for the Revolution). No patriotic objections were raised against accommodating these politically significant minorities. States were even more likely to cater to minority needs. Before World War I, bilingual education was common in areas where nonanglophone groups enjoyed political clout. During the 19th century, state laws, constitutions, and legislative proceedings appeared in languages as diverse as Welsh, Czech, Norwegian, Spanish, French, and of course, German.

At other times, Americans have imposed restrictive language policies. California rewrote its state constitution in 1879 to eliminate Spanish language rights. In 1897, Pennsylvania made English proficiency a condition of employment in its coal fields, a none-too-subtle way to exclude Italians and Slavs. Security fears during the World War I era led to unprecedented bans on public use of the German language—in schools, on the street, during religious services, and even on the telephone.

So it is impossible to characterize any American "tradition" on the official language question. History is rarely so cooperative. Our responses to diversity have ranged from accommodation to tolerance to discrimination to repression, usually determined by factors that have little to do with language. These have included a minority group's race, religion, numbers, political clout, and cultural distinctiveness, as well as the majority group's feelings of prosperity, stability, or paranoia.

One thing we can say with certainty: Language diversity has always been with us. As early as 1664, when the island of Manhattan was ceded from the Dutch to the British, 18 different tongues were spoken there, not counting any of the hundreds of Native American languages spoken in North America at the time. In the 1790 census, German Americans accounted for 8.6 percent of the population—a proportion comparable to that of Hispanic Americans, 9.0 percent, exactly two centuries later. Certainly, there are more languages spoken in the U.S.A. today than in 1790. (The 1990 census reported 323—surely an undercount.) But this is a quantitative, not a qualitative, change.

Proportionally speaking, the language-minority population was larger **10** at the turn of the 20th century, when immigration reached its highest levels in U.S. history, than at the turn of the 21st. In the 1890 census, there were 4.5 times as many non-English speakers than in the 1990 census (with its superior capabilities for counting such groups). In 1910, 23 percent of foreign-born whites, 39 percent of Japanese, 41 percent of Chinese, and 66 percent of other immigrants spoke no English, as compared with less than 10 percent of foreign-born residents in 1990. A decade before New Mexico became a state in 1912, two-thirds of its residents remained monolingual speakers of Spanish or Native American languages. Meanwhile, significant enclaves of French speakers remained intact in Louisiana and northern New England. German still predominated in large areas of the upper Midwest. These groups gradually became Anglicized—not through legislation, but through social changes due to industrialization, migration, roadbuilding, electrification, mass media, and the passing of isolated rural life.

These assimilative forces are even more powerful today. There is no evidence that bilingual accommodations slow down English acquisition. Absolutely none has been marshalled by English Only advocates—only unsupported claims about ethnic separatism and immigrants' disinclination to learn English unless forced to do so.

Demographic research shows that now, more than ever, language patterns in America are a case of "Babel in reverse."[1] A massive shift to English continues. This trend has been somewhat masked by rising immigration levels over the past two decades, following half a century of restrictive quotas. So it is not suprising that many Americans have trouble grasping the paradox: While the number of minority language speakers is increasing, so is the rate of linguistic assimilation. All available evidence suggests that today's newcomers are learning English—and losing their native tongues—more rapidly than ever before. English was far more "threatened" in earlier times; yet it survived quite nicely without official status.

About a third of the world's nation-states have official language provisions in their constitutions. But few of these designate a single language for government. Some do so at enormous cost to civil liberties—Turkey, for example, has criminalized minority language usage in many contexts. Others elevate a single national language for purely symbolic, ceremonial purposes. But a larger number of constitutions include explicit provisions for minority rights, giving official status to more than one language. In

---

1. Einar Haugen, *The Ecology of Languages* (Stanford, Calif.: Stanford University Press, 1972).

practice, some of these guarantees are faithfully observed; some are ignored. Elsewhere language laws serve a planning function, for example, in
post-colonial nations that remain linguistically diverse. Or they may seek
to mediate ethnic rivalries.

In sum, it is impossible to generalize about the meaning of an official
language. Political contexts vary enormously. It would mean one thing for
a small "unilingual" country—Iceland, let's say—to declare an official language as an emblem of national pride. It would mean quite another for the
United States to do so, where the political impact would be to restrict and
denigrate minority tongues that already are subordinate to English. And
recently, it meant something else again when the colony of Puerto Rico
ended its official bilingualism, imposed by military force in 1902, in favor
of Spanish as its sole official language. (The new policy lasted barely two
years, an indication of its unique political subtext: combat between Puerto
Rico's statehood and "commonwealth" forces.)

15   All this is not to say the United States should have no language policy.
Quite the contrary. Now more than ever we need a comprehensive plan for
managing language resources and ensuring language rights. But such a
policy involves much more than simply designating an official tongue.

REFLECTING AND INTERPRETING

1. What strategy does Crawford use to open his argument?

2. How does this opening affect the tone?

3. When did Congress first consider English-only official language legislation?
   Who introduced the amendment?

4. When was the English proficiency requirement for citizenship enacted?

5. How did the early states and Continental Congress treat minority language
   needs?

6. What does Crawford assert with certainty?

7. Were you surprised by any of the points he makes in paragraph 10? Give an
   example.

8. When did New Mexico become a state? What proportion of the residents
   spoke English then? Why was this number so low?

9. What claim does Crawford make about the rate that immigrants learn English today? What medium has greatly facilitated the learning of English?

10. Does Crawford believe that the USA should continue with no language
    policy?

A WRITER'S RESPONSE

How do you stand on the "English as an official language" question? Write an
essay stating your position and reasons. You may quote from the three essays or
consult other sources. (For help with organizing an argument, see chapter 19.)

IN PLAIN ENGLISH: LET'S MAKE IT OFFICIAL

CHARLES KRAUTHAMMER

Born in Uruguay, Charles Krauthammer grew up in Montreal, Canada. He earned a political science/economics degree at McGill University, then became a Commonwealth Scholar at Balliot College, Oxford. Later he moved to the United States, obtained an MD from Harvard Medical School, and practiced as a psychiatrist at Massachusetts General Hospital. In 1978 he worked in President Carter's psychiatric research planning unit and began writing for *The New Republic*. He assisted Walter Mondale as a speech writer and later penned "The Reagan Doctrine." In 1987 Krauthammer was awarded the Pulitzer Prize for commentary. Now he serves as a guest commentator on *Fox News*. His columns and essays appear in the *Washington Post*, *Time*, *The Weekly Standard*, *The Irish Times*, and others. The following argument was published in *Time* magazine. June 12, 2006.

Growing up (as I did) in the province of Québec, you learn not just the 1 joys but also the perils of bilingualism. A separate national identity, revolving entirely around "Francophonie," became a raging issue that led to social unrest, terrorism, threats of separation and a referendum that came within a hair's breadth of breaking up Canada.

Canada, of course, had no choice about bilingualism. It is a country created of two nations at its birth, and has ever since been trying to cope with that inherently divisive fact. The U.S., by contrast blessed with a single common language for two centuries, seems blithely and gratuitously to be ready to import bilingualism with all its attendant divisiveness and antagonisms.

One of the major reasons for America's great success as the world's first "universal nation," for its astonishing and unmatched capacity for assimilating immigrants, has been that an automatic part of acculturation was the acquisition of English. And yet during the great immigration debate now raging in Congress, the people's representatives cannot make up their minds whether the current dominance of English should be declared a national asset, worthy of enshrinement in law.

The Senate could not bring itself to declare English the country's "official language." The best it could do was pass an amendment to the immigration bill tepidly declaring English the "national language." Yet even that was too much for Senate Democratic leader Harry Reid, who called that resolution "racist."

Less hyperbolic opponents point out that granting special official sta- 5 tus to English is simply unnecessary: America has been accepting foreign-language-speaking immigrants forever—Brooklyn is so polyglot it is a veritable Babel—and yet we've done just fine. What's the great worry about Spanish?

The worry is this. Polyglot is fine. When immigrants, like those in Brooklyn, are members of a myriad of linguistic communities, each tiny and discrete, there is no threat to the common culture. No immigrant presumes to make the demand that the state grant special status to his language. He may speak it in the street and proudly teach it to his children, but he knows that his future and certainly theirs lie inevitably in learning English as the gateway to American life.

But all of that changes when you have an enormous, linguistically monoclonal immigration as we do today from Latin America. Then you get not Brooklyn's successful Babel but Canada's restive Québec. Monoclonal immigration is new for the U.S., and it changes things radically. If at the turn of the 20th century, Ellis Island had greeted teeming masses speaking not 50 languages but just, say, German, America might not have enjoyed the same success at assimilation and national unity that it has.

Today's monoclonal linguistic culture is far from hypothetical. Growing rapidly through immigration, it creates large communities—in some places already majorities—so overwhelmingly Spanish speaking that, in time, they may quite naturally demand the rights and official recognition for Spanish that French has in French-speaking Québec.

That would not be the end of the world—Canada is a decent place—but the beginning of a new one for the U.S., a world far more complicated and fraught with division. History has blessed us with all the freedom and advantages of multiculturalism. But it has also blessed us, because of the accident of our origins, with a linguistic unity that brings a critically needed cohesion to a nation as diverse, multiracial and multiethnic as America. Why gratuitously throw away that priceless asset? How mindless to call the desire to retain it "racist."

10   I speak three languages. My late father spoke nine. When he became a naturalized American in midcentury, it never occurred to him to demand of his new and beneficent land that whenever its government had business with him—tax forms, court proceedings, ballot boxes—that it should be required to communicate in French, his best language, rather than English, his last and relatively weakest.

English is the U.S.'s national and common language. But that may change over time unless we change our assimilation norms. Making English the official language is the first step toward establishing those norms. "Official" means the language of the government and its institutions. "Official" makes clear our expectations of acculturation. "Official" means that every citizen, upon entering America's most sacred political space, the voting booth, should minimally be able to identify the words President and Vice President and county commissioner and judge. The immigrant, of course, has the right to speak whatever he wants. But he must understand that when he comes to the U.S., swears allegiance and accepts its bounty, he undertakes to join its civic culture. In English.

REFLECTING AND INTERPRETING

1. Where is the main idea of the argument located?
2. What does the term "Francophonie" suggest in regard to this bilingual province?

3. Although the United States is becoming bilingual in many areas, how does it differ from Quebec?

4. What factor does the author attribute to the USA's "great success as the world's first 'universal nation'"?

5. In your own words, summarize in one sentence a popular argument that opponents offer?

6. How does the author answer that claim?

7. What would be the result of official recognition of two languages?

8. What does the author cite as the chief benefit that an official English amendment would yield?

9. What does "official English" mean?

10. The author says that making English the official language is the first step toward establishing assimilation norms. What does he mean?

A WRITER'S RESPONSE

Have you had any experience with bilingualism in your area? If so, how would you describe the assimilation of immigrants there? Do you see any problems now or in the future? Write a paragraph setting forth your comments.

SPEAKING ENGLISH PRESERVES OUR NATIONAL HERITAGE

NATHAN TABOR

Nathan Tabor earned a BA in psychology at St. Andrews Presbyterian College and an MA in public policy at Regent University. Currently, he is a political activist, based in Kernersville, North Carolina, and a contributing editor for the Web site *The Conservative Voice.com.* He has written *The Beast on the East River* (2006) and dozens of essays. Tabor also speaks periodically on the radio. The following column was posted on December 5, 2004 at <lincolntribune.com>.

Today we have a large and rapidly growing population of immigrants, both legal and illegal, surging into the United States, many of them Hispanic. As a result, some well-meaning folks are advancing the idea that our schools should teach classes in Spanish to accommodate those who don't know English.

America, the modern politically correct theory goes, should become a multilingual culture to reflect the multicultural backgrounds of the various ethnic groups who now live here. Thus our election ballots, laws, public records, court proceedings, etc., should all be conducted in at least two languages and possibly more.

This misguided idea represents the epitome of enlightened liberalism. I believe that such a move would be a cultural disaster because it would result in the Balkanization of American society. After all, there are currently more than 300 different languages spoken by various groups within America.

It is true that we are a "nation of immigrants," and that the proverbial American "melting pot" contains individuals from a variety of different cultural backgrounds. It is also legitimate for people to remember and preserve many of their ancient traditions and their ethnic heritage. However, the essence of immigration has always been assimilation into the larger American society. People flocked to our shores en masse because America alone promised them freedom and the opportunity for a better life than they had elsewhere. While they might speak their native languages at home, in public they did business in English so that they could flourish and prosper in this new land.

5   To become naturalized American citizens, these newcomers had to learn our language and our history, and then take a solemn oath to obey our laws and defend our way of life. In other words, they had to change and adapt to the new common culture they desired to join. They might retain their own personal cultural distinctions, but their new national identity made them all uniquely Americans.

"There is no room in this country for hyphenated Americans," pronounced President Theodore Roosevelt a century ago. "The one absolutely certain way of bringing this nation to ruin, of preventing all possibility of its continuing to be a nation at all, would be to permit it to become a tangle of squabbling nationalities. We have but one flag. We must also learn one language and that language is English," TR shrewdly observed.

Roosevelt's authoritative proclamation came at a high tide of American immigration, when literally hordes of immigrants from Eastern as well as Western Europe were flooding America's shores and filling her cities and factories with the raw human resources of the Industrial Revolution. He saw the dangers as well as the blessings of this massive influx of humanity. Today there is an effort afoot to pass legislation declaring English to be the official language of the United States. This was not done by the Founding Fathers, because back then there was no reason to pass a law mandating what was already true in fact. The overwhelming majority of settlers in colonial America came from what Winston Churchill later famously called "the English-speaking peoples." Thanks to the navies of the British Empire, the English language has encircled and dominated the globe.

Declaring English to be the official language of America today would mean that official government business at all levels must be conducted solely in English. This includes all public documents, records, legislation and regulations, as well as hearings, official ceremonies, public meetings and election ballots.

Today twenty-seven states have some form of "Official English" law, and there is an ongoing effort in Congress to pass national legislation. Of course, the ACLU opposes this idea, despite the fact that 82 percent of adult Americans favor it, according to the latest Zogby poll. An Official English law will not only preserve our cultural heritage, historical documents, and uniquely American way of life, it will also enable immigrants to fit in and flourish here. At a bare minimum, Official English legislation would:

1. Promote unity within the society;

2. Empower immigrants to prosper in the community;

3. Produce efficient, common-sense government.

"I believe we are being dishonest with language minority groups if we tell them they can take full part in American life without learning the English language," said S. I. Hayakawa, the founder of U.S. English, Inc., the leader in promoting Official English.

Hayakawa's sentiments thus agree with those of President Ronald Reagan, without question the most respected and beloved American leader of the 20th Century. "By emphasizing the importance of a common language, we safeguard a proud legacy and help to ensure that America's future will be as great as her past," Reagan said.

For both our great nation and her diverse people, Official English makes good sense.

REFLECTING AND INTERPRETING

1. What does Tabor do in paragraphs 1 and 2?

2. What shift occurs in paragraph 3? What does he predict?

3. What is the "melting pot" policy that the United States has been known for in the past?

4. What were the early requirements for citizenship in the USA?

5. Summarize the belief of former President Theodore Roosevelt.

6. If English were to be declared the official language of the USA, what would the law likely require?

7. Tabor lists three benefits to be derived from a national official English law. What are they?

8. What statement did the late Senator S. I. Hayakawa make?

9. Do you disagree with any of Tabor's points? If so, why?

10. What types of evidence does Tabor provide to support his argument?

A WRITER'S RESPONSE

What changes are occurring in your community or your state as a result of an influx of immigrants? Have they affected housing, employment, social services, or other community elements? If so, consider both the positive and negative effects. How might these trends affect our nation?

Short Stories

JUMPER DOWN   DON SHEA

Don Shea has published over fifty stories and has been nominated for the Pushcart Prize twice. His stories have appeared in *The North American Review, The Utne Reader, Gettysburg Review, Nebraska Review*, and *The Quarterly*, to name a few. NPR has aired his writing. Several well-known anthologies have included his work. Shea's stories are stark but elegant; every detail serves to advance the plot. "Jumper Down" first appeared in *High Plains Review* (1997), then later in *Flash Fiction Forward* (2006).

1   Henry was our jumper up expert—had been for years. When the jumper was up, by which I mean when he or she was still on the building ledge or the bridge, Henry was superb at talking them down. Of all the paramedics I worked with, he had the touch.

When the call came in "jumper up," Henry always went, if he was working that shift. When the call was "jumper down," it didn't matter much which of us went—we were all equally capable of attending to the mess on the ground or fishing some dude out of the water.

The university hospital we worked out of got more than its share of jumpers of both varieties because of its proximity to the major bridges—Manhattan, Brooklyn, and Williamsburg. Over the years, dealing with his jumpers and the other deranged human flotsam the job threw his way, Henry got a tad crusty—you might even say burned out—although he was still pretty effective with the jumper ups. He always considered them a personal challenge.

Henry was retiring. On his last shift, we threw him a little party in the lounge two doors down from the ER, even brought some liquor in for the off-duty guys, although that was against the rules. Everyone was telling their favorite jumper stories for Henry's benefit; he'd heard them all before, but that didn't matter. Big John told the story of the window cleaner who took a dive four stories off his scaffolding. They got him in the bus, started a couple of IV lines, and John radioed ahead to the ER, "Bringing in the jumper down." Now this guy was in sad shape, two broken legs, femur poking through the skin, but he sits right up and says with great indignation, "I did *not* jump, goddamnit! I *fell*!"

Just as Big John finished this story, a call came in. Jumper up on the 5 Brooklyn Bridge. Everyone agreed it was meant to be, it was Henry's last jumper, and I went along since it was my shift too.

The pillar on the Manhattan side of the Brooklyn Bridge is over water. Our jumper up had climbed the pillar on the Brooklyn side, which is over land. By the time we got there, the police had a couple of spotlights on him, and we could see him clearly, sitting on a beam about a hundred feet up, looking pretty relaxed. Henry took a megaphone and was preparing to climb up after him when the guy jumped.

It looked like a circus act. No exaggeration. Two half gainers and a backflip, and every second of it caught in the spotlights. The guy hit the ground about thirty yards from where we were standing, and Henry and I were over there on the run, although it was obvious he was beyond help.

He was dead, but he hadn't died yet. His eyes were open, and he looked somewhat surprised by what he had done to himself. Henry leaned in close and bellowed in his ear.

"I know you can hear me, 'cause hearing's the last thing to go. I just gotta tell ya, I wanted you to know, that jump was fucking *magnificent*!"

At first I considered Henry's parting shot pretty insensitive. Then I 10 thought about it some. I mean, it was clearly not the occasion to *admonish* the jumper, who had obviously suffered enough defeats and rejections in his life. Why should he spend his last few seconds on this earth hearing how he blew it once again?

Seems to me if I was a jumper on the way out, right out there on the ragged edge of the big mystery, I might, indeed, upon my exit, find some last modicum of comfort in Henry's words, human words of recognition and congratulation.

REFLECTING AND INTERPRETING

1. In paragraphs 1 and 2, what do you learn about the main character?

2. How does a "jumper up" differ from a "jumper down"?

3. Do you see any foreshadowing?

4. Who is the narrator? Which case of pronouns does he use? What is the effect of telling the story this way?

5. What do you notice about the narrator's voice and attitude? Why might he talk this way?

6. Can you find the shift from the background to the first scene? Do you notice anything ironic?

7. Where does the shift to scene 2 occur? How would you describe the change in tone?

8. Can you find a simile? Why is this description significant?

9. Where does scene 3 begin? What two surprises occur here?

10. How would you state the theme?

A WRITER'S RESPONSE

In this story there is no explicit blood or gore. Euphemisms veil reality. Although this is a tale of suicide, nowhere are those words used. What other indirect terms do you see? Why might the paramedics talk this way? How does this usage affect the story? Write a paragraph or a short paper discussing this aspect of "Jumper Down."

SCHEHERAZADE   CHARLES BAXTER

A prolific writer, Charles Baxter is also an instructor at the University of Minnesota. Baxter is the author of five novels, *Shadow Play* (1994), *First Light* (1995), *The Feast of Love* (2001), *Saul and Patsy* (2003), and *The Soul Thief* (2008). He has also written poems, essays, and four collections of short stories: *A Relative Stranger* (1991), *Harmony of the World* (1997), *Believers* (1998), and *Through the Safety Net* (1998). Five of his stories have been selected for *Best American Short Stories*. "Scheherazade," which appears here, was first published in *A Relative Stranger*.

1   She leaned down to adjust his respirator tube and the elastic tie around his neck that kept it in place. "Don't," he said, an all-purpose warning referring to nothing in particular, and she heard Muzak from down the hall, a version of "Stardust" that made her think of cold soup. A puddle outside his window reflected blue sky and gave the ceiling of his room a faint blue tint.

He was looking sallow and breathing poorly; she would have to lie again to perk him up.

"Do you remember," she said, sitting in the chair next to his chair, "my goodness, this would have been fifty years ago, that trip we made to Hawaii?"

"Don't remember it," he said. "Don't think I've been there."

5   "Yes, you have," she said, patting his hand where the wedding ring was. "We took the train, it had 'Zephyr' in its name somewhere, one of those silver trains that served veal for dinner. We had a romantic night in the Pullman car; I expect you don't remember that."

"Not just now," he said.

"Well, we did. We took it to Oakland or San Francisco, I forget which, and from there we took the boat to Honolulu."

"What boat? I don't remember a boat. Did it have a name?"

She leaned back and stared at the ceiling. Why did he always insist on the names? She couldn't invent names; that always caused her trouble. And her bifocals were hurting her. She would have to see that nice Dr. Hauser about them. "The name of the ship, dear, was *Halcyon Days,* not very original, I must say; we were on the C deck, second-class. The first night out you were seasick. Then you were all right. The ship had an orchestra and we danced the fox-trot. You flirted with that woman whose room was down the hall. You were quite awful about it."

The outline of a smile appeared on his face. "Who?"

She saw the smile and was pleased. "I don't remember," she said. "Why should I remember her name? She was just a silly woman with vulgar dark-red hair. She let it fly all over her shoulders."

"What was her name?"

"I told you I don't remember."

"Please," he said. His mouth was open. His filmy eyes looked in her direction.

"All right," she said. "Her name was Peggy."

"Peggy" he said, briefly sighing.

"Yes, Peggy," she said, "and you made yourself quite ridiculous around her, but I think she liked you, and I remember I once caught you two at the railing, looking at the waters of the Pacific go by as the ship churned westward."

"Was I bad?"

"You were all right, dear. You were just like any man. I didn't mind. Men are like that. You bought her drinks."

"What did she drink?"

"Old-fashioned," she said, but she felt herself going too far and hauled herself back in. "What *I* minded was that she would not always close the door to her stateroom. You would look in, and there she was."

"Yes," he said. "There she was."

"There she was," she continued, "in her bathrobe, or worse, with that terrible red hair of hers billowing down to her shoulders. In her white bathrobe, and you, standing in the hallway like any man, staring at her."

"You caught me."

"Yes, I did, but I didn't blame you. You were attractive to women."

"I was?"

"Yes, you were. You were so handsome in those days, and so witty, and when you sat down at the piano and sang those Cole Porter tunes, it was hard for women to resist."

"Could I play the piano?" He was smiling, perhaps thinking of the Pacific, or Peggy.

"Very well, dear. You could play and sing. Though I've heard better, I have certainly heard worse. You sang to me. You'd sing to anybody."

"To Peggy?"

"To anyone," she said. When she saw his smile fade, she said, "And to her, too. In an effort to charm. You sang 'You're the Top.' I daresay she liked it. Who knows what trouble you two got into? I was not a spy. All I know now is, it's been over fifty years."

He closed his eyes and stretched his thin legs. She saw a smile cross his face again and was pleased with herself.

"In Hawaii," she said, "we stayed at the Royal Palm Hotel." Although she had once been on a ship, she had never been in Hawaii and was speaking more slowly now as she tried to see the scene. "It was on the beach, the famous one with the name, and the sands were white, as white as alabaster. We played shuffleboard."

"I remember that," he said.

35   "Good. We drove around the island and climbed the extinct volcano, Mount Johnson. There's a lake inside Mount Johnson, and you went swimming in it, and there were large birds, enormous blue birds, flying over our heads, and you called them the archangel birds and said that God had sent them to us as a sign."

"A sign of what?"

"A sign of our happiness."

"Were we happy?"

"Yes," she said. "We were."

"Always?"

40   "It seems so to me now. Anyway, Mount Johnson was one day, and on another day we went diving for pearls. You found an oyster with a pearl in it. I still wear it on a pin."

He looked over at her and searched her face and chest and arms.

"Just not today," she said. "I'm not wearing it today."

The sound of the oxygen hissing out of the respirator tube fatigued her. She would not be able to continue this much longer. It was like combat of a subtle kind. She hurried on. "On the island we picked enormous flowers, and every evening we sat down for dinner by the water, and you put a gardenia in my hair one night. We ate pineapples and broke open coconuts, and at moonrise the sea breezes came in through the window of our room where we were lying on the bed. We were so in love. We had room service bring us champagne and you read poetry to me."

45   "Yes," he said. "What did you look like?"

She clasped her hands in her lap. "I was beautiful." She paused. "You said so."

"The sound," he said.

"What sound?"

"There was a sound."

50   "I don't remember a sound," she said.

"There was one," he insisted.

"Where?"

"In the room."

"Yes?"

55   "It came in through the window," he whispered.

"From where?"

"From the sea. Do you hear it?"

"No."

"Listen."

She sat listening. The Muzak from the hallway had fallen silent. From 60
outside there was a faint, low humming.

"Hear it?"

"Yes," she said faintly.

"I heard it first there. In Hawaii."

"So did I."

"I feel a little better," he said. "I feel sleepy." 65

"Go to sleep, dear," she said. "Take a little nap."

"You'll be back?"

"Yes, tomorrow."

"Where else did we go?"

"We went," she said, "to Egypt, where we crawled through the pyra- 70
mids. We went through the fjords in Norway. We saw wonders. We saw
many wonders."

"Tell me tomorrow."

"I will." She kissed him on the forehead, stood up, and walked to the
doorway. She looked back at him; he seemed to be about to fall asleep, but
he also seemed to be listening to the sound. She gazed at him for a moment, and then went down the hallway, past the nurses, bowing her head
for a moment before she went out the front door to the bus stop, thinking
of tomorrow's story.

REFLECTING AND INTERPRETING

To understand the allusion in the title of "Scheherazade," the reader needs to
know that it alludes to the *Arabian Nights,* a collection of 200 folktales. The *Arabian Nights* begins with a story about King Shahriyar, who has vowed to marry
a new wife every night and have her beheaded in the morning. When Scheherazade becomes his bride, however, she tells him a tale that is so entertaining he
lets her live another day so that she can finish it. Her storytelling continues for
one thousand and one nights. By that time the king is so in love with her that he
lets her live.

1. Describe the setting of "Scheherazade." (Consider the weather outside as
   well as the atmosphere inside.)

2. What in the story indicates that the old man is terminally ill? (Hint: Think
   about the title.)

3. Why does the old woman tell her husband the tale about their going to
   Hawaii? Is this the first time that she has lied to him?

4. With a dictionary, look up the meaning of the names of the train and the
   ship. How do these names form a connection to the setting and the old man?

5. What direction did the ship head? What other connections do you see to this
   direction? What is the significance of this direction?

6. What are the archangel birds a sign of? Was the marriage always a happy one?

7. Examine the description of Hawaii. Do you notice any symbolism?

8. What does "It was like combat of a subtle kind" refer to? Who (or what) was the old woman's adversary?

9. What does the old woman's tale reveal about her?

10. What element of this story lends a note of universality?

A WRITER'S RESPONSE

The author is very careful to name objects but not the main characters. What is the effect of calling them *she* and *he* rather than giving their names? Does this detract or enhance the image of the hospital room for you? Why?

THE STORY OF AN HOUR   KATE CHOPIN

A prolific writer, Kate Chopin (1850–1904) did not start writing until age thirty-eight, when she wrote her first poem "If It Might Be" and began the story "Euphrasie." She married at age twenty and had six children before her husband died in 1882. In 1889 the poem and two stories, "Wiser than a God" and "A Point at Issue," were published and well received. In 1890 her novel, *At Fault*, appeared in print. She was unable to find a publisher for another novel, *Young Dr. Gosse*, and destroyed the manuscript. Other successful writing— "Désirée's Baby" (1893), *Bayou Folk* (1894), "Athénaise" (1895), and *A Night in Acadie* (1897)—made her acclaimed in St. Louis, where she lived. In 1899, however, the reviews of *The Awakening* were scathing. Critics deemed it "immoral," and her popularity faded. In the past few decades, her writing has again gained favor in the United States.

1   Knowing that Mrs. Mallard was afflicted with a heart trouble, great care was taken to break to her as gently as possible the news of her husband's death.

It was her sister Josephine who told her, in broken sentences: veiled hints that revealed in half concealing. Her husband's friend Richards was there, too, near her. It was he who had been in the newspaper office when intelligence of the railroad disaster was received, with Brently Mallard's name leading the list of "killed." He had only taken the time to assure himself of its truth by a second telegram, and had hastened to forestall any less careful, less tender friend in bearing the sad message.

She did not hear the story as many women have heard the same, with a paralyzed inability to accept its significance. She wept at once, with sudden, wild abandonment, in her sister's arms. When the storm of grief had spent itself she went away to her room alone. She would have no one follow her.

There stood, facing the open window, a comfortable, roomy armchair. Into this she sank, pressed down by a physical exhaustion that haunted her body and seemed to reach into her soul.

She could see in the open square before her house the tops of trees [5] that were all aquiver with the new spring life. The delicious breath of rain was in the air. In the street below a peddler was crying his wares. The notes of a distant song which some one was singing reached her faintly, and countless sparrows were twittering in the eaves.

There were patches of blue sky showing here and there through the clouds that had met and piled one above the other in the west facing her window.

She sat with her head thrown back upon the cushion of the chair, quite motionless, except when a sob came up into her throat and shook her, as a child who has cried itself to sleep continues to sob in its dreams.

She was young, with a fair, calm face, whose lines bespoke repression and even a certain strength. But now there was a dull stare in her eyes, whose gaze was fixed away off yonder on one of those patches of blue sky. It was not a glance of reflection, but rather indicated a suspension of intelligent thought.

There was something coming to her and she was waiting for it, fearfully. What was it? She did not know; it was too subtle and elusive to name. But she felt it, creeping out of the sky, reaching toward her through the sounds, the scents, the color that filled the air.

Now her bosom rose and fell tumultuously. She was beginning to rec- [10] ognize this thing that was approaching to possess her, and she was striving to beat it back with her will—as powerless as her two white slender hands would have been.

When she abandoned herself a little whispered word escaped her slightly parted lips. She said it over and over under her breath: "free, free, free!" The vacant stare and the look of terror that had followed it went from her eyes. They stayed keen and bright. Her pulses beat fast, and the coursing blood warmed and relaxed every inch of her body.

She did not stop to ask if it were or were not a monstrous joy that held her. A clear and exalted perception enabled her to dismiss the suggestion as trivial.

She knew that she would weep again when she saw the kind, tender hands folded in death; the face that had never looked save with love upon her, fixed and gray and dead. But she saw beyond that bitter moment a long procession of years to come that would belong to her absolutely. And she opened and spread her arms out to them in welcome.

There would be no one to live for during those coming years; she would live for herself. There would be no powerful will bending hers in that blind persistence with which men and women believe they have a right to impose a private will upon a fellow-creature. A kind intention or a cruel intention made the act seem no less a crime as she looked upon it in that brief moment of illumination.

And yet she had loved him—sometimes. Often she had not. What did [15] it matter! What could love, the unsolved mystery, count for in face of this possession of self-assertion which she suddenly recognized as the strongest impulse of her being!

"Free! Body and soul free!" she kept whispering.

Josephine was kneeling before the closed door with her lips to the keyhole, imploring for admission. "Louise, open the door! I beg; open the door—you will make yourself ill. What are you doing, Louise? For heaven's sake open the door."

"Go away. I am not making myself ill." No; she was drinking in a very elixir of life through that open window.

Her fancy was running riot along those days ahead of her. Spring days, and summer days, and all sorts of days that would be her own. She breathed a quick prayer that life might be long. It was only yesterday she had thought with a shudder that life might be long.

20   She arose at length and opened the door to her sister's importunities. There was a feverish triumph in her eyes, and she carried herself unwittingly like a goddess of Victory. She clasped her sister's waist, and together they descended the stairs. Richards stood waiting for them at the bottom.

Some one was opening the front door with a latchkey. It was Brently Mallard who entered, a little travel-stained, composedly carrying his gripsack and umbrella. He had been far from the scene of accident, and did not even know there had been one. He stood amazed at Josephine's piercing cry: at Richards' quick motion to screen him from the view of his wife.

But Richards was too late.

When the doctors came they said she had died of heart disease—of joy that kills.

REFLECTING AND INTERPRETING

1. Might there be more than one kind of "heart trouble" involved?

2. Often denial is the first stage of grief. How does Mrs. Mallard react to the news?

3. Describe the scene outside her open bedroom window. How does that scene symbolize what she is experiencing?

4. As she sits, facing the window, Mrs. Mallard feels ambivalent. Why? (Consider the lines in her face and "fearfully.")

5. How does her outlook on life change? How does this change affect her behavior?

6. Reread the story. Do you see any foreshadowing?

7. Do you notice any changes in the way the narrator refers to the main character? What is the significance of these various forms?

8. How does the staircase function in the story?

9. How is the story ironic?

10. What is curious about the use of "abandonment" and "abandoned"? How do these words relate to the ending—or do they?

A WRITER'S RESPONSE
Essay or Small Group: Consider that this story was written in 1894. How do you think it might have been received by the general public if it had been published then? What is your reaction to the story?

STILL OF SOME USE JOHN UPDIKE

In an interview for *Salon* magazine, Dwight Garner wrote: "There is indeed something snow-capped and oddly angelic about [John] Updike; he seems to hover over the contemporary literary scene like an apparition from another era, the last great American man of letters." In 1981 John Updike (1932–) won the Pulitzer Prize for *Rabbit Is Rich*, the third of a series of Rabbit novels. Over four decades Updike has won numerous awards for his books (more than fifty), which include novels, collections of short stories, poems, and criticism. Some of his best-known works include *Rabbit Run* (1960), *Pigeon Feathers* (1962), *Couples* (1968), *Bech: A Book* (1970), *Bech Is Back* (1982), *In the Beauty of the Lilies* (1997), *Bech at Bay: A Quasi-Novel* (1998), *Gertrude and Claudius* (2000), *Seek My Face* (2002), and *Villages* (2004). The following short story was first published in *Trust Me* (1987).

When Foster helped his ex-wife clean out the attic of the house where 1 they had once lived and which she was now selling, they came across dozens of forgotten, broken games. Parcheesi, Monopoly, Lotto; games aping the strategies of the stock market, of crime detection, of real-estate speculation, of international diplomacy and war; games with spinners, dice, lettered tiles, cardboard spacemen, and plastic battleships; games bought in five-and-tens and department stores feverish and musical with Christmas expectations; games enjoyed on the afternoon of a birthday and for a few afternoons thereafter and then allowed, shy of one or two pieces, to drift into closets and toward the attic. Yet, discovered in their bright flat boxes between trunks of outgrown clothes and defunct appliances, the games presented a forceful semblance of value: the springs of their miniature launchers still reacted, the logic of their instructions would still generate suspense, given a chance. "What shall we do with all these games?" Foster shouted, in a kind of agony, to his scattered family as they moved up and down the attic stairs.

"Trash 'em," his younger son, a strapping nineteen, urged.

"Would the Goodwill want them?" asked his ex-wife, still wife enough to think that all of his questions deserved answers. "You used to be able to give things like that to orphanages. But they don't call them orphanages anymore, do they?"

"They call them normal American homes," Foster said.

His older son, now twenty-two, with a cinnamon-colored beard, of- 5 fered, "They wouldn't work anyhow; they all have something missing. That's how they got to the attic."

"Well, why didn't we throw them away at the time?" Foster asked, and had to answer himself. Cowardice, the answer was. Inertia. Clinging to the past.

His sons, with a shadow of old obedience, came and looked over his shoulder at the sad wealth of abandoned playthings, silently groping with him for the particular happy day connected to this and that pattern of colored squares and arrows. Their lives had touched these tokens and counters once; excitement had flowed along the paths of these stylized landscapes. But the day was gone, and scarcely a memory remained.

"Toss 'em," the younger decreed, in his manly voice. For these days of cleaning out, the boy had borrowed a pickup truck from a friend and parked it on the lawn beneath the attic window, so the smaller items of discard could be tossed directly into it. The bigger items were lugged down the stairs and through the front hall; already the truck was loaded with old mattresses, broken clock-radios, obsolete skis and boots. It was a game of sorts to hit the truck bed with objects dropped from the height of the house. Foster flipped game after game at the target two stories below. When the boxes hit, they exploded, throwing a spray of dice, tokens, counters, and cards into the air and across the lawn. A box called Mousetrap, its lid showing laughing children gathered around a Rube Goldberg device, drifted sideways, struck one side wall of the truck, and spilled its plastic components into a flower bed. A set of something called Drag Race! floated gently as a snowflake before coming to rest, much diminished, on a stained mattress. Foster saw in the depth of downward space the cause of his melancholy: he had not played enough with these games. Now no one wanted to play.

Had he and his wife avoided divorce, of course, these boxes would have continued to gather dust in an undisturbed attic, their sorrow unexposed. The toys of his own childhood still rested in his mother's attic. At his last visit, he had crept up there and wound the spring of a tin Donald Duck; it had responded with an angry clack of its bill and a few stiff strokes on its drum. A tilted board with concentric grooves for marbles still waited in a bushel basket with his alphabet blocks and lead airplanes—waited for his childhood to return.

10   His ex-wife paused where he squatted at the attic window and asked him, "What's the matter?"

"Nothing. These games weren't used much."

"I know. It happens fast. You better stop now; it's making you too sad."

Behind him, his family had cleaned out the attic; the slant-ceilinged rooms stood empty, with drooping insulation.

"How can you bear it?" he asked, of the emptiness.

15   "Oh, it's fun," she said, "once you get into it. Off with the old, on with the new. The new people seem nice. They have *little* children."

He looked at her and wondered whether she was being brave or truly hard-hearted. The attic trembled slightly. "That's Ted," she said.

She had acquired a boyfriend, a big athletic accountant fleeing from domestic embarrassments in a neighboring town. When Ted slammed the kitchen door two stories below, the glass shade of a kerosene lamp that, though long unused, Foster hadn't had the heart to throw out of the window vibrated in its copper clips, emitting a thin note like a trapped wasp's song. Time for Foster to go. His dusty knees creaked when he stood. His ex-wife's eager steps raced ahead of him down through the emptied house. He followed, carrying the lamp, and set it finally on the bare top of a bookcase he had once built, on the first-floor landing. He remembered screwing the top board, a prize piece of knot-free pine, into place from underneath, so not a nailhead marred its smoothness.

After all the vacant rooms and halls, the kitchen seemed indecently full of heat and life. "Dad, want a beer?" the bearded son asked. "Ted brought some." The back of the boy's hand, holding forth the dewy can, blazed with fine ginger hairs. His girl friend, wearing gypsy earrings and a NO NUKES sweatshirt, leaned against the disconnected stove, her hair in a bandanna and a black smirch becomingly placed on one temple. From the kind way she smiled at Foster, he felt this party was making room for him.

"No, I better go."

Ted shook Foster's hand, as he always did. He had a thin pink skin and silver hair whose fluffy waves seemed mechanically induced. Foster could look him in the eye no longer than he could gaze at the sun. He wondered how such a radiant brute had got into such a tame line of work. Ted had not helped with the attic today because he had been off in his old town, visiting his teen-aged twins. "I hear you did a splendid job today," he announced.

"They did," Foster said. "I wasn't much use. I just sat there stunned. All these things I had forgotten buying."

"Some were presents," his son reminded him. He passed the can his father had snubbed to his mother, who took it and tore up the tab with that defiant-sounding *pssff.* She had never liked beer, yet tipped the can to her mouth.

"Give me one sip," Foster begged, and took the can from her and drank a long swallow. When he opened his eyes, Ted's big hand was cupped under Mrs. Foster's chin while his thumb rubbed away a smudge of dirt along her jaw which Foster had not noticed. This protective gesture made her face look small, pouty, and frail. Ted, Foster noticed now, was dressed with a certain comical perfection in a banker's Saturday outfit—softened blue jeans, crisp tennis sneakers, lumberjack shirt with cuffs folded back. The youthful outfit accented his age, his hypertensive flush. Foster saw them suddenly as a touching, aging couple, and this perception seemed permission to go.

He handed back the can.

"Thanks for your help," his former wife said.

"Yes, we do thank you," Ted said.

"Talk to Tommy," she unexpectedly added, in a lowered voice. She was still sending out trip wires to slow Foster's departures. "This is harder on him than he shows."

Ted looked at his watch, a fat, black-faced thing he could swim under water with. "I said to him coming in, 'Don't dawdle till the dump closes.'"

"He loafed all day," his brother complained, "mooning over old stuff, and now he's going to screw up getting to the dump."

30   "He's very sensi-tive," the visiting gypsy said, with a strange chiming brightness, as if repeating something she had heard.

Outside, the boy was picking up litter that had fallen wide of the truck. Foster helped him. In the grass there were dozens of tokens and dice. Some were engraved with curious little faces—Olive Oyl, Snuffy Smith, Dagwood—and others with hieroglyphs—numbers, diamonds, spades, hexagons—whose code was lost. He held out a handful for Tommy to see. "Can you remember what these were for?"

"Comic-Strip Lotto," the boy said without hesitation. "And a game called Gambling Fools there was a kind of slot machine for." The light of old payoffs flickered in his eyes as he gazed down at the rubble in his father's hand. Though Foster was taller, the boy was broader in the shoulders, and growing. "Want to ride with me to the dump?" Tommy asked.

"I would, but I better go." He, too, had a new life to lead. By being on this forsaken property at all, Foster was in a sense on the wrong square, if not *en prise.* He remembered how once he had begun to teach this boy chess, but in the sadness of watching him lose—the little furry bowed head frowning above his trapped king—the lessons had stopped.

Foster tossed the tokens into the truck; they rattled to rest on the metal. "This depresses you?" he asked his son.

35   "Naa." The boy amended, "Kind of."

"You'll feel great," Foster promised him, "coming back with a clean truck. I used to love it at the dump, all that old happiness heaped up, and the seagulls."

"It's changed since you left. They have all these new rules. The lady there yelled at me last time, for putting stuff in the wrong place."

"She did?"

"Yeah, it was scary." Seeing his father waver, he added, "It'll only take twenty minutes." Though broad of build, Tommy had beardless cheeks and, between thickening eyebrows, a trace of that rounded, faintly baffled blankness babies have, that wrinkles before they cry.

40   "O.K.," Foster said. "You win. I'll come along. I'll protect you."

REFLECTING AND INTERPRETING

"Still of Some Use" is a rather puzzling story because so much that is important is left unsaid. The reader must watch for clues and listen to the nuances of dialogue to detect the turbulent emotions beneath the calm exterior of the main characters. As you make inferences, be sure to base each one on evidence from the story. Qualify your statements to make them tentative as you discuss the questions that follow.

1. Only one of Foster's family members is named. What does the lack of names imply?

2. What does Foster discover as he flips the games down to the truck?

3. Why are Foster's old toys and bookcase significant in the story? (Consider their condition.)

4. What does Foster's sarcastic response to his ex-wife indicate?

5. How does Foster feel about his ex-wife? What signs do you see?

6. Why might Foster's wife drink beer when she does not like it? What does her sharing her drink with him indicate?

7. What change does Foster show in his conversation with Tommy?

8. How are the title, the first paragraph, and the last sentence linked?

9. What is the analogy that underlies this story?

10. What themes do you see?

SMALL GROUP DISCUSSION

With your group, discuss the change in societal attitudes toward divorce. In the 1930s, divorce was relatively rare and viewed askance. Now at the start of the twenty-first century, divorce is commonplace, with nearly half of all marriages disintegrating. What causes have contributed to the change? What subtle changes often occur in the way children are regarded and treated after divorce? Should any changes be made in laws regarding marriage and divorce?

THE HANDBOOK

A Guide to Grammar, Punctuation, Mechanics, and Usage

INTRODUCTION

This concise handbook is a handy guide to frequently asked questions about standard written English. You won't find complicated explanations of rarely used rules. Instead, basic information, examples, and common errors are explained. Whether you write essays, papers, letters, reports, or other documents, you can easily find answers to almost all of your usage questions either in this reference section or in related parts of the textbook.

What Is the Best Way to Use This Handbook?

www.mhhe.com/dietsch
To assess the skills you
need the most help with,
go to:
Editing>Diagnostic Tests

To find quick answers to usage questions, first turn to the Handbook Directory, which appears on the opposite page. Next, scan the headings to locate the section you need and the page number, such as *H-2.* Then turn to that page and scan until you find the appropriate rule. Or you may wish to brush up on all of the rules in a particular section. If you desire more help, look for cross-references in the handbook that direct you to other explanations and examples in chapters of this text. You can also consult the *subject index* in the back of the book.

Should a Writer Ever Break a Rule?

If you deliberately break a stylistic rule, it should be done to promote effective writing. To estimate how effective a change might be, consider the rhetorical situation (chapter 1). Two key questions will help in predicting the result:

- What do readers expect?
- Is the writing appropriate for the occasion?

If readers expect traditional usage and you punctuate creatively, they may think you are uneducated. As a result, your ideas may not receive the attention they deserve. When in doubt about usage, consult this book, your instructor, the campus writing center, or an online site:

- *The American Heritage Book of English Usage* Covers grammar, diction, style, words, gender, and pronunciation <http://www.bartleby.com/64/>
- *Guide to Grammar and Writing* <http://ccc.commnet.edu/grammar>
- *Merriam-Webster's Collegiate Dictionary* <http://www.m-w.com/dictionary>

1. Grammar and Usage

English grammar classifies words into eight major parts of speech: *nouns, pronouns, adjectives, verbs, adverbs, prepositions, conjunctions,* and *interjections.* Other constructions such as gerunds, phrases, and clauses also serve as minor parts of www.mhhe.com/dietsch

For further coverage of the parts of speech, visit: Editing>Parts of Speech

speech. This section defines these terms and provides examples of structures that often cause problems and raise questions. The guidelines presented here are generally used for college composition in the United States, although some instructors may vary them slightly to fit various rhetorical situations. If you are in doubt, check with your instructor.

1a. Nouns

A noun is the name of a person, place, or thing. Nouns serve as the subject of a sentence, object of a verb (also called a direct object), and object of a preposition. For explanations of these three structures, see chapter 7.

▶ The *hammer* is in the tool chest. [subject]

▶ Hank hit the *ball* over the back fence. [object of verb]

▶ The ball rolled under a lilac *bush.* [object of a preposition]

Note: For *specific nouns,* see "Moving from General to Specific," chapter 8.

1b. Pronouns

www.mhhe.com/dietsch

For online coverage of pronouns, go to: Editing>Pronouns

A pronoun is a handy substitute for a noun. By using a pronoun, you can avoid unnecessary repetition of the noun. Notice that a pronoun needs an *antecedent*— a noun to directly precede to avoid confusion. If there is another intervening noun, do not use a pronoun to refer to the first noun.

Exception: Once in a while the pronoun *it* is clear and needs no antecedent: *It* is snowing!

1.   **Make sure that what each pronoun refers to is clear.**

A pronoun needs a clear antecedent (sometimes called referent). The meaning of a pronoun is clear only when the reader or listener knows to what or to whom the pronoun refers.

www.mhhe.com/dietsch

For more examples of pronouns and antecedents, visit: Editing>Pronoun-Antecedent Agreement

UNCLEAR

❯ The law firm of Creager and Colvin failed after *he* withdrew the operating capital and fled to Switzerland.

❯ Teresa proofread my paper, but she didn't find a single *one.*

❯ He believes in reincarnation, but he does not believe that *they* appear to the living.

❯ *It* said in the newspaper that the election would be close.

CLEAR

▶ The law firm of Creager and Colvin failed after *Colvin* withdrew the operating capital and fled to Switzerland.

▶ Teresa proofread my paper, but she didn't find a single *error.*

▶ He believes in reincarnation, but he does not believe that *the dead* appear to the living.

▶ The newspaper reported that the election would be close.

2.   Use the correct case of pronouns.

Because pronouns have different uses, they have different forms. A pronoun that is the subject of a sentence is in the *subjective* case. A pronoun that shows ownership is in the *possessive* case. A pronoun that acts as an object is in the *objective* case.

Case of Pronouns

	Subjective	Possessive	Objective
Singular			
First person	I	my, mine	me
Second person	you	you, yours	you
Third person	he, she, it	his, her, hers, its	him, her, it
Plural			
First person	we	our, ours	us
Second person	you	your, yours	you
Third person	they	their, theirs	them

Use the subjective case for the following:

SUBJECTS OF MAIN OR SUBORDINATE CLAUSES

▶ *I* will act as chairman during Brad's absence. [subject of main clause]

▶ Hope's party was the best that *I* have ever attended. [subject of subordinate clause]

APPOSITIVES THAT IDENTIFY WORDS IN THE SUBJECTIVE CASE

▶ Only two people—*Ray and I*—decided to go.

SUBJECT COMPLEMENTS FOLLOWING LINKING VERBS (BE VERBS, SEEM, APPEAR, FEEL, ETC.)

▶ The winners were *he* and Joan.

Use the possessive case to designate ownership and before a gerund (see section 1j):

▶ The hat is *hers.*

▶ The committee was late in finishing *its* report.

▶ *Your* not writing upset Mother. (*writing* is the gerund)

▶ *Her* drum playing angers the neighbors. (*playing* is the gerund)

Use the objective case for direct objects, indirect objects, and objects of prepositions (see sections 1a and 1f):

▶ Bradley reimbursed *him* for the roll of stamps. [direct object]

▶ Jack sent *her* flowers. [indirect object]

▶ The letter was addressed to *me*. [object of preposition]

Use the objective case in an appositive that identifies the object:

▶ The club elected two new members, Erin and *her*.

Note: An *appositive* is a noun or pronoun, often with modifiers, that follows another noun or pronoun to identify it. (*Appositive:* Erin and her.)

Use the pronoun case that correctly completes your meaning after *than* or *as*:

▶ My mother understands my sister better than *I*. ("than I do")

▶ My mother understands my sister better than *me*. ("than she understands me")

Note: *We* or *us* before a noun takes the same case it would if you dropped the noun.

▶ *We* students have complained to the administration about this problem before.

▶ It is difficult for *us* registered Independents to affect the primary process.

3.   **Use the correct person of pronouns.**

First person

First person *I* and *we* refer to the individual who is speaking (*I* sold my old car). *My, mine, our,* and *ours* show ownership. *Me* and *us* are used as objects.

▶ *I* will leave soon. *We* will meet at the inn. [subjective case]

▶ *My* suitcase is packed. *Our* children are going, too. [possessive case]

▶ Rick will pick *them* up at the airport. [objective case]

▶ I brought Tim and let *him* ride up front. [objective case]

Second person

Second person *you* refers to the individual spoken to (*You* will be in charge). *Your* and *yours* show ownership. Sometimes a subject in *second person* is omitted; this usage is called *understood you* (also see chapter 11).

▸ *You* are very thoughtful [subjective case]

▸ [*You*] Clean the bathroom before turning on the computer. [understood you]

▸ The supermarket is right on *your* way home. [possessive case]

▸ Where did the rubber band hit *you?* [objective case]

Third person

Third person refers to the people or things mentioned by the preceding noun that agrees with it in person, number, and gender.

▸ Neil planned to bring *his* running shoes but forgot. [possessive case]

▸ Kristin had intended to put *them* in the big suitcase. [objective case]

▸ *They* both thought to bring *their* tickets for the dinner. [subjective, possessive case]

4. Avoid inappropriate shifts of person.

A careless shift in person can confuse your reader and disrupt the flow of the sentence. Maintain a consistent point of view by writing in the same person. If you make a shift in person, do so skillfully for a purpose.

INAPPROPRIATE

I always spend the morning hours on work that requires mental effort, for *your* mind is freshest in the morning.

REVISED

I always spend the morning hours on work that requires mental effort, for *my* mind is freshest in the morning.

5. Make pronouns and their antecedents agree in gender, person, and number.

Pronouns must have the same gender, number, and person as the word they refer to. Because gender and person seldom pose problems with pronouns (but see section 1b.6 on sexist usage), the discussion here is limited to agreement in number. The rule is simple: Use plural pronouns to refer to plural antecedents. Use singular pronouns to refer to singular antecedents.

RECOGNIZING SINGULAR PRONOUNS [Tip: *One* is the clue.]

▸ *Anyone* who intends to go should be prepared to stay overnight.

▸ *Everybody* who is coming needs to make a reservation. [Think: *Each one.*]

▸ *Neither* one brought matches to light the campfire.

Most indefinite pronouns indicate number. The plural forms seldom pose problems, but the singular forms are confusing, sometimes violating logic. For example, the word *everyone* means all, but *everyone* is singular and *all* is plural. Listed below are the most common *singular* pronouns:

anyone	everybody	somebody
anybody	everyone	one
either	someone	each
neither	no one	

An easy way to recall these eccentricities of usage is to remember that any pronoun containing *one* or *body* is singular. If you have trouble with *either, neither,* or *each,* then mentally add *one* and think *either one, neither one, each one.* Likewise, in a word that has the suffix *body,* substitute *one.* For *anybody,* think *anyone.* For *somebody,* think *someone.*

USING INDEFINITE PRONOUNS CORRECTLY

COMPOUND ANTECEDENTS AND PRONOUNS

Use a singular pronoun to refer to *singular* antecedents linked by *or* or *nor:*

▸ A cat or a dog needs *its* own bowl of fresh water, especially during the summer.

Use a plural pronoun to refer to *plural* antecedents linked by *neither* and *nor:*

▸ Neither friends nor family members gave *their* approval to the marriage.

Use a plural pronoun to refer to compound antecedents linked by *and:*

▸ Kerry and Daniel are taking *their* time.

Exception: Use a singular pronoun and a singular verb when a compound antecedent is preceded by *each* or *every:*

▸ Every cafe and restaurant in town *has seen its* business suffer.

▸ Each beauty salon and barber shop owner *has paid his* or *her* license fee.

6. **Avoid sexist use of pronouns.**

Since the early 1970s, we have become more aware that the English language discriminates against women in many ways. Some people object to word forms that contain the generic form *man* (meaning all people—the human race) and the use of the pronoun *he* when the referent could be female, as in "Everyone brought *his* cell phone." Below are two possible ways to handle the problem:

Use *he or she* and *his or her* sparingly.

One *he or she* or one *his or her* will not disrupt the flow of a sentence, but the repeated use of these terms can distract the reader. Instead, rewrite sentences, avoiding male and female pronouns. You can omit the third-person pronoun and repeat the noun. Consider the following correct examples:

▶ If a person is insincere, chances are that *his or her* insincerity will be detected.

▶ If a person is insincere, chances are that *the* insincerity will be detected. (preferable)

Write in the plural.

▶ If *people* are insincere, chances are that *their* insincerity will be detected. (preferable)

Some folks misuse *their* when referring to a singular subject. This colloquial usage is heard in sentences such as "*Everyone* should remember to take *their* ground cloth and hunting knife." For most writing, this sentence would be considered incorrect. Standard English is as follows:

USING *THEIR* CORRECTLY

• *Everyone* should remember to take *his* or *her* ground cloth and hunting knife.

• *All* should remember to pack *their* rain gear.

• Not *one* of the runners felt *she* had run *her* best. [All are female.]

---

7. Use relative pronouns correctly.

There are only six relative pronouns. You can easily memorize them as the "five *W*'s and a *T*." The six are *who, whom, whose, which, what,* and *that*.

Use *who* and *whom* correctly in questions.

▶ *Who* is calling? [subject]

▶ *Whose* gerbil is that? [possessive]

▶ *Whom* did Shelley call? [direct object]

▶ To *whom* am I speaking? [object of preposition]

▶ Will you give the message to *whomever* answers? [object of preposition]

Use *which* and *that* correctly.

That always introduces an essential clause and provides emphasis. *Which* carries less emphasis and can introduce either an essential or a nonessential clause. In the first sentence below, *that* introduces the *essential* adjective clause— no commas are needed. In the second example, *which* introduces the *nonessential* adjective clause and requires commas. Since a nonessential clause just gives extra information, the clause is enclosed by a pair of commas.

▶ The dog *that is wearing the collar* is mine. [essential clause]

▶ A dog, *which had no collar,* followed me home. [nonessential clause]

CASES OF RELATIVE PRONOUNS

Most relative pronouns have different case forms. When you write, choose the correct form of a pronoun, according to its use in the sentence—as a subject, object, or possessive.

Subjective	Objective	Possessive
who	whom	whose
which	which	whose
that	whom or which	whose
what	what	what

NOTE: Who and *whom* generally refer only to people. *That* can refer to anything. *Which* can refer to animals, places, or things. Sometimes *who* is used to refer to animals with names, but such usage is unusual.

1c. Adjectives

www.mhhe.com/dietsch

For online coverage of adjectives, check out: Editing>Adjectives and Adverbs

Adjectives modify nouns and pronouns. An adjective may modify in any of three ways: (1) by identifying the kind (*taupe* leather), (2) by indicating something (*this* cat, *that* dog, *those* men), (3) by stating how many (*nine* players, *few* customers). Usually, an adjective directly precedes the word it modifies.

▶ Jenny is wearing a *two-carat* diamond in *that* necklace.

▶ The *tall, elderly* man limped along.

Exceptions:

▶ Ian is *precocious.* [predicate adjective]

▶ The moon, *full* and *bright,* lighted our path. [stylistic reason]

www.mhhe.com/dietsch

You can find additional material on articles at: Editing>Articles

A, an, and the

These three little words are similar to adjectives because they modify nouns. *A* and *an* are actually classified as *indefinite articles*—they are not specific. *The* is classified as a *definite article* because it points to one certain item or person. *A* is used to precede words beginning with consonants. *An* precedes words that begin with vowels.

▶ *a* kitten   (general, nonspecific)

▶ *an* apricot   (general, nonspecific)

▶ *the* tiger-striped kitten   (one specific kitten)

1d. Verbs

Most verbs show action. These verbs can be written in the *active* or *passive voice*, although the active voice is generally used. *Be* verbs do not show action; they relate to our existence, to our being here on earth.

1. **Use the active voice of verbs unless there is a good reason for using the passive voice.**

When the subject performs the action, the verb is in the active voice. The passive voice occurs when the subject is not the doer of the action expressed by the verb.

▶ Sergei Grinkov *won* an Olympic gold medal twice. [active voice]

▶ Twice an Olympic gold medal *was won* by Sergei Grinkov. [passive voice]

Note: For a detailed explanation of active and passive voice, see chapter 7.

2. **Make subjects and verbs agree in number.**

Use singular verbs with singular subjects; use plural verbs with plural subjects. Verb agreement is sometimes a problem, particularly for international students. Although adding an *s* to a noun makes it plural, the opposite is true of verbs. Adding an *s* to a verb makes it *singular*, as shown here:

Singular	Plural
is	are
was	were
has	have
skates	skate
drives	drive

Words between the subject and verb

Words and phrases that appear between the subject and the verb sometimes mislead. In the following sentence, the verb is plural to agree with the plural subject:

▶ The letters, along with the package, *were* mailed today.

The word *package* is not the subject. But because *package* comes immediately before the verb, it may seem natural to use *was.* But this usage is incorrect. In the following sentences, *were* is correct:

▶ The letters and the package *were* mailed this morning.

▶ The package and the letters *were* mailed this morning. [preferable]

Compound subject linked with *or* or *nor*

Another troublemaker is the sentence that has a singular and a plural subject without *and*. Then the *subject nearest the verb* determines the agreement of the verb:

▶ Neither the cookies nor the fruitcake *was* fresh.

▶ Neither the fruitcake nor the cookies *were* fresh.

Inverted word order

In questions and in statements beginning with *there,* the subject usually follows the verb. Be careful that the verb agrees with the subject in such constructions.

▶ *Is* the box labeled and ready to go? (box *is*)

▶ There *are* three cashiers on duty right now. (cashiers *are*)

Relative pronoun subjects

In a clause beginning with a relative pronoun—*who, which,* or *that*—look for the antecedent of the pronoun to decide whether the verb is singular or plural.

▶ People who *litter* should be fined heavily. (people *litter*)

▶ This house, which *needs* some work, could be a bargain. (house *needs*)

3. **Use the correct tense of a verb.**

Most verbs pose no problem in regard to tense. But several require cautious use. Those verbs are the ones we focus on here. (If you have a question about the tense of a verb, consult your dictionary. Be aware that two or more forms are sometimes considered acceptable.)

Four verbs—*can, may, will,* and *shall*—are frequently misused because the tenses are mixed improperly. The lists below will help you keep the tenses straight.

Present Tense	Past Tense
can	could
may	might
will	would
shall	should

Six verbs—*lie, lay, sit, set, rise, raise*—commonly cause havoc for inexperienced writers. The following chart and explanation will help you use them correctly. Perhaps the best advice is to say the tenses for each verb aloud so that you become used to hearing each one correctly.

Six Troublesome Verbs

Present Tense	Past Tense	Past Participle
lie (to recline)	lay	(have) lain
lay (to place an object)	laid	(had) laid
sit (to take a seat)	sat	(has) sat
set (to place an object)	set	(have) set
rise (to get up)	rose	(had) risen
raise (to list)	raised	(has) raised

To use the "troublesome six" correctly, just remember that *lay, sat,* and *raise*—when used in the active voice—all require direct objects. *Lie, sit,* and *rise* do not take objects. In the examples below, the direct objects are italicized.

Direct Objects

Please lay the *book* there.

Sharon laid her *coat* on the bed.

Barry set his *briefcase* on my desk.

Connor raised the *blind.*

No Direct Objects

Lie down, Rags.

Jada has lain in the sun two hours.

Harry sat there.

The sun rises at 6:30 a.m.

4. **Use the correct helping verb according to number and tense.**

Helping verbs assist other verbs in showing action or making a statement. Two or more verbs used together make up a *verb phrase.* The parts of a verb phrase may have intervening words.

▶ The bomb *had been concealed* underneath a cart of melons.

▶ The soldier *would* not *submit* to an anthrax vaccination. (*would submit* is the verb phrase)

Helping verbs must agree in number (be singular or plural) with the main verb and show the same tense.

The verbs below can work either alone or with other verbs as helpers. When these verbs are used alone, they are not helping verbs.

am	did	may	would
are	do	shall	will
is	has	has been	might
was	had	have	might have
were	can	could	

COMMON HELPING VERBS

5.   Use verb forms correctly.

It is not uncommon for individuals to grow up hearing incorrect verb forms. To them, standard verb forms sound strange. If you are in doubt about the correct verb form, check it out in a recent dictionary. A few usages have changed over time.

All verbs have four basic forms. These principal parts are the *infinitive, present participle, past,* and *past participle.* These basic forms can be varied by the addition of helping verbs or the preposition *to. To* indicates the infinitive, which is in the present tense (see page H-18).

Four Principal Parts

Infinitive	Present Participle	Past	Past Participle
(to) live	(is) living	lived	(has, have, or had) lived

Principal parts of irregular verbs

The following list of irregular verbs and their principal parts is based on the *American Heritage Dictionary,* 3rd edition. These verbs are used with helping verbs (such as *is, are, was, were, have, has, had, have been*) to form various tenses.

Present	Present Participle	Past	Past Participle
bear	(is, are) bearing	bore	(has, have, had) borne
beat	beating	beat	beaten
become	becoming	became	become
begin	beginning	began	begun
bite	biting	bit	bitten
blow	blowing	blew	blown
break	breaking	broke	broken
bring	bringing	brought	brought
burst	bursting	burst	burst
buy	buying	bought	bought
catch	catching	caught	caught
choose	choosing	chose	chosen
come	coming	came	come
cut	cutting	cut	cut
creep	creeping	crept	crept
dive	diving	dived	dived, dove

Present	Present Participle	Past	Past Participle
do	doing	did	done
draw	drawing	drew	drawn
drink	drinking	drank	drunk
drive	driving	drove	driven
eat	eating	ate	eaten
fall	falling	fell	fallen
find	finding	found	found
fling	flinging	flung	flung
fly	flying	flew	flown
forget	forgetting	forgot	forgot, forgotten
freeze	freezing	froze	frozen
get	getting	got	gotten, got
give	giving	gave	given
go	going	went	gone
grow	growing	grew	grown
hang (suspend)	hanging	hung	hung
hang (execute)	(is being) hanged	hanged	hanged
hit	hitting	hit	hit
hurt	hurting	hurt	hurt
keep	keeping	kept	kept
know	(is) known	knew	known
lead	leading	led	led
leave	leaving	left	left
lend	lending	lent	lent
let	letting	let	let
pay	paying	paid	paid
lose	losing	lost	lost
ride	riding	rode	ridden
ring	ringing	rang	rung
rise	rising	rose	risen

Present	Present Participle	Past	Past Participle
run	running	ran	run
say	saying	said	said
see	seeing	saw	seen
shake	shaking	shook	shaken
shine (the sun)	shining	shone	shone
shine (to polish)	shining	shined	shined
sing	singing	sang or sung	sung
sink	sinking	sank or sunk	sunk
speak	speaking	spoke	spoken
spring	springing	sprang, sprung	sprung
stand	standing	stood	stood
steal	stealing	stole	stolen
sting	stinging	stung	stung
strike	striking	struck	struck
swear	swearing	swore	sworn
swim	swimming	swam	swum
swing	swinging	swung	swung
take	taking	took	taken
teach	teaching	taught	taught
tear	tearing	tore	torn
tell	telling	told	told
throw	throwing	threw	thrown
wear	wearing	wore	worn
write	writing	wrote	written

6. Use *be* correctly.

The verb *be* should not be used as if it were a complete verb. Except in a few special instances (see the discussion of the subjunctive mood in the next section (1d.7), some other form of *be* or a helping verb such as *will* is required.

NONSTANDARD

I *be* a college student.

I *be* going there.

Mrs. Beck, you *be* leaving soon?

STANDARD

I *am* a college student.

I *am* going there.

Mrs. Beck, *will* you *be* leaving soon?

7. **Use the subjunctive mood correctly.**

Verbs may show three moods: *indicative* (almost all verbs are in the indicative mood), *imperative* (expresses a request or command), or *subjunctive*. The subjunctive mood is commonly used in two ways: to express (1) a situation contrary to fact (unreal condition) or (2) a request, suggestion, wish, or order. Once in a while, the subjunctive mood is used to introduce a few idioms.

UNREAL CONDITIONS

▶ My husband acted as though he *were* an expert at ironing until he scorched a shirt.

▶ In Chicago's traffic jams, I felt as if I *were* having a bad dream.

▶ Terry could fix that leak if he *were* here.

REQUESTS, SUGGESTIONS, WISHES, OR ORDERS

▶ Her boss asked that she *remain* in the building during her coffee break.

▶ I wish I were going to Chicago with my friends.

▶ The company requires that I *be* on duty at 6:30 a.m.

▶ The committee agreed that Jane *be* given extra time to complete the project.

▶ Henry moved that the meeting *be* adjourned.

Note: *That* usually introduces the clauses above.

A FEW IDIOMS

▶ If this *be* true

▶ *Come* what may

▶ Far *be* it from me

▶ Long *wave* the stars and stripes!

8. **Avoid inappropriate shifts of tense, voice, or mood.**

Inappropriate shifts in the tense, voice, or mood of verbs can be distracting and even confusing for the reader.

INAPPROPRIATE

▷ Before he *went* to class, he *drinks* three cups of coffee. [needless shift from past to present tense]

▷ A cocoon was sighted on a liatris plant, and in the spring a beautiful moth crept out. [needless shift from active to passive voice]

> *Go* to school, and *you* *should* take an umbrella. [needless shift from imperative to indicative mood]

APPROPRIATE

▶ Before he *goes* to class, he *drinks* three cups of coffee. [Both verbs are in the present tense.]

▶ On a liatris plant, I *found* a cocoon; and in the spring a beautiful moth *crept* out. [Both verbs are in the past tense and active voice.]

▶ *Go* to school and *take* an umbrella. [Both verbs are in the imperative mood.]

1e. Adverbs

www.mhhe.com/dietsch

For online coverage of adverbs, visit: Editing>Adjectives and Adverbs

An adverb is a word that modifies a verb, an adjective, or another adverb. An adverb may express how, where, when, to what degree, or under what conditions. *Not* is an adverb that makes an exception. Since adverbs are flexible, they may appear at various spots in a sentence. The usual place is after a verb or before an adjective or adverb.

▶ Tanya is *not* the one who threw the snowball. [adverb modifies verb; makes an exception]

▶ *Tomorrow* Riley will arrive. [adverb modifies verb; tells when]

▶ *Quickly,* Troy stepped out into the darkness. [adverb modifies verb; tells how]

▶ Kaia is a *very* good singer. [adverb modifies adjective; tells degree]

▶ Wade studied *quite* often and aced the exam. [adverb modifies adverb: tells how often]

Conjunctive adverbs

These adverbs link elements of equal rank. They can show addition, similarity, contrast, effect or result, time, emphasis, or example.

▶ We had intended a simple cookout; *however,* my sister brought all sorts of goodies.

▶ Shawn wrote an outstanding report; *in fact,* he edited it without staff help.

▶ Rags is well trained; *for example,* he will not accept food from strangers.

1f. Prepositions

A preposition usually precedes a noun or pronoun to make a prepositional phrase, as *for her.* In the phrase, the noun or pronoun is the object of the preposition. Sometimes a prepositional phrase also has other words:

▶ *under* the chair

See chapter 7.

▶ The cupboard *above the refrigerator* is hard to reach.

▶ *Near the barn* stood a large buck deer.

about	around	beside	from	on
above	at	between	in	over
across	before	beyond	like	past
after	behind	by	near	to
against	below	down	of	until
among	beneath	except	off	up

COMMON PREPOSITIONS

1g. Conjunctions

A conjunction is a word that connects words, phrases, or clauses. There are three types of conjunctions: *coordinating, correlative,* and *subordinating.* For detailed explanations, see chapter 7, "Restyling Sentences."

1. **Use coordinating conjunctions to join words, phrases, or main clauses.**

   ▶ Jan invited several neighbors, including you *and* me. [connects two pronouns]

   ▶ Over the bridge *and* through the tunnel, we go. [connects two prepositional phrases]

   ▶ Most of us sang carols on the ride home, *but* grandpa slept. [connects two main clauses]

2. **Use correlative conjunctions to join elements of equal grammatical importance.**

   Notice that correlative conjunctions always work in pairs.

   ▶ Ryan was *not only* the tallest player on the squad *but also* the best.

   ▶ *Either* we leave in plenty of time to reach the airport early *or* I'm not going.

3. **Use a subordinating conjunction to join a minor clause to a main clause.**

   ▶ Dustin bought municipal bonds *because* they are triple tax free.

   ▶ We stayed in the basement *until* the tornado had passed.

   Note: For *conjunctive adverbs,* see section 1e, "Adverbs."

1h. Interjections

An interjection is a word or phrase that conveys emotion yet has no grammatical connection to the sentence. Interjections are followed by an exclamation point or a comma, depending on the degree of emotion expressed.

▶ *Oh!* We just missed our train.

▶ *Ouch!* A splinter went into my finger.

▶ *Oh dear,* we are out of sugar.

1i. Infinitives

An infinitive is a verb form that is preceded by *to.* An infinitive can be used as a noun or a modifier.

▶ *To travel* to Switzerland would be fascinating! [infinitive as the subject]

▶ However, my husband does not want *to go.* [infinitive as the object of a verb]

▶ Bret's motive for late-hours trading was *to gain* quick profits. [infinitive as a predicate nominative]

▶ She had the foresight *to reject* his offer. [infinitive acts as an adjective; modifies *foresight*]

▶ All her life Carrie has studied *to learn.* [infinitive modifies the verb *studied*]

Notes:

1. **When complements or modifiers are added to an infinitive, an** *infinitive phrase* **results:**

   ▶ *To save money,* she clips coupons.

2. **Notice that an infinitive phrase differs from a prepositional phrase. A prepositional phrase never contains a verb.**

Split infinitives

When a word intrudes between the parts of an infinitive, the result is a *split infinitive.* Authorities disagree about the use of a split infinitive. Since it sometimes impedes the flow of a sentence and offends readers, many instructors prefer that students avoid this construction. In rare cases, if the traditional use of the infinitive is unclear or awkward, then split the infinitive.

UNTRADITIONAL

▶ *To properly work,* a curling iron needs to heat for a few minutes. [split infinitive]

TRADITIONAL

▶ *To work* properly, a curling iron needs to heat for a few minutes.

1j. Gerunds and Gerund Phrases

A gerund is a *verbal noun,* formed by adding *-ing* to certain verbs. For example, if you add *-ing* to *drive,* you have *driving,* which can be used as a noun, as in

"*Driving* can be dangerous." You can tell when the same word is used as a verb because it requires a helping verb, as in "He *is driving* a new car."

1. Use a gerund as you would a noun.

Like a noun, a gerund can be used as a subject, object of a verb, object of a preposition, or predicate nominative.

▶ *Coasting* down a high hill on a sled is fun. [subject]

▶ Haley quietly watched his *juggling* of five balls. [object of a verb]

▶ The neighbors objected to his *practicing* on the drums outside. [object of a preposition]

▶ Happiness for Rachel was *winning!* [predicate nominative]

2. Use a gerund phrase as you would a noun.

A gerund phrase consists of a gerund and its modifiers or complements. A gerund phrase can be used in four ways:

▶ *Finding a four-leaf clover* is thought by some folks to bring good luck. [subject]

▶ Caitlin and Michael went *mushroom hunting.* [object of verb]

▶ Nikki's goal in *fishing for bass* was to catch enough for supper. [object of preposition]

▶ Happiness for Jerry was *winning the race.* [predicate nominative]

1k. Dangling Participles and Other Misplaced Modifiers

Dangling participles interfere with clarity and logic. Other modifiers such as misplaced participial phrases, adverb clauses, and adverbs can also cause problems. These errors can be found not only in student writing but also in advertisements, newspaper articles, and other media.

1. Avoid dangling modifiers.

Dangling modifiers are phrases that lack a referent. The noun or pronoun needed to make the phrase clear and logical has been omitted or placed somewhere else in the sentence. Usually, a dangling modifier clings precariously at the beginning of a sentence with an incorrect subject following it.

www.mhhe.com/dietsch
For additional coverage of modifiers, check out:
Editing>Dangling Modifiers

Dangling participles and participial phrases

A *participle* is a verb form that ends in *-ing* or *-ed*. When used with other words as a modifier, the result is a *participial phrase.* Whenever you begin a sentence with a participle or participial phrase, check to see that the correct subject follows.

INCORRECT

▶ *Lifting her over the fence,* her coat caught on the barbed wire. (Who is lifting her?)

> After standing up well under the two-year exposure test, the *manufacturers* were convinced that the paint was sufficiently durable. (The manufacturers stood up well?)

> Absorbed in a mystery novel, the oven timer went unheard. (Who is absorbed?)

REVISED

▸ As *he lifted* her over the fence, her coat caught on the barbed wire.

▸ After *the paint* stood up well under the two-year exposure test, the manufacturers were convinced that it was sufficiently durable.

▸ Absorbed in a mystery novel, *he did not hear* the oven timer.

Dangling adverb clause

INCORRECT

> When only a youngster in grade school, *my father* instructed me in the art of boxing. (Who was in grade school?)

REVISED

▸ When *I was* only a youngster in grade school, my father instructed me in the art of boxing.

2.   Avoid other misplaced modifiers.

Misplaced modifiers are simply out-of-place words or phrases. They sneak into places they do not belong. For example, *only* is an impudent pest that cuts into line ahead of other words. Although *only* may seem small and harmless in the wrong place, don't overlook its misbehavior. Yank it back to where it belongs, close to the word it limits. Consider some examples:

MISPLACED

> "Who says kids *only* like junk food?" (ad for spaghetti)

> "If *only* your feet could talk." (ad for podiatrist)

> "If you *only* inspect your draft sentence by sentence, you can easily overlook how its parts work together." (a textbook)

REVISED

▸ Who says kids like *only* junk food?

▸ If your feet could *only* talk.

▸ If you inspect your draft *only* sentence by sentence, you can easily overlook how its parts work together.

The adverbs *almost* and *even* are other frequent offenders. Like *only,* they should precede the word they modify:

MISPLACED

▸ She *almost* used the entire bottle of bath oil for one bath.

▸ I *even* felt worse after I took the medicine.

REVISED

▸ She used *almost* the entire bottle of bath oil for one bath.

▸ I felt *even* worse after I took the medicine.

Clauses and phrases may also be misplaced in sentences, leading to humorous misreadings:

MISPLACED

▸ Faith wore a flower in her hair that was pink. (What was pink?)

▸ Jerry kept an odd-shaped piece of jade in his jacket pocket, *which he considered lucky.* (What was lucky?)

▸ I easily spotted the rare bird *using highly powered binoculars.* (Was the bird using binoculars?)

REVISED

▸ In her hair Faith wore a flower that was pink. (Or: pink flower)

▸ Jerry kept an odd-shaped piece of jade, which he considered lucky, in his jacket pocket.

▸ Using highly powered binoculars, I easily spotted the rare bird.

Note: Probably the best way to find such tangled syntax is to read your writing aloud and listen carefully. Does each sentence make sense? Beware of answering in the affirmative too quickly. Writers know what they mean. *The question is whether each sentence will be clear and logical to readers.*

1l. Using *Like* Correctly

1. **Use *like* as a preposition.**

   ▸ Jenny looks *like* her aunt.

   ▸ *Like* me, Bill enjoys jazz.

   ▸ It is not *like* him to be late.

   ▸ I feel *like* resting.

2. **Use *like* as an adjective, meaning "similar, equal, or alike."**

   ▸ I used one-half cup of butter and a *like* amount of flour.

   ▸ My grandmother used to say, "*Like* father, *like* son."

3. Use *as if,* not *like,* as a conjunction to connect two independent clauses.

    INCORRECT

    ▶ None of the teenagers lit their cigarettes *like* they were used to smoking.

    ▶ Lola acted *like* she was angry with me.

    CORRECT

    ▶ None of the teenagers lit their cigarettes *as if* they were used to smoking.

    ▶ Lola acted *as if* she were angry with me.

1m. Sentence Fragments

www.mhhe.com/dietsch

If you want more information on sentence fragments, go to:
Editing>Sentence Fragments

A fragment is a portion of a sentence that is punctuated as if it were an entire sentence. Lacking a subject, a verb, or both, a fragment is an incomplete thought. A fragment may be a word, a phrase, a dependent clause, or any combination of words that deviate from the basic requirement of a subject and verb (or verb-subject) needed for a complete sentence.

Traditionally, sentence fragments have been frowned on and complete sentences advocated except in dialogue, conversation, and other informal situations. In formal writing, fragments are avoided in all but a few special circumstances.

USING FRAGMENTS FOR A PURPOSE

To be effective, a fragment should have a purpose consistent with the rhetorical situation. The writer who uses fragments carelessly risks not only appearing unknowledgeable but also being misunderstood. The most important special uses of the fragment are exclamations, requests, commands, or answers to questions.

- *No! Not really!* **[exclamation]**
- *Please, no smoking.* **[request]**
- *Ready, get set, go!* **[command]**
- [When is the next meeting?] *Thursday at 2:30 p.m.* **[answer to a question]**

1. Avoid using *-ing* words or *infinitives* as main verbs, thus creating a fragment.

    INCORRECT

    ▶ *Driving* 100 miles a day to and from classes, *doing* complex assignments, and *raising* a family. I found that my undergraduate days were exhausting. [The first group of words is a fragment.]

    ▶ Owen and Shane stayed home last night. The reason *being* that they were broke. [The second group of words is a fragment.]

> First, the proper equipment *to get* out on the lake or pond. A canoe with a paddle or chest waders will do the job. [The first group of words is a fragment.]

CORRECT

▶ *Driving* 100 miles a day to and from classes, *doing* complex assignments, and *raising* a family, I found that my undergraduate days were exhausting. [Join the fragment to the sentence with a comma.]

▶ Owen and Shane stayed home last night *because* they had no money. [The fragment and the sentence could be joined with a comma, but the result would be wordy.]

▶ First, *gather* the proper equipment to get out on the lake or pond. Either a canoe with a paddle or chest waders will do the job. [Add a verb to the first word group; the subject is understood to be *you*, meaning "you gather."]

2. **Avoid treating phrases that merely add additional details as complete sentences.**

   INCORRECT

   > Then there is the high-speed driver. *A real maniac.*

   > Brayden called his father collect last night. *To ask for a loan.*

   > The company refused to honor the warranty. *Even though I purchased the lawn mower only six months ago.*

   CORRECT

   ▶ Then there is the high-speed driver, a real maniac.

   ▶ Brayden called his father collect last night to ask for a loan.

   ▶ The company refused to honor the warranty even though I purchased the lawn mower only six months ago. [The fragment is added to the complete sentence that precedes it.]

3. **Avoid treating dependent clauses as complete sentences.**

   INCORRECT

   > *After I learned the market price for comparable antique tables.* I decided to rescue mine from the attic and refinish it.

   CORRECT

   ▶ After I learned the market price for comparable antique tables, I decided to rescue mine from the attic and refinish it. [The introductory adverb clause is made a part of the sentence with a comma.]

2. Punctuation

The purpose of punctuation is to clarify the meaning of a sentence. Even punctuation so small as a comma can be significant. The omission of a comma in a contract can change the interpretation—possibly leading to a loss or a lawsuit. In the following sentence, notice how the insertion of punctuation changes the meaning:

▸ Woman without her man is nothing.

▸ Woman: without her, man is nothing.

Unnecessary punctuation can obscure the meaning, distract, and annoy. To improve your writing, learn the basic rules and use punctuation for a purpose.

2a. Comma (,)

www.mhhe.com/dietsch

For online coverage of commas, go to: Editing>Commas

The primary task of the comma is to clarify by indicating sentence structure. Commas should be used for a reason. (The old general rule to insert a comma for a pause does not always work.) In fact, many comma errors are due to unnecessary commas. To guide you, here are three "Don'ts":

❭ Do not place a comma before a parenthesis.

❭ Do not place a comma between a verb and a direct object.

❭ Do not insert a comma if you lack a reason.

1. **Use a comma to separate a series of coordinate words, phrases, and clauses.**

    ▸ The Delany children were named *Lemuel, Sarah, Elizabeth, Julia, Henry, Lucius, Manross, Hubert, Laura, and Samuel.* [a series of nouns]

    ▸ A 1994 book by Sadie and Bessie Delany *made the best-selling nonfiction list, ran as a successful play,* and *won several awards.* [a series of verb phrases]

    ▸ Sarah "Sadie" Delany, *by completing normal school, graduating from Columbia University's Teachers College,* and *circumventing prejudice,* gained a teaching position in an all-white New York City school during the Depression. [a series of participial phrases]

    ▸ *If Sadie had accepted the stereotypes of the times, if she had succumbed to the racial barriers, if she had rejected the long hours of work and study,* she would have remained in the South, uneducated and unknown. [a series of adverb clauses]

    (For more information and examples of coordination, see "Parallel Items in a Series," chapter 7.)

2. **Use a comma to separate addresses, dates, and titles.**

    ▸ In the late 1890s Henry and Nanny Delany lived with their ten children in a small house on the campus of *Saint Augustine's School, Raleigh, North Carolina.*

▸ Elizabeth "Bessie" Delany was born on *September 3, 1891.*

▸ In 1918 Henry Beard Delany, *Jr.,* encouraged his sister to become a dentist, too.

▸ Bessie Delany, *DDS,* became the second black woman licensed in New York City to practice dentistry.

3. **Place a comma before a coordinating conjunction that joins independent clauses (clauses that could be complete sentences).**

The coordinating conjunctions are *for, and, nor, but, or, yet, so.* (See chapter 7 for more on joining independent clauses.)

▸ In 1869 the territory of Wyoming granted women the right to vote, *but* Amendment 19 to the Constitution did not become law until August 1920.

4. **Use a comma to separate an introductory subordinate clause from the main part of the sentence.**

When the introductory clause is short and will not be misread, the comma may be omitted. (See chapter 7 for more on subordinate clauses.)

▸ *After Victoria Claflin Woodhull became one of the first two female stock-brokers in the United States,* she became, in 1872, the first woman to run for the presidency.

5. **Use a comma after an introductory participial phrase or infinitive phrase.**

▸ *Living in Tasmania and southern Australia,* wombats are marsupials that feed on roots, leaves, and vegetables.

▸ *To see a wombat,* you must look at night.

6. **Use a comma after two or more introductory prepositional phrases or a long introductory prepositional phrase (a good rule of thumb is four words or more).**

▸ *In the icy waters of the North Atlantic,* the savage wolf fish grows up to three feet long. *Along the sea bottom,* the sea robin walks on its breast fin rays, looking for food.

7. **Use commas to set off transitional expressions and conjunctive adverbs.**

Transitional expressions include phrases such as *in fact* and *for example.* Conjunctive adverbs include words such as *however, consequently,* and *therefore.*

▸ *Finally,* the floodwaters receded after ten days of rain.

▸ It was, *in fact,* the worst flooding on record in the region.

▸ Flooding is common in the area; *consequently,* people are being discouraged from rebuilding homes there.

8. **Use commas to set off nonessential (nonrestrictive) elements.**

Use a comma to set off tag words such as *well, yes,* and *isn't it* at the beginning or end of a sentence.

▶ *Yes,* you really did win a new Lexus.

▶ You are a very lucky fellow, *aren't you?*

Use a *pair* of commas to set off nonessential phrases and clauses that interrupt the flow of a sentence.

▶ One department head, *working late,* inadvertently erased the weekly sales report.

▶ Ricardo Alvarez, *a business owner,* joined our Toastmasters' Club last week.

▶ Our students, *who come from surrounding counties,* usually commute daily.

9. **Use a comma to set off a contrasting expression.**

▶ My billfold is lying on the dresser, *not the chair.*

10. **Use a comma to prevent misreading.**

Sometimes a comma is needed for clarity.

▶ Inside, the stereo was going full blast.

▶ Outside, the children were roaring around the house on their motorbikes.

11. **Use commas to set off a speaker tag or source tag from a direct quotation.**

A speaker tag or source tag identifies the speaker or writer and includes a verb of saying, such as *said, called, asked,* or *wrote.*

▶ *Derek yelled,* "Get out! The rear tire is on fire!"

▶ "The law must be stable," *wrote Roscoe Pound,* "but it must not stand still."

Note that when the speaker tag follows a quotation or part of a quotation, the comma preceding it is placed inside the quotation marks.

2b. Semicolon (;)

www.mhhe.com/dietsch

For more help using semicolons, visit: Editing>Semicolons

Basically, the semicolon has only two uses. If you understand the rules governing it, you should be able to use the semicolon with confidence. Remember that the semicolon is a stronger mark of punctuation than the comma and that it is used for the *larger* divisions within a sentence.

1. Use a semicolon to connect two closely related independent clauses not joined by a comma and a coordinating conjunction (*and, but, or, nor, for, so,* and *yet*). (See "Compound Sentences," chapter 7.)

   ▶ Representatives from every state attended the Democratic Convention; the majority voted against "open rule."

2. Use a semicolon between two independent clauses joined by a conjunctive adverb or other transitional expression.

   ▶ Sue is an accounting major; *however,* she plans to switch to engineering.

   ▶ Kevin was not feeling well; *nonetheless,* he went to the dance.

   Note that using a comma instead of a semicolon before a conjunctive adverb such as *nevertheless, however,* or *therefore* at the junction of two independent clauses results in an error called a comma splice. (For more on comma splices, see the box in chapter 7, "Avoiding Comma Splices and Fused Sentences.")

3. Replace commas with semicolons for clarity when items in a series already contain commas.

   ▶ Here is our new slate of officers: *Jean Henson, president; Mike Henry, vice president; Scott Trainor, treasurer; and Mary Wiley, secretary.*

4. If there are commas within the independent clauses of a sentence, use a semicolon rather than a comma before the coordinating conjunction.

   ▶ The Harvest House, a new restaurant on Center Street, features ethnic foods; and the crowds, surprisingly large for a small town, flock in.

2c. Colon (:)

A colon is used after an independent clause to signal that something will follow.

www.mhhe.com/dietsch
To learn more about colon use, check out:
Editing>Colons

1. Use a colon to precede a list or series that does not fit smoothly into a sentence.

   ▶ Sue ordered the following items: *one pair of scissors, two yards of denim, one thimble, and one tape measure.*

   ▶ Nanette will need these tools: *needle-nose pliers, a monkey wrench, a claw hammer, and a hacksaw.*

   Note: Do not use a colon after a verb or preposition.

   INCORRECT

   ▶ My grocery list included: zucchini, papaya, mangoes, and sunflower seeds. [The colon is not needed.]

2. **Use a colon to introduce a formal quotation.**

   ▶ My point can be summarized in the words of Edward Haines: "With every civil right there has to be a corresponding civil obligation."

3. **Use a colon between independent clauses when the second explains the first.**

   ▶ Jim has a real problem: his hair started falling out last month.

   ▶ "Let the world slip: we shall ne'er be younger." (William Shakespeare, *The Taming of the Shrew*)

4. **Use a colon in biblical references, in expressions of time, and after salutations in business letters.**

▶ Psalm 27:3	▶ 6:05 p.m.	▶ Dear Ms. Brown:

2d. Apostrophe (')

www.mhhe.com/dietsch
For additional coverage of apostrophes, go to:
Editing>Apostrophes

The little apostrophe is one of the most abused marks of punctuation. Often apostrophes are inserted where they are unneeded. The apostrophe has *three* basic uses: to form possessives, to form a few plurals, and to indicate certain omissions.

1. **Use an apostrophe with *s* to form the possessive of singular nouns and irregular plural nouns not ending in *s*.**

▶ today's fashions	▶ children's toys
▶ men's clothing	▶ the city's attractions
▶ my mother's life	▶ mice's life spans

   Note:　When adding *s* to form the possessive sounds awkward in speech, some writers add only an apostrophe in writing: *Mr. Rogers' neighborhood, Charles' sons.* But it is never incorrect to add both an apostrophe and *s* for such words. Whichever practice you adopt, be consistent.

2. **Add only an apostrophe to form the possessive of a plural noun ending in *s*.**

▶ boys' jeans	▶ horses' manes	▶ butterflies' wings

3. **Indefinite pronouns (*anyone, everyone, everybody, nobody, one*) in the possessive case are treated like singular nouns and require an apostrophe before *s*.**

   ▶ Everyone's invitation was mailed.

   ▶ Anybody's guess is as good as mine.

   ▶ Someone's coat was left outside.

   ▶ Each one's jacket was labeled.

▸ No one's car was ticketed.

▸ Nobody's name was omitted.

4. **To show joint possession and to show possession with hyphenated terms and names of organizations, make only the last word possessive.**

   ▸ Bill and Thad's boat   ▸ father-in-law's car

   ▸ Cutter and Holt's Welding Company

5. **To show individual possession, use an apostrophe with each name.**

   ▸ Sue's and Joan's themes are late.

6. **Use an apostrophe to form the possessive of words referring to time or to amounts of money.**

   ▸ a minute's rest   ▸ two years' time

   ▸ two hours' work   ▸ one cent's worth

   ▸ three days' pay   ▸ two dollars' worth

   ▸ a week's wages   ▸ a dime's worth

   ▸ one month's rent

7. **Use an apostrophe to form the plurals of numbers, letters, symbols, and words referred to as words. (Sometimes the apostrophe is omitted if there is no problem of clarity.)**

   ▸ My house number is simply three 7's, or 777.

   ▸ *Occasionally* is spelled with two *c*'s and one *s*.

   ▸ How many ='s should there be in this equation?

   ▸ Ashley had three *and*'s in one sentence.

8. **Use an apostrophe to replace omitted letters or numbers in a contraction.**

   ▸ They don't know when they'll be called back to work. [*do not; they will*]

   ▸ Terry can't go until tomorrow. [*cannot*]

   ▸ It's his turn. [*It is*]

   ▸ The class of '89 is planning a reunion. [*1989*]

   Note: Do not confuse *it's* with the possessive pronoun *its*, which does not require an apostrophe: "The cat lost its catnip mouse." (*Its*, like *his* and *hers*, is in the possessive case.)

2e. Dash (—)

Dashes, parentheses, and brackets share a basic function: to set off information from the rest of the sentence. But these marks of punctuation differ in effect.

www.mhhe.com/dietsch

If you want to learn more about using the dash, check out:
Editing>Dashes

Dashes emphasize material whereas parentheses de-emphasize. Brackets are generally used to enclose clarifying information in direct quotations.

The dash is informal punctuation that indicates an interruption of a sentence. A dash can signal a break in thought or provide special emphasis. Often used in pairs, dashes are bold and dramatic—as long as they are used sparingly. (If your keyboard lacks a dash, use two hyphens without spacing.)

1. **Use a dash or a pair of dashes to emphasize an appositive or other explanatory material.**

   ▶ "Soon members of the PMAC—referred to as the Derg—were dispatching their 'enemies' without trials."

   ▶ "There was not—and never had been—a Communist Party in Ethiopia: the country was linked to the West and dependent on free-world aid."

   ▶ "Soon he realized that his one hope was to make contact with two notorious smugglers who might guide him out—an idea fraught with risk."

   ▶ "He had to do this—regardless of the consequences."

   Note: The preceding examples of dashes are taken from "Escape from Ethiopia," by Trevor Armbrister.

2. **For clarity, use a dash or a pair of dashes to set off nonrestrictive (nonessential) elements containing commas.**

   ▶ The Kincaid triplets—Jane, Janice, and Jeanette—enrolled in Miss Hickman's first-grade class.

3. **Use a dash or a pair of dashes to set off interrupters or to indicate a pause.**

   ▶ Sarah has twenty—yes, twenty—Angora cats!

   ▶ That cat is a nuisance—just a big, fat freeloader.

2f. Parentheses ( )

www.mhhe.com/dietsch

For further coverage of parentheses, visit:
Editing>Parentheses

You might think of the parenthesis as a whisper whereas the dash is more like a shout. For a discussion of the basic functions and different effects of parentheses and dashes, see the first paragraph of section 2e in this handbook.

1. **Use parentheses to enclose (and de-emphasize) nonessential material.**

   ▶ The United States two-cent piece (issued in 1864) was the first coin with the motto "In God We Trust."

2. **Use parentheses to enclose explanations or definitions.**

   ▶ According to the National Association of Insurance Commissioners (NAIC), faked car accidents and phony insurance claims have been increasing.

▶ The NAIC says that the increase in fraud claims is partly the result of no-fault auto insurance (requires insurers to pay up to $250,000, regardless of the cause).

▶ Semicolons have only two basic uses (see section 2b).

3. **In some documentation styles, use parentheses to enclose reference information such as page numbers or dates.**

▶ In *The Laughter Prescription,* Dr. Lawrence J. Peter advises making "yourself the target of your own quips" (146).

(For more information on documentation styles, see chapter R-4.)

4. **Occasionally an entire sentence or more is enclosed in parentheses as a kind of aside.**

▶ "In a Pullman berth, a man can truly be alone with himself. (The nearest approach to this condition is to be found in a hotel bedroom, but a hotel room can be mighty depressing sometimes, it stands so still.)"

Note: The preceding sentence is from E. B. White, "Progress and Change."

2g. Brackets [ ]

1. **Use brackets to insert explanatory material in a quotation:**

▶ E. B. White wrote: "In a Pullman berth [a curtained bunk on a sleeping car of a train], a man can truly be alone with himself. . . ."

▶ Euripides wrote: "This is courage in a [person]: to bear unflinchingly what heaven sends." The original passage says "man." It was updated to avoid sexism.

2. **For clarity, use brackets instead of parentheses to enclose material already within parentheses.**

▶ We should be sure to give Emanuel Foose (and his brother Emilio [1812–1882] as well) credit for his role in founding the institute.

(For more on using brackets in quoted material, see chapter R-3.)

2h. Hyphen (-)

www.mhhe.com/dietsch
To learn more about hyphen use, go to:
Editing>Hyphen

1. **Use a hyphen to divide a word at the end of a line.**

At least one syllable of three or more letters should be before the division: *con-sequently.*

2. **Use a hyphen in spelled-out compound numbers from twenty-one through ninety-nine.**

3. **Use a hyphen in spelled-out fractions.**

▶ one-fourth   ▶ five-eighths

▶ two-thirds   ▶ four and one-third

4. **Use a hyphen between two or more words used together as a modifier before a noun (unless the first word ends in *ly*).**

    ▶ thought-provoking speech   ▶ all-out effort

    ▶ problem-solving quiz   ▶ on-the-job training

    ▶ rosy-cheeked baby   ▶ up-to-date data

    ▶ lightly salted peanuts   ▶ highly rated programs

    Exception: Do not hyphenate when such modifiers do not precede the noun they modify.

    ▶ The quiz was about problem solving.

    ▶ The baby was rosy cheeked.

    ▶ Training was conducted on the job.

    ▶ The data were up to date.

5. *Rule of Suspension:* **Use suspended hyphens (hyphens followed by a space or by punctuation and a space) in a series of compounds having the same main elements.**

    ▶ Ann organized her essay in most- to least-important order.

    ▶ The first- and second-grade students no longer have a recess.

    ▶ Our local preschool accepts two-, three-, and four-year-old children.

    ▶ Nineteenth- and twentieth-century American literature can provide insight into the emancipation of women.

6. **Use a hyphen with certain prefixes.**

    These include *ex-* and *self-* with the exceptions of *selfless* and *selfsame.* There is no hard-and-fast rule about other prefixes such as *anti-, co-, pre-, pro-, re-,* and *well-.* Check an up-to-date dictionary, and if given a choice, be consistent.

    ▶ anti-intellectual   ▶ pre-election

    ▶ co-owner   ▶ self-denial

    ▶ ex-president   ▶ well-being

    Note: Always use a hyphen when the word to be prefixed begins with a capital as in *pro-American, non-British,* or *mid-July.*

7. **Use a hyphen to avoid doubling a letter and to avoid confusion.**

    ▶ semi-invalid [avoids *semiinvalid*]

    ▶ re-enlist [avoids *reenlist*]

    ▶ re-form [avoids confusion with *reform*]

2i. Slash (/)

1. In certain situations, such as highly informal writing or technical papers, use a slash to replace *or*, which is ordinarily required to show alternatives.

▶ all ready/already   ▶ radio/television   ▶ to/too/two

Note: Many readers object to the use of *and/or*. Often *and* or *or* is sufficient.

2. Use a slash to separate elements in certain expressions.

▶ Dates: 1998/99   ▶ Fractions: 1/4

▶ Places: Dallas/Fort Worth

3. Use slashes (with a space on each side of the slash) in prose to indicate divisions between lines of poetry.

▶ Shakespeare writes: "Like as the waves make towards the pebbled shore, / So do our minutes hasten to their end. . . ."

(See "Preparing an Analysis of a Poem," chapter 23.)

2j. Quotation Marks (" ")

www.mhhe.com/dietsch
For additional information on quotation marks, go to:
Editing>Quotation Marks

Although quotation marks have more than one use, they usually indicate the beginning and end of someone's exact words. Dialogue requires quotation marks. Citations require quotation marks (see chapter R-3). Quotation marks may also be used to indicate words used in special ways. Titles of short written works or parts of works are enclosed with quotation marks.

1. Use quotation marks in dialogue to enclose the exact words of a speaker.

▶ Phoebe called, "Sparky, bring that shoe back here!"

▶ "Come on, Sparky," she cajoled, "bring the shoe back, and I'll give you some Teeny Bits."

2. Use quotation marks to enclose short direct quotations.

Short is defined differently in different documentation styles. The most commonly used style in English, that of the Modern Language Association (MLA), defines *short* as four lines or less. (Long quotations are indented. For more on quoting sources, see chapter R-3.)

▶ In *The Conduct of Life,* Emerson wrote as follows: "The art of conversation, or the qualification for a good companion, is a certain self-control, which now holds the subject, now lets it go, with a respect for the emergencies of the moment."

3. Use quotation marks to enclose the titles of parts of books and periodicals.

Because this rule is often confused, here is an informal guideline that will help you remember the principle: Underline (italicize) the title or name of a whole item; use quotation marks around the title of a part. The lists below indicate how the guideline applies:

Underline "Whole" Items	Use Quotation Marks for "Parts"
book title	chapter or story title
songbook title	song title
poetry book title	poem title
title of a very long poem (e.g., *Paradise Lost*)	
name of a newspaper	comic, article, or feature title
name of a magazine	article, feature, or story title
pamphlet title	speech, short report
name of a plane, ship, or train	
title of a film, painting, record album, television or radio program	title of an episode of a radio or television series

Finally, a writer does not underline or use quotation marks with his or her own title at the beginning of a work. (See also section 2k on italics [underlining].)

4. **Use single quotation marks to enclose a quotation within a quotation.**

If a quotation occurs within a quotation already marked with double quotation marks, enclose the inside quotation in single quotation marks. This will sometimes result in three quotation marks at the end of the quotation.

▸ "You must have read Eiseley's 'The Real Secret of Piltdown,'" Bill's friend observed.

Note: In ordinary American usage, the only exceptions to the use of double quotation marks for main, or outside, quotations are long quotations (block quotations), which are not placed within quotation marks because they are indented. (See chapter R-3.)

5. **Traditionally, quotation marks were used to enclose words discussed as words. However, many writers now prefer italics for this purpose (see also section 2k, "Italics").**

▸ "Computer" is derived from the Latin verb *computare.*

6. **Use quotation marks to enclose words used in a special or ironic sense.**

▸ What chain of events caused the sinking of an "unsinkable" ship such as the *Titanic?*

Note: Do not use quotation marks for emphasis. The effect can be unintentionally ironic and humorous: Jordan Bailey, "President"; "I'm sure your 'wife' will enjoy the ring you bought at our store."

7.   **Use other punctuation with quotation marks correctly.**

Commas and periods always go *inside* closing quotation marks (except in one documentation situation). Colons and semicolons always go *outside* closing quotation marks. The rule for all other punctuation is that if the punctuation is part of the quotation, it goes inside, and if it is not part of the quotation, it goes outside.

▶ "Reading *Space Technology* gives me the insider's view," he says, adding, "It's like having all the top officials sitting in my office for a discussion."

▶ He said, "I will pay the full amount"; this certainly surprised us.

▶ She has two favorite "sports": eating and sleeping.

2k.   *Italics* (Underlining)

Italics is a typeface that slants to the right (*Moby Dick*). If your keyboard does not have italics, underline instead. Italics and underlining can indicate foreign words; special names of vehicles, vessels, or artworks; words used as words; and titles of long works. Since many foreign words have been adopted into English, check a dictionary to see whether or not they should be italicized. Direct quotations in another language are not italicized.

> www.mhhe.com/dietsch
>
> For more information about the use of italics, visit:
>
> Editing>Italics

1.   **Use italics (underlining) for titles of long works.**

For a discussion of when to use italics and when to use quotation marks in titles, see section 2j.3 of this handbook. The treatment of titles differs from one documentation style to another. (For more information on titles of sources in research papers, see chapter R-3.) Listed here are the most common kinds of works with italicized titles:

- **books:** *A Tale of Two Cities*
- *Exception:* Do not use italics (or underlining) for the names of sacred books: the Bible (or the Holy Bible), the New Testament, the Koran, and so forth.
- **long poems:** *Paradise Lost; The Iliad; The Wasteland*
- **newspapers and magazines:** the *New York Times; National Geographic*
- **pamphlets:** *Letters from an American Farmer*
- **vessels (planes, trains, ships, spacecraft):** the *Titanic;* the *Burlington Zephyr; Challenger*
- **plays:** *Hamlet; The Music Man*
- **comic strips:** *Doonesbury*
- **films and television and radio programs:** *Aladdin; Lost; A Prairie Home Companion*
- **albums and long musical works:** *Thriller;* Mahler's *Symphony No. 9*

- **paintings and sculpture:** da Vinci's *Mona Lisa;* Michelangelo's *David*
- **software:** *Windows XP; PageMaker 7.*

2. **For clarity, use italics for words discussed as words, particularly when quotation marks are used in the same sentence for another purpose.**

▶ The word *boudoir* comes from an Old French verb, meaning "to pout or sulk."

3. **Use italics for emphasis, but do so sparingly.**

▶ Trust me—take Route 315, *not* Route 23.

▶ What is the *evidence* for that position?

21. Ellipsis (. . .)

An ellipsis is a set of three spaced dots that indicate an omission. When an omission occurs at the beginning of a quotation, an ellipsis is *not* necessary; but an omission in the middle or at the end requires an ellipsis. To shorten a quotation, you can use an ellipsis as long as you do not distort the meaning. When omitting a word, phrase, sentence, or more, be guided by integrity: Is the result fair to the author? Is it grammatically correct?

Although the fifth edition of the *MLA Handbook* included the use of brackets to distinguish between your ellipses and the spaced periods that sometimes appear in works, the sixth edition of the *MLA Handbook* has reverted to the traditional use of ellipses, shown in earlier editions. Your instructor may decide to follow either style. The examples that follow reflect *traditional* usage. The first two are based on an excerpt from Linda Ryberg's "The Midwest Salutes Its Swedish Roots" in *Midwest Living* June 1996.

ORIGINAL

A harsh first winter on the windswept Illinois prairie in 1846 couldn't stop a tiny group of Swedish immigrants from prospering in the town they founded and named Bishop Hill. After all, they'd crossed the Atlantic, sailed the Great Lakes, and walked 160 miles southwest from Chicago to get there.

1. **Use an ellipsis to show an omission in the middle of a quotation.**

▶ Tracing the history of an Illinois town, Linda Ryberg writes: "A harsh first winter . . . in 1846 couldn't stop a tiny group of Swedish immigrants from prospering in the town they founded and named Bishop Hill."

2. **Use an ellipsis to show an omission at the end of a quotation.**

▶ Linda Ryberg, tracing the history of Bishop Hill, Illinois, explains that in 1846 a small band of Swedish settlers "crossed the Atlantic, sailed the Great Lakes, and walked 160 miles southwest from Chicago. . . ."

▶ Linda Ryberg, tracing the history of Bishop Hill, Illinois, explains that in 1846 a small band of Swedish settlers "crossed the Atlantic, sailed the Great Lakes, and walked 160 miles southwest from Chicago . . ." (40).

Note: Since there is no parenthetical reference in the first example, the sentence period is placed flush against the last word within the quotation marks. In the second example, however, the sentence period is placed after the parenthetical reference of this short quotation. (For information on using ellipses in long quotations, see chapter R-3.)

3. **Use an entire line of ellipsis points to indicate omission of a line or more in quoted poetry.**

    ▶ William Wordsworth was a poet of the city as well as the countryside. While crossing Westminster Bridge, in London, he wrote:

    Earth has not anything to show more fair:
    Dull would he be of soul who could pass by
    A sight so touching in its majesty:
    . . . .
    Ne'er saw I, never felt, a calm so deep!

4. **Use an ellipsis to indicate a pause or hesitation, but use this device sparingly.**

    ▶ Don't swim in this water . . . unless you're fond of sharks.

2m. Period (.)

1. **Use a period at the end of statements, mild commands, and indirect questions.**

    ▶ The temperature in the cave is a constant 58 degrees.

    ▶ As you tour the cave, please stay on the marked trail.

    ▶ Many people have asked how the cave was first discovered.

2. **Use a period (or periods) with some abbreviations.**

    If an abbreviation comes at the end of a sentence, use only one period. (For more on abbreviations, see section 4 of this handbook.)

3. **Use a period as a decimal point in numbers.**

    ▶ 1.06   ▶ 0.910   ▶ $149.95

2n. Question Mark (?)

1. **Use a question mark at the end of a direct question or request.**

    ▶ Will you please pick up a roll of stamps on your way?

    ▶ A group of citizens discussed the question, "Does our town need a city manager instead of a mayor?"

2.   **Use a question mark after each elliptical question in a series.**

▶ Should obscenity be controlled on the Internet? If so, by whom? How?

3.   **Use a question mark in parentheses after an item that is of doubtful accuracy.**

▶ The tunnel from his cell, disguised by a huge poster, was started in 2001(?) but was discovered only after he had fled.

2o. Exclamation Point (!)

An exclamation point indicates strong emotion: pain, fear, surprise, indignation, or excitement. An exclamation point cannot bolster a weak statement or make an argument more convincing. Use exclamation points sparingly; otherwise, they lose their power.

1.   **Use an exclamation point to add force to a command or expression of emotion.**

▶ "Ouch!"

▶ "Help!" Jimmy screamed. "The horse is standing on my foot."

▶ WATCH OUT! Deer Crossing

2p. Comma Splices and Fused (Run-on) Sentences

www.mhhe.com/dietsch

Want online coverage of fused sentences and comma splices? Go to:
Editing>Fused Sentences
Editing>Comma Splices

Beginning writers sometimes omit punctuation between clauses in a compound sentence. This error results in a *fused sentence,* sometimes called a *run-on sentence.* A related error is the *comma splice,* which occurs when two clauses are joined (spliced) with a comma. (See chapter 7 for more on compound sentences.)

1.   **Punctuate sentences correctly to avoid comma splices.**

Never use the comma alone to punctuate a long compound sentence. If you use a comma, you must also have a coordinating conjunction. Note, too, that a semicolon is required before a conjunctive adverb such as *however* or *therefore.*

INCORRECT

▶ Terrariums are costly at a flower shop, they are inexpensive to make at home.

▶ Terrariums are costly at a flower shop, however, they are inexpensive to make at home.

CORRECT

▶ Terrariums are costly at a flower shop, *but* they are inexpensive to make at home. [coordinating conjunction and a comma]

▶ Terrariums are costly at a flower shop; however, they are inexpensive to make at home. [semicolon]

2. **Punctuate sentences correctly to avoid fused (run-on) sentences.**

   INCORRECT

   ❯ The ordinance won wide support it was passed by a two-thirds vote.

   CORRECT

   ▶ The ordinance won wide support; it was passed by a two-thirds vote. [semicolon]

3. Capitalization

If you become lost in the thicket of capitalization, first consult an up-to-date dictionary. If you should find more than one way to capitalize, then let your audience be your guide. In other words, when you are writing for an employer, follow conventional business and technical usage. When writing a college research paper, follow the style your instructor recommends.

> **www.mhhe.com/dietsch**
> You'll find additional help regarding capitalization at: Editing>Capitalization

For example, leading dictionaries capitalize both "Roman numerals" and "Arabic numerals." But the *MLA Handbook for Writers of Research Papers*, 6th edition, and the APA *Publication Manual*, 5th edition, do not capitalize "roman numerals" or "arabic numerals."

Once you master the following standard rules of capitalization, you will be able to capitalize most words without consulting other sources.

1. **Capitalize the first word of a sentence.**

   ▶ The sentence above is an example; so is this one.

   Note: In most writing, capitalization of a sentence following a colon is optional, but be consistent. Some documentation styles specify whether such sentences should be capitalized, so if you are writing a research paper following a particular documentation style, see the appropriate guidelines. The Modern Language Association specifies that the second sentence is capitalized if it enunciates a rule or principle, but not if it simply elaborates on the first sentence.

2. **Capitalize proper nouns and trade names.**

   Capitalize the names of people; places; political, racial, and religious groups; institutions and organizations; sacred writings; brand and trade names; ships, planes, and trains; monuments; awards; and specific academic degrees and courses.

   ▶ Lily O'Neill   ▶ the South

   ▶ the Dead Sea Scrolls   ▶ Congress

   ▶ the Bible (or the Holy Bible)   ▶ Calculus 101

   ▶ Twenty-first Street   ▶ University of Michigan

   ▶ Colorado River   ▶ Catholic, Protestant, Jewish

▶ the Koran

▶ United States Post Office

▶ the Spirit of St. Louis

▶ Purina Cat Chow

▶ League of Women Voters

▶ Master of English Education

Exceptions: Do not capitalize directions, ideologies, or philosophies (unless derived from the name of an individual—Marxism, for example).

▶ After Caleb left Philadelphia, he drove *south.*

▶ Ava is an *idealist.*

▶ Many Russians feel they were better off under *communism.*

3. **Capitalize proper adjectives and abbreviations.**

Capitalize adjectives and abbreviations derived from proper nouns.

▶ the French language

▶ Cooper's hawk

▶ Japanese maple

▶ IRS

▶ Palestinian soldiers

▶ Appalachian quilt

▶ Boston terrier

▶ UCLA

Note: There are exceptions: for example, *Venice* but *venetian blind, French door* but *french fry.* If in doubt, check a dictionary. See also section 4, "Abbreviations."

4. **Capitalize official and personal titles.**

Capitalize a title (or rank) immediately before the name of a person.

▶ Dr. Stephanie Winters

▶ Justice Sandra Day O'Connor

▶ General Colin Powell

▶ Mr. Jacob Turner

▶ Professor Celia Kincaid

▶ President Dwight Eisenhower

▶ Reverend Jamison

▶ Ms. Shannon Maguire

Exception: When no name is given, do *not* capitalize a title.

▶ The professor encouraged the class to share their opinions.

▶ The president of the United States visited flood victims.

5. **Capitalize titles of literary and other artistic works.**

Ordinarily, capitalize the first and last words as well as all major words in the title of a literary or artistic work.

▶ Last week Mason read the autobiography of William O. Douglas, *Go East, Young Man: The Early Years.*

▶ Erma J. Fisk's *The Peacocks of Baboquivari* is an unusual story of an elderly woman who lived alone for five months in the foothills of Arizona, recording and banding birds.

▶ At the Louvre, we saw Leonardo Da Vinci's *The Mona Lisa.*

Note: Rules for capitalizing titles of works differ from one documentation style to another. If you are writing a research paper and following a particular style, check the appropriate guidelines.

6. **Capitalize calendar items and historical periods.**

Capitalize months, special weeks, days, holidays, and historical periods.

▶ April   ▶ New Year's Day

▶ Tuesday   ▶ Right-to-Read Week

▶ Easter   ▶ Middle Ages

▶ the Renaissance   ▶ the Great Depression

Exceptions: Do not capitalize seasons or centuries.

▶ our spring break   ▶ the twentieth century   ▶ in the winter

7. **Capitalize events and documents.**

Capitalize wars, treaties, constitutions, and other important events and documents.

▶ World War II   ▶ Treaty of Versailles

▶ World Series   ▶ United States Constitution

▶ Rose Bowl game   ▶ Magna Carta

▶ the Louisiana Purchase ▶ Battle of Gettysburg

Exceptions: Do not capitalize laws, theories, or hypotheses:

▶ nature's laws   ▶ theory of relativity

▶ code of Hammurabi   ▶ Mendelian principles

4. Abbreviations

When writing, avoid unnecessary abbreviations and use them appropriately. Use only conventional abbreviations that can be easily understood. Except for addresses and documentation, spell out the names of countries, states, and possessions in the United States. In desk dictionaries and many other reference sources, you will find a key to the abbreviations used, in either the front or the back of the publication. (For abbreviations used in MLA works-cited entries and in APA entries, see chapter R-4.)

www.mhhe.com/dietsch
You'll find more help using abbreviations at:
Editing>Abbreviations

4a. Guidelines for Using Abbreviations

Abbreviation styles may differ significantly from one dictionary to another or from one documentation style to another. If you are writing a research paper and following a particular style, check the appropriate guidelines. *Generally, use abbreviations in a table and a list of works cited, but not in the text of a research paper.* If you do use an abbreviation in the text, be sure to define it. The examples that follow are based upon the *MLA Handbook for Writers of Research Papers*, 6th edition, by Joseph Gibaldi.

1. **Use no periods or spaces between abbreviations of most letters that are capitalized.**

FBI	IBM	MD	BA
PSAT	PhD	RN	AD
IRS	EST	DNA	BC

SOME EXCEPTIONS:

U.S.S.	Scott Felder, Jr.	Mr. Daley
N.P.	S.S.	
J. R. Smith	Ms. Jones	

2. **Use a period after each lowercase letter of most abbreviations that represent a word.**

p.m.	ed.	i.e.
a.m.	r.s.v.p.	e.g.
n.p.	p.p.a.	

THERE ARE MANY EXCEPTIONS:

2nd	mph	rpm

3. **Use a period after most abbreviations that end with lowercase letters.**

govt.	Eng.	wk.	Wed.	assn.
dept.	mkt.	mo.	Mar.	biog.
Mar.	obs.	yr.	fig.	introd.
adj.	arch.	ed.	def.	cont.

4b. Common Abbreviations and Reference Terms

AD	*anno Domini* (in the year of the Lord). Precedes numerals (AD 16). Follows centuries (eighth century AD).
arch.	archaic
BC	before Christ. Follows numerals (23 BC).
c., ca.	*circa*: "about"; used with approximate dates
comp., comps.	compiled by, compiler(s)

Cong.	Congress
Cong. Rec.	Congressional Record
e.g.	*exempli gratia:* "for example"
et al.	*et alii:* "and others"
ex., exs.	example(s)
DA, DSI	Dissertation Abstracts, Dissertation Abstracts International
diss.	dissertation
doc.	document
H. Doc.	House of Representatives document
ibid.	*ibidem:* "in the same place"
i.e.	*id est:* "that is" (set off by commas)
ips	inches per second (refers to tape recordings)
LC	Library of Congress
ms., mss.	manuscript(s)
par.	paragraph
pref.	preface, preface by
pt.	part
rept., repts.	reported by, report(s)
rpt.	reprint, reprinted by
S. Doc.	Senate document
sec., sect.	section
sic	thus in the source (place in square brackets as an editorial note, otherwise in parentheses)
S. Rept.	Senate report
var.	variant

5. Numbers

Roman numerals and two basic systems of arabic numbers—ordinary style and technical style—are explained here. Choose the style that is appropriate for your purpose, audience, and occasion. All three systems call for consistency and specify numerals (figures) in certain situations. General guidelines for the ordinary style and the technical style are also shown. (Dictionaries capitalize "Arabic" and "Roman" numerals, but the MLA and APA style do not. For research papers, do not capitalize these terms.)

www.mhhe.com/dietsch

If you want more coverage of using numbers in your writing, visit:
Editing>Numbers

5a. Roman Numerals

1. **When citing pages from a book with lowercase roman numerals, cite the number as written.**

   ▶ page xxvii

   ▶ pages xv–xxiii (range of pages)

2. **When the divisions of a play are written in roman numerals, you may cite as written unless your instructor prefers decimals (see section 5c.2).**

   ▶ King Lear III.i (Act 3, scene 1)

3. **Use uppercase roman numerals for the major divisions of a formal outline (see chapter 5) and after the names of persons in a series.**

   ▶ King Henry IV

   ▶ William A. Dixon III

5b. Ordinary Style of Arabic Numbers

When writing about a topic that requires few numbers, you may use ordinary style. Using this style, you spell out numbers written in two words or less. Use numerals, however, for numbers requiring three or more words.

- One or two words: ten million, four thousand, one hundred, sixty-five, ten, one-half
- Three or more words: 1,537; 101; 5½

Exceptions: Special uses such as in dates, time, addresses, and precise measurements require the use of numerals.

5c. Technical Style of Arabic Numbers

In technical style, numbers are usually written as numerals. If you write a report or paper that requires many numbers, use the technical style. This style is used to express statistical findings and describe scientific projects. For charts, figures, and tables, the technical style is required. Decimals are often used to express precise measurements, but decimals should not be used for data that is normally expressed in fractions.

1. **Express all numbers 10 and above as figures.**

   ▶ seven members   ▶ 10 officials

   Exceptions: Numbers preceding a unit of measurement, as shown below.

2. **Use figures for numbers that precede specific measurements.**

   ▶ 3 miles   ▶ 7 hours   ▶ 6 feet

   ▶ 28½ cubic inches (If the keyboard does not have a fraction key, add a hyphen.)

3. **Unless a unit of measurement is quite short, abbreviate it when preceded by a figure.**

    ▶ 150 hp (horsepower)   ▶ 125 ppm (parts per million)

    ▶ 65 mph (miles per hour)   ▶ 90 wpm (words per minute)

5d. General Guidelines for Ordinary Style and Technical Style of Arabic Numbers

1. **Begin sentences with spelled-out numbers.**

    Never use figures to begin a sentence. Either spell out the number or invert the sentence if the number is large.

    ▶ Seventy-five students were enrolled in CM 111 last quarter.

    ▶ Last quarter 250 students were enrolled in CM 110.

2. **Use numerals in pages and divisions of written works (also see section 5a.2).**

    ▶ page 33   ▶ lines 30–36   ▶ part 5   ▶ chapter 3

    ▶ Act 3   ▶ scene 1   ▶ King Lear 3.1

3. **Spell out round numbers (tens, hundreds, thousands, etc.), estimates, and approximations.**

    ▶ Experts estimate we have enough coal to last two hundred years.

    ▶ Our home cost about thirty thousand dollars to build in 1964.

    ▶ Over eight hundred persons were homeless in Columbus, Ohio, in October 2004.

4. **Use numerals to express decimals and other precise measurements.**

    ▶ 0.625

    ▶ The average age of our students is 27.5 years.

    ▶ The temperature was 98 degrees.

5. **Combine numerals and words to avoid very large figures with many zeros.**

    ▶ 25 million   ▶ 300 billion   ▶ 100 trillion

6. **Spell out the smaller number when two numbers immediately follow in a phrase.**

    ▶ 10 eight-inch planks   ▶ three 5-man crews

7. **If two numbers occur together, either spell out the smaller number or else recast the sentence to separate them.**

UNCLEAR

▷ In 2004, 3,532 students registered for fall quarter.

CLEAR

▶ In fall quarter 2004, there were 3,532 students registered.

8. **Use numbers correctly in addresses.**

Except for the house number *one*, express house numbers as numerals. If a street name is a number less than eleven, spell out the number. If the street name is number eleven or higher, use a hyphen preceded and followed by a space to separate the house number from the street number.

▶ One Blaine Avenue   ▶ 9 Blaine Avenue

▶ 454 East Fifth Street   ▶ 4310 - 12th Street

9. **Use numerals in dates and times of the day.**

▶ April 1936   ▶ 15 March 2005

▶ March 15, 2005 (not March 15th)

▶ the 1990s   ▶ the 90s (or: the nineties)

▶ 1893-97 [Use a range of years in same century.]

▶ 1897-1907 [Write both years in full for two centuries.]

▶ 15 BC   ▶ AD 375

Exceptions:

▶ six o'clock [When the word *o'clock* is used, spell out the number.]

▶ the twentieth century

▶ nineteenth-century literature

10. **Use numerals with abbreviations or symbols.**

▶ 7 KB   ▶ 10:30 a.m.   ▶ $6

▶ 4 lbs.   ▶ 125 rpm   ▶ 32° centigrade

11. **For percentages, use the percent symbol or spell out percent as appropriate.**

In a sentence, spell out the word *percent* when preceded by a figure. Use the symbol for percent in charts and tables.

▶ 50 percent [in a sentence]   ▶ 50% [in charts and tables]

12. **Ordinarily, use numerals for sums of money.**

▶ $1.38   ▶ $454.06   ▶ $1,564

▶ $5   ▶ $10 [Zeros can be omitted for even amounts.]

▸ eighty-nine cents [amounts less than one dollar in ordinary style]

▸ $0.89, 89¢, or 89 cents [technical style]

Special usage: In legal documents, spell out the sums of money and then write the figures in parentheses:

▸ I agree to pay a monthly rental fee of one hundred and ten dollars ($110).

13. **Be consistent in writing numbers in parallel construction. Write related numbers, such as items in a series, in the same style.**

- Ordinary style: Kaya bought five books, six pens, and two notebooks.
- Technical style: The owner hired a crew of 1 plumber, 4 carpenters, 8 laborers, 1 foreman, and 2 masons.

14. **If a small number is used in the same sentence with a larger number but in a different context, spell out the smaller number.**

▸ Those two technicians are operating machines that cost $105,000 each.

6. Spelling

6a. Spelling Tips

Many people feel inferior because they are poor spellers. They feel less intelligent than people who spell accurately. But not all very bright people are good spellers. For example one ninth-grader, a physician's daughter, was a brilliant student except for her spelling. Her essays were filled with misspelled words. Once, after she had corrected a theme, a word was misspelled in a different way. When asked why she hadn't used a dictionary, she replied, "Oh, I asked Dad." This example illustrates the need for spelling tip number one: *Use a dictionary; don't ask someone how to spell a word.*

The mystery of poor spelling has not been completely solved. But we do know that incorrect pronunciation sometimes leads to incorrect spelling. Students who mispronounce words frequently misspell those same words. The left list below contains some words that are commonly misspelled due to mispronunciation:

www.mhhe.com/dietsch
For online spelling assistance, go to:
Editing>Spelling

Incorrect	Correct
Artic	Arctic
congradulations	congratulations
discribe	describe
goverment	government
enviroment	environment
convience	convenience

secratary	secretary
wreck havoc	wreak havoc
pitchur	picture
then (used in comparison)	than

If you are unsure of the spelling or pronunciation of a word, look it up in a dictionary. Then practice writing and saying the word correctly. One way is to keep a list of words that you misspell frequently and practice writing them. (Chances are there will be fewer than a dozen.) After you look up the correct spelling of each word on your list, write each one at least a dozen times. That practice will strengthen your mental image of the word.

6b. Association Aids to Improve Spelling

One way to improve spelling is to devise an association that will help you recall the correct spelling. For example, one student who had difficulty with the word *occasion* could not remember whether it had two *c*'s and one *s* or vice versa. She looked the word up several times until she devised this sentence: "Twenty-one is a special occasion." Twenty-one (21) reminded her that occasion had 2 *c*'s and 1 *s*. Listed below are some other associations to help you recall certain spellings.

▶ A *secretary* is a keeper of *secrets*. [An *e* follows the *r* in both words.]

▶ *Separate* has *a rat* in it. [An *a* follows the *p*.]

▶ *there, their, they're*
   there: Without the *t*, *there* becomes *here*. [Both words refer to location.]
   their: Without the *t*, *their* becomes *heir*. [Both words refer to ownership.]
   they're: This is a contraction of *they are*. [The apostrophe indicates that *a* has been omitted.]

▶ *principal and principle:* The following sentence should help you remember that *principal* refers to someone or something of importance: "The *principal* points of his speech were. . . ." On the other hand, *principle* refers to a code, law, or doctrine.
   • The *principal* of our school was a *pal* to the students.
   • The Tenth Commandment is a difficult *principle* to follow.

▶ *prejudice:* Just remember that *prejudice* means to *pre-judge* something.

▶ *stationery* and *stationary:*
   Remember that you write on an envelope. [Both *envelope* and *stationery* have *e*'s.]
   Something *stationary* stays in one place. [two *a*'s]

▶ *maneuver:* When you are riding a horse, the mane is in front of you. Just remember that the *mane* is before the *u*.

You may want to devise your own association aids for words that give you trouble.

6c. Other Spelling Aids

▶ **Only one English word ends in** *-sede: supersede.* **Only three words end in** *-ceed: exceed, proceed, succeed.* All other words of similar sound end in *-cede.*

▶ **Drop the final** *e* **in most words when the suffix begins with a vowel:** *chang(e)ing, hop(e)ing, purchas(e)able.*

▶ **Keep the final** *e* **when the suffix begins with a consonant:** *hopeful, vengeful, homeless.* In some instances, however, the *e* is kept: *changeable, knowledgeable, peaceable.* And some words have two spellings: *salable/saleable, livable/liveable,* and others.

▶ *Pre* **means "before."** *Preschool:* before school

▶ *Per* **means "through, to, for, by each," or "by means of."** *Perceive:* to become aware of directly through any of the senses

▶ *Pro* **means "in favor of" or "acting as."** *Procapitalism:* in favor of capitalism or private ownership of production

Plurals of words ending in *y* are formed as follows:

▶ **When a consonant precedes the final** *y,* **change the** *y* **to** *i* **and add** *es: company/companies, lady/ladies, cherry/cherries.*

▶ **When a vowel precedes the** *y,* **keep the** *y* **and add** *s: monkeys, attorneys, byways.*

Exceptions: Plurals for proper names such as the *Berrys, Kellys,* or *Malinys.*

▶ **To form the plural of nouns ending in** *ch, s, sh, x,* **and** *z,* **add** *es: matches, gases, bushes, taxes, buzzes.* This rule also applies to the singular forms of verbs ending in these letters. (Just remember to use *es* for plurals that have the *z* sound.)

6d. Six Ways to Improve Spelling

Probably the biggest factor in any improvement is motivation. If you resolve to refine your spelling skill and follow a plan, you will become a better speller. Here are six techniques to aid you:

1. **Use a dictionary to check words if you are unsure of their spelling.** Carry a spelling checker or pocket dictionary and keep a desk dictionary in a convenient place at home. But remember that computer spelling checkers are limited in their helpfulness. (See "Glossary of Usage," pages H-50– H-58, for similar words that are commonly confused.)

2. **Pronounce words correctly.** If you leave out letters or syllables in pronunciation, you may leave them out when writing the word.

3. **Compile your own spelling list.** Review this daily for a few weeks. Look at each word. Then shut your eyes and see if you can spell it correctly.

4. **Write misspelled words correctly several times so that you can visualize their correct spelling in your mind.**

5. **Familiarize yourself with the memory association aids.** Then devise some aids of your own.

6. **As a last resort, if you cannot recognize misspelled words, ask someone to mark them. Then get out the dictionary and correct the spellings yourself. With practice, your spelling ability will improve, and you will be able to catch more of your errors.**

7. Glossary of Usage

Some words in the English language are commonly confused because they look or sound alike. Other words used in conversation are sometimes mistaken for standard usage. This glossary will help you select the appropriate word for your college and business writing. The recommendations here are based on usage listed in current dictionaries. For clarity, misspellings and other unaccepted variations are listed after the standard word.

a, an Use *a* before words starting with a consonant sound. Use *an* before words starting with a vowel sound.

- a bristlecone pine, a history, a quail, a sinkhole
- an aardvark, an egg, an infant, an honorable man

accept, except *Accept* means "to believe," "to approve," or "to take" (as take an offered gift). *Except* means "without" or "excluding."

- Can he *accept* constructive criticism?
- All the children *except* Jane are here.

access, excess The noun *access* is the "ability or right to enter, to use, or to approach." The verb *access* is used in a technological sense, as "to locate data." *Excess* means "too much" or "exceeding that which is normal and sufficient."

- It is impossible to gain direct *access* to the freeway from here.
- Lucinda can *access* those files easily.
- She stored the *excess* bread dough in the refrigerator.

adapt, adept, adopt *Adapt* means "to make suitable for a specific situation." *Adept* means "very skilled; proficient." *Adopt* means "to take up and use as one's own," as an idea, word, or the like. *Adopt* also refers to the process of child adoption.

- Do you think you can *adapt* the part to make it fit?
- Jeff is *adept* at programming.
- When customers complain, Sarah *adopts* the tactic of "A soft answer turneth away wrath."

adverse, averse *Adverse* means "harmful or unfavorable." *Averse* means "unwilling" or "disinclined."

- William has surmounted *adverse* circumstances before.
- Mike is *averse* to risk taking.

advice, advise *Advice* is a noun that means "a view, opinion, or judgment." *Advise* is a verb that means "to counsel," "to inform," or "to recommend."

- His *advice* was to look for another job.
- I really don't know what to *advise*.

affect, effect *Affect* is a verb meaning "to change" or "to influence." *Effect* is usually used as a noun to mean "result." As a verb *effect* means "to make" or "to implement."

- How will that *affect* your decision?
- What will be the *effect* of that decision?
- Can you *effect* an improvement in that procedure?

all ready, already *Already* refers to time, meaning "previously." *All ready* means "prepared" or "available for action."

- Did you *already* clock out?
- Are you *all ready* to leave?

all right *All right* means "satisfactory" or "proper." *Alright* is a common misspelling.

- It is *all right* to go in the kitchen; the floor is dry.

all together, altogether *All together* means "in a group." *Altogether* means "completely."

- The birds huddled *all together* to keep warm.
- Joe's answer was not *altogether* right.

allot, a lot *Allot* means "to parcel out" or "to give a certain portion." *A lot*, used to mean "a large extent, amount, or number," is informal. *Alot* is a common misspelling.

- The government *allots* only one per family.
- He has *a lot* of confidence.
- Jill's grandmother is *a lot* better.

allusion, delusion, illusion An *allusion* is "a reference" (often to a literary work). A *delusion* is a "mistaken idea." An *illusion* is "an erroneous perception of reality."

- He made an *allusion* to Hamlet.
- He suffers from the *delusion* that he is immortal.
- The ghost was an *illusion*, created with special lighting.

altar, alter *Altar* is a noun meaning a table or platform used in worship. *Alter* is a verb meaning to change or adapt.

- On the *altar* are two large candelabra.
- Can you *alter* these pants by Saturday?

among, between Use *among* when referring to three or more units or people. Use *between* when referring to only two.

- Let's keep this secret *among* our family members.
- *Between* you and me, I like his beard.

amount, number *Amount* refers to a quantity or weight. *Number* refers to a numeral, unit, or indefinite quantity of items or individuals.

- The recipe called for a small *amount* of black pepper.
- The crowd *numbers* in the thousands.

an, a See *a, an.*

any, any other *Any* can mean "one, some, every," or "all." *Any other* is used in a comparison. Do not substitute *any* (by itself). The following examples are correct:

- Brian was faster than *any other* runner in his age group.
- You may select *any* of the top prizes.

anyone, any one *Anyone* is a pronoun that means "any person" or, in some instances, "everyone." *Any one* means "whichever one (just one) of a group." *Any one* can refer to a person or a thing.

- *Anyone* may come, not just members.
- *Any one* of the band members can carry the flag.

appraise, apprise *Appraise* means "to evaluate or estimate the value." *Apprise* means "to give notice to or inform."

- Will you *appraise* this emerald ring for me?
- Did you *apprise* the prisoner of his rights?

assure, ensure, insure *Assure* means "to inform positively." *Ensure* means "to make sure or certain." *Insure* means "to cover with insurance." *Insure* also means "to make certain, especially by taking precautions."

- I *assure* you that every precaution will be taken.
- Checking the map beforehand will *ensure* that you find the right road.
- Did you *insure* the contents of your house?

averse See *adverse, averse.*

awhile, a while *Awhile* is an adverb that means "a short time." *A while,* which consists of an article and a noun, means "a period of time." (The preposition *for* may be used with *a while.*)

- He stopped *awhile* to rest. (not *for awhile*)
- Don't rush off—stay for *a while.*

beside, besides *Beside* means "next to." *Besides* means "also."

- The scissors are lying *beside* my sewing basket.
- *Besides* my fishing equipment, I'm taking a picnic lunch.

between See *among, between.*

bloc, block *Bloc* is a noun meaning a group of people or nations. *Block* is a noun meaning a solid piece of material.

- The conservative *bloc* voted against a tax increase.
- He chopped the *block* of wood into kindling.

breath, breathe *Breath* is a noun; *breathe* is a verb. Both refer to inhalation and exhalation.

- The speech instructor advised taking a deep *breath* before starting to speak.
- *Breathe* deeply as you work out.

capital, capitol *Capital* refers to the "official place or city of government" or an "amount of money." *Capitol* refers to the "building that houses the official government offices."

- Denver is the *capital* of Colorado.
- We need more *capital* to fund the project.
- Sue visited the *capitol* building during her trip to the state *capital.*

carat, caret *Carat* (or *karat*) is a noun used to measure the weight of gems or the quality of gold. *Caret* is a noun, a small pointed mark that indicates where a printed insert goes.

- The diamond in Ashley's engagement ring must weigh over a *carat.*
- Where should I put the *caret* to mark the insertion of this phrase?

censor, censure *Censor* is "to examine books, films, or other materials to remove or suppress what is considered objectionable." *Censure* is "to criticize severely or blame."

- The school board plans to *censor* books purchased for the school.
- The editorial *censured* a city council member for his failure to attend meetings regularly.

cite, sight, site *Cite* means "to quote." *Sight* refers to the ability to see or view. *Site* refers to location, as a building site.

- Can you *cite* his exact words?
- Can you *sight* Venus above the evening horizon?
- They selected a lovely wooded *site* for their new home.

complement, compliment *Complement* means "to complete or bring to perfection." *Compliment* means "to express praise."

- That floral arrangement *complements* your table setting.
- Brad *complimented* Cindy on her new shoes.

comprise, compose *Comprise* is a verb meaning to contain, to form, or to consist of. *Compose* is a verb meaning: (1) to create, to make, or to constitute; to put parts together to form a whole; (2) to set type; or (3) to calm oneself, to settle one's emotions.

- The USA *comprises* fifty states.
- Fifty states *compose* the USA.
- The Linotype operator *composed* type for a newspaper years ago.
- Before seeing my next client, I must *compose* myself.

conscience, conscious *Conscience* is "the awareness of a moral or ethical aspect of one's conduct" and the desire "to prefer right over wrong." *Conscious* refers to "awareness of one's environment and existence."

- Jeannette returned the wallet to its owner to relieve her *conscience.*
- Is the patient *conscious* yet?

continual, continuous *Continual* means "recurring regularly or often." *Continuous* means "uninterrupted."

- Uncle Jake's *continual* complaining made our visit unpleasant.

- The flow of fresh air throughout the building is *continuous.*

council, counsel *Council* refers to a group of people who are delegated "to serve in an administrative, legislative, or advisory capacity." *Counsel,* as noun or verb, refers to advice.

- Anthony is a member of the town *council.*
- The admissions office *counsels* students.
- Lawyers charge for their *counsel.*

criteria, criterion A *criterion* is a "standard, rule, or test upon which a judgment or decision can be based." *Criteria* is the plural of *criterion.*

- She gave only one *criterion* for the job: a strong back.
- He stated six *criteria* for the upcoming performance evaluation.

delusion See *allusion, delusion, illusion.*

effect, affect See *affect, effect.*

elicit, illicit *Elicit* is a verb meaning to draw out, to evoke. *Illicit* is an adjective meaning unlawful, illegal.

- The police interrogation *elicited* important information.
- Littering is an *illicit* act.

emigrate, immigrate When people *emigrate,* they leave their homeland to reside elsewhere. When they *immigrate,* they enter a different country to reside.

- My paternal ancestors, five brothers, *emigrated* from Wales in the late 1700s.
- They *immigrated* to the United States and traveled to the territory that later became Ohio.

eminent, imminent *Eminent* means "of high rank, station, or quality." *Imminent* means "about to occur, impending."

- Today is the birthday of that *eminent* inventor Thomas A. Edison.
- Skating on thin ice poses an *imminent* danger.

enthusiastic *Enthusiastic,* meaning to have great excitement or interest, is standard usage. *Enthused* is used only colloquially.

- Cody was *enthusiastic* about traveling to the Rocky Mountains.

except See *accept, except.*

excess See *access, excess.*

explicit, implicit *Explicit* means "fully and clearly expressed; leaving nothing implied." *Implicit* means "implied or understood though not directly expressed."

- The doctor's directions were *explicit:* "Take one tablet with a full glass of water after meals."
- The company president has *implicit* trust in Sheila's judgment.

farther, further *Farther* refers to "physical distance" and *further* to a nonphysical dimension such as distance in time.

- We drove *farther* than usual the second day of our trip.
- If we go *further* back a few generations, we find other family members who also suffered from breast cancer.

fewer, less *Fewer* is used in comparisons to refer to "individual units, things that can be counted." *Less* is used in comparisons to mean a smaller amount or "a mass of measurable extent."

- *Fewer* people attended the state fair this year than last year.
- Opals cost much *less* than diamonds of the same size.

flaunt, flout *Flaunt* means "to parade or display ostentatiously." *Flout* means "to show contempt for" or "to scorn."

- Lorrie *flaunted* her new engagement ring.
- Timothy *flouted* the dress code.

further See *farther, further.*

garner, garnish *Garner* is a verb meaning to collect or to gather. *Garnish* is a verb meaning to decorate, enhance, or embellish. *Garnish* can also be used as a substitute for *garnishee*, which means to attach one's wages (for a debt owed) through a court order.

- The Lone Ravens have *garnered* rave reviews for their performances.
- The poached fish was *garnished* with parsley.
- His salary was *garnished* for unpaid child support.

get *Get* means "to receive" or "to bring." Avoid the many colloquial uses of *get* in college and business writing. (See a dictionary for other examples of colloquial usage.)

- Standard: Will you *get* a gallon of milk when you go out?
- Colloquial: I hope the frost doesn't *get* our garden.
- Colloquial: That really *gets* to me!

good, well *Good* is an adjective meaning "positive or desirable." *Well* is often used as an adverb to mean "satisfactorily or sufficiently" or "skillfully or proficiently." *Well* is also used as an adjective to mean "a satisfactory condition; right or proper."

- Jerry received *good* news this morning.
- Jeremy did *well* on his calculus exam.
- Henry is *well;* he has completely recovered from pneumonia.
- The project is going *well.*

hanged, hung People are *hanged.* Objects are *hung.*

- The convicted murderer was *hanged.*
- Derek *hung* the painting over the fireplace.

idea, ideal An *idea* is "a thought." An *ideal* is "a principle" or "a conception or model of something in its absolute perfection."

- Suddenly he had a delightful *idea.*
- Her *ideal* husband would be a wonderful father.
- Always be true to your *ideals.*

illusion See *allusion, delusion, illusion.*

implicit See *explicit, implicit.*

its, it's *Its* is the possessive form of *it. It's* is a contraction of *it is.*

- The dog has lost *its* collar.

- *It's* over seventy miles to the next town.

leave, let *Leave* means "to go out or away from." *Let* means "to permit or allow."

- Will you *leave* Jiffy at the kennel when you go to the lake?
- Please *let* me help you with those packages.

less See *fewer, less.*

let See *leave, let.*

loose, lose *Lose* is a verb meaning "to mislay." *Loose* is an adjective meaning "not tight" or "unconfined."

- Did you *lose* an earring?
- My watchband is too *loose.*
- An orangutan was *loose* in the park.

medium, media *Medium* is (1) an "intermediate course," the midpoint between two extremes; (2) a way that something is "transmitted or carried"; (3) "an agency by which something is accomplished or conveyed or transferred." *Media* is the plural of *medium* and takes a plural verb.

- The Internet is a *medium* that relays daily stock market reports.
- The *media* frequently refer to the escapades of the royal family.

moral, morale *Moral* is an adjective that refers to "judgment of the goodness or badness of human action and character." *Morale* is a noun that means "the state of the spirits of a person or group."

- The *moral* code of society seems to be changing.
- Employee *morale* is high at XYZ Company.

notable, notorious *Notable* is an adjective meaning distinguished or remarkable. *Notorious*, an adjective, refers to being well-known, but the word carries negative connotations.

- David is *notable* for his ability to play and sing Irish folk songs.
- That actress is *notorious* for posing for centerfolds.

number See *amount, number.*

passed, past *Passed* is a verb that means "having moved on; proceeded." *Past* as an adverb means "beyond" and as a noun or adjective refers to time that is over. Do not write "*past* history" because all history is past.

- Jerry *passed* the bakery without stopping.
- Jerry drove *past* the bakery without stopping.
- Let's forget the *past* and look to the future.

patience, patients *Patience* is the ability to "bear pain, provocation, or annoyance with calmness." *Patients* refers to people who "receive medical attention, care, or treatment."

- *Patience* is a quality that is learned.
- The physician saw thirty-seven *patients* yesterday.

peak, pique *Peak* is a verb meaning to reach the highest point or capacity. *Pique* is a verb meaning to annoy, irk, or inflame.

- In 2006 the DJIA *peaked* in December.
- Hilary was *piqued* by Ryan's insolence.

personal, personnel *Personal* refers to the private matters of an individual. *Personnel* refers to a group of people who work for an organization. (Note that *personnel* has two *n*'s and two *e*'s.)

- Please don't ask *personal* questions.
- Their *personnel* are very courteous.

precede, proceed *Precede* means "to go before." *Proceed* means "to go" or "to continue."

- The Rose Bowl game *precedes* the Orange Bowl game.
- Let's *proceed* with the meeting.

principal, principle See "Association Aids to Improve Spelling," page H-48.

quiet, quite *Quiet* means "free of noise." *Quite* means "very; entirely."

- Our dorm is rarely *quiet.*
- Your homemade apple pie is *quite* tasty.
- It is *quite* all right to park there.

quotation, quote *Quote* is a verb that means "to repeat or copy the words of [another]," usually citing the source. *Quotation* is a noun meaning "the act of quoting" or "a passage quoted."

- Do you plan to *quote* John F. Kennedy in your speech?
- A *quotation* from Winston Churchill might make an effective introduction.

real, really *Real* is an adjective meaning "genuine or authentic," "free of pretense or falsehood." (Avoid using *real* to mean "very.") *Really* is an adverb meaning "truly; genuinely."

- Her diamond is *real.*
- *Really,* I can't go with you.

regardless *Regardless* means "in spite of everything; anyway." *Irregardless* is redundant and nonstandard.

- Many people neglect to buckle their seat belts, *regardless* of the danger.

sight See *cite, sight, site.*

sometime, some time, sometimes *Sometime* means "an indefinite or unstated time." *Some time* refers to an amount of time. *Sometimes* means "occasionally."

- Stop in *sometime.*
- I haven't seen him for *some time.*
- *Sometimes* I feed the elephants at the city zoo.

stationary, stationery *Stationary* means "not moving" or "not capable of being moved." *Stationery* refers to writing materials.

- The tables in that restaurant are *stationary.*
- Would you like some monogrammed *stationery* for Christmas?

than, then *Than* is a conjunction indicating a comparison. *Then* is an adverb indicating time.

- Harrison likes pistachio ice cream better *than* chocolate.
- I will meet you *then*.

their, there, they're *Their* is the possessive form of *they*. *There* is an adverb that refers to place. (*There* can also be used in several other ways.) *They're* is a contraction of *they are*.

- *Their* cars are parked on the street.
- Do you see that ten-dollar bill lying *there* in the grass?
- *They're* the third couple from the left.

to, too, two *To* is a preposition meaning "toward," "in contact with," "in front of," or "constituting"; or it can be the sign of an infinitive. *Too* means "also" or "more than enough." *Two* is the whole number following *one;* a couple.

- I walked *to* the town square.
- *To* ensure you arrive safely, check the cable that is towing your glider.
- May I go, *too?*
- *Two* robins built a nest.

try to *Try to* means "to attempt." *Try and* is not generally accepted usage.

- *Try to* pull up the cap of the bottle after the arrows meet.

two See *to, too, two*.

wangle, wrangle *Wangle* is a verb meaning to finagle or to contrive. *Wrangle* is also a verb, but it means to dispute loudly or to quarrel.

- Jason *wangled* a job as a radio announcer although he had no experience in broadcasting.
- The couple *wrangled* over his not helping with the children.

which, who Use *which* when referring to an object or an animal. Use *who* when referring to a person. (For more information about usage, see section 1b.7 on pronouns.)

- The black horse, *which* is near the barn, belongs to Stanley.
- *Who* did you say is calling?

who, whom *Who* is in the subjective case, *whom* in the objective case.

- These are the men *who* you thought were responsible. [*who* were responsible]
- These are the men *whom* you chose for the job. [you chose *whom*]

who's, whose *Who's* is a contraction of *who is* or *who has*. *Whose* is the possessive form of *who*.

- *Who's* the best candidate for the position?
- *Whose* dalmatian is that?

your, you're *Your* is the possessive form of *you*. *You're* is the contraction of *you are*.

- Will you take *your* car?
- *You're* the winner of a trip to Tahiti.

Credits

Levine, Dan. "Wal-Mart's Big City Blues" by Dan Levine reprinted from the November 24, 2003 issue of *The Nation*. For subscription information call 1-800-333-8536. Portions of each week's magazine can be accessed at *http://www.thenation.com*.

Lewis, C. S. "We Have No 'Right' to Happiness" from *God in the Docks* by C. S. Lewis, copyright © C. S. Lewis Pte. Ltd. 1970. Extract reprinted by permission.

MacLeish, Archibald. "Ars Poetica" from *Collected Poems 1917–1982* by Archibald MacLeish. Copyright © 1985 by the Estate of Archibald MacLeish. Reprinted by permission of Houghton Mifflin Company. All rights reserved.

Malanga, Steven. "The War on Wal-Mart." This article, reprinted from the *Wall Street Journal* (4/7/04) was adapted from the Spring 2004 issue of the Manhattan Institute's *City Journal* (*www.city-journal.org*) where Steven Malanga is a contributing editor.

Mannes, Marya. "How Do You Know It's Good?" from *But Will It Sell?* by Marya Mannes. Copyright © 1962 by Marya Mannes. Copyright © renewed 1990.

McCarthy, Bernice. "A Tale of Four Learners." Copyright © 1997 by Bernice McCarthy. Reprinted by permission of the author.

Ramirez, Robert. "The Barrio." Copyright © Robert Ramirez. Reprinted by permission.

Raspberry, William. "The Handicap of Definition" from *Instilling Positive Images* by William Raspberry. Copyright © 1982 by The Washington Post Writer's Group. Reprinted with permission.

Raymond, David. "On Being 17, Bright and Unable to Read." *The New York Times*, 4/25/76. Copyright © 1976 by The New York Times Co. Reprinted by permission.

Roiphe, Anne. "Why Marriages Fail" by Anne Roiphe. Reprinted by permission of International Creative Management, Inc. Copyright © 1983 by Anne Roiphe.

Samuelson, Robert. "Fun Ethic vs. Work Ethic" from *Newsweek*, 9/10/2001. Copyright © 2001 Newsweek, Inc. All rights reserved. Used by permission. *www.newsweek.com*.

Sandburg, Carl. "Grass" from *Cornhuskers* by Carl Sandburg, copyright 1918 by Holt, Rinehart and Winston and renewed 1946 by Carl Sandburg. Reprinted by permission of Harcourt, Inc.

Shea, Don. "Jumper Down" originally appeared in *High Plains Literary Review*. Copyright © 1997 by Don Shea. Reprinted by permission of the author.

Sierra Club Sequoia Task Force. "Logging in Giant Sequoia National Monument." Reproduced with permission of the Sierra Club. Copyright © 2007 Sierra Club. All Rights Reserved.

Sollisch, James. "Fruitful Questions," *Chicago Tribune Magazine*. Reprinted by permission of The Chicago Tribune.

Sone, Monica. "The Stubborn Twig: My Double Dose of Schooling" from *Nisea Daughter* by Monica Sone. Copyright © 1953 by Monica Sone. Copyright renewed 1981 by Monica Sone. By permission of Little, Brown and Company (Inc.) and Brandt & Hochman Literary Agency.

Sora. "The Barley Field" from *An Introduction to Haiku* by Harold G. Henderson. Copyright © 1958 by Harold G. Henderson. Used by permission of Doubleday, a division of Random House, Inc.

Sullivan, Andrew. "The Pursuit of Happiness: Four Revolutionary Words." Copyright © 2002 by Andrew Sullivan. First published in *Forbes*, 2001. Reprinted with the permission of the Wylie Agency, Inc.

Tabor, Nathan. "Speaking English Preserves Our National Heritage." *The Conservative Voice*. Copyright 2004. Reprinted by permission of the author.

Tan, Amy. "Mother Tongue" copyright © 1990 by Amy Tan. First appeared in *The Threepenny Review*. Reprinted by permission of the author and the Sandra Dijkstra Literary Agency.

Terkel, Studs. "Dolores Dante" from *Working* by Studs Terkel. Copyright © 1974 by Studs Terkel. Reprinted by permission of Donadio & Olson, Inc.

Updike, John. "Still of Some Use" from *Trust Me* by John Updike. Copyright © 1987 by John Updike. Used by permission of Alfred A. Knopf, a division of Random House, Inc.

Vest, Jason, Warren Cohen and Mike Tharp. "Road Rage" (June 2, 1997). Copyright © 1997 *U.S. News and World Report*, L.P. Reprinted with permission.

Weiss, Phillip. "How to Get Out of a Locked Trunk" by Phillip Weiss. Copyright © 1992 by Harper's Magazine. All rights reserved. Reproduced from the 1992 issue by special permission.

Photo Credits

PO-1 © John Lund/Digital Vision/Getty Images
PO-2 © StockByte/Punchstock
PO-3 © Royalty-Free/Corbis
PO-4 © Guy Crittenden/Images.com/Corbis
PO-5 © Steve Cole/Digital Vision/Getty Images
PO-6 © Claudia Rehm/Westend61/Getty Images

Author-Title Index

Note: Student writers and works are indicated by an asterisk.*

Subject Index